MANJŪ

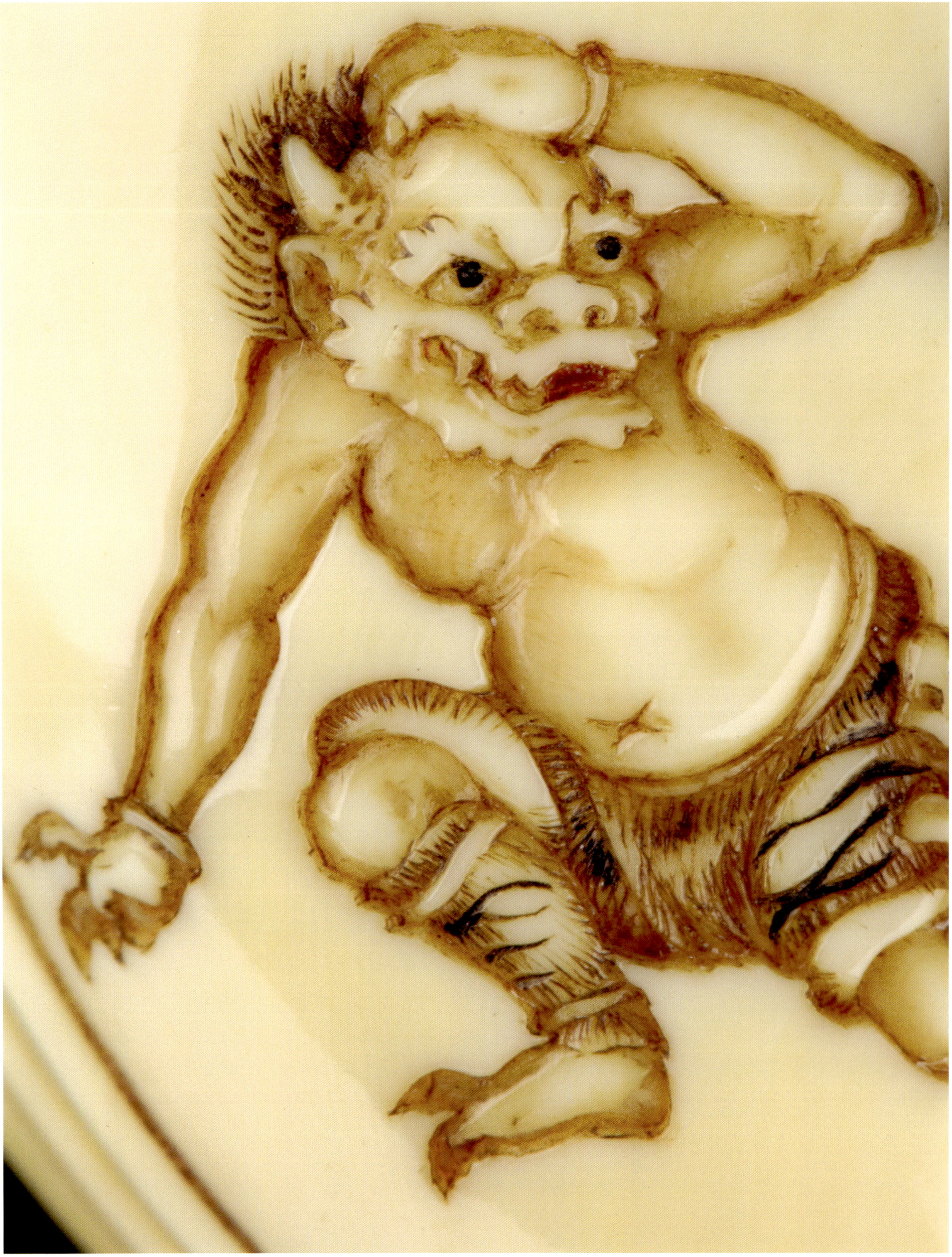

JOYCE SEAMAN

MANJŪ

Netsuke from the Collection of the Ashmolean Museum

Photography by David Gowers

ASHMOLEAN
MUSEUM OF ART AND ARCHAEOLOGY UNIVERSITY OF OXFORD

2013

Manjū: Netsuke from the Collection of the Ashmolean Museum

British Library Cataloguing in Publications Data
A catalogue record for this book is available
from the British Library

EAN 13: 978 1 85444 279 6

Catalogue designed by Stephen Hebron
Printed and bound in Malta by The Gutenberg Press

Frontispiece: Oni running away (cat. no. 46, detail)

For further details of Ashmolean titles please visit:
www.ashmolean.org/shop

ASHMOLEAN
MUSEUM OF ART AND ARCHAEOLOGY UNIVERSITY OF OXFORD

Contents

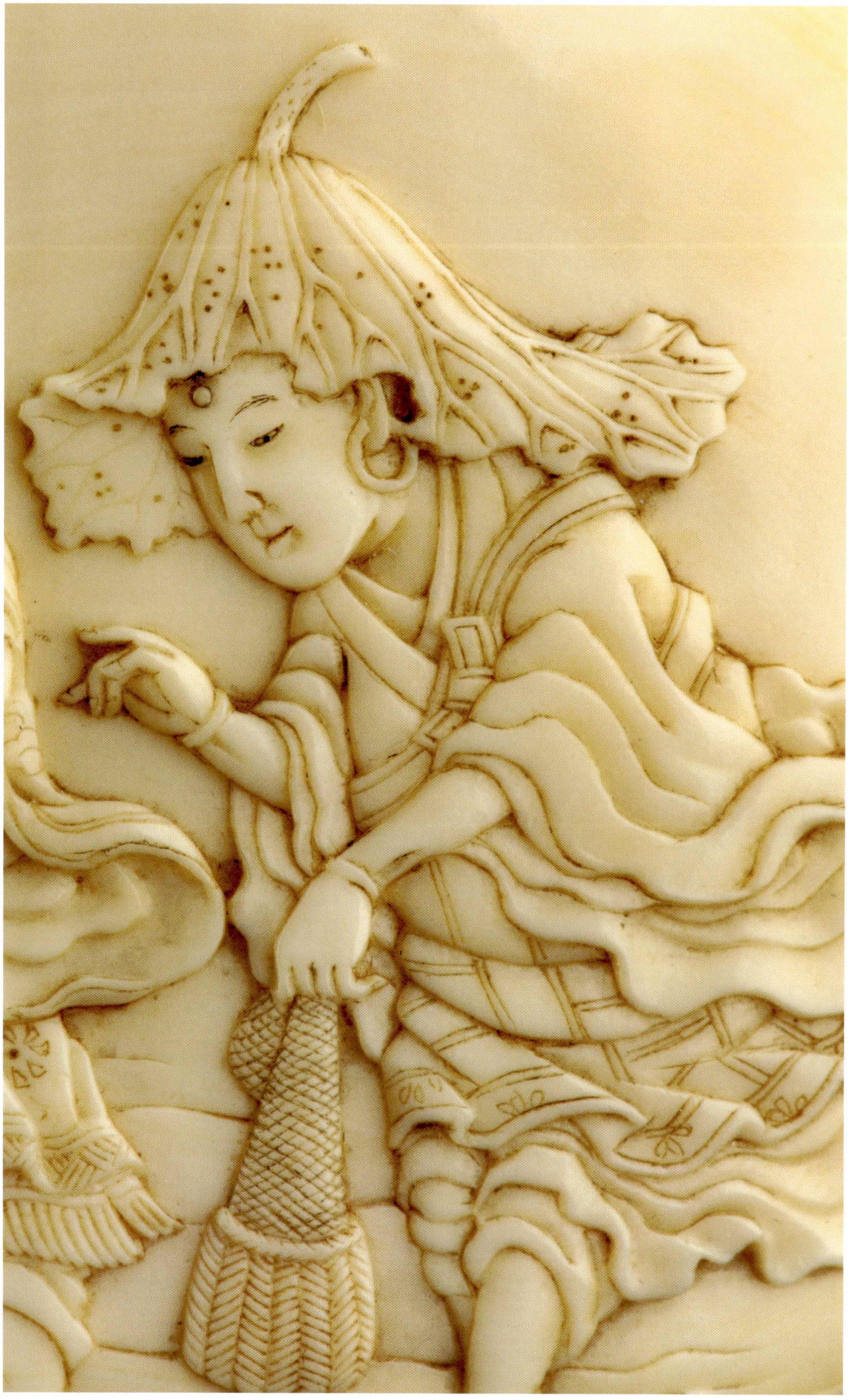

Cat. no. 25 (detail)

Acknowledgements

This exhibition could never have come into being without the help and encouragement of a great many people. I extend my grateful thanks to the following:

Dr Oliver Impey, the Keeper of Japanese Art until his retirement in 2003 and his untimely death two years later, for giving me the opportunity to work with the Japanese Collections for so many years. Dr Clare Pollard for her enthusiastic support, suggestions and scholarship throughout the whole project. Kiyoko Hanaoka for patiently translating and deciphering signatures. Dr James McMullen for assistance with translation and interpretation. Neil Davey for his help over subject matter. Rosemary Bandini and Max Rutherston for their scholarship. Jonathan Gestetner, Michael Dean and Douglas Wright for their reminiscences of Dr Monica Barnett. Dr Helen Loveday from the Baur Collection, Geneva; Clare Caless from the Maidstone Museum, Kent; Angie Simonds from the Museum of Fine Arts, Boston; Hwai-ling Yeh-Lewis and Imtikar Ally from the Metropolitan Museum of Art, New York; Karina Corrigan, Eric Wolin and Dave O'Ryan from the Peabody Essex Museum, Salem, Mass. for giving me access to their collections. Also, the staff at the Victoria and Albert Musuem and the British Museum, London, for allowing me to look at their collections. Mrs Ohara at Sagemonoya and the Chinese Bodleian Librarians for their help in identification of themes. Unity Coombes for her drawing.

The librarians at The National Diet Library and Waseda University Library for approving the use of their images. The Pitt Rivers Museum, Oxford and the Museum Kunst Palast, Düsseldorf for providing images of works in their collections.

At the Ashmolean Museum, David Gowers in the photographic studio, Liz Gardner, Dana Norris and in the conservation laboratory, and the staff in the Eastern Art Study Room, Sigolene Loizeau and Alessandra Cereda, Sarah Mitchell, and Aimée Payton of the Eastern Art department. Declan McCarthy in the publications department and Amy Taylor from the picture research department.

Sara Bryant for laboriously proof-reading and to Stephen Hebron for his patience and skill in design. Dr Patrizia Jirka-Schmitz, Eva Sweet, Dr Monika Bincsik and many others, too numerous to mention, who have helped in so many different ways to bring this project to completion.

Joyce Seaman

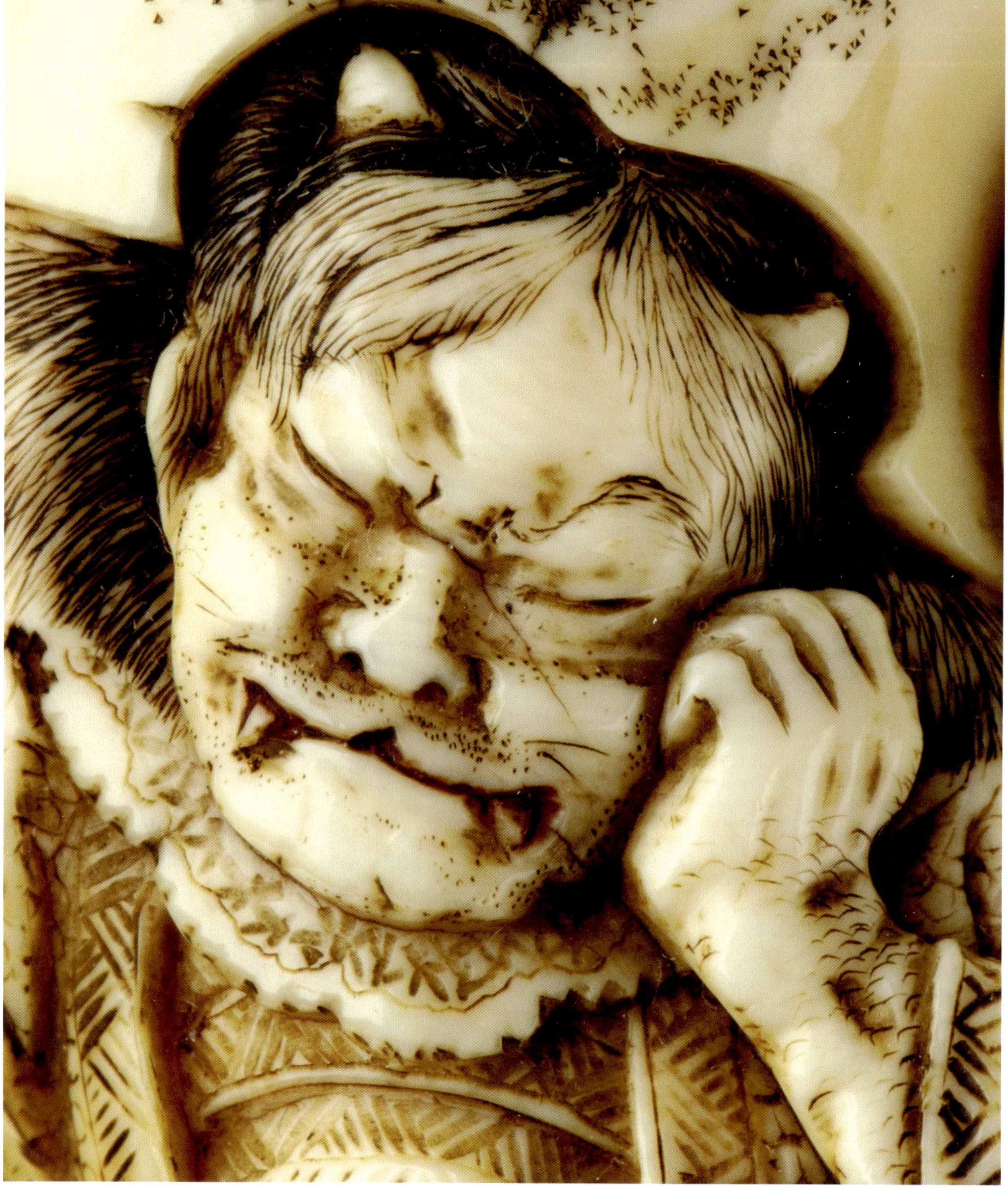

Cat. no. 78 (detail)

Director's Foreword

The traditional Japanese garment, the kimono, has no pockets, so small personal items were carried in containers hung from the sash and secured with small toggles called netsuke. Carved from materials such as wood, ivory and horn, netsuke became particularly fashionable with the merchant class during the Edo period (1600-1868). This is a catalogue of the Ashmolean Museum's collection of a particular type of netsuke, the *manjū,* which is named after a round, sweet bean-paste filled bun. These *manjū* netsuke illustrate scenes from Japanese history, religion, folklore and everyday life. They display carving of remarkable skill and bring us a fascinating glimpse of Japanese culture during the late Edo and early Meiji (1868-1912) periods. Yet they have been little studied in comparison with the arguably more accessible sculptural or *katabori* netsuke. This catalogue, which accompanies an exhibition of *manjū* in the Ashmolean's Eastern Art Galleries, aims to redress this imbalance

Japanese netsuke have been enthusiastically collected by Westerners since the opening of Japan to foreign trade in the 1850s. The introduction of Western dress which began to take place in the 1870s caused many netsuke to become redundant, for personal items could now be put into suit pockets, instead of being hung from the waist. The result was that many fine netsuke came onto the market for sale and a large number of these left Japan for Europe and America. At this time, few Japanese took an interest in netsuke as works of art, considering them to be everyday functional objects. By the early twentieth century their use in Japan was restricted to special events when traditional Japanese dress was still worn.

The Museums of the University of Oxford - the Pitt Rivers, the Museum of the History of Science and the Ashmolean Museum - have received netsuke from several collectors over the last hundred years, giving each one interesting and varied holdings. In 1956 a large gift which included netsuke came to the Ashmolean from Sir Herbert Ingram. These accompanied many other Japanese objects, which the Ingrams bought on their honeymoon in Japan in 1908, and included some *manjū* netsuke. Subsequently the Hildburgh, Christie-Miller, Oppenheim and Biegun gifts, almost all of *katabori* netsuke, augmented the Ashmolean's collection and a large gift from Hermann Gunther in 1980 was divided between the Pitt Rivers Museum and the Museum of the History of Science. A selection of netsuke from all three museums was published in 1993 in a small book entitled *Japanese Netsuke in Oxford* written by Dr Oliver Impey, the former curator of Japanese art at the Ashmolean Museum.

In 2001 the netsuke collection of Dr Monica Barnett, a graduate of St. Anne's College, Oxford, was bequeathed to the Ashmolean Museum. This collection consisted of more than eighty *manjū* and transformed the Museum's holdings of this type of netsuke. Dr Barnett's approach to collecting was systematic and scholarly, assisted by a large library of books on Japanese art which was presented to the Museum with her collection. Indeed, much of the research for this catalogue has been done with the aid of her library. Dr Barnett's *manjū*, along with those from the Hildburgh, Christie-Miller and Oppenheim gifts, have been included in this catalogue, which will be the first ever book devoted to the subject of the *manjū* netsuke.

This authoritative catalogue has been compiled by Joyce Seaman who is a Research Assistant in the Department of Eastern Art. I would like to take this opportunity to thank her for her profound commitment to the museum and its Japanese collections over many years.

Professor Christopher Brown, CBE
Director, Ashmolean Museum

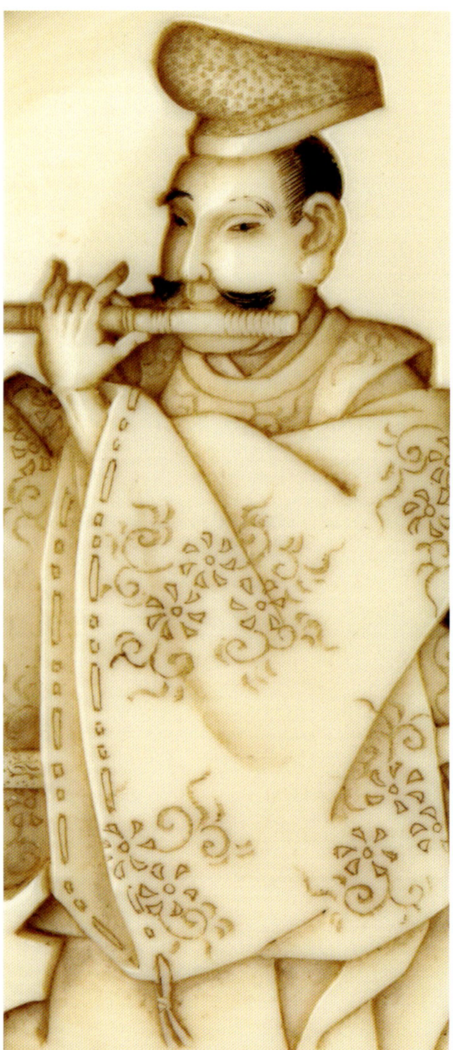

Cat. no. 73 (detail)

Foreword

by David Battie, FRSA

Many people will be familiar with the Japanese netsuke, made of a variety of materials and carved as figures, animals, vegetables or, seemingly, anything else. But there was another, less familiar form, the *manjū*, which resembled the eponymous rice cake. Netsuke were worn by all strata of society: samurai, farmers, peasants, artisans and merchants and their status (in that descending order) bore no indication of their wealth; one could be a lowly, but very rich, merchant or a high status, but impoverished, samurai.

The great Shogun, Tokugawa Ieyasu (ruled 1603-1605) would not have been familiar with the *manjū* netsuke as it had yet to be developed. The sixteenth century was a time of internecine strife with the samurai of one fiefdom under its *daimyō* (lord) slaughtering the inhabitants of the next-door territory. This left little time for the development of works of art. It was clear to Ieyasu that the wealth of Japan was being squandered and he determined to bring peace to the country. He succeeded and it was to last two hundred years.

The samurai, deprived of a use for their swords, turned themselves into objects of display. Gold, silver, complex amalgams of metals and the finest chasing embellished their swords, scabbards and fittings. Over time, what was formerly a practical iron *tsuba* (sword guard) morphed into a soft copper simulacrum, easy to decorate but useless, as it was unable to stop a blow from an opponent's sword. While the *inrō, ojime* and netsuke had to match the metalwork in quality, the set was often complementary in decoration, frequently in lacquer. The samurai might choose from his large collection of individual pieces, making up the set before strutting his stuff, much as a woman might select the right pieces of jewellery for her mood for that day. In an 1876 edict, the Emperor banned the wearing of swords. Without their swords the samurai's elaborate costume was redundant and it had the effect of the Japanese adopting western dress, which has pockets, making the *inrō* etc. surplus to requirements. They were sent to the west and were sold from barrels of good and not-so-good in, for example, Liberty of London, at sixpence and one shilling. There is little doubt that the sixpenny barrel would have contained *manjū* netsuke, for in the late nineteenth century the contemporary aesthetic would have held that three dimensions were far superior to two, hence the neglect of the *manjū* for over a century. But discriminating early Western collectors of netsuke in the 1870s and 1880s did not eschew *manjū* and they appear illustrated in the books of collections as well as, for example, Henri L. Joly's *Legends in Japanese Art* (1908). It is impossible to allocate a fine *manjū* to one layer of society or another and surviving *manjū* provide a false picture of the scope of the quality that was available. The western collectors, with bulging wallets, bought the best, as this catalogue demonstrates. The middle range also sold, but the bottom end did not: there are very few poor *manjū* in existence. By 1900, there was a number of collectors of taste and prices rose. This led to the production of forgeries, most poor, but some difficult to detect, amongst them *manjū* and *kagamibuta* in celluloid, which had the alternating dark and light lines of ivory built in. The alternating lines visible on genuine ivory are tubules, tiny tubes which run the whole length of the tusk and which contain a wax which gives ivory its fine polish. Oddly, unlike most copies of works of art, Japanese ivory netsuke made around the turn of the twentieth century can be fine quality and are collectable,

While the netsuke allowed the carver free rein to imagine whatever subject took his fancy, what appears at first sight a more simple form, the *manjū*, was at the time equally popular. In fact, the smooth form of the *manjū* makes it easier to slip up under the *obi* and less likely to snag.

The distribution of raw materials for netsuke was curious. Raw ivory was the monopoly of wholesalers who bought tusks and sawed them into discs which were then quartered and each piece weighed. The ivory blank was given to a carver and the details noted. When the finished netsuke was handed back it was weighed again and the loss in weight had to be paid for. For this reason, most netsuke retain their original, conical form. Given the distances involved, it might be assumed that the tusks came mainly from the Indian subcontinent but the sheen and colour of most Japanese ivory suggests that it was African.

It might be worth pointing out that the word ' carve' applied to ivory conjures up the wrong image. Distinct from a sharp blade and the Sunday joint, ivory cannot be cut. It can be sawn, drilled, sanded, filed and scraped and this last is most commonly used. *Manjū* would have been turned on a lathe and the image released by scraping. Most *okimono* netsuke depict animals or figures in frozen animation. The carvers of *manju* had much more freedom and could treat the surface as if it were a drawing or a scroll, (and many took these as inspiration) the figures could chase one another from the front to the back of the *manjū*. Great skill is needed in planning and carving the *manjū*, the most common subject of which is a pursuit between a protagonist on the front and a cowering victim on the rear. Shōki, the Demon Queller on the front and his devils, (*oni*), on the rear, are frequently depicted. Some *manjū* extend the subject into three parts by introducing a further scene on the interior of a *manjū*, often a scene of a sexual (*shunga*) nature, which splits peripherally. More often than not, the carver signed his work.

During the reign of the Meiji Emperor, Tokyo School bronzes and the ivory figures (*okimono*) are often depicted with an *inrō, ojime and* netsuke and the *manjū* appears far more often than the three dimensional *katabori* netsuke. It might be assumed that it would be logical to take a cross-section slice through a tusk to form the beginnings of a *manjū*, but the majority of *manjū* netsuke are formed from a longitudinal slice. There is good reason for this. The cross-section would always have a central black or brown dot, which is the remnant of the nerve canal and which could be disfiguring, whereas the longitudinal slice would have the attractive light and dark stripes which often form a grounding for the carved design.

No wearer of a *manjū* could be unaware of the similarity of his toggle to the moon which, legend has it, was home to the 'Hare which Pounds the Elixir of Life'. By extension, the *manjū* conferred old age on the wearer.

While interest in *manjū* has been growing, they still deserve greater recognition and this catalogue and exhibition will help to bring the 'Japanese Rice Cake' to a wider audience.

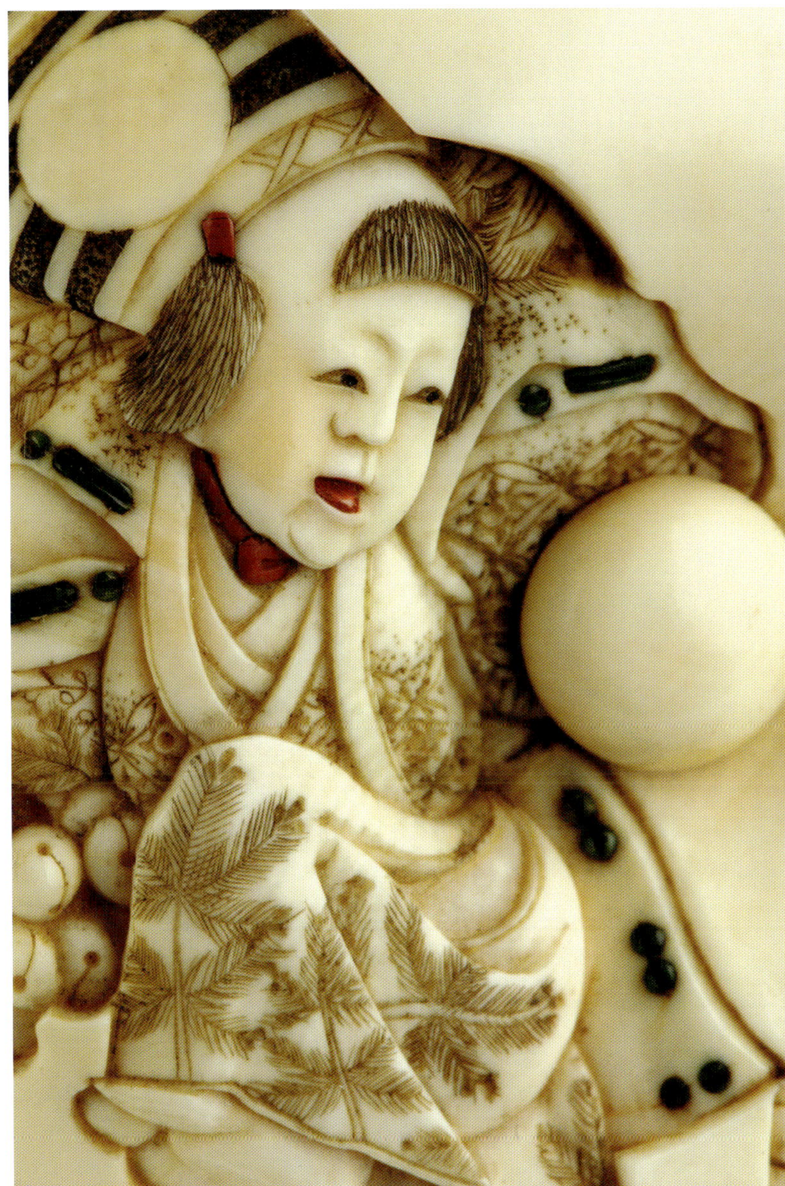

Cat. no. 49 (detail)

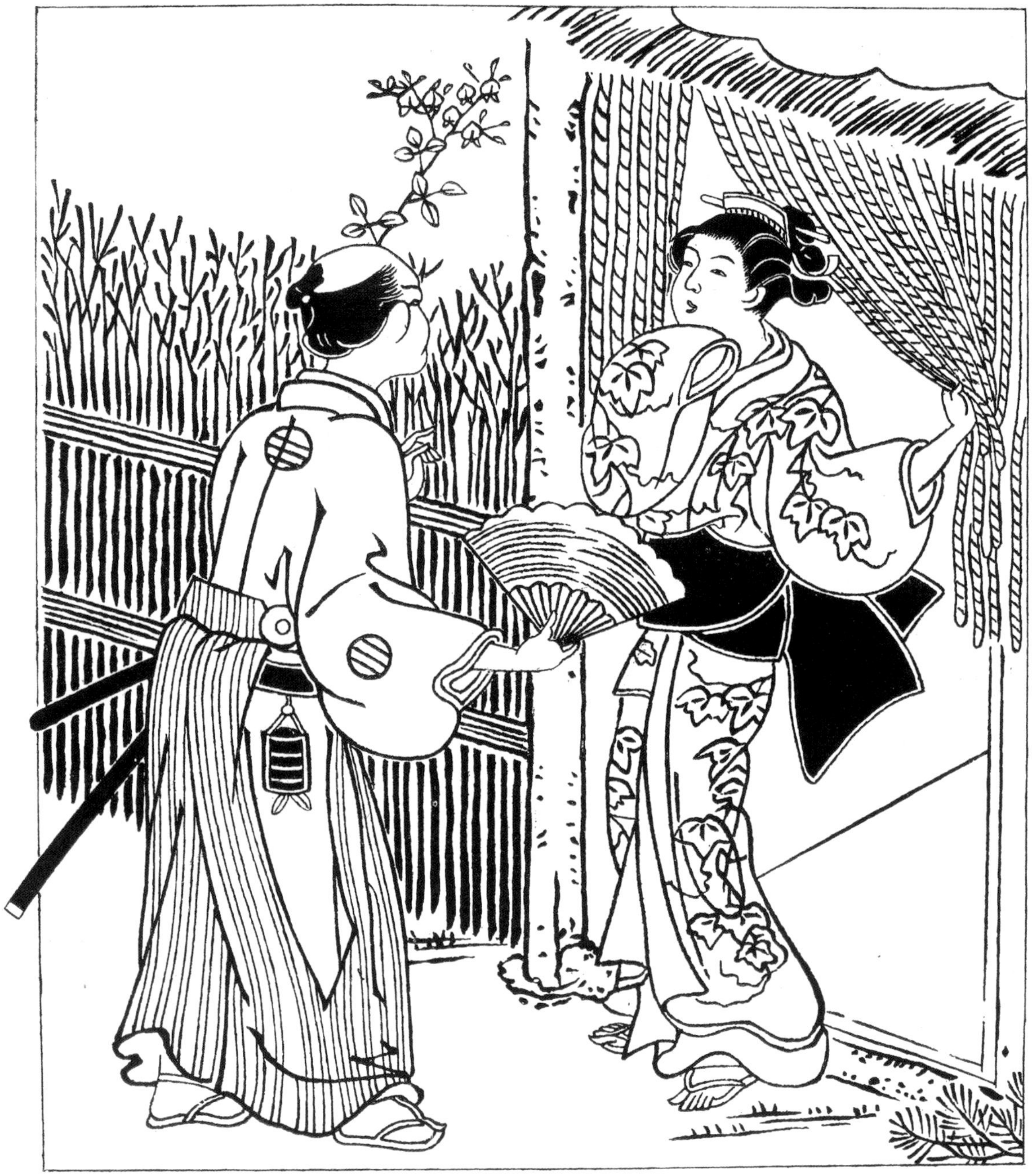

Fig. 1 Illustration from *Ehon chiie no Miyama* by Shimokawabe Jūsui, showing a man wearing an *inrō* ensemble

Introduction

When the question 'Do you know what a Japanese netsuke is?' was posed to a random selection of visitors to the Ashmolean Museum one morning, it revealed that at least two-thirds of those asked had never heard the word 'netsuke' and of those who had, only very few volunteered an accurate description.

The first purpose of this catalogue therefore, is to bring to a wider audience this art form in general and the *manjū* in particular, detailed knowledge of which is still only in the realms of the specialist. The *manjū*, which is named after a round, sweet bean-paste filled bun, has in the past few decades been virtually ignored, suffering as the poor relation of the *katabori* (carved in the round) netsuke. Various critics have been less than polite about them, which has not helped their cause. Perhaps one of the most damning was Jack Hillier's description of *manjū* as 'circular uninspiring buttons that seem the negation of all the qualities that we look for in a netsuke'.[1] This catalogue aims to point out the delights of these 'uninspiring buttons' and to encourage enthusiasm and marvel in the mind of the viewer, student or collector.

In 2001, a year after her death, the Ashmolean Museum received a very generous bequest of one hundred and three netsuke from the estate of Dr Monica Barnett, a collector for thirty years. Of these, eighty-nine were of the *manjū* type. This collection almost doubled the museum's existing netsuke holdings, most of which were of the *katabori* type. The imminent major refurbishment of the Ashmolean Museum afforded little time to study the new collection before it was all packed away in boxes for several years. When it finally emerged, after the museum's re-opening in December 2010, the idea of a small exhibition and a catalogue of *manjū* netsuke evolved. Around twenty *manjū* given by different collectors, some of whose gifts date back to the early part of the last century, have been gathered together with the Barnett pieces to form this catalogue.

In 1984 Dr Monica Barnett was invited by Eskenazi Ltd of London to contribute an essay on *manjū* for the catalogue of their October exhibition. Her description of a *manjū* netsuke is as apt today as it was then, so an excerpt has been included here.

> The manju is a netsuke of distinctive form, in the shape of the cake or bun of this name. In origin it was circular, but it can also be oval, square, rectangular or hexagonal. It usually is slightly convex and can sometimes be domed. Like all netsuke it can be made of wood, ivory, metal, metal alloy, lacquer, pressed horn etc. Sometimes the manju is two-part, split horizontally, the two pieces fitting together, the lower half having a central hole for the cord to pass through to an eyelet in the upper half. The manju can also be solid, the fastening being effected by means of a peg *(mekugi)* with a hole in its lower end, the peg sitting

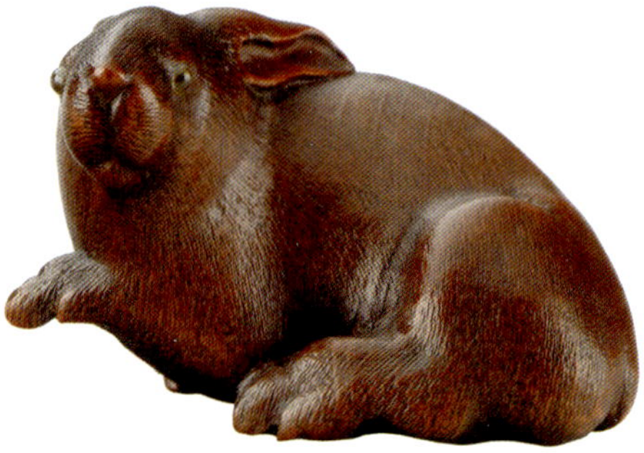

Fig. 2 *Katabori* netsuke of a hare by Shōmin (EA1996.24)

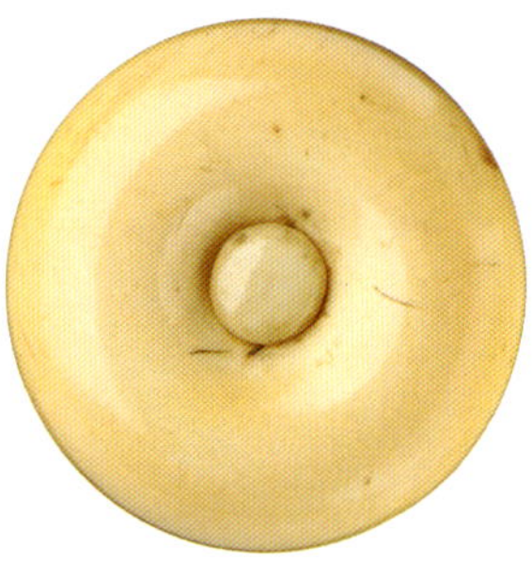

Fig. 3 A plain solid *manjū* netsuke with central peg (cat. no. 123)

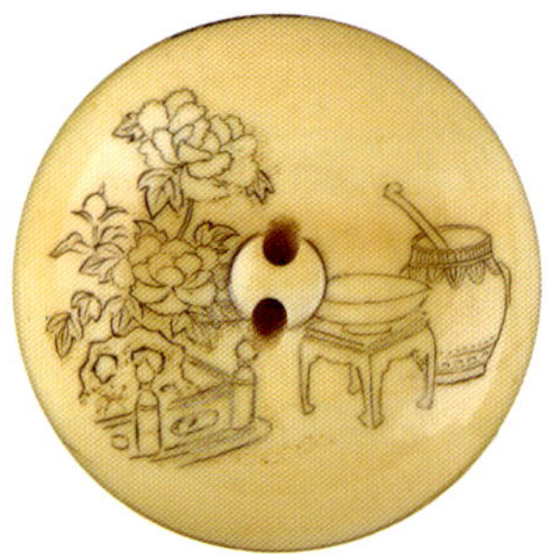

Fig. 4 *Manjū* reverse showing *himotōshi* (cat no. 7)

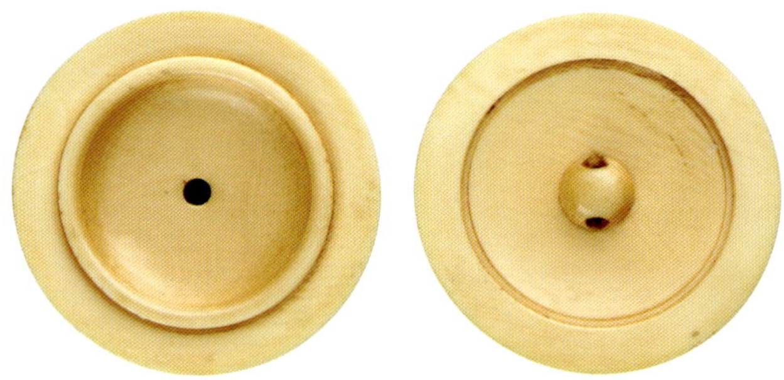

Fig. 5 Cat. no. 68 showing interior fixing arrangement

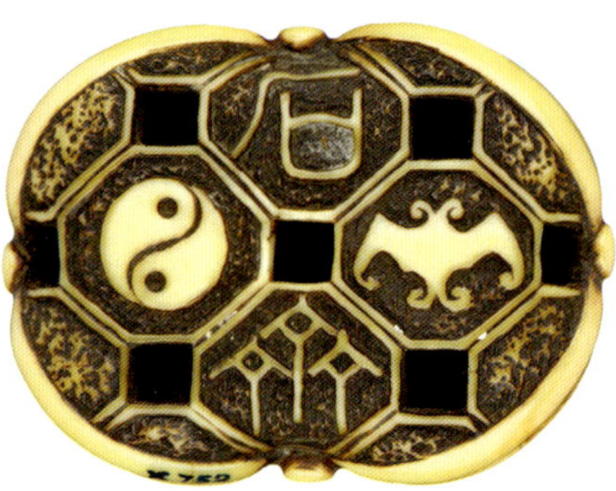

Fig. 6 *Ryūsa* netsuke (cat. no. 107)

in a round hole drilled in the centre of the manju. The top of this peg is sometimes decorated. Another means of fastening a solid manju is a two-channel hole (*himotōshi*); in older netsuke the two openings are usually of a good size and unequal, the larger accommodating the cord knot. Finally a manju can be attached to a chain by means of a ring.

The *Ryūsa* manju is named after the carver who invented the technique. It is made of wood or ivory which is hollowed or perforated. The *Ryūsa* too can be of different sizes and shapes, and fastened like a manju Sometimes the *Ryūsa* has a metal motif which fits snugly into the space it adorns. This insert (*kanamono*) has an eyelet on the reverse through which the cord is fastened. The manju differs from the netsuke not only in shape but in its rendering of the subject. It is nearly always two-dimensional whereas the netsuke is three-dimensional. The obverse of the manju can be carved in high or low relief (*ukibori*) or deeply undercut (*sukashibori*). The reverse often continues the scene or incident shown on the obverse or shows some other object connected with the same hero. Occasionally the reverse bears no apparent thematic link with the obverse.'[2]

What are the qualities we look for in a netsuke? They need to be tactile, inviting you to fondle them in the hand; they must be compact with no protrusions and the skill of the carver's knife must be apparent. It is fair to say that a hare with amber eyes may have more charm and instant appeal than a battle scene meticulously carved on a 'bun'. The excitement of a *manjū* comes on another level, the knowledge of the stories or themes these carvings represent and the elucidation of a scene by an extra hint on the reverse. The carver's skill must not be discounted either, as we shall see later.

Fig. 7 *Kagamibuta* netsuke. Takeuchi no Sukune on a boat receiving the sacred jewels from Ryūjin by Ozawa Shūraku (EA2001.120)

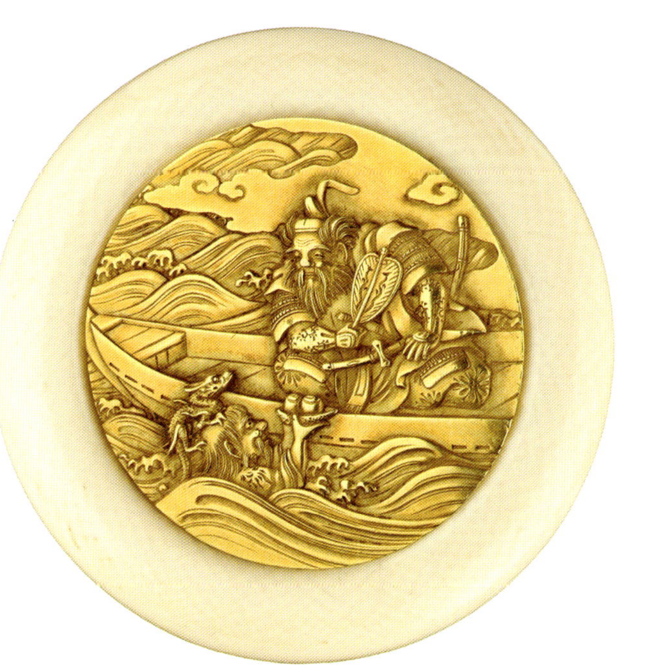

Netsuke come in a myriad of different shapes and sizes. They are divided into a number of groups, the most frequently encountered amongst them being: the *katabori* netsuke (fig. 2); the *manjū*, which is sometimes of one solid piece with a central peg (fig. 3), or with *himotōshi* (fig. 4), or divided into two (fig. 5) with a hoop for the cord inside; *Ryūsa* netsuke, which are carved with a perforated design and are grouped in the *manjū* category (fig. 6); and *Kagamibuta* netsuke, which have a flat metal plate inserted into a bowl of another material (fig. 7).

Netsuke should not be studied in isolation, for the netsuke formed part of a set and it is interesting that Dr Barnett makes no mention of the things to which a *manjū* might have been attached. For centuries people across the world and in particular across the Asian continent have carried essential objects at their waists in bags or pouches hanging from cords,

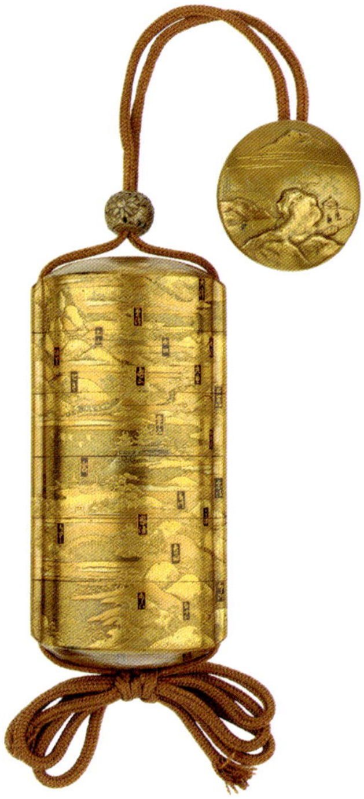

Fig. 8 *Inrō* ensemble depicting the Fifty-three Stations of the Tōkaidō (cat. no. 61)

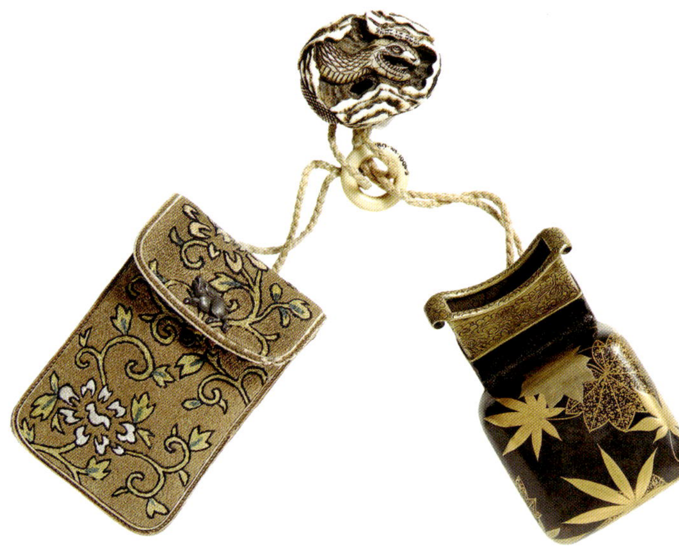

Fig. 9 Purse and a most unusual *metsubishi*, a device which held powder to blow in the eyes of an attacker, in order temporarily to blind him, with ivory *manjū* (Pitt Rivers Museum, Oxford 1980.34.1040)

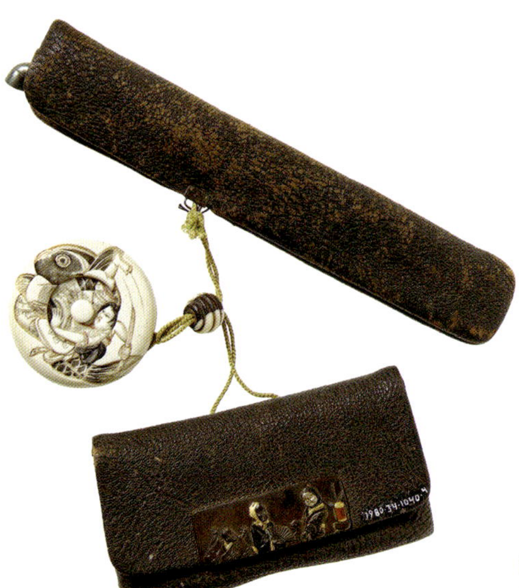

Fig. 10 Tobacco pouch, pipe case and ivory *manjū* (Pitt Rivers Museum, Oxford 1980.34.1040)

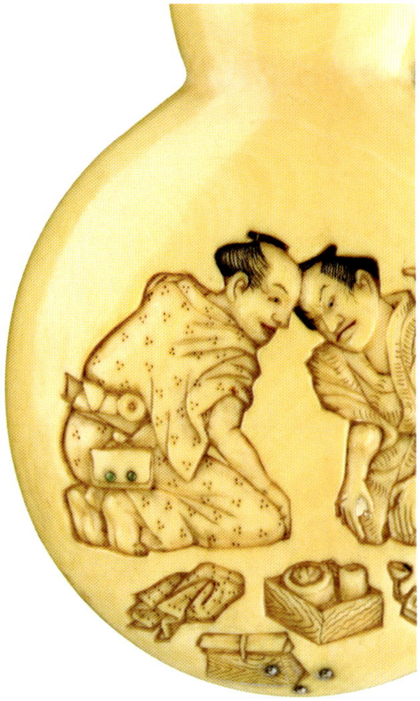

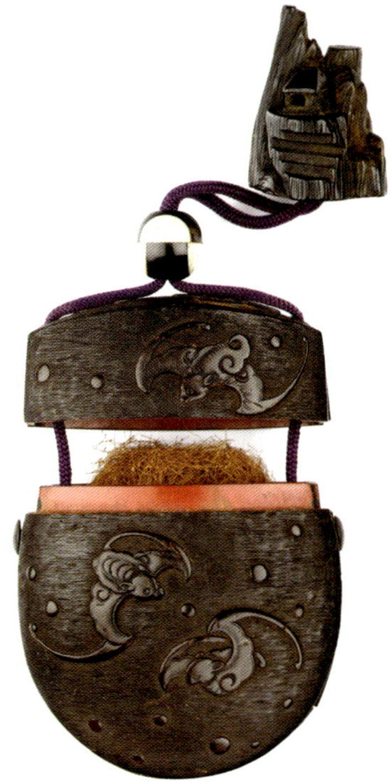

Above left: Fig. 11 A make-up case showing a *tabako-ire* worn with *manjū* (EA2001.39 close-up)

Above right: Fig. 12 This box, made with a veneer of coconut shell, is decorated with bats and still has very finely cut tobacco inside (EA1978.147)

strings or belts. The netsuke's function was to act as a toggle to hold in place 'hanging things' (*sagemono*) which were suspended from the waist sash. These included medicine boxes (*inrō*) (fig. 8), purses (*kinchaku*) (fig. 9), and tobacco pouches (*tabako-ire*) and pipes (*kiseru*) (fig. 10). Fig. 11, from a make-up case, shows a *tabako-ire* worn with *manjū*. Tobacco was also kept in a *tonkotsu* (tobacco box), which was usually made of wood in the style of an *inrō* with one compartment, and also had cords running through the sides. This was attached to a netsuke or a pipe case or sometimes to both (fig. 12).

In Japan, the first objects used to secure these *sagemono* were rudimentary items such as natural roots, nuts, wooden sticks, shells, stones or small gourds. They were insignificant, practical objects, which gradually, over several hundred years, evolved into miniature works of art to display wealth and status. Around the beginning of the seventeenth century these randomly shaped toggles began to evolve into ring-shaped pieces of metal or ivory, through which the waist sash (*obi*) could be threaded. Genre screens from the early Edo period (1603–1868) show these attached to an assortment of shaped pouches and bags, frequently more than one piece hanging from the same ring. From this ring-shaped netsuke, a solid circular slice of ivory with a central hole came into being and its further evolution brought about the *manjū* netsuke. It sat on top of the *obi* and the cord slipped behind it next to the kimono, the container hanging below. This new arrangement allowed the wearer to keep his sash tied should he have need to remove the ensemble. Between the netsuke and the *sagemono*, a bead (*ojime*) was fitted, which slid up and down the cords and held the bag or pouch closed or the layers of an *inrō* pressed tightly together.

Background

Edo period Japan (1600–1868) was a society ruled by the Tokugawa Shoguns and structured along Neo-Confucian lines into four socially distinctive layers: samurai or warriors, farmers, artisans and merchants. The imperial family were above all in the hierarchy, but were powerless, conducting only ceremonial duties. The seat of government moved from Kyoto to Edo (Tokyo) at the beginning of the seventeenth century. Because the samurai and their overlords (*daimyō*) were required by the Tokugawa regime to live in Edo in alternate years leaving their wives and heirs in the capital (*sankin kōtai*), a great deal of expenditure was required for the upkeep of two estates and the travelling back and forth to their domains with, in some cases, several hundred attendants. This soon began to deplete the financial reserves of some families. Artisans and merchants benefitted from this system as they were the providers of the food, the clothing and the many accoutrements necessary for the samurai class. They were also the money changers and lenders. By the end of the Edo period there were many impoverished samurai, while the merchants had grown rich at their expense.

In various seventeenth century publications, we learn that by the middle of the century hanging accessories were common amongst men, whereas women tucked their small essential items into the front folds of their kimono. *Inrō* are mentioned as early as the fourteenth century in dictionaries, diaries and illustrated encyclopaedias of clothing accessories.[3] Among these items hung from the waist were containers for seals and seal paste for signing documents, a practice which originated in China. All samurai were required to use a seal on official documents in the early Edo period, later all documents needed to be sealed. Originally *inrō* were only carried by the samurai class. As the *inrō* developed, so its use expanded and changed principally into a holder for powdered medicines. In *Takaragura* (Treasure House), a collection of stories written in 1660, the poet Yamaoka Genrin (1631–1672) states 'Inro are good for carrying paper prayers when visiting shrines and also good for holding alms to give to beggars along the way. One can put medicine in them too, for one's own emergencies or for others. They are useful for holding ointment for the eyes and preserving bits of cooked food. Although they are small, their uses are unlimited. They are about three inches long ...'[4] By 1777 *Shikigusa* (Grasses of the Four Seasons), Ise Sadatake's book on historical precedent, reports that 'these days, even common people are wearing *kinchaku* (purse) and *inrō* suspended from the sash, but they do not use them for carrying medicine. They just like the exotic effect such articles have. These objects have become nothing more than ornament to show off to other people. Now they have lost their function and are mere popular trifles.'[5]

The tobacco pouch (*tabako-ire*) and the tobacco box (*tonkotsu*) were, however, not 'mere popular trifles'.[6] By the middle of the eighteenth century one or other had become an essential for all townsmen, farmers and artisans who could possibly afford to smoke. Tobacco was introduced into Japan by the Portuguese in the late sixteenth century and by the first decade of the

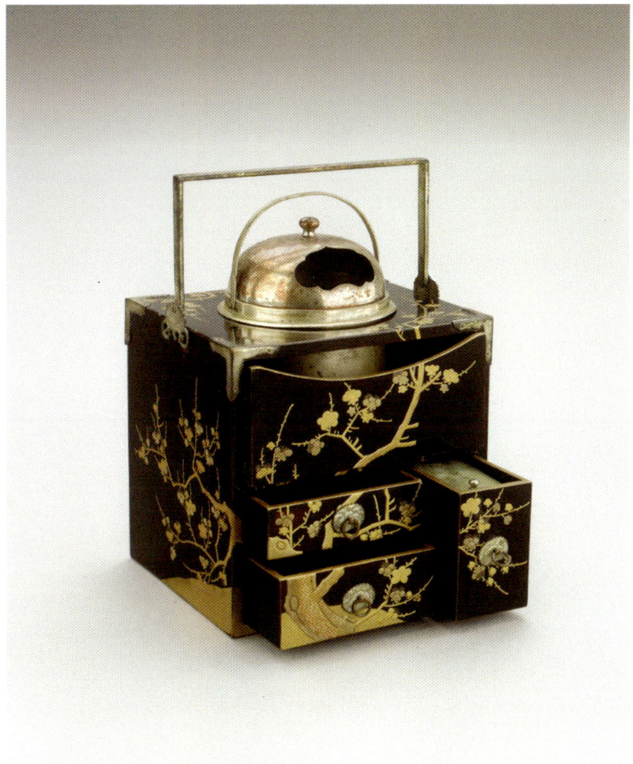

Fig. 13 Tobacco box (EAX.1148)

seventeenth century was being grown in Japan, immediately making it more affordable than imported tobacco. The addictive power of the 'fragrant weed', as the nineteenth century British Japanologist, Basil Hall Chamberlain referred to it,[7] had soon taken its hold on the nation. Both men and women throughout the country and across all strata of the social hierarchy were smokers. The Tokugawa government tried to issue laws to forbid its use, deeming it unclean and a drain on the economy. But people would smoke in the privacy of their homes and flout the rules in public. Proving impossible to enforce, the laws were relaxed in 1667 and were finally repealed in 1716.

Tobacco was originally kept wrapped in folded papers and slipped inside the kimono, but as the eighteenth century progressed, tobacco boxes (*tonkotsu*), attached in the same way as an *inrō*, and *tabako-ire* became *de rigeur* for fashionable townsmen (*chōnin*) and were made with ever more expensive, often imported fabrics and exotic leathers. The various smoking accessories including pipes and pipe cases were produced in large numbers, and these too became extravagant luxury items. Until the 1750s a host would provide tobacco for his guest, using a box similar in shape to that shown in fig. 13. The pipe and everything the guest needed was contained within the box (*tabako-bon*). After that the custom changed and a man carried his own tobacco at his waist, hung from a netsuke. Samurai did not carry tobacco, as their servants carried and prepared it for them. A smoker might have several of each component of the tobacco smoking set, including a selection of *manjū*, and would match them according to the occasion or the season or simply to provide a

Below: Fig. 14 Illustration from *Ehon imayō sugata* by Utagawa Toyokuni (1769–1825) showing a geisha smoking a long pipe (EA2012.148)

Right: Fig. 15 The Actor Onoe Hatsusuke holding a pipe. Colour woodblock print by Katsukawa Shunshō (1726–1793) (EAX.4823)

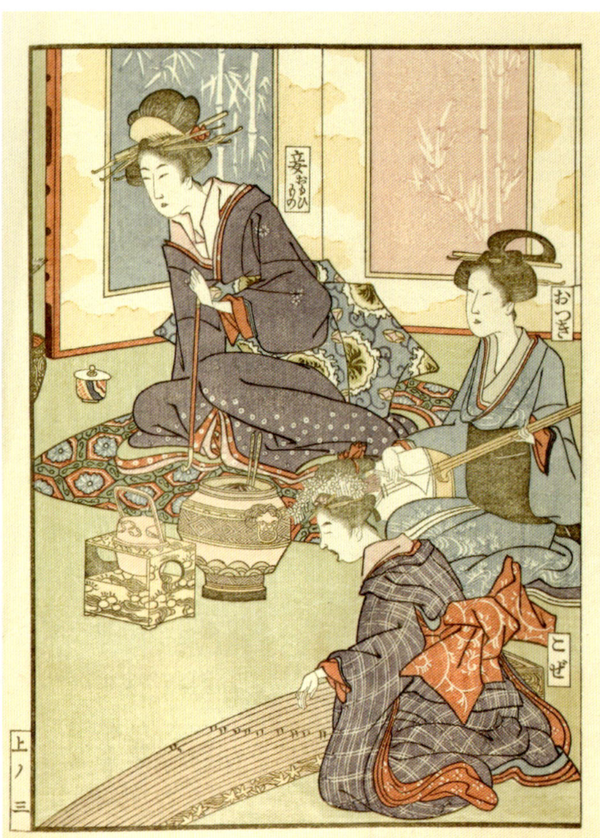

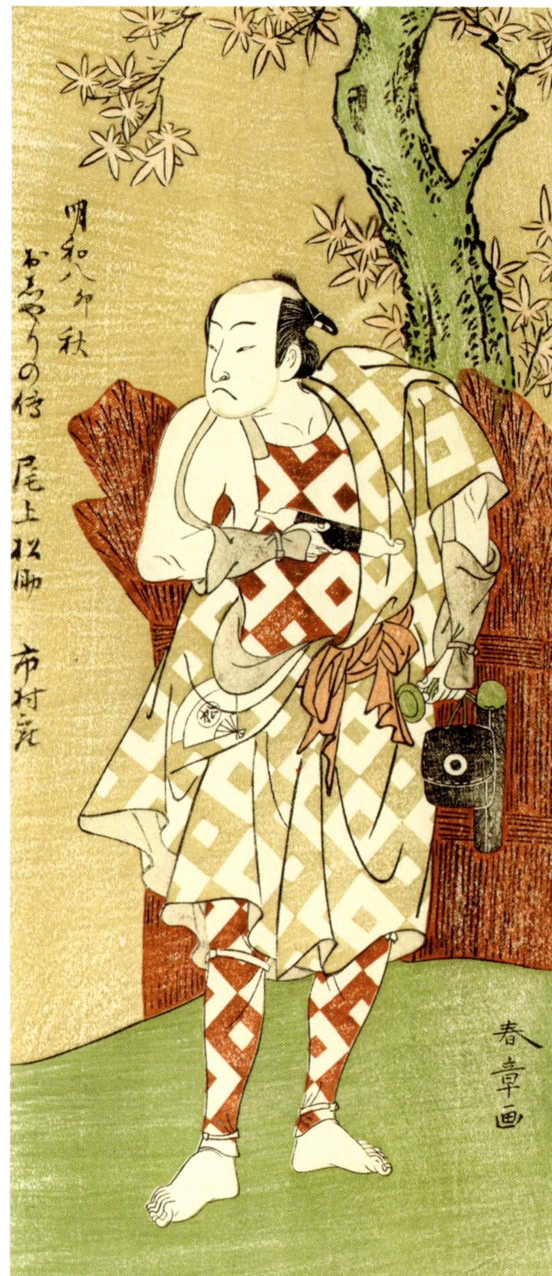

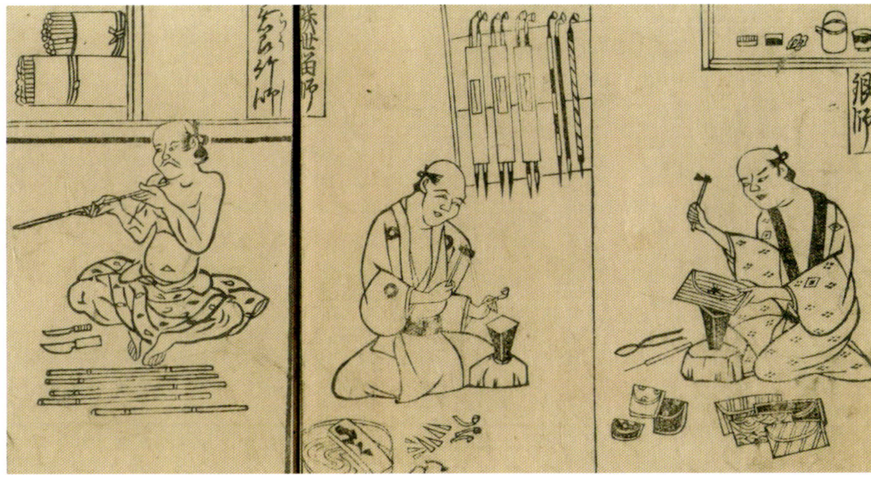

Fig. 16 Pipe, purse and pouch makers, from *Jinrin kinmō zui* (Illustrated Instructions for Proper Behaviour), vol. 5 p. 11 (National Diet Library, 292592443/11 and 12)

conversation piece. Many shops selling these various accoutrements sprang up in Edo to meet the demand. Even after the introduction of Western dress in the 1870s, there were still about a thousand pouch shops in Edo, by then known as Tokyo.[8]

To support the weight of most of these pouches, the larger *manjū* or *kagamibuta* netsuke were the chosen anchor. Smoking was probably the single most important impetus for the making and continuation of *manjū* netsuke. As more and more people could afford to smoke, the demand for smoking paraphernalia increased. The pipe evolved from the impractical length of about one metre, when it was used communally (fig. 14), to something much more portable, about one third of that length (fig. 15). The bowl was very small allowing only about two or three puffs. Sometimes the pipe case was attached with cords or chains directly to the tobacco pouch, which was tucked inside the top of the sash without using a netsuke.

All this smoking equipment could be very costly and involved several artists: the leather worker, the cord makers, the metalworkers who produced the pouch fittings, the pipes and – where a *kagamibuta* type of netsuke was used – the plates, and the netsuke carver who might also make the bowl (fig. 16).

Who were the craftsmen who made *manjū*? The Edo period witnessed a great 'flowering' as it is often called, of all aspects of the decorative arts. Netsuke as an art form were relatively new in the early seventeenth century, but by the closing decade '*Jinrin kinmō zui*' (Illustrated Instructions for Proper Behaviour) which is divided into six sections – arts, industry, merchants, artisans, work and austerities – records that netsuke makers could be found in the Teramachi area of Kyoto and also elsewhere.[9] Many of the finest *katabori* netsuke were made in the Kansai area (around Osaka and Kyoto) and in the regional centres such as Iwami, on the northwest coast; Hida, the area around Takayama; Tanba, north of Kyoto; and in Nagoya. However, the *manjū* featured in this catalogue were made considerably later than this in the nineteenth century in Tokyo or

Osaka. The first book to devote a significant amount of space to netsuke was a seven-volume publication of 1781 treating swords and sword makers as its focus. *Sōken Kishō's*[10] final volume is devoted to netsuke carvers. It lists over fifty carvers and illustrates many figures, mostly of Chinese immortals and historical figures who were the subject matter of many early netsuke. These late eighteenth century craftsmen were figural not *manjū* carvers. At that time *katabori* netsuke were more likely to have been carved by the makers of Buddhist sculptures working in wood, or the plectrum makers using ivory.

The system in Japan for artists and craftsmen was one of apprenticeship, sometimes starting in the early teenage years. A master could have several pupils, perhaps his own son or an adopted son to whom he would slowly, over many years, teach his techniques and secrets. His hope would be to hand on the workshop and its reputation to the next generation. Little personal knowledge is available on the *manjū* carvers, with a few notable exceptions.

Several 'schools', as they were referred to by early Western collectors, feature prominently in the Ashmolean Museum's collection; four pieces in the collection are signed by various carvers of the Kikugawa group, many of whom signed only 'Kikugawa' on their work, making it hard to pinpoint a particular maker on the signature alone. Another five pieces are by the master craftsman Meikeisai Hōjitsu, about whom we know a little more and some of whose pupils were given characters from his name once they had satisfied their teacher that they were skilled enough to carry on the high reputation of his workshop: for example Hōichi and Ippōsai took the character '*hō*' 法 and Meisai and Meijitsu chose or were given '*mei*' 明 to use in their name. Moritoshi Kōsai's work and that of his workshop is sometimes followed by a distinctive circular 'crane' *kakihan* (stamp) after his signature, which also identifies other carvers with whom he was connected. Several pieces from his workshop appear in this catalogue. Ono Ryōmin, another skilled netsuke and *okimono* (small ornamental sculpture) maker, also had many pupils, all of whose names began with '*Ono*'. Fortunately the collection has three pieces by Ono Ryōmin, but is lacking the work of his students. Artists' profiles, where known, will be added to the catalogue text, in the signature section.

Materials

The vast majority of *manjū* in this collection are made of ivory, the other materials used being various metals and metal alloys, lacquer, wood, stag antler, pressed horn, tagua nut and coral. This does not necessarily mirror the proportions of *manjū* made in the Edo period, for many fine lacquer *inrō* were made en suite with lacquer *manjū*, but there happens to be only one of these sets in the Ashmolean's collection (cat. no. 61). It just happens that Dr Barnett particularly favoured ivory carving. *Manjū*, could be made from so many different materials that the list becomes very long if all the indigenous and exotic woods are included.

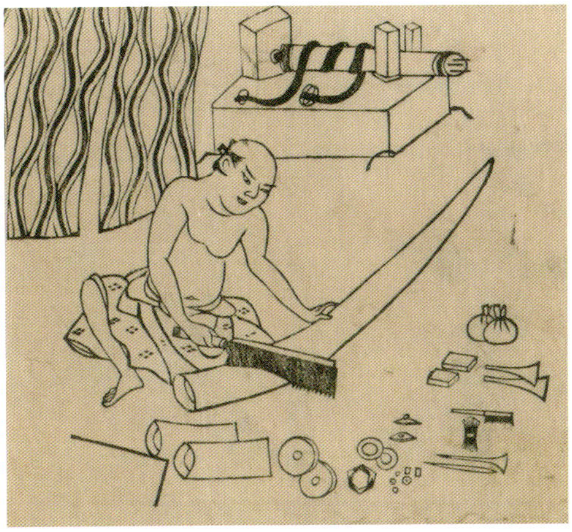

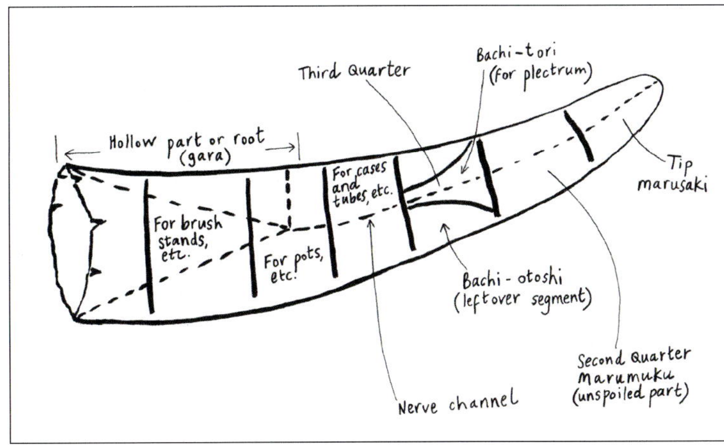

Left: Fig. 17 The ivory craftsman from *Jinrin kinmō zui* (Illustrated Instructions for Proper Behaviour), Vol. 5 p.9 (National Diet Library, 2592443/10)

Right: Fig. 18 The division of a tusk (Drawing by Unity Coombes)

Elephant tusks from India and Africa were imported into Japan throughout the Edo Period. Indian elephant ivory is whiter than the creamy coloured African tusk. The tusk is an upper incisor tooth with one third, the root, buried within the head of the animal. This part has a conical-shaped soft pulpy centre which gradually tapers away as the tusk grows outside the skull. With skill, this central part of the section of tusk being worked can be positioned to coincide with the central peg hole of the *manjū*.

Fig. 17 shows an illustration of an ivory carver cutting lengths of an elephant's tusk, which would be used for different purposes, one of which was the *manjū* netsuke. On the ground in front of him are several shapes that he has been able to make, including two thick rings with small holes suitable for *manjū*. In the background can be seen the hand-driven lathe operated by pulling on the rope.

Fig. 18 shows how the tusk is divided up. Ivory is a dense, hard substance, but is soft enough to be worked with the carver's tools and a fine smooth surface can be achieved with polishing. Patina comes with age and with handling which results in ivory of a rich deep golden colour, seen on some of the *manjū*. Others have been stained all over (cat. no. 97) to create the aged look. Once the basic shape had been cut, the lathe was used to refine the contours. The split type was probably made from a piece of the tusk nearer to the end, where the ivory is solid.

Under a magnifying glass, it is possible to see a pattern of lines, sometimes known as Schreger lines, which criss-cross within the material, and by examining the angles at which they cross, it is possible to determine the part of the tusk from which the section comes (fig. 19, overleaf). The nearer to the centre of the tusk, the sharper are the angles of intersection. Ivory was a luxury material so the carver would be anxious not to waste any of the tusk. Items such as the central pegs (*meguki*), and *ojime* could be made from smaller pieces.

Walrus tusk was also used (cat. no. 12). It is heavier than other ivories and becomes a rich amber colour with time. It also has a crystalline or marbled centre, which carvers sometimes tried to disguise with decoration.

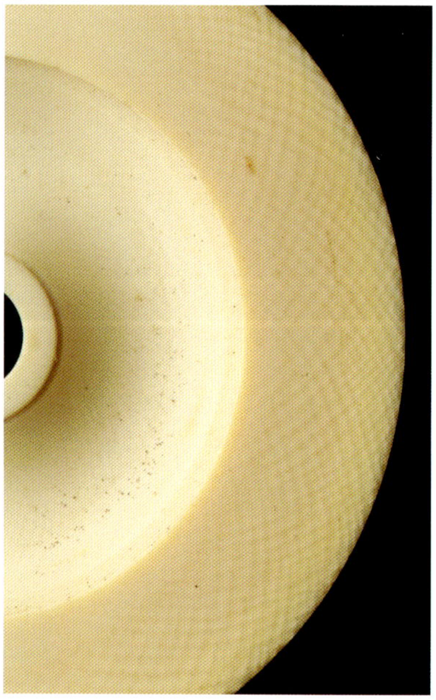

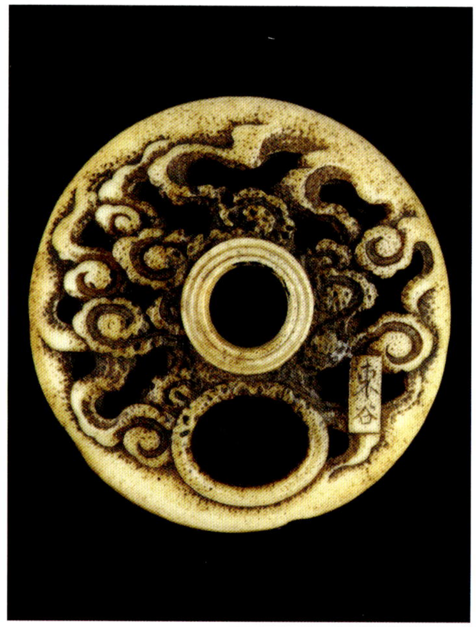

Left: Fig. 19 Schreger lines (cat. no. 48, detail)

Right: Fig. 20 Stag antler (cat. no. 23, reverse)

Stag antler was the favoured material of the carvers who worked in the Asakusa area of Tokyo towards the end of the nineteenth century. Antlers have a porous centre and multiple small capillary holes can often be seen on the surface of stag antler netsuke (fig. 20). The Asakusa carvers made many perforated *ryūsa* type netsuke to which this material was well suited, for the porous centre could be hollowed out. It is harder than ivory and therefore more difficult to work with, however the advantage was that it was cheap and readily available, for the stag sheds his antlers every year.

The tools of an ivory carver were numerous: many different sized and shaped gouges, chisels and knives for the carving and dozens of other abrasive tools and equipment for the polishing. Over two hundred different tools might be owned and used by one carver. Two diagrams showing thirty six of the Meiji period carver Gyokuzan's tools, artistically arranged around a central point, label each tool with a different name. No doubt this was only a small selection from his array.[11] Polishing was done in stages beginning with coarse sandpapers proceeding to fine black emery paper – sometimes special leaves were used at this stage – and finally various fine grit powders. Wax could be used to bring up a glossy surface.

Netsuke are often stained, sometimes only partially in highlights, but the old stain recipes seem to have been kept as safely guarded secrets (fig. 21). In the well-known carver Masatoshi's book on carving, which was translated by Raymond Bushell and published in 1992, the craftsman mentions fumigation with burning incense *(ibushi)* which cannot be relied on to give an even distribution of colour, *yashadama* (cones from alder trees), a mixture made from gardenia berries (*gamboge*) and black ink (*sumi*) for hair and highlights.[12] Modern carvers may use the liquid of black walnut or pecan shells. All these processes need very careful preparation and application, as Masatoshi explains in the

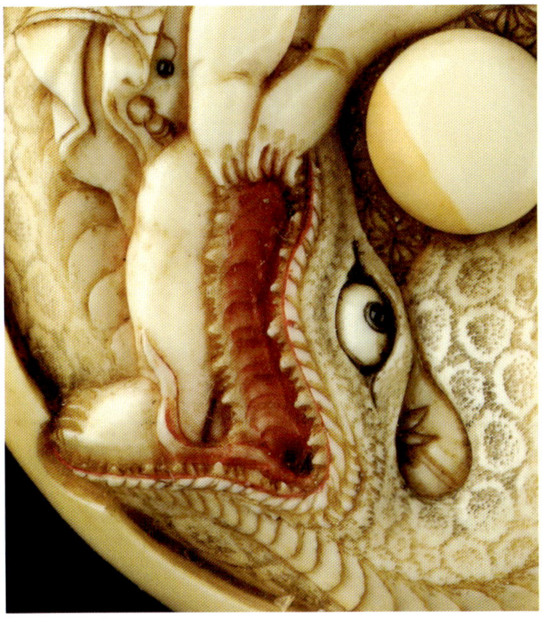

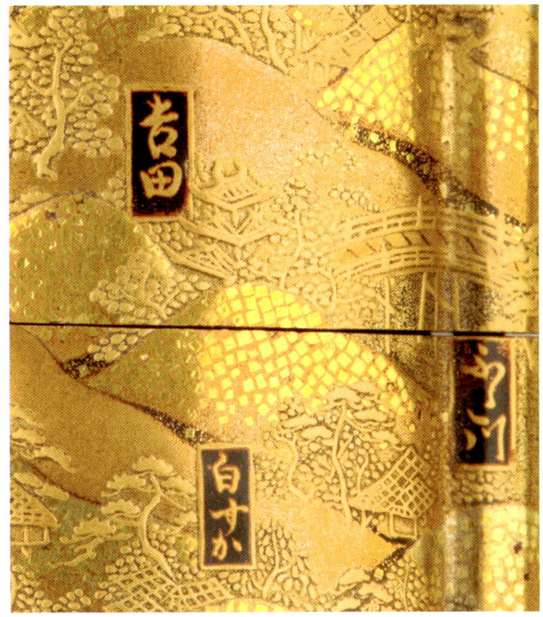

Left: Fig. 21 Detail of red and black staining (cat. no. 61, detail)

Right: Fig. 22 *Kirikane* (cat. no. 79, detail)

book. Three methods of ivory carving are demonstrated in this collection. Sunken relief *shishiaibori* is most commonly found carved on the front of a *manjū*. The design is carved beneath the surface. *Ukibori* is the opposite, where the design sits proud of the surface. Frequently found on the reverse of *manjū* is a sketchier rendering of the theme, done in fine lines, like an etched drawing. This is known as *kebori*.

Lacquer *manjū* were made in much the same way as *inrō*, the process being far less complicated by reason of the simple domed circular shape. This would have had a base made of either a light cypress wood, leather or fabric. Onto this base the lacquerer would apply the many layers of lacquer, each one requiring drying and polishing in between. Once satisfied with the coating, the *maki-e* (sprinkled picture) artist, possibly the same person, would apply his design with *tsutsu* (hollow bamboo tube) and different grades of metal powders. Sometimes, as in the case of fig. 22, minute squares of gold leaf (*kirikane*) would be set into the wet lacquer surface to enhance the richness of the decoration. In the process known as *tsuishu* the carver used his tools to carve into the layers of red lacquer, in a technique which dates at least as far back as the Sung period in China. (cat. nos. 19 and 20).

Two *manjū* came to the collection catalogued as 'pressed horn' (cat. nos. 80 and 85). These, according to Arende H. Kempers, were made from horses' hooves[13] and Alain Ducros says that imported Indian buffalo hooves were used.[14] Whichever it was (or perhaps both were used) the horn was powdered, boiled and pressed into a mould. The mould could be used several times and although it is not known how many times, it is not unusual to see several of the same design. Subjects are almost always historical. Alain Ducros says they were the first manufactured netsuke of the Meiji period. Norman Sandfield has had some of his 'pressed horn' netsuke tested by the scientific firm, McCrone and this has revealed that they are made of cross-linked casein[15] Further scientific research is therefore required for the two netsuke in the Ashmolean Museum.

The kernel inside the nut of the tagua palm tree *(phytelephas macrocarpasis)* has a dark brown skin over a hard, white, cellulose centre, which can be carved and was occasionally used for netsuke. It grows in the tropical forests of South America. The *manjū* seen in cat. no. 117 is made of this natural material and embellished with silver.

Woods native to Japan vary in density and colour enormously but even without this it is not always easy to identify them and certainly not with the naked eye. Exotic woods were imported into Japan. After carving some were stained, making colour an unreliable marker. A study of grain, density and weight helps with identification. The solid little ebony figure of Hotei enveloped in his sack, for example (cat. no. 36) is very heavy for its size and the wood grain very close, whereas the plain wood disc inlaid with cloisonné enamel (cat. no. 122) is the opposite, light and relatively coarse-grained. Alain Ducros illustrates an array of these woods with colour photographs.[16] Coral came from the South Seas and was a luxury material. It was seldom used for *manjū* netsuke; the piece described in cat. no. 104 has probably been adapted from a Chinese pendant. An article written in 1917 reported that Japan was turning to a new tourist industry in coral, for previously about half of Japan's crude coral was exported to Italy and 'there the workmen carved it into the various forms popular with the tourists'.[17]

Sources of themes and designs

'The Japanese look to China as we look to Italy and Greece: for them it is the classic land, the source from which their art has drawn not only methods, materials, and principals of design, but an endless variety of theme and motif'; so states Laurence Binyon, Keeper of Oriental Prints and Paintings at the British Museum from 1892–1933.[18]

Japan's virtual isolation from the outside world during the Edo period had a profound effect on the decorative arts. In the late fifteenth and sixteenth centuries Japan had undergone almost one hundred years of civil war until it was united under the Tokugawa government when peace finally prevailed and Tokugawa Ieyasu became the first of a long line of Tokugawa shoguns who ruled for almost two hundred and fifty years. During the period of Tokugawa rule the country was almost completely isolated from the outside world. Trade with Portugal, which had brought tobacco to the shores of Japan during the sixteenth century, ceased. Christianity arrived with Jesuit missionaries in the sixteenth century and by the early seventeenth century was beginning to take a hold on parts of the country, which the Tokugawa government considered threatening to the stability of the nation. Christians began to be persecuted and killed and many fled, but continued to worship clandestinely. From 1639 all foreigners except a handful of Dutch and Chinese were expelled. Both groups of foreign nationals had to live and trade in Nagasaki and their activities were very carefully monitored.

Printed foreign books also came under a government ban from 1640, until in 1720 they were finally allowed to enter the country again. This lifting of the ban brought a new intellectual curiosity which filtered right down through the social system. Dutch scientific books began to be studied but those that had the greatest influence on netsuke came from China.

In the centuries before the Tokugawa shoguns took charge, scrolls, paintings, carvings and sutras brought back from China by monks sent there to study had provided information and inspiration to Japanese artists.

An important source for early netsuke carvers was *Liexian quanzhuan* (Illustrated Accounts of Immortals) which described and illustrated over five hundred deities and was so popular that it was translated into Japanese as *Yūshō ressen zenden* (Complete Illustrated Lives of Immortals) in 1650. Many early netsuke figures can be traced to these images.

Sanguozhi pinghua (The Romance of the Three Kingdoms) a novel about the events which took place during the Han dynasty (206 BC–AD 220), when the Chinese Empire was divided into three warring states, was another source of ideas for subject matter. It drew on historical accounts, drama and poetry. It became an important illustrated Chinese epic and spread through Korea to Japan where it was translated. It reflects the Confucian values of loyalty to family, superiors and friends, and self-denial. This sat well with the Tokugawa government's Neo-Confucian system of thought.

Many of the religious figures and folklore heroes from these books were given Japanese names and were integrated into the Japanese pantheon and into the cultural life of Japan.

The *Konjaku Monogatari* (An Anthology of Tales from the Past), a compilation of mostly folkloric tales from India, China and Japan published in the late Heian Period (794–1185), was a very important source of subject matter as were the books recounting the exploits of the founders of the island race of Japan which are told in a combination of historical and mythical events in the early historical accounts, *Nihongi* (Japanese Chronicles) and *Kojiki* (Record of Ancient Matters). Shintō rituals are described, as well as the important beginnings of the imperial line which has continued throughout the centuries until the present.

During medieval times, when Japan suffered long periods of conflict, war heroes emerged whose stories were told and retold until they too entered the realms of myth and legend. *Heike Monogatari* (The Tale of the Heike) charted the rise and fall of the Taira clan (Heike) and its final defeat at the hands of the Minamoto (Genji). It provided ideas for many *manjū* artists. Many of these tales were written as Nō plays and later were acted out on the kabuki stage. Tales of Japanese heroes and folklore are especially suited to the *manjū*, for the surface is treated as a canvas, the carver's knife being wielded in the same way as the painter's brush. Scenes using perspective and distance can easily be executed on the flattish surface, devices that would not be possible in *katabori* netsuke. The reverse surface can either conclude the scene on the obverse or occasionally the complete design will wrap uninterrupted around the edges. Key events in the calendar were also immortalised in paintings and illustrated books which were produced in Japan from the early seventeenth century onwards and provided both plastic and print artists with inspiration for their work.

In 1979 Jack Hillier gave a talk entitled 'Source-Books for Japanese Craftsmen', which focused on their relevance to netsuke carving. It outlines and illustrates many of the source books that were used by netsuke artists. He points out that *Sōken Kishō* (Appreciation of Superior Sword Fittings), dated 1781, was the earliest Japanese writing on netsuke carvers until in 1942 Ueda Reikichi wrote *Netsuke no Kenkyū* (A Study of Netsuke). This indicates that until relatively recently the Japanese were not very interested in netsuke as an art form, simply regarding them as everyday functional objects, much as we might view a button. For the early carvers there were no illustrated 'How To' manuals. Carving was a skill passed from master to pupil and its secrets were closely guarded. The Japanese were however, fascinated by books illustrating people at work and showing how things were made and done. Books illustrating social customs and showing craftsmen at work seem to have been a source of fascination for the Japanese. *Jinrin kinmō zui* (Illustrated Instructions for Proper Behaviour) published in 1690, is one of these (see figs. 16 and 17). Another book, published almost a century later in 1770, *Saiga shokunin burui* (Polychrome Pictures of Craftsmen) by Tachibana Minko, shows various craftsmen at work and was used by Ryūchin, when he was composing his *manjū* design on the *piece* shown in cat. no. 17.[19] The artist Hōjitsu, whose large number of pupils made *manjū*, is known to have made use of designs by Hanabusa Itchō (1652–1724), which appear in *Itchō gafū* (An Album of Paintings by Hanabusa Itchō) for *manjū* (cat. no. 15). *Shoshoku ekagami* (Mirror of Drawings for Craftsmen) by the print artist Masayoshi Kitao makes no pretence at anything other than an aid for artists which Ippōsai, a pupil of Hōjitsu, uses for another depiction of Shōki, the Demon Queller (cat. no. 14).

In some of the fifteen volumes of *Hokusai Manga* (Hokusai's Sketches) there are numerous small vignettes, playfully executed and perfect for transferring onto the *manjū* surface. Landscapes, animals, birds and flowers are all included and many of these designs or parts of them were slavishly copied by netsuke artists. In this collection one image has been plucked directly from its pages (cat. no. 3), while in others there is an element strongly suggestive of the designs. In *Banshoku zukō* (Designs for all Artisans) published in 1850 Hokusai's follower Katsushika Taito presented some of his designs in circular cartouches.

Criticism has been levelled at the netsuke carvers who copied these images, for their lack of artistic originality. However, the skill of transferring a design from a flat page onto the domed circular surface of the *manjū* requires an extraordinary level of ingenuity and ability. Searching for the source of a design is an endless task and delight for the netsuke specialist and many more discoveries will, it is hoped, be made for this collection in the future.

In the disastrous Ansei-Edo earthquake of 1855, when almost twenty thousand people perished, many netsuke were lost in the fire and destruction that followed it. Ueda and others have suggested that there followed a surge in production of *manjū* netsuke, as they were quicker to make than *katabori* pieces. There may be an element of truth in this, but the details and skill of *shishiaibori* carving, which can be seen in this collection, could surely consume as many hours as a carving in the round.

Notes

1 Jack Hillier. *Source-Books for Japanese Craftsmen*. A Lecture given at the London Convention 1978 entitled "Netsuke in Japanese Art". Han-Shan Tang Ltd, 1979, p. 40
2 With the kind permission of Eskenazi Ltd.
3 Hirokazu Arakawa. *The Gō Collection of Netsuke*. Tokyo National Museum. Kodansha International Ltd, 1983, p. 188
4 Ibid. p. 189
5 Ibid. p. 191
6 Ibid p. 191
7 Basil Hall Chamberlain. *Japanese Things. Being Notes on Various Subjects Connected with Japan*. Charles E. Tuttle. Rutland Vermont & Tokyo, Japan, 1971 (Paperback)
8 '*Shoga Kotto Zasshi*' Issue No. 68, February 1924. '*Netsuke no Kenkyū*' by Takeuchi Kyuichi. Translated into English in the Journal of the International Netsuke Collectors' Society, Vol. 7, No. 3
9 Makieshi Genzaburō, illustrated by. *Jinrin Kinmō zui*' 人倫訓蒙圖彙 (Illustrated Instructions for Proper Behaviour) 7 volumes, 1690
10 Inaba Tsūryū Shin'emon. *Sōken Kishō* 装剣奇賞 (Appreciation of Superior Sword Fittings), 1781.
11 The Shoto Musuem of Art. *History of Japanese Ivory Carving. Ge-bori-okimono and Shibayama of the Meiji Period*. Tokyo, 1996, p. 12
12 Masatoshi as translated by Raymond Bushell. *The Art of Netsuke Carving*. Weatherhill, New York, Tokyo, 1992
13 'Once upon a time.... The Story of Endō Morito and Kesa Gozen'. *Andon* 56. 1997, Society for Japanese Arts, p. 7
14 Alain Ducros. Netsuke. *Art, magie et médecine. Une étude basée sur la collection Marco Cuturi.* Editions Cum Turri, 2006
15 For a discussion on this material see the website of the International Netsuke Society http://netsuke.websitetoolbox.com/post/Authentic-Plastic-Netsuke-5413347
16 Alain Ducros. Materials used in Netsuke. *Netsuke Kenkyukai Journal*, vol. 9, nos 3 & 4, 1989
17 *The Art World,* Vol. 3, No. 3, December 1917, p. 248
18 Laurence Binyon. *Painting in the Far East.* Arnold, London, 1923
19 Tachibana Minko. *Saiga shokunin burui* 彩画職人部類 (Polychrome Pictures of Crafsmen), published in 1784

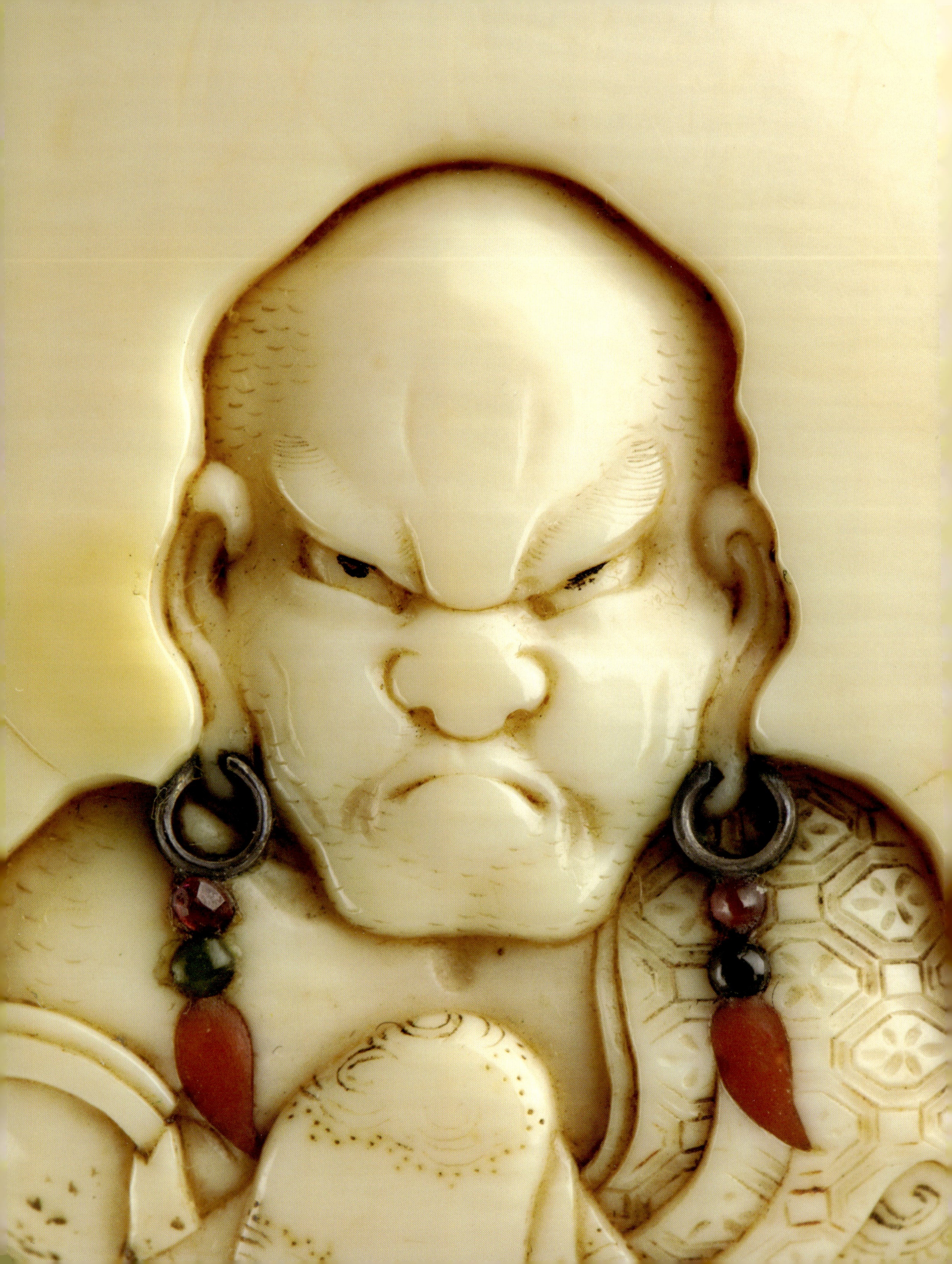

CATALOGUE

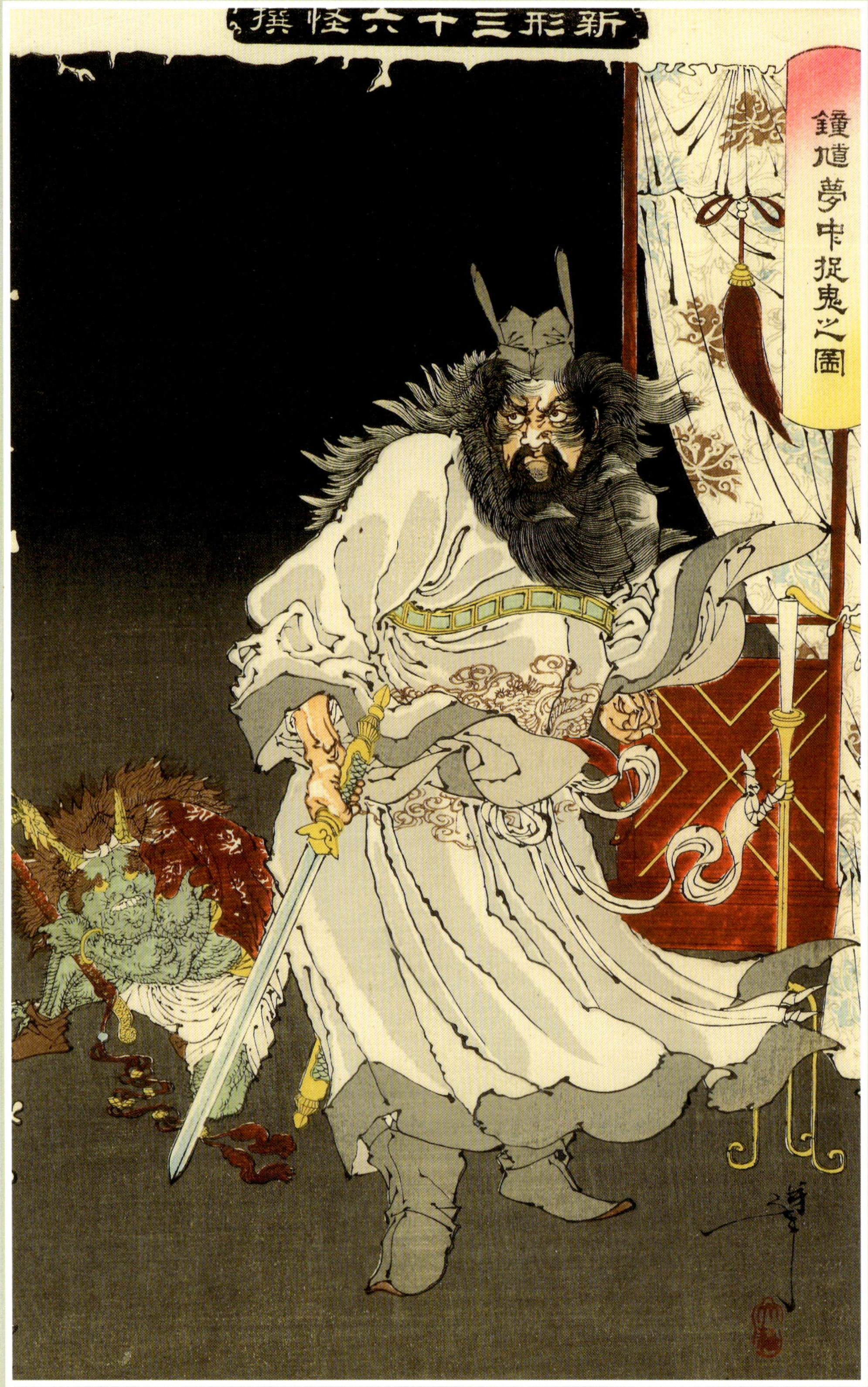

Fig. 23 Shōki the Demon Queller in a Dream. Colour woodblock print by Tsukioka Yoshitoshi (1839–1892) (EA1971.186)

Chinese heroes and folktales

China has long provided the source of much that prevails in Japanese culture. Religion played a major part in the transference of ideas and philosophical thought. The most fundamental of these influences came from Daoism, an indigenous religion, developed in China between the fourth and third centuries BC, from the thoughts of Confucius, and from Buddhism, which arrived from India several centuries later. Daoism was thought to originate with the writings of Laozi, author of the *Dao de jing* (Classic of the Way and its Power), the 'way' or '*dao*' providing its name. Unlike Buddhism, in which statues of the various incarnations of the Buddha and his attendants were worshipped, early Daoism eschewed iconography. The aim of Daoists was to maintain cosmic harmony and to seek personal immortality. The secret of achieving this was thought to be hidden in the fabled 'elixir', a mixture of natural herbs and minerals. This quest was tackled through various exercises, abstentions and an alarming array of medicinal concoctions. Those who had reached this state were known as immortals (Ch. *xianren*, Jap. *sennin*) and were thought to inhabit one of Five Sacred Peaks, one for each of the four cardinal directions and one in the centre. Japanese representations of these figures were based on illustrations taken from Chinese illustrated books, in particular the sixteenth century *Liexian quanzhuan* (Jap. *Yūshō ressen zenden)* (Complete illustrated lives of Chinese immortals), which reached Japan in the middle of the seventeenth century. Ink paintings from the Muromachi period (1336–1576), which were heavily influenced by Chinese artists of the Song period, were a further source for Japanese artists. There are many different *sennin*, some of whom have special attributes and can therefore easily be identified.

1

Bashikō performing acupuncture on a dragon

Verso: waves and clouds

Ivory, gold with dark staining
Signed: Meikōsai Hōichi 明光斎法一 with *kakihan*[1]
Mid-19th century
Diam: 4.5 cm; H: 1.7 cm
EA2001.104
Bequest of Dr Monica Barnett

Design illustrated in:
Henri L. Joly. *Legend in Japanese Art*. London. Kegan Paul, Trench, Trubner and Co. 1967. p. 71

Ex W. C. Alexander Collection

The Daoist immortal Ma Shihuang (Jap. Bashikō) was a celebrated Chinese physician and equine veterinarian who lived around 2600 BC during the reign of the Emperor Huang Di. Legend relates that when a sick dragon with drooping ears and jaws hanging open with exhaustion presented itself to him, he applied a form of acupuncture, which he had successfully used to treat horses. The result was miraculous and the dragon made a quick recovery. So grateful was the beast for the cure that it agreed to carry Bashikō, whenever he was ready to go, to the realms of paradise, home of the Immortals. One morning the dragon took Bashikō on his back and bore him away.

A bearded Bashikō with an expression of kindly concentration on his face, instrument at the ready in his hand, approaches the sick dragon to perform with pinpoint accuracy his healing treatment. Waves, which continue on the reverse, swirl about the animal, which has emerged from the sea for its cure. The carving on this piece is superbly detailed: on the reverse clouds and waves are outlined in the fine lines typical of the *kebori* technique, while a tiny glint of inlaid gold enhances the dragon's eye. This design with a few minor variations was used by Hōichi's teacher, Meikeisai Hōjitsu.[2]

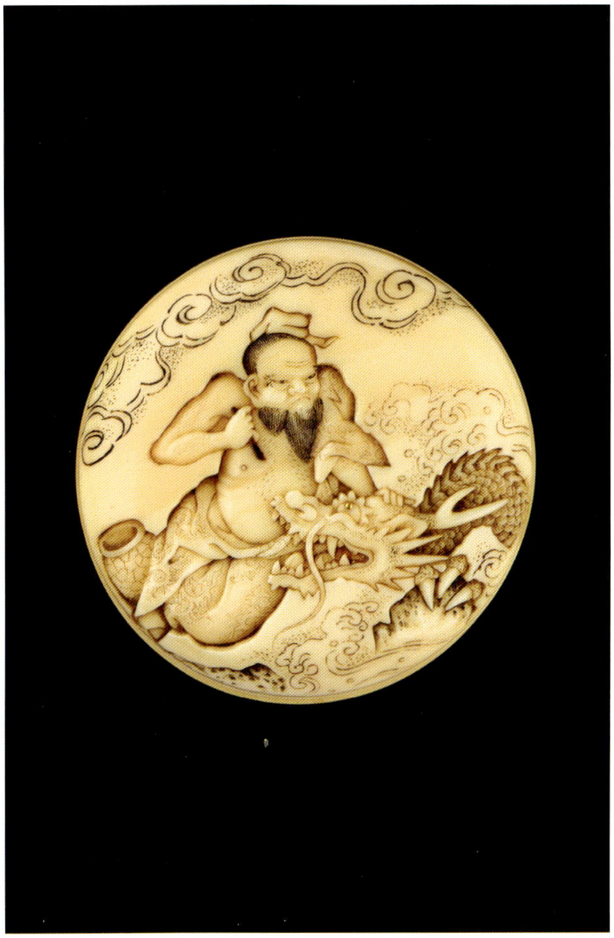

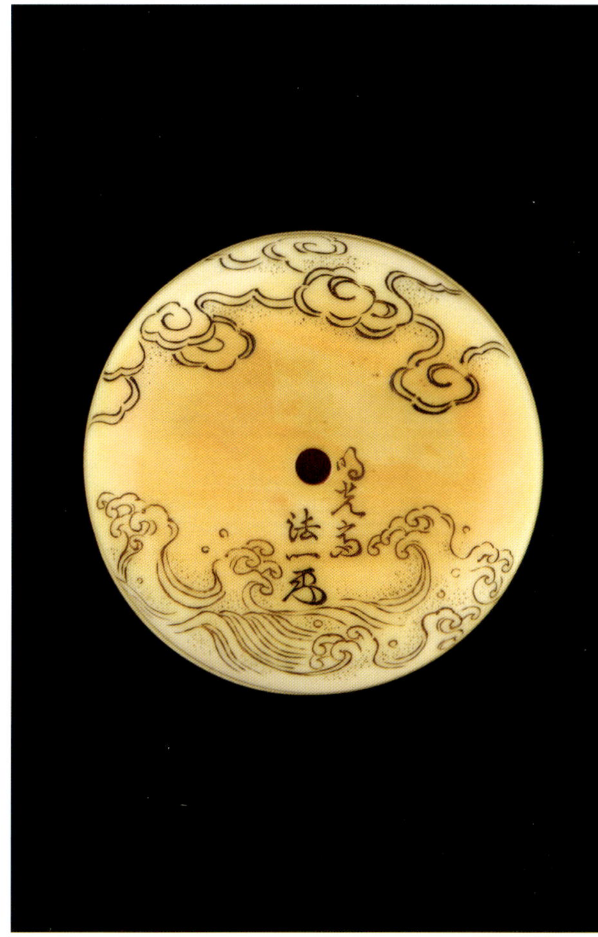

2

Zhang Guolao (Jap. Chōkarō Sennin)

Verso: His horse looks back as it gallops away

Ivory
Signed: Ippōsai 一法齋 with *kakihan*
Mid- to late 19th century
Diam: 4.5; H: 1.85 cm
EA2001.53
Bequest of Dr Monica Barnett

Illustrated in:
Egerton Ryerson. *The Netsuke of Japan. Legends, History, Folklore and Customs.* G. Bell and Sons, Ltd, London 1958. Plate 6.
See The Baur Collection, Geneva. C 151 for an identical piece by Ippōsai.

Bought from Douglas J. K. Wright Ltd. Oriental Art, 34 Curzon Street, London W1Y 1AE on 22/09/71

Zhang Guolao, one of the group singled out as the Eight Daoist Immortals, is said to have lived in China in the eighth century. A hermit, he was the most eccentric of the eight and many legends relate his expertise in magical practices, not least of them his ability to stage his own convincing death and to revive again when it suited him. When summoned to the imperial palace he impressed the Emperor Xuanzong, so much so that the emperor invited Zhang Guolao to stay there and to marry his daughter. He even had the hermit's portrait hung in his palace. Zhang Guolao however, eschewed membership of the imperial court and returned to the mountains to live. This popular legend describes Zhang Guolao with his horse, on which he was able to travel huge distances in a day without food or water. When they came to rest, Zhang Guolao was able to fold up the animal into the gourd hanging from his waist and later restore it to its original form by sprinkling it with a few drops of water. Japanese depictions almost always show Zhang Guolao with a horse, rather than a mule, which is sometimes referred to in Chinese texts.

Zhang Guolao is carved with great skill in *shishiaibori* by Ippōsai, another pupil of the Meikeisai Hōjitsu, and on the reverse a few simple lines *(kebori)* portray the horse, looking back and galloping away having been released from Zhang Guolao's gourd. The Japanese expression *'Hyōtan kara koma ga deru'*, which translates as 'from a gourd comes a foal', means that even events that may seem to be unthinkable can occasionally happen.

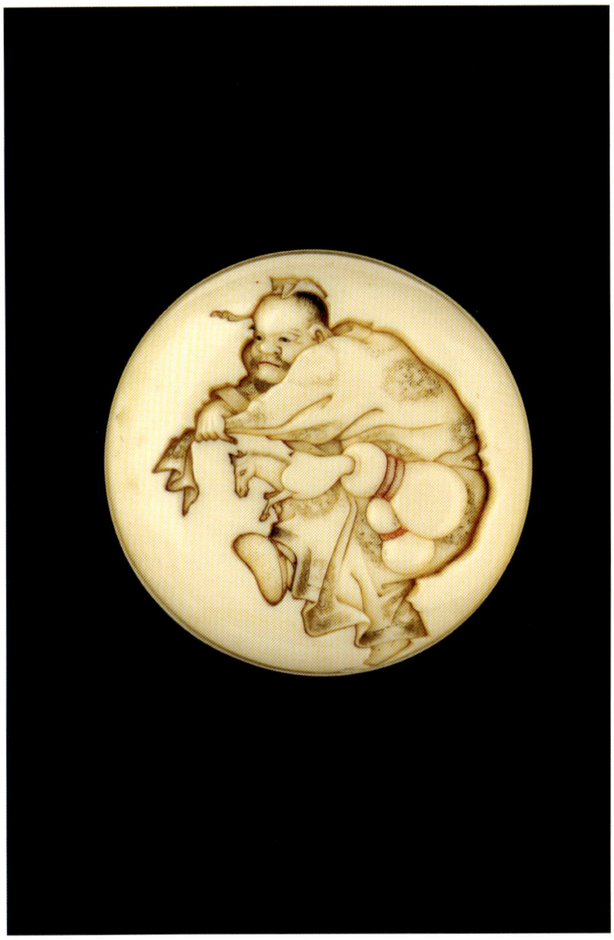

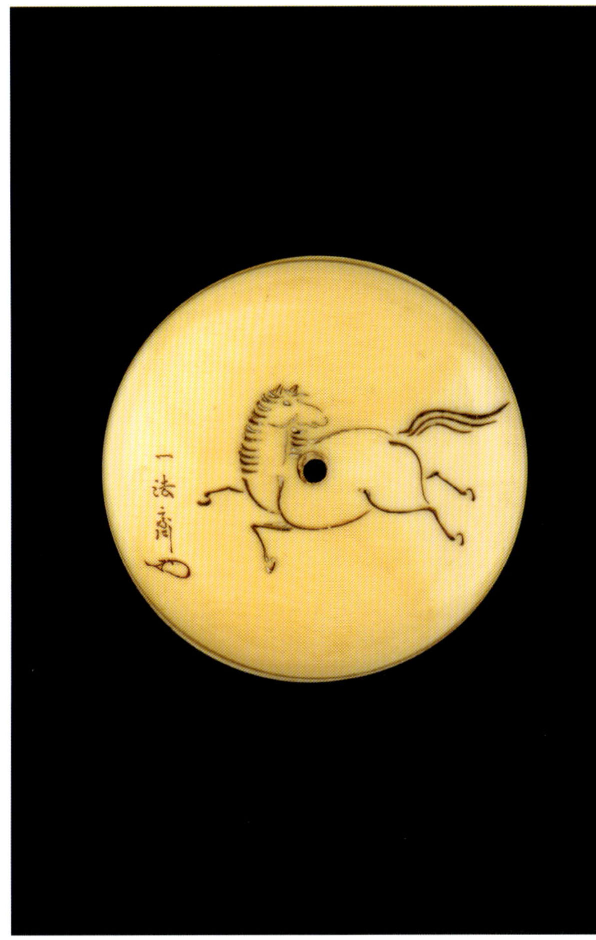
一法斎

3

Chinese *sennin* playing the *shō*

Verso: Moon and clouds

Ivory
Unsigned
Mid-19th century
Diam: 4.0; H: 2.1 cm
EA2001.77
Bequest of Dr Monica Barnett

Bought from Nihon Token 31/12/80

In volume three of the *Hokusai Manga* (Hokusai's sketches) there is an almost identical design labelled 'Baifuku 梅福', the name of a Daoist immortal. Flying towards him is a phoenix, his attribute, missing on this netsuke (fig. 24).

This simply carved unsigned *manjū* is possibly the work of a pupil of one of the large workshops where there was likely to be a copy of the *Manga* by Katsushika Hokusai (1760–1849). Hokusai began working on the *Manga* in 1814, producing 12 volumes by the time he died in 1849 and a further three volumes were published posthumously. These books are packed with sketches of plants, animals, landscapes and people in hundreds of different poses and occupations and were frequently drawn upon by lacquer, netsuke and metal artists.

Mei Fu (Jap. Baifuku) lived during the Han Dynasty (206 BC – AD 220) and was governor of one of the Chinese provinces, but, disgusted with the corruption of certain officials, he resigned in 14 BC and, according to the Han histories, retired to the mountains to devote himself to reciting books and cultivating his mind. Eventually he was said to have found and tasted the elixir of immortality and was swept up into the Daoist immortals' realm.

The *shō* (Ch. *sheng*) is a type of mouth-organ consisting of seventeen bamboo pipes with metal reeds set in a wooden body

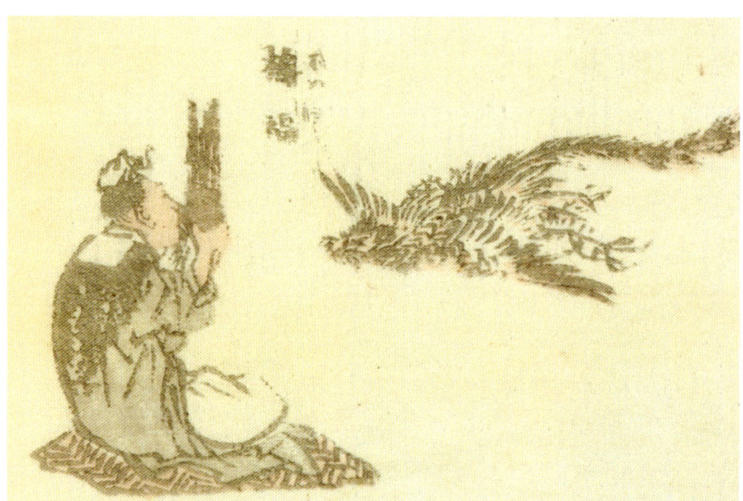

Fig. 24 Illustration from *Hokusai Manga*, Vol. 3, p. 13 (EA2012.22)

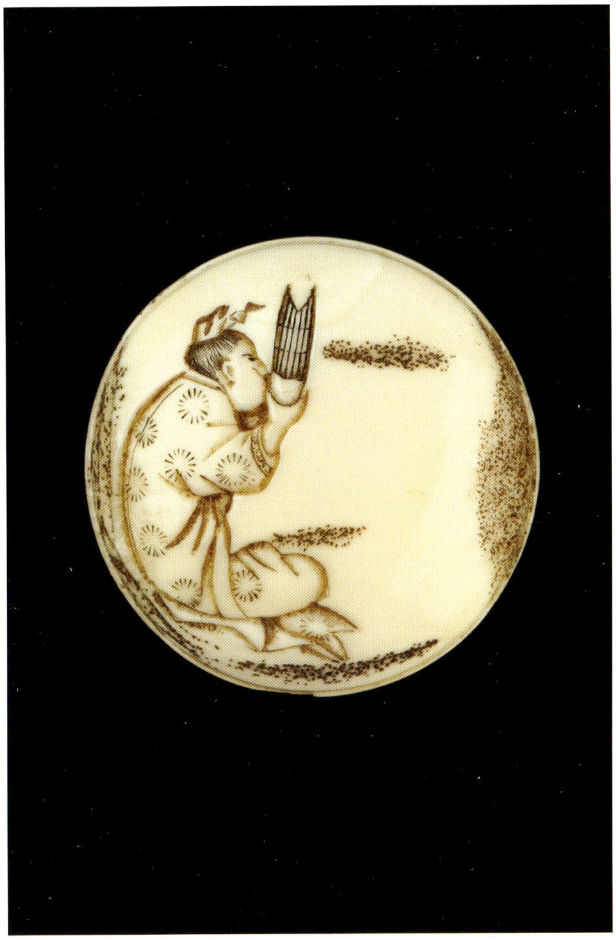
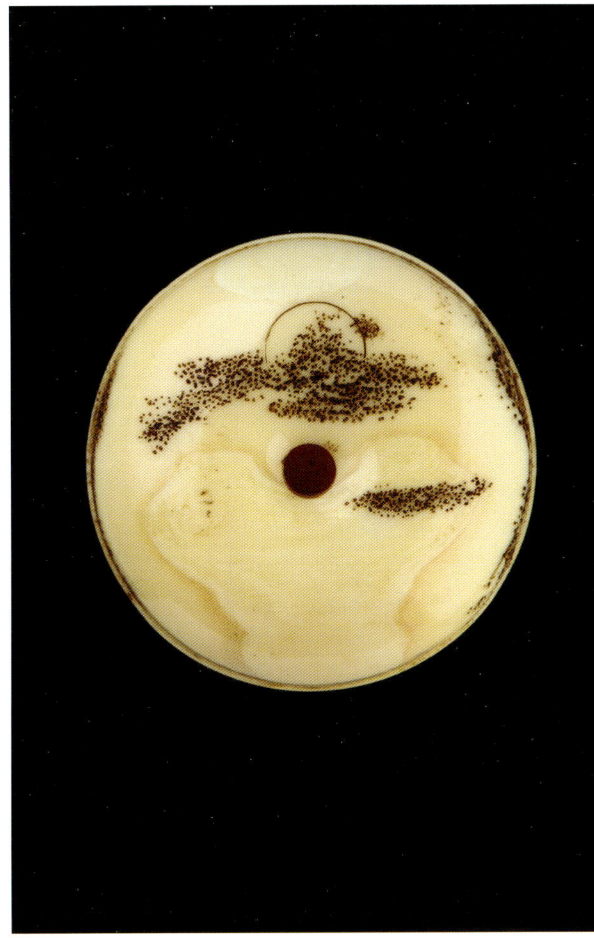

which vibrates when breathing in and out through it. The sound produced is like the drone of a bagpipe. It was an instrument of the Chinese court with ancient origins which reached Japan in the eighth century AD, when it was one of the instruments used in *gagaku*, the musical accompaniment to the ritual *bugaku* dances held in the court.

4

Kume Sennin

Verso: Sennin descending from the clouds

Ivory with red and black staining
Signed: Masatoshi 正壽
Early 19th century
Diam: 4.2; H: 1.95 cm
EA2001.117
Bequest of Dr Monica Barnett

The fantastic tale of Kume, the only native Japanese immortal to feature in this collection, is told in the *Konjaku monogatari* (Anthology of Tales from the Past), a collection of stories of Japan, China and India, compiled during the late Heian period (794–1185 AD). This story is in Chapter 11, Section 24.

Kume, who lived in a temple in the Yoshino area near Kyoto, had been studying hard in order to achieve transcendency, which would enable him to fly. At last he mastered the technique and having reached his goal decided to practise his new skill. However, while soaring over the Yoshino River he looked down and saw a young maiden washing lengths of cloth in the river. In order not to wet her kimono, she had tucked her hem into her sash, thus revealing her bare legs. The sight of these legs was too much for Kume, 'carnal thoughts'[3] entered his mind, he lost concentration and crashed to the ground in front of her. The two, so the story goes, fell in love immediately and after a short while they were married.

Many years later, the emperor decided to build a new capital at Takaichi. The timber chosen came from a forest far away. Kume had joined the workforce as a labourer but when it was discovered that he had once been able to fly, the supervisors entreated him to help move the timber by air. Kume pleaded that married life had cost him his transcendent power and he doubted if he could regain it. However, he volunteered to try and retreated to a quiet place to concentrate. After seven days, there appeared to be no progress, but on the eighth day, thunder, lightning and torrential rain hit the forest. Suddenly it cleared and the timber could be seen rising from the ground and heading through the air in the direction of Takaichi, where it landed successfully, ready for

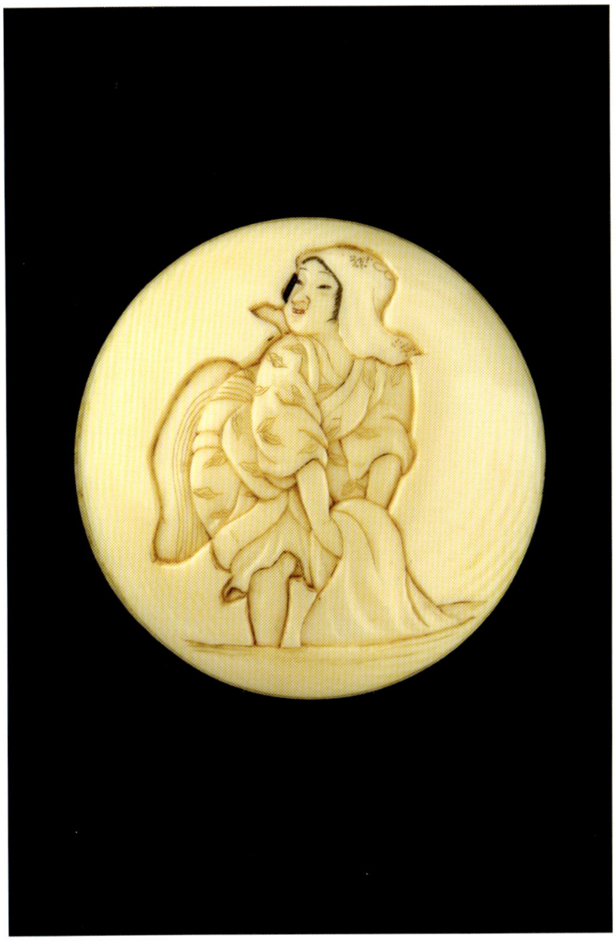

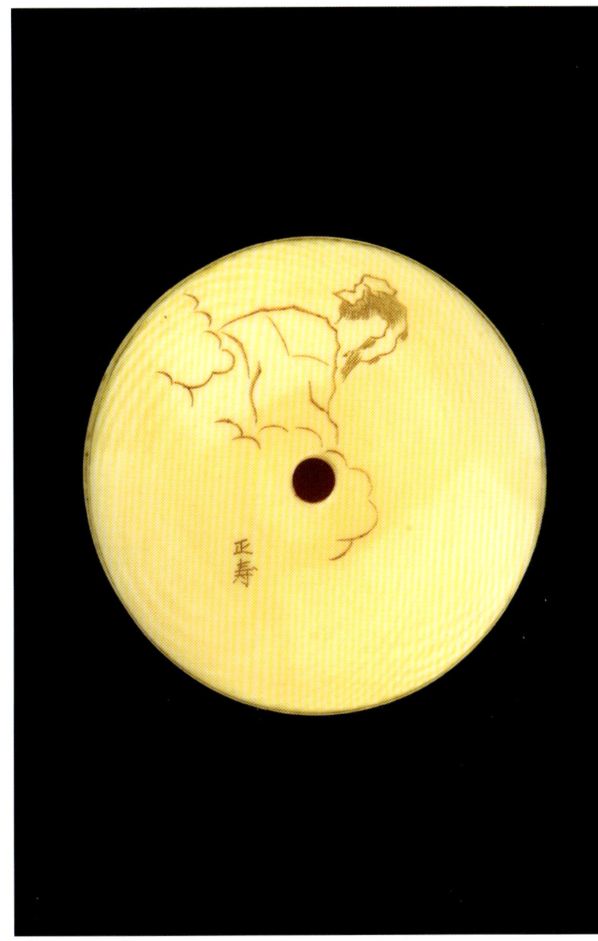
正寿

use. When the emperor heard of this miracle, he awarded Kume a large parcel of land. In gratitude to the Buddha, without whose help he could not have achieved this feat, Kume built a temple and called it '*Kumedera*' (The temple of Kume).

Masatoshi contrasted two techniques, carving the main image, in delicate *shishiaibori*, of the maiden exposing only one bare leg, which proved to be Kume Sennin's undoing, and for the ethereal sage on the reverse, using a simple *kebori* sketch of the bearded figure steering himself through the air amid clouds.[4]

'The Romance of the Three Kingdoms'

The next few netsuke illustrate legendary stories that involve Chinese historical figures. Many of these tales are found in the fourteenth century book, *Sanguozhi yanyi* (Jap. *sangokushi engi*) or 'The Romance of the Three Kingdoms'.[5] This was based on the earlier historical 'Records of the Three Kingdoms' (Ch. *Sanguozhi*) attributed to Luo Guanzhong, which describes in vivid detail the political unrest of the kingdoms of Wu, Wei and Shu, all battling for supremacy in the third century.

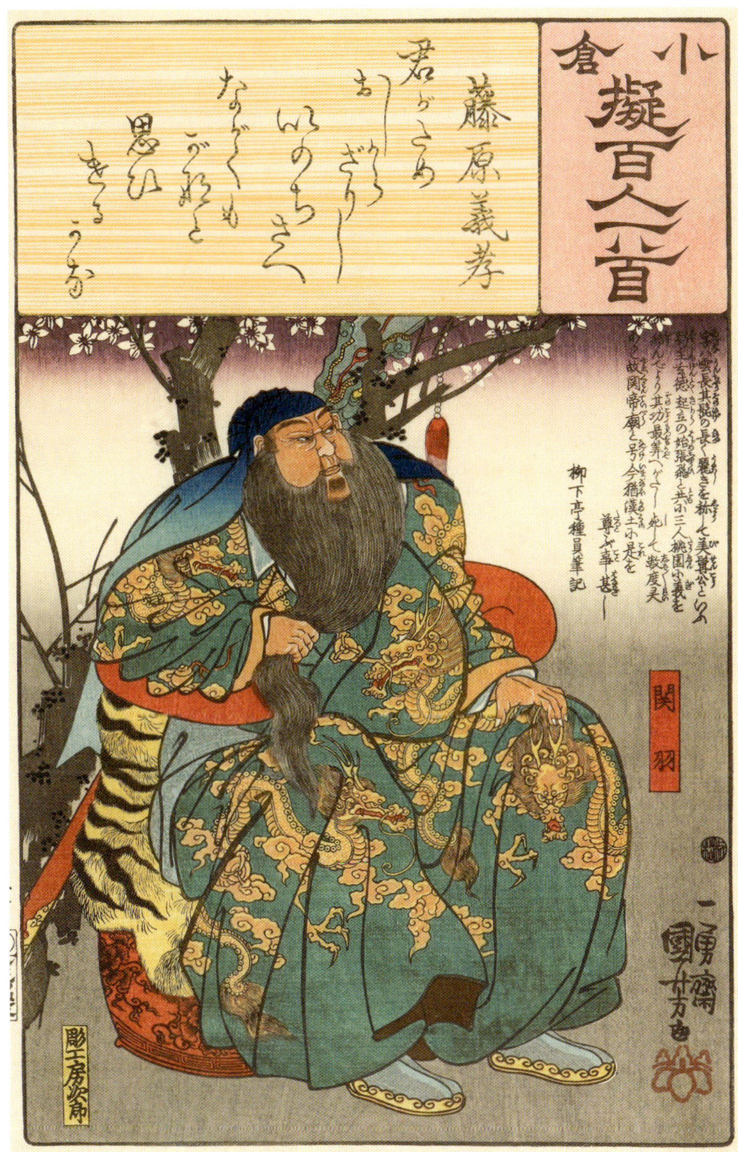

Fig. 25 Kan'u. Colour woodblock print by Utagawa Kuniyoshi (1797–1862) (EA1971.113)

5

Yu Rang (Jap. Yojō) stabbing Zhao Wuxu's cloak

Verso: plain

Ivory and red staining
Signed: Ichiyūsai 一遊蔡
Mid-19th century
Diam: 4.0; H: 1.8 cm
EA2001.97
Bequest of Dr Monica Barnett

At the end of the Warring States period in China (476–221 BC), Yu Rang (Jap. Yojō) was in the service of Zhi Yao (Jap. Chikaku), an avaricious and scheming man but one who nonetheless treated Yu Rang well. When a man called Zhao Wuxu brutally murdered Zhi Yao and made his skull into a drinking cup, Yu Rang was determined to avenge his master. Being a novice swordsman, his first attempt failed, but fortunately he was pardoned by Zhao Wuxu. Determined to succeed, he tried again, but on his second bungled attempt, Zhao Wuxu said he would pardon him no more. Yu Rang made a last request and asked Zhao Wuxu if he would spare him his own cloak. In a frenzied pretence at a third attempt to kill his master's murderer, he stabbed at it furiously with his sword and then took his own life.

Yu Rang is usually depicted with non-Chinese features despite being Chinese. The reason for this may be that in order to disguise himself before his attempts to assassinate Zhao Wuxu, he is said to have disfigured himself.

Loyalty to one's master was one of the most valued virtues in medieval Japan. The samurai code of ethics, heavily influenced by Confucian values, demanded loyalty, wisdom, courage,

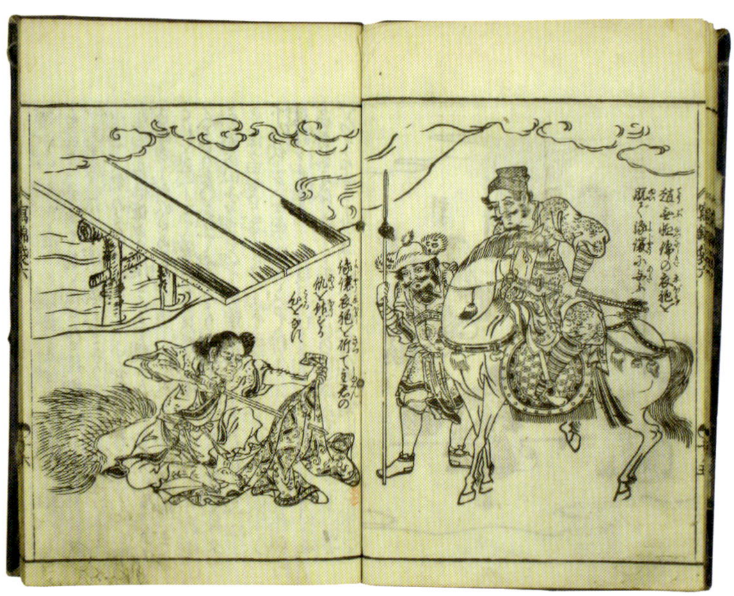

Fig. 26 This incident is illustrated in *Ehon shahōbukuro* 絵本写宝袋 (Picture book, treasure-bag of sketches) by Tachibana Morikuni 1770 (1st ed. 1720), Book 10, p. 12 (Waseda University Library, Tokyo, bunko06 01293-(6))

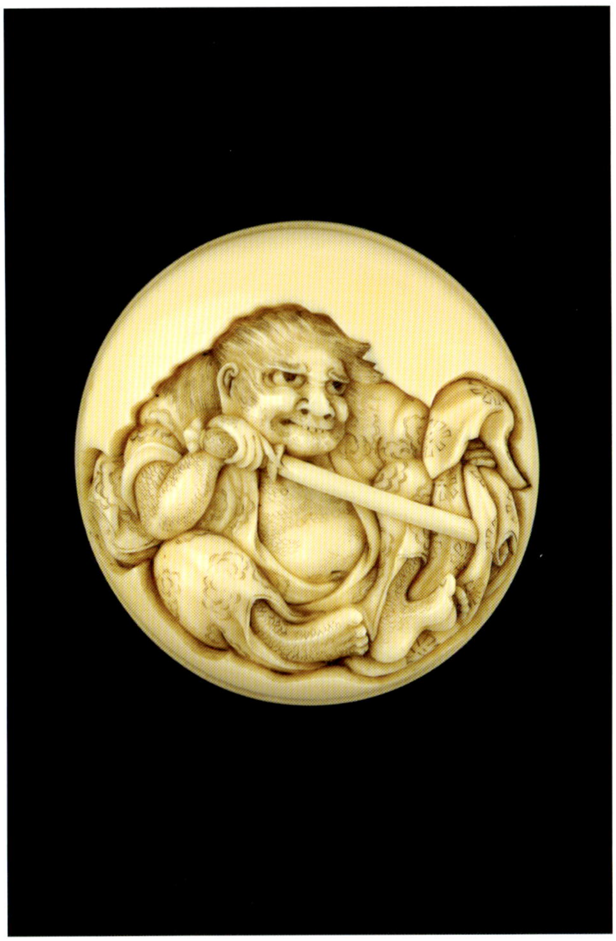

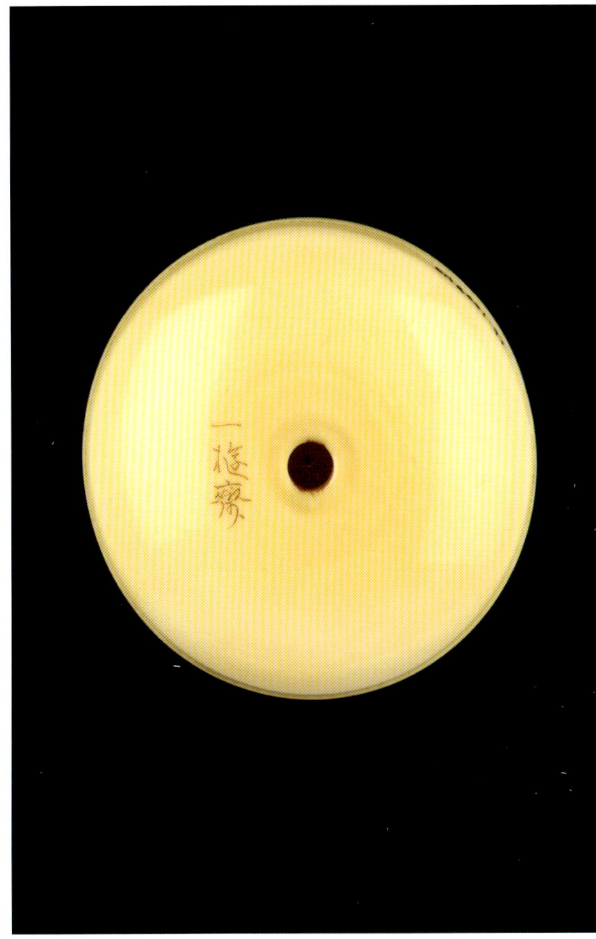

benevolence, disdain for one's own life, impassivity under duress and above all the maintenance of personal honour.

The story of Yu Rang is recorded in the chapter 'Biographies of the Assassins' of the *Shi ji* (Records of the Grand Historian) by Sima Qian (ca. 145 or 135–86 BC), historian to the emperor.

6

Zhang Liang (Jap. Chōryō) returns Huangshi Gong's (Jap. Kōsekikō) shoe from beneath a bridge

Verso: Scroll

Ivory with brown staining
Unsigned
Mid-19th century
Diam: 4.5; H: 1.6 cm
EA2001.72
Bequest of Dr Monica Barnett

Bought from Nihon Token

Zhang Liang (Jap. Chōryō) (262–189 BC) was a strategist and statesman and one of the founding heroes of the Han Dynasty. This story takes place at a time when he was being hunted down after a failed attempt to assassinate the Emperor Qin Shi Huang.

One day when Zhang Liang was walking across a bridge, an old man crossed his path and deliberately dropped his shoe beneath the bridge. He asked Zhang Liang to go and fetch it and although slightly surprised, Zhang Liang complied. 'Put it on my foot' said the old man. Again the elder's attitude astonished Zhang Liang, but because the man was so much older, he obeyed. Complete with both shoes, the old man walked away, saying nothing. Zhang Liang was shocked, but shortly after, the old man turned around and instructed Zhang Liang to meet him in five days' time. The meeting duly took place but the old man chided Zhang Liang for being late and told him to return in another five days. Again he arrived later than the elder. Another meeting was proposed and this time Zhang Liang was presented with a scroll by the old man, who revealed himself as Huangshi Gong (Jap. Kōsekikō), a famous Daoist scholar and military strategist, also known as the Yellow-Stone Elder. 'Read this' he entreated, 'and you will become the teacher of princes and in ten years' time you will begin to rise'. Zhang Liang opened the scroll and discovered that it contained a secret treatise on military strategy and the art of war. He studied it until he knew it by heart. Some sources say that Huangshi Gong wrote the treatise himself. Years later he imparted its secrets to Liu Bang, the future Emperor Gaozu, to whom he had become a trusted general.

This unsigned piece is carefully carved with attention to the details of the robes and faces of the two gentlemen. As if to emphasise its importance, the single rolled scroll adorns the reverse.

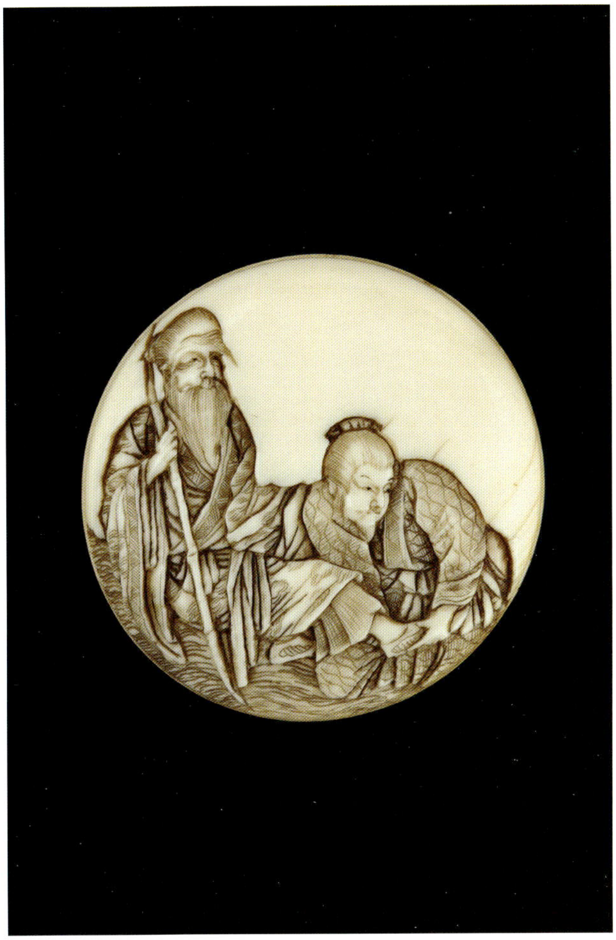
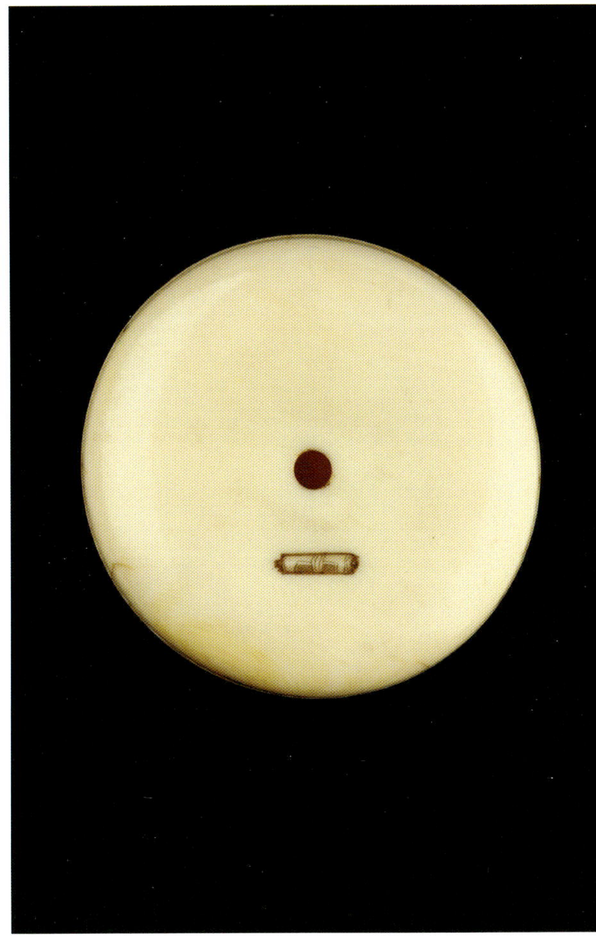

7

Fan Kuai (Jap. Hankai)

Verso: The corner of a terrace beside which grows a flowering peony. On the right is a table on which sits a bowl and beside that a wine jar and ladle.

Ivory with staining
Unsigned
19th century
Diam: 5.3; H: 2.65 cm
EA2001.50
Bequest of Dr Monica Barnett

Published in:
Wilhelm, G. *Manjū exégèse et appréciation.* Bulletin Association Franco-Japonaise. No. 54. Octobre 1996. Fig: MB3

Bought from Fairclough 01/07/1971

As a boy, Fan Kuai (Jap. Hankai) (242–189 BC) lived in the same village as Liu Bang, whom he befriended and who eventually became the first emperor of the Han dynasty, Han Gaozu (Jap. Kan no Kōso). Fan Kuai married Liu Bang's sister-in-law and was appointed as his aide and bodyguard. While fighting for Liu Bang, Fan Kuai greatly distinguished himself on the battlefield.

Around the year 206 the treacherous Xiang Yu, who was engaged in a long power struggle with Liu Bang, was intent on assassinating his enemy and destroying his army. He organised a feast ostensibly to entertain Liu Bang, but in fact it was a plot to kill him. This became known as the Feast of Hong Gate. The statesman Zhang Liang (Jap. Chōryō) (cat. no. 6) was also invited as he was a supporter of Liu Bang. During the banquet, Zhang Liang sensed the plot and raised the alarm by going outside to find Fan Kuai, on duty as bodyguard. Moments later, Fan Kuai burst into the banquet in a most uncouth fashion, breaking down the door and carrying it in with him under his arm. In spite of verbally chiding Xiang Yu for contemplating this evil deed and bravely extolling Liu Bang's virtues, he was invited to join in the feast and was placed next to his master Liu Bang, given food and wine and treated courteously. While eating, however, they hatched their own plot. Liu Bang would leave the hall and pretend to go and relieve himself. Fan Kuai would accompany him and, with great haste, fetch a horse on which Liu Bang could ride away to safety. They managed to pull off the daring plot and Liu Bang survived.

The artist of this solid *manjū* paid great attention to the details of Fan Kuai's armour and to the door he is carrying. On the back the details are much sketchier, with the central *himotōshi* holes encircled to give the effect of a peg.

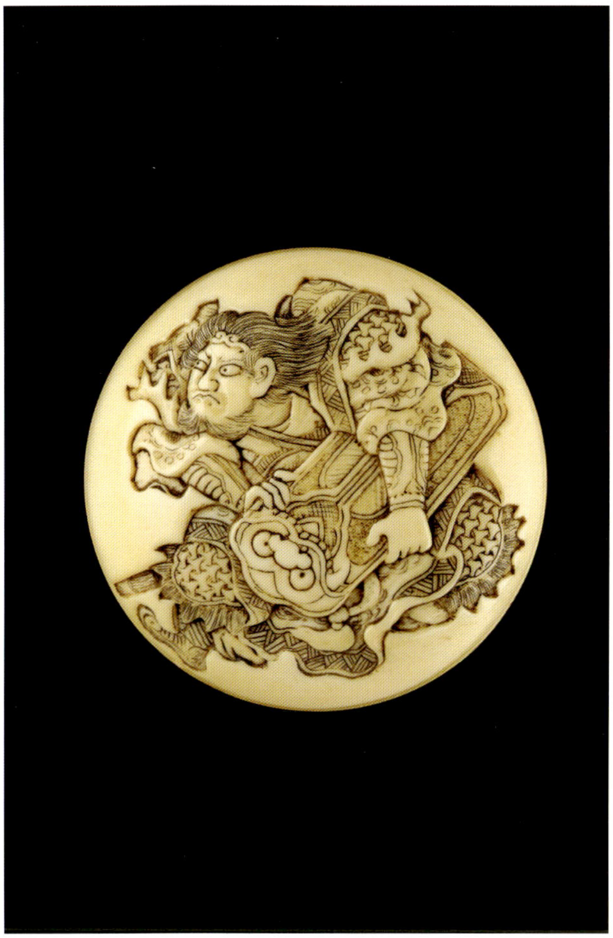

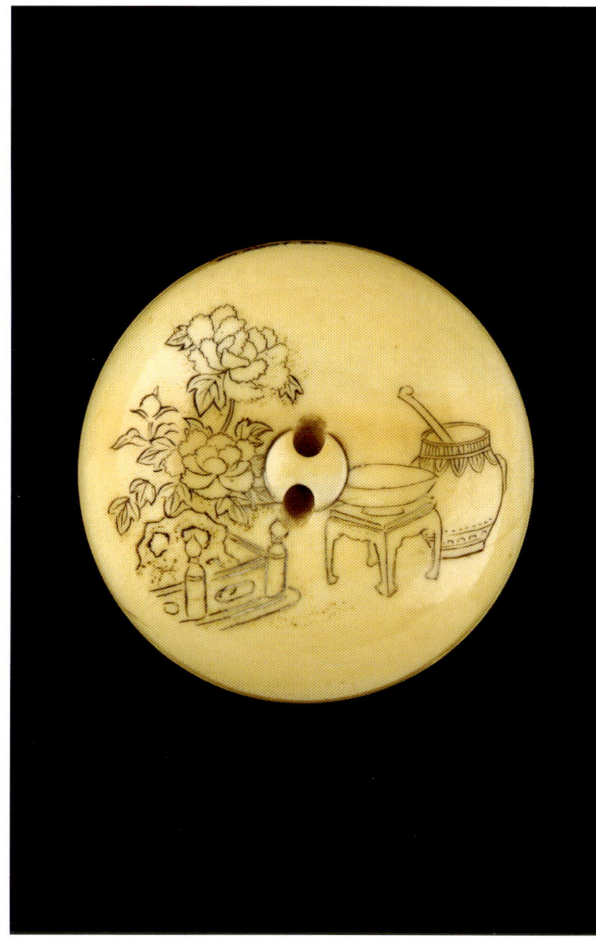

8

Han Xin (Jap. Kanshin)

Verso: a brigand laughs and points mockingly at Han Xin; a basket containing a fish is on the ground behind him

Ivory
Signed: Kōju 光寿 with *kakihan*
Edo period: 19th century
Diam: 5.0; H: 2.96 cm
EA2001.124
Bequest of Dr Monica Barnett

Illustrated in:
Frederick Meinertzhagen. Ed. George Lazarnick. *MCI. Meinertzhagen Card Index on Netsuke in the Archives of the British Museum*, Alan R. Liss, Inc., New York., Vol. 1, p. 362
Henri L. Joly. *Legend in Japanese Art*. Charles E. Tuttle Company Limited Vermont and Tokyo. Japan. 1967, p. 253

Ex W. L. Behrens Collection No. 1261
Illustrated in Behrens Plate. XXIII
Ex W W Winkworth collection 1944

Accordng to Frederick Meinertzhagen, this piece was bought from the Behrens sale in 1913 for £3.50. When it sold again in 1995 at Sotheby's it made £2,300. See Sotheby's *The Carlo Monzino Collection of Netsuke, Inro and Lacquer. The Property of a Private Trust*. London 21/06/1995. Lot 278

Han Xin, who died in 196 BC, lost his father when he was a child, leaving him destitute and forced to beg for food. One day a woman found him in a desperate state and gave him food. Because of her kindness, he vowed to repay her once his circumstance improved. She laughed at him. This netsuke illustrates an occasion when Han Xin was confronted in the marketplace by ruffians, one of whom challenged him either to fight him or to crawl between his legs. Han Xin decided to humiliate himself by choosing the second option. The other two ruffians mocked him with laughter. This story is told in the Romance of the Three Kingdoms. The expression 'Han Xin's crawling between the legs' refers to this incident, and indicates patience, forbearance and perseverance.

Throughout his youth Han Xin had studied treatises on military strategy and finally he rose through the ranks to become a great military leader. Through loyalty to Liu Bang, who around AD 202 finally became the Emperor Gaozu, Han Xin was made 'King of Chu'. Now in a position of regional power, he sought out the woman who had fed him and rewarded her with gold and the ruffian he appointed as one of his lieutenants.

These expressive figures are carved in shallow *shishiaibori* on both back and front by one of Meikeisai Hōjitsu's pupils about whom we know nothing else. He was mainly a carver of *manjū*.

The ivory is slightly worn and bears a good patina.

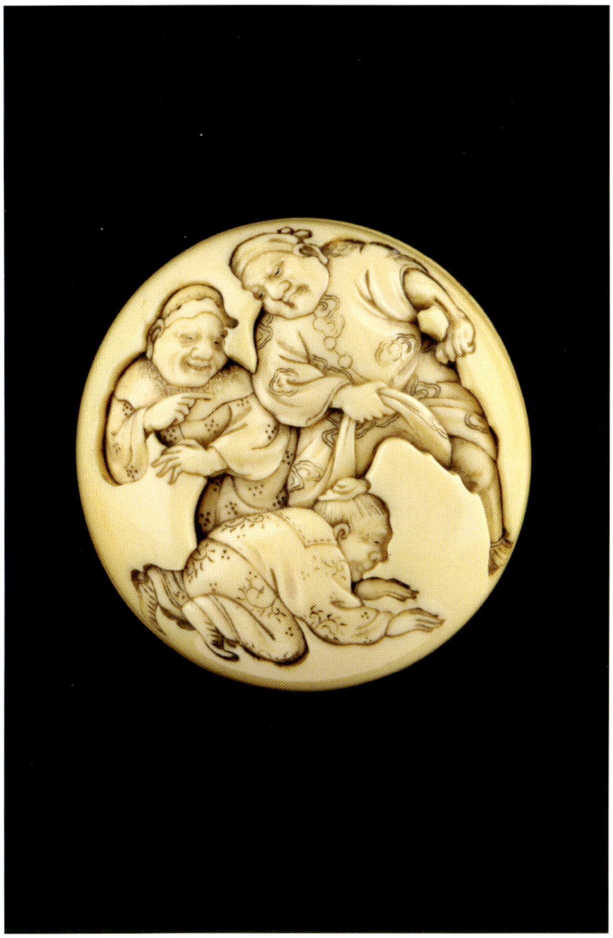

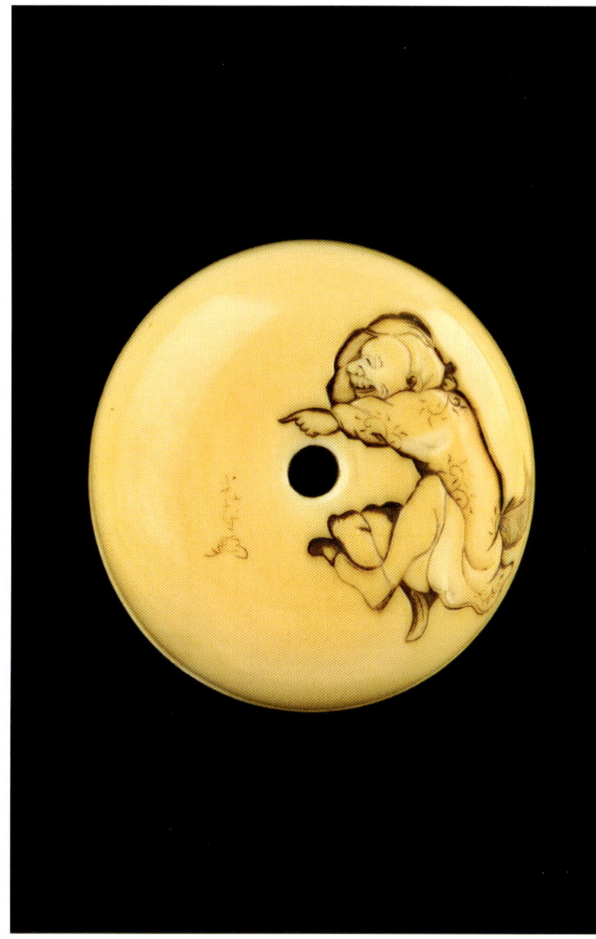

9

Zhang Fei (Jap. Chōhi) and Guan Yu (Jap. Kan'u)

Verso: Geometric outer and inner bands

Ivory
Signed: Genryōsai Minkoku 玄了齋民谷
Early 19th century
Diam: 5.8; H: 2.39 cm
EA2001.45
Bequest of Dr Monica Barnett

Signature illustrated in:
Neil K. Davey, *Netsuke A comprehensive study based on the M.T. Hindson collection*, Faber & Faber Limited, London, in association with Sotheby Parke Bernet Publications, 1974, p. 104

Ex W. L. Behrens Collection

Bought from Douglas J. K. Wright Ltd, 13/11/1970

These two men are Guan Yu (Jap. Kan'u) and Zhang Fei (Jap. Chōhi), who together with Liu Bei (Jap. Ryūbi) are referred to as the 'Three Sworn Brothers of the Peach Garden'. Promising loyalty to one another, their aim was to enable Liu Bei to take his place as legitimate successor to the throne of Shu, the westernmost of the three states vying for power in China after the fall of the Han dynasty in AD 220. After many fierce battles they succeeded and finally Liu Bei became the Emperor Xuande (Jap. Gentoku) of the state of Shu Han.

Guan Yu, in front of Zhang Fei, looks calm, determined and scholarly, holding a scroll in his hands. By contrast Zhang Fei looks fierce, focused and ready for battle, a spear in his hand. Both these men died shortly after seeing their ambition realised. Guan Yu was executed for refusing to renounce his loyalty to Liu Bei and Zhang Fei was assassinated in his sleep. Guan Yu was later deified as the god of war, not for his military might but for his loyalty and sense of brotherhood, virtues much admired by both the Chinese and the Japanese.

Genryōsai Minkoku II carved the men in low relief against a background of a hexagonal diaper[6] pattern which continues on the reverse. A similar background pattern and the treatment around the cord hole (*himotōshi*) occur on Chinese style carved lacquer *manjū* (Cat. Nos. 19 and 20). Genryōsai's father taught his son who followed his father in carving very detailed and carefully executed figures and *manjū* in ivory. They worked in Edo in the mid-19th century.

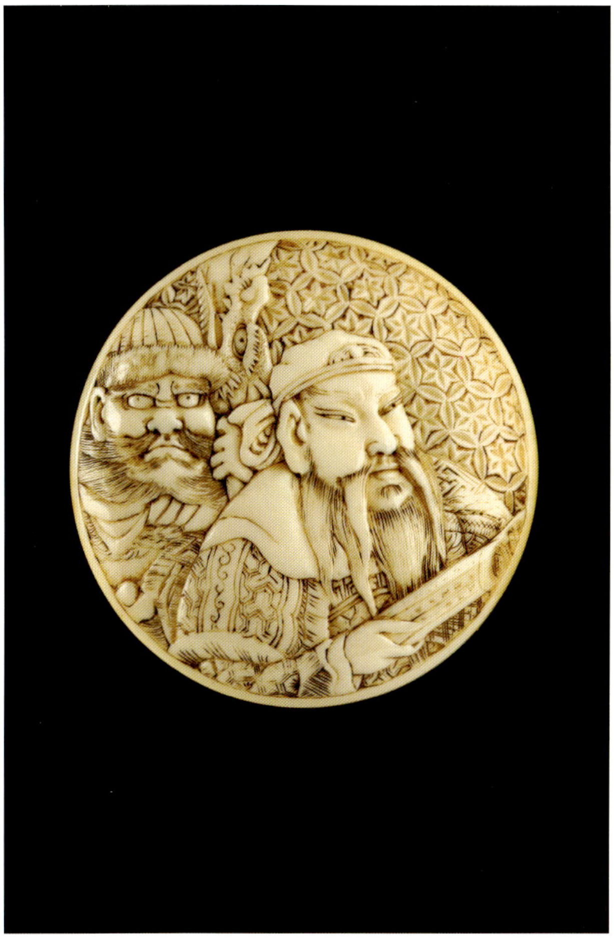

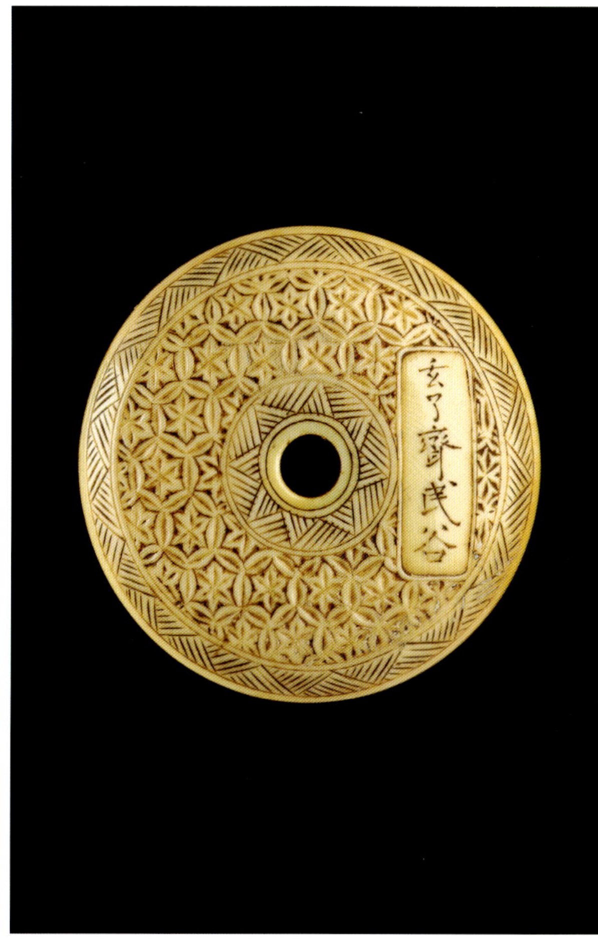

10

The Spirit of the Plum Tree

Verso: Plum wine pot and a wine cup

Ivory with black and red staining and silver beads
Signed: Kogetsu 古月 (unrecorded)
Mid- to late 19th century
Diam: 5.1; H: 2.5 cm
EA2001.74
Bequest of Dr Monica Barnett

See Christie's, London, 04/03/1980. Lot 140
Bought from Eskenazi Ltd.

The poet Zhao Shixiong (589–618) was climbing Mount Luofu in Southern China, in order to view the flowering plum trees. He stopped to refresh himself at a wine shop. There he met a beautiful woman with whom he sat down to drink some wine and subsequently they exchanged wine cups. That night the beautiful woman returned to him in a dream and when he awoke he was beneath a plum tree in full bloom. Realising that he had been visited by 'The Spirit of the Plum Tree' he composed a poem 'In the moonlight under the trees a beautiful woman comes' (Jap. *getsumei rinka bijin majiru).*

The woman is lavishly dressed in several layers of Chinese clothing to indicate the chill of the season, late winter or early spring, when plum trees are in full bloom. She also wears a necklace and tiara. The square pot used for wine on the reverse is of a shape made in China in the 19th century.

In the Ashmolean Museum's collection there is a woodblock print by Utagawa Kuniyoshi dated 1843, which shows a woman dressed in Japanese kimono holding a Chinese vessel with a large flowering plum bough in a vase behind her, very similar to the artist's rendering on this *manjū*.

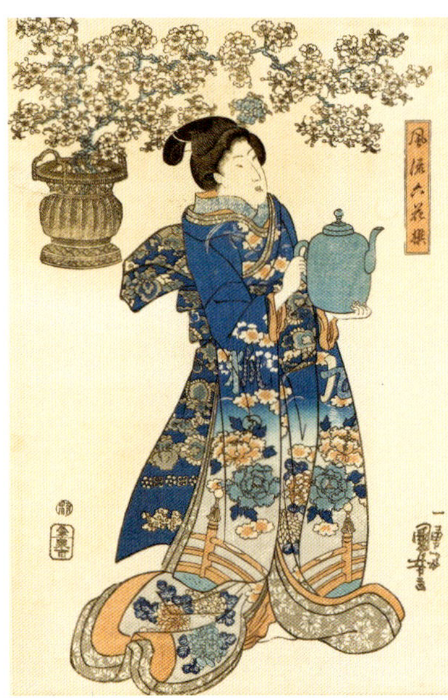

Fig. 27 Beauty from the series *Fūryū rokkasen*. Colour woodblock print by Utagawa Kuniyoshi (1797–1862) (EAX.5293)

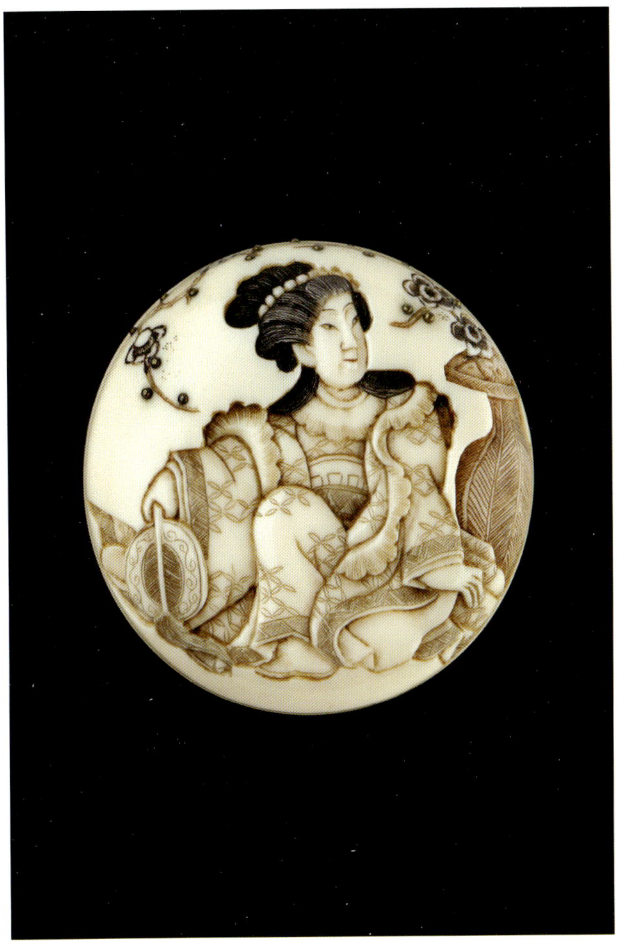

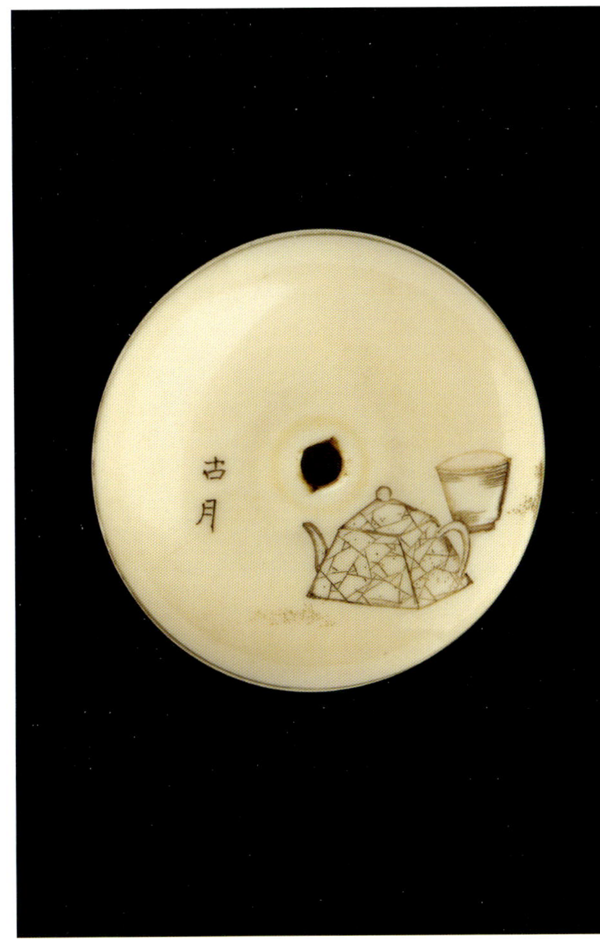
古月

This netsuke came to the museum catalogued as 'Seiōbo, The Queen Mother of the West'. However, this is unlikely as Seiōbo is associated with peaches.

Kogetsu is unrecorded and in this case it is likely that the simple characters 古 and 月 were added later to make it more saleable in a market where foreigners were unlikely to be able to read signatures, let alone verify them. It is well known that there were a few unscrupulous antique dealers, who sold to unsuspecting foreigners in the Meiji period.

11

Yang Guifei plays the flute with the Emperor Xuanzong

Verso: plain

Shakudō, gold and silver.
Signed: Naotoshi 直壽 with kakihan
Around 1850
Diam: 3.22; H: 2.1 cm
EA2001.68
Bequest of Dr Monica Barnett

Wilhelm, G. *Manjū exégèse et appréciation*. Bulletin Association Franco-Japonaise. No. 54. Octobre 1996. Fig. MB26

When the Chinese Emperor Xuanzong (Jap. Gensō) (685–762) who reigned from 713–756, first set eyes on the beautiful Yang Yuhuan he fell hopelessly in love with her. Soon she was given the name Guifei (Precious concubine). In this position Yang Guifei (Jap. Yōkihi) (719–756) managed to use her influence at court to extend the imperial favour to members of her family. The Emperor's infatuation soon distracted him from his duties and encouraged him to make some unwise decisions, which resulted in a rebellion in 756 led by An Lushan. One night, as the troops approached Xian, the Emperor and Yang Guifei were forced to flee the capital. However, on the way the imperial bodyguards mutinied and demanded the death of members of Yang's clan and of Yang Guifei herself. She was strangled with a silken rope while the distraught emperor looked on.

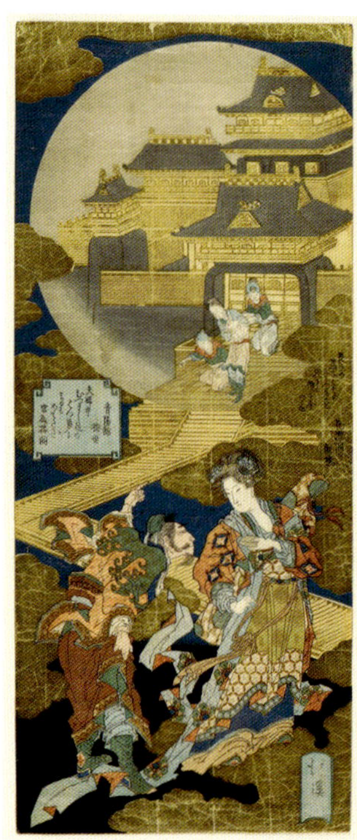

Fig. 28 Yang Guifei before the Palace of Heaven sending her message to the Emperor Xuanzong, her lover. *Surimono* by Totoya Hokkei (1780–1850) (EAX.4571)

The story lived on in China in the long epic poem by Bai Juyi (772–846) known as 'The Song of Unending Sorrow' (Jap. *Chōgonka*). It reached Japan in the ninth century, where it was instantly popular, and during medieval times the

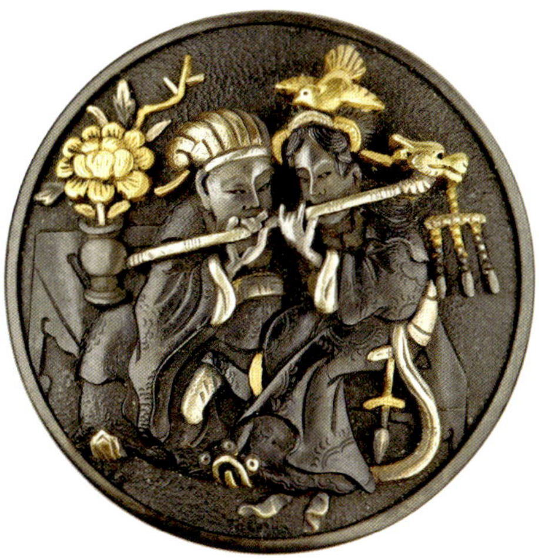

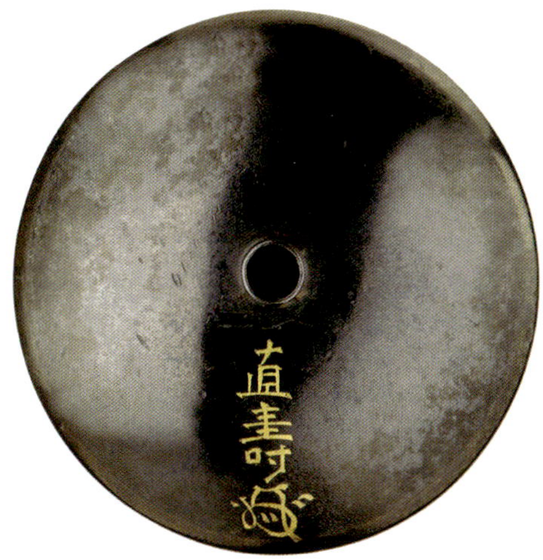

story was continually re-written until it even contained several fictitious characters. The fifteenth century Nō play *Yōkihi*, in which Yang Guifei's spirit is re-united with the soul of the aged emperor by a Daoist priest, was enthusiastically received. During the Edo period Yōkihi's plight continued to be portrayed in songs, paintings, prints and other forms of decorative art.

'The Song of Unending Sorrow' ends with the lines:

> Earth endures, heaven endures; some time both shall end,
> While this unending sorrow goes on and on for ever.'
>
> (Translated by Witter Bynner)

12

Zhong Kui (Jap. Shōki) the Demon Queller

Verso: Rocky outcrop with plants and clouds above an inscription in *sōsho* script reading:

Oni no iru	鬼のいる	Who would live
Tokoro ni sumu ya	ところにすむや	In a place
Shi yoki	志よき	where there are *oni*
Ka na	かな	Shōki surely?[8]

Walrus ivory
Signed: Hidemasa 秀政 (in an irregular reserve)
Late 18th or early 19th century
Diam: 4.2 cm; H: 1.9 cm
EA2001.59
Bequest of Dr Monica Barnett

Illustrated in:
Neil K. Davey. *Netsuke. A comprehensive study based on the M.T. Hindson collection.* Faber & Faber Limited, London, in association with Sotheby Parke Bernet Publications. 1974. p. 19, No. 13

Sold at Sotheby's to D.J.K. Wright for £65 in the sale of M.T.Hindson Collection of Important Netsuke. 11/10/1967. Lot 179. It then reappeared in Sotheby's 23/10/1972. Lot 2, when it sold to Marchant & Son for £100. It was then bought by Dr Barnett from Marchant & Son on 6/12/1972

A bust portrait of Zhong Kui (Shōki) shows him looking angrily about for demons *(oni)* to capture to fulfil his promised task. The character of Zhong Kui, the Demon Queller, first appeared in eighth century China. He featured in a dream of the ailing Emperor Xuanzong (see cat. no. 11), in which a small demon *(oni)* came into the palace and stole Yang Guifei's embroidered perfume bag and the emperor's own jade flute. The demon then began to dance around the palace grounds flaunting his loot. The emperor went to him and demanded an explanation, to which the demon replied that he was stealing for fun, replacing man's joys with sorrow. The emperor was infuriated and was about to call in his bodyguards when there appeared a large figure who grabbed the thief, scratched his eyes out, tore him in pieces and ate him. This was Zhong Kui, the Demon Queller, who then explained that he had failed his exams and had committed suicide because of the disgrace. Out of respect, the emperor at the time had given him the honourable burial of a court official of

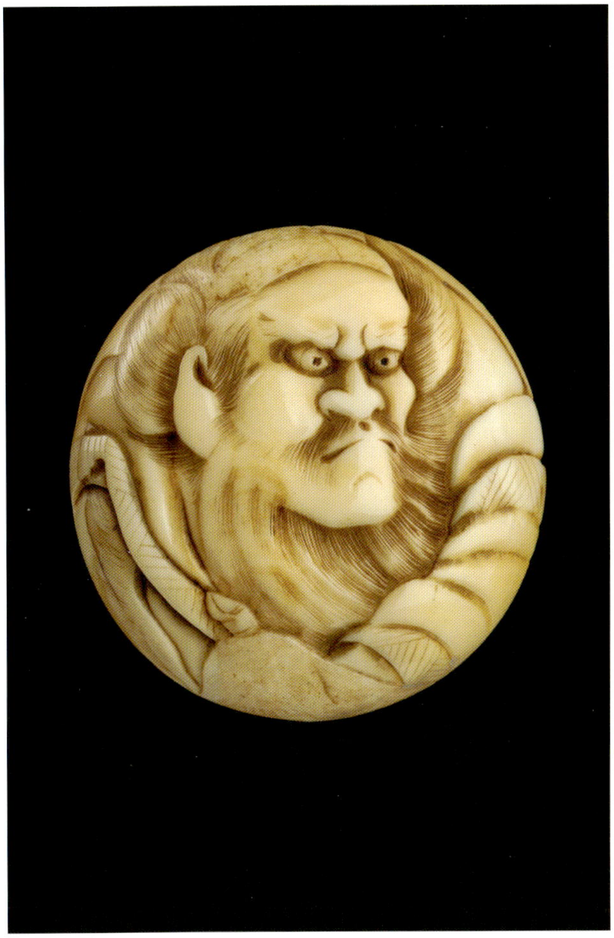

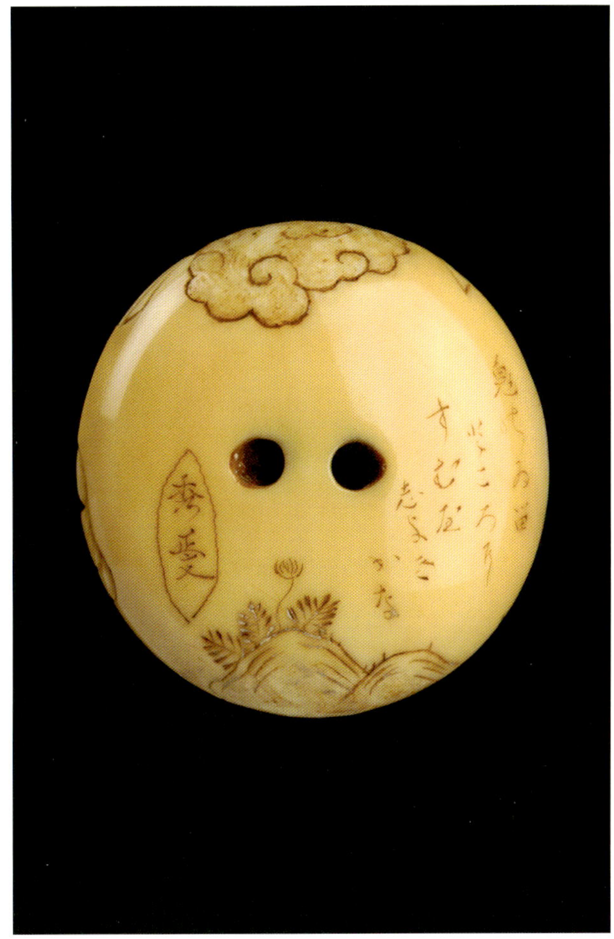

Ex M.T. Hindson Collection

Published in:
Francesco Moreno, Ed., *Giappone, Terra di Incanti, Di Linea e Di Colore (Japan the Land of Enchantment, Line and Colour)*. Firenze Musei (Palazzo Pitti). Sillabe. 2012. No. 98

the green robe rank; in gratitude Zhong Kui had vowed thereafter to rid the world of the pestilence and evil of demons. When Emperor Xuanzong awoke, he was well again.

Hidemasa carved this fierce portrait of Zhong Kui in low relief. His eyes stare with intense concentration and his beard blows in the wind. Hidemasa carved almost exclusively in ivory and most frequently made *katabori* netsuke of figures, paying special attention to the details of their robes. This is an unusual departure from his regular form. He worked in Osaka in the late eighteenth and early nineteenth century. The signature is written in an unusual way with the '政' (masa) character split vertically, maybe a 'playful' way to present it, entirely in keeping with Japanese images of Shōki.

13

Zhong Kui, (Jap. Shōki) the Demon Queller on the prowl, sword at the ready and a frightened-looking *oni* peering through the window of a thatched hut.

Verso: Back view of the *oni* looking through the window.

Ivory
Signed: Isshinsai 一心斎 with *kakihan*
Mid-19th century
Diam: 5.9; H: 2.3 cm
EA2001.130
Bequest of Dr Monica Barnett

See Sotheby's, New York. From the Collection of Philip Schneider 21/03/1997. Lot 392

In this piece Zhong Kui (Jap. Shōki) is easily recognisable wearing the robes and hat of a Chinese scholar. In Japanese art of the Edo period, Zhong Kui is often depicted in a humorous way, chasing demons who tease him and often get the upper hand by escaping. This rendering makes him look as if he really means business, and the *oni* appears suitably frightened. However, in a similar version of this design in the Museum of Fine Arts, Boston, the *oni* has a very self-satisfied grin on his face.

Isshinsai Masayuki was an artist thought to have worked in Osaka in the mid-nineteenth century. Here he uses only one name, though on other pieces he occasionally signed both Isshinsai and Masayuki followed by this *kakihan*. He used wood and ivory for his *manjū* and also carved groups of masks. The Tokyo carvers Gyokkōsai Morimasa, Suzuki Kōsai and Kōmin all used this or a similar design.

See cat. no. 12 for the story of Zhong Kui

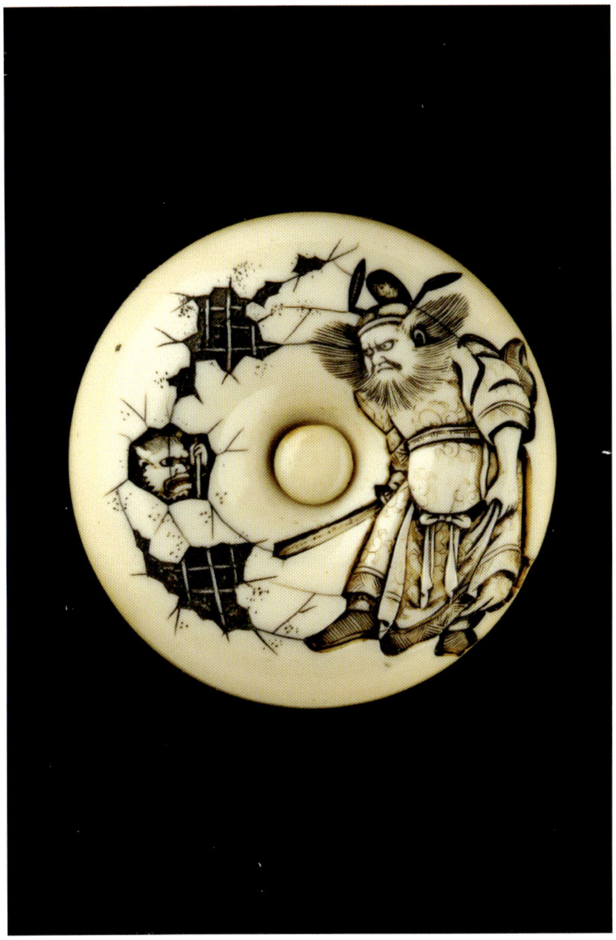

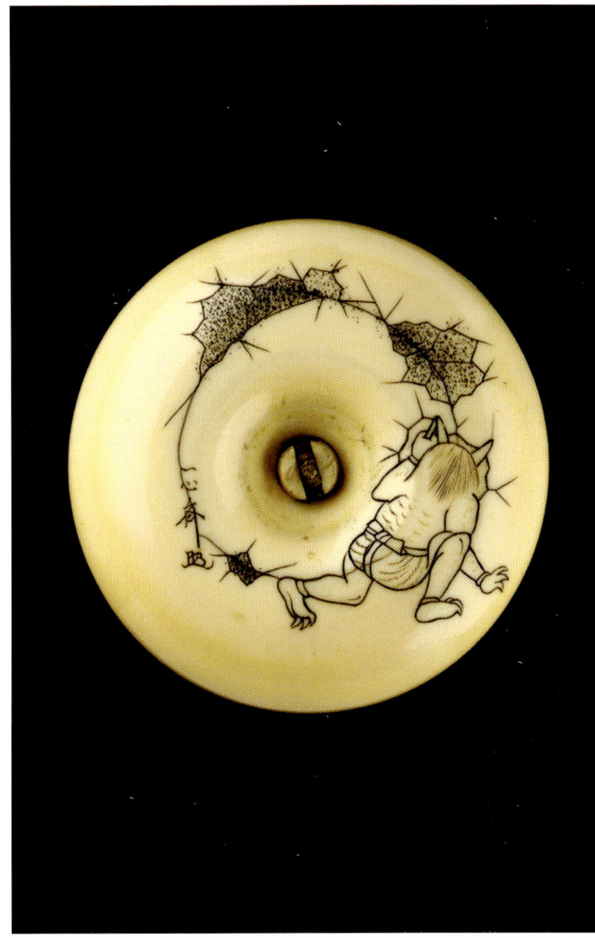

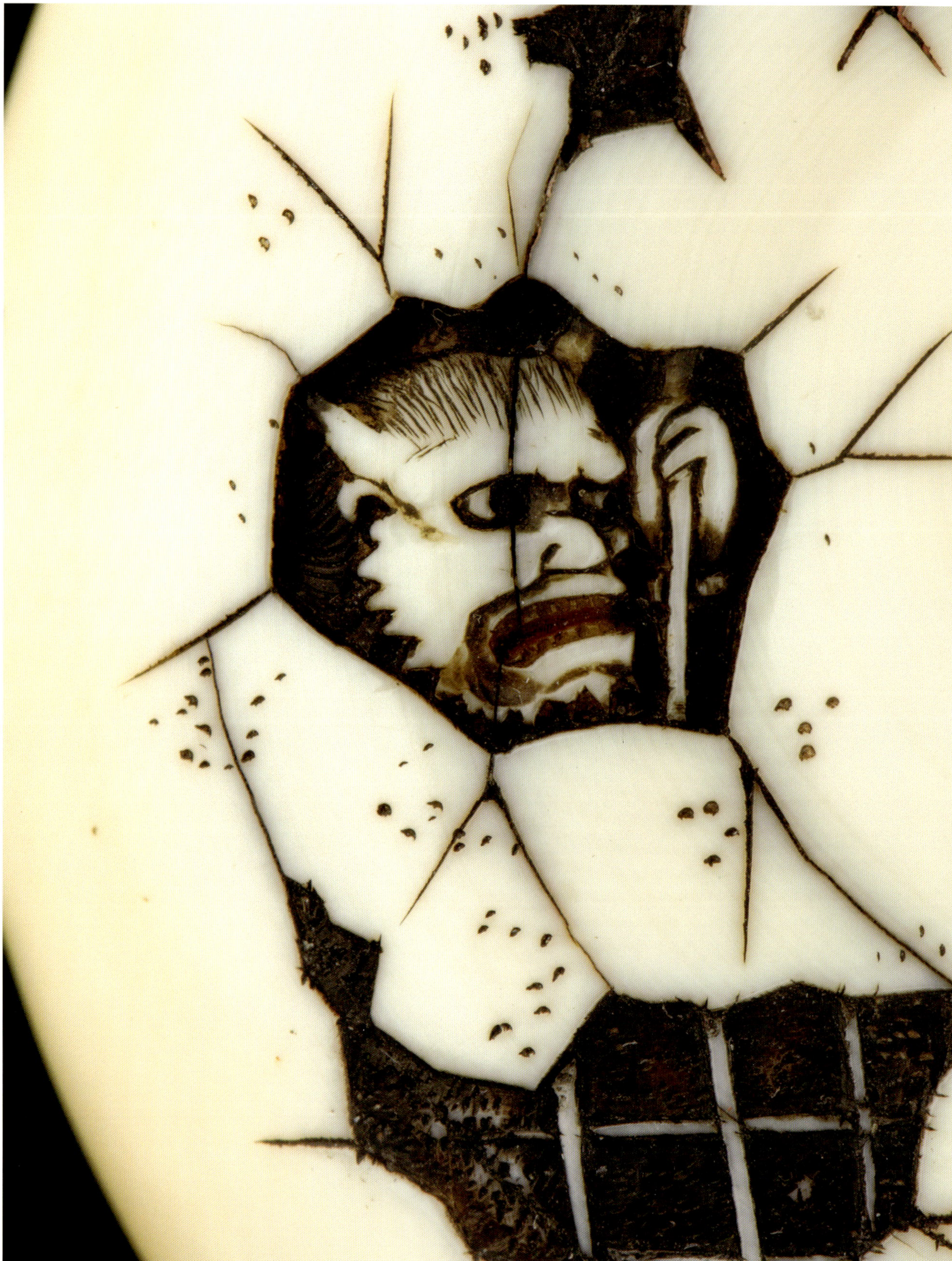

Cat. no. 13 (detail)

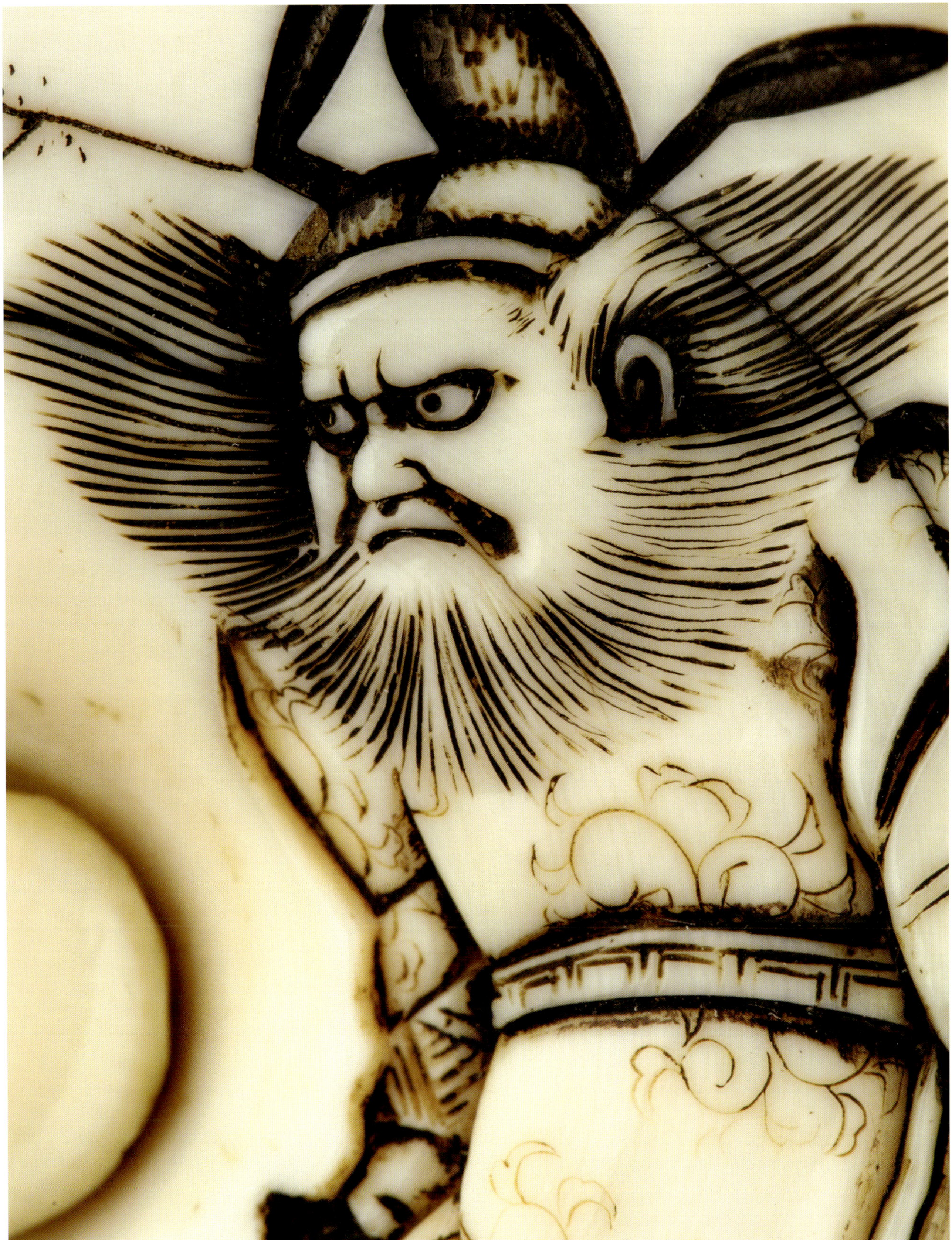

Cat. no. 13 (detail)

14

Zhong Kui (Jap. Shōki) kneeling by a rock with his double-edged sword (*ken*) at the ready

Verso: Oni runs away hidden under a bundle of straw

Ivory with black, red, brown and grey staining
Signed: Ippōsai 一法斎 with *kakihan*
Mid-19th century
Diam: 5.1; H: 2.7 cm
EA2001.85
Bequest of Dr Monica Barnett

Illustrated in:
Frederick Meinertzhagen. Ed. George Lazarnick. *MCI The Meintertzhagen Card Index on Netsuke in the Archives of the British Museum*. New York. Alan R. Liss Inc. 1986. No. 1481C which states Ex Hawkshaw and Gaskell Collections

Sold at Glendining's in January 1911 with a three-case inlaid Shibayama *inrō* for £12.10s (£12.50) where the netsuke was described as 'very beautiful work'. The Collection of J.C. Hawkshaw, Esq. of Hollycombe, Liphook. Lot 304

Sold at Sotheby's, London, 13 &14/06/1985. Lot 503

See Arakawa, Hirokazu. *The Gō Collection of Netsuke*. Tokyo National Museum. Kodansha International Ltd. Tokyo, New York and San Francisco. 1983. No. 132 for an almost identical design by Hōjitsu.

Zhong Kui (Jap. Shōki) was one of the most popular figures from Chinese legend and a cult figure in Japan. In the seventeenth century, amulets depicting the Demon Queller were carried at the annual celebration of the Boys' Festival on the fifth day of the fifth month. Many homes displayed banners of Zhong Kui, for he was thought to be able to ward off disease. In China this day was traditionally considered 'one of the most unlucky and pestilential days in the Chinese calendar',[9] a notion which carried over into Japan. Gradually the idea of encouraging manliness and a sense of competition in young boys became the major concern of the day.

This depiction of the Demon Queller, sharpening his sword on a rock ready to take on any mischevious *oni*, was based on an original design by Hanabusa Itchō (1652–1724). A piece from the Scott Meredith Collection by Meikeisai Hōjitsu gives him credit on the reverse.[10] Later, Kita Masayoshi included a version of it in *Shoshoku ekagami* (Mirror of Images for All Arts) which was published in 1794 in Osaka. Ippōsai has remained quite faithful to the image (left-hand page, top-left image).

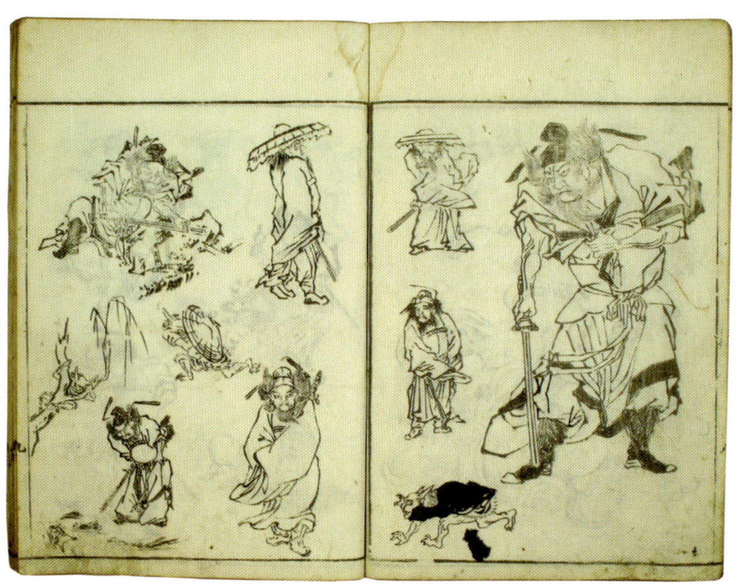

Fig. 29 Illustration from *Shoshoku ekagami* Vol. 1, p. 11 (Waseda University Library, Tokyo, chi04 06282)

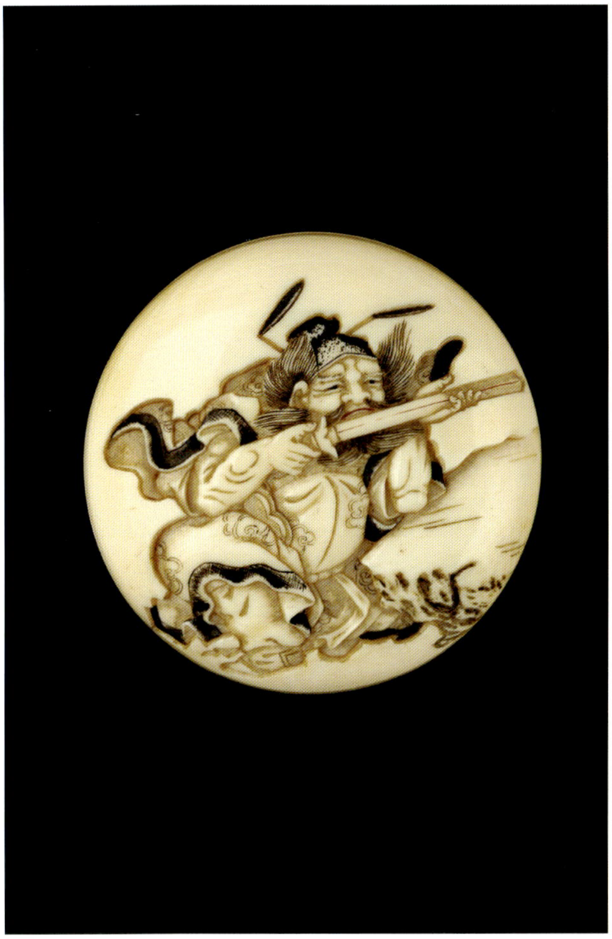

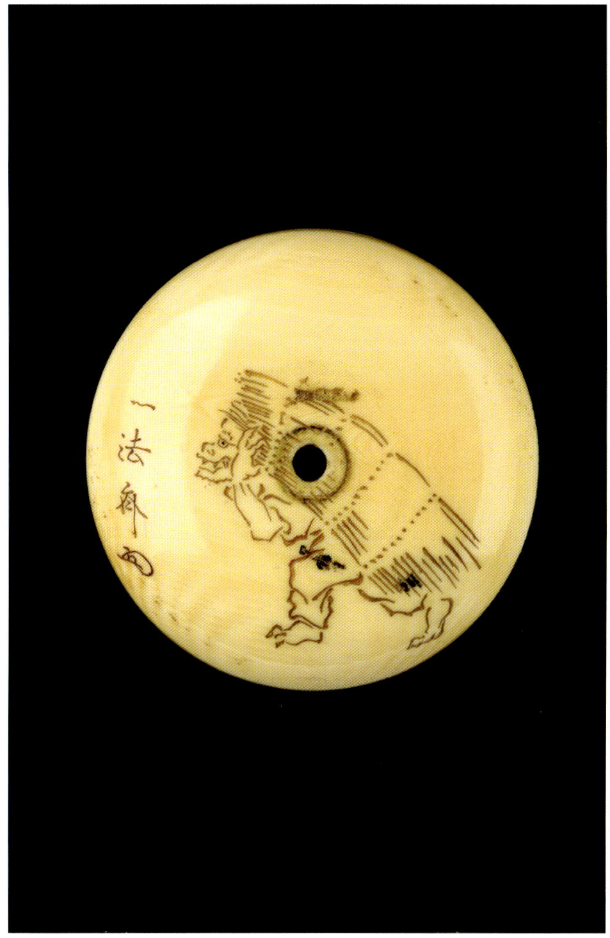

15

Zhong Kui (Jap. Shōki) the Demon Queller

Verso: Oni escaping up a tree, which grows on the bank of a fast-flowing river.

Ivory with black and red staining
Signed: Meikeisai Hōjitsu 明鶏齋法實 in raised rectangular reserve
Mid-19th century
Diam: 5.15; H: 2.6 cm
EA2001.90
Bequest of Dr Monica Barnett

Wilhelm, G. *Manjū exégèse et appréciation*. Bulletin Association Franco-Japonaise No. 54. Octobre 1996. Fig. MB6

Zhong Kui (Jap. Shōki), sword in hand, has captured an *oni* and has it by the chin, tucked under his arm; another, clutching its head, runs away behind him. Meikeisai Hōjitsu (*c.* 1800–1872) was regarded as the best netsuke carver of his time in Edo, excelling in his renderings both of *katabori* and *manjū* netsuke. He lived and worked in Edo and witnessed the social upheaval of the Meiji period and all its implications for craftsmen. He was a prolific carver of fine netsuke. As fashions changed in the Meiji period and collectors from the West began to buy netsuke, he put new skills to work, using different materials and woods as inlays, particularly on his *katabori* pieces (see fig. 38). He appears to have overseen a large workshop, with many students. Over twenty years after his death, a ceremony was held in 1894 at the Nichiren Sect temple, Renkyūji, to erect a tombstone in his memory and on it were carved the names of some of his pupils; Ippōsai, Hōichi, Kōjitsu, Hōkyō, Hōmin and Hōgyoku, works by the first three of whom are represented in this collection. He made netsuke for the *daimyō* of Tsugaru and was a retainer of the Tokugawa government and it is also possible that he even carved for the shōgun. During his life Hōjitsu developed such a high reputation that it appears that less skilled carvers used his signature, but these are clearly not work of his high standard. Sekido Kengo, however, does not believe these to be the work of his pupils either.[11]

For the story of Zhong Kui (Jap. Shōki), see cat. no. 12.

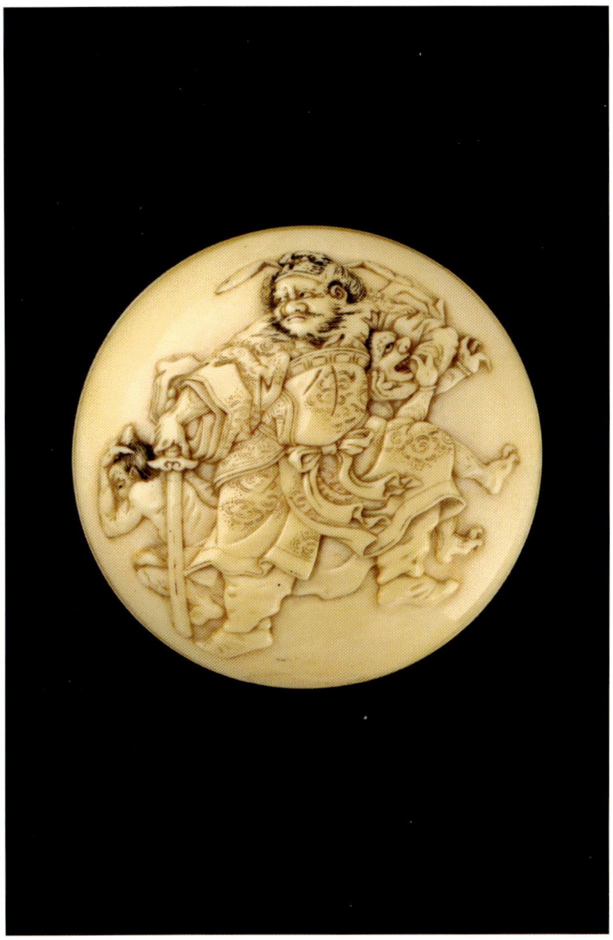

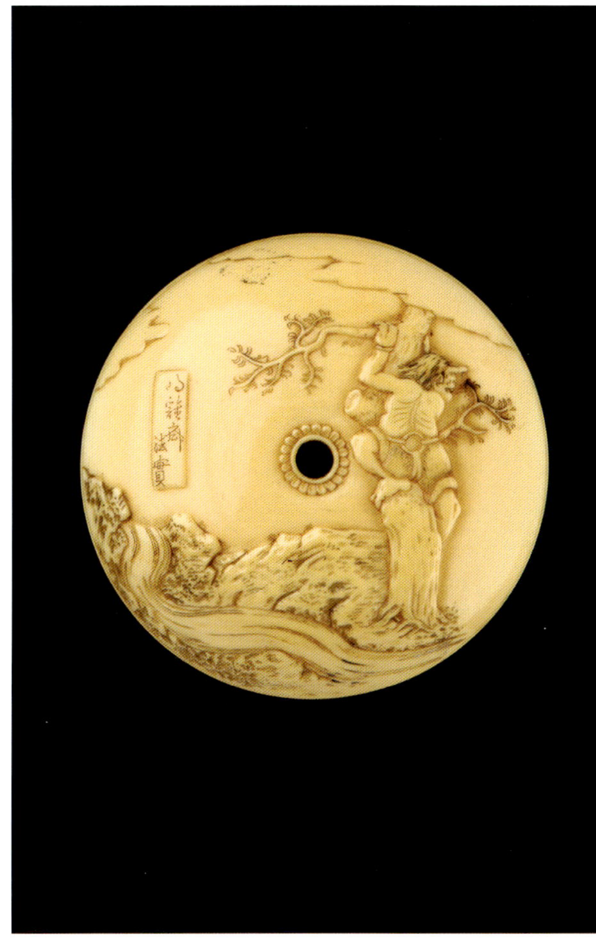

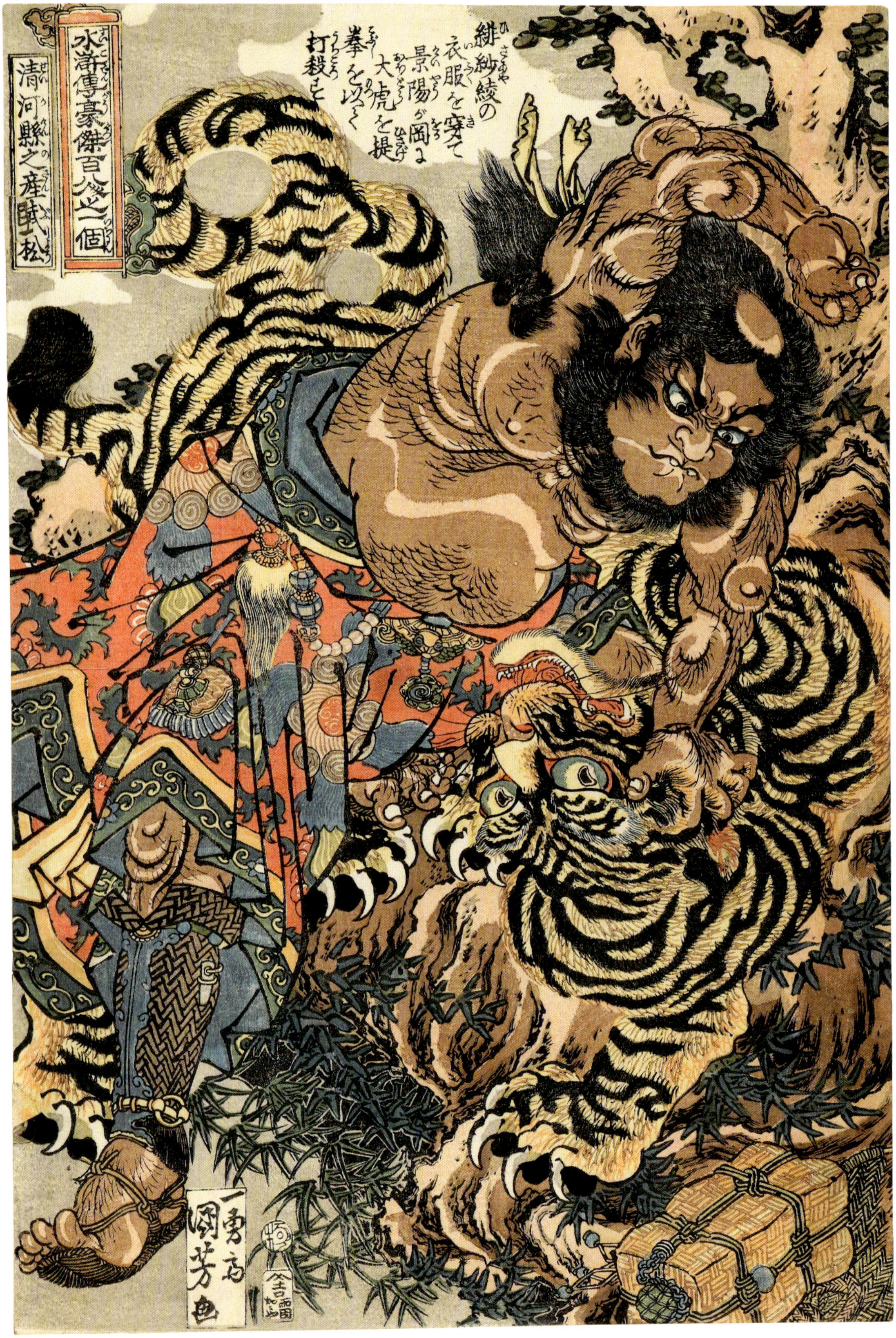

水滸傳豪傑百八人之一個
清河縣之産武松
緋紗綾の衣服を穿て景陽が岡に大虎を提拳をもつて打殺せし
一勇斎國芳画

Heroes of the Water Margin

The Chinese fourteenth century semi-historical novel *Shuihu Zhuan* (Outlaws of the Marsh) recounts the exploits of a group of brigands in China who, 'bound together by superhuman strength, phenomenal accomplishment in the martial arts and a disdain for the constraints of conventional society',[12] find themselves resorting to violence in their struggle for justice against official corruption. The novel which is known in Japanese as *Suikoden* (The Water Margin) was reworked and translated in 1805 by Takizawa Bakin (1767–1848) and illustrated by Katsushika Hokusai (*Shinpen Suikogaden*). In 1805 the new edition of *Suikoden* appeared in print in a form of written Japanese (*furigana*) made easier for the masses to read, thus expanding its readership to a much wider audience. Several more publications of the book were produced causing somewhat of a '*Suikoden* fashion' and provided inspiration to Japanese artists of the 19th century. The Tokugawa regime was draconian, meting out harsh punishment to those in Edo who did not toe the line. Tales of Chinese heroes standing up to a corrupt and bullying government appealed enormously to the lower classes in the social hierarchy.

The wood-block print artists produced detailed and lively renderings of these episodes with explanations of the stories beside the picture. In 1827 Utagawa Kuniyoshi published a series of 108 Chinese heroes entitled *Tsūzoku Suikoden gōketsu hyakuhachinin no hitori* based on this book. He followed this enormously successful series with a corresponding set of 108 Japanese hero prints.[13]

Opposite: Fig. 30 Sanbushō (Wu Song) killing the tiger. Colour woodblock print by Utagawa Kuniyoshi (1797–1862) (EAX.4202)

Below: Cat. no. 17 (detail)

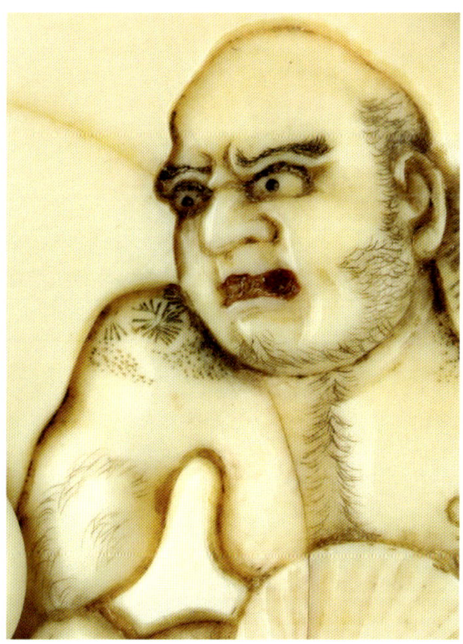

16

Wu Song (Jap. Sanbushō)

Verso: plain

Walrus ivory and staining
Unsigned
Diam: 4.74; H: 1.5 cm
1800–1820
EA2001.109
Bequest of Dr Monica Barnett

A wild-looking Sanbushō is about to deliver the fatal blow with his bare hand to a tiger.

This story comes from Chapter 23 of the *Shuihu zhuan* (Outlaws of the Marsh). Wu Song (Jap. Sanbushō) had fled his home county of Qinghe because he had struck a man and killed him, or so he thought. A gentleman known as 'Lord Chai', from a village far from Wu Song's home, generously invited him to stay in his house. The fugitive stayed for a year, until Chai's generosity ran out, for Wu Song was a drunkard and became abusive to his host. He was asked to leave and so decided to return home to visit his brother. On the way he stopped at an inn and yet again drank too much. Despite the warning given to him by the innkeeper, that a tiger was at large, and had killed almost thirty people on the Jingyang Ridge, Wu Song staggered out into the night. Shortly he came across a notice, sealed with an official seal, announcing the presence of the tiger, which concluded 'to single travellers at any time, the ridge is closed, lest the tiger take their lives. Let this be known to all'.[14] Wu Song had disbelieved the innkeeper and now he ignored the sign. He continued along the ridge in the darkness. Emboldened by the effects of the wine he asked himself,

Below left: Fig. 31 Detail from pair of screens by Kishi Ganku (*c.* 1750–1839) painted around 1820 (EA2002.61). Kishi Ganku and his followers made particularly fine and realistic portraits of tigers in the wild, whereas this beast looks more comical than fierce.

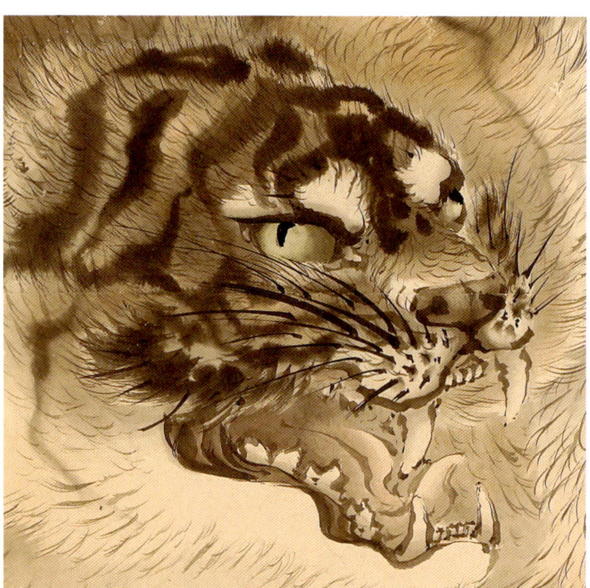

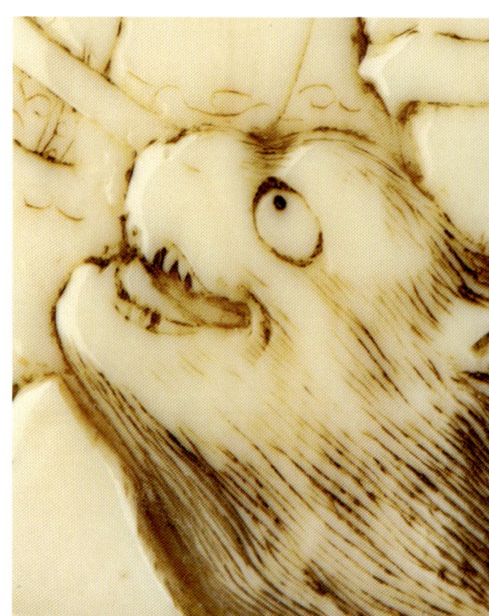

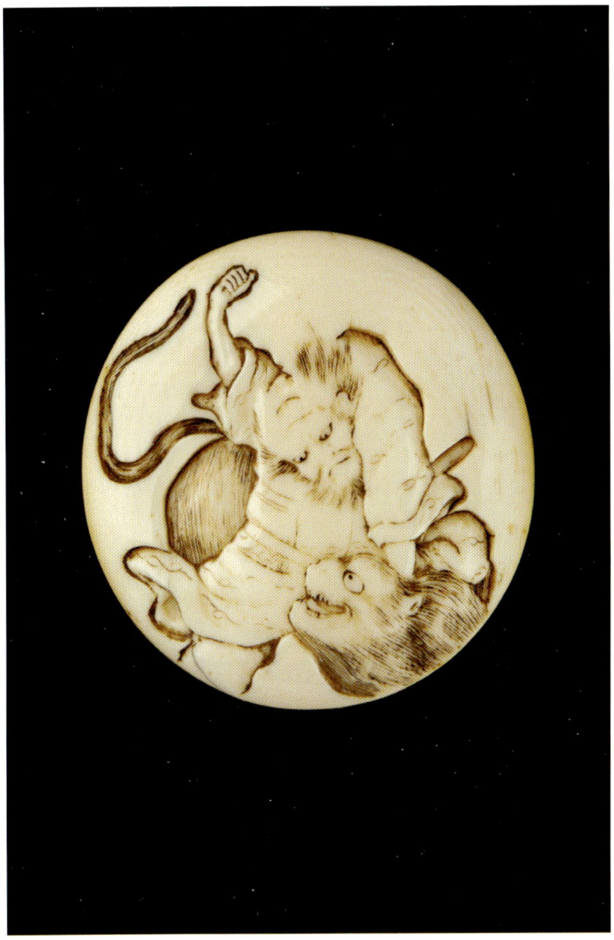

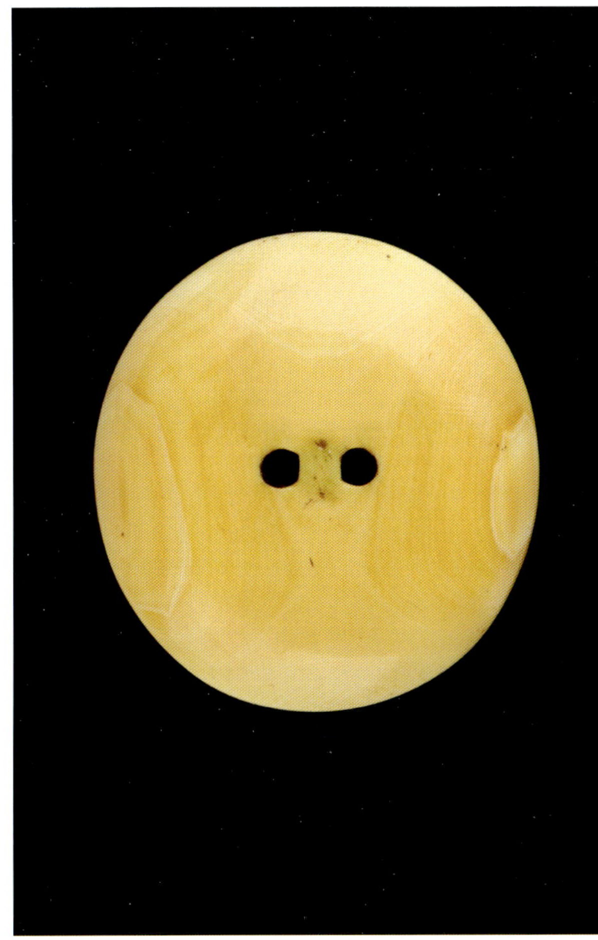

'What is there to be afraid of?' Soon his question was answered. Out of a thicket came a huge tiger which immediately pounced upon Wu Song. A fierce and bloody battle ensued, which almost resulted in Wu Song's demise, but in a final effort, he delivered to the tiger's head a blow with his bare fist, 'big as an iron mallet',[15] and the animal fell to the ground, lifeless.

This depiction of the tiger follows earlier models painted by artists of the Kanō school who had never seen the real animal in the flesh – and nor, probably, had this artist. The first realistic paintings of tigers had appeared a few decades before this carving was done.

17

Xue Yong (Jap. Byōtaichū Setsuei) and Mu Chun (Jap. Shōsharan Bokushun)

Verso: Hexagonal bowl of food on a round plate

Ivory with red and black staining
Signed: Kōsai Moritoshi 光斎守寿 with *kakihan*
Mid-19th century
Diam: 5.8; H: 2.1 cm
EA2001.84
Bequest of Dr Monica Barnett

Sold at Sotheby's London 13 & 14/06/1985. Lot 497

It is not clear which story from the *Water Margin* this netsuke represents, but Dr Barnett labelled it as Sotheby's had suggested in the catalogue of the sale from which she bought it, as Chapter 35 of *Shuihu zhuan* (Outlaws of the Marsh).[16]

Xue Yong was an itinerant medicine seller, seen here on the left with the tattooed body. After arriving in a village Xue Yong did not pay his respects to the brothers Mu Hong and Mu Chun, the village heads. Thus Mu Chun told the villagers not to buy Xue Yong's medicine. However, a man named Song Jiang was travelling through the village and disobeyed, deliberately purchasing medicine from Xue Yong. Mu Chun moved in to fight Song Jiang but the medicine seller intervened and took on Mu Chun himself, winning with ease. Eventually the dispute was settled and perhaps what this *manjū* shows is a quieter moment of reflection after the fight when Xue Yong and Mu Chun sit down together to talk things over.

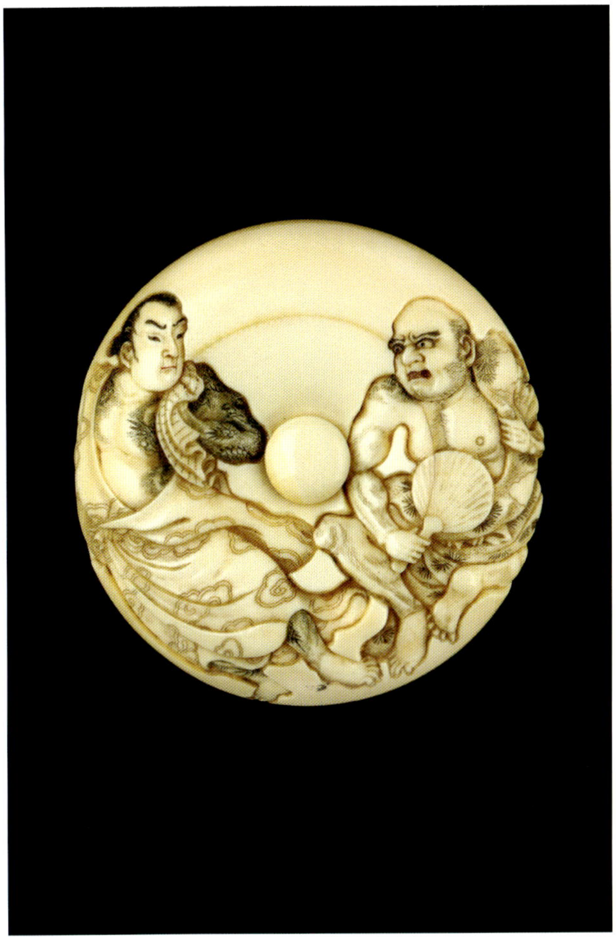

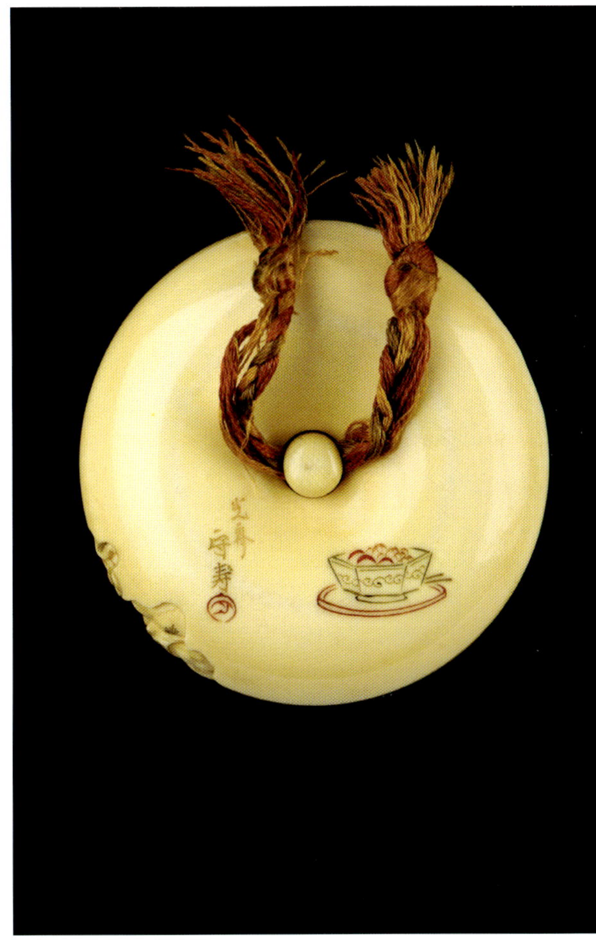

18

Qian Ao

Verso: plain

Ivory with staining
Unsigned
Mid-19th century
Diam: 5.2; H: 2.0 cm
EA2001.78
Bequest of Dr Monica Barnett

A rich Chinese man, Qian Ao, is seated on a low stool, scattering beans on the ground in front of a poor man who grovels on his knees. This netsuke illustrates a Chinese saying, *'Bu shi jie lai zhi shi'* (不食嗟来之食) 'do not eat food handed out in contempt', for disrespect is held in very low esteem.

During the Spring and Autumn period (770–476 BC) of the Eastern Zhou dynasty, when there was a serious famine in the State of Qi, a very rich and arrogant man named Qian Ao, thought he would look generous if he handed food to refugees arriving from the neighbouring state, starving from lack of sustenance. A man, so weak with hunger that he could barely open his eyes, came crawling along the road. When the rich man shouted at him 'Here, come and eat this food', and threw him some beans, the man refused it. The poor, hungry refugee felt that the food was being offered with such contempt that his dignity was offended. To preserve his self-respect, he decided he would rather die than be despised.

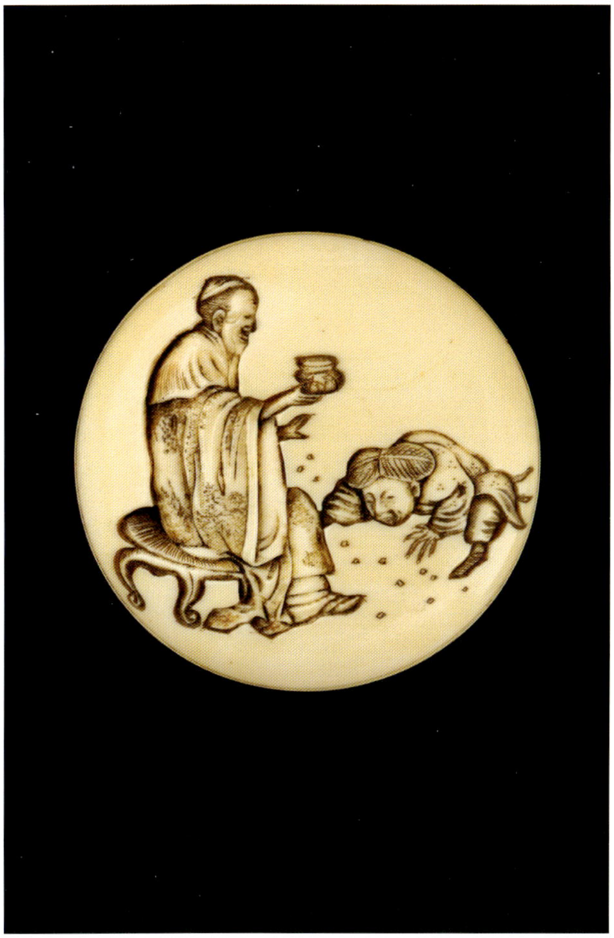

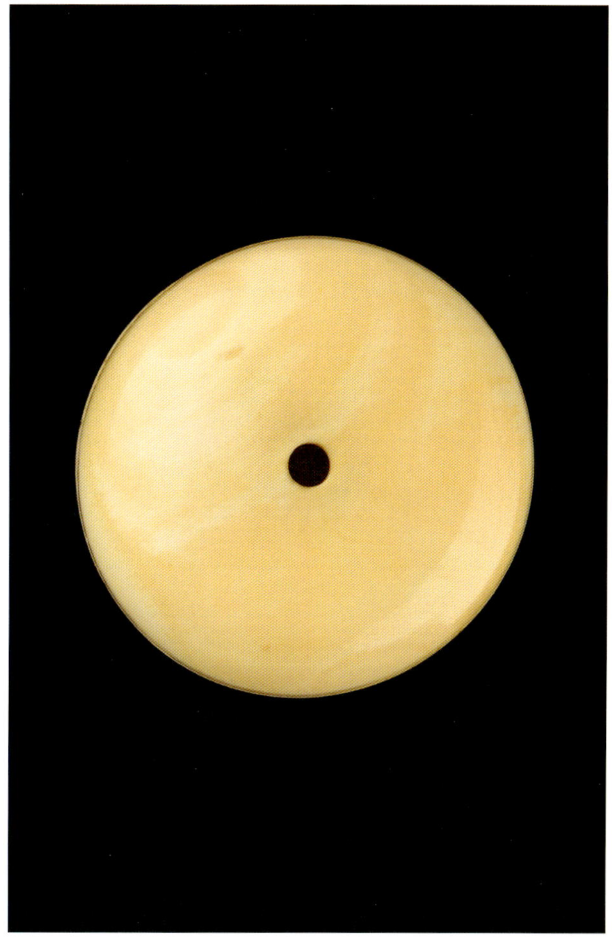

19 and 20

Karako (Chinese boys)

[19]
Red lacquer
Unsigned
1750-1825
Diam: 4.43; H 2.1 cm
EAX.1340
Oppenheim gift

[20]
Red lacquer
Unsigned
1750-1825
Diam: 4.1; H: 2.1 cm
EA1956.3223
Presented by Sir Herbert Ingram

Scholars and Chinese boys playing in landscapes. These two netsuke were made in the latter half of the eighteenth or the early nineteenth century. This style of carved lacquer originated in China in the late thirteenth century and began to be copied in Japan soon after. It is known as *tsuishu* (piled-up red) and was the speciality of one school of lacquerers in Japan who took the name Yōsei. (See cat. no. 112 for a signed example.) The base consists of up to a hundred layers of lacquer, applied, dried and then smoothed by polishing before the application of the next layer. The designs are on two distinct levels: the highest would be tackled first and then the diaper background would be carved later, using chisels and fine knives. Themes on this type of netsuke are invariably Chinese in nature. Sages and their attendants going about their leisurely pursuits in a garden are perhaps the most common. Chinese children playing musical instruments and dancing are also a frequent subject. Where there is a group of five children it represents the accumulated advantages that numerous sons will bring to a family. These netsuke would probably have been made en suite with an *ojime* and *inrō*, similarly carved with Chinese themes.

The book *Irohabiki monchō* いろは引紋帳 (Book of crests and designs) by Tanaka Kikuo, published in 1881, illustrates both family and purely decorative crests. On this page an explanation of how to go about drawing this diaper pattern is explained.

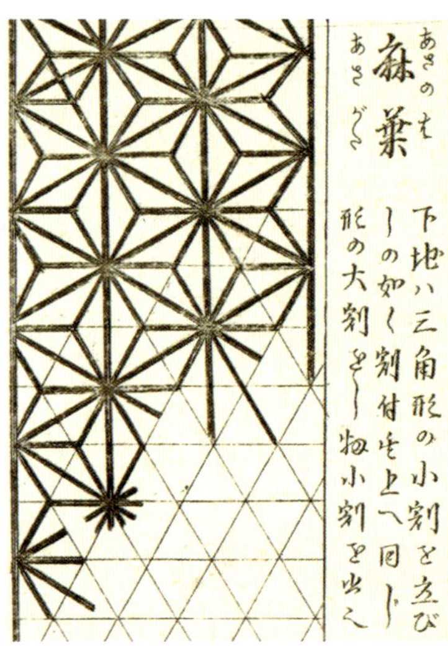

Fig. 32 Illustration from *Irohabiki monchō*. *Asa-no-ha* pattern (EA2012.168)

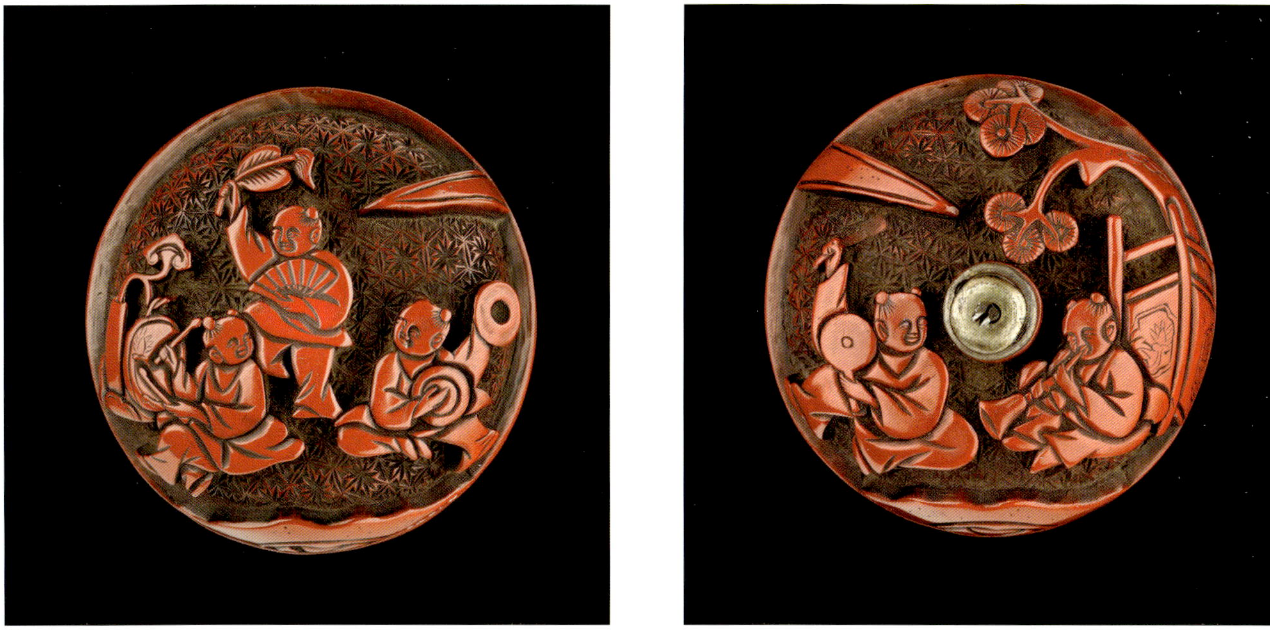

Cat. no. 19

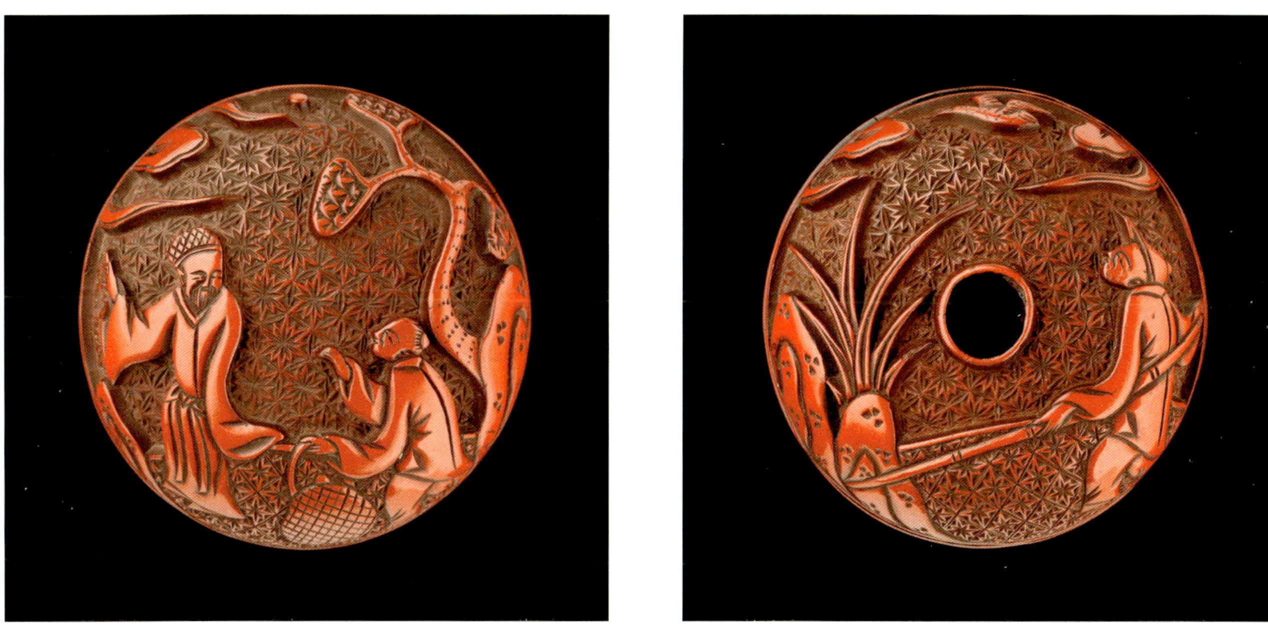

Cat. no. 20

21

Ashinaga and Tenaga

Verso: plain

Bamboo
Signed: Jugyoku 寿玉 with inlaid red lacquer seal reading Ren (Ryūkōsai Jugyoku II)
Edo period: 19th century
Diam: 4.4; H: 2.5 cm
EA2001.123
Bequest of Dr Monica Barnett

Illustrated in:
Frederick Meinertzhagen. *MCI. The Meinertzhagen Card Index on Netsuke in the Archives of the British Museum.* Edited by George Lazarnick. Part 1, 1986. p. 278
Ex. F. Meinertzhagen collection.

Ex W.W. Winkworth collection, bought from Frederick Meinertzhagen.
Ex Carlo Monzino collection which sold at Sotheby's in London on 21/06/1995. (Lot 249)

See Wolf, Richard. *Die Welt der Netsuke.* F.A. Brockhaus. Wiesbaden 1970. p. 132 for the ivory version

The characters Ashinaga (long legs) and Tenaga (long arms) are sitting side by side no doubt on the shore of the Chinese coast, whence they were thought to originate. Their facial features are those of South Sea island coral fishermen, who were usually portrayed by the Japanese with a mane of long curly hair. Japan's virtual isolation from the outside world from the beginning of the seventeenth century meant that non-Asian faces were rarely seen, except perhaps in one of the rare books which filtered into the country through the Dutch and Chinese traders. The fascination with foreigners began in the sixteenth century, when the Portuguese brought trading ships to Nagasaki, and continued well into the early nineteenth century, until Japan was opened up to foreign trade on a larger scale. Ashinaga and Tenaga are mentioned in two eighteenth-century encyclopaedias, the *Wakan sansai zue*[17] (Illustrated Sino-Japanese Enclycopaedia) which records that they lived in two provinces to the east of the Shakusui River,

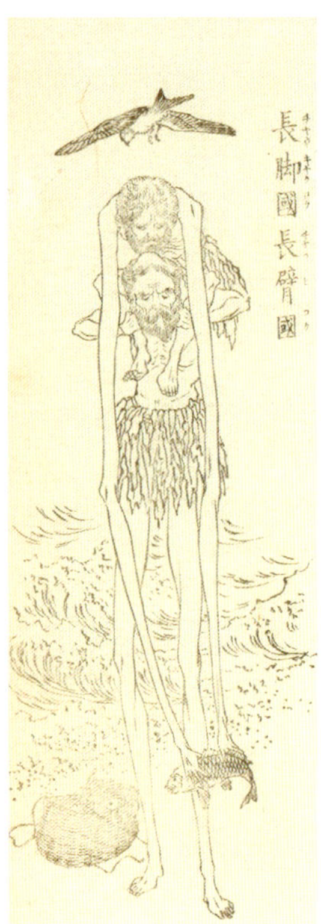

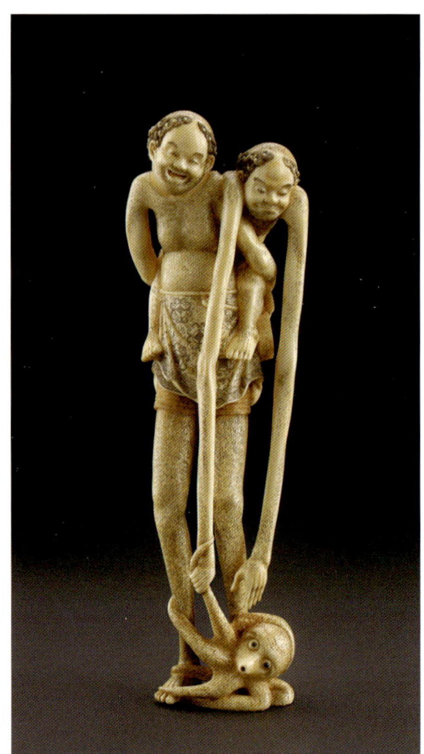

Right: Fig. 33 Illustration from *Banbutsu hinagata gafu*, vol. 3. Ashinaga and Tenaga fishing (EA2012.15)

Far right: Fig. 34 Illustration of Ashinaga and Tenaga. Ivory *okimono* (EA1956.3319)

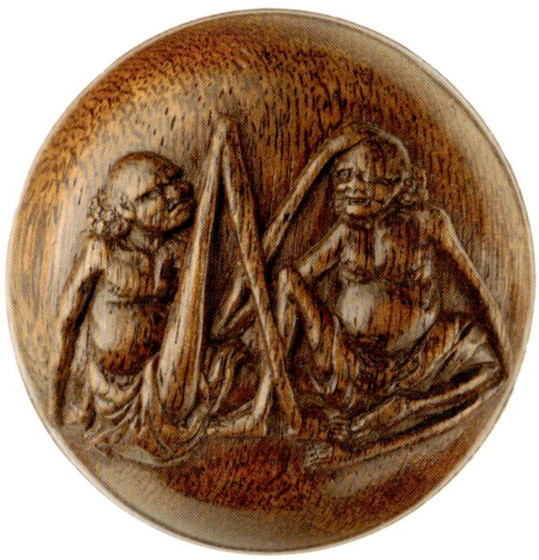

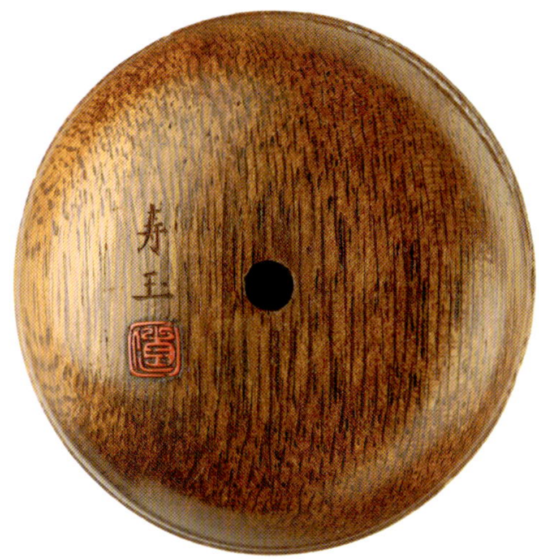
寿玉

Ashinaga in the long-leg province and Tenaga close by in the long-arm province. Hence they symbolise mutual co-operation: two people working in perfect harmony.

Because of Ashinaga's long legs, many early netsuke figures of these two fishermen were long and thin, with Tenaga sitting on Ashinaga's shoulders and reaching down into the sea with his elongated arms. In Jugyoku's unusual depiction, they are sitting side by side on the beach, a pose which perfectly suits the circular surface of the *manjū*. This versatile artist experimented with many different materials, making an ivory version of this design, which was in the Brokhaus collection.[18]

22

Coral Fisherman

Verso: formal scrolling of clouds

Ryūsa-type *manjū*
Ivory, stained to a reddish brown colour
Unsigned, Asakasa school, Tokyo
Circa 1850
Diam: 4.2; H: 1.8 cm
EA2001.89
Bequest of Dr Monica Barnett

Published in:
Francesco Moreno, Ed., *Giappone, Terra di Incanti, Di Linea e Di Colore (Japan the Land of Enchantment, Line and Colour)*. Firenze Musei (Palazzo Pitti). Sillabe. 2012. No. 93

This design was carved several times by one or more of the Asakusa school artists and the figure in the centre has been variously described as Raiden, the God of Thunder, a *sennin*, a dwarf, or a *koronbojin* (a native of Colombo, Sri Lanka) which more generally meant a foreigner with dark skin. When this was exhibited at the Palazzo Pitti, in Florence, Max Rutherston made a case for a South Sea-island fisherman, surrounded by a long rope, sitting beside a bifurcate piece of coral (on the left). What were often thought of as clouds around the edge easily convert into breaking waves. Coral was a luxury material in Japan during the Edo period, when it was occasionally sparingly used for netsuke, often in conjunction with ebony to portray these coral-fishing foreigners. It is interesting to compare the faces of Ashinaga and Tenaga (cat. no. 21) with this fisherman. They all have the generic 'foreign' face which the pre-Meiji Japanese artists used to portray people from the South Seas.

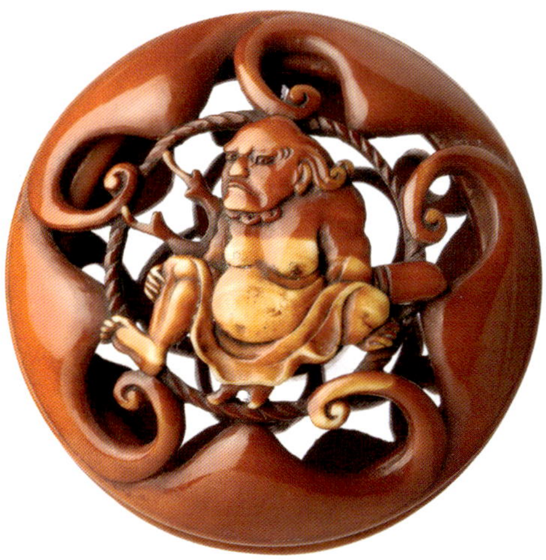

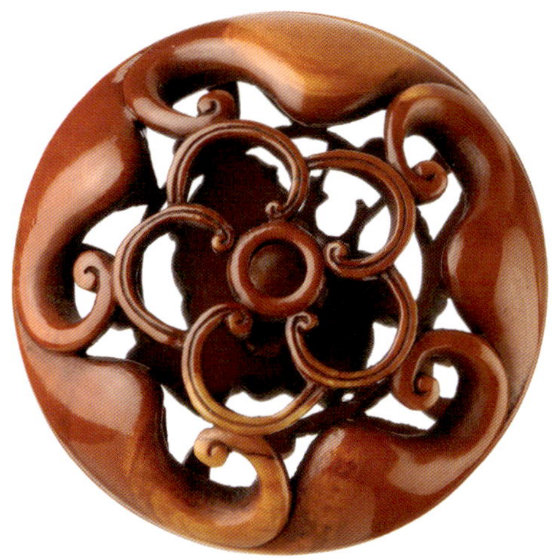

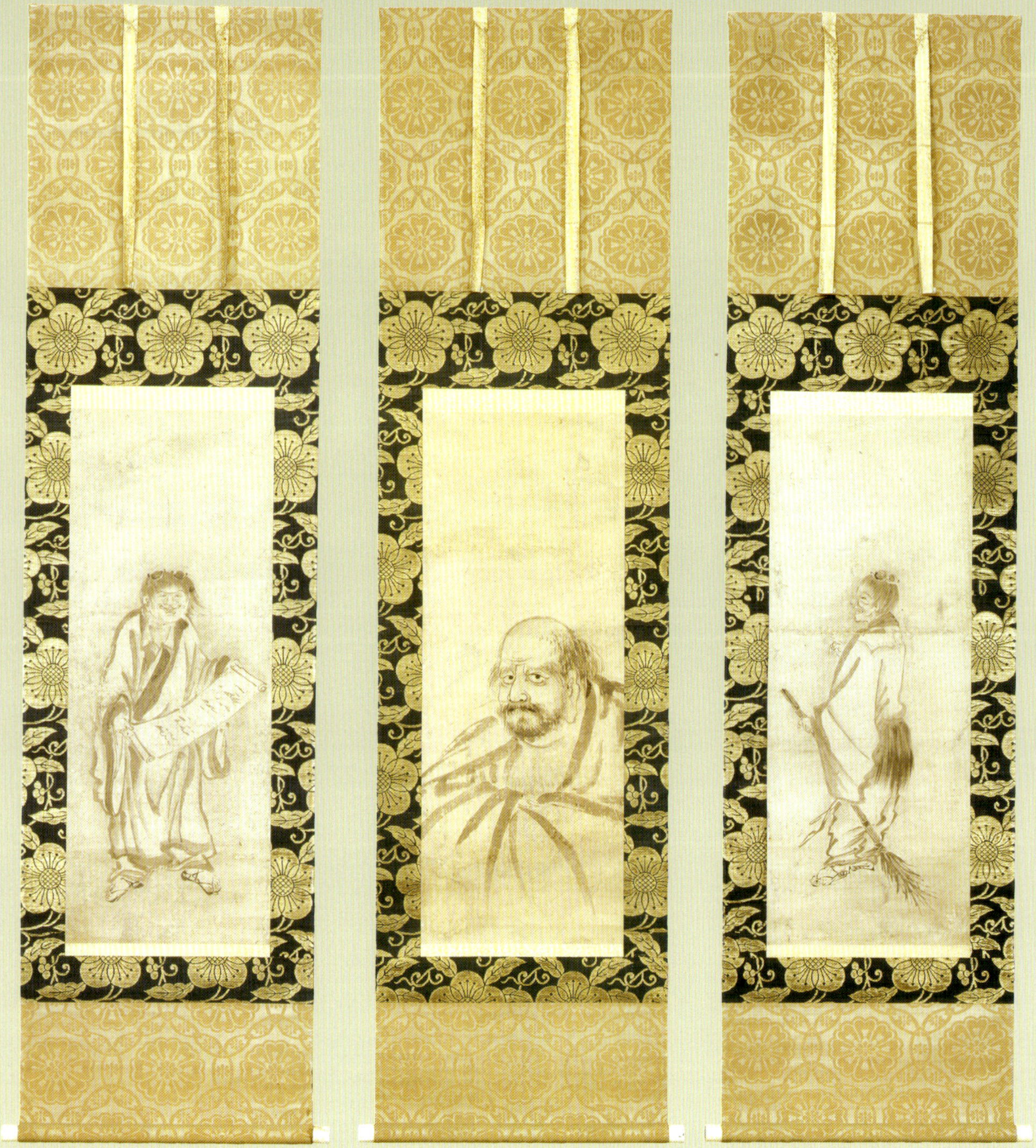

Fig. 35 Daruma flanked by Kanzan and Jittoku. Hanging scrolls, ink on paper, 16th century (EA1962.114–115)

Religious Subjects

Buddhism reached Japan from India via China and Korea in the sixth century. Based on the teachings of Siddhartha Gautama, the historical Buddha, it offered personal salvation and an escape from the endless cycle of suffering and rebirth. It quickly became established in Japan, where it was enthusiastically embraced. The Buddha, who achieved enlightenment and was therefore not subject to rebirth, appointed various disciples to assist human beings to live their lives according to his doctrine. Images of the Buddha do appear in Japanese paintings and sculpture but much more common are images of his attendants, who have various roles assigned to them, several of whom are illustrated in this collection.

Buddhism divided into a number of sects, each one following the words of a different sutra or interpreting doctrines in a different way and emphasising different images for their particular form of worship. The sect to have the greatest impact on Japan was 'Chan' Buddhism, known as 'Zen' in Japan. Monks from Japan were sent to study at the five important Chan monasteries of southern China and returned with the new doctrine and associated works of art to aid their teaching. They built the five Zen monasteries of Kamakura and Kyoto (*gozan*), modelling them on their Chinese predecessors. Early Zen Buddhism eschewed the worship of images of the Buddha in favour of chanting sutras, meditation and working on catechetics (Jap. *kōan*), often of a very obtuse nature. The first Zen patriarch was *Bodhidharma*, known in Japan as Daruma. He was the subject of many serious protraits in China and Japan but was also treated very playfully by the Japanese, particularly by netsuke carvers (see cat. no. 33).

In the mid-17th century, Zen was given a new impetus when the priest Ingen, a member of the Zen Ōbaku sect and a refugee after the fall of the Ming Dynasty in China, was invited by the Japanese emperor to build a Zen temple at Uji, near Kyoto. Named, Manpukuji and finished in 1661, it became a centre for Chinese cultural pursuits, which slowly filtered further afield into Japan.

23

Tennin (heavenly being)

Reverse: Stylised clouds

Ryūsa-type *manjū*
Stag Antler
Signed: Tōkoku 東谷
Mid- to late 19th century
Diam: 3.9; H: 1.2 cm
EAX.626

Tennin are Buddhist celestial beings or 'angels' who are said to live in Amida Buddha's Western Paradise, where those who have escaped the circle of transmigration are able to reside on their way to attaining Buddhahood. *Tennin* originated in India where they are known as *apsara* and are usually portrayed as beautiful young women. Various versions of these creatures emerged in art all over Asia. In Japan they are generally seen flying through the firmament, with long scarves flowing around them.

Tōkoku has carved a broad-faced female and dressed her in the traditional flowing robes and long scarves, with a necklace and an elaborate tiara. The reverse is made up of swirling stylised clouds around two uneven *himotōshi*. She nurses a large lotus blossom, a symbol of purity in Buddhism, across her breast.

24

Two *tennin*

Ryūsa-type *manjū*

Ivory
Signature is illegible
Late 19th century
H: 2.5; W: 3.45; D: 1.7 cm
EAX.753

Two *tennin* are ingeniously woven into the perforated surfaces of this *manjū*, one holds a lotus and the other plays a *shō*, an instrument associated with heavenly musicians. Their long scarves flow around conveniently making the network for the pierced ivory design.

Both *tennin* are holding lotus flowers.

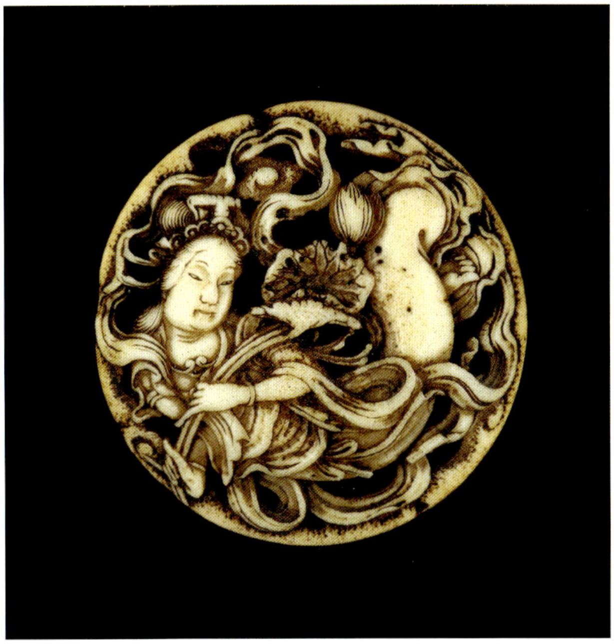

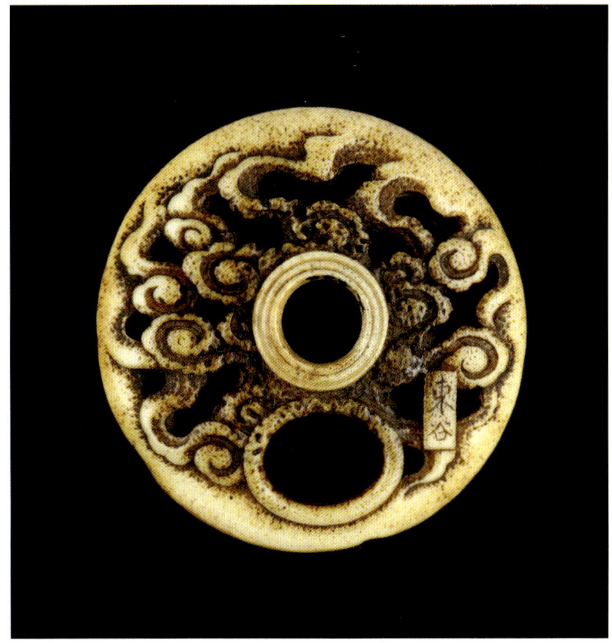
東谷

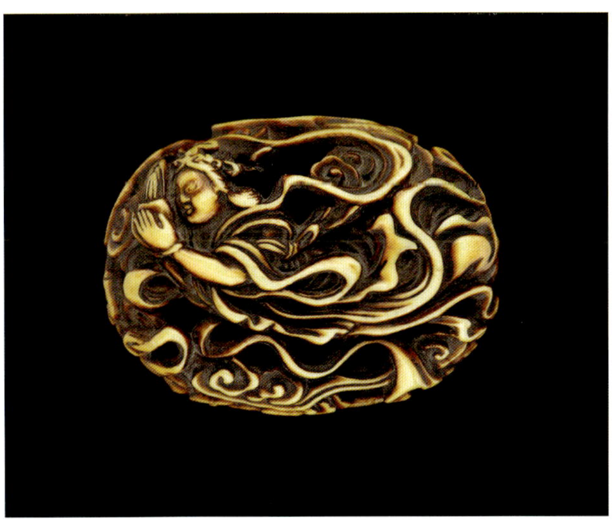

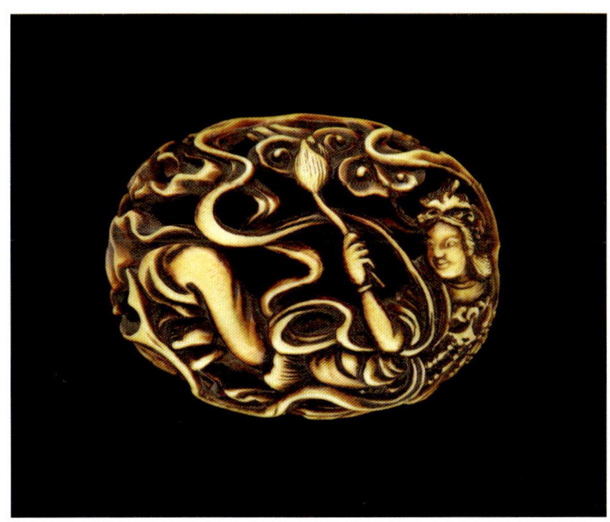

25

Enma-ō and Jizō Bosatsu crossing the river Sanzu.

Verso: Horse-headed attendant bringing Enma-ō's archaic shoes, slung over a staff carried across his shoulder.

26

Enma-ō and Jizō Bosatsu crossing the river Sanzu.

Verso: Horse-headed attendant bringing Enma-ō's archaic shoes, slung over a staff carried across his shoulder.

[25]
Ivory with green stone inlay
Signed: Ono Ryōmin 小野陵民
with *kakihan*
1860–1880
Diam: 4.8; H: 2.0 cm
EA2001.107
Bequest of Dr Monica Barnett

[26]
Ivory
Signed: Ono Ryōmin 小野陵民
with *kakihan*
1860–1880
Diam: 5.4 H: 2.25 cm
EA2001.133
Bequest of Dr Monica Barnett

See Patrizia Jirka-Schmitz. *Netsuke. Gürtelschmuck aus Japan. Die sammlung Trumpf*. Linden-Museum Stuttgart. Staatliches Museum für Völkerkunde. Arnoldsche Art Publishers for a similar example by Ono Ryōmin, dated 1864. No. 106

EA2001.107 sold at Sotheby's, London on 20/02/1986. Lot 24

In these two delightful designs Enma-ō grimaces as he accompanies the gentle *bodhisattva*, Jizō, on a fishing trip in the River of Souls.

Enma-ō is the Japanese Buddhist form of the Hindu god of death, Yama. He wears a crown with the simple identifying character 王 (*ō*), meaning king. He was incorporated into the Japanese Buddhist pantheon as the King of the Underworld and Judge of the Dead. His job is to assign souls to one of the six realms of hell, which include hungry ghosts, animals and fighting demons, all determined by their earthly deeds. There they remain until their rebirth, unless saved by the prayers of the living, which can hasten their progress to earth or to a heavenly paradise. Enma-ō's usual countenance is intended to put fear into the eye of the beholder. Lafcadio Hearn describes a statue of him in Kamakura, kept hidden behind a curtain, 'A Face, tremendous, menacing, frightful … The wonder of the creation is not in the tiger frown, nor in the violence of the terrific mouth, nor in the fury and ghastly color of the head as a whole: it is in the eyes, – eyes of nightmare'.[19] In this parody, Ono Ryōmin has almost made it look as if Enma-ō is enjoying himself with his companion. Parody pictures (*mitate-e*) usually poked fun at authority – in this case Buddhism.

A *bodhisattva* (Jap. *bosatsu*) is one of the Buddha's disciples destined to attain enlightenment (*bodhi*) but who has postponed this in order to help others on earth. In theory, in the doctrine of Mahayana Buddhism, which is practised in Japan (as opposed to Theravada Buddhism, favoured in many countries in South East Asia), anyone who aspires to enlightenment and performs the requisite practices is regarded as a *bodhisattva*. Jizō is a *bodhisattva*, entrusted with the task of escorting human souls at their death to the Pure Land of Amida Buddha. In particular, he is the protector of children's souls. Usually portrayed in monk's clothing

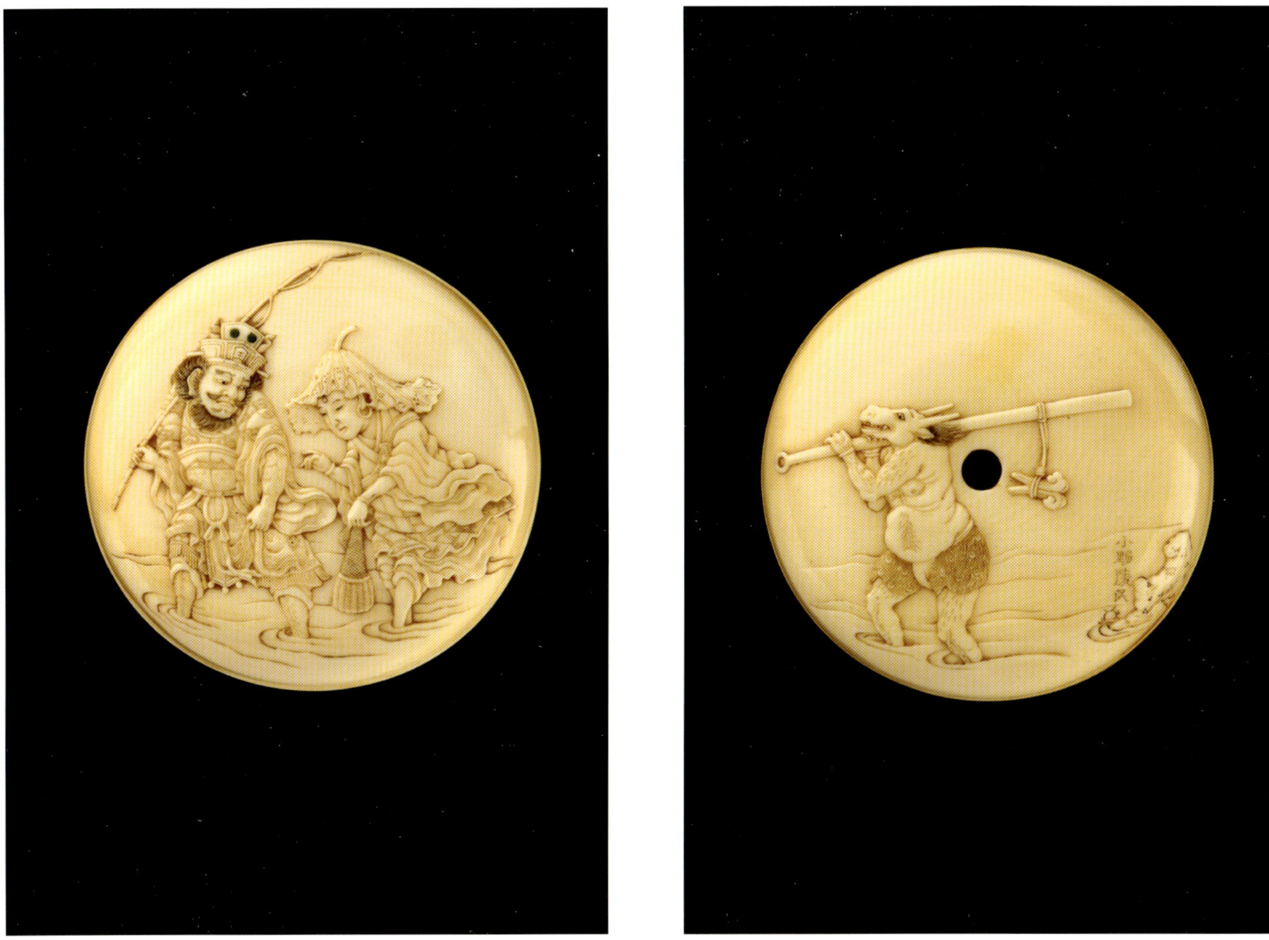

Cat. no. 25

with a shaven head, standing upon a lotus pedestal, here he has plucked a large leaf from his pedestal and uses it as a fetching hat. The lotus is also associated with rituals of death and the transformation of new souls in the Buddhist heaven.[20]

When approaching hell, the first obstacle is the crossing of the Sanzugawa, or the River of Souls, the Buddhist equivalent of the Styx. Those whose minor misdeeds merit an easy passage are allowed to cross at the shallow ford. Enma-ō and Jizō, robes tucked up above their knees, have no difficulty with the crossing. On the reverse a horse-headed creature, one of the two chiefs of hell, is depicted bringing up the rear, carrying Enma-ō's archaic shoes slung over Jizō's staff which he carries across his shoulder.

It is interesting to compare these two *manjū* by Ono Ryōmin, who has sought inspiration from different sources for his subject. The design on the front of cat. no. 26 is illustrated in *Itchō gafū*.[21] In Hanabusa Itchō's print, Enma-ō and Jizō are followed by two attendants, one bull-headed, the other, with a horse's head, carrying the pair's luggage piled over Jizō's staff. A *manjū* by Ono Ryōmin in the Trumpf collection, has a horned *oni* (demon) carrying the luggage on the reverse.[22] The source of cat. no. 25 is unknown, and may simply be the artist's own interpretation of the subject. Ryōmin carved with great delicacy, which prompted Luigi Bandini of Eskenazi, to write of this *manjū*, 'such fine craftsmanship is rarely seen in a manjū'. [23] The details on one are executed in slightly raised relief and on the other in shallow sunken relief.

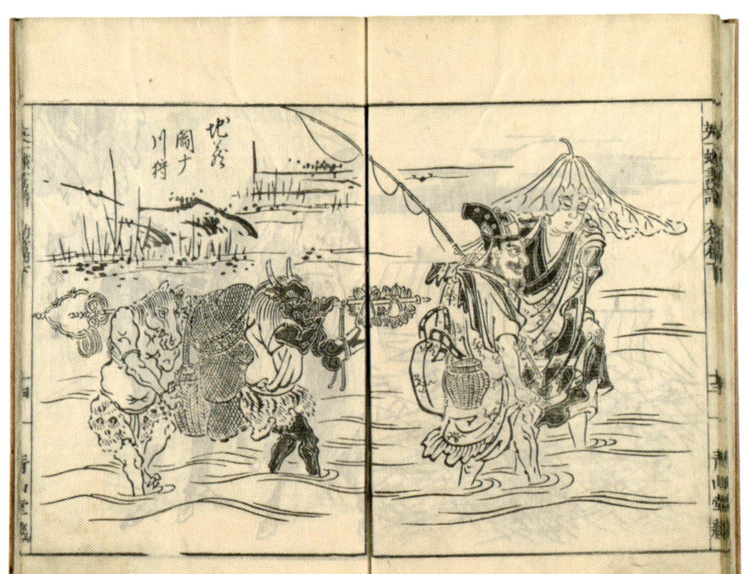

Fig. 36 Illustration from *Itchō gafū* ,vol. 3 (National Diet Library, Tokyo 2554324/16)

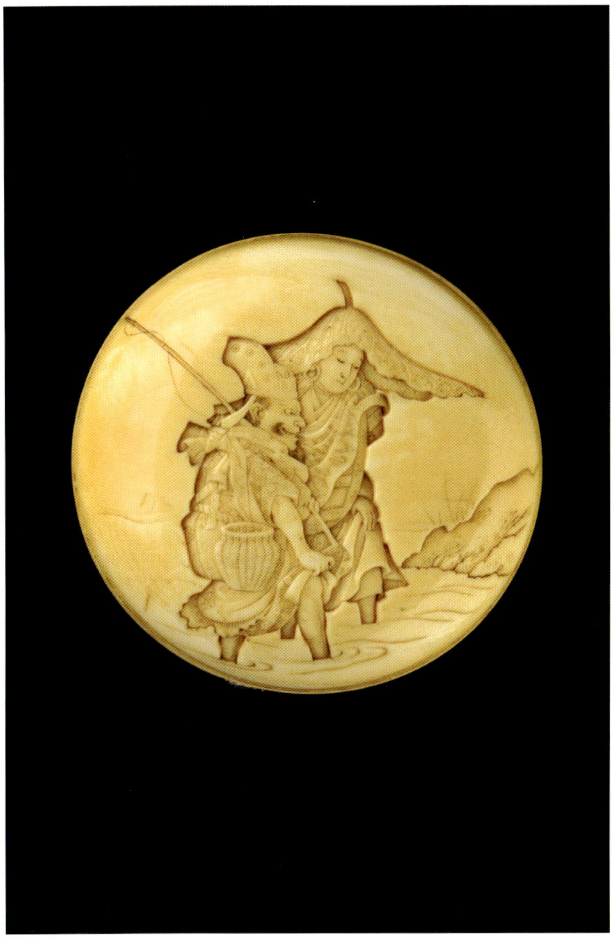 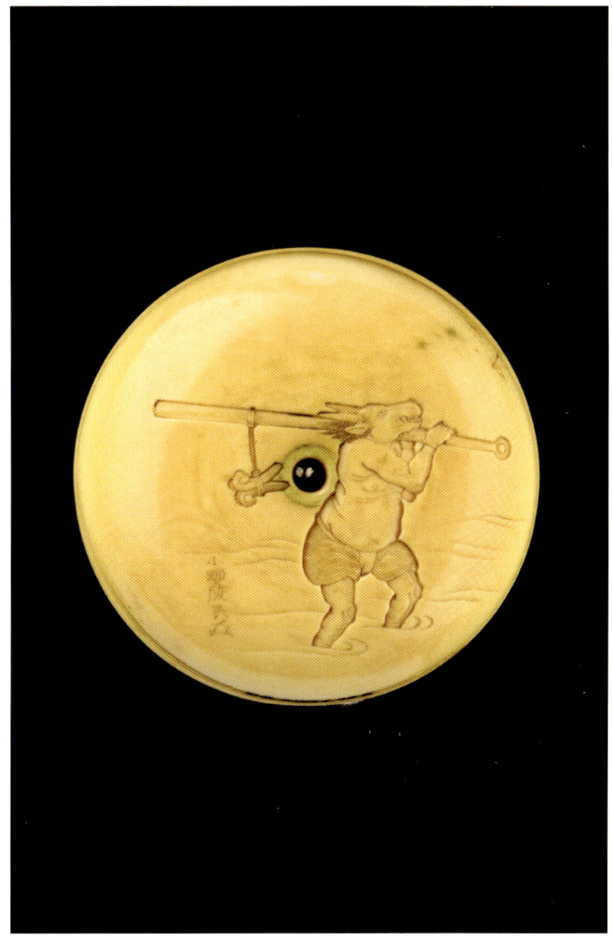

Cat. no. 26

27

Rakan

Verso: Stylised breaking waves

Ivory with metal, red and green glass and lacquer
Signed: Ikkōsai Kōjitsu 一光斎孝實 with *kakihan*
Mid- to late 19th century
Diam: 4.45; H: 2.1 cm
EA2001.52
Bequeathed by Dr Monica Barnett

For similar pieces see:
Seymour Trower Collection. No 396, Plate V by Kōju which was sold at Sotheby's Chicago in the sale 'Fine Netsuke Including Property from the Collection of Alan R. Liss'. September 02/09/1993, Lot 148
In the same sale (Lot 286) the subject is carved by Kōju and it bears a label from the Red Cross Exhibition of Japanese art, London 1915, No. 122
For an example by Ikkōsai Hōraku (一光斎法楽) with a very similar *kakihan* see George Lazarnick, *Netsuke and Inro Artists, and How to Read their Signatures.* Reed Publishers, Honolulu. 1981., p. 489.
For examples by Ikkōsai Kōjitsu see Neil K. Davey. *Netsuke. A comprehensive study based on the M.T. Hindson collection.* Faber & Faber Limited. London, in association with Sotheby Parke Bernet Publications. 1974. p. 153, No. 455. and Akkerman, P. (introd.), Sale exhibition of: The Buzaglo Collection of Fine Netsuke (comprising 545 items collected in Japan between 1950–1960) 29/11/ – 21/12/1985. Aalderink, Amsterdam, Holland. No. 519 p. 48 Ex Behrens collection.
Suzuki Kōsai carved a version with the same reverse showing breaking waves which is now in the Maidstone Musuem, Kent (42.1979.M23)

Bought from Douglas J K Wright 28/08/1971

Rakan (Sk. *Arhat,* Ch. *lohan*) are disciples of the Buddha, who at his death were chosen to continue his teaching and to protect the Buddhist rule of law. Chinese artists portrayed them in paintings individually, in groups of five hundred, but more often as the sixteen or eighteen who were specially selected from amongst the throng. Japanese painters and netsuke artists then continued the tradition.

This frontal depiction of a *rakan* is more comical than serious. His domed bald head is surrounded by a large halo and his Indian features, pinched into a ridiculous expression of concentration are augmented by elongated earlobes, adorned with elaborate dangling earrings. His hands are clasped together in front of his chest beneath his priestly robe. Ikkōsai has paid great attention to the textile patterns on both robe and *kesa* (monk's overgarment, traditionally made up of fragments of brocade) but seems to be poking fun at the venerable disciple. In the eighteenth and nineteenth centuries paintings of *rakan* were widely used as teaching aids for Zen Buddhist acolytes.

Ikkōsai Kōjitsu (1833–1893) was one of the most talented pupils of Meikeisai Hōjitsu. Here he has put his own interpretation on this subject, and there exist several other similar versions by members of Meikeisai Hōjitsu's school. He has carved the ivory in deep *shishiaibori* for the portrait and added metal for the rings, red and green glass for the beads and coral for the droplets of the earrings. The reverse has a large breaking wave, carved with fluid *kebori* lines.

This design was used, with slight variations, by Kōju, Suzuki Kōsai, Ikkōsai Hōraku and more than once by Ikkōsai Kōjitsu, all of whom belonged to the same workshop.

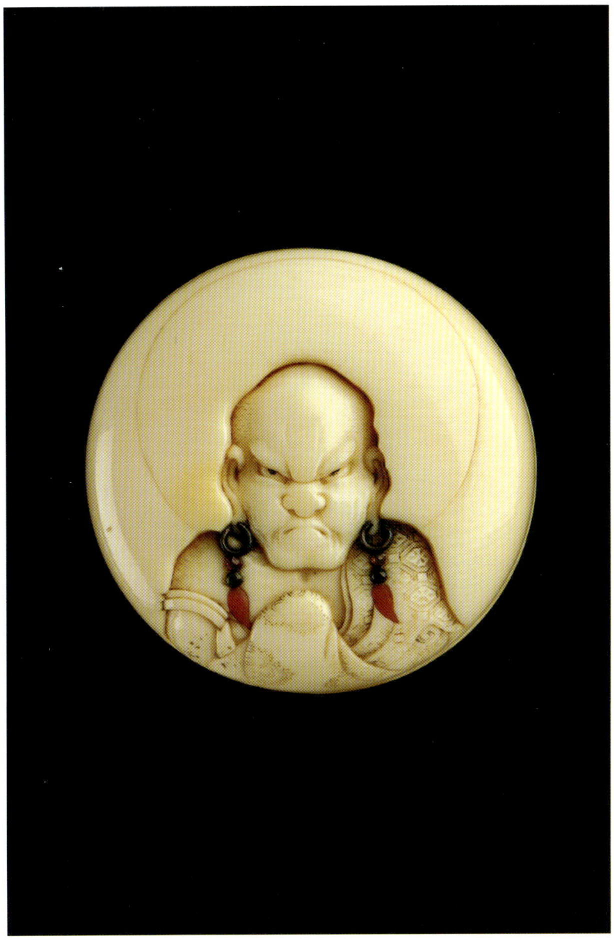

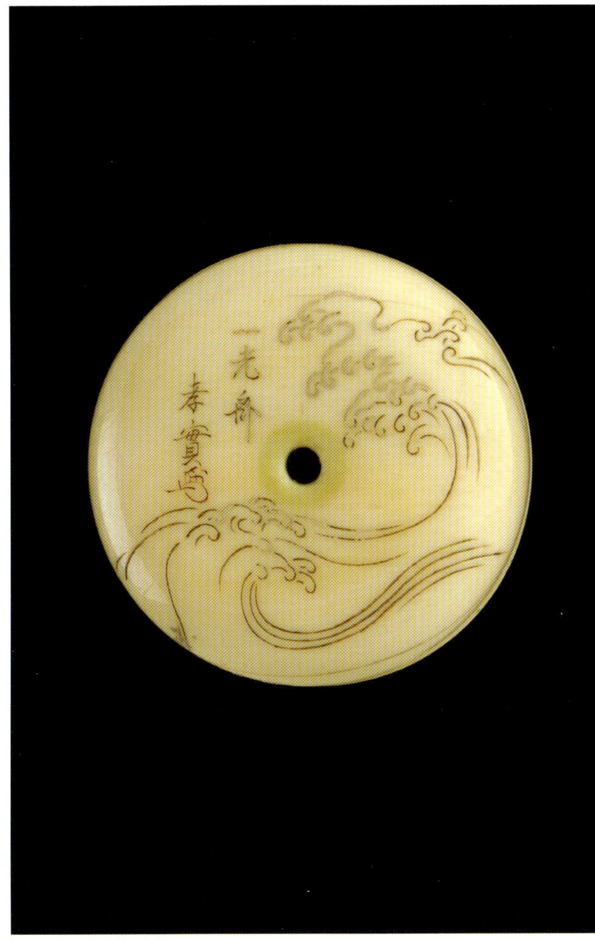

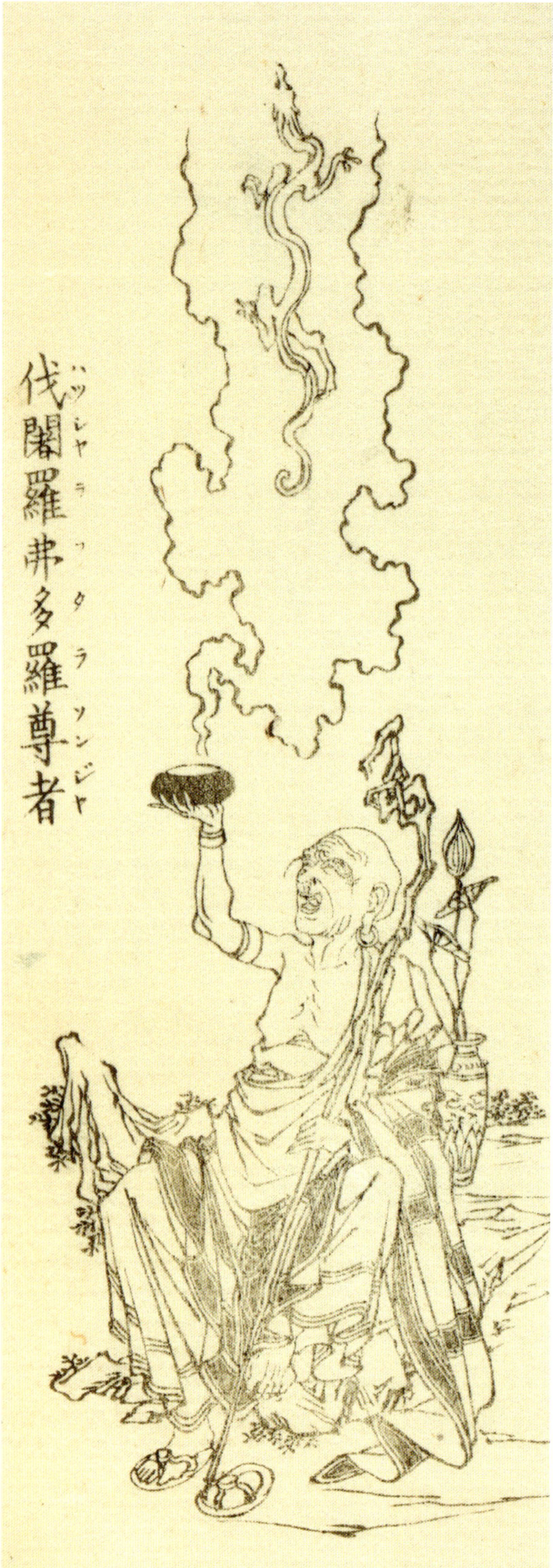

Fig. 37 Illustration from *Banbutsu hinagata gafū* of the *rakan* shows clearly the sinuous dragon, hidden on the top edge of cat. no. 28 (EA2012.13)

Handaka Sonja

This *rakan* is one of the élite group of sixteen. He has Indian features and is usually shown with shaven head and long earlobes. He sits on a rock dressed in the robes of a Buddhist monk and is said to be able to conjure from his alms bowl a dragon, seen appearing at his side in cat. no. 29 and issuing forth in a sinuous s-shape around the top of cat. no. 28.

28

Handaka Sonja sitting beneath an old pine tree holding up his bowl

Verso: Pine tree, *hossu*, flare and dragon flying around the edge

Ivory; Signed: Kōsai 光斎; 19th century
Diam: 4.8; H: 2.15 cm; EA2001.99
Bequeathed by Dr Monica Barnett

Sold at Sotheby's. London 24/07/1985. Lot 23. Illustrated in Plate 1

The signature of Kōsai 光斎 without a *kakihan* makes it impossible to know who carved this *manjū*. Moritoshi Kōsai used these characters and had several pupils who used them too, mostly adding a distinctive 'crane' *kakihan* (see cat. no. 91)

29

Handaka Sonja

Verso: A three-clawed hind leg of a dragon and a luxurious swishing tail disappearing around the edge.

Stag antler
Signed: Morimasa 守正 with 巴 *(tomoe)* *kakihan*
Mid-19th century
Diam: 5.2; H: 1.9 cm
EA1976.26
Presented anonymously

Sold at Christie's, New York. 26/03/1991. Lot 46

Stag antler is notoriously difficult to carve because of the blood capillary passages which show up as tiny holes on the surface. Morimasa has managed to disguise these, positioning them where they help to make a craggy rock look very natural. He has cleverly contrived to use an area with a clear smooth surface for the *rakan's* halo.

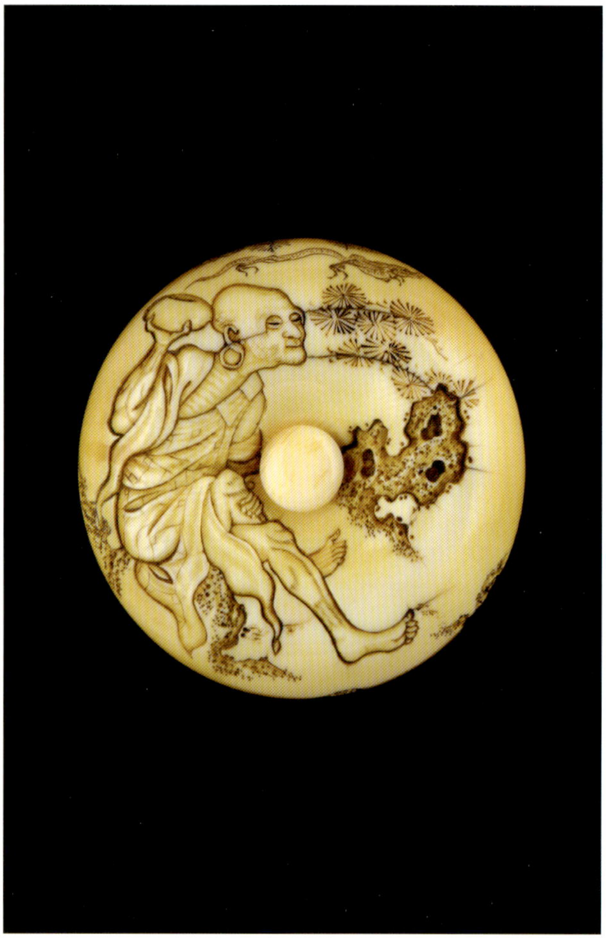

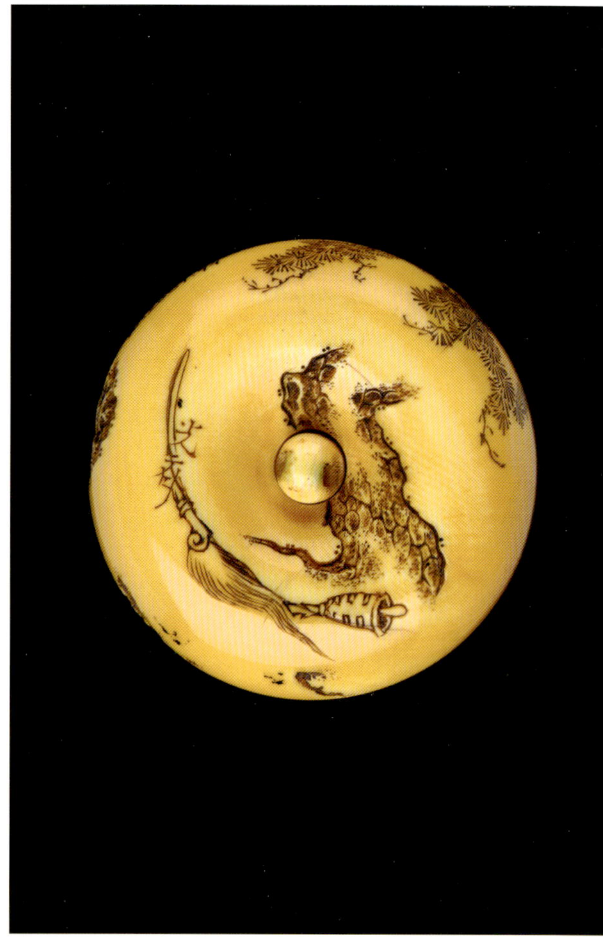

Cat. no. 28

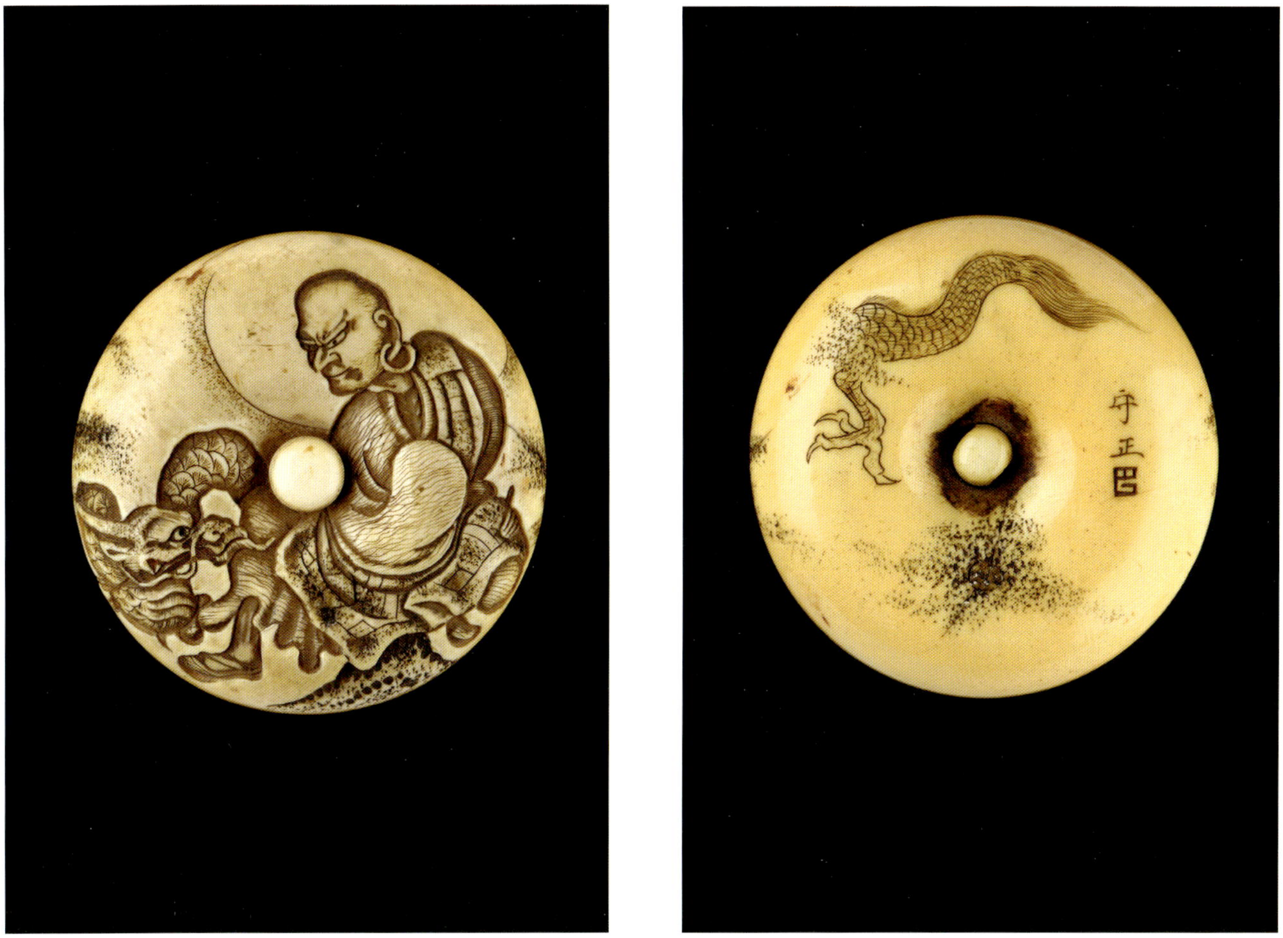

Cat. no. 29

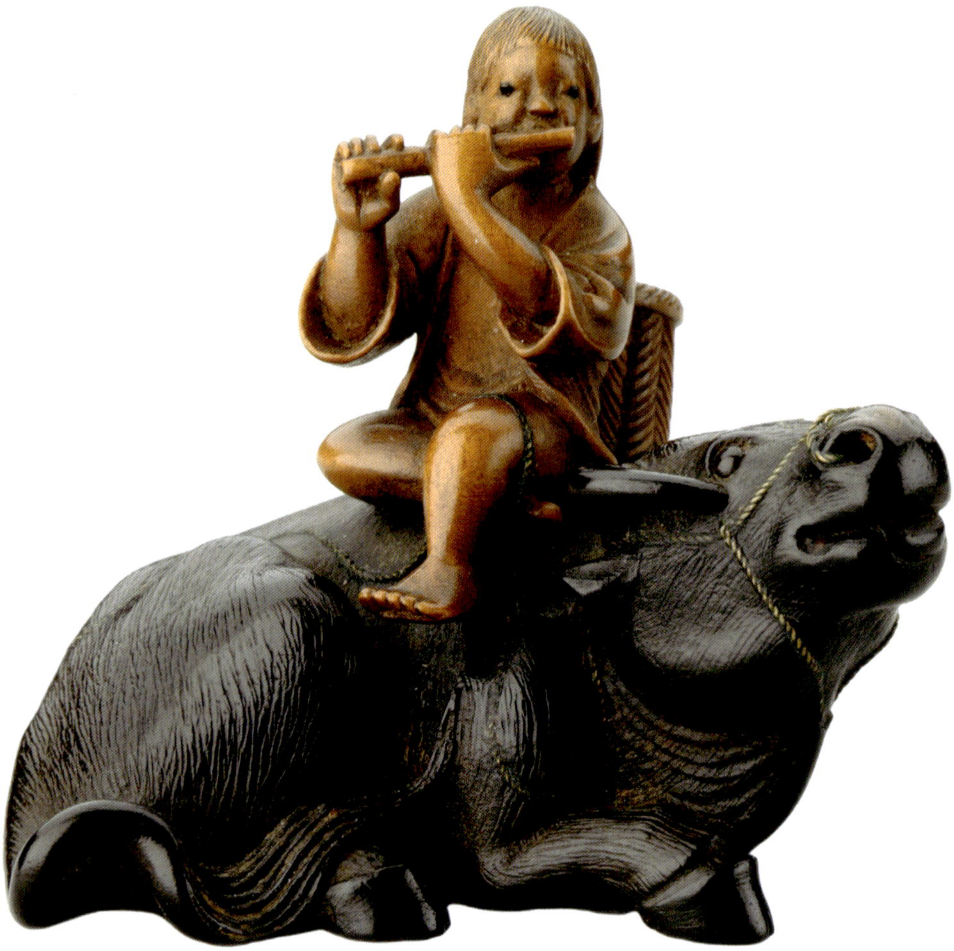

Fig. 38 Wood netsuke by Meikeisai Hōjitsu (*c.* 1800–1872). Ox and herdboy. Gift of Mrs Anna Beigun. (EA1996.25)

Ten Ox-herding Pictures

Parables provided an aid towards enlightenment in Zen Buddhism. One of these parables was a series of paintings known as the Ten Ox-herding Pictures (Jap. *Jūgyūzū*) each of which provides an image of one of ten illusions which need to be dispelled before enlightenment can be achieved. An ox-herd, representing Man, is shown negotiating the arduous mental journey towards enlightenment and the perfection of wisdom. The ox represents the mind. The originals of these ten stages were painted by Chinese artists around the middle of the twelfth century; they were later printed in woodblock book form. These were then brought to Japan and were copied by Japanese artists.

These two *manjū* illustrate two stages of the Ten Ox-herding Pictures. The struggle towards enlightenment begins with the ox-herd looking for his ox (his inner understanding) which has disappeared (Stage 1). He sees its footprints and begins to understand where it might be (Stage 2). In Stage 3 he sees the ox, representing a clearing of the confusion of his mind and in Stage 4 he catches the ox, but it is hard to keep control of it. He is beginning to gain control over the wanderings of his mind (see cat. no. 30). In Stage 5 he is able to lead the ox towards home, for it is calmer and he is more in control. By Stage 6 his struggle is over and he has enough mental control to be able to ride the ox (see cat. no. 31), and is usually seen playing a joyful tune on his flute. See fig. 39 which is also by Ichiyūsai.[25]

In the final four stages the ox-herd and the ox have become one and no longer have worldly attachments. His mind 'has transcended all manifestations of the transitory world'[26] and he eventually emerges as a manifestation of Miroku, the Buddha of the Future.

30

A young ox-herd clambers onto the back of his ox, as it crosses a river

Verso: a wintry branch in a basket with a sickle beside it

Ivory with red pigment
Mid-19th century
Diam: 4.65; H: 2.05 cm
Ichiyūsai 一遊齋 with *kakihan*
EA2001.54
Bequeathed by Dr Monica Barnett

Bought in October 1971 from 'Irene'. (Label No. 140 inside)

The similarity between this *manjū* and the piece in the Werdelmann Collection raises the question of whether Ichiyūsai attempted to carve all ten of the ox-herding pictures onto *manjū*.

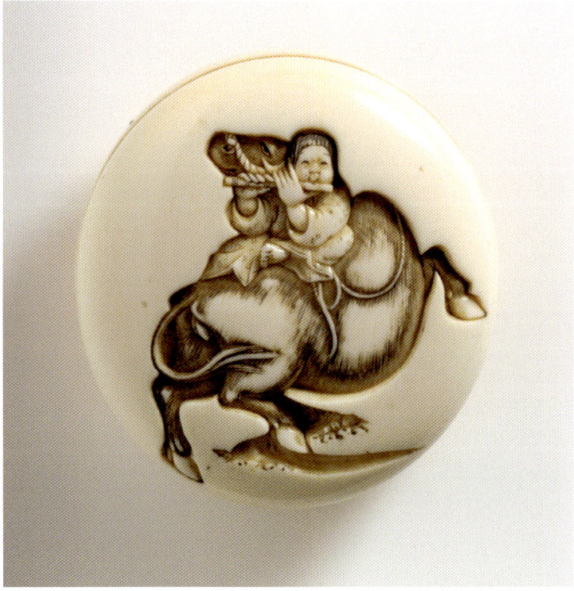

Fig. 39 *Manjū* Netsuke. Ox and Herdboy signed Ichiyūsai and *Kaō*. Ivory, Diam. 5.3 cm. Düsseldorf, Stiftung Museum Kunstpalast. Inventory number: P2005-568. Photo: © Stiftung Museum Kunstpalast – ARTOTHEK

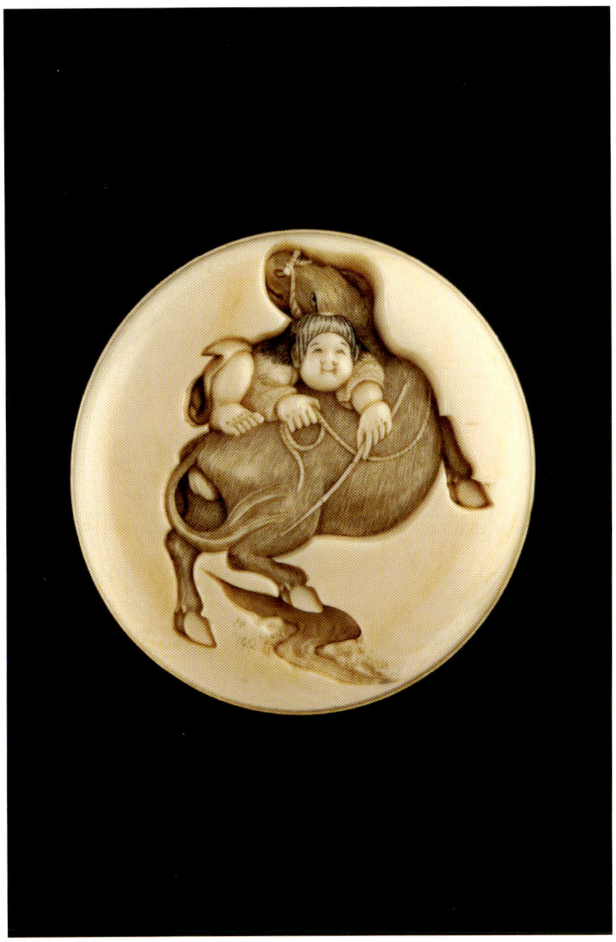

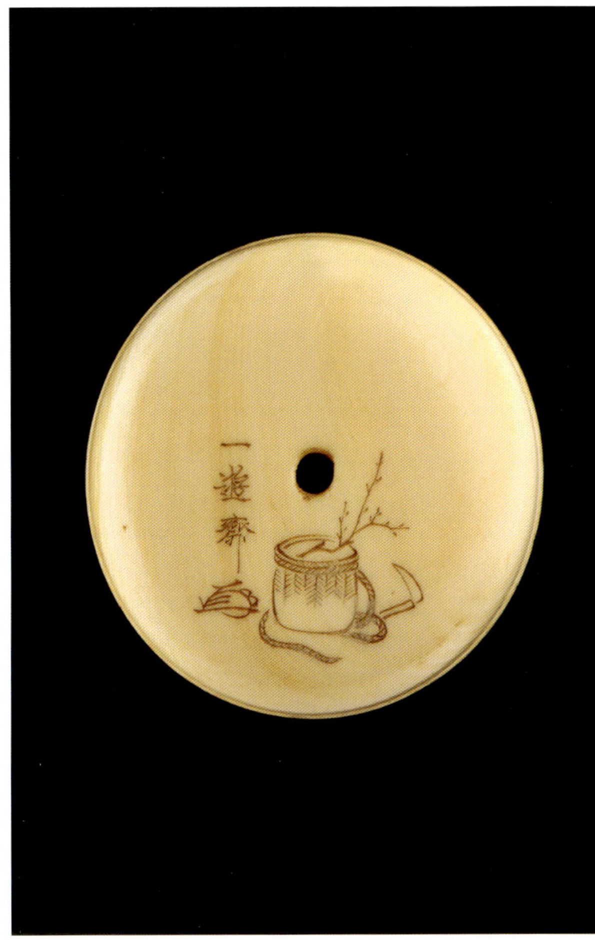
一遊齋

31

Ox-herd riding his ox. A bird has landed on the end of his staff

Verso: Basket and sickle on the ground with two birds in flight against an *'ishime'* ground

Copper with *shakudō*, gold and silver
Signed: Yoshimori 美盛 in a rectangular reserve
Late 19th century
Diam: 4.55; H: 2.0cm
EA2001.119
Bequeathed by Dr Monica Barnett

The body of this *manjū* is of copper, the ground hammered to give the effect of stone (*ishime*). Onto this the artist has inlaid a lively figure of an ox in *shakudō*, the ox-herd riding upon his back in gold with a silver face and *shakudō* hair. His stick is silver with a small *shakudō* bird perched on the end. Small tufts of gold grass give a sense of depth to the background. On the reverse Yoshimori shows the path, representative of the journey towards enlightenment, taken by the ox-herd, and on it lies his basket and sickle, abandoned in his effort to capture the ox. Two birds speed through the air above. This face shows Yoshimori's skill with the chisel, creating lines of different thickness to resemble a painting in the technique known as *katakiri-bori*.

This may be one of Unno Yoshimori's (1864–1919) earlier works, made while there was still a demand for netsuke.

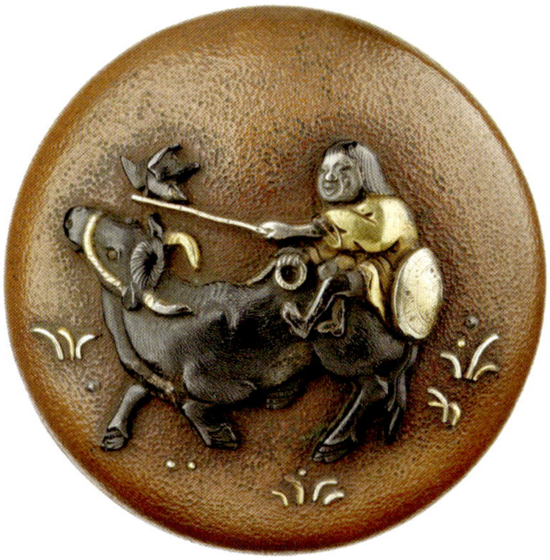

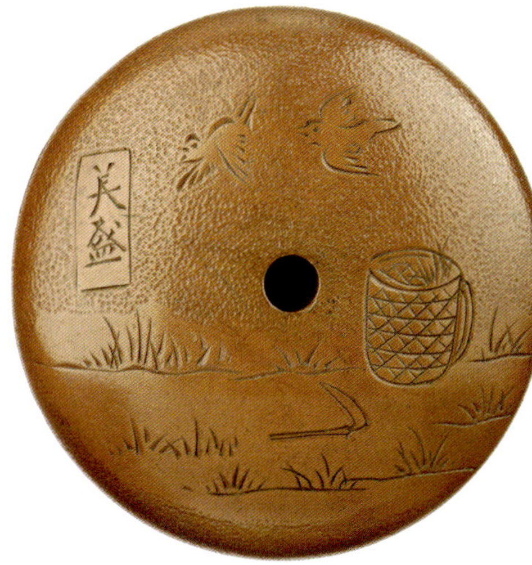

Daruma

Bodhidharma, known in Japanese as Daruma, is a legendary Indian sage, the 28th patriarch of Buddhism after the historical Buddha (who lived in the fourth century BC) and the first patriarch of Zen Buddhism. He is credited with transmitting Zen Buddhism beyond India to China whence it reached Japan via Japanese monks who, after studying there, returned home to spread Zen teaching. Zen was to have a profound influence on future generations, for much of Japanese cultural life is steeped in its traditions. Meditation and philosophical debate are practised with the aim of reaching enlightenment – within Zen the ultimate truth in this life. Daruma is admired for his extraordinary self discipline, resoluteness and self-reliance. These were all qualities that the Japanese samurai warrior wished to emulate.

Perhaps the most common depiction of Daruma (Sk. *Bodhidharma*) is during the nine gruelling years he spent sitting facing a wall in meditation. He looks stern, his bearded Indian features peering from beneath the red robe that covers his head. During this time his legs were said to have atrophied completely, a fact of which the little roly-poly self-righting dolls of Daruma, so commonly seen in Japan, remind us. Sometimes he is stretching or yawning while trying to keep his concentration. Comical portrayals of Daruma were also favourites of the netsuke craftsmen. Zen Buddhism delights in humour and the netsuke makers drew

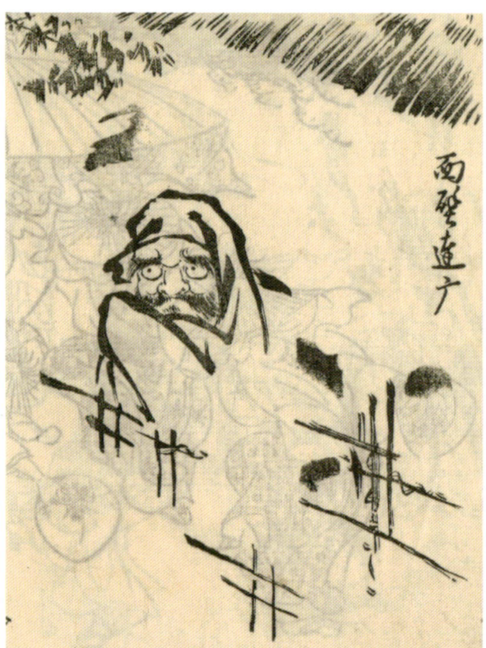

Fig. 40 Illustration of Daruma from *Itchō gafū* (National Diet Library, Tokyo, 2554323/11)

Opposite: Cat. no. 33 (detail)

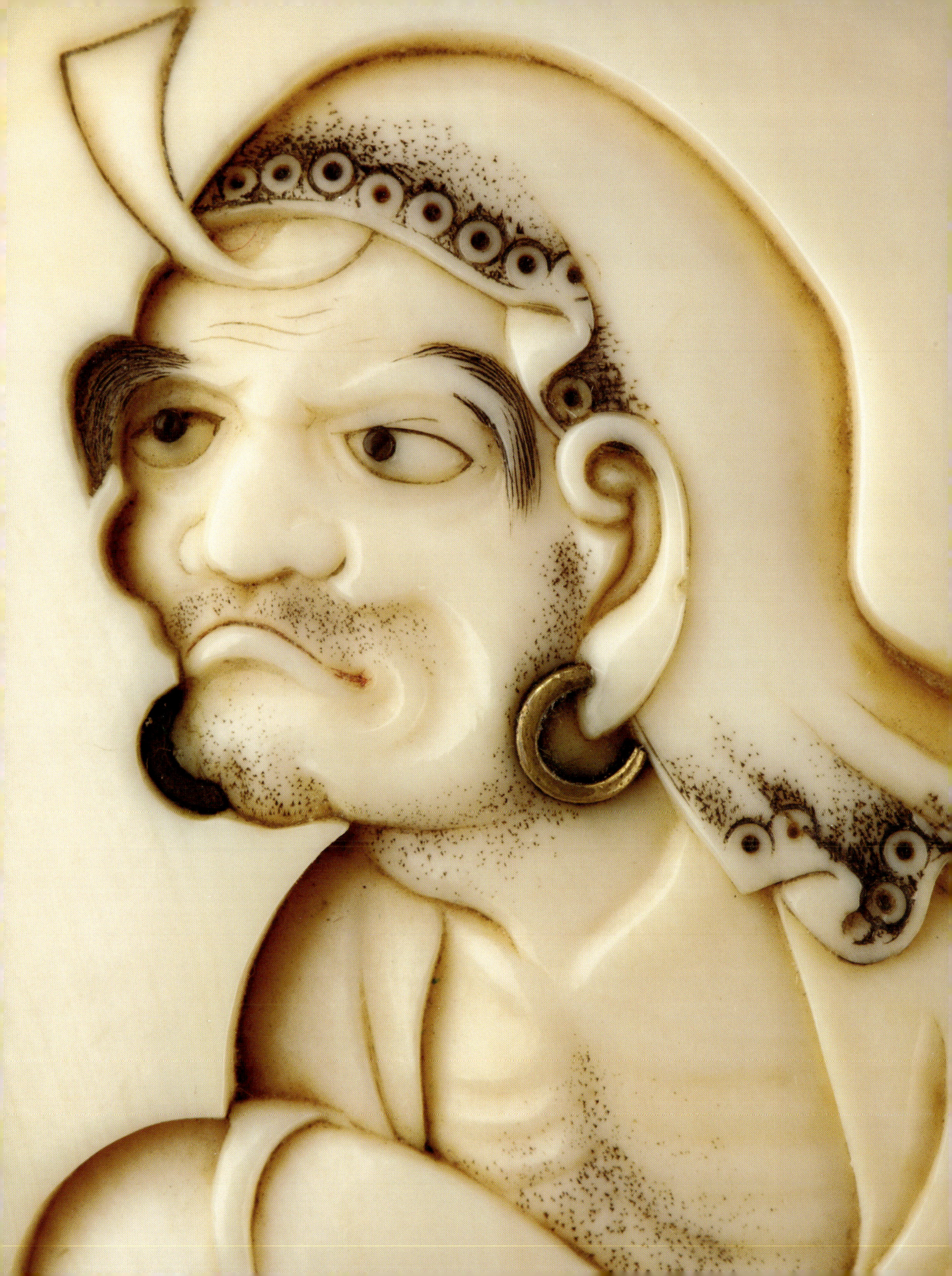

on cariacatures and parodies for their inspiration. Ukiyo-e artists too portrayed him seductively masquerading as a courtesan or in the company of courtesans of the Yoshiwara district of Edo, for one meaning of the word '*daruma*' is prostitute. There were good reasons for this use of humour which Conrad Hyers explains: 'By comparison with the tragic vision of life Zen may be said to be fundamentally comic. The Zen uses of humor share the comic inclination to move toward reducing tensions, overcoming conflicts and including opposites in some larger unity. In doing so, Zen reflects both the traditional Indian critique of dualism and the Chinese vision of harmony of opposites, as in the *yin/yang* cosmology.'[27]

32

Daruma stretching

Verso: Hossu (Buddhist fly whisk) carved in *kebori*

Ivory:
Signed: Kōsai 光齋
19th century
H: 1.35; W: 3.85; D: 3.95 cm
EA2001.48
Bequeathed by Dr Monica Barnett

Daruma is stretching and yawning while trying to keep his concentration, the pain of inactivity apparent on his face. Kōsai presented this agonised moment within a cartouche against a diamond-shaped diaper background and on the reverse, drawn in fine *kebori* lines, the *hossu*. This fly-whisk carried by Zen Buddhist priests is made of bamboo and hair and is a symbol of the authority of a Zen master to pass on the teachings of *Bodhidharma*. It can also be used to flick away insects without causing them harm.

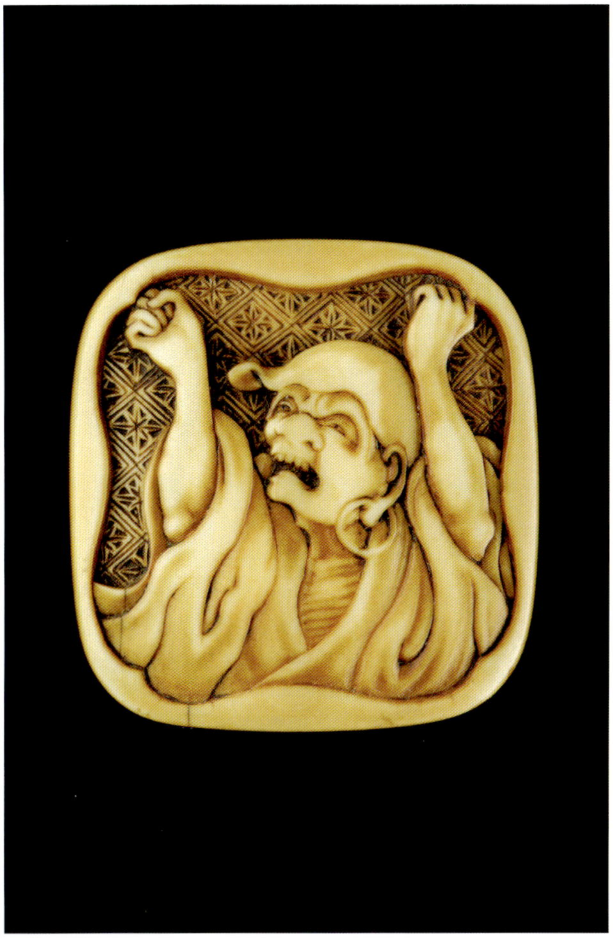

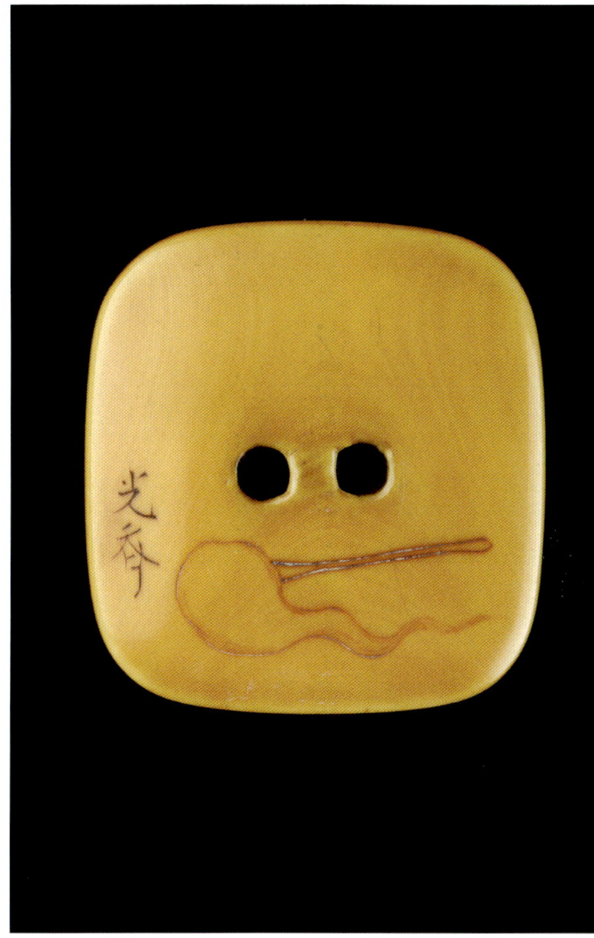

33

Daruma playing *kamifuki*

Verso: Hossu (Buddhist fly whisk)

Ivory
Signed: Kikugawa 菊川 with *kakihan*
19th century
Diam: 4.6; H: 2.0 cm
EA2001.61
Bequeathed by Dr Monica Barnett

Wilhelm, G. *Manjū exégèse et appréciation*, Bulletin Association Franco-Japonaise. No. 54. Octobre, 1996. Fig. MB11

Eskenazi: 06/02/1973

On this *manjū* we have a comical portrayal of Daruma playing the simple children's game *kamifuki*, in which each player has a piece of paper slipped under his hat, or whatever he is wearing on his head. He has to blow so hard that the paper folds back under the headgear. Here Daruma is almost going cross-eyed with the effort of watching the paper.

The Kikugawa school of carvers specialised in *manjū* netsuke, frequently signing the name Kikugawa followed by the appropriate *kakihan* as seen on this piece. They were closely connected to the carvers surrounding Moritoshi Kōsai, some of whom used the same *kakihan*.

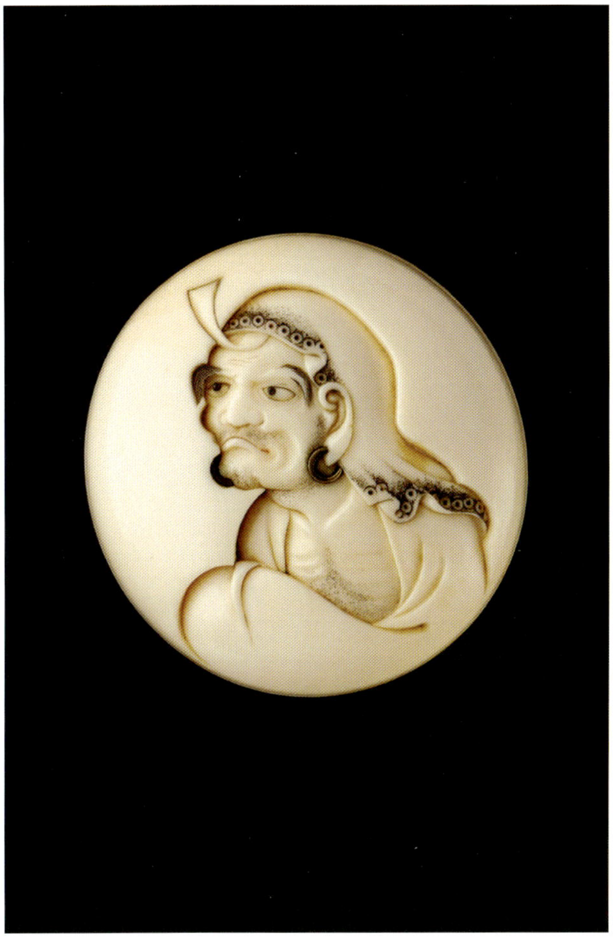

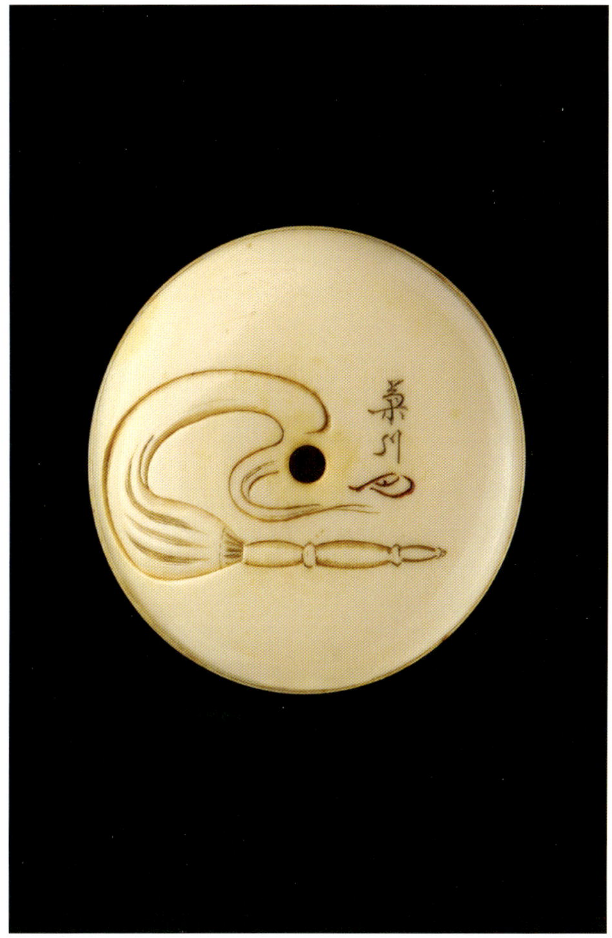

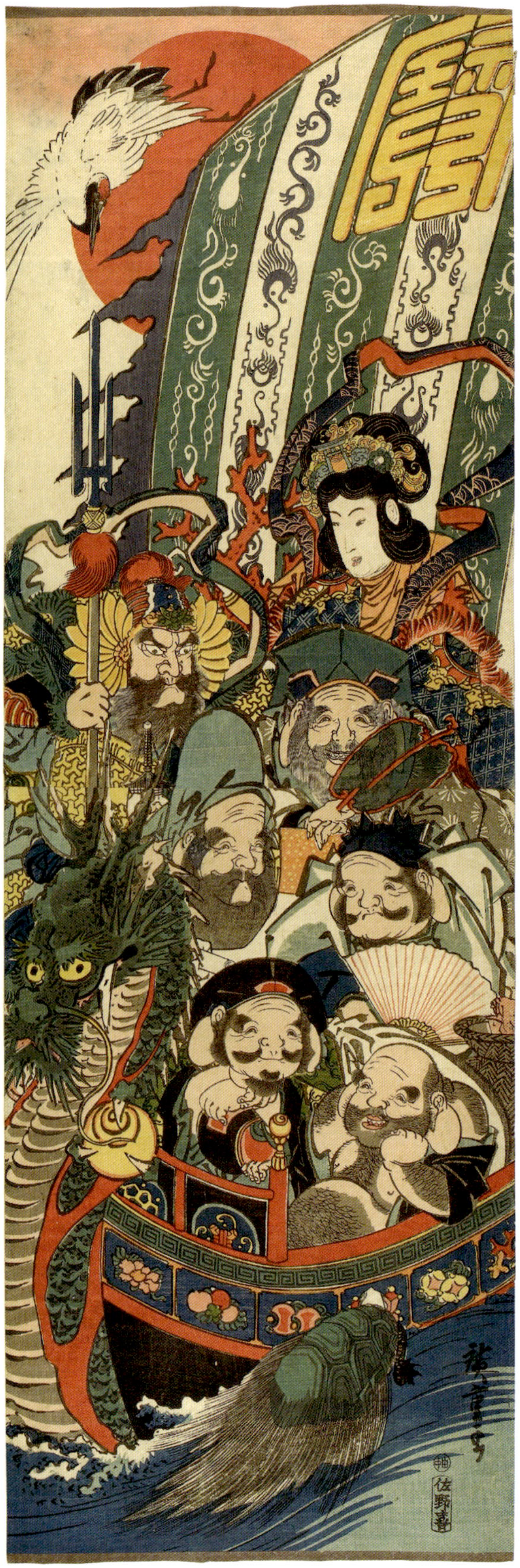

Fig. 41 The Seven Gods of Good Fortune in their Treasure Boat. Colour woodblock print by Utagawa Hiroshige (1797–1858) (EAX.4243)

The New Year and Shichifukujin (Seven Gods of Good Fortune)

The next few netsuke illustrate a group of gods brought together from diverse origins. Collectively they are called the *Shichifukujin* (Seven Gods of Good Fortune), Daikoku, Ebisu, Hotei, Fukurokuju, Jurōjin, Bishamonten and Benten. All but one are Chinese with either Buddhist or Daoist origins and Ebisu is native to Japan. They were brought together as a group in Japan during the late Muromachi period (1336–1573) and became popular in all forms of Japanese art. They are worshipped throughout the country and shrines dedicated to each of them have appeared over the centuries to accommodate the many people who pray to them for good fortune, long life, prosperity in business and wisdom, all of which they symbolise. At the New Year they are said to sail into port in their treasure ship *(takarabune)* laden with these symbolic treasures which they distribute to all. The only one not represented in the collection is Bishamonten, the guardian deity.

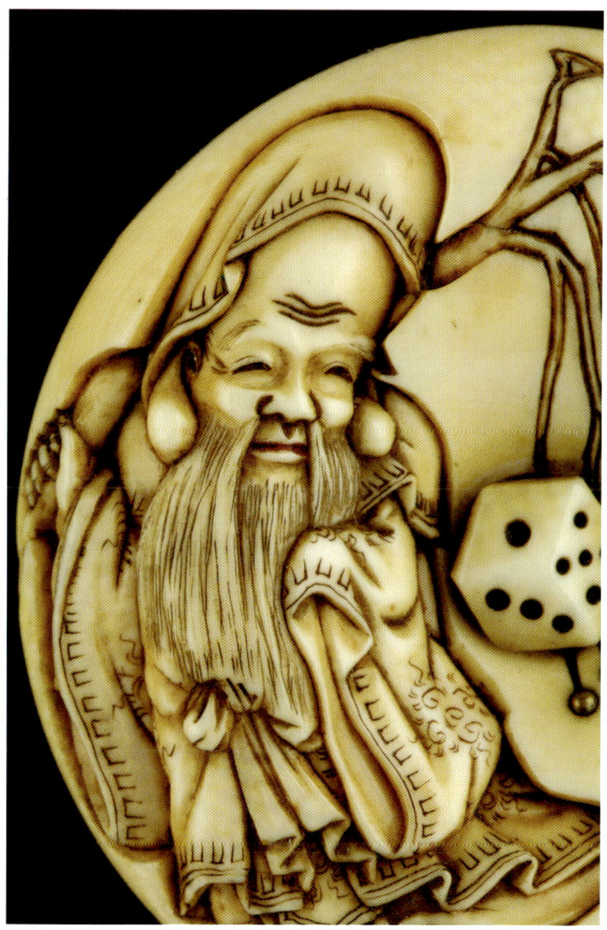

Cat. no. 43 (detail)

34

Treasure Ship *(Takarabune)*

Verso: Pillow, pipe and alms bowl with a wisp of smoke issuing from the pillow indicating a dream.

Ivory
Signed: Meisai 明斎
19th century
Diam: 5.0; H: 2.65 cm
EA2001.127
Bequeathed by Dr Monica Barnett

Sold at Christie's, London 14/11/94, Lot 18

This imaginary ship is said to arrive on New Year's Eve loaded with *takaramono* (precious things). It has many forms; here it has a dragon-headed prow and makes its journey through the waves with the wind behind a large sail decorated with the interlocking circle design known as *shippō tsunagi,* which represents the seven treasures; gold, silver, pearl, agate, crystal, coral and lapis lazuli. Sometimes the *Shichifukujin* are on board, but this ship simply carries representative treasures, each one a symbol of good fortune: Ebisu's basket with a fish emerging from the top, Daikoku's mallet and Hotei's treasure sack, accompanied by a coral branch to ward off malign influences, a flat fan *(uchiwa),* a symbol of authority, three sacred gems contained in a bowl, the key to the storage house of the gods, a *hossu,* the hammer of chaos (*konton no tsuchi*), the hat of invisibility, two crossed rhinoceros horn cups, cloves, and Bishamonten's staff. The design of a pillow on the reverse refers to the Edo period custom of placing a picture of the *takarabune* under one's pillow on the second night of the New Year in order to induce auspicious dreams which would bring good fortune throughout the coming year.

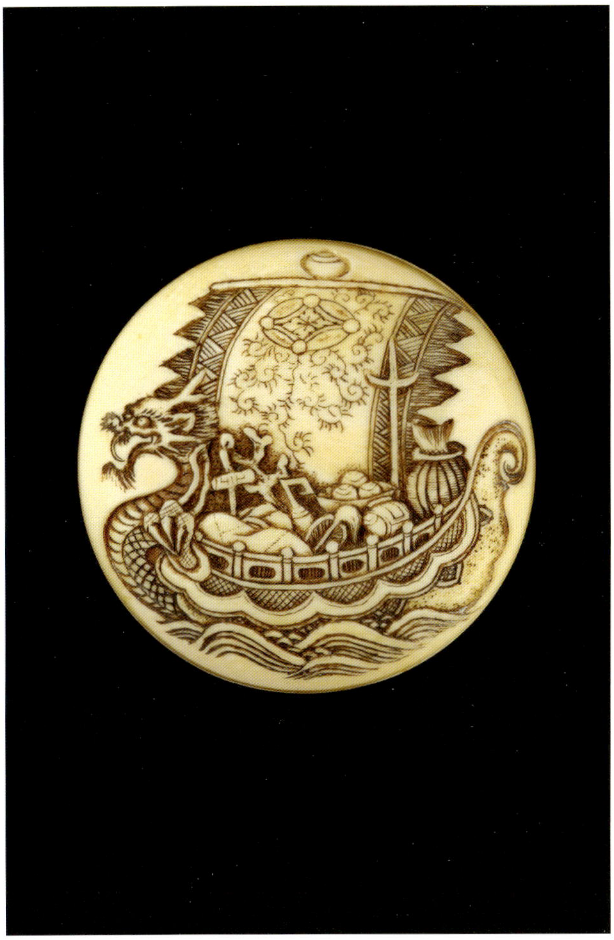

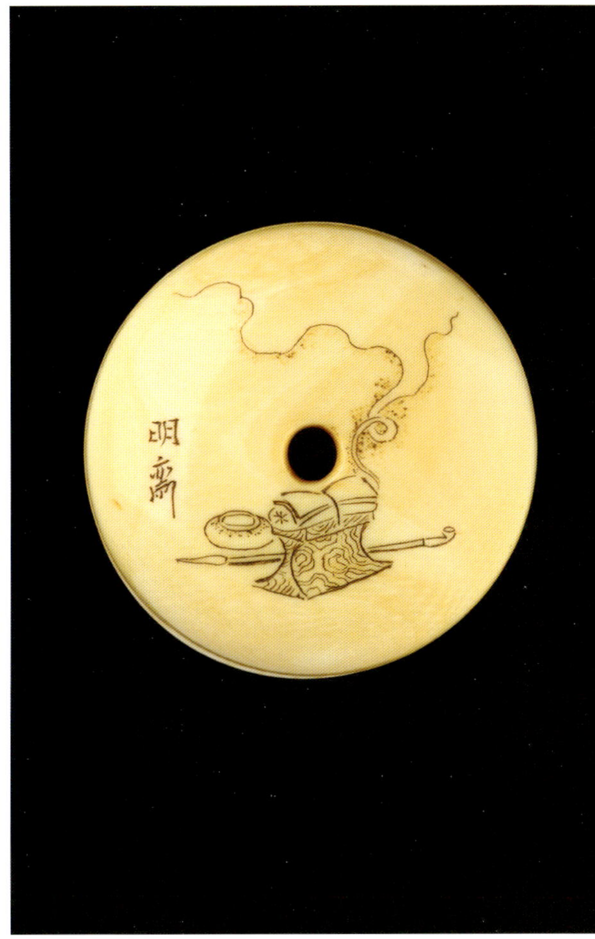
明斎

35

Takarazukushi (Set of Precious Things)

Verso: Plain

Ivory with red and gold lacquer
Signed: Kajikawa saku 梶川作 (made by Kajikawa) with a red pot seal reading 'Ei'
19th century
Diam: 4.3; H: 1.3 cm
EA2001.62
Bequeathed by Dr Monica Barnett

Bought from Eskenazi 06/02/1973

This delicate netsuke displays the *takaramono* associated with the *Shichifukujin*, carefully lacquered in black, gold and red onto the ivory surface in the technique known as *maki-e*, literally, 'sprinkled picture', in which metal powders are sprinkled onto the wet lacquer surface and then polished. Several of these treasures have a black lacquer base, built up of many layers, each requiring polishing in between.

This *manjū* would have been made to complement an *inrō*, decorated with a theme to celebrate the New Year and possibly also made in the Kajikawa workshop.

The Kajikawa family had a long and distinguished history dating from the early seventeenth century as *maki-e* lacquer artists to the Tokugawa shogunate. The signature Kajikawa saku 梶川作 with a red pot seal reading 'Ei' was used by several of the Kajikawa family. In his book of *inrō* artists, Edward Wrangham[28] mentions almost fifty by name, starting in the seventeenth century.

This netsuke has a dealer's coded label inside reading:

ナカ
オモ

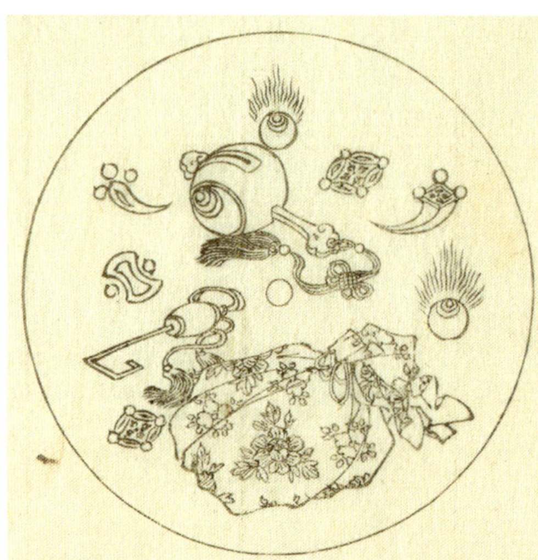

Fig. 42 Illustration from *Banbutsu hinagata gafū* Vol. 2, p. 7, showing the kind of woodblock printed image that netsuke artists might copy faithfully or use as a guide for their designs (EA2012.14)

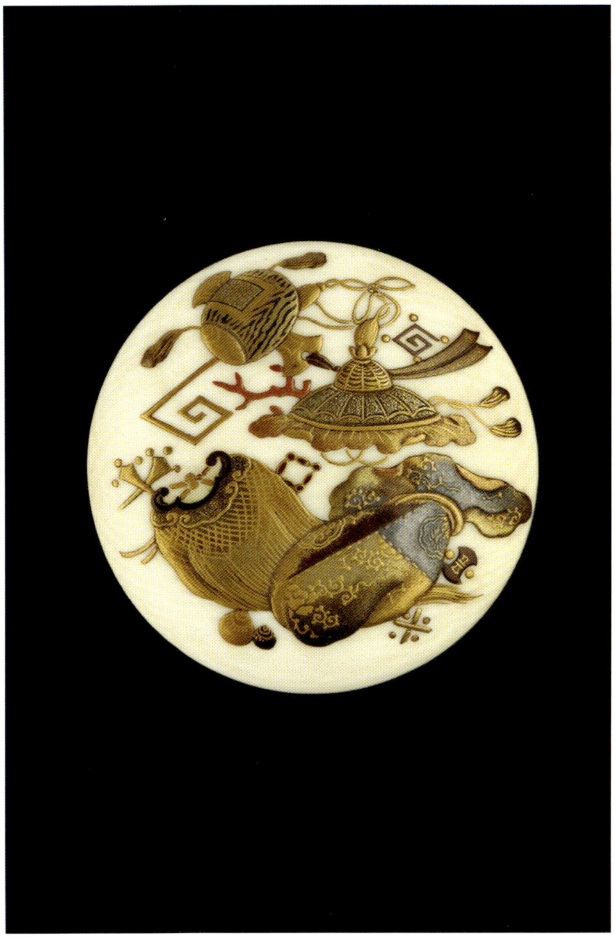

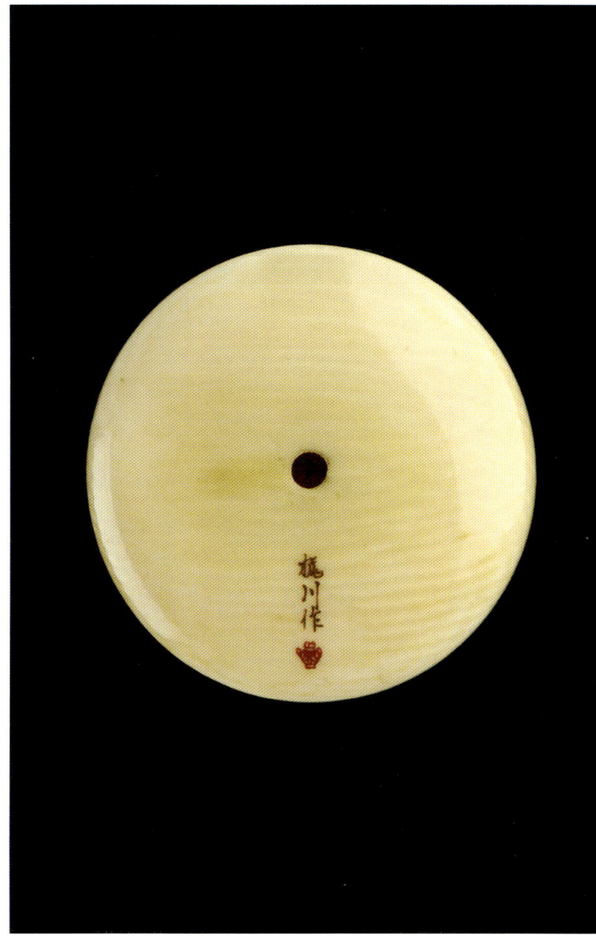
楓川作

Hotei

Hotei (Ch. Budai) was a tenth century mendicant monk who was thought by some to be a manifestation of Maitreya (Jap. Miroku), the Buddha of the Future. By the time the group of *Shichifukujin* had formed in Japan he had become a large, corpulent and benevolent figure, epitomising contentment and magnanimity. He is often depicted accompanied by children to whom he would give small gifts from the sack he carried on his back. His name translates as 'cloth sack'. As a monk his sack carried his few posessions, but now, as a god of happiness, it is full of material wealth which he is pleased to distribute to others.

36

Hotei peering out from within his sack

Ebony
Unsigned
1840-1860
H: 2.81; W: 4.482; D: 3.57 cm
EA2001.35
Bequeathed by Dr Monica Barnett

A laughing Hotei peeps from his sack, in which he is completely enveloped. It is tied above his head as a *furoshiki*, (cloth for carrying parcels and gifts) and his fan is attached within the fold of the knot.

An almost identical piece sold at Butterfield, San Francisco, 16/06/2007, Lot 6062

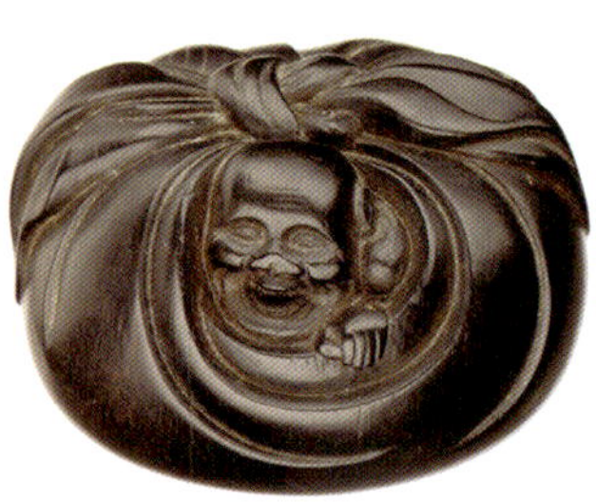

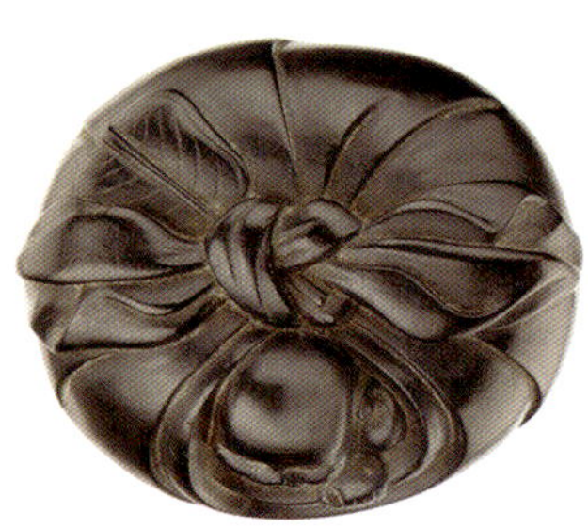

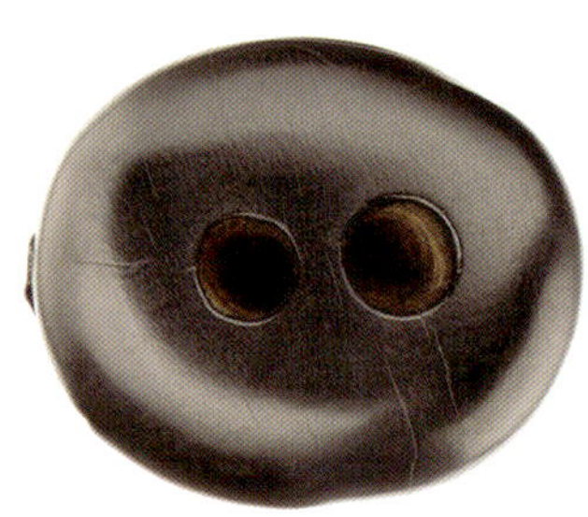

37

Hotei peering out from within his sack

Shakudō and gilt metal
Diam: 3.4; H: 1.7 cm
Signed: Yoshiaki 好明 or Kōmin with *kakihan*
Early 19th century
EA2001.56
Bequeathed by Dr Monica Barnett

See Barry Davies Oriental Art. *Netsuke Classics*. June 1990. London. No. 75. for a similar piece.

Bought from Douglas J. K. Wright 17/05/1972

In another version of this popular design Hotei's smiling face looks out from the folds of his sack. He holds a jewel (*tama*) and his fan (*uchiwa*).

On the reverse of a piece almost identical to this, which was in the collection of the late Edward Wrangham,[29] is the inscription *'motte Yasuchika no zu, Yoshiaki kore o cho'* (designed by Yasuchika, carved by Yoshiaki). *Tsuba Taikan* shows a similar design by Yasuchika on a *tsuba* (sword guard), No. 309, in which Hotei's face is set to one side to avoid the central opening and which may have provided the inspiration for Yoshiaki.[30] Haynes includes a metalworker Yoshiaki who worked around 1800.[31]

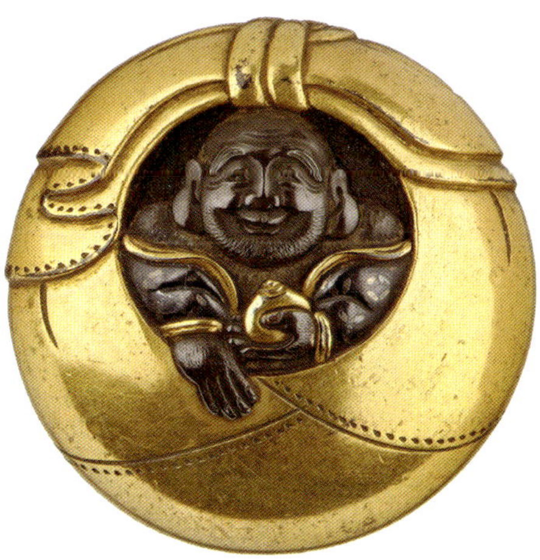

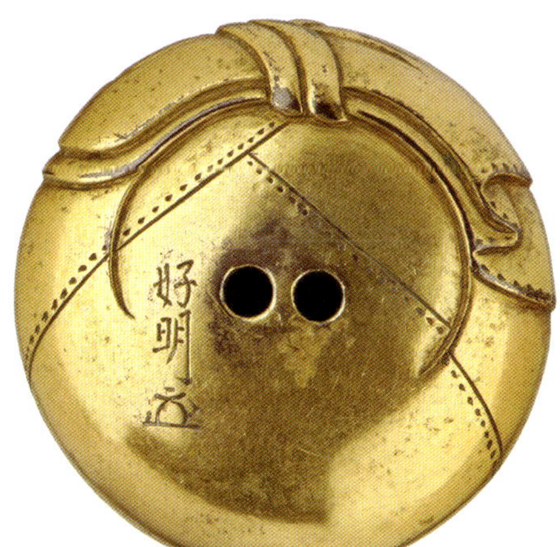

38

Karako walking along with Hotei's sack on a pole slung over his shoulder

Verso: plain

Ivory (chain *kanamono* attached)
Signed: Naohiro 直廣
19th century
Diam: 3.7; H: 1.8 cm
EA2001.58
Bequeathed by Dr Monica Barnett

Bought from Sotheby's via Douglas J. K. Wright 26/07/1972

Children dressed in Chinese clothing are known as *karako* in Japanese. Typically they wear richly patterned baggy trousers, a shirt with an elaborate ruff around the neck and have two twists of hair either side of their heads. Hotei was often accompanied by a group of small children, to whom he distributed small presents from his sack. A *karako* carries Hotei's sack full of small treasures over his shoulder and appears to be skipping along sharing Hotei's benevolent mood.

There is a visible stripe across the back of this netsuke, which has appeared with age, the darker part indicating the outer part of the elephant tusk.

Attached to this piece is a plaited string on which are arranged some transparent and black glass beads, two green jade beads and an old metal coin, all probably amulets which must have had special significance for the owner.

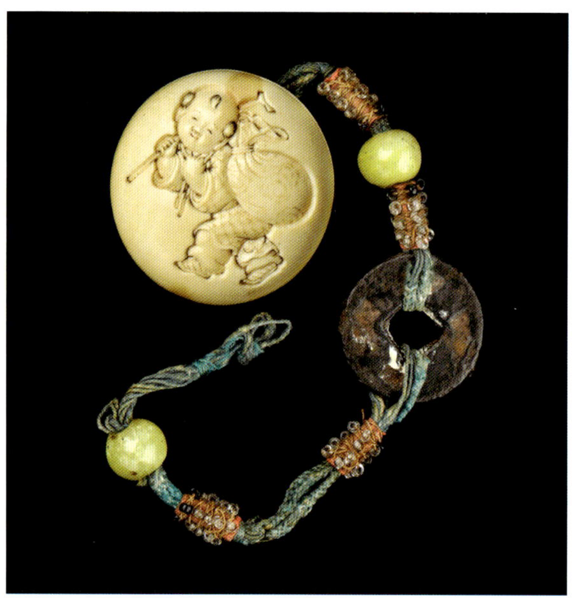

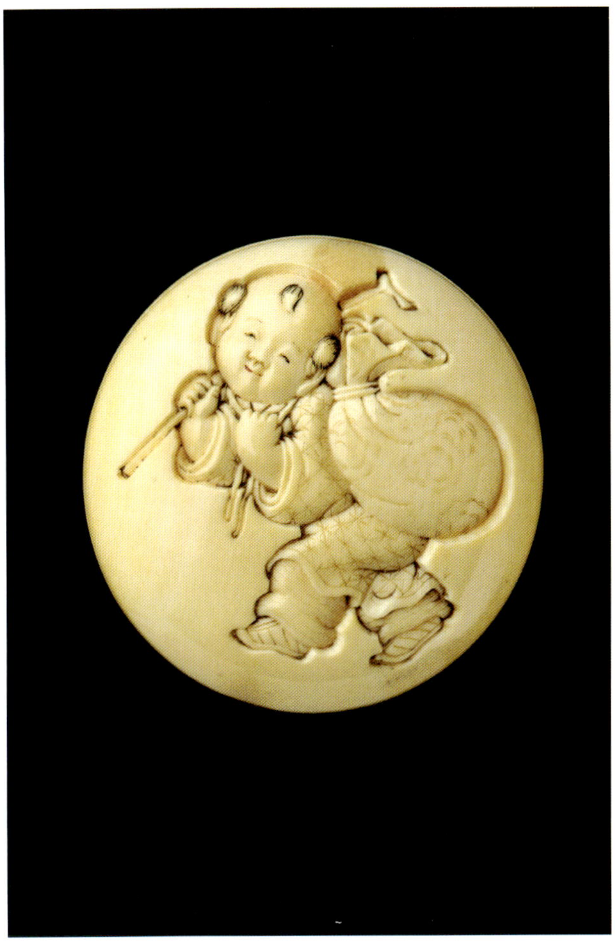

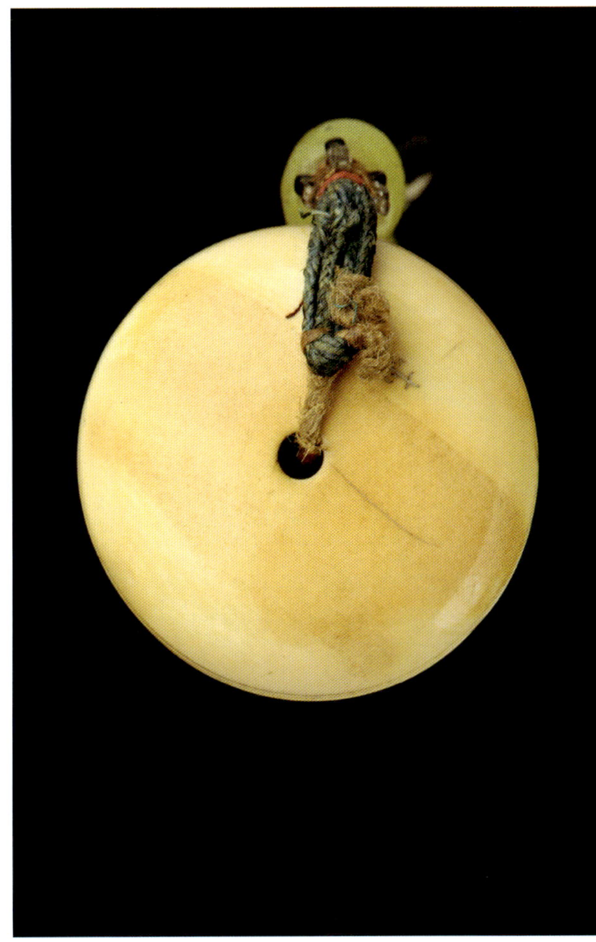

39

Daikoku and Ebisu: Daikoku is shaking his mallet to shower Ebisu with gold coins which tumble over the top

Verso: Ebisu holds out his fish basket to catch the coins

Ivory
Signed: Shunkōsai 春江齋 (Shunkōsai Chōgetsu)
Late 19th century
Diam: 5.1; H: 2.0 cm
EA2001.64
Bequeathed by Dr Monica Barnett

Here are two of the *Shichifukujin,* Daikoku, a household god who particularly watches over the kitchen and represents wealth and prosperity, and Ebisu, the patron of fishermen and merchants.

On this *manjū* Daikoku stands upon two rice bales, a large sack slung over his left shoulder. In his right hand he holds his magic mallet *(tsuchi)* and each time he shakes it out fly coins which Ebisu scrambles to catch in his fishing basket on the reverse.

At the 1984 London International Netsuke Convention, Dr Monica Barnett led a workshop entitled 'In Praise and Defence of the Manjū' and used the reverse of this piece, which she had by then owned for ten years, as the illustration on the brochure. It is finely carved in the *shishiaibori* technique that she so admired.

40

Daikoku and Ebisu dressed as *Manzai* dancers with two sacred jewels at their feet

Verso: plain

Ivory
Signed: Ikkōsai Kōjitsu 一光斎孝實 and *kakihan*
Mid- to late 19th century
Diam: 4.8; H: 2.2 cm
EA2001.100
Bequeathed by Dr Monica Barnett

Manzai dancing originated in China and has been performed in Japan since the eighth century, at first only at court, but after the thirteenth century it became a widespread tradition of the New Year, which corresponded to the beginning of spring. It was not until around 1400 that the performers were granted permission to wear the hat *(eboshi)* and robes *(hitatare)* normally reserved for people of higher status. Traditional *manzai* was a 'narrative performance given by two repesentatives of a shrine or temple, one of them in the role of the "wit" *(tayū)* the other the "straight man" *(saizō)*'.[32] The two dancers make their way from house to house, shouting '*Manzai, manzai!*', one holding a fan while the other beats his drum *(kotsuzumi).*

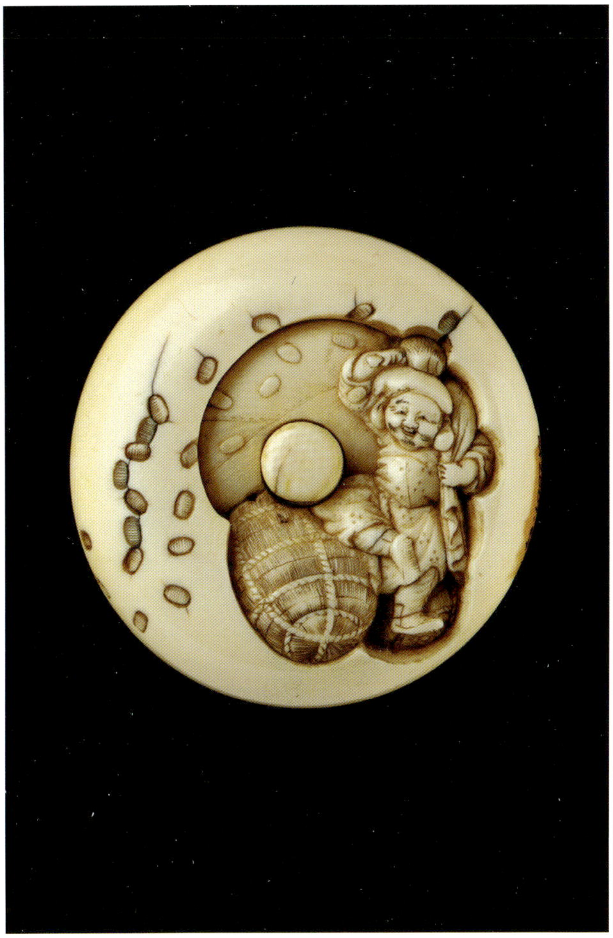

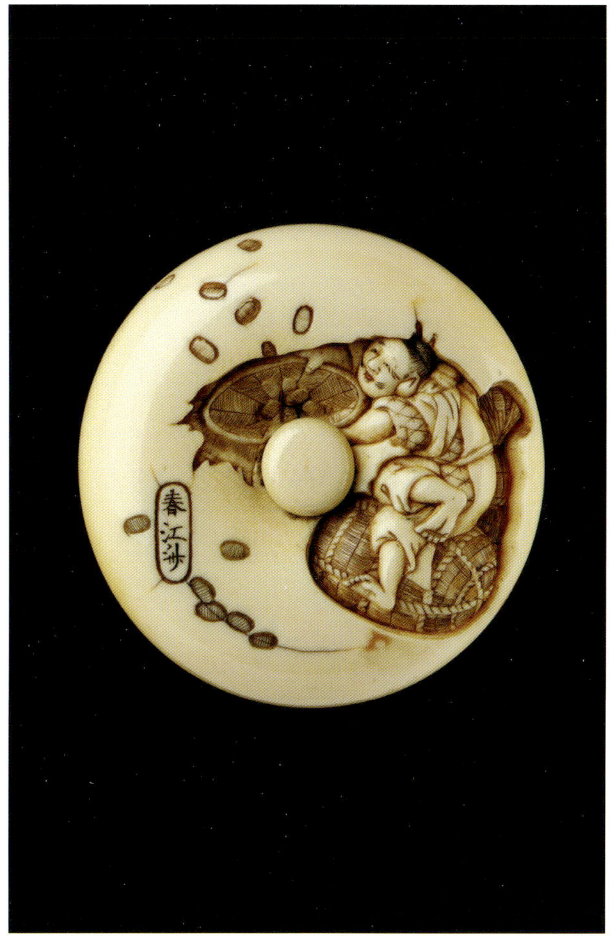

Cat. no. 39

Here Daikoku and Ebisu provide the comic duo, Ebisu wearing the traditional mask and carrying the fan of the *saizō,* and Daikoku, who is playing the part of the *tayū,* his wish-granting mallet tucked into his belt, beating the hand-drum (*kotsuzumi*) and stamping his feet while perhaps shouting '*Manzai, Manzai*', a promise of long life and prosperity to all who watch.

There were more than one hundred types of street entertainment practised during the Edo period at the many festivals that peppered the annual calendar. *Manzai* is one form that has survived to this day in certain parts of the country.

The pairing of Daikoku and Ebisu dates back to the medieval period and was a popular motif in all forms of art. This rendering of the two gods is loosely based on a design by Hanabusa Itchō (1652–1724) in the woodblock printed book, *Itchō gafū* (fig. 43).

Prints of *manzai* dancers were hung up at the New Year in the hope that this would bestow longevity and prosperity upon the household.

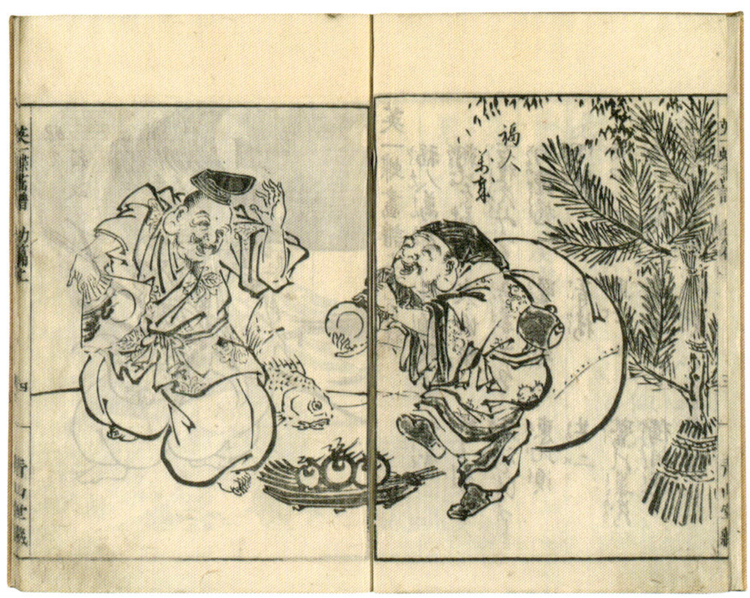

Fig. 43 Illustration of *Itchō gafū*, Vol.1, p. 6 (National Diet Library, Tokyo, 2554322/6)

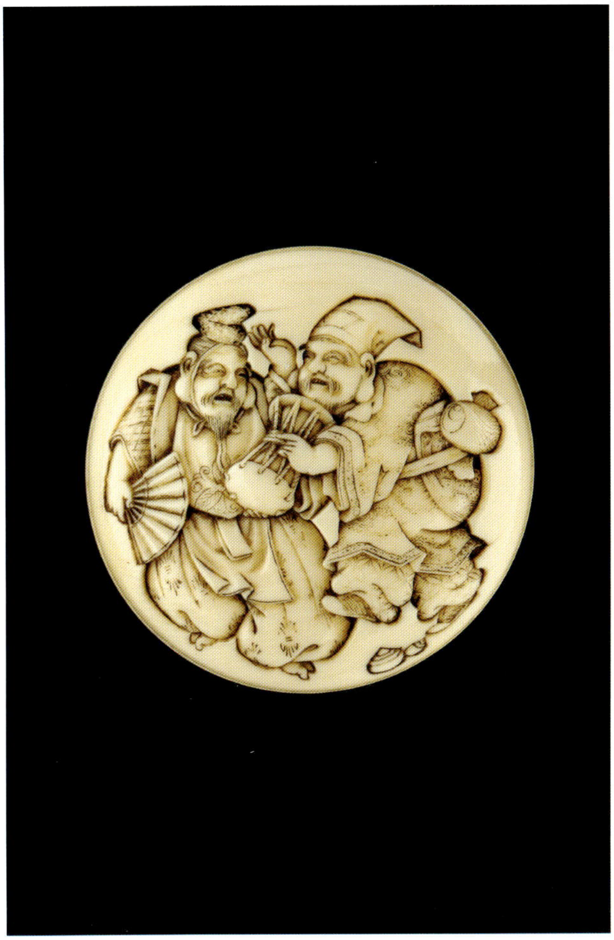

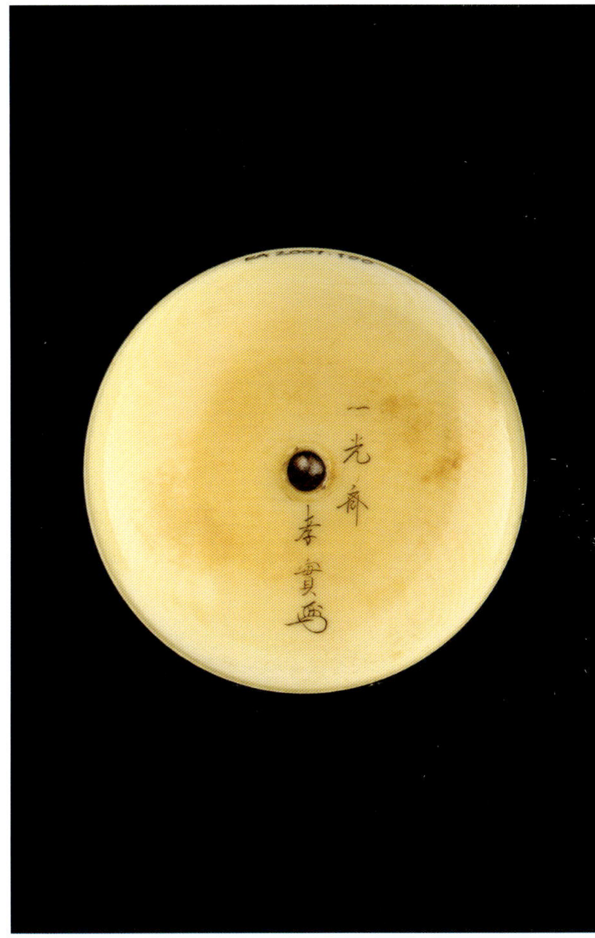

Cat. no. 40

41

Manzai dancers beside *kagami mochi* (rice cakes) on a *sanbō* (stand). Their kimonos are decorated with bamboo and sparrows and stylised snowflakes

Verso: large *kadomatsu* decoration with lobster and a *sake* kettle and cup

Ivory with staining
Signed: Meikeisai Hōjitsu 明鶏齋法實 with *kakihan*
19th century
Diam: 6.35; H: 2.2 cm
EA2001.131
Bequeathed by Dr Monica Barnett

All the decorative elements on this *manjū* celebrate the New Year. *Kadomatsu* (literally 'gate pine'), in this case made up of evergreen pine, lobster and fern, are placed on either side of the entrance to a house, to welcome ancestral spirits or the gods of the harvest. They remain there for the first seven days of the year and their removal marks the end of festivities. Each element has deep symbolic meaning: the pine (*matsu*) represents continuity; the bent back of the lobster *(ebi)* is suggestive of old age and longevity; and the fern (*shida*), whose fronds have multiple branches, represents prosperity. A kettle and cup sitting on a lacquered stand are filled with special sweet spiced *sake (o-toso)*, to which medicinal herbs have been added. This is served to all members of the family at the New Year, the youngest first and the oldest last, in order to rid the family of the previous year's maladies and to hope for a long life. On the front rice cakes (*kagami mochi*), one large and one small, made from steamed, pounded rice, and shaped to resemble mirrors *(kagami),* sit on top of sheets of clean white paper on a stand *(sanbō)*. During the festivities these cakes are divided up and eaten by all.

In Japan the New Year is not just a date in the calendar but has deep spiritual significance. It is a time when 'the gods permit humanity a fresh start, and if properly propitiated will bestow their protection'.[33]

In the hands of the master carver Meikeisai Hōjitsu this scene, full of vitality, conveys the festive spirit of the New Year.

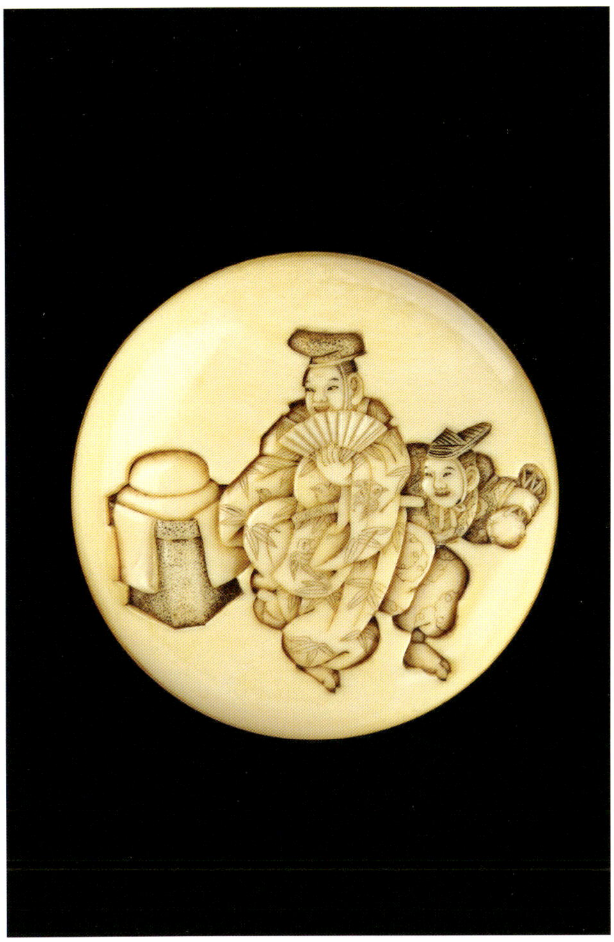

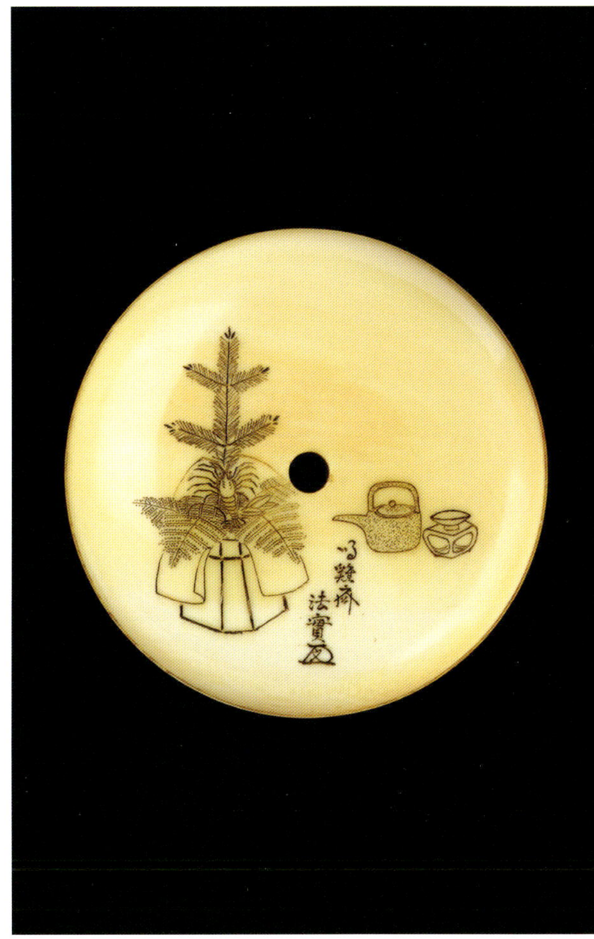

42

Daikoku's rat: A plump ivory turnip (*kabu*) with tortoiseshell leaves

Verso: a rat in mother-of-pearl

Wood, ivory, tortoiseshell and mother-of-pearl
Unsigned
Around 1800
Diam: 3.5; H: 1.91 cm
EAX.633

The festival of the Seven Herbs (*nanakusa no sekku*) takes place on the seventh day of the New Year. A mixture of seven herbs, of which the green leaves of the turnip (*kabu*) are one, are put onto a board, and in a small ritual ceremony, conducted facing in an auspicious direction, they are chopped. During this process a special chant is droned, which varies according to the region, as can the available herbs. The chopped herbs are then made into a gruel with rice (*nanakusa-gayu*) and eaten in order to bring longevity and good health in the coming year.

The rat is a companion of Daikoku, whose mallet brings forth riches aplenty. It is also a symbol of wealth, for it only appears when food is in plenteous supply. Westerners on the whole dislike rats, whereas in Japan they are welcomed as auspicious creatures, associated with industry and intelligence.

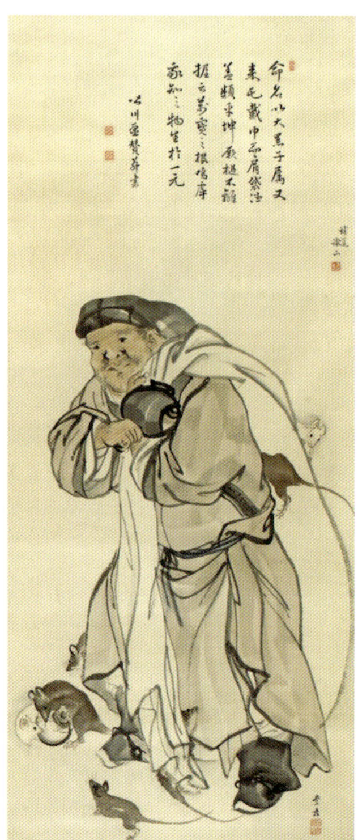

Fig. 44 Daikoku besieged by rats, two of whom play with a turnip. Hanging scroll, ink and colour on paper by Mori Tetsuzan (1775–1841) and Okamoto Toyohiko (1773–1845) (EA1965.136)

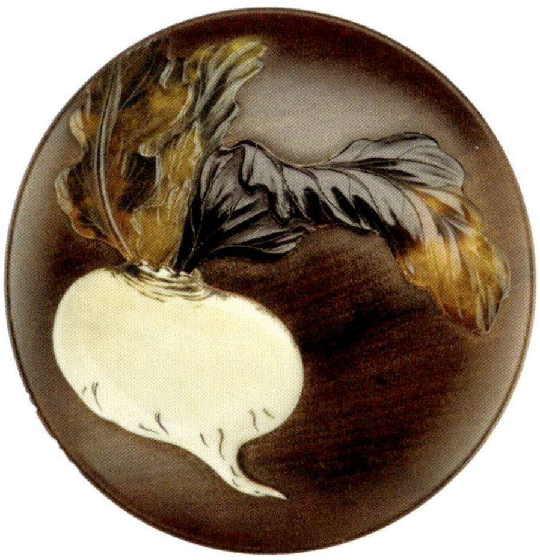

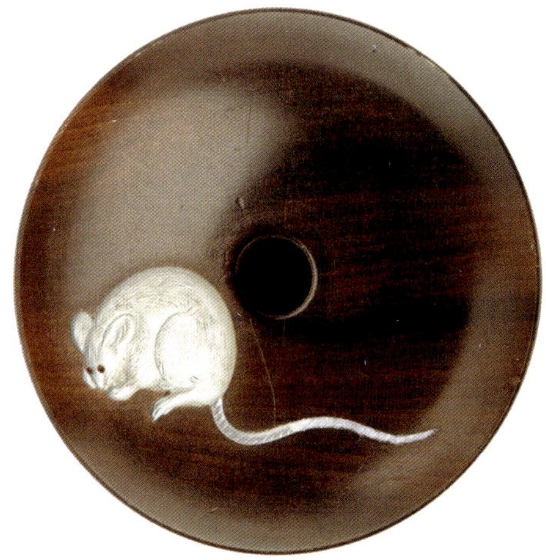

43

Fukurokuju

Verso: Hagoita and shuttlecock

Ivory and silver
Signed: Hidechika 秀親 with *kakihan*
Early 19th century
Diam: 5.2; H: 1.9 cm
EA2001.65
Bequeathed by Dr Monica Barnett

Wilhelm, G. *Manjū exégèse et appréciation*. Bulletin Association Franco-Japonaise. No. 54. Octobre, 1996. Fig. MB8

Bought at Sotheby's 28/01/1974

The three characters forming this god's name, *fuku* 福 *roku* 禄 *ju* 寿, translate as wealth, happiness and longevity, all of which Fukurokuju is said to be able to bestow upon believers.

He is a benevolent old man with a long beard and a very high forehead indicating his superior intelligence. He was originally a popular deity in China and was thought to embody the South Pole Star. Fukurokuju holds a willow branch laden with toys for distribution at the New Year (*mayudama*). Nowadays this is usually decorated with small red and white rice balls, instead of toys. The toys on this piece include a bag, a boat, coins, a shuttlecock, an old-fashioned merchant's account book, 大福帳 (*daifuku-chō*) and silver beads hanging from the ends of many of the branches. The peg is shaped as a die showing the sides with one, three and five spots.

The *hagoita* is a paddle or bat used in the game of battledore and shuttlecock (*hanetsuki*), played at the New Year. The bamboo decoration on it is an auspicious symbol of strength, endurance and resilience.

The depiction of Fukurokuju on this piece is very similar to a *katabori* netsuke of Fukurokuju, Ofuku and a small child in the Gō Collection, Tokyo National Museum, illustrated as Nos. 314 and 315 in the catalogue[34] and signed Chōunsai Hidechika, the artist's full name. The treatment of his face, robe and particularly the fabric covering his head look very similar. He carries a similar selection of toys and the account book, and between the two adult figures is a die.

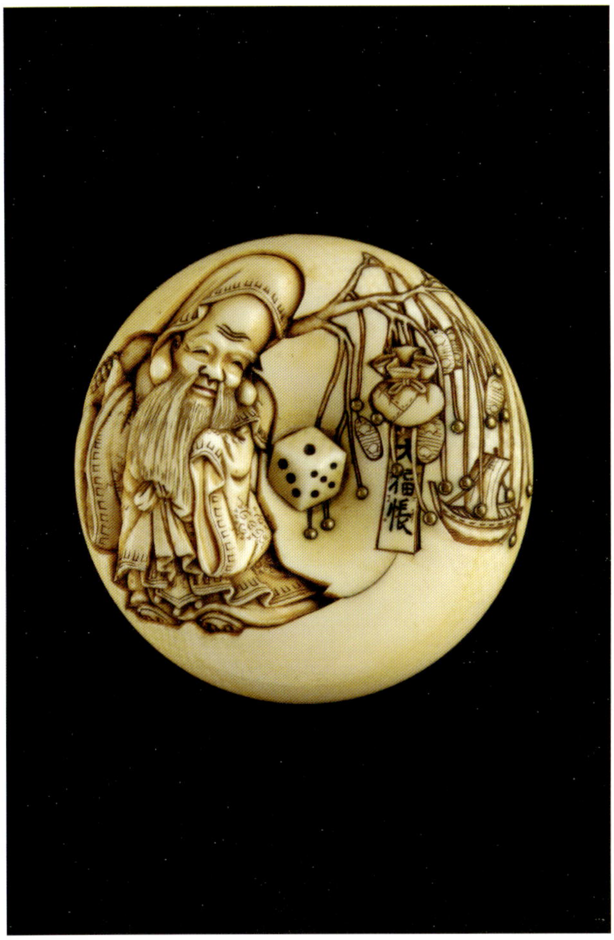

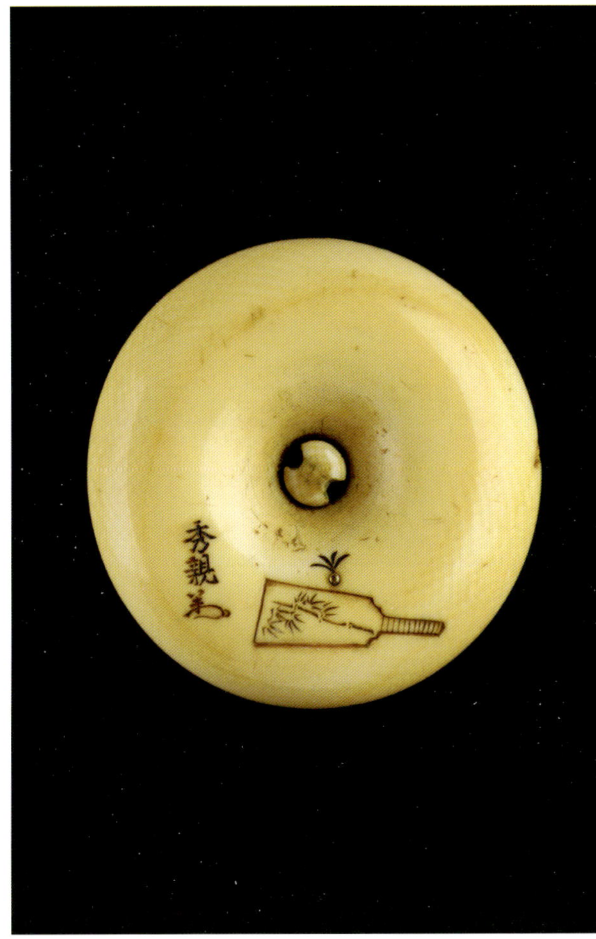
秀親

44

Child riding a sacred deer

Verso: Two birds in flight above a sacred tree tied around with a *shimenawa*

Ivory with red and black staining
Signed: Hōjitsu 法實 with *kakihan*
Mid- to late 19th century
Diam: 4.9; H: 1.6 cm
EA2001.79
Bequeathed by Dr Monica Barnett

Sold at Sotheby's, London. 16/11/1983. Lot 26.

This Japanese child either poses as the Daoist sage Jurōjin (Ch. *Shoulao*), or has borrowed the old man's messenger companion, to transport him and the sack he is carrying (possibly for Hotei). Jurōjin is numbered amongst the *Shichifukujin* and is not unlike Fukurokuju to look at; he is depicted as a wise old man who is almost always accompanied by a deer, said to be 1500 years old. The deer is sacred in Japan and is believed to be an intermediary between the gods and human beings; it is symbolic of longevity, as is Jurōjin. The deer is the only animal said to be able to find the fungus of immortality, sought by Daoist immortals to prolong their lives and youthfulness. The *shimenawa* tied around the tree on the reverse denotes a sacred place. It is a rope decoration with cloth streamers representing offerings to the spirits of the Shintō gods believed to dwell within it.

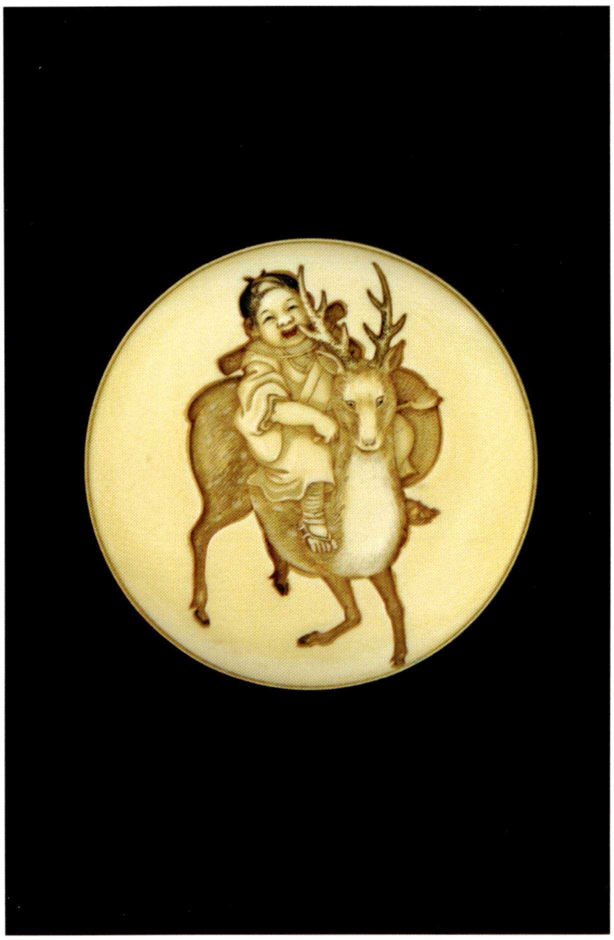

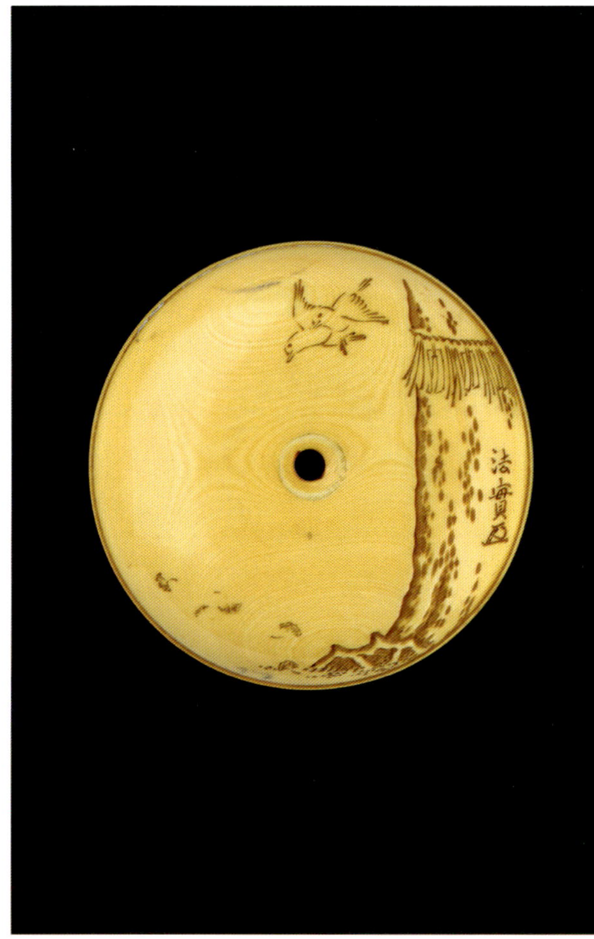

45

The Goddess Benten

Verso: stylised chrysanthemum flowers and scrolling clouds

Ryūsa-type *manjū*
Ivory
Signed: Koku 谷
Asakusa School
Late 19th century
Diam: 4.65; H: 2.0 cm
EAX.627

Benten, the only female amongst the *Shichifukujin*, is accompanied by a dragon said to be one of her incarnations. In her hand she holds a *'ruyi'* sceptre, which is a token of good fortune and was given as a gift in China because of its auspicious connotations. Benten originated in India as the goddess Sarasvati, named after the river in India from which a dragon emerged, giving rise to the notion that she was part-dragon (see cat. no. 89). She is worshipped in many shrines in Japan as a goddess of love and a giver of wealth. When depicted with the *Shichifukujin* she is often shown playing a *biwa*, a stringed musical instrument not dissimilar to the lute.

Ozeki Kokusai's signatures are as original as the netsuke he carved. He used the single *'koku'* character on many pieces, usually cut in raised seal script. Here it is incised. The indomitable collector Anne Hull Grundy, whose collection is now in the British Museum, wrote of Kokusai's signatures '… some are raised, others engraved, and they appear in or out of any shaped reserve; some shaded as a negative, and each stylised to suit his prevailing mood – and these are only his everyday signatures! On those occasions when he is feeling more subtle … he only puts on the engraved suggestion of a fleeting stylized 'Koku' and leaves it to us to complete the diagnosis by scrutinizing his style of carving'.[35]

This subject matter is very much in keeping with the Asakusa School of carvers who were 'strongly influenced by classical Chinese Buddhist symbolism'.[36]

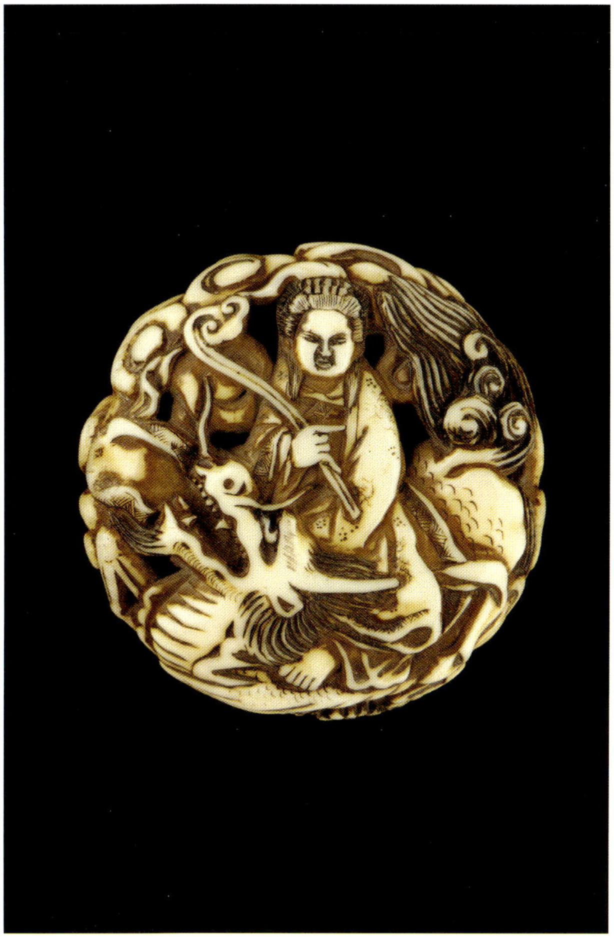

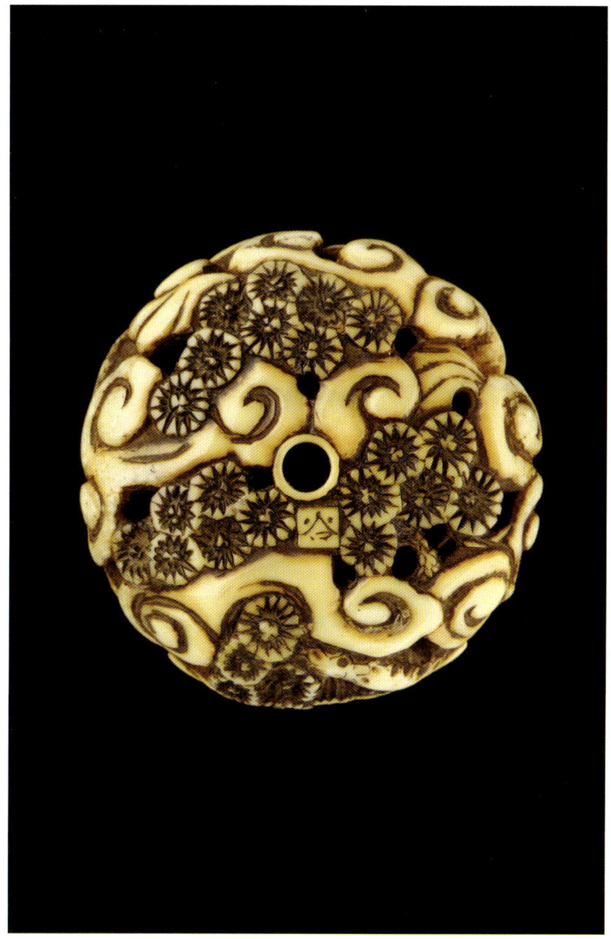

46

Setsubun festival: young boy throwing beans

Verso: Three fleeing *oni* dressed in tiger-skin loin cloths

Ivory
Signed: Meikeisai Hōjitsu 明鶏齋法實 with red lacquer seal reading Hōjitsu
Mid-19th century
Diam: 4.1; H: 2.4 cm
EA2001.126
Bequeathed by Dr Monica Barnett

Illustrated in:
Frederick Meinertzhagen. Ed. George Lazarnick. *MCI. Meinertzhagen Card Index on Netsuke in the Archives of the British Museum*, Alan R. Liss, Inc., New York. p. 175
Barry Davies Oriental Art, 100 *Selected Pieces from the Scott Meredith Collection and 50 from another Private American Collection*. London. 08–15/08/1995. No. 138
Hōzan (法山) copied this design on a *manju* netsuke, illustrated in Frederick Meinertzhagen. Ed. George Lazarnick. *MCI. Meinertzhagen Card Index on Netsuke in the Archives of the British Museum*, Alan R. Liss, Inc., New York.p. 203

This piece sold at Glendinning's in January 1937 for £2.21 (according to Meinertzhagen)
See Sotheby's, London. 13 & 14/06/1985. Lot 502

It is the winter solstice (nowadays 3 February), the festival known as *Setsubun*, when homes were ceremoniously cleansed of devils. This was celebrated in the old lunar calendar as the New Year. A young boy dressed in traditional costume hurls soy beans to drive out the devils, seen on the reverse running away under a hail of these missiles. The accompanying chant '*oni wa soto, fuku wa uchi*' ('Out with the devils and in with good fortune') rings out.

The specially prepared beans are held in a box mounted on an offering tray (*sanbō*) used in Shintō ceremonies. On the side beneath the *oni* is a sprig of holly and a dried salted sardine (*iwashi*) head, which according to U. A. Casal was 'hung up as a further talisman against the ghosts of hunger'.[37]

This is one of the finest *manjū* from Dr Barnett's collection. Meikeisai Hōjitsu was considered by many to be the greatest *manjū* carver of the nineteenth century.

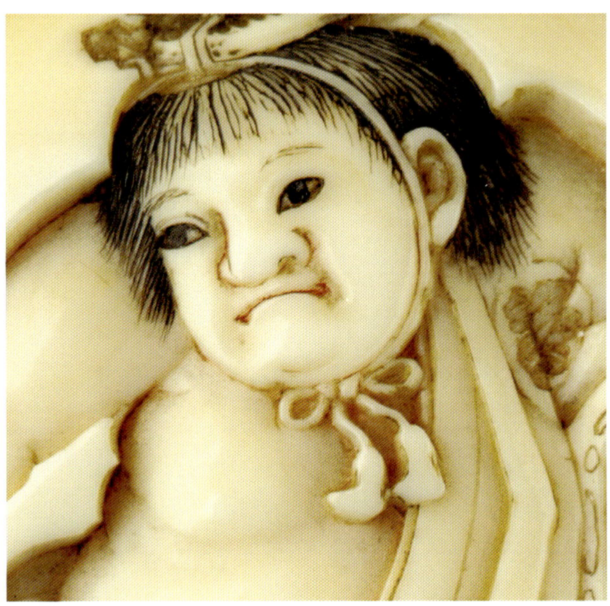

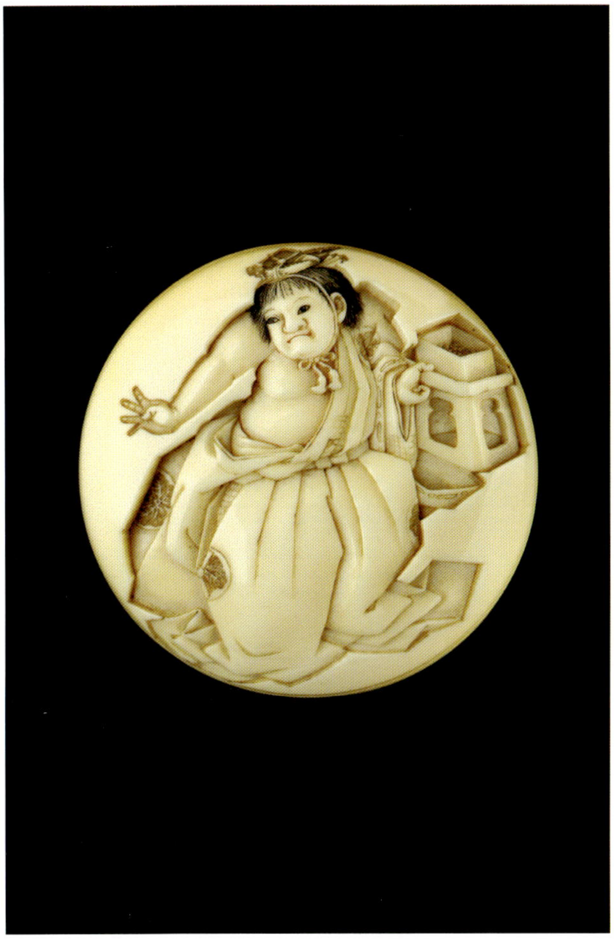

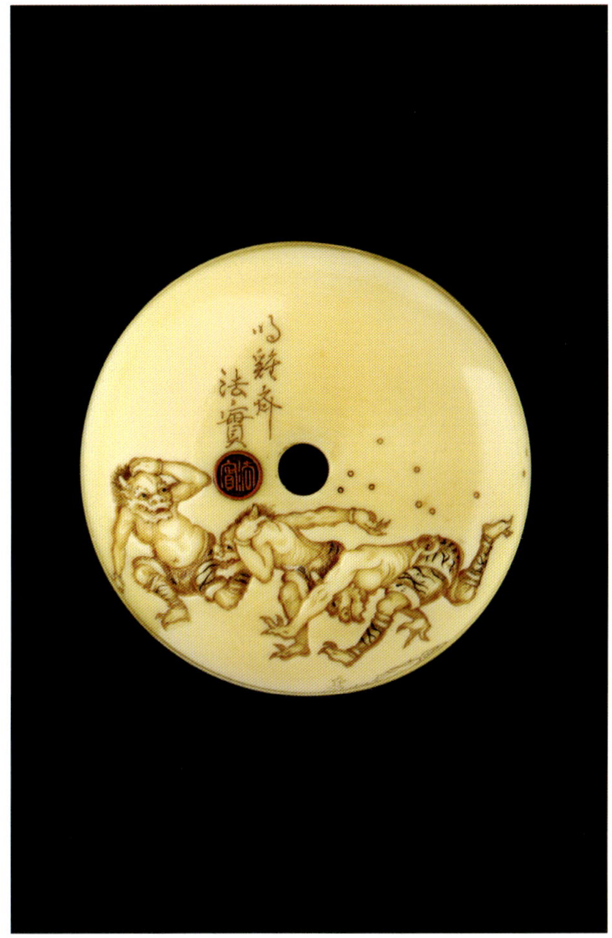

47

Setsubun: Young boy chasing away two oni

Ivory with black staining
Signed: Moritoshi 守寿 with crane *kakihan*
19th century
Diam: 5.31; H: 1.95 cm
EA2001.37
Bequeathed by Dr Monica Barnett

This netsuke celebrates the New Year, and illustrates *Setsubun* (see cat. no. 46). Moritoshi has wrapped the design uninterrupted around the side of this *manjū* which shows a young boy flourishing a plaited whip and chasing away two *oni*, one sitting, mouth open possibly in shock or supplication, the other cowering, with head on the ground begging forgiveness.

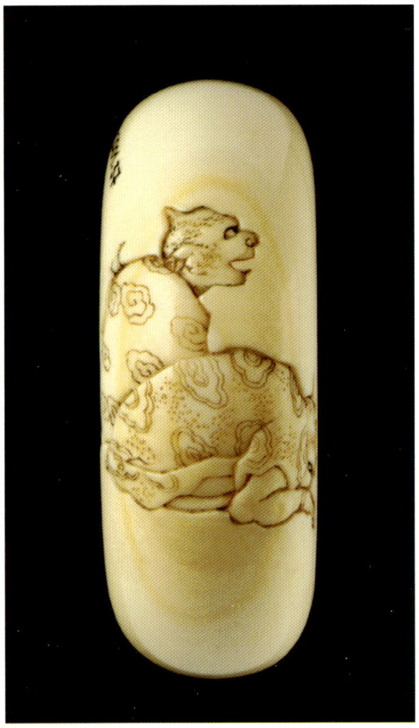

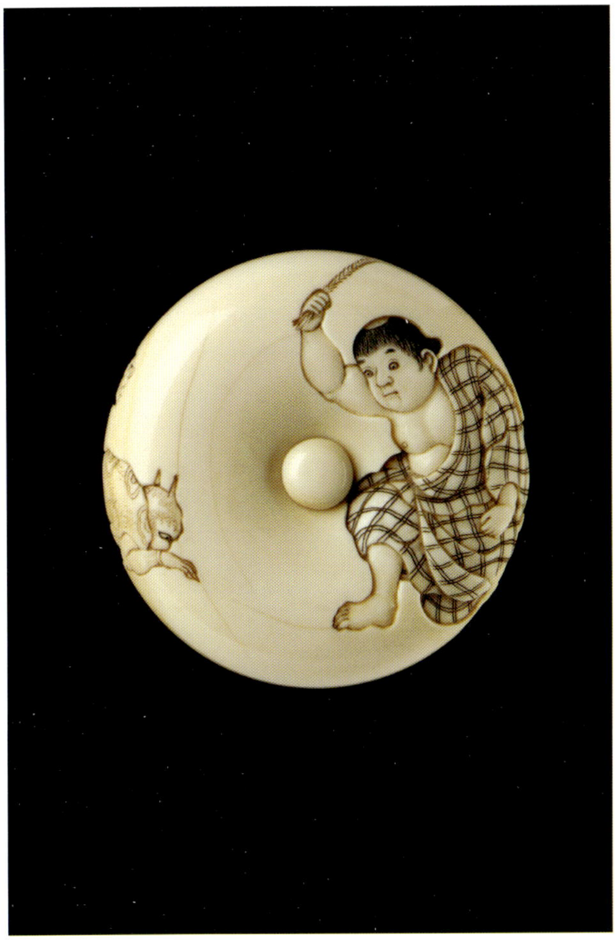

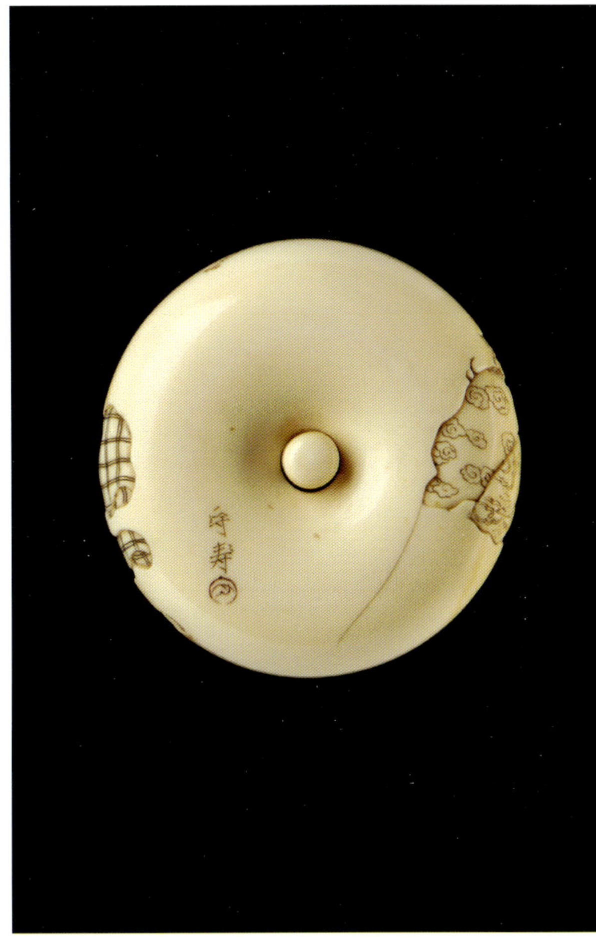

48

Okina: The mask-box bearer and Sanbasō dancing

Verso: A seated Okina, with pine branch and curtain

Ivory with staining
Signed: Ikkōsai 一孝斎
Mid-late 19th century
Diam: 6.4; H: 2.76 cm
EA2001.103
Bequeathed by Dr Monica Barnett

Okina (The Old Man) is a type of Nō performance, a combination of Nō and Kyogen, which was produced as a prelude to the traditional full day's programme of five Nō plays, performed during the Edo period. Nowadays, it is reserved for the New Year or very special occasions. Three main performers take part: two Nō actors, Okina and Senzai and a Kyōgen actor, Sanbasō. It is described as a religious ritual dance, for all performers undergo rigorous abstention and purification rituals beforehand.

Okina's dance celebrates long life and is an invocation for peace and harmony and a plentiful harvest. Senzai, whom we do not see on this netsuke, is the first to dance, requesting the presence of the gods. Before Okina appears, his white mask (*haku-shikijō*) is brought onto the stage in a lacquer box by the mask bearer, seen sitting on the right. Okina dons his mask on the stage (the only Nō play in which this happens) and nowadays this is considered to be his moment of apotheosis, when from human he becomes god.[38] His dance is stately and slow. He wears the costume of the nobility, (*kariginu*) decorated with the linked hexagonal pattern, reminiscent of turtle shell and by association a symbol of longevity and good fortune. In contrast the Sanbasō dancer who completes the performance wears a costume of the samurai class decorated with cranes and pines, also symbols of longevity and the New Year. His tall lacquered conical hat has twelve horizontal stripes, one for each month of the year and two large discs, the red representing the sun and the white disc the moon. He wears a black mask (*koku-shikijō*). His dance is lively and noisy; the dance of the earth. He stamps his feet, mimicking the planting and harvesting of rice and shakes his bell rattle (*suzu*) to attract the attention of the god who has the power to give life to the rice and thus a plentiful harvest.

Ikkōsai 一孝斎 has been faithful to details of the costumes in this performance, indicating that this was either commissioned by a devotee of Nō or that he himself was familiar with this sophistocated New Year ritual. Nothing is known about this nineteenth century artist whose '*kō*' character in Ikkōsai is different from that of Ikkōsai Kōjitsu.

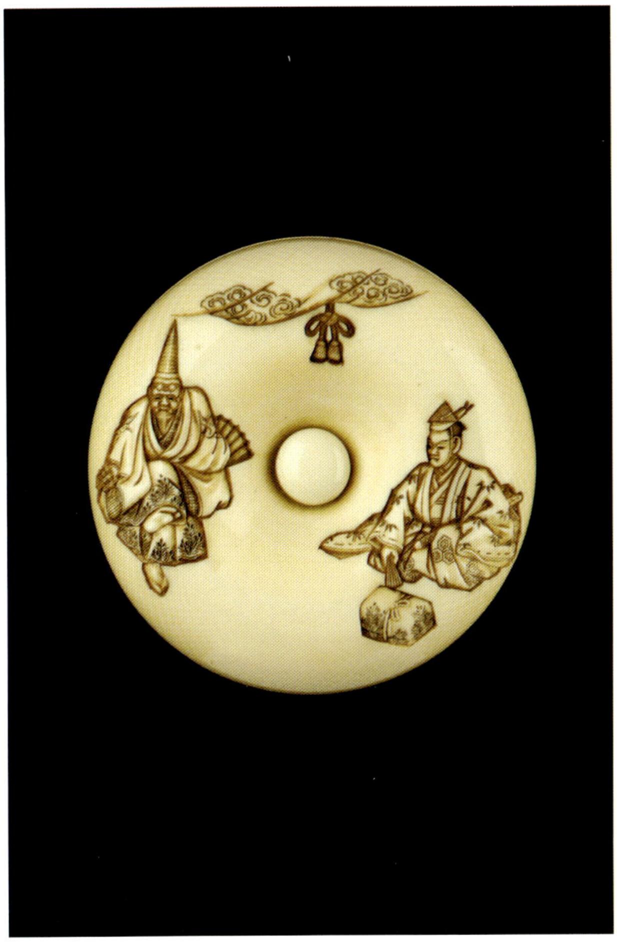

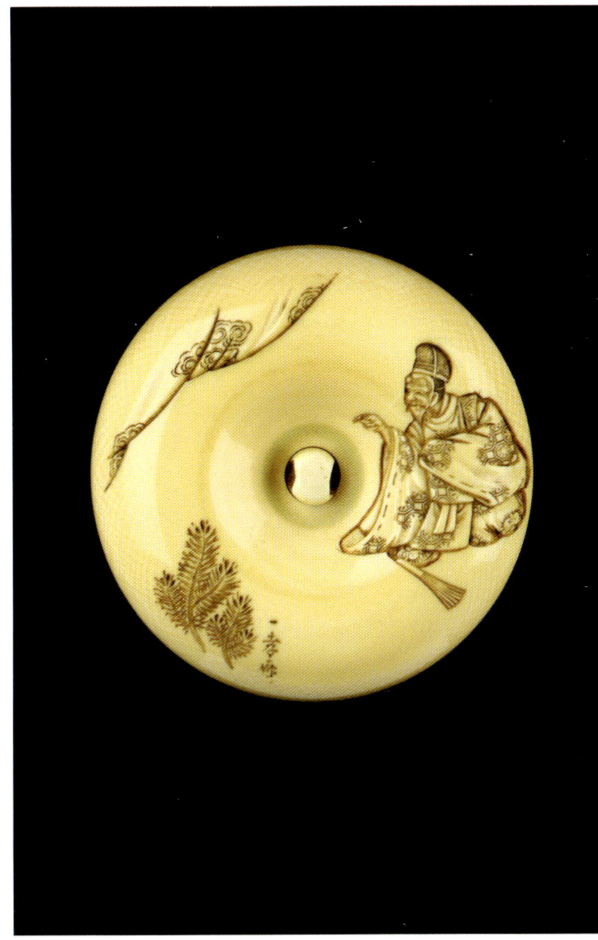

49

Sanbasō dancer

Verso: An uprooted pine sapling

Ivory with inlaid red and green lacquer or malachite
Signed: Kikugawa 菊川 with red *tomoe* seal
1820–1860
Diam: 5.15; H: 2.1 cm
EA2001.41
Bequeathed by Dr Monica Barnett

Bought from S.Marchant on 26/08/1970

This is a charming depiction of two young boys, one impersonating the Sanbasō dancer in the performance of Okina (see cat. no. 48) while the younger of the two, a mere toddler, is the guardian of Okina's mask, contained in the box in front of him.

The young uprooted pine sapling on the reverse represents an imperial ceremony, known as *ne no hi no asobi* (Entertainment of the Day of the Rat), dating back at least to the ninth century. A hill outside Kyoto was chosen to which courtiers would proceed and enjoy a picnic in the open air. They would then uproot young pine saplings, bring them back and plant them in the imperial garden as a good omen. As U. A. Casal puts it, these young saplings 'predicted all the beauty, vigour and happiness of the mature tree. As they would grow, so should the family's and country's prosperity grow'.[39]

Another *manjū* in this collection signed Kikugawa bears the added *tomoe* seal without a red border. In the Ferenc Hopp Museum in Budapest, the enclosed seal is used on a *manjū* by Kikugawa Ryūgoku, so we can speculate that this piece is also by him.

Meinertzhagen describes Kikugawa Ryūgoku as 'the greatest master of "*cavo-rilievo*"' work, selecting his subjects to suit his style' and says that he brought the carving and decoration of 'manjū netsuke to its highest perfection'.[40] To enhance the deep *shishiaibori* carving, the artist has added lacquer details in red, green and black to the kimono on which he has described the auspicious symbols of the New Year in fine *kebori* lines. Children, with or without their mothers, frequently appear on *manjū* made by this workshop.

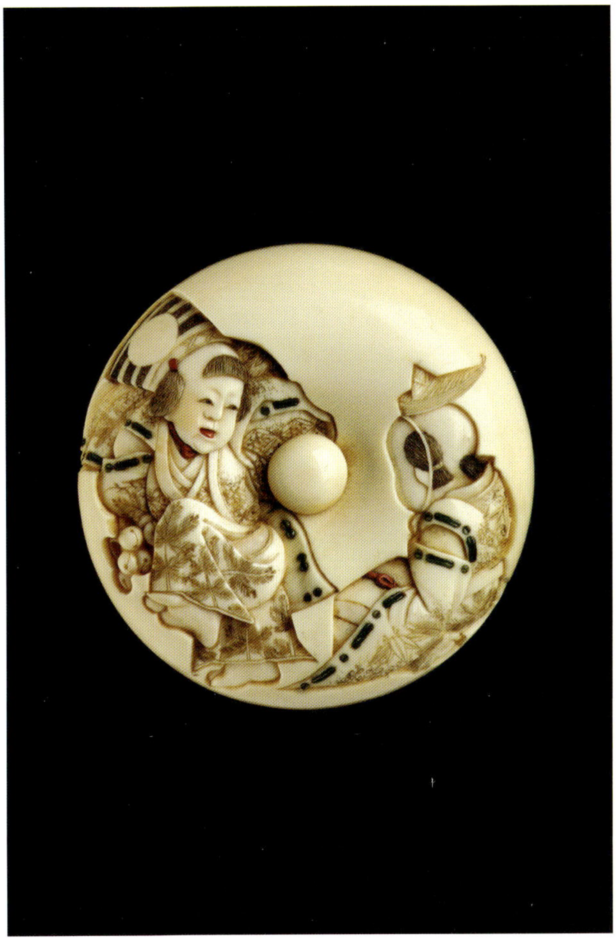 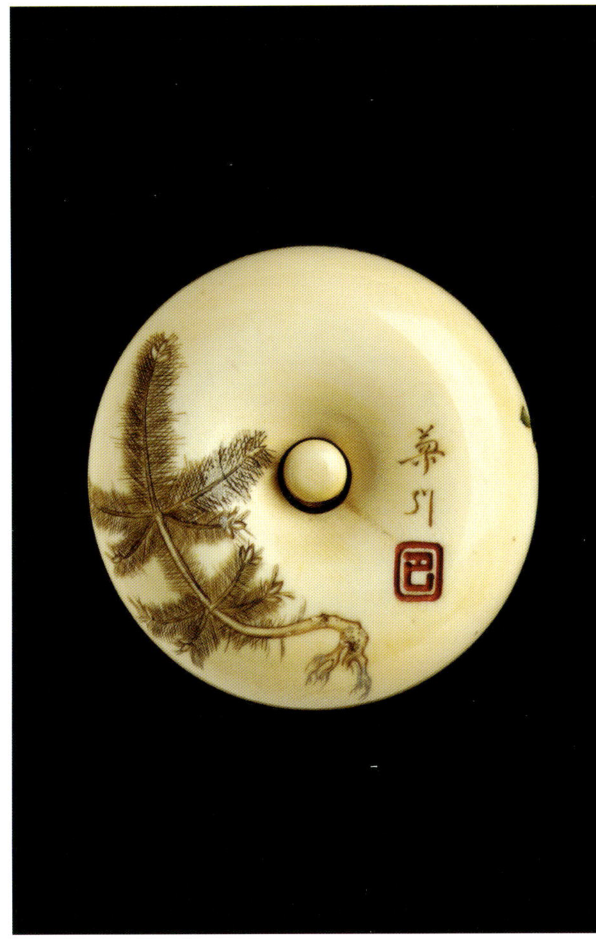

50

Sacred horse

Verso: Monkey tugging at the rope

Ivory with tortoiseshell
Signed: Doshō 道笑 with *kakihan*
Osaka school
1850–1868
Diam: 5.2; H: 1.8 cm
EA2001.93
Bequeathed by Dr Monica Barnett

Published:
Wilhelm, G. *Manjū exégèse et appréciation*. Bulletin Association Franco-Japonaise. No. 54. Octobre, 1996. Fig. MB7 (the attribution to Hidechika is incorrect).

In Japan the monkey has been considered the guardian of horses since ancient times, having the ability to protect them from illness. Horses have ancient religious significance as mediators between humans and gods and act as mounts for the gods. Horses were originally donated to Shintō shrines as offerings, a practice which slowly evolved from a gift of a live horse, through a wooden model, then to paper horses and finally to pictures of horses, which are known as *ema*. Today, small wooden *ema* (literally 'picture horse') can be bought at all shrines, bearing either the zodiac animal of the year or an image related to the particular shrine. The custom is to write a message to the resident *kami* (god) either expressing thanks or asking for something such as good health, safe delivery of a baby, success in examinations and various other personal requests. These are then hung up in the shrine precinct and later, usually at the following New Year, undergo a ritual burning.

The role of the monkey as protector and guardian of horses gave rise to the practice of monkeys performing dances in front of sacred horses in shrine stables on festival days and particularly

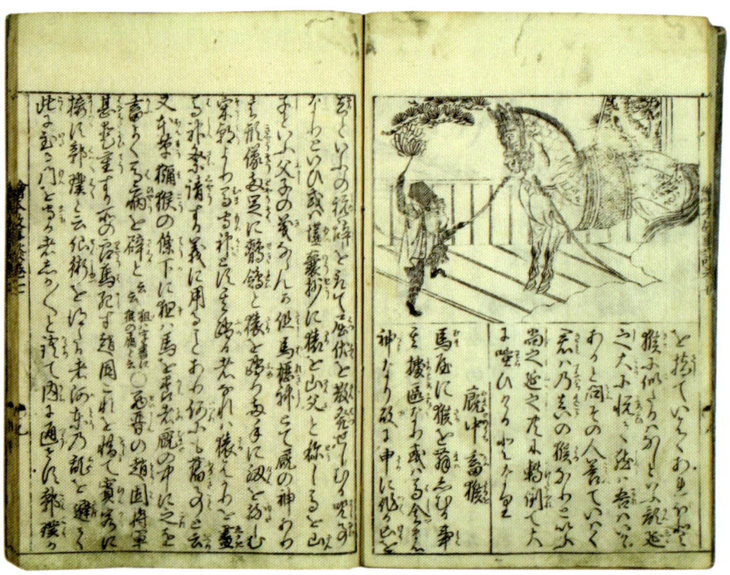

Fig. 45 Illustration from *Ehon kojidan*, Vol. 7, p. 10. Monkey performing a *sambasō* dance for a sacred horse (Waseda University Library, Tokyo, bunko 06 0025–(7))

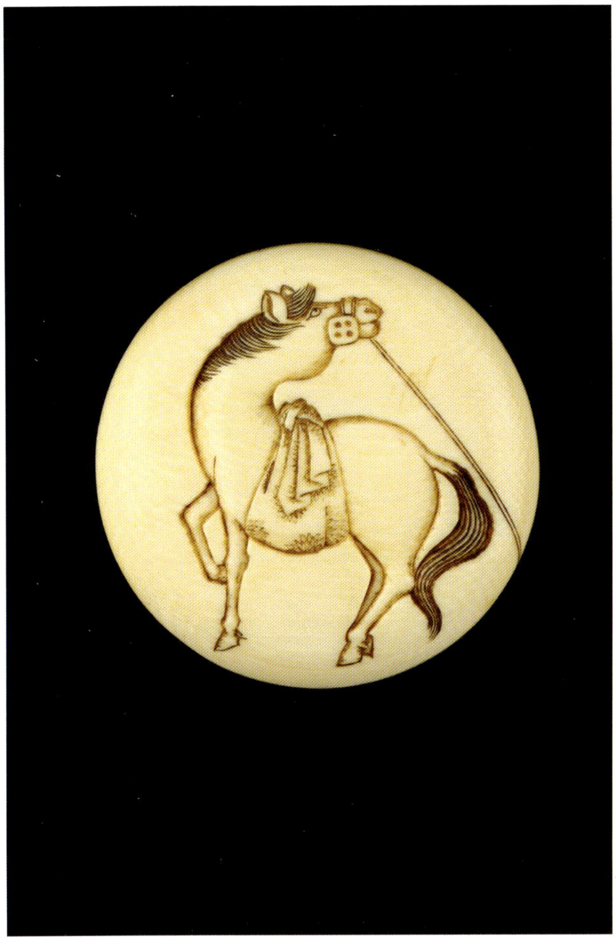

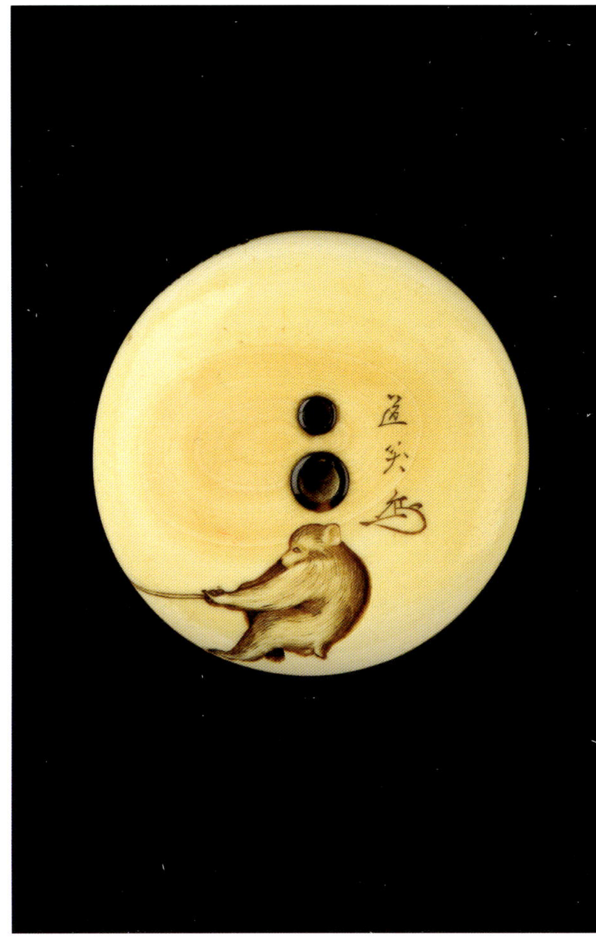

at the New Year. During the Edo period, monkey dances were performed both at the stables of the Imperial Palace in Kyoto and at those of the court of the shōgun in Edo.[41] The *sanbasō* dance was frequently part of the ritual.

Here Dōshō's horse also wears a festive cloth, decorated with chrysanthemums. Its reluctance to move, head drawn backwards, creates a perfect shape for the circular 'canvas' of the *manjū*. It is not until you look at the reverse that a determined monkey, tugging at the horse's halter, is revealed. The catalogue of the Inrō Museum in Takayama, (now closed), has a very similar piece with the same subject signed Doshōsai. This monkey is more gently persuasive than the one on the Ashmolean piece.[42] The *himotōshi* is lined with tortoiseshell.

51

Raiden, the thunder god

Verso: a back view of Raiden peering through a hole in the clouds

Pottery with green, blue, red and gold enamels
Signed: Teiji 貞二
1850–1880
H: 1.7; W: 3.5; D: 3.4 cm
EA1956.3198
Presented by Sir Herbert Ingram

Raiden, the thunder god, peers timidly at the world through a gap in the clouds. On the reverse his back view reveals his drum, slung over his shoulder. It has emblazoned on it the *tomoe mon* representing *yin* and *yang*, the opposite forces of nature. He was often portrayed with his accomplice, Fujin the wind god. Netsuke portrayals of these gods were frequently comical. On this *manjū*, the formidable strength of Raiden, who was capable of producing a fearsome noise, seems to have left him.

Teiji enjoyed making fun of religious figures in this style of *manjū*. On a piece now in the Weston Collection, he has had the idea of disturbing Daruma during his long years of meditation. A rat jumps up and bites his ear and the patriarch, cocooned in a tumbledown thatched hut cries out in pain.[43]

Kawamoto Teiji was a potter whose work included combinations of clay and wood. He was active in the mid-nineteenth century at a kiln set up in the grounds of the *daimyō* Matsudaira Yoshitake's Edo residence.

This *manjū* was bought by Herbert Ingram in Japan in 1908 and is listed in his catalogue as 'porcelain netsuke – demon looking through window'. Unfortunately these are the only details we

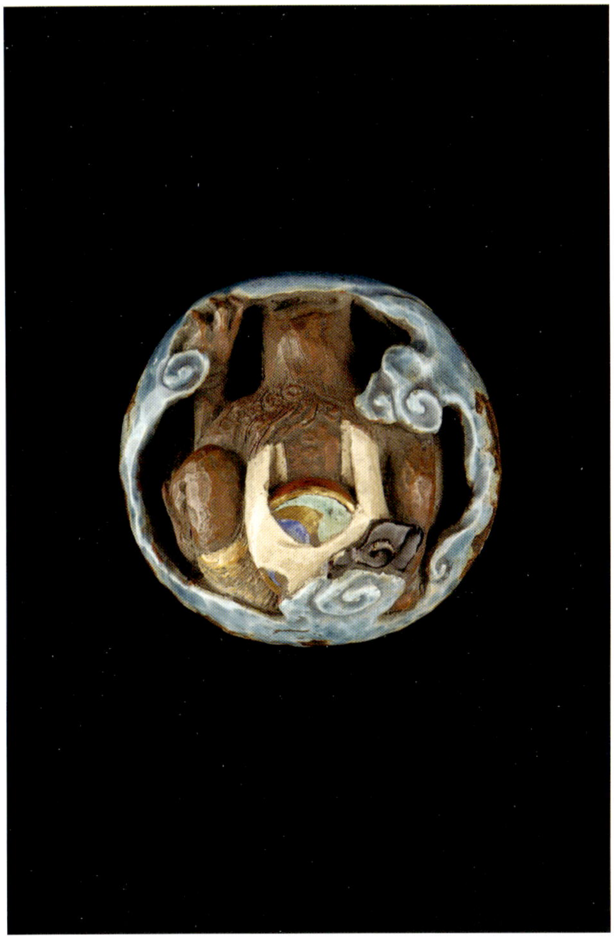

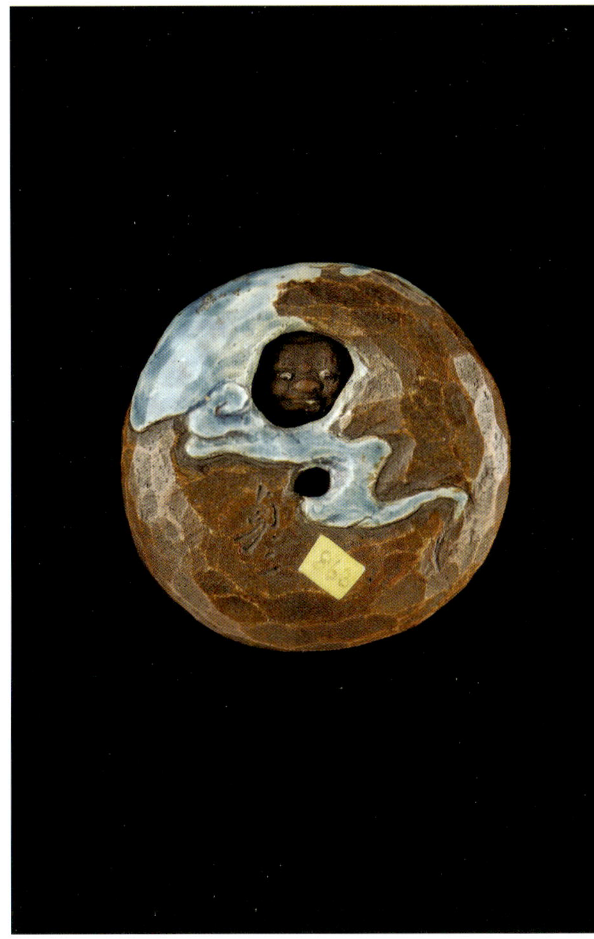

have of its purchase, unlike other objects in his collection which have prices paid and shop names attached to them. In those days he was able to buy netsuke for between one and two yen, the equivalent of two to four shillings each.

Several very similar versions of this *manjū* exist, two of which are in the Gō Collection, Tokyo National Museum[44] and another is in the Toledo Museum of Art, in Ohio.[45]

52

Shishi rolling on its back while playing ball. Edge with geometric motif

Verso: plain

Ivory with light staining
Signed: Shōseki tō 蕉石刀
(Carved by Shōseki)
Circa 1860
H: 1.5; W: 4.2; H: 2.7 cm
EA2001.47
Bequeathed by Dr Monica Barnett

Bought from Douglas J.K. Wright
21/01/1971

Shishi, which means 'lion-dog', is the Japanese name for an animal which looks more like a Tibetan spaniel than either a lion or a dog. *Shishi* first appeared in China as guardians of the Buddhist faith. When positioned in pairs either side of the entrance to a Buddhist temple, they act as protectors.

This *shishi*, playing with a ball while holding a smaller one in its mouth, is symbolic of an empire at peace. *Shishi* also represent courage and strength. The fur of the *shishi* on this *manjū* is carefully depicted and the animal has the splendid curly mane and tail in keeping with tradition. The fret pattern carved around the outside of the platform on which the *shishi* is playing also reminds us of its Chinese origins and harks back to eighteenth century netsuke carving, when Chinese lion-dogs (*karashishi*) were fashioned sitting on a platform, the base of which was carved to form a seal. The uneven *himotōshi* on this unusually shaped solid oval *manjū* imitates these eighteenth-century netsuke.

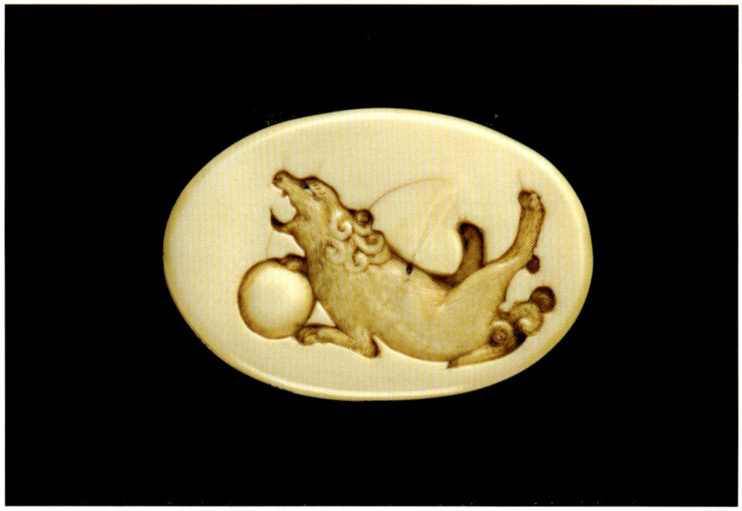

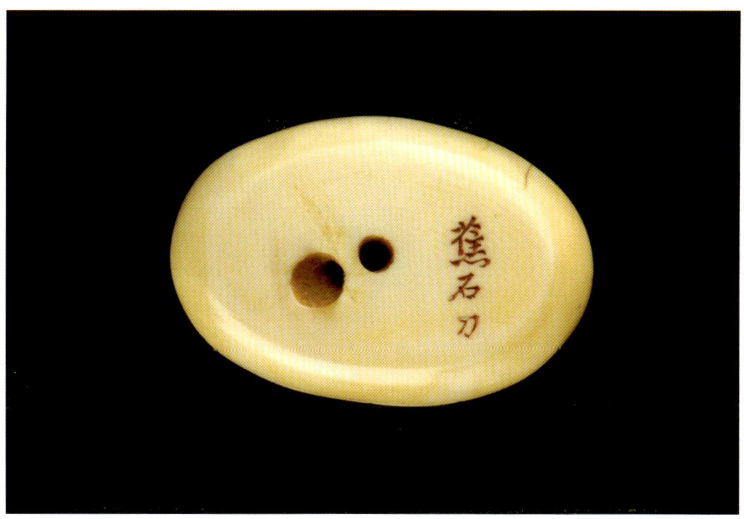
蕉石刀

53

Shishi

Verso: altar vase containing lotus flowers and *mokugyō*

Ryūsa-type *manjū*
Ivory and silver
Signed: Harumichi 治道 (unrecorded artist)
Late 19th century
Diam: 4.0; H: 2.3 cm
EAX.628

A silver *shishi* is superimposed on an ivory pierced *manjū* shape with Buddhist altar vases, lotus flowers and leaves. A *mokugyō,* a type of wooden gong, hit with a stick as an aid to keep rhythm during the chanting of Buddhist sutras, bears the signature of this unrecorded ivory artist. The metalwork of the *shishi* is unsigned. It was not unusual for *kanamono* artists, who made metal fittings for tobacco pouches amongst other things, to collaborate with *manjū* netsuke carvers in the second half of the nineteenth century. The most common joint efforts were those which created *kagamibuta*-type netsuke, a type of netsuke which are mostly formed with a central disc, usually of metal, inserted into a rounded frame made of ivory, wood, lacquer or horn.

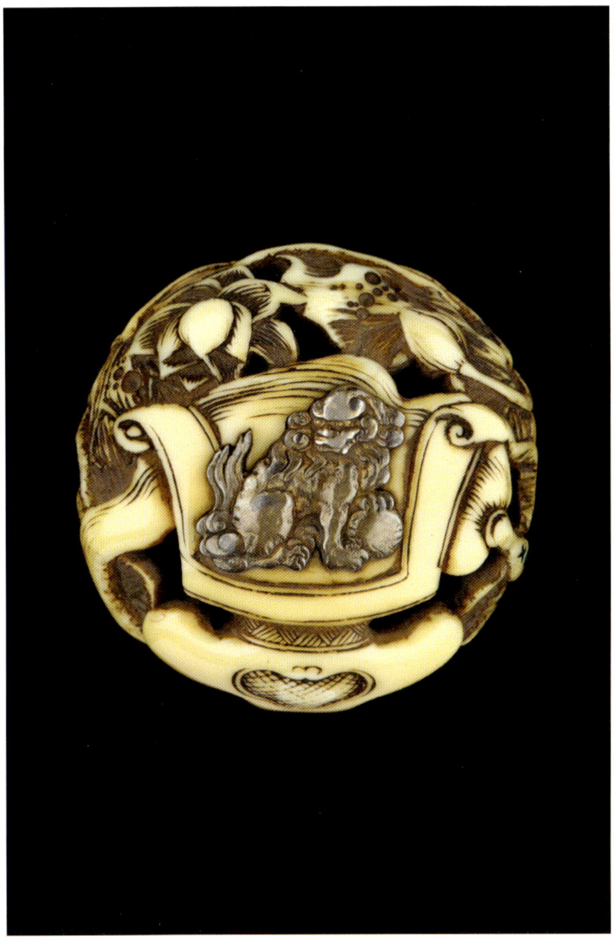

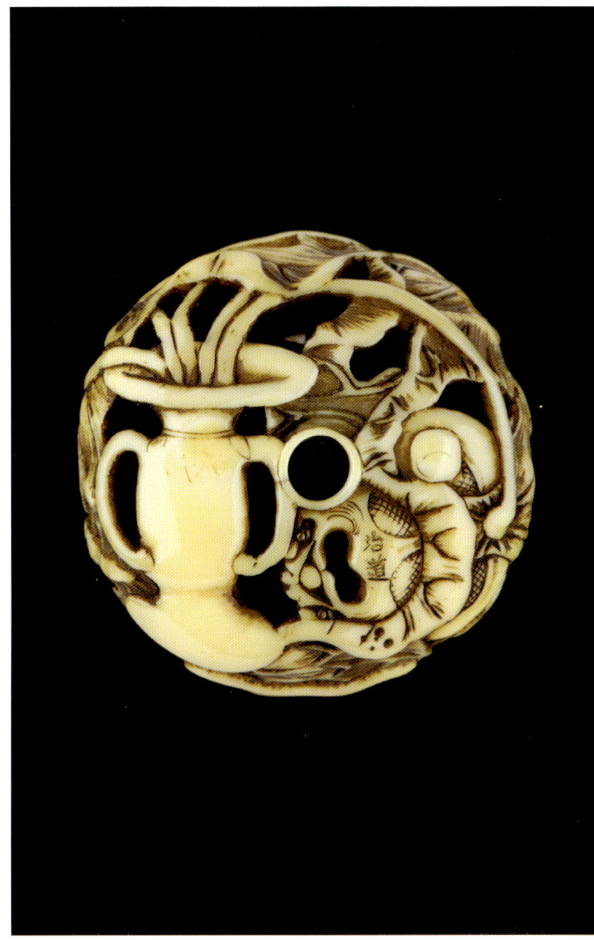

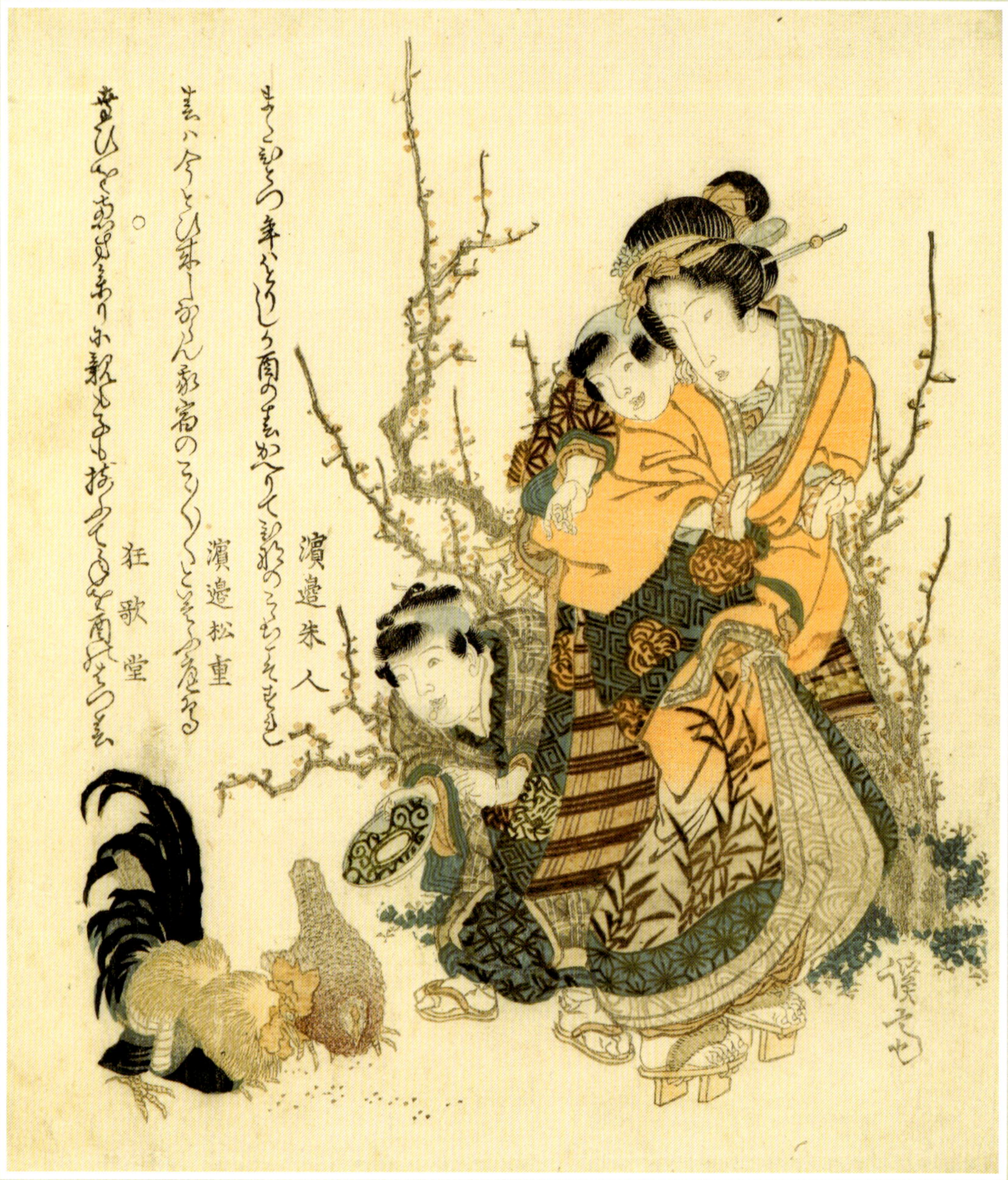

Fig. 46 *Surimono* of mother and children by Keisai Eisen (1795–1848) (EAX.4610)

Daily Life

Netsuke carvers delighted in portraying ordinary people going about their work, play and leisure activities. A particular moment, frozen in animation, might be chosen to amuse or to show something unusual. Young children, traditionally depicted as *karako* (Chinese children) were celebrated at two festivals during the year. Boys' Day on the fifth day of the fifth month and Girls' Day on the third day of the third month provided an occasion to wear an appropriately decorated netsuke. The Kikugawa school in particular often featured *karako* and mothers with young children. Illustrations of craftsmen at work were also a source of fascination to nineteenth century townsmen and merchants. These were the subject of printed books and were a source of inspiration for the *manjū* carvers.

During the Edo period travel increased enormously, in part due to the *sankin kōtai* system which required samurai to reside in Edo in alternating years, leaving their families in the home domain. Some took a retinue of hundreds of retainers each time they travelled back and forth to the new capital. Inns sprung up around the staging-posts along the various highways, where all types of traveller could stay, for leisure travel also increased dramatically. The production of guide books to famous places (*meisho*) and towns along the main routes helped encourage travellers to venture forth. Some were on religious pilgrimage to temples and shrines, others travelling purely for pleasure and curiosity. Along the Tōkaidō, the road which ran between Tokyo and Kyoto, there were many of these *meisho*. Whereas the well-known print designers such as Hiroshige and Hokusai drew each staging post along the route in a landscape, the netsuke carvers might only pick a small detail to complement the design of a whole ensemble, *inrō*, *ojime* and netsuke (see cat. no. 61).

54

Toddler balancing a spinning top on his outstretched finger

Verso: A top and spinner

Ivory
Signed: Kōrin 孝林 with kakihan
19th century
Diam: 4.65; H: 1.6 cm
EA2001.36
Bequeathed by Dr Monica Barnett

See Sotheby's, New York 02/02/1990 for a similar piece. Lot 145

And for an almost identical piece by Kōrin see Bushell Collection sale at Sotheby's, London. 18/11/1999. Lot 176.

Young children in Japan have traditionally enjoyed much attention from their mothers and grandparents, the three generations often living within the same household. Indulged but respectful of their elders, once children start school their lives change as they take on the serious responsibility of education.

This charming study shows a very small boy entertaining himself with a spinning top. Some Japanese toys were gender specific and the spinning top was always played with by boys. A huge selection of simply crafted, brightly coloured tops can still be found in shops around Japan.

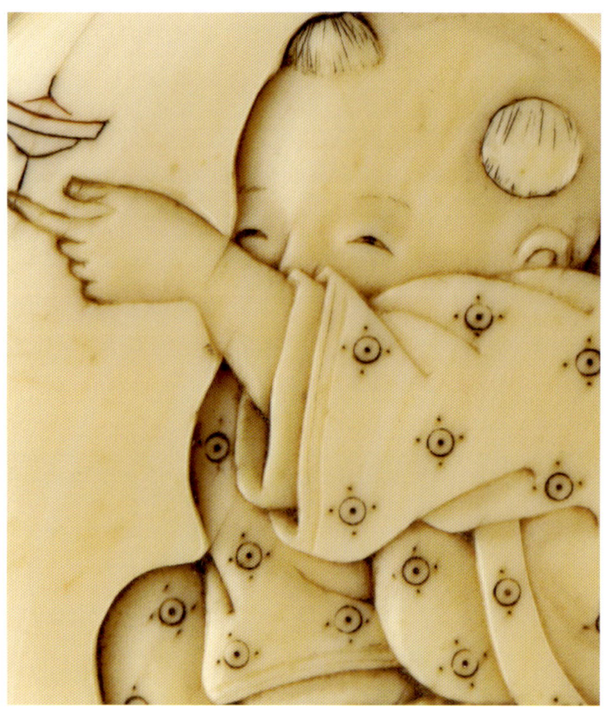

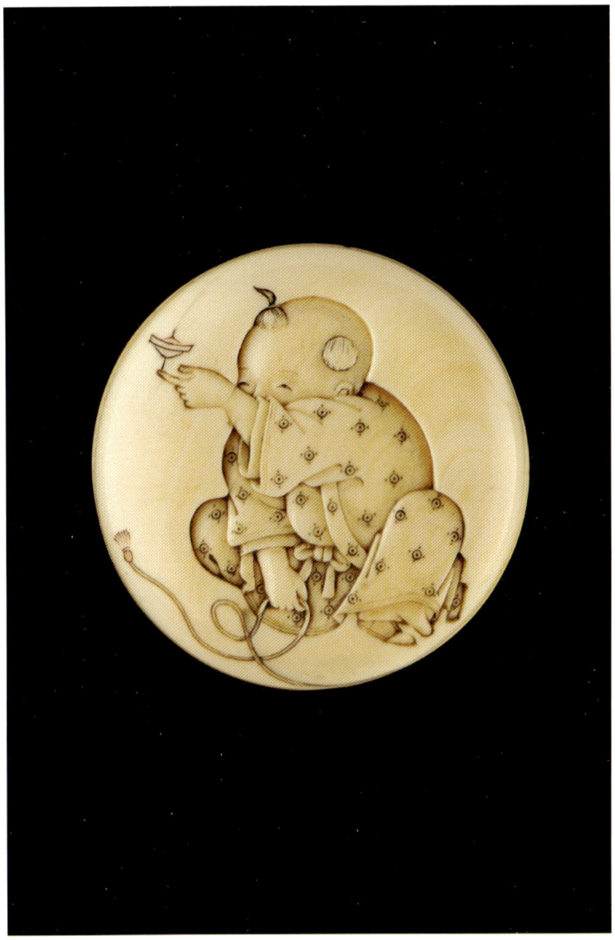

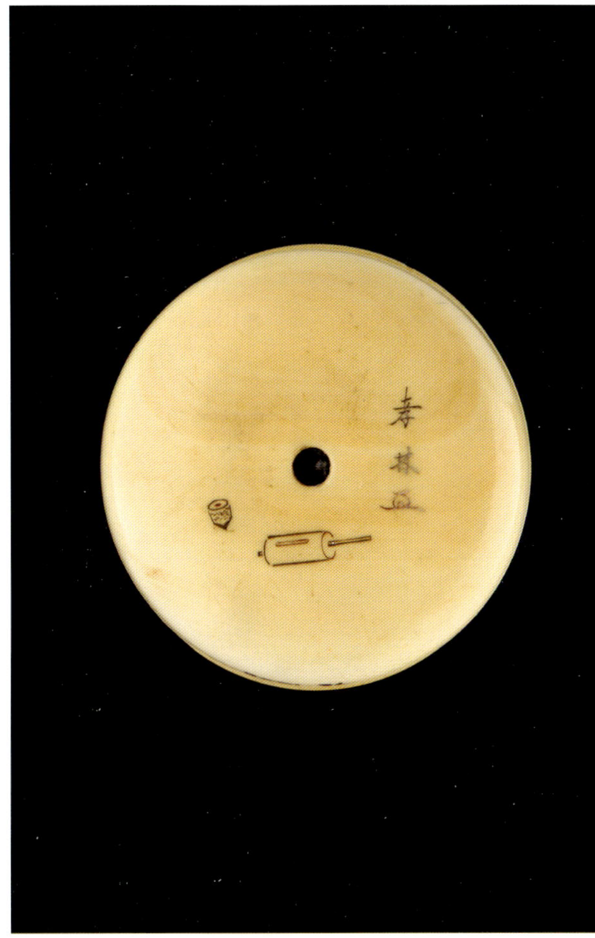

55

Mother feeding a child

Verso: a toy duck on wheels and a bamboo branch

Ivory with black and red staining, and metal beads
Signed: Kikugawa Masamitsu 菊川正光 with kakihan
Mid- to late 19th century
Diam: 4.7; H: 2.2 cm
EA2001.116
Bequeathed by Dr Monica Barnett

See Christie's, London. 12/12/ 1973. Lot 117. Bought by Mendelson for £280
Sold at Sotheby's, New York, May 23–25/05/1979. Lot 1135
Sold at Sotheby's New York 24 & 25/04/1991. Lot 323

A mother wearing a kimono decorated with a winter design of bamboo and snow is feeding her child and twisting a drum-on-a-stick (Jap. *den-den taiko)* in her left hand to amuse him. The noise made by the two dangling balls hitting the tiny drum are said to have the added advantage of warding off evil spirits. Beside them are other toys, including a *pin-pin sakana*, a small bow with a fish which travels up and down. Two of the toys have been intentionally coloured red, an auspicious colour.

Kikugawa Masamitsu is thought to be the founder of the Kikugawa line which was active in Tokyo throughout the second half of the nineteenth century. Many pupils signed only 'Kikugawa' and used this *kakihan*. The school specialised in large, boldly carved *manjū* of warriors, folktales, children, and everyday domestic scenes.

An example with a similar subject by Hōgyoku sold at Christie's, London. 16/05/2007. Lot 123.

Another *manjū* of Yamauba playing with Kintarō and toys by Kikugawa Ryūgoku with *tomoe* seal is in the Ferenc Hopp Museum of Eastern Asiatic Arts, Budapest. No. 457.[46]

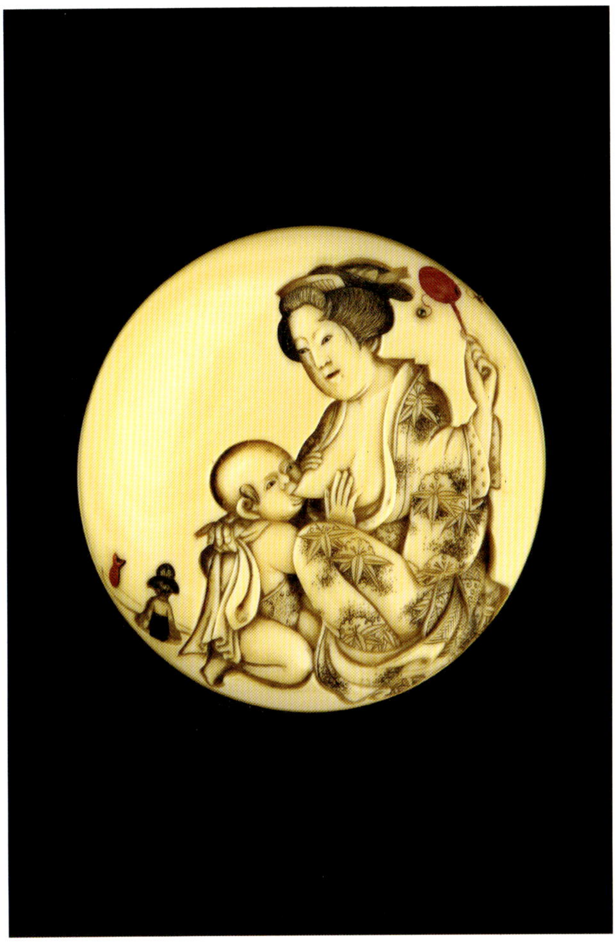

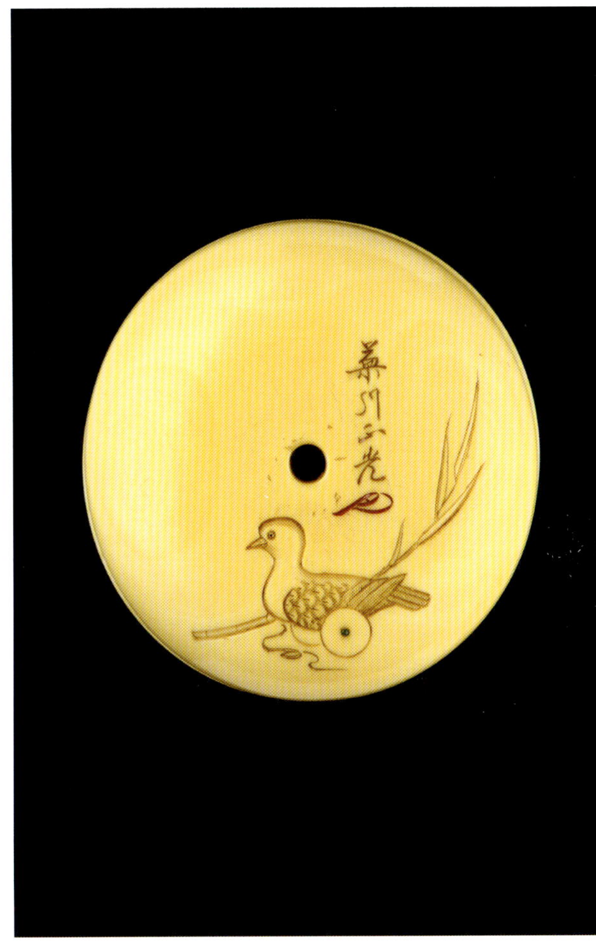

56

Toys: Faces peering out of a roundel in the centre

Verso: Various toys and a long-nosed mask

Ryūsa-type *manjū* in *kagamibuta* form
Ivory
Unsigned
Around 1860
Diam: 4.2; H: 1.55 cm
EA2001.134
Bequeathed by Dr Monica Barnett

Sold at Christie's, London. *The Raymond and Frances Bushell Collection of Netsuke Part II*, on 17/10/1988. Lot 189

This shows a range of toys from different regions of Japan, including a bird-shaped kite, a fish, a *hagoita* (shuttlecock bat), an origami *tachibina* doll, a book, a rabbit, a drum, a fish, spinning tops, an animal with tongue poking out wearing a *sanbasō* hat and a mask with distorted human features.

Named after the first artist to popularise the technique, the *ryūsa* type of netsuke lends itself well to groups of objects packed together in the round against a hollow background and separated by pierced openings which are the distinguishing feature of *ryūsa*. This piece is shaped in imitation of the type of netsuke known as *kagamibuta* (see fig. 7).

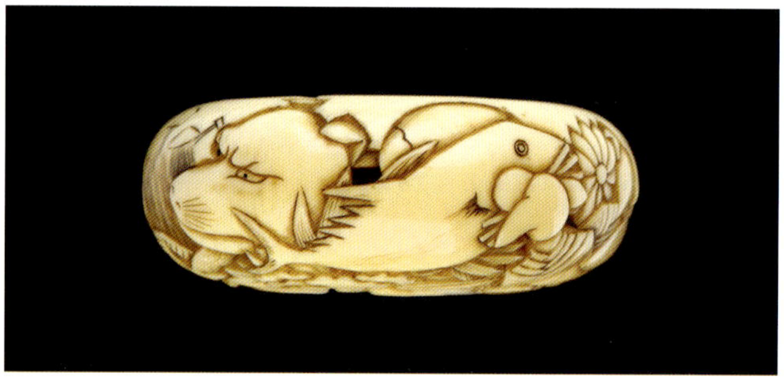

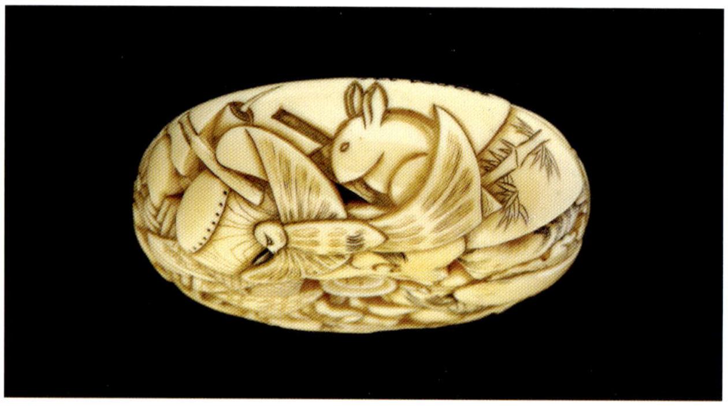

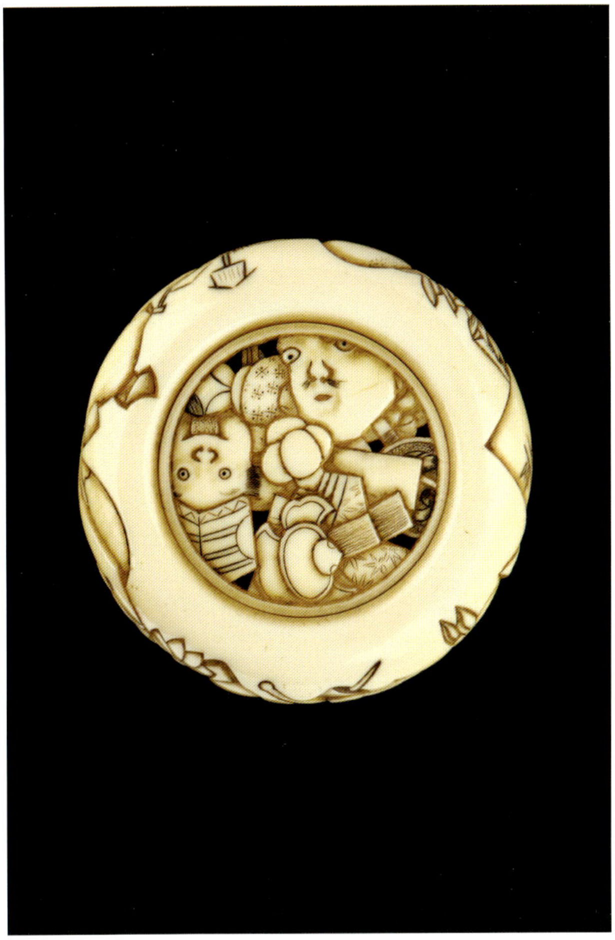

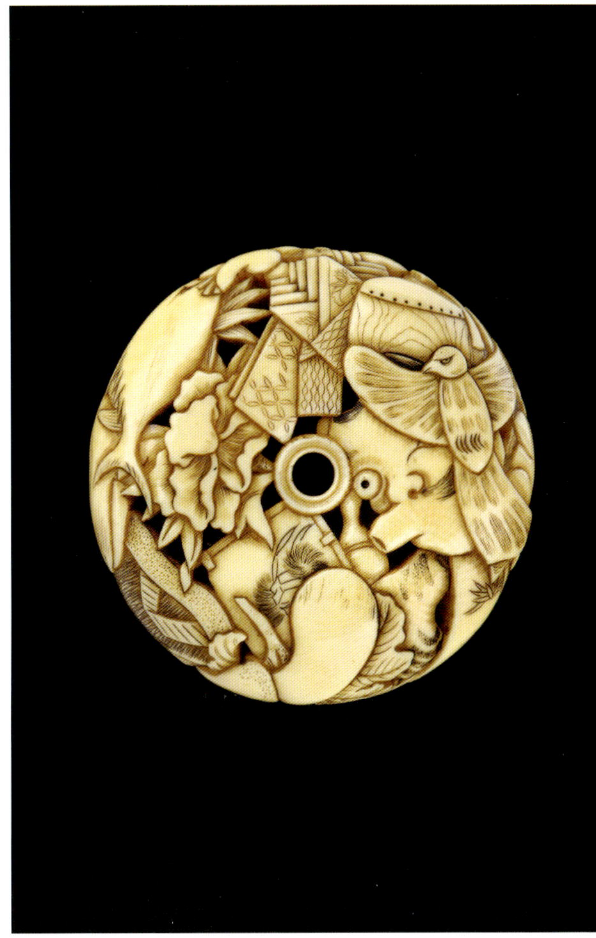

57

Brush-maker

Verso: Rock garden in a circular dish

Ivory
Signed: Ryūchin 竜珍 with red seal reading Ryūchin (Gyokuhōsai)
Around 1850–1860
Diam: 4.6; H: 1.85 cm
EA2001.121
Bequeathed by Dr Monica Barnett

Illustrated in:
Eskenazi. *Japanese Netsuke from the Carré Collection.* 15/06 –09/07/1993
Signature is illustrated in George Lazarnick. *Netsuke and Inro Artists, and How to Read their Signatures.* Reed Publishers. Honolulu. 1981. p. 889.
Neil K. Davey. *Netsuke. A comprehensive study based on the M.T. Hindson collection.* Faber & Faber Limited. London, in association with Sotheby Parke Bernet Publications, 1974. p. 125, No.367

Published:
Wilhelm, G. *Manjū exégèse et appréciation.* Bulletin Association Franco-Japonaise. No. 54. Octobre, 1996. Fig. MB12

Ex M.T. Hindson Collection and bought by Carré in the Hindson Sale at Sotheby's (Part IV) 09/07/1968. Lot 584

The brush-maker is sitting at a low table testing the flexibility of a brush and peering through round spectacles.
Painters, calligraphers and lacquerers all needed high quality brushes to execute their various trades. The brush-maker therefore played an important role in their lives, supplying brushes of varying thickness, length and type. Hair from goats, wolves, badgers and rats among many others were used, the different parts of the pelt providing brushes for specific tasks. The brushes themselves are works of art.

This design is based on that of the brushmaker in Tachibana Minkō's *Saiga shokunin burui* (Coloured Pictures of Classified Artisans), published in 1770 (fig. 47).[47] Above the illustration in the book is a poem by Fujiwara no Teika from the collection *Shūi gushō* which roughly translates as:

> Who are you?
> Unseen worlds portrayed,
> Your image is made by the play of the brush.

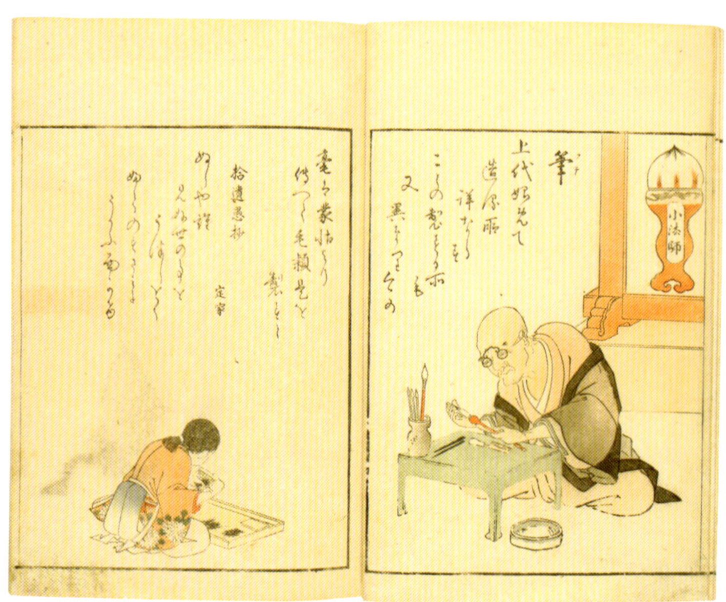

Fig. 47 Illustration from *Saiga shokunin burui* (National Diet Library, Tokyo, 1286831/6)

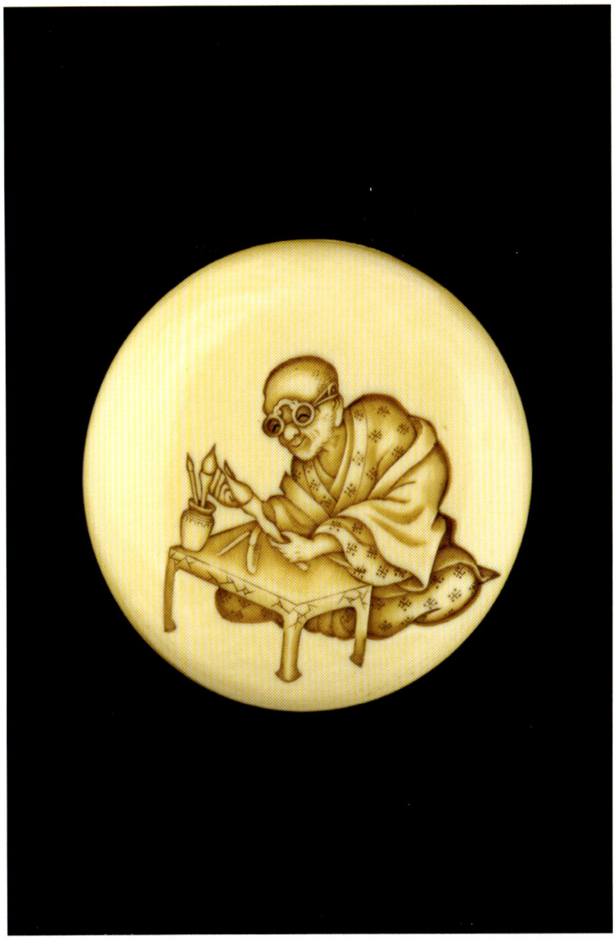

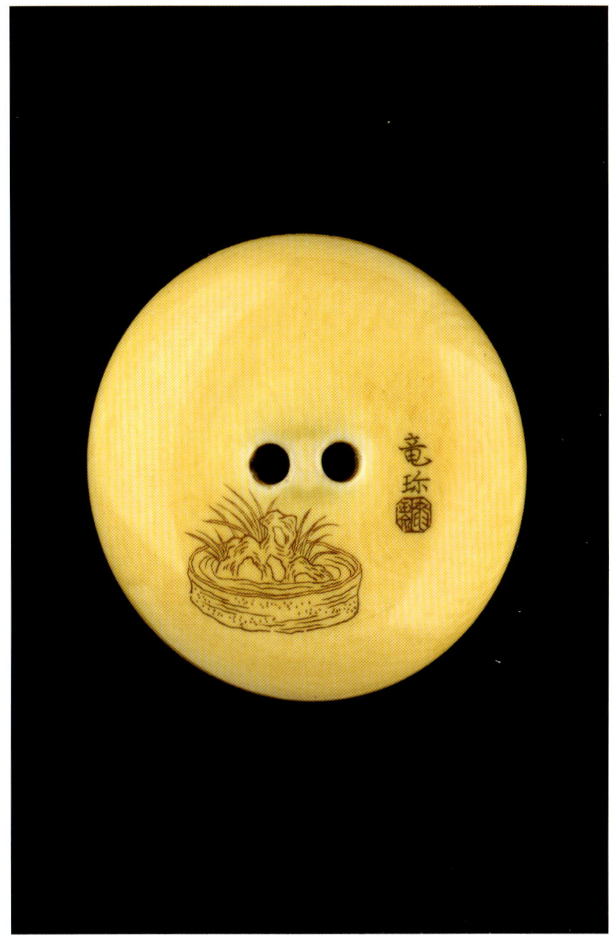
竜珎

58

Tooth Blackening

Verso: Ingredients for the tooth blackening recipe

Ivory with staining
Signed: Hōjitsu 法實
Mid-19th century
Diam: 3.85; H: 1.8 cm
EA2001.80
Bequeathed by Dr Monica Barnett

A woman is leaning over a basin (*tsunodarai*) with a small bowl (*hagurowan*) balanced on top of it, blackening her teeth.

The custom of tooth blackening has a long history in Japan. It was used as prevention against decay and to indicate status. In the Edo period members of the imperial family and married women practised the habit. A young bride-to-be would be given the ingredients by seven close friends in order to dye her teeth for the first time before her wedding ceremony. Courtesans in the pleasure quarters also blackened their teeth.

The recipe for the tooth blackening mixture was complicated and its preparation laborious. Two powders, gallnut and tannin, were added to acetic acid and mixed with iron to make the black paste that was applied, preferably daily, but certainly every other day, to maintain the effects.[48]

Despite a government ban on the practice in 1870, some women continued to use the dye until the Meiji Empress appeared in public in 1873 with white teeth, after which the custom faded.

Meikeisai Hōjitsu also used this design on a squarish *hako*-type netsuke which is now in the collection of the Museum of the History of Science, Oxford.[49]

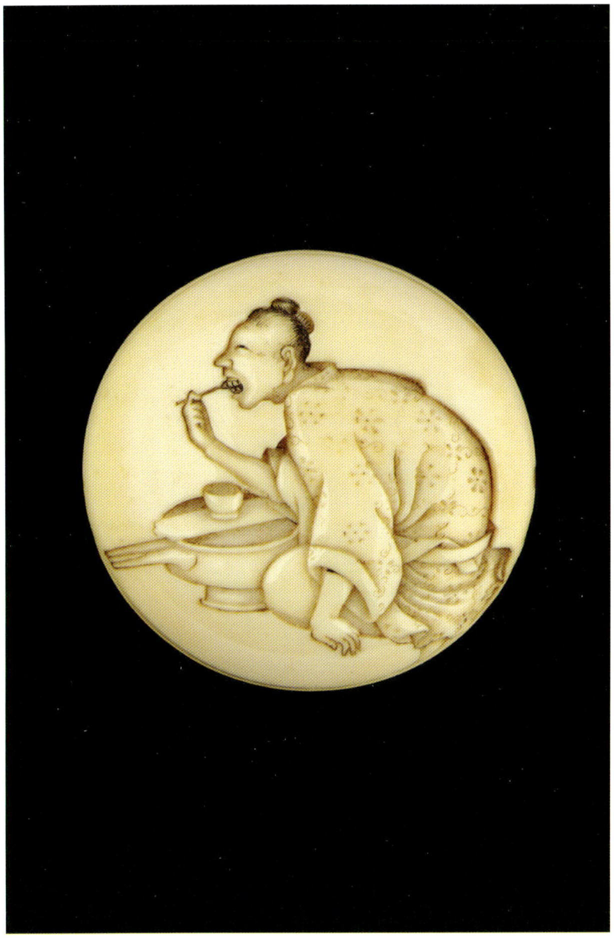

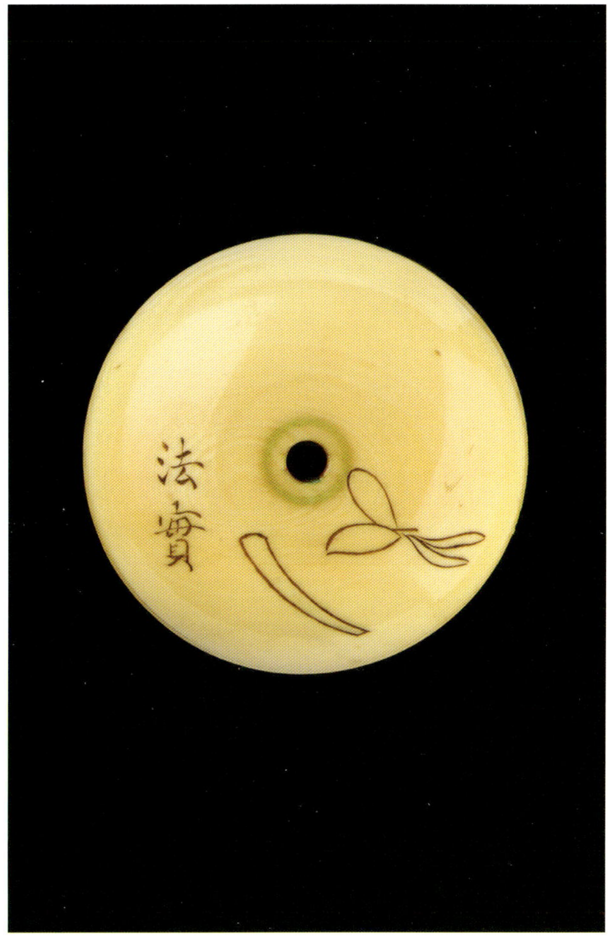
法實

59

Shintō shrine attendant

Verso: mushrooms

Ivory with black and red staining
Unsigned
Mid-19th century
Diam: 4.1; H: 1.7 cm
EA2001.86
Bequeathed by Dr Monica Barnett

Wearing a lacquered hat (*ebōshi*) and Shintō robes (*saifuku*), and wielding a besom, the attendant carries out one of the many duties that fall upon those living and working at Shintō shrines. Keeping the grounds tidy and the gardens well tended, and preparing food for offerings at festivals and ceremonies are all duties to be carried out by young priests and attendants. Here it is autumn and the red maple leaves are falling. Judging by the expression on the man's face, he is maybe thinking of the passing of the seasons and and feeling the melancholy which autumn brings. On the reverse are mushrooms which are harvested in the autumn.

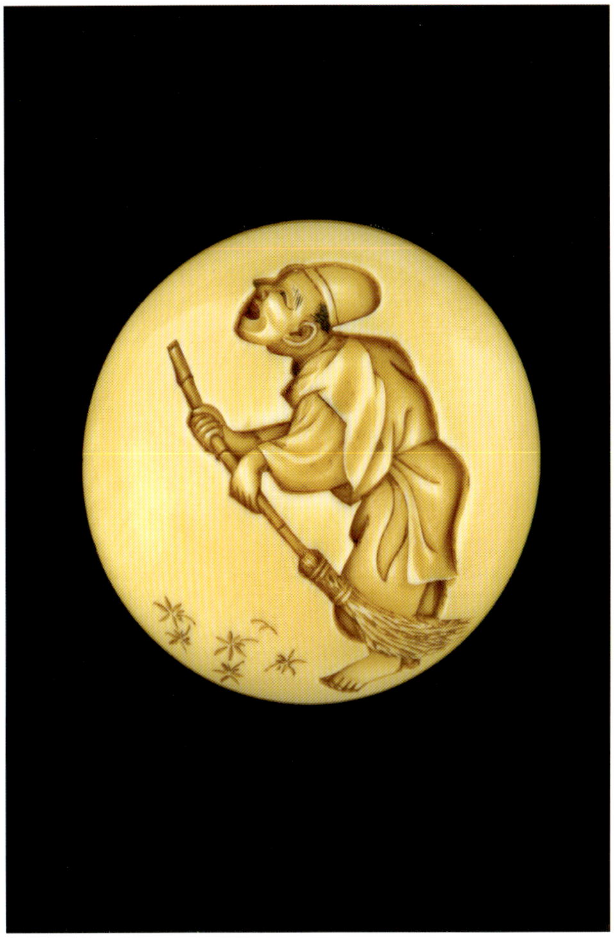

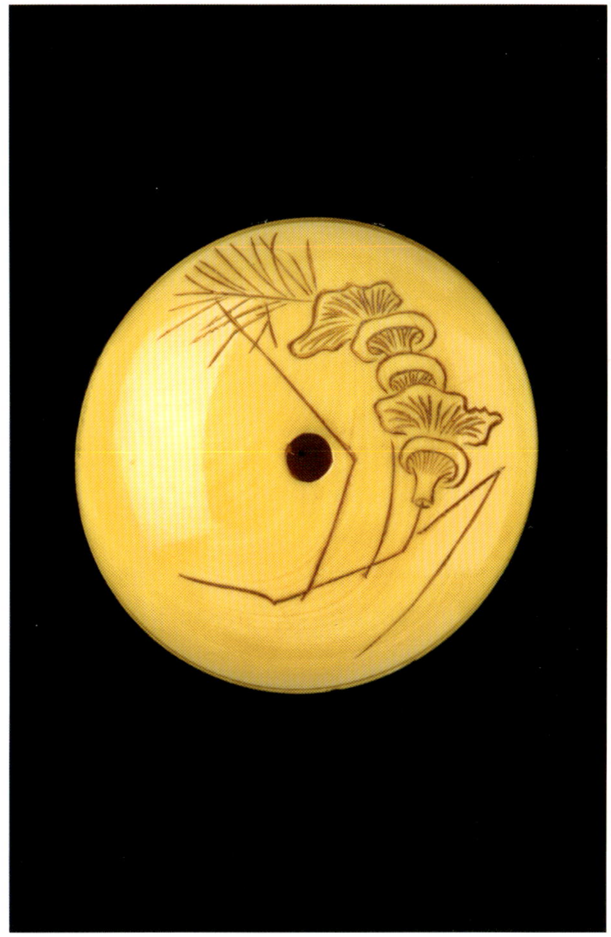

60

Priest preparing *fugu*

Verso: a root vegetable possibly *wasabi*

Ivory with red and black staining
Signed: Ichiyūsai 一遊 祭 (with a variant of the *yū* character) Naomitsu
Mid-19th century
D: 5.1; H: 1.9 cm.
EA2001.73
Bequeathed by Dr Monica Barnett

For other examples of this variant of Ichyūsai's signature see cat. nos. 5 and 88.

Puffer fish (*fugu*) is a great delicacy in Japan, but must be prepared with the utmost care, for ingesting the tiniest remnant of tetrodotoxin, which occurs in several parts of the fish's body, can cause a swift and painful death through paralysis. Careful preparation is essential, for not only must the toxic parts be removed, but no toxin must contaminate any of the edible parts. Although the laughter on this priest's face suggests he is not taking his duties seriously, once the knife is inserted, he must surely concentrate on this most responsible of jobs.

Engelbert Kaempfer (1651–1716) in his '*History of Japan*' published posthumously in 1727, tells of no fewer than five people in Nagasaki who died from eating *fugu* and also of a neighbour who was suffering the 'Pox' and who wished to use *fugu* as a means of suicide. He does however quote a saying, 'foolish it is to eat *fugu*, foolish not to eat it' so delicious is its flesh.[50]

In Kaempfer's time military men were forbidden to eat the fish and still to this day the rule applies to the Emperor of Japan.

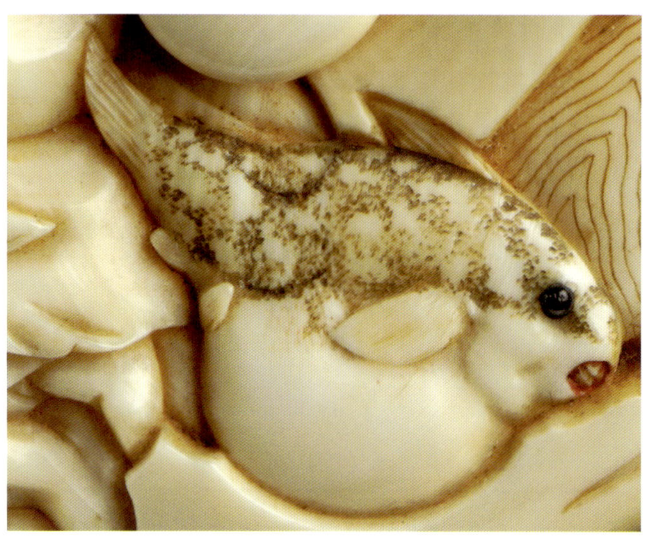

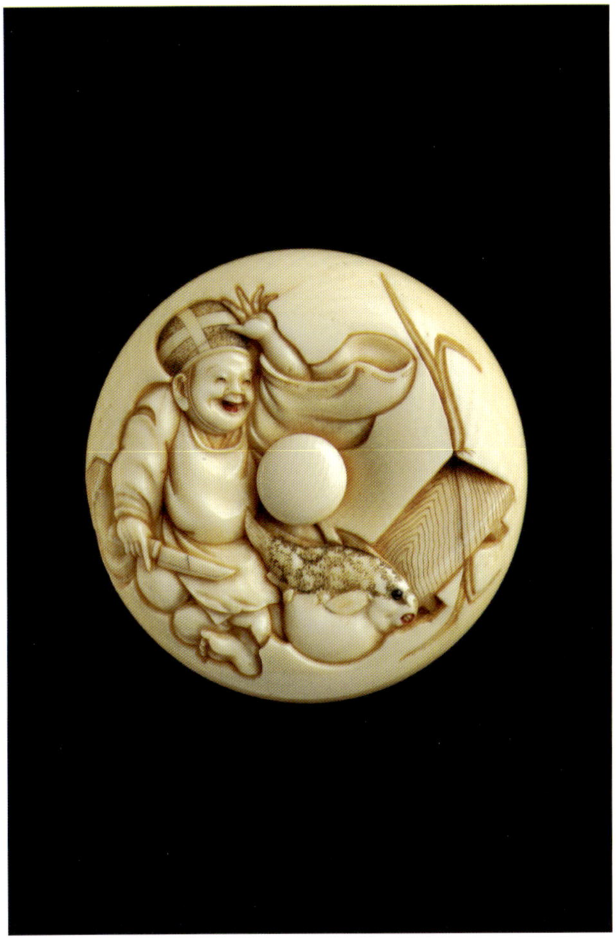

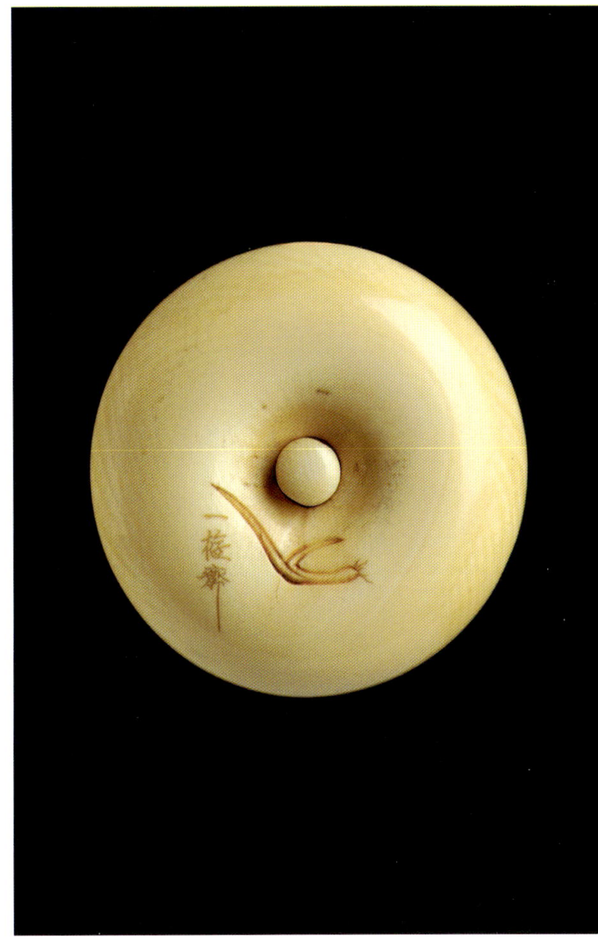

61

Travellers along the Tōkaidō

Verso: a single boat sails across a stretch of water

Lacquer, gold, silver, bronze and copper
Unsigned
Late eighteenth century
Diam: 3.5; H: 1.4 cm
EAX.608

The *inrō* attached to this *manjū* illustrates the Fifty-three Stations of the Tokaidō, the ancient road which runs between Kyoto and Edo (Tokyo). Each station is marked in gold letters on a black ground in a rectangular cartouche. (See fig. 8 in the Introduction.)

The netsuke shows travellers sitting and chatting beyond a large rocky outcrop and admiring the view across the water to a hill in the distance. A porter approaches carrying packages on a pole slung across his shoulders. A bamboo shelter has been erected nearby for less clement days. The reverse shows a single boat loaded with cargo sailing acoss the water.

This lacquer *manjū* is decorated on a *kinji* ground with gold, silver, *aokin* (alloy of gold and silver) and red lacquer in *takamaki-e* and *hiramaki-e*, *kakiwari* (lines in gold and *aokin*), small squares and long strips of gold foil (*kirikane*) and *sengaki* (thin lines drawn in lacquer).

Travel along the Tokaidō required passing through the domains of a number of *daimyō*. Identification papers had to be produced at the checkpoints which marked these boundaries. The journey is around three hundred miles long and took days or sometimes weeks to complete, depending on the method of transport. During the Edo period the road was very busy, for there were many people travelling for reasons of trade, pilgrimage, sight-seeing or on account of the *sankin kōtai* system, which required participation in *daimyō* processions. Accommodation was plentiful along the way, scrupulously divided for suitability according to the rank of the traveller. There were also many resting places for refreshments. The terrain along the route was far from easy, but the main obstacle was the rivers, some of which could be waded through while others needed to be crossed by ferry (see cat. no. 65). When there had been heavy rain to swell the rivers, traffic was temporarily halted. A *manjū* by Nanka is inscribed with the whole of the 'Song of Travel Hints' which warns, 'when on the road, never expect to be free of of cares – you can only be carefree if you prepare for inconveniences'.[51]

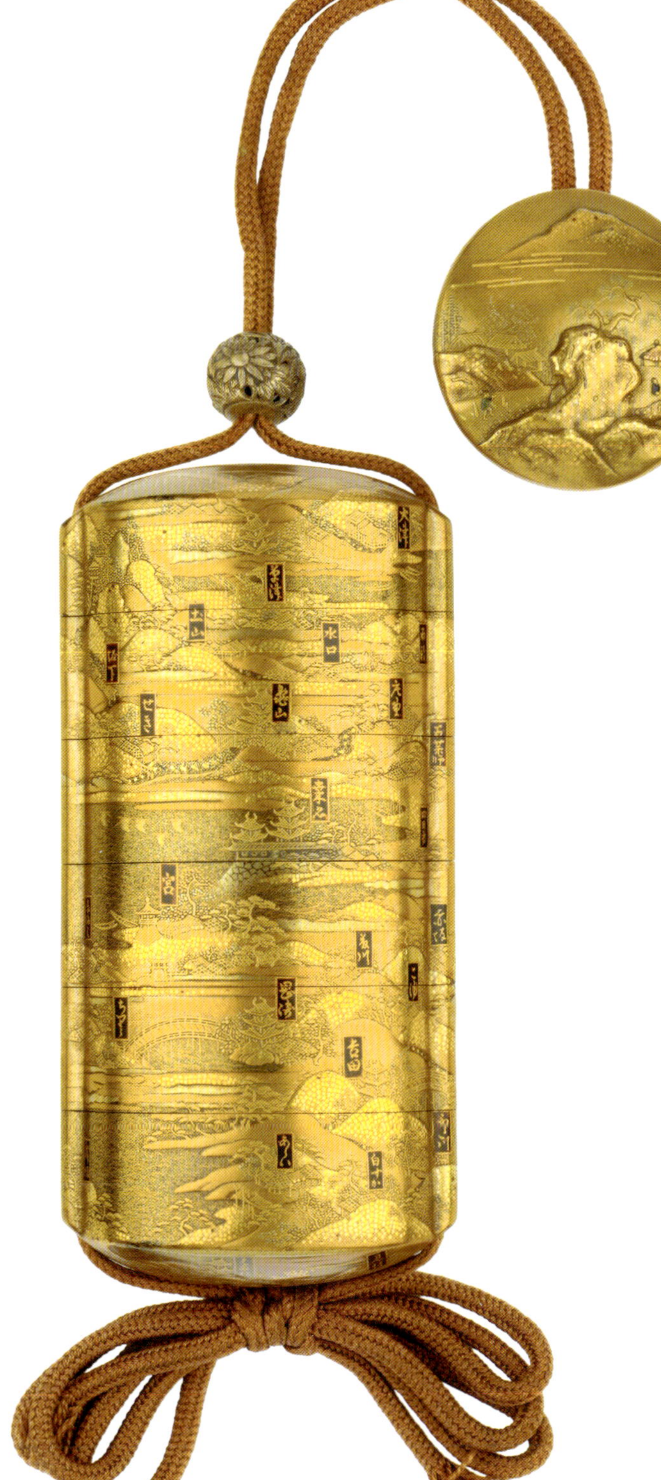

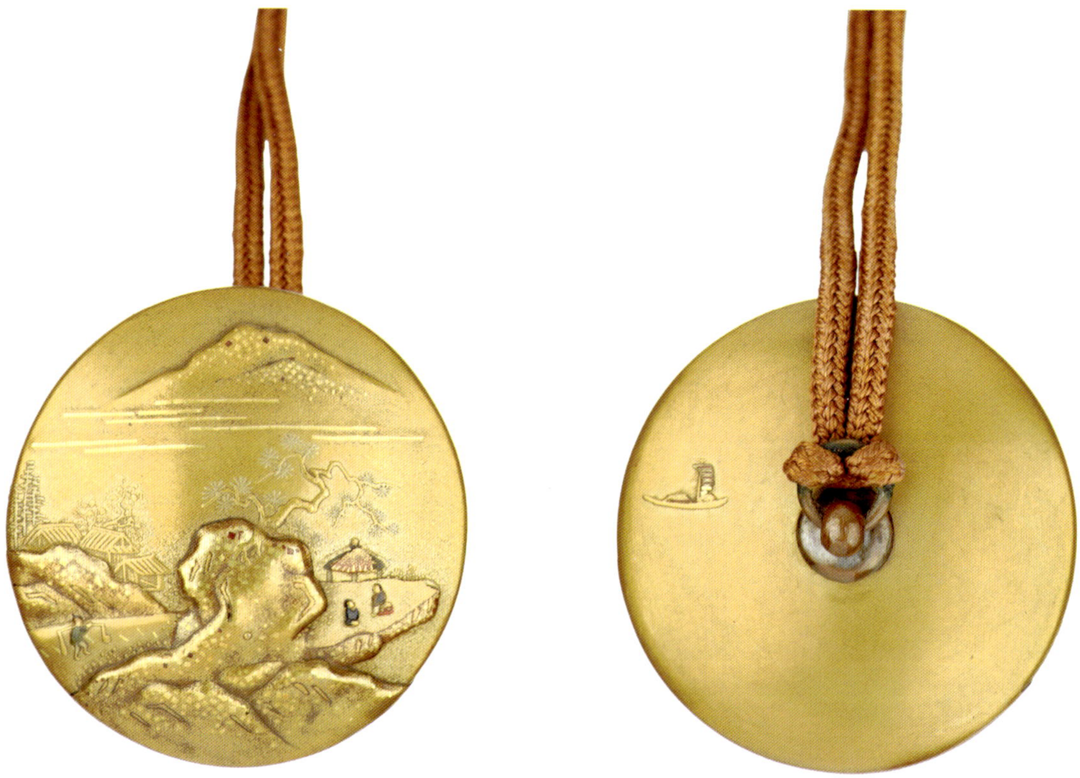

Cat. no. 61

62

Folded mat

Verso: Three further *mon*

Ivory
Signed: Gyokuyōsai 玉陽斎
Early 19th century
W: 3.3 cm; H: 3.4 cm
EA2001.135
Bequeathed by Dr Monica Barnett

Sold at Sotheby's, London, 26 October 1981. Lot 225
See Raymond Bushell, *Netsuke Familiar and Unfamiliar*. No. 290 which came up at Christie's, New York, 23/04/1991 Sale, Lot 49. 'Four folded teapot mats (*Chabin Shiki*)' Ivory, signed Gyokuyōsai. Mid-19th century, 3.5cm wide, with age cracks.
For an example of the folded letter shape see Metropolitan Museum, New York, 10.211.419 (attached to a lacquer *inrō*).

This netsuke is in the shape of folded length of fabric or as Raymond Bushell describes it, a teapot mat *(chabin shiki)*.[52] On it are scattered various *mon* (crests) including a snowflake, a paulownia flower, a fan, a hexagon, a bean and a cherry blossom all decorated in a variety of textile patterns in low relief. Gyokuyōsai frequently used textile patterns as backgrounds for his netsuke and made at least one other of this shape. Another shape he used and decorated in this style was the folded letter.[53] The main body of his work however, was *katabori* netsuke in ivory. He paid great attention to details, and sometimes created tiny detailed scenes inside a hollowed-out vegetable.

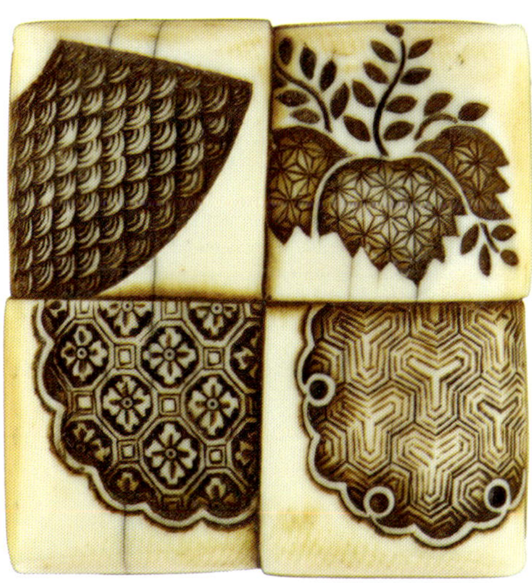

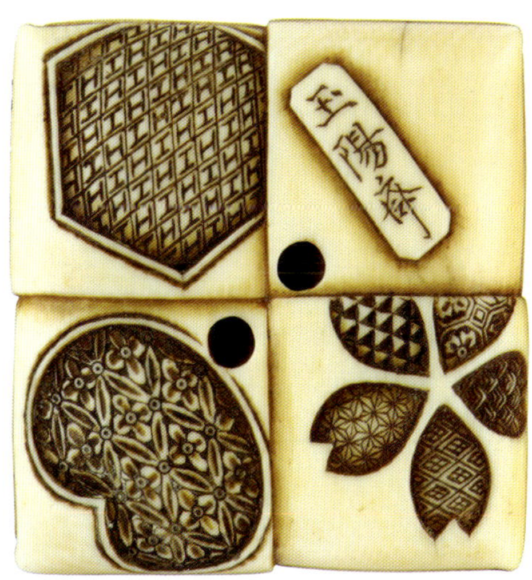

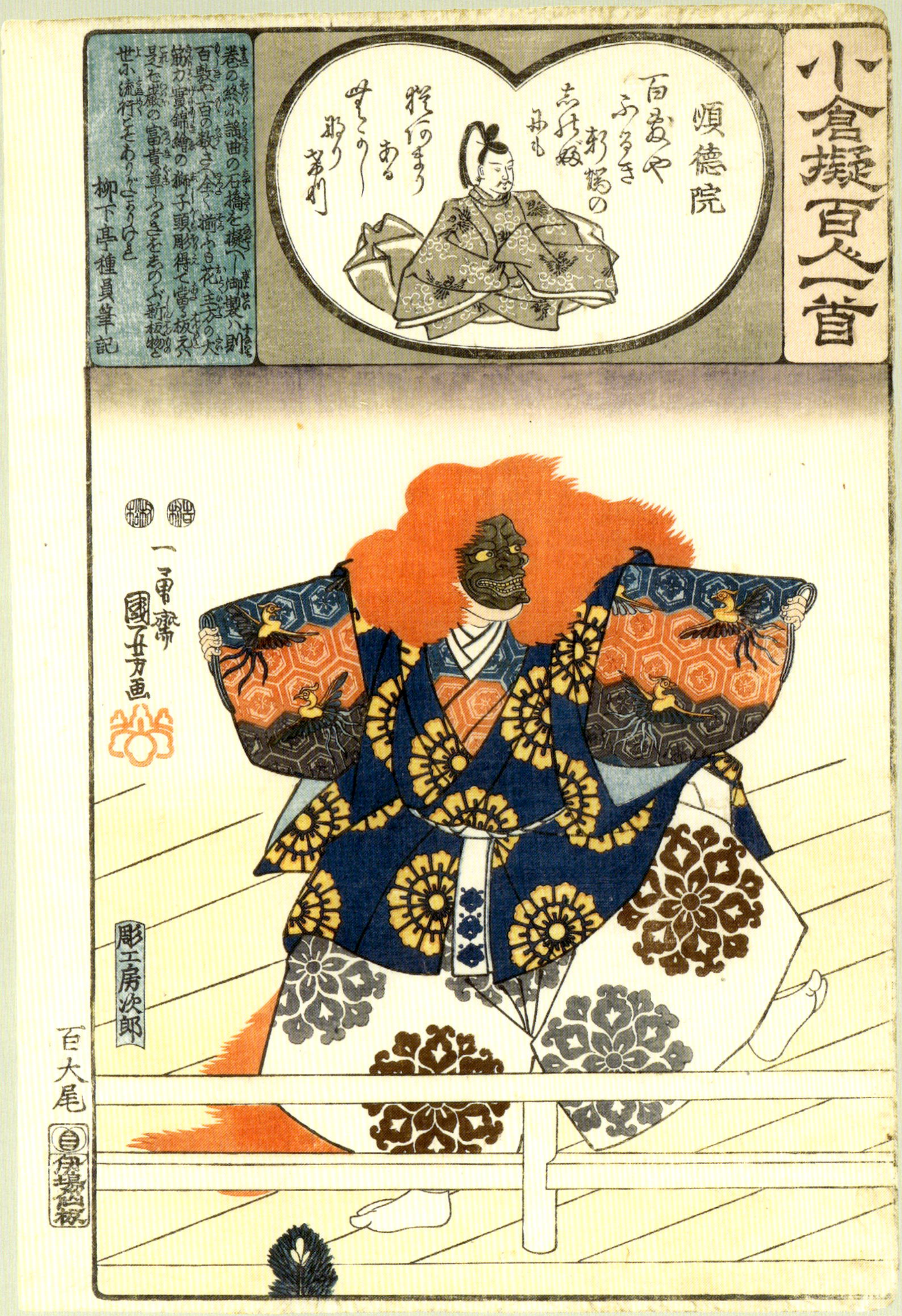

Fig. 48 Lion dancer from the Nō play *Shakkyō*. Colour woodblock print by Utagawa Kuniyoshi (1797–1862) (EA1971.130)

Literature and Theatre

Characters from Japanese literature going back to the earliest historical records of the creation of the Japanese islands, from Nō drama and from the popular kabuki theatre are all to be found in netsuke. A subtle poetic reference can be the single clue to subject matter, leaving the viewer to rely on his knowledge of the classics. For merchants who held the nation's purse strings in the latter part of the Edo period and who strove to become as educated as the aristocracy, choosing an obscure theme needing interpretation gave them a sense of belonging to an élite group. A number of Nō masks, dancers and poets appear amongst the carvings on the Ashmolean's *manjū*.

63

Rokkasen (The Six Immortal Poets), in various attitudes, within shaped cartouches, one for each poet

Ryūsa-type *manjū*
Ivory
Signed: Issen 一泉
Mid- to late 19th century
H: 2.0; W: 4.3; D: 3.75 cm
EA2001.106
Bequeathed by Dr Monica Barnett

For other versions of the *rokkasen* see:
Raymond Bushell. *Netsuke Familiar and Unfamiliar*. No. 570 by Hakuun

Sotheby's, London. 16 & 17/11/1995. Lot 563 by Hakuunsai
Sotheby's, 17/06/1998, Dr Walter Heihs Collection. Lot 770 by Hakuunsai
Sotheby's, New York 03/12/1993 for a square version by Minkoku
Sotheby's, 11/03/1988, Lot 99 for a similar piece by Genryōsai Minkoku II
Bonham's, 12/11/2008, Lot 434 by Hakuunsai, showing coloured staining. (This may be one of the previous examples returning for sale).

For centuries the Japanese have been inspired to write verse to express the emotions aroused by the passing of the seasons or the complications of love. Originally poetry was written in Chinese, but when the *kana* syllabary came into being, around AD 800, the writing of *waka*, 31-syllable poems, became an essential and popular pastime of the Heian court. Competitions were held and a courtier displaying extraordinary skill at this highly refined form of literature could improve his or her chances of advancement in the court hierarchy. The first imperial anthology of *waka* written in Japanese was the *Kokin wakashū* (Collection of Poems of Ancient and Modern Times).[54]

Compiled in AD 905, it was written by members of the court and the poems were selected by Ki no Tsurayuki (872–945). From the poets whose work he chose, he singled out a group of six poets, five men and one woman, who became known as the *rokkasen* or The Six Immortals of Poetry. Although portraits of the poets were probably never made in their lifetime, throughout the ages each has acquired features which are recognisable.

Sōjō Henjō (815–890) was a courtier, serving the Emperor Ninmyō, but after the Emperor's death in 850, Henjō took holy orders and became a priest.

Ono no Komachi, the only woman in the *rokkasen*, was said to have been very beautiful and to have had many love affairs but ended her life as a lonely old woman. She wrote of love and

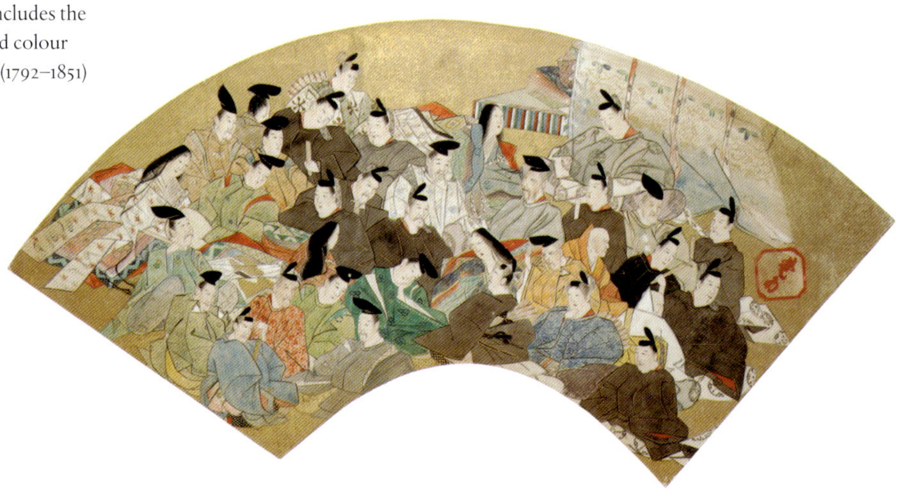

Fig. 49 A later group of the Thirty-six Immortals of Poetry, which includes the *Rokkasen*. Fan painting, ink and colour on paper, by Ōnishi Chinnen (1792–1851) (EAX.5426)

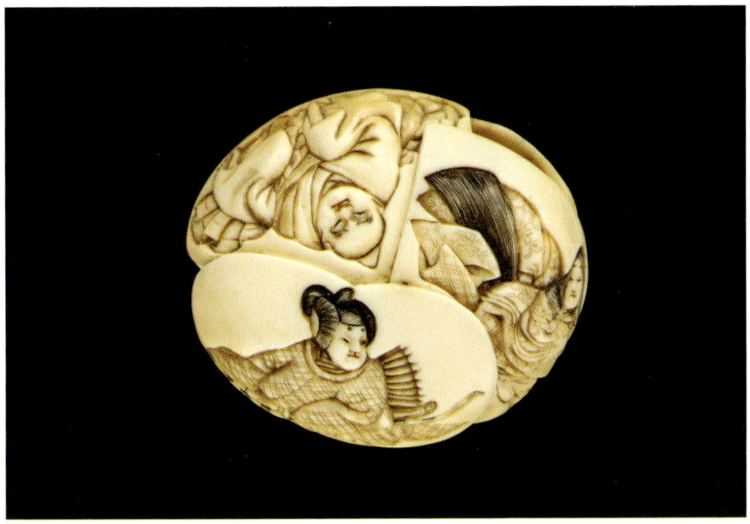

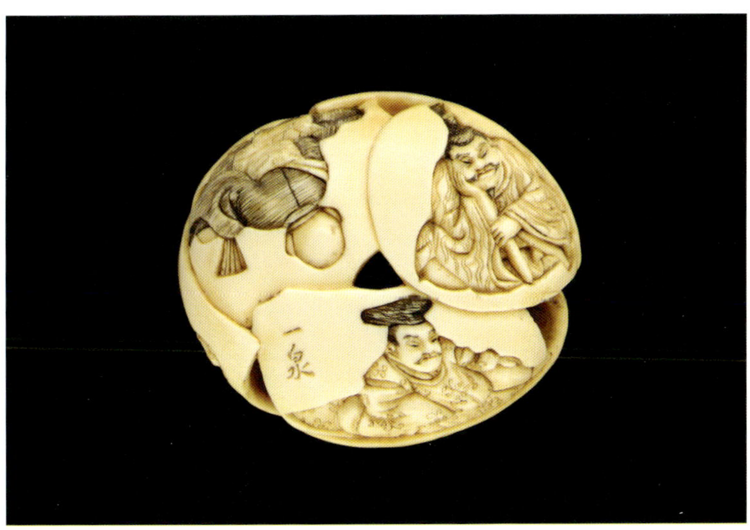
一泉

loneliness in her poems. She was the subject of Nō plays and was also a favourite of netsuke carvers who portrayed her both in her youth and in the misery of her old age.

Ariwara no Narihira was a handsome noble with loose morals. His amorous exploits were written down in the *Ise Monogatari* which includes some of the poems from the *Kokin wakashū*.

Of the lives of the other three, Ōtomo no Kuronushi, Kisen Hōshi and Fun'ya no Yasuhide, very little is known.

Issen's work is rare. For this *ryūsa* netsuke he used a design that Hakuunsai and Minkoku had used before him. His *katabori* netsuke are small, neat and detailed and include a group of the *rokkasen* now in the Gō Collection, Tokyo National Museum, No. 567 and another of two poets in the Museum of Fine Arts, Boston. (11.23263).

64

Ono no Tōfū: a frog stands beneath a willow tree holding an umbrella

Reverse: The broad trunk of the willow

Ivory
Unsigned
Mid-19th century
H: 4.0; W: 4.1; D: 1.3 cm
EAX.757

For another similar square version signed Dōzan see Bonham's, London. 11/05/2010. Lot 219

This little sketch illustrates a story about the calligrapher Ono no Tōfū, otherwise known as Ono no Michizane (894–964). In his early years he was, at best, a mediocre calligrapher and was slow to progress through the ranks at court.

One summer day he was out walking during a shower and noticed a tree-frog trying to leap from a pond onto an overhanging willow branch. The tiny creature jumped many times, always falling back into the pond, until finally, near exhaustion, it managed to hang onto the branch and climb it.

Seeing this diminutive animal's perseverance had a profound effect on Ono no Tōfū and he went back to his studies. After much hard work and practice he succeeded in producing some of the finest calligraphy of his age. He was appointed calligrapher to the Emperor Daigo and remained in the post during the reigns of Daigo's two successors, Emperors Suzaku and Murakami. By the time of his death Ono no Tōfū was one of the three most revered calligraphers in Japan.

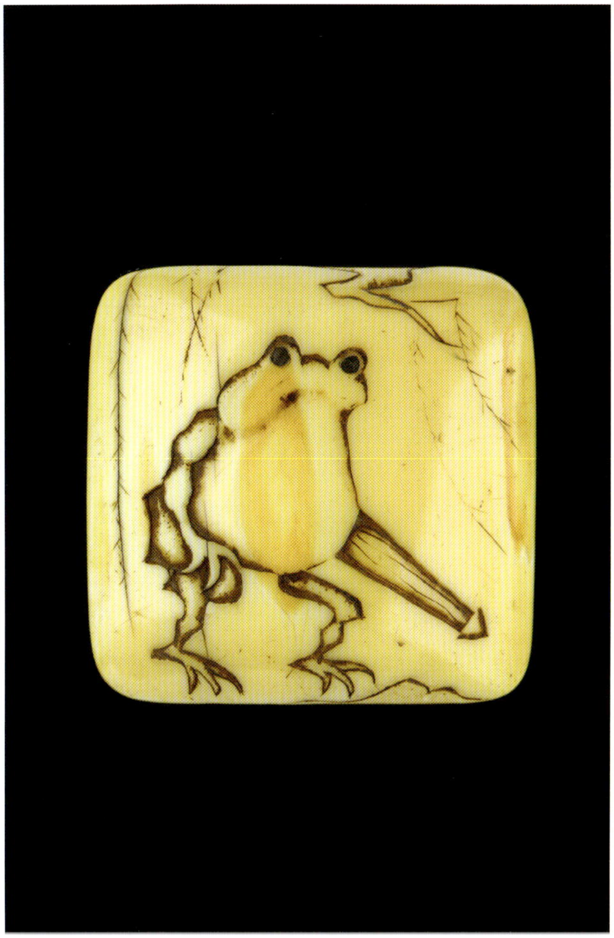
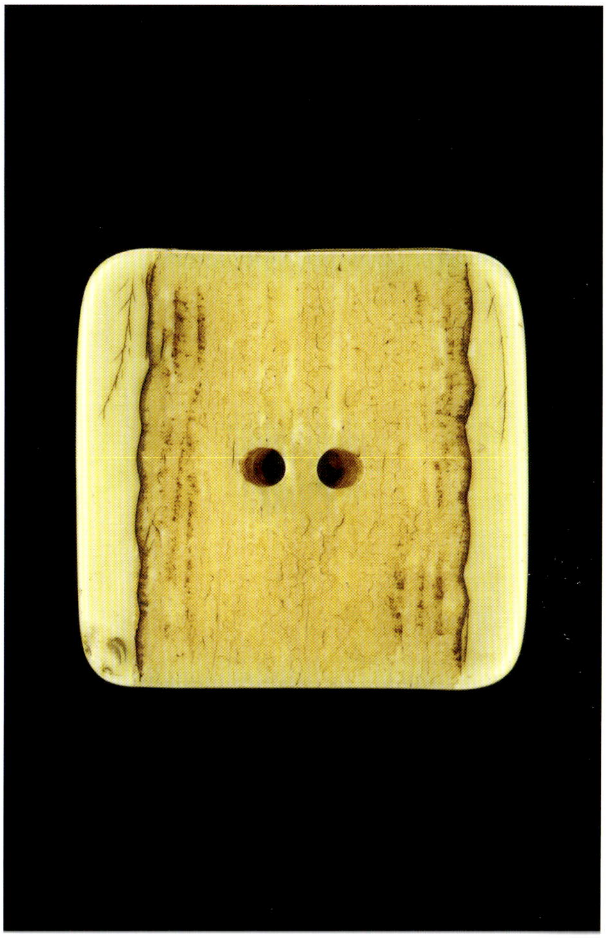

This *manjū* gives a playful interpretation of the subject with the frog standing beneath a willow tree holding an umbrella. Those who knew this story would immediately make the connection with Ono no Tōfū.

For a similar piece, see Ferenc Hopp Collection. No. 460[55]

65

Saigyō Hōshi in a ferry

Verso: boatman poling from the stern

Ivory with dark staining
Signed: Hakuyōsai 白陽蔡 with *kakihan*
(Hakuyōsai Kōgyoku 白陽蔡孝玉)
Around 1830
Diam: 5.0; H: 2.4 cm
EA2001.102
Bequeathed by Dr Monica Barnett

For an example of a *manjū* with a similar subject by Suzuki Kōsai see the Gō Collection, Tokyo National Museum, No. 349 [57]

This design shows the priest Saigyō Hōshi (1118–1190) on his travels, crossing a river in a ferry. Travel around the mountainous country of Japan was mainly carried out on foot, except for warriors who rode on horseback. Many rivers and streams needed to be crossed and bridges were few and far between, so the ferry was the transport of choice. In the Edo period, as well as being a means of getting from place to place, ferries also provided a neutral space where people of all social levels were able to mix freely with one another, without worrying about class distinctions.

Saigyō is seen here sitting between two entertainers in a ferry. He was a nobleman who at the age of twenty-two became a monk. Thereafter he undertook many journeys particularly in Northern Honshū, during which he wrote poetry. The name Saigyō means 'western journey', a reference to the Buddhist Western Paradise. This poem was composed shortly after he took the tonsure and retired from the world:

wata no hara	わたのはら	Across the wide sea's sweep
haruka ni nami o	遙に波を	From afar the waves
hedate kite	へだて来て	Come one by one;
miyako ni ideshi	都にいでし	When the capital I left
tsuki o miru kana	月を見るかな	That is the moon I saw.[56]

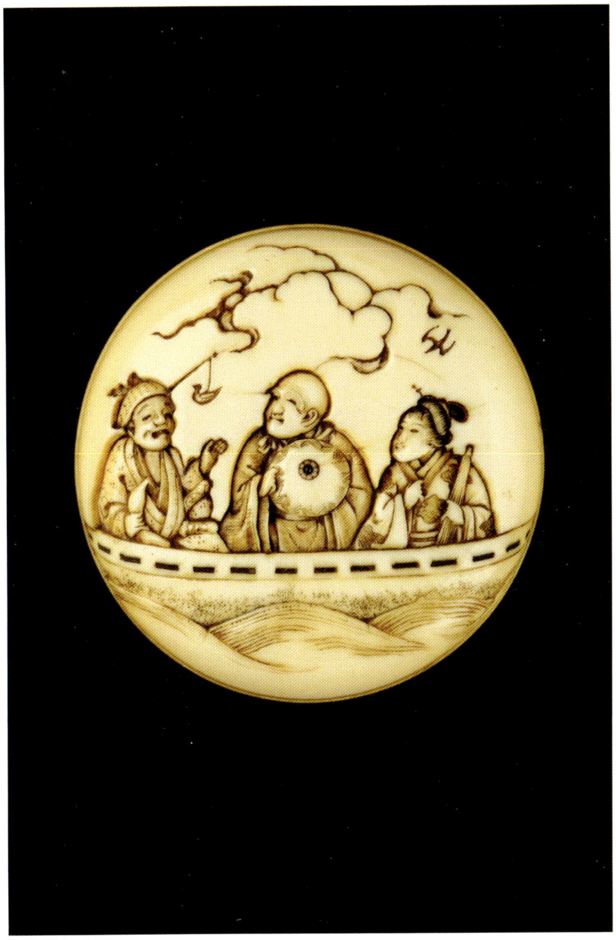

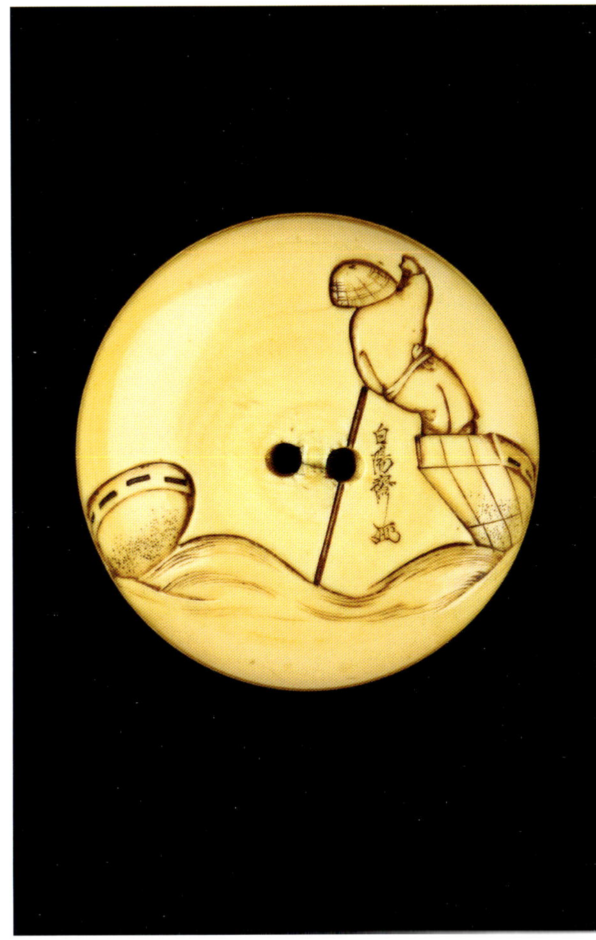

66

Dōjōji: Temple drum with detachable *Hannya* mask

Ivory, stained
Signed: Ryūraku 龍楽
1820–1850
Diam: 4.1; H: 2.45 cm.
EA2001.118
Bequeathed by Dr Monica Barnett

The design on this netsuke alludes to the tragic tale of rejection and revenge told in the Nō play *Dōjōji*. Kiyohime was the young daughter of an innkeeper who lived in a village on the pilgrim route between the three Holy Places of Kumano, in present day Wakayama prefecture. A priest named Anchin made annual visits to these temples and on his journey stayed at the inn. He would play with the young daughter and brought her small gifts. When she grew older she fell hopelessly in love with Anchin and begged him to marry her, which he was unable to do. She pursued him several times to his temple Dōjōji, and finally at his wits end, he hid inside the temple bell, which was on the ground for repair. That night, the girl swam across the river to the temple and on the way she was slowly transformed into a dragon, a consequence of the rage of the unrequited love that burned within her. She discovered Anchin inside the bell and enveloped it with her scaly coils, breathing fire upon the metal until it became white-hot. Together they were reduced to dust amongst the molten metal.

In the Nō play the actor playing the part of Kiyohime puts on the Hannya mask, a fiercesome horned visage with piercing evil

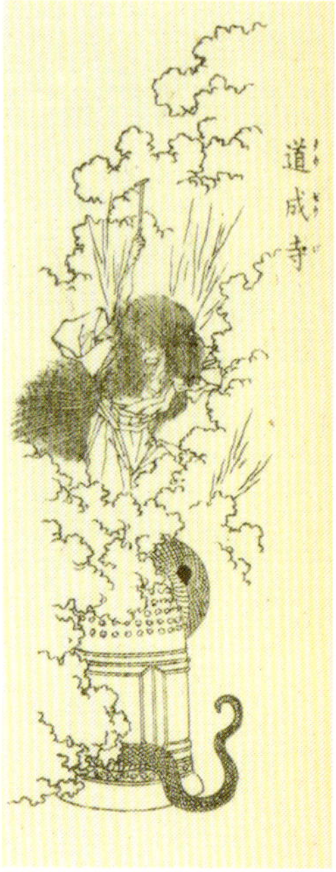

Fig. 50 Illustration from *Banbutsu hinagata gafū*, Vol. 2, p. 12. Kiyohime wrapping herself around the Dōjōji bell (EA2012.14)

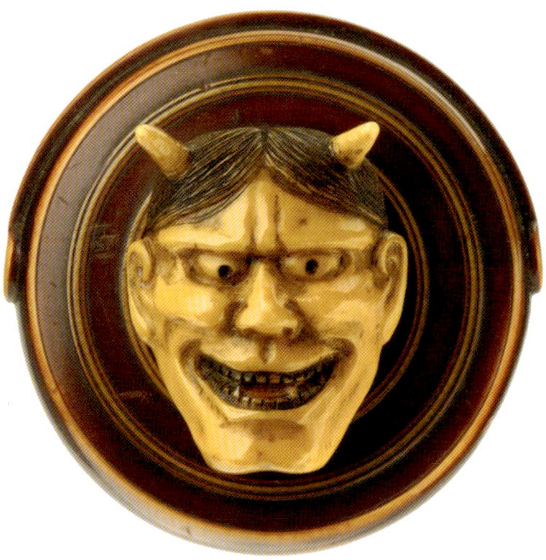

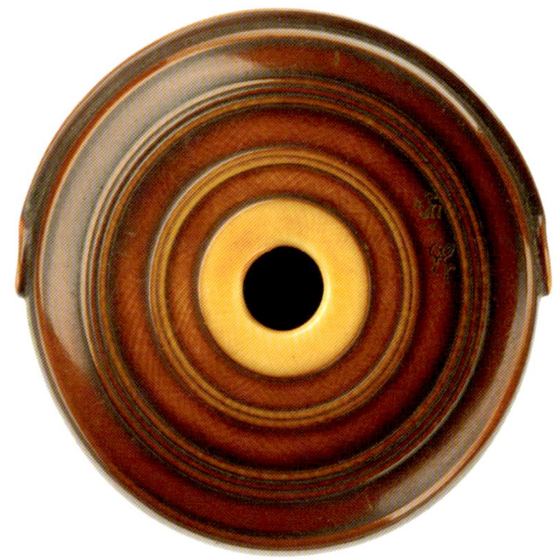

eyes, as she slowly metamorphoses into the dragon. There are other plays in which Hannya masks are used to represent women possessed with a vengeful or jealous spirit, for example the noblewoman turned demon at the maple viewing picnic, *Momijigari* (cat. no. 72); and the old woman who at night goes out in search of the blood of young girls wears it in the play *Adachigahara* (cat. nos. 70 and 71). It is also famously worn by the actor playing Lady Rokujō in the play *Aoi no Ue* which tells the story of Prince Genji's discarded lover who becomes so jealous when she hears that Genji's wife, Lady Aoi, is expecting a baby that she goes mad and finally her jealous spirit causes the death of Lady Aoi.

67

Lion dancer from the Nō play *Shakkyō*

Verso: A flowering peony bush and part of the Nō stage

Ivory with red, green and brown staining
Signed: Moritoshi 守寿 with crane kakihan
Mid-19th century
Diam: 4.4; H: 2.0 cm
EA2001.38
Bequeathed by Dr Monica Barnett

Bought from Crichton 06/05/1970

The Nō play *Shakkyō* tells the story of a scholar-poet who, after the untimely death of his wife, took the tonsure and became a priest named Jakushō (*c.* 962–1034). On a pilgrimage to the holy places of China, he reached the entrance of the holy mountain, said to be the realm of Manjusri (Jap. *Monju Bosatsu*) the *bodhisattva* of wisdom. (Manjusri is typically shown either seated upon a lion or in the form of a young child). Its entrance was marked by a Stone Bridge *(Shakkyō)*, which crossed a deep ravine with a waterfall crashing down into it.

As the priest was about to cross the stone bridge a child appeared and warned him that only priests who had undergone years of rigorous ascetic training and who had received help from the Buddha could cross this bridge. The child then departed hinting that if the priest waited a while he would witness something remarkable.

Within a short time Manjusri's messenger, a lion, emerged and danced a lively and colourful dance amid the peonies growing beside the bridge. The auspicious combination of lion and peony provides an uplifting ending to the play, leaving the audience with a very positive feeling for the outcome of the priest.

Moritoshi and his school were principally *manjū* carvers. The artist has carefully chosen a pose during the dance which fits perfectly the round shape of the *manjū* form.

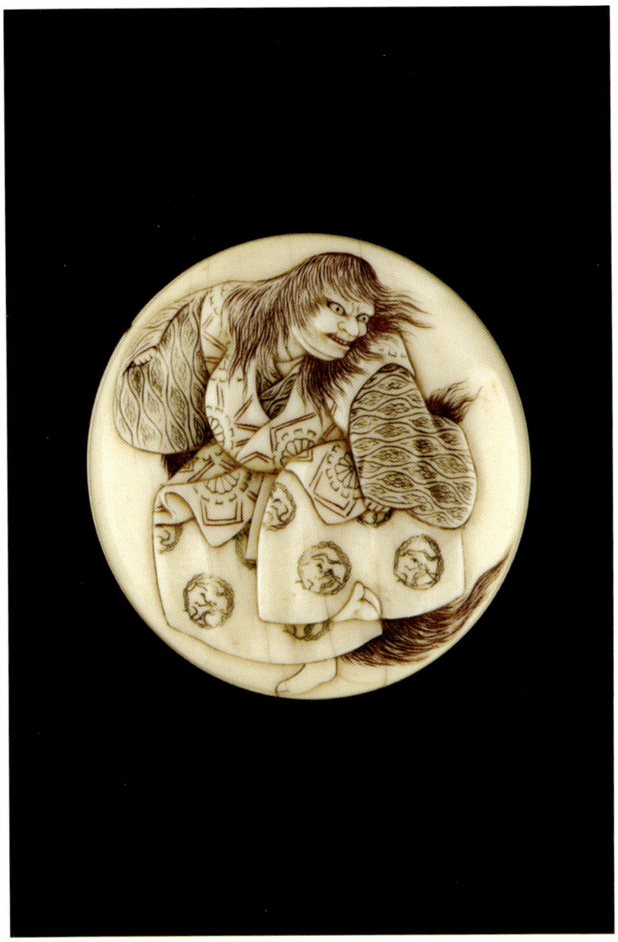

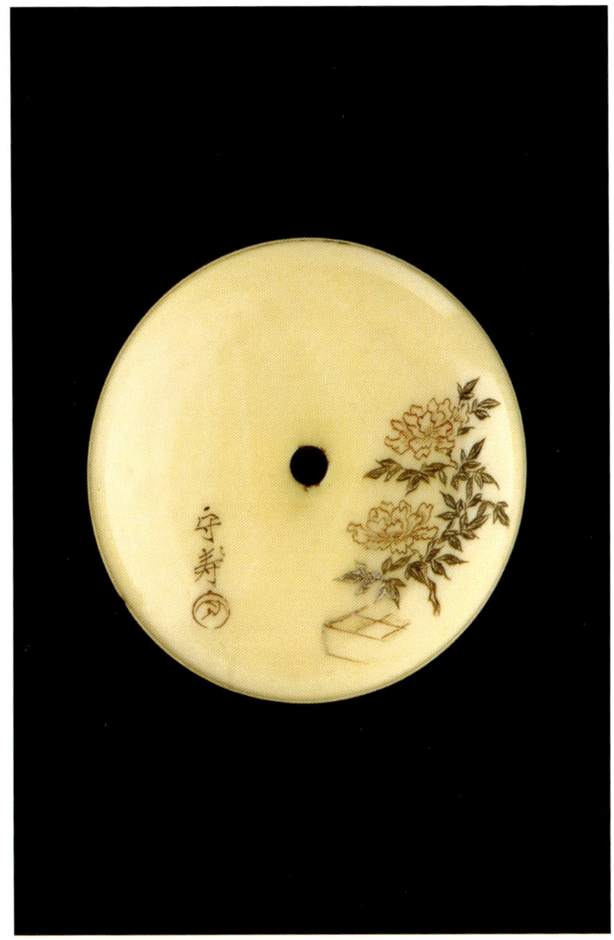
守寿

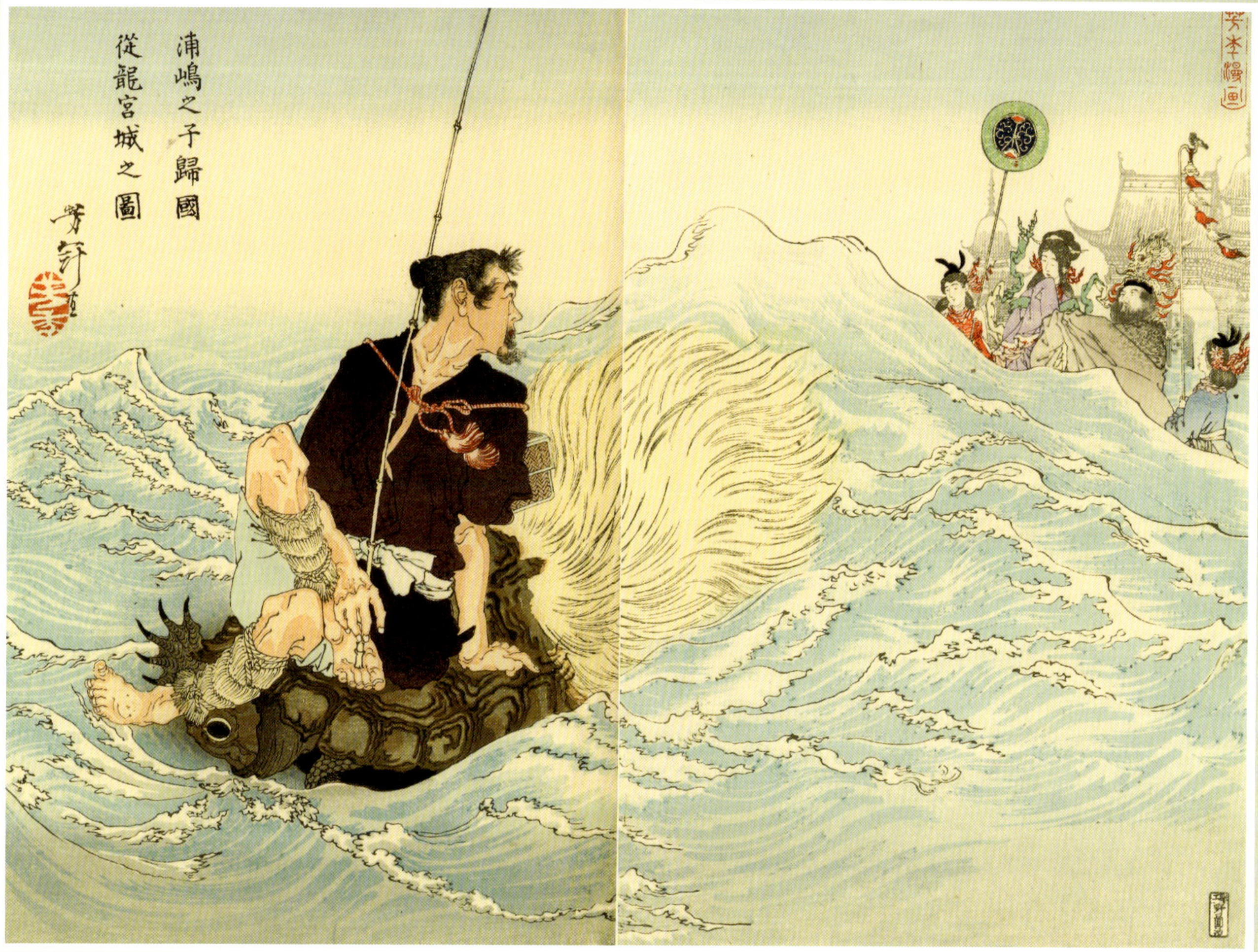

Fig. 51 Urashima Tarō leaving the Palace of the Dragon King of the Sea. Colour woodblock print by Tsukioka Yoshitoshi (1839–1892) (EA1971.204)

Folktales

The establishment of the Japanese syllabic script (*kana*) in the early Heian period (794–1185) brought the possibility of reading to many more people and particularly women, who were not supposed to study Chinese, previously the official written language of Japan. Early handscrolls interspersing text with pictures began to be produced to tell tales of religious figures. These developed over the years into tales dealing with every topic in the story teller's repertoire. Historical figures joined creatures from the realms of the supernatural. Itinerant story tellers would go from village to village telling short stories, many of which had a didactic purpose. By the mid-Edo period, many of these tales were very well known even to those who could not read and for those who could, printed books provided a rich source. Demons, ogres and shapeshifting animals all served netsuke carvers with material for dramatic designs, some of which they took directly from picture books (*ehon*).

68

Urashima Tarō returning home on the back of Otohime disguised as a *minogame*

Verso: treasure box amid reeds

Ivory with light staining and black and red highlights
Signed: Suzuki Kōsai 壽々木孝斎 with *kakihan*
Mid- to late 19th century
Diam: 4.7; H: 2.2 cm
EA2001.139
Bequeathed by Dr Monica Barnett

Urashima Tarō was out fishing one day when he caught a female turtle in his net, which he released back into the sea. A few days later she reappeared out of the waves to thank Urashima Tarō for his life-saving gesture and issued him with an invitation to visit her home under the sea. He accepted and off they went together, he riding upon her back. When they arrived he found himself in the palace of Ryūjin, the Dragon King of the Sea; and his new friend was none other than Otohime, Ryūjin's daughter. Urashima Tarō was invited to stay for a while. Gradually the two fell in love and were married.

Three years later, Urashima Tarō wanted to return home to visit his parents. Otohime consented but on one condition. She presented him with a sealed box which she forbade him to open until he returned to her. Again she took on the guise of a turtle and transported him back to the shore near his village. When he arrived his parents were not there and nothing seemed to be the same. He was very upset not to see his mother and father, wondering what could possibly have happened to them. He was still carrying the box Otohime had given him and in his confused state, decided to open it. A thin vapour began to rise from the box and as he watched it, his strength started to ebb, his hair turned

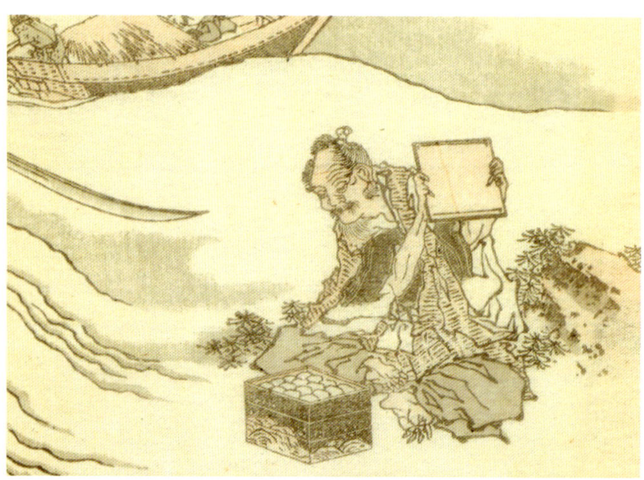

Fig. 52 Illustration from *Hokusai manga* Vol. 15 page 5. Urashima Tarō as a wrinkled old man opening the treasure box (*tamatebako*) (EA2012.22)

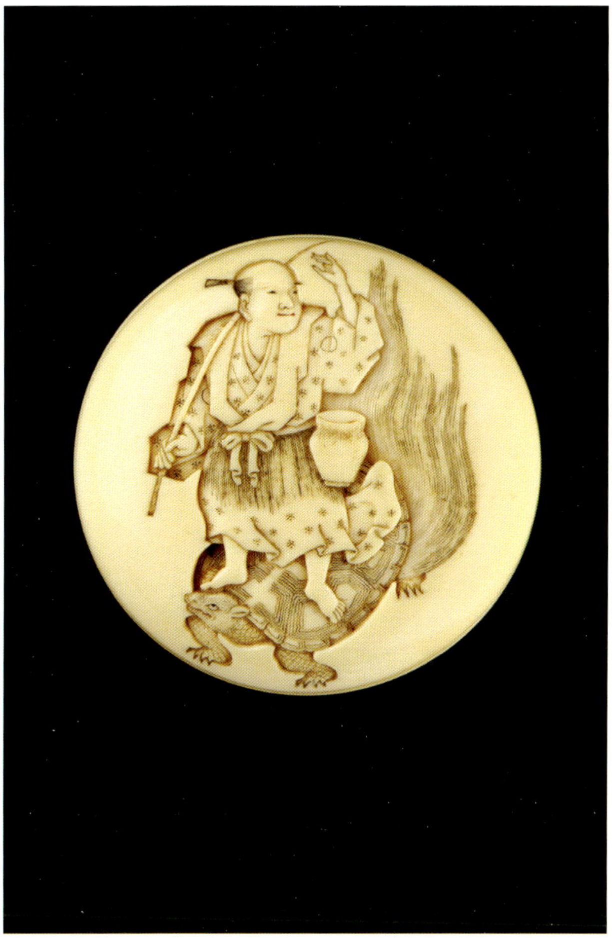

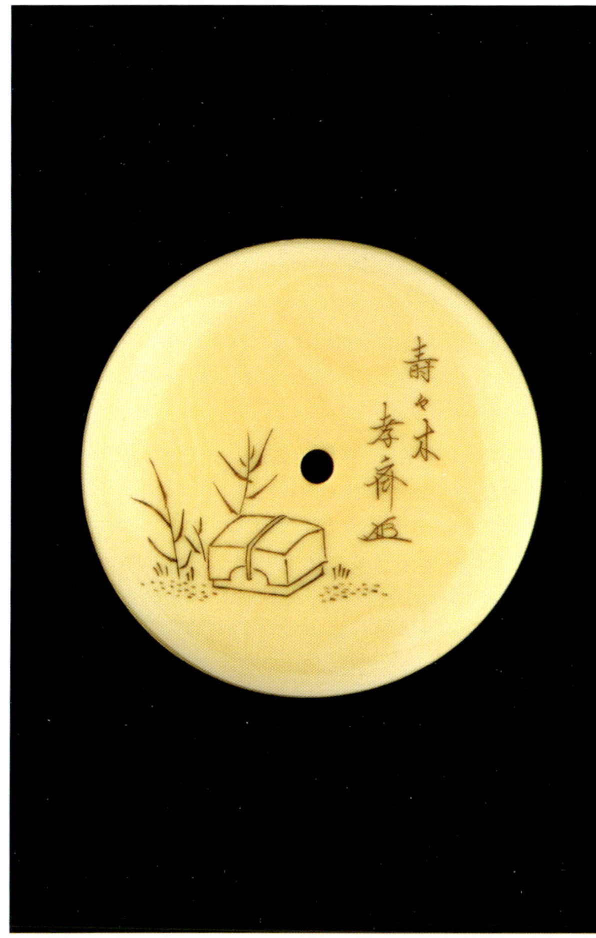
壽々木
孝齋匠

white and his skin began to wrinkle like that of an old man, for unbeknown to him, three hundred years has passed since he had left home (fig. 52).

Suzuki Kōsai has displayed his skill in detailed *shishiaibori* carving on the front of this *manjū* contrasting it with a simple sketch of the box beside reeds on the shore on the reverse.

69

Kappa

Verso: plain with a beaded collar surrounding the *himotōshi*

Ivory with dark staining
Signed: Mitsuo 光雄 with seal reading *tomo*
Around 1840
H: 2.0; W: 4.3; D: 3.35 cm
EA2001.55
Bequeathed by Dr Monica Barnett

Illustrated in:
Frederick Meinertzhagen. Ed. George Lazarnick. *MCI. Meinertzhagen Card Index on Netsuke in the Archives of the British Museum*, Alan R. Liss, Inc., New York. Vol. 1, p. 522

Ex J. Fairley collection. No. 259. Feb 1933

Bought from Crichton. May 1972

The *kappa* is a mischevious water goblin of Japanese folklore. It is one of the best known Japanese mythical creatures, being part-human, part-turtle, with webbed feet and is about the size of a small child.

Featured in folktales throughout Japan, the *kappa's* behaviour and shape differ from region to region. However, all agree that its most important feature is a depression on the top of its head, filled with a fluid from which it gains strength. Should the fluid spill out, the *kappa* will collapse. Both mischief and wickedness have been associated with *kappa,* one of its more nefarious deeds being the drowning of horses, cattle and even humans, by dragging them into water. The advice, were one to meet a *kappa*, is that a low bow will produce the same response in return, for despite all its mischief, it is a polite creature. This trick will be its undoing for the fluid will escape and it will be forced to desist from malign deeds.

Executed in the high-relief carving technique known as *takanikubori,* a benign-looking *kappa* sits astride its favourite food, a cucumber. In days gone by, after a mysterious drowning when the *kappa* was a prime suspect, cucumbers were thrown into the water in the hope of preventing a further occurrence.

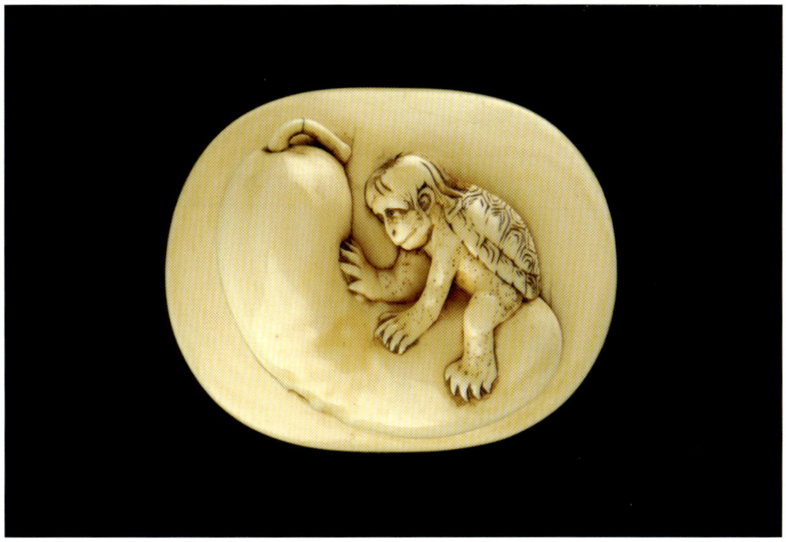

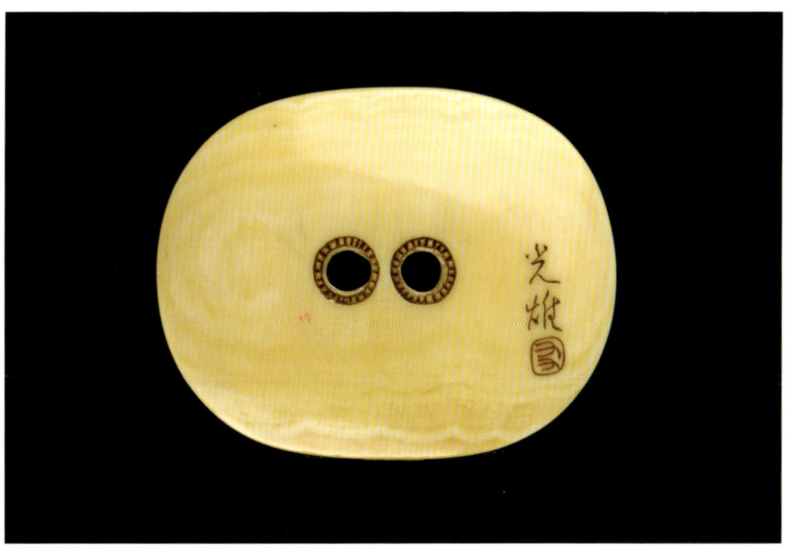

70

Young girl pleading to be spared by the Witch of Adachigahara

Verso: a fan, a bamboo screen and a bowl containing a steaming witch's brew

Ivory with brown and black staining, red highlights
Unsigned
Mid-19th century
Diam: 5.05; H: 1.9 cm
EA2001.111
Bequeathed by Dr Monica Barnett

Sold at Sotheby's, London 19& 20/06/1989. Lot 28

This gruesome story, which fortunately has a happy ending, is about a woman said to be of high rank, who was in the service of the *daimyō* whose domain covered the moor of Adachi. He had become ill with a serious and unusual disease, which it was said, could only be treated with the blood of female children, born in a certain month. Desperate to see her master cured, the woman decided to go in search of the healing medicine. She operated from a hut on the lonely moor of Adachi. One evening she was visited by a pilgrim, looking for shelter for the night. After much persuasion from the visitor, she grudgingly consented and showed him his room, insisting that he look no further around the hut. That night she left to collect firewood. When she did not return, the pilgrim became suspicious and his curiosity got

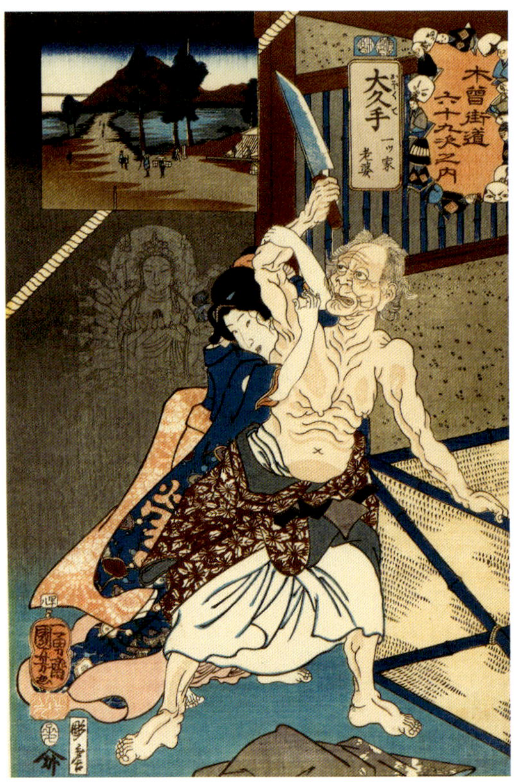

Fig. 53 Witch of Adachigahara. Colour woodblock print by Utagawa Kuniyoshi (1797–1862) (EA.1971.93)

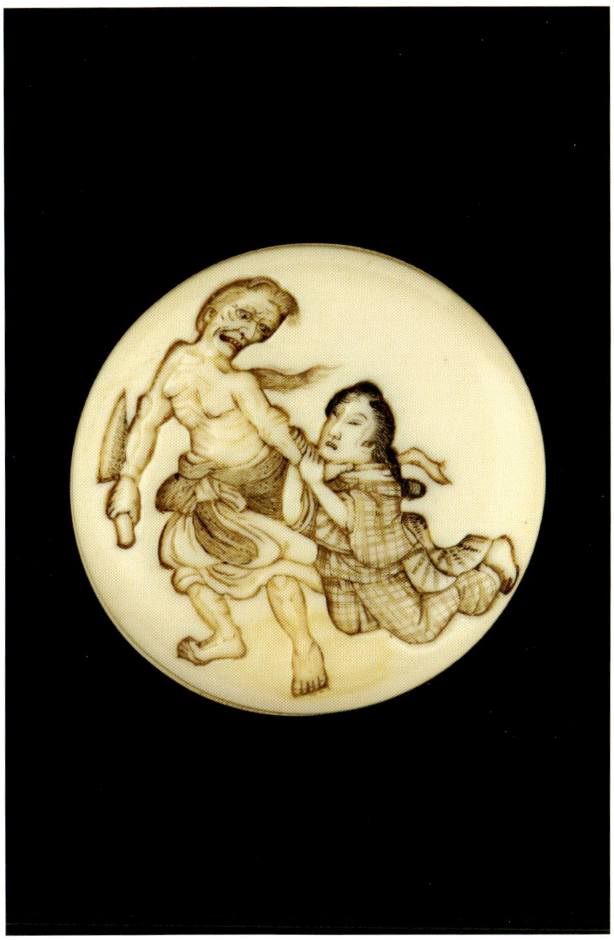

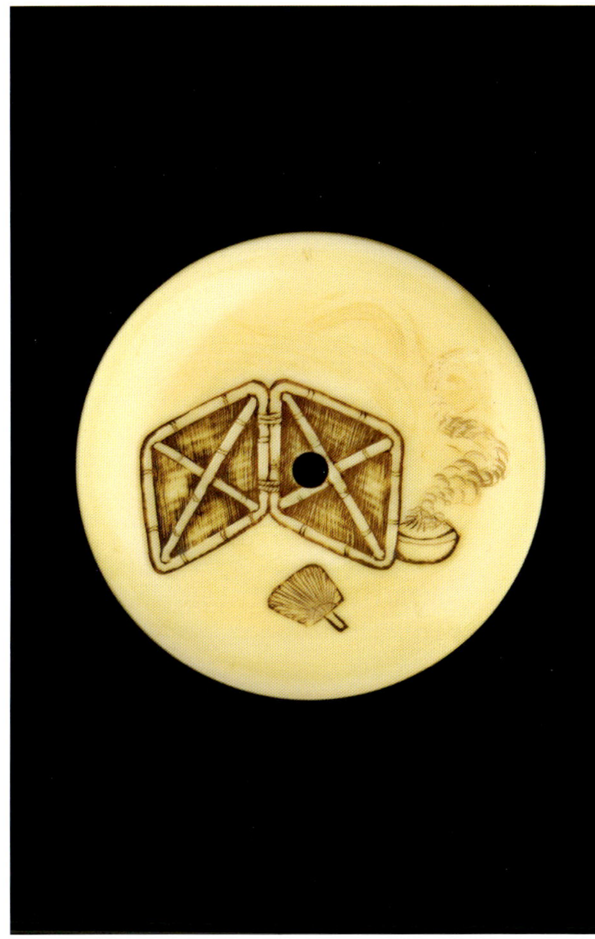

the better of him. He peeped into her room and there saw horrendous evidence of her deeds. Shocked and horrified, he was hastily preparing to leave when she returned and caught him. He looked up and found himself staring at the figure of a witch. He dashed across the moor as fast as he could and when he eventually returned to his senses, reported her deeds.

In the meantime, the *daimyō* made a full recovery after a few doses of the dreadful medicine supplied by the woman. On hearing that her master was well again, the woman confessed. Despite the horror of her deeds, she was immediately pardoned for showing such unswerving loyalty to her lord and master, a quality held in the very highest esteem.

Kuniyoshi's print of this scene appears to have supplied elements of the design. A shadowy figure of the eleven-headed kannon of mercy in the background provides a protective presence for the girl (fig. 53).

71

Witch of Adachigahara attempting to kill a young girl with a knife

Verso: Pilgrim's satchel and straw hat

Ivory with black, brown and red staining
Signed: Meijitsu 明實 with *kakihan*
1830-1870
Diam: 4.2; H: 1.4 cm
EA2001.60
Bequeathed by Dr Monica Barnett

For another piece on the same subject, but a different design by Meijitsu see Sotheby's, London 11/03/1988. Lot 18

Bought from S. Marchant and Son 06/12/72

Meijitsu's interpretation of this subject brings it much closer to the viewer than in cat. no. 70 and conveys with dramatic effect the plight of the poor girl who may be dead within seconds. In one of her hugely muscular arms the witch holds an alarmingly large knife and is attacking with grim determination, while the helpless girl tries to push her away. The generous application of black dye for the girl's hair adds greatly to the drama of this gruesome moment.

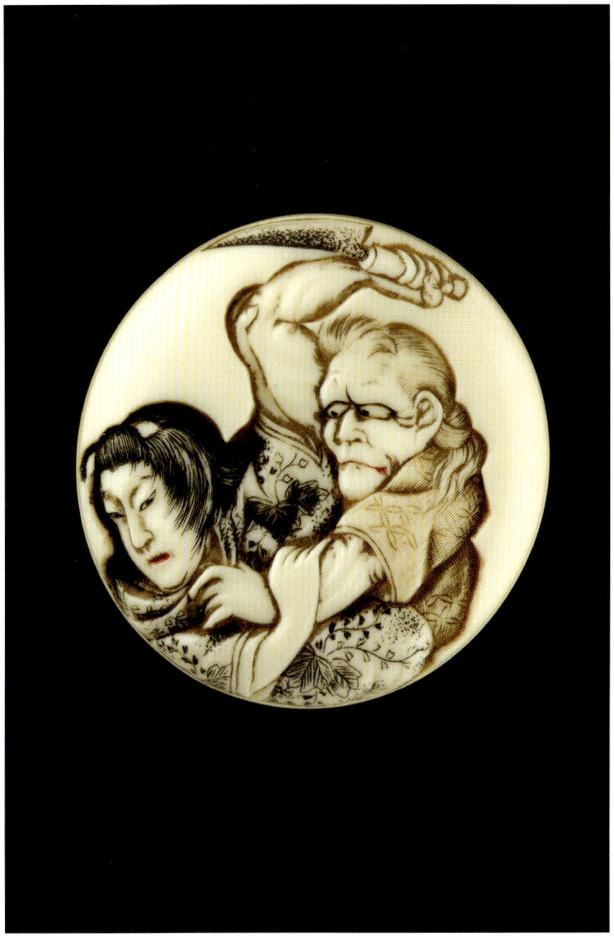

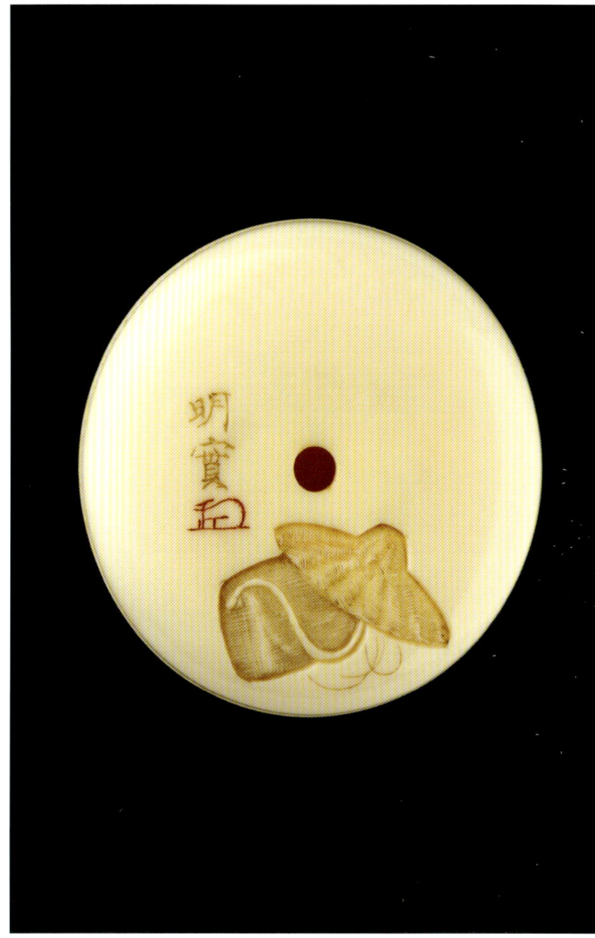
明賓

72

Taira no Koremochi and a demon

Verso: maple leaves blowing in the wind

Ivory with black and red staining
Signed: Ichiyūsai Naoharu 一遊斎直春 with *kakihan*
1860–1890
Diam: 5.6; H: 2.3 cm
EA2001.75
Bequeathed by Dr Monica Barnett

See Neil Davey, Netsuke. A comprehensive study based on the M.T. Hindson collection. No. 83 for a very similar piece signed by Ichiyūsai's pupil.

Sold at Sotheby's, London. 29/05/1980. Lot 6
Sold at Christie's, London. 9/06/1986. Lot 367

A demon was haunting the deity Hachiman on Mount Togakushi, near Kyoto. On the orders of the emperor the famously brave warrior Taira no Koremochi (883–953) was sent to look into the problem. The warrior set off, ostensibly to look at the autumn colours on Mount Togakushi. There were many people picnicking, viewing the maple leaves, and as he walked among them he met the Princess Sarashino, whose beauty he thought had an almost ethereal quality. She courteously invited Koremochi to join her party. All enjoyed a very relaxed picnic and much drinking, the effects of which caused Koremochi to fall asleep.

In a dream, the god Hachiman's retainer appeared to him, warning him of the true nature of the princess. He then presented Koremochi with a sword from Hachiman. Suddenly Koremochi awoke, looked up and was confronted by a terrifying spectre dressed in the princess's robes, descending towards him. Quick as a flash, he drew Hachiman's sacred sword and managed to dispatch the monstrous creature in an instant.

This story was told in the *Konjaku monogatari*, and was then written as a Nō play, *Momijigari* (Autumn Foliage Viewing) in the Muromachi period. Such was its popularity that it was also performed on the kabuki[58] stage, its début being in 1887, possibly around the time when this netsuke was made.

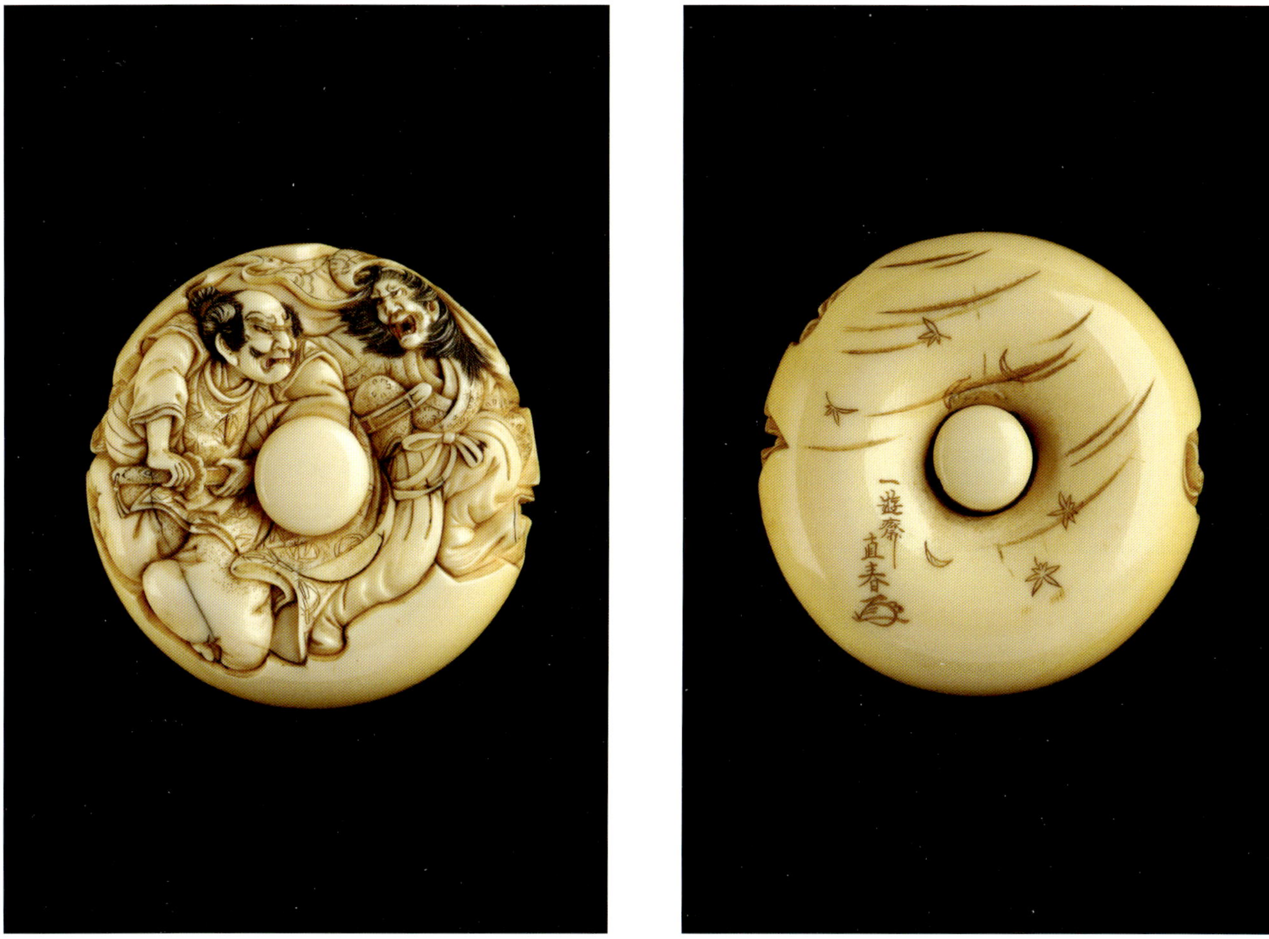

Cat. no. 72

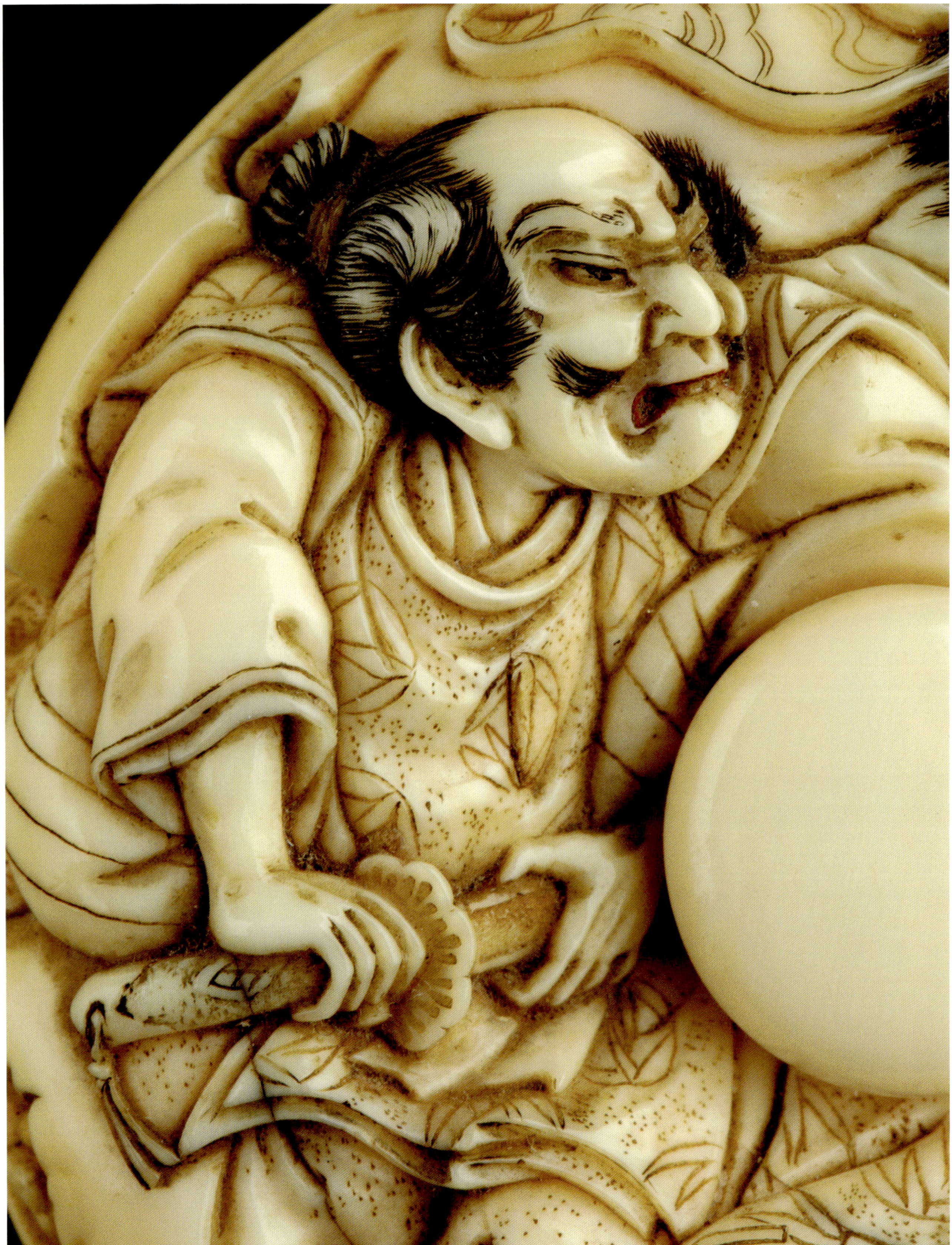

Cat. no. 72 (detail)

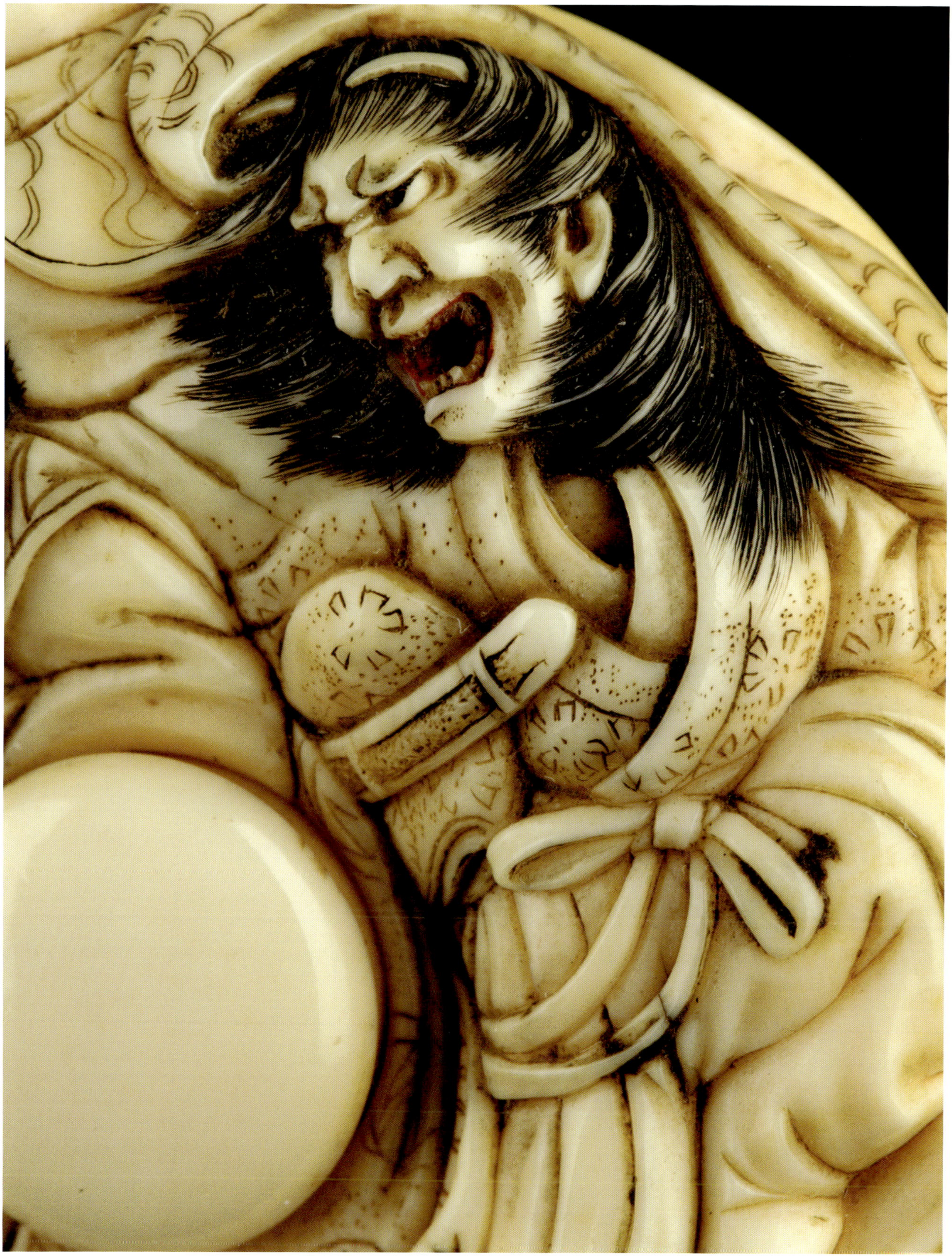

Cat. no. 72 (detail)

73

Yasumasa and Hakadamare

Verso: Moon appearing from the clouds

Ivory with black and brown staining
Signed: Ono Ryōmin 小野陵民 with *kakihan*
Late 19th century
Diam: 5.0; H: 2.0 cm
EA2001.95
Bequeathed by Dr Monica Barnett

Illustrated in:
Henri L. Joly. Legend in Japanese Art. London. 1908 p. 404

Ex Behrens collection. No. 1223

The same design can be seen on the plates of several *kagamibuta*. One is illustrated in *The Raymond and Frances Bushell Collection of Netsuke, A Legacy at the Los Angeles County Museum of Art*. 2003. No. 538 and another is in the Baur Collection, Geneva. C 376

The bandit Hakadamare was renowned as 'a man without match in the realm, bold of heart and great in strength, swift of foot, skilled of hand and wise in judgement. His trade consisted of stealthily seeking his opportunity and robbing innumerable men of their possessions.'[59]

On this crisp moonlit night, Hakadamare needed a robe to keep him warm. Along the road came a man dressed in formal court hunting attire, *kariginu*, the elaborately patterned robe with draw-strings on the flowing sleeves and *sashinuki*, the long 'puff-ball' trousers, gathered up at the hem, to prevent damage to the fabric. He played a flute, apparently unaware that he was being followed. Hakadamare crept up behind him and just as he was about to challenge the man, he was suddenly overcome with fear. So he followed the flautist, who still ignored him. Finally, Hakadamare drew his sword, at which Fujiwara no Yasumasa turned around and calmly asked 'What kind of person are you?' He confessed to being a 'clothes robber' and announced his name as 'Hakadamare'. Yasumasa said quietly, 'Come with me' and took Hakadamare to his house and gave him a thick cotton robe saying 'From now on, when you need this sort of thing, come here'. Hakadamare was overcome as he realised he was in the house of Fujiwara no Yasumasa, the former Governor of Settsu and a fine warrior. Some sources hint that the nobleman treated the bandit kindly because the two were in fact brothers.

This story is told in *Konjaku monogatari* (Anthology of Tales from the Past) Chapter XXVI Number VII and in '*Uji shūi monogatari*' (Tales gleaned from Uji). It was also made into a kabuki dance by the famous actors Ichikawa Danjurō VII and Onoe Kikugorō III in 1822. It was again performed forty years later around the time that Ono Ryōmin was carving in Tokyo.

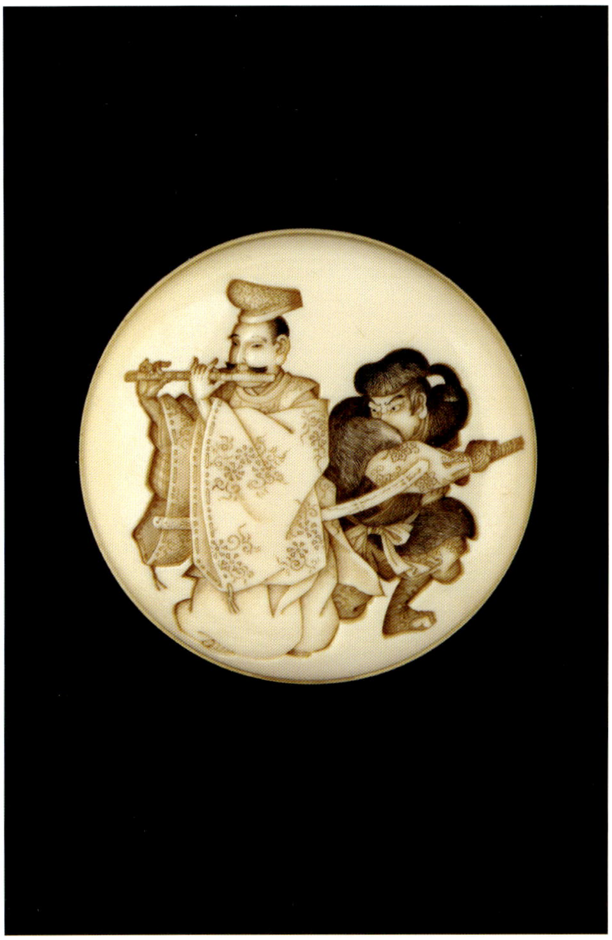

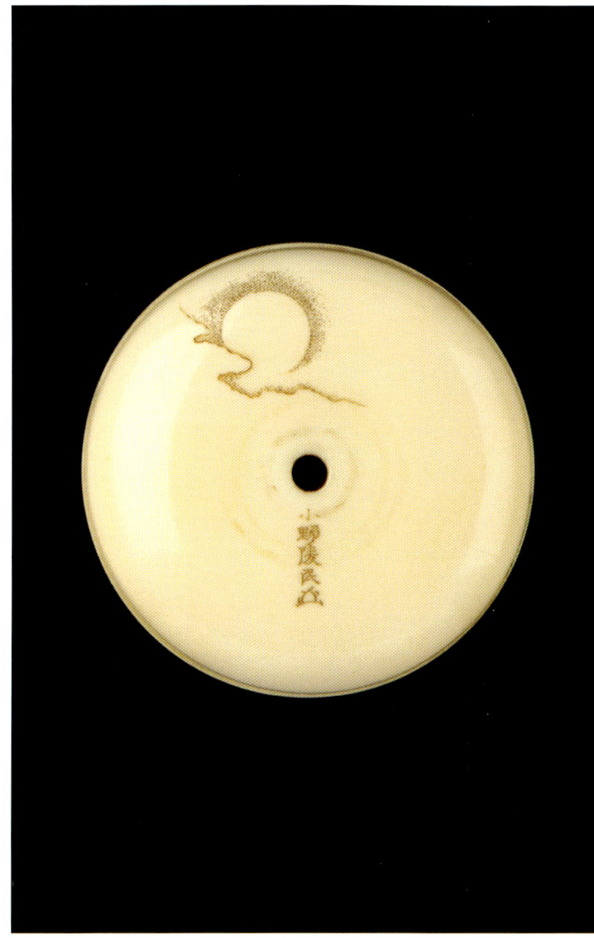

74

Tsuchigumo (Earth Spider)

Verso: plain

Ivory
Signed: Munetoshi 宗利 (unrecorded artist)
19th century
Diam: 4.9; H: 1.8 cm
EA2001.105
Bequeathed by Dr Monica Barnett

Illustrated in:
Bulletin Franco-Japonaise No. 20. Avril 1988. Sales report.

The *'tsuchigumo'* or 'Earth Spider' was a 'creature with a horned head, six arms, two legs, eyes bright as mirrors, and teeth like saws, capable of spinning threads strong enough to entangle man and beast and invulnerable against sword or arrow. Such was the monster that was said to have appeared in Yamato (an ancient name for Japan) at the time of the Emperor Jimmu 660–585 BC'.[60] Terror surrounded this beast, which was eventually hunted down, trapped in a cave and smoked to death. Sixteen centuries later the *'tsuchigumo'* reappeared in a similar form and was finally dispatched by Minamoto no Yorimitsu (Raikō) (944–1021) and his retainers (cat. no. 75).

75

One of Minamoto Yorimitsu's retainers tries to kill one of an array of goblins in the Earth Spider's entourage

Verso: spider's web and goblins

Ryūsa-type *manjū*
Ivory
Signed: Gyokuhōsai 玉宝齋 within an oval reserve
1830–1860
H: 1.4; W: 4.3; D: 4.0 cm
EA2001.122
Bequeathed by Dr Monica Barnett

Published in:
Wilhelm, G. *Manjū exégèse et appréciation*, Bulletin Association Franco-Japonaise. No. 54. Octobre, 1996. Fig. MB18

See Sotheby's, London, 29/4/1968. Lot 319 and Sotheby's, New York. The Cornelius V.S. Roosevelt Collection of Netsuke. 02/06/1992. Lot 279

Minamoto no Yorimitsu (948–1021), known as Raikō (Sino-Japanese reading of Yorimitsu), was head of a branch clan of the Genji (Minamoto), a high-ranking member of the Fujiwara court and a martial arts expert. As with many of these historical figures, tales of his feats and adventures have become embellished over the centuries to give him supernatural powers. With his four trusted retainers, Watanabe no Tsuna, Kintoki no Sakata, Usui no Sadamitsu and Urabe no Suetake, he was involved in all kinds of improbable escapades, this story being one of them.

By the Meiji period the original tale of the *'Tsuchigumo'* would have been well known through the *Heike Monogatari* and Nō and kabuki plays. To give the story further exposure, Utagawa Kuniyoshi designed the woodblock print 'Minamoto Raikō and

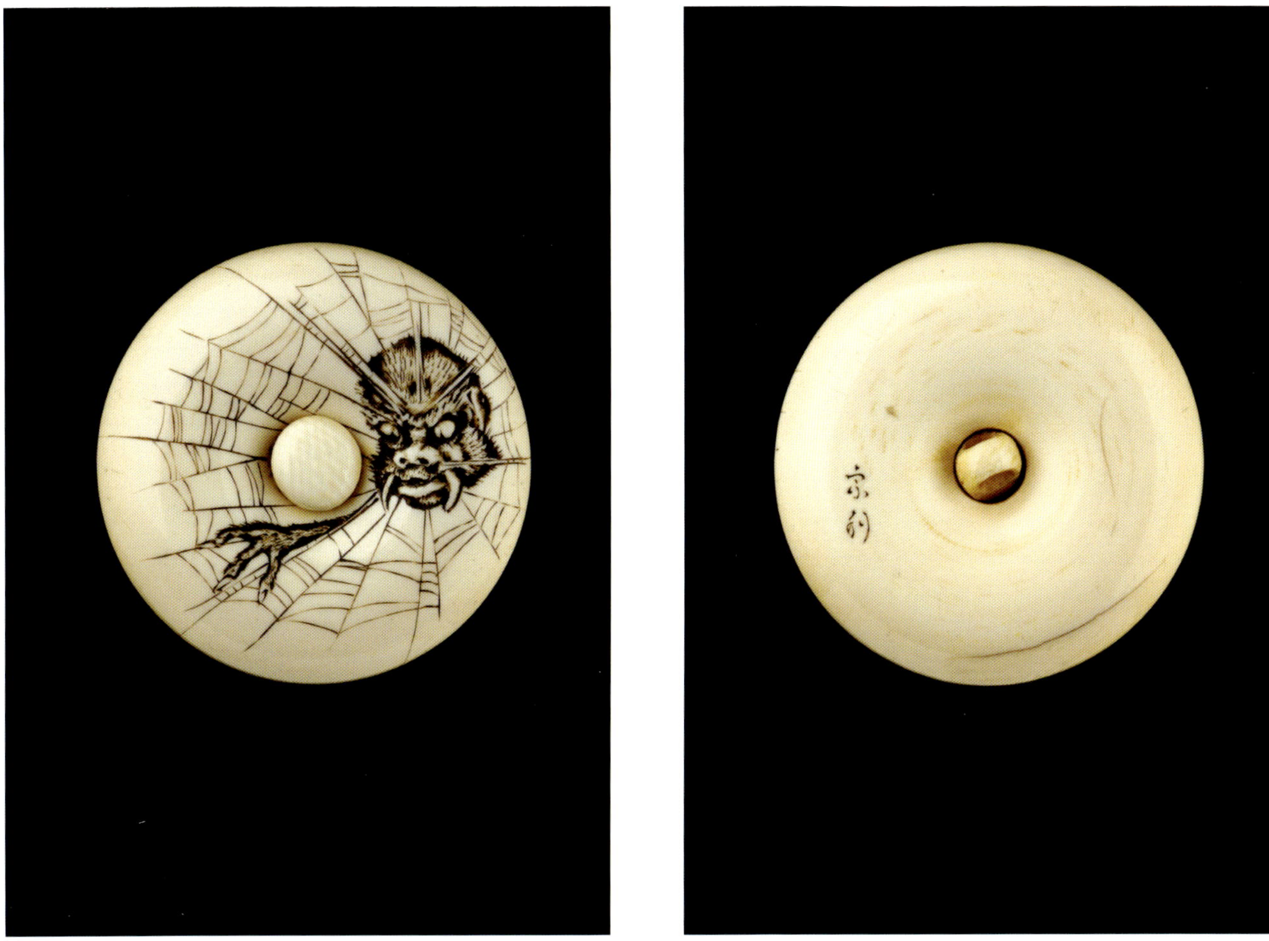

Cat. no. 74

the Earth Spider' in 1843 (see fig. 54), which satirised the Tenpō reforms implemented by the Tokugawa Government and caused outrage and near incarceration for the artist.[61]

The story begins with Raikō who was haunted by a monstrous spider. Medicine failed to help. He was visited by a Buddhist monk, but after a while he watched in horror as the trusted bonze slowly metamorphosed into a spider and tried to envelop the ailing warrior in its web. He lashed out at it with his sword, but it just managed to escape, despite being injured. Raikō then sent his four retainers out to capture the creature, following its trail of blood which led them to a cave in which the wounded monster spider was hiding. With one slash of a sword the monster was slain. It is no surprise that Raikō was already on the path to recovery when the victorious retainers returned. The sword was then named *Kumokiri* (spider slasher).

Belief in the supernatural has permeated Japanese culture from ancient times. Ghosts and demons abound and appear in many folktales. Ceremonies are regularly performed to exorcise, or at least to appease the troubled spirits represented by them. In the nineteenth century there was a huge increase in the popularity of supernatural themes, particularly in woodblock prints. These designs were then used by netsuke carvers as sources of inspiration.

On the front of this *manjū* one of Raikō's retainers is trying to destroy a one-eyed creature with a blow to the head, while on the reverse, with the spider and its web threatening to engulf them, Gyokuhōsai has incorporated his own array of transfigured

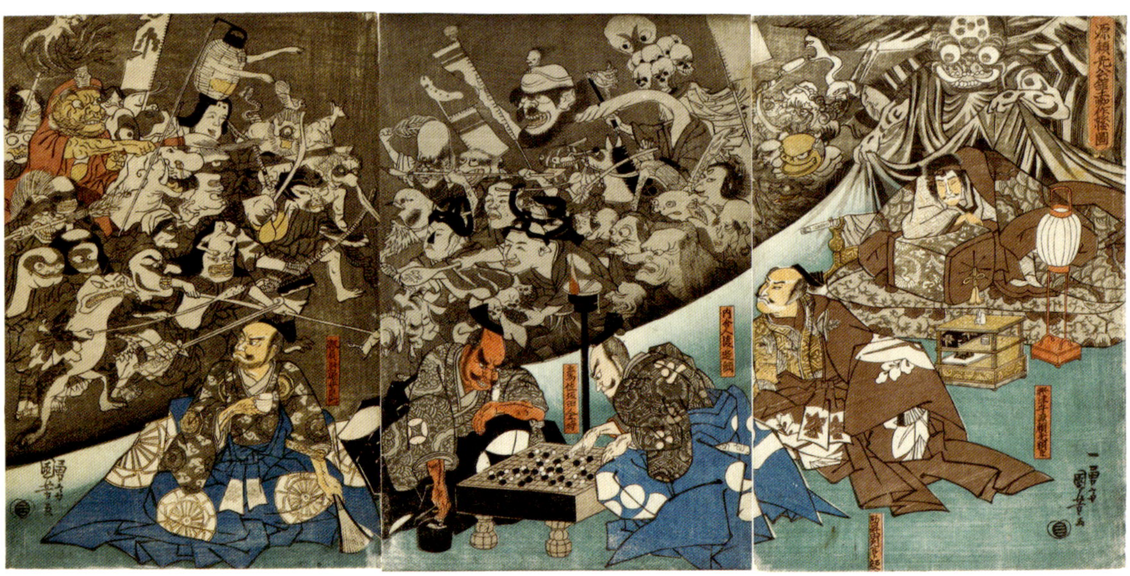

Fig. 54 Minamoto Raikō and the Earth Spider. Colour woodblock print by Uragawa Kuniyoshi (1797–1862) (EA1971.164)

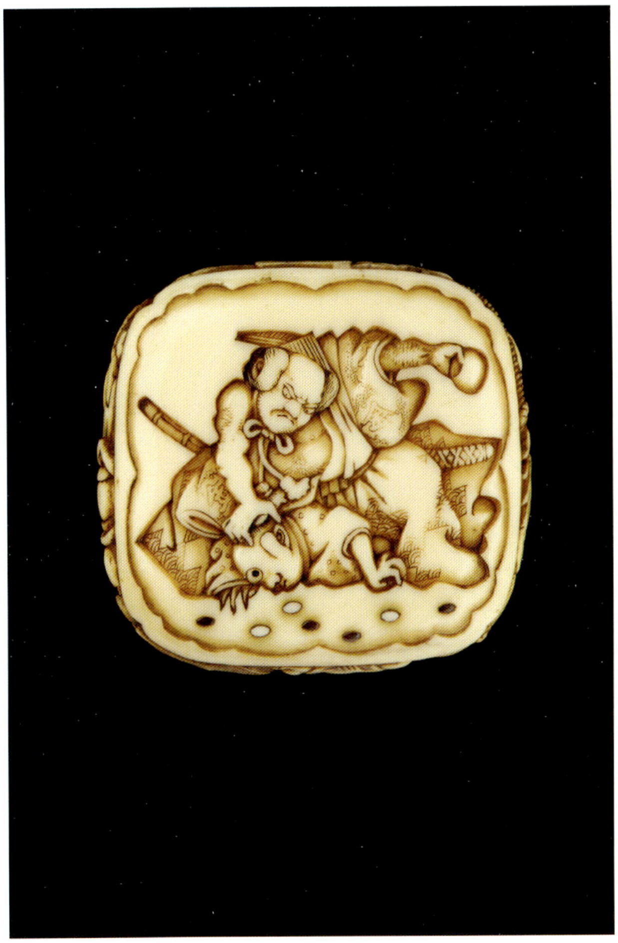

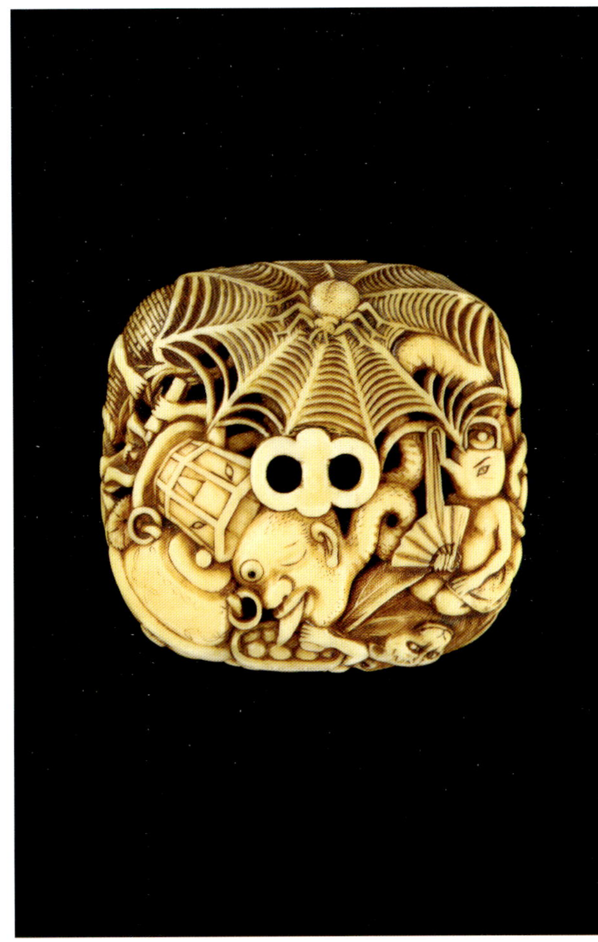

Cat. no. 75

objects: a long-necked one-eyed monster *(ichimoku)* accompanies a teapot with a human body, and a bucket that has acquired eyes and a long tongue, all jumbled together with fans, scrolls and other objects.

In Japanese folklore, utensils which have been discarded change into animate beings after one hundred years. They are known as *tsukumogami* and their vengeful spirits can cause all manner of trouble and on occasion, have even been known to eat human flesh. They are most frequently seen in illustrated scrolls of 'night processions of one hundred demons' (*hyakki yakō emaki*).[62]

This unusual shape and style, pierced on the reverse and carved on a flat surface on the front may be Gyokuhōsai Ryūchin's own design. Another piece in the Art Gallery of Greater Victoria, Canada, which depicts Ōishi Kuranosuke, leader of the Forty-seven Rōnin with an assortment of umbrellas, fans, trees, flowers and a lantern on the reverse (2007.016.034), is in the same style.

76

Slaying a *bakemono*

Verso: Leaves blowing in the wind and part of a blind (*sudare*)

Ivory
Signed: Moritoshi 守寿 with crane *kakihan*
19th century
Diam: 4.4; H: 1.7 cm
EAX.629

A warrior, possibly Sakata no Kintoki, one of Minamoto no Yorimitsu's retainers who were known as 'The Four Guardians' (*Shitennō*), is about to dispatch yet another monstrous looking creature (*bakemono*) whom he has pinned down to the ground.

Moritoshi Kōsai's workshop produced many *manjū* of this type in ivory, illustrating Japanese folktales and events.

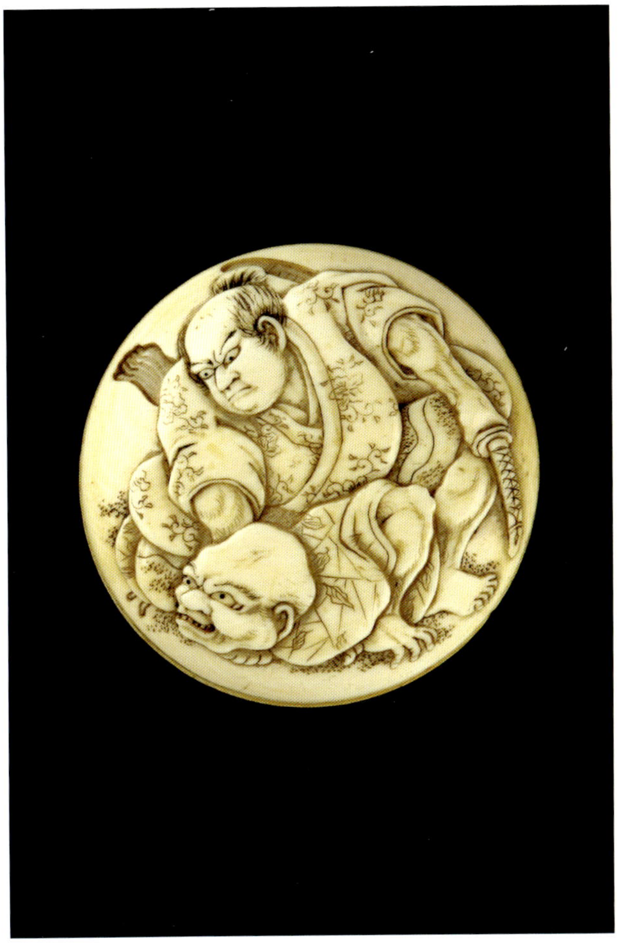

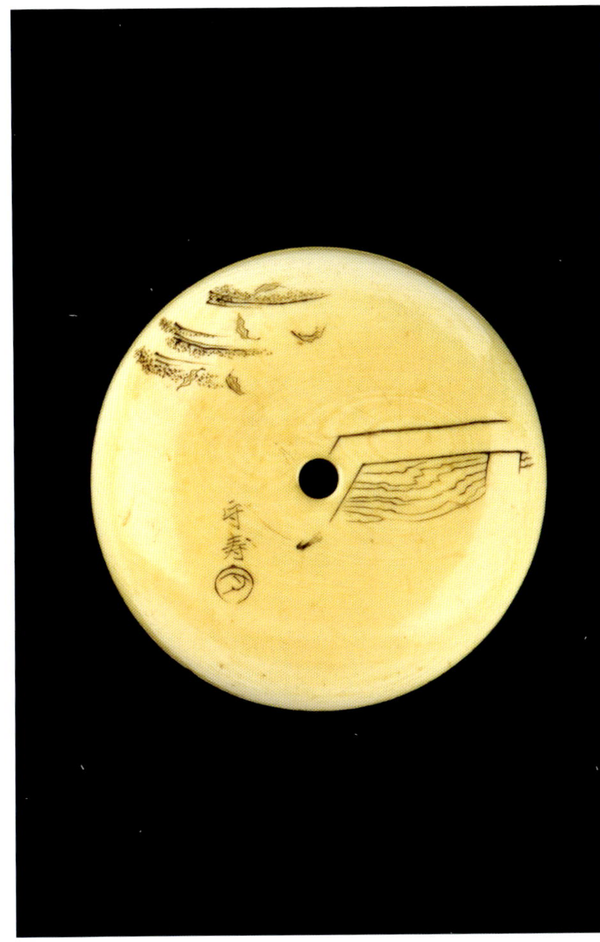

77

Watanabe no Tsuna and the Ibaraki Demon

Verso: Scabbard of a sword used to cut off the demon's arm with Mount Atago behind

Ivory
Signed: Ittokusai 一徳斎
Around 1820
Diam: 7.5; H: 3.25 cm
EA2001.66
Bequeathed by Dr Monica Barnett

Published:
Wilhelm, G. *Manjū exégèse et appréciation.* Bulletin Association Franco-Japonaise, No. 54. Octobre, 1996. Fig. MB4

This large netsuke illustrates another legend. The Ibaraki Demon (*Ibaraki dōji*), one of the assistants of the *Shuten dōji* (cat. no. 78), was sent to harass people trying to pass through the Rashōmon gate in the south of Kyoto. Many people had been assaulted and domestic animals had been seized by this demon. So much trouble did it cause that Minamoto no Yorimitsu, (Raikō), sent his loyal retainer, Watanabe no Tsuna (953–1025) to deal with the problem. Watanabe approached the gate on horseback and after what seemed to be an interminable wait, a ghastly demonic creature appeared coming at him over the roof. Watanabe drew his sword, and in the ensuing fight only managed to sever the arm of the demon, which let out a blood-curdling yell and vanished screaming out that it would return. Watanabe grabbed the arm and fled with it. When he arrived home he locked it in a chest. He then spent the next seven days reciting sutras and praying to the Buddha.

A few days later his Aunt Mashiba paid him a visit and, curious to hear about his exploits with the demon, she asked to see the arm. Watanabe went over to the chest and as he opened it her features slowly transformed into the very creature he had fought. Before he could do anything, she snatched the arm and raced away. So shaken was Watanabe that he could not give chase. Fortunately, this was the end of the Ibaraki Demon and never again were the citizens of Kyoto troubled by it.

This is another story which was told in both the *Heike Monogatari* (Book 11) and the *Taiheki* (Book 32), the two versions differing slightly. The story became well-known through the Nō play '*Rashōmon*'. In 1883 a kabuki version '*Ibaraki*' was first performed and a dramatic painting of the hideous creature by Shibata Zeshin was commissioned for the theatre billboard.

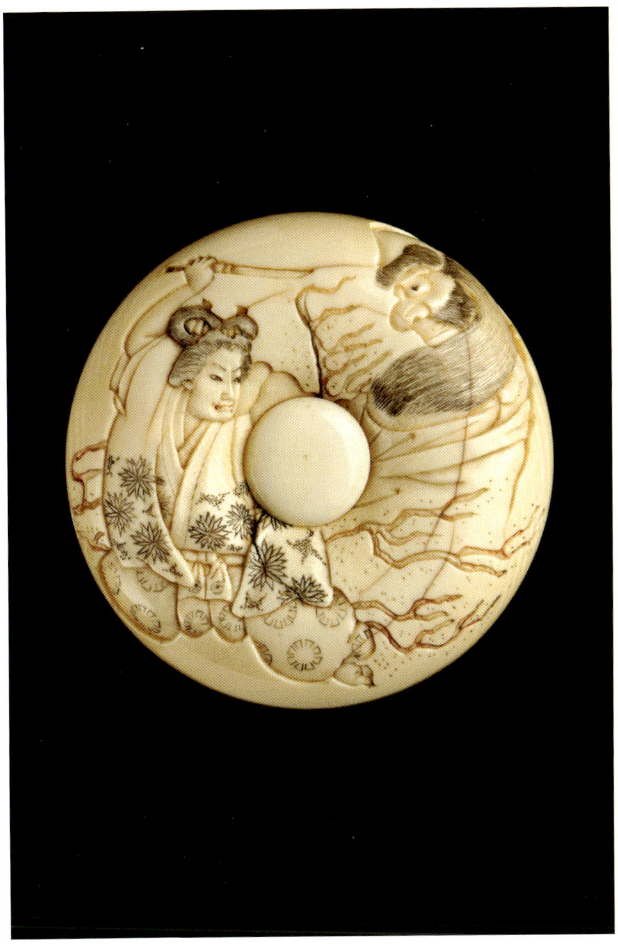

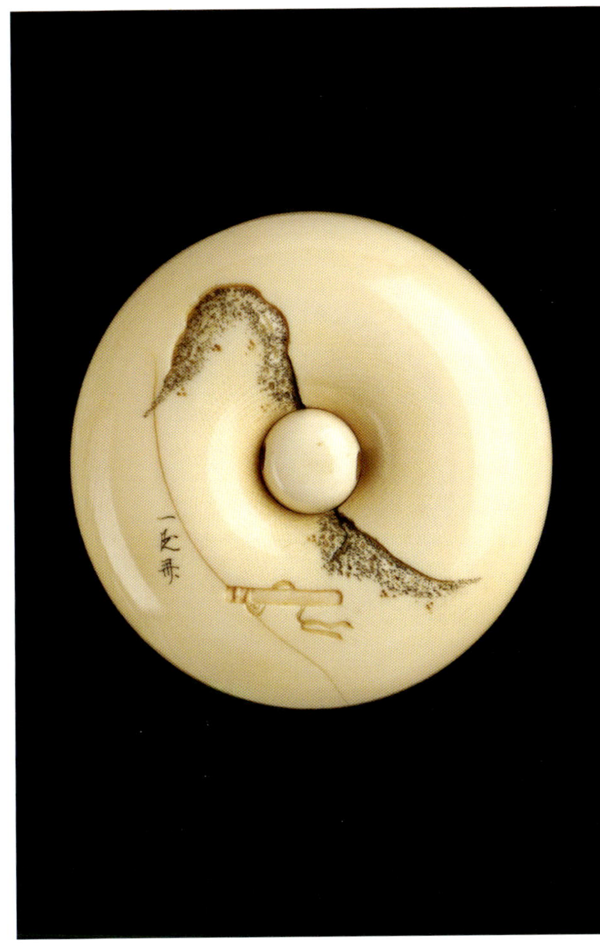

78

The *Shuten dōji* (Drunken demon)

Verso: Partially unrolled blind in the palace interior

Ivory with agate, mother-of-pearl and coral
Signed: Tōto kōjin (eastern capital skillful technician) Shinryūsai Chikahiro 東都巧人眞龍齋親廣 with inlaid shell *kakihan* 本人 Honnin (I am the very one)
1850–1870
Diam: 7.7 H; 3.1 cm.
EA2001.76
Bequeathed by Dr Monica Barnett

Ex Behrens Collection. No. 1207
Ex Brockhaus collection

Illustrated in:
George Lazarnick. *Netsuke and Inro Artists, and How to Read their Signatures.* Reed Publishers, Honolulu. 1981. Vol. 1, p. 327
Henri L. Joly, *Legend in Japanese Art*, London, 1908, Opposite p. 413
Frederick Meinertzhagen. Ed. George Lazarnick. *MCI. Meinertzhagen Card Index on Netsuke in the Archives of the British Museum*, Alan R. Liss, Inc., New York. Vol. 1, p. 22 (Okada dates this piece from the Tempo period: 1830–1844.) 'Fine powerful work circa 1820'. Sold to Stafford Cripps December 1929 for ten pounds

Published:
Wilhelm, G. *Manjū exégèse et appréciation*, Bulletin Association Franco-Japonaise. No. 54. *Octobre*, 1996. Fig. MB1

Depicted on this *manjū* is another gruesome legend which relates the exploits of Minamoto no Yorimitsu (Raikō) and his band of faithful warriors who were charged by the emperor to find and kill the ogre responsible for kidnapping and eating young maidens from the capital, Kyoto. There are two versions of the story; in this one the monster, *Shuten dōji* (drunken demon) lives on Mount Oe.

After much discussion, Raikō and his warriors, one of whom was Watanabe no Tsuna (see Ibaraki demon story, cat. no. 77), decided to disguise themselves as mountain ascetics. They began their mission with prayers, first to the gods at the Shrines of Kumano, Yahata and Sumiyoshi and then to the Buddha. Dressed as priests, with their armour concealed in their panniers, they set off up Mount Oe. Along the way they came across three men, distressed relatives of abducted maidens, who said that they were not brave enough to go any further up the valley to the *Shuten dōji*'s palace. Having heard of the *Shuten dōji*'s propensity for wine, the men gave Raikō some special *sake*, for he insisted the warriors continue their journey. They set off again and slowly it began to dawn on them that the three men were in fact the three deities to whom they had prayed. Encouraged by this thought they pressed on. With cunning and fast talking they got past the guards and into the *Shuten dōji*'s 'magnificent palace, with rows of roofs and bejeweled screens'.[63] There they were entertained with a meal of human flesh accompanied by the blood of the captured maidens. This they ate trying not to show their disgust. Then they returned the hospitality, offering their special *sake*. The *Shuten dōji* became suspicious, thinking that they looked horribly like the band of warriors in Kyoto who had caused much trouble to *Ibaraki dōji*, one of his henchmen. Raikō skilfully managed to laugh off the accusation and finally the *Shuten dōji* became so drunk that he retired to bed. At night his appearance changed from human to demon. Once all the attendants were similarly intoxicated, the visitors found their way to the *Shuten dōji*'s bedroom but just as they were about to slay him, he awoke. A fierce fight broke out in which Raikō eventually managed to sever the demonic head. The maidens who had not yet been killed were released and returned to the capital, along with the head of the *Shuten dōji* borne aloft on a stretcher. The emperor was both relieved and pleased and Raikō and his men were well rewarded.

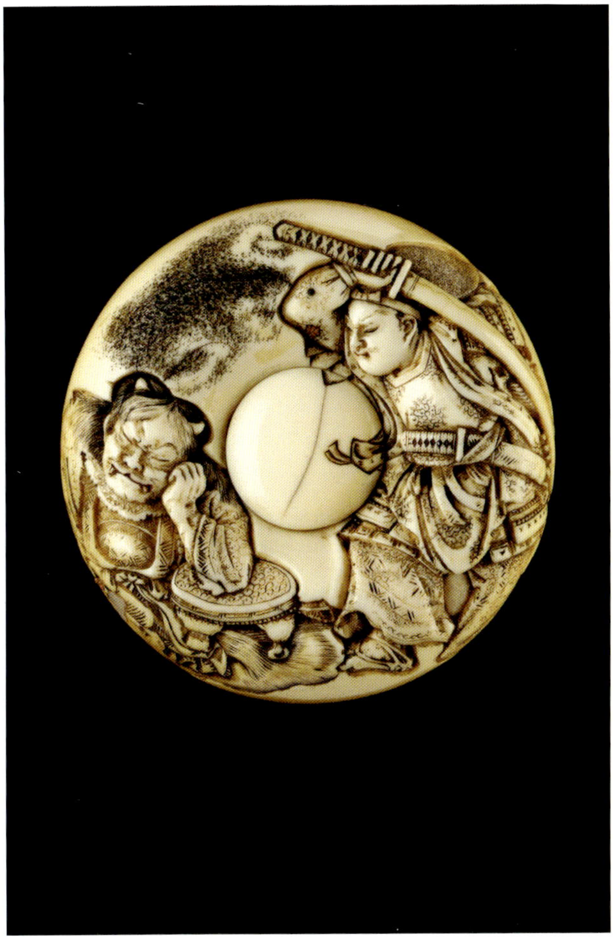

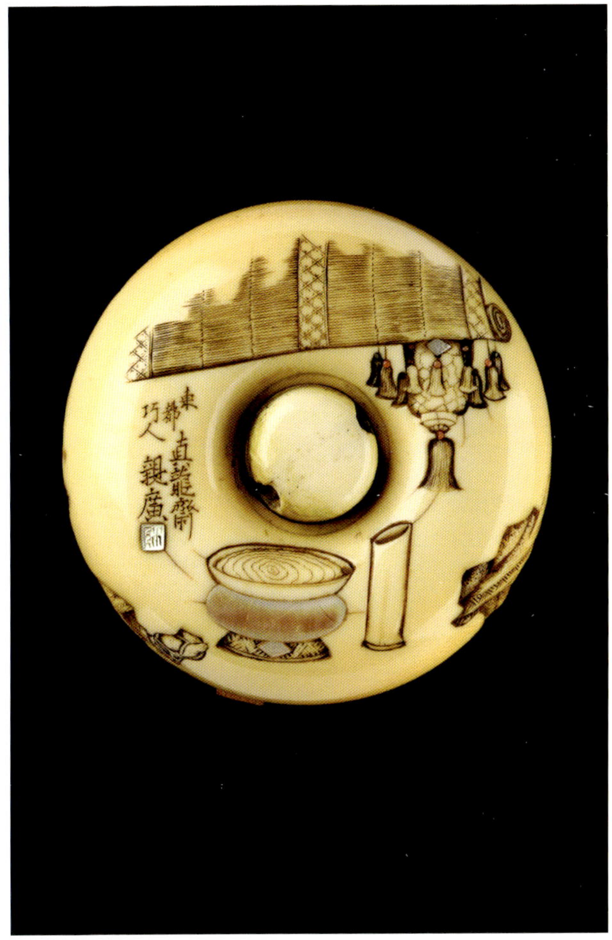
東
都直龍齋
巧人
親廣

This tale is of a type known as '*otogi zōshi*' which were written from the fourteenth to the seventeenth centuries for the purpose of entertainment and moral or religious edification. 'The 'Shuten dōji' story reveals how warriors faithful to the Buddha and to Shintō deities can defeat even the most monstrous of villians'.[64]

79

Kintarō

Verso: maple leaves blowing away

Ivory, coral, malachite, mother-of-pearl inlay and red and black colouring
Signed: Meijitsu 明實 with *kakihan*
(Hōryūsai Meijitsu 法龍斎明實)
Mid-19th century
Diam: 5.7; H: 1.85 cm
EA2001.83
Bequeathed by Dr Monica Barnett

Illustrated in:-
Bulletin Association Franco-Japonaise, No. 10, Septembre 1985, sales report by G. Wilhelm.

For similar examples:
See Eskenazi catalogue Oct. – Nov. 1984 for a *manjū* of the subject by Hōryūsai Meijitsu

See Sotheby's, Chicago. 02/09/1993. Lot 165
Sold at Sotheby's, London 13 & 14/06/1985. Lot 495

Kintarō, which means 'golden boy', is the name given to Sakata no Kintoki, a retainer of Minamoto no Yorimitsu. Kintarō was involved in the slaying of the *Shuten dōji*. (cat. no. 78). He is said to have been brought up by a kind mountain hermit named Yamauba. His supernatural strength was legendary and many tales were told of his extraordinary feats. In this dynamic carving the young Kintarō forces open the mouth of a giant snake as he grapples with it, muscles rippling in his huge arms. It seems a little incongruous for this super-strong boy to be playing with the toy fish, which is falling to the ground, but it is purely symbolic to stress his young age. Kintarō's emblem, a large hatchet, lies amongst autumn leaves on the reverse.

This woodblock print by Utagawa Yoshitsuya (fig. 55) must surely have served as the model for this design which Meijitsu has skilfully adapted to the circular shape of the *manjū*.

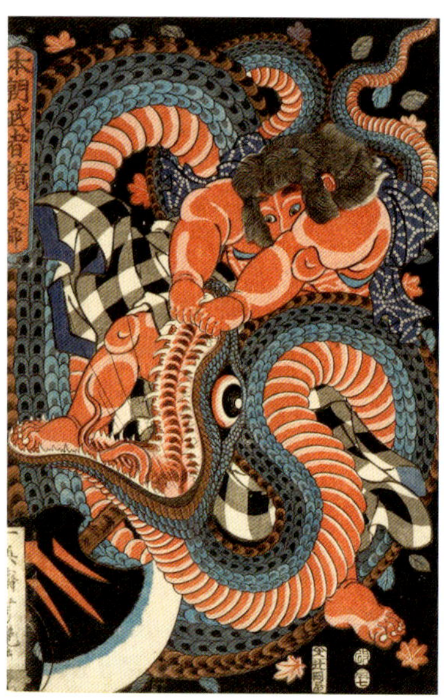

Fig. 55 Kintarō and a giant snake. Colour woodblock print from the Series *Honchō musha kagami* by Utagawa Yoshitsuya (1822–1866) (EA1971.220)

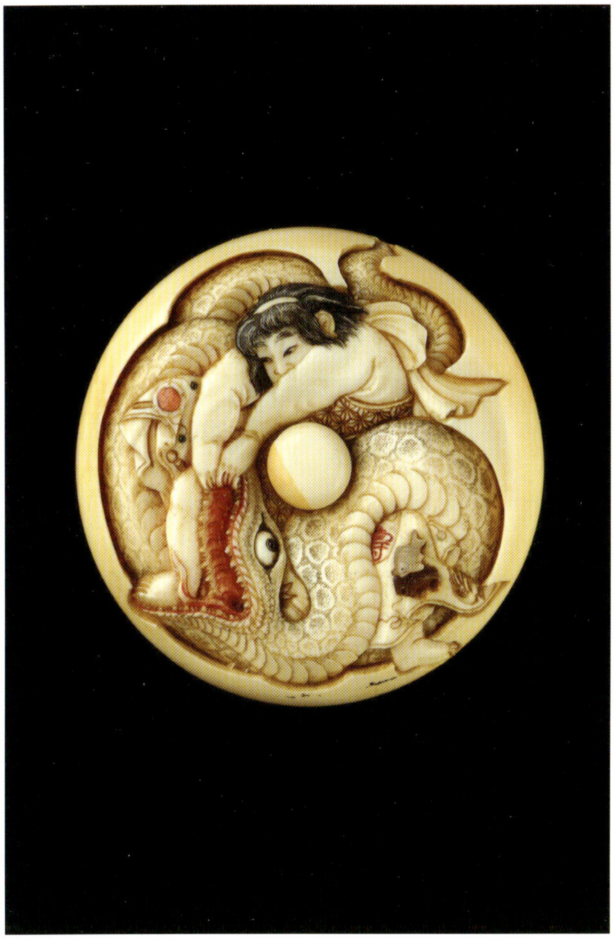

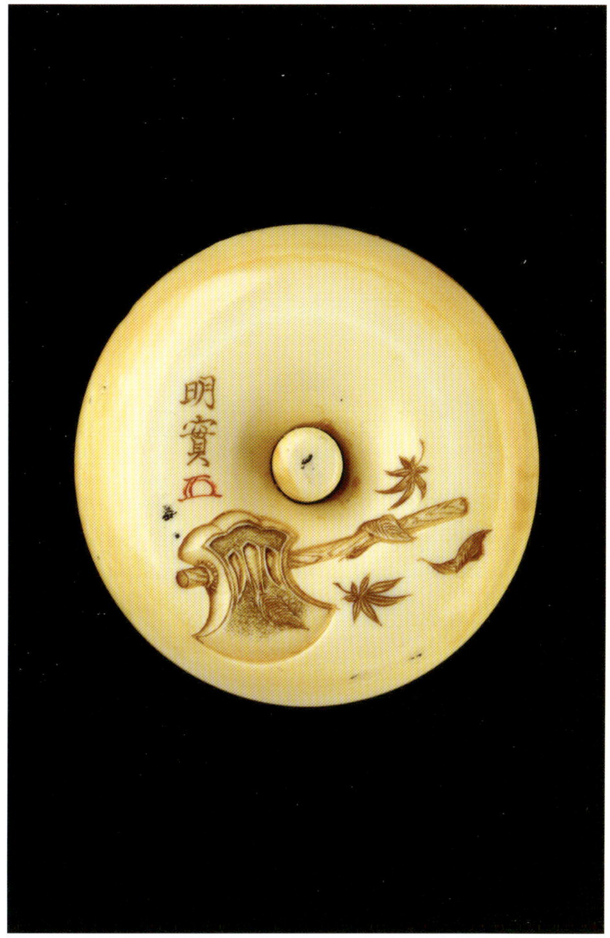

80

Endō Moritō

Verso: Kongara and Seitaka descending among clouds

Pressed horn (or cross-linked casein)
Unsigned
Late 19th century
Diam: 4.2; H: 2.0 cm
EA2001.136
Bequeathed by Dr Monica Barnett

For articles illustrating the design of this *manjū*, see *Andon, Society for Japanese Arts*, No. 56 (with a follow up article in No. 58).

Endō Moritō was a warrior who lived in the twelfth century. He grew up alongside his cousin, Kesa, who married Watanabe Wataru, an imperial palace guard, and she became Kesa Gozen (The Lady Kesa). After many years Endō Moritō met her again and fell madly in love with her but his attentions were not reciprocated. He became obsessed and even threatened to kill her family if he could not be with her. In desperation Kesa Gozen pretended to enter into a plot in which Moritō would kill her husband, so that they could be together. On the appointed night, Moritō crept into the sleeping Watanabe's bedroom. With one flourish of his sword, Moritō severed Watanabe's head, grabbed it and rushed out, now free, as he thought, to take his beloved for himself. He held up his prize… and collapsed in grief, for what he saw was Kesa Gozen, her hair cut to resemble her husband's (fig. 56). She had made the ultimate sacrifice by taking his place in the bedroom, while he was away.

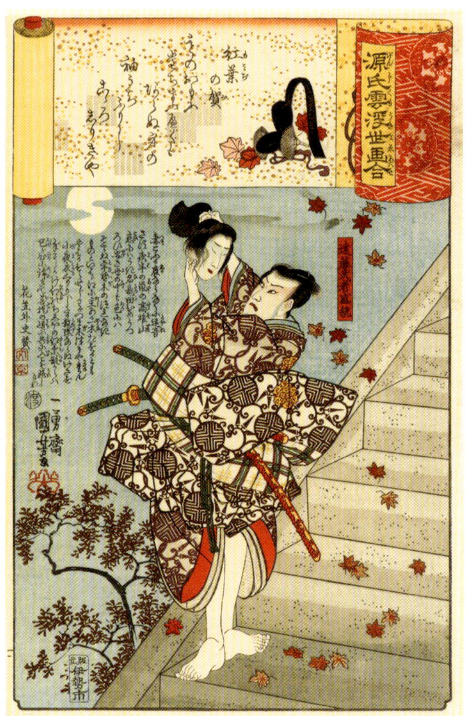

Fig. 56 Endō Moritō realising what he has done. Colour woodblock print by Utagawa Kuniyoshi (1797–1862) (EA1971.141)

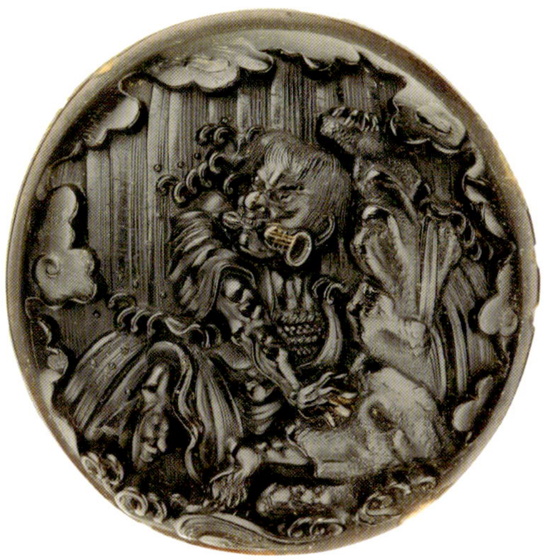
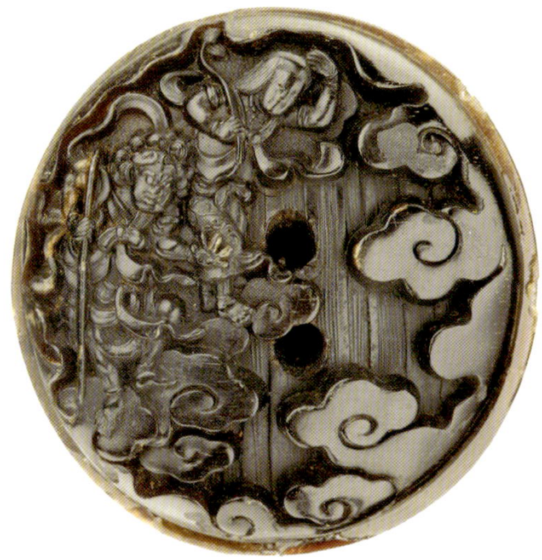

Endō Moritō was so overcome with guilt, grief and admiration for her courage, that he took the tonsure, and the name, Mongaku Shōnin. To atone for his murderous act, he undertook a number of austerities. On this netsuke he is shown sitting beneath the icy waters of the Nachi waterfall (in modern Wakayama Prefecture) reciting, for three weeks, invocations to Fudō Myōō (the Buddhist Immovable King of Light), while his body slowly begins to freeze. Had it not been for the intervention of Fudō Myōō's two attendants, Seitaka and Kongara, (seen on the reverse), he would have perished. In his teeth he holds a *vajra* (Jap. *kongōsho*), a ritual object of Esoteric Buddhism which symbolises the destruction of passion and carnal desire.

The austerities of Mongaku and his salvation by Fudō Myōō and his attendants are told in the thirteenth century chronicle *Heike Monogatari*.[65]

Pressed horn *manjū* are made from horses' hooves (according to Arende H. Kempers in *Andon*), and from buffalo horn imported from India (according to Alain Ducros). The horn was boiled and then pressed into a mould. The mould was used several times and although it is not known how many times, it is common to see more than one piece of the same design. Subjects are almost always historical. Ducros says they were the first manufactured netsuke of the Meiji period.[66] Norman Sandfield has had some of his 'pressed horn' netsuke tested by the scientific firm Mc Crone, and this has revealed that they are made of cross-linked casein'.

Tamamo no Mae

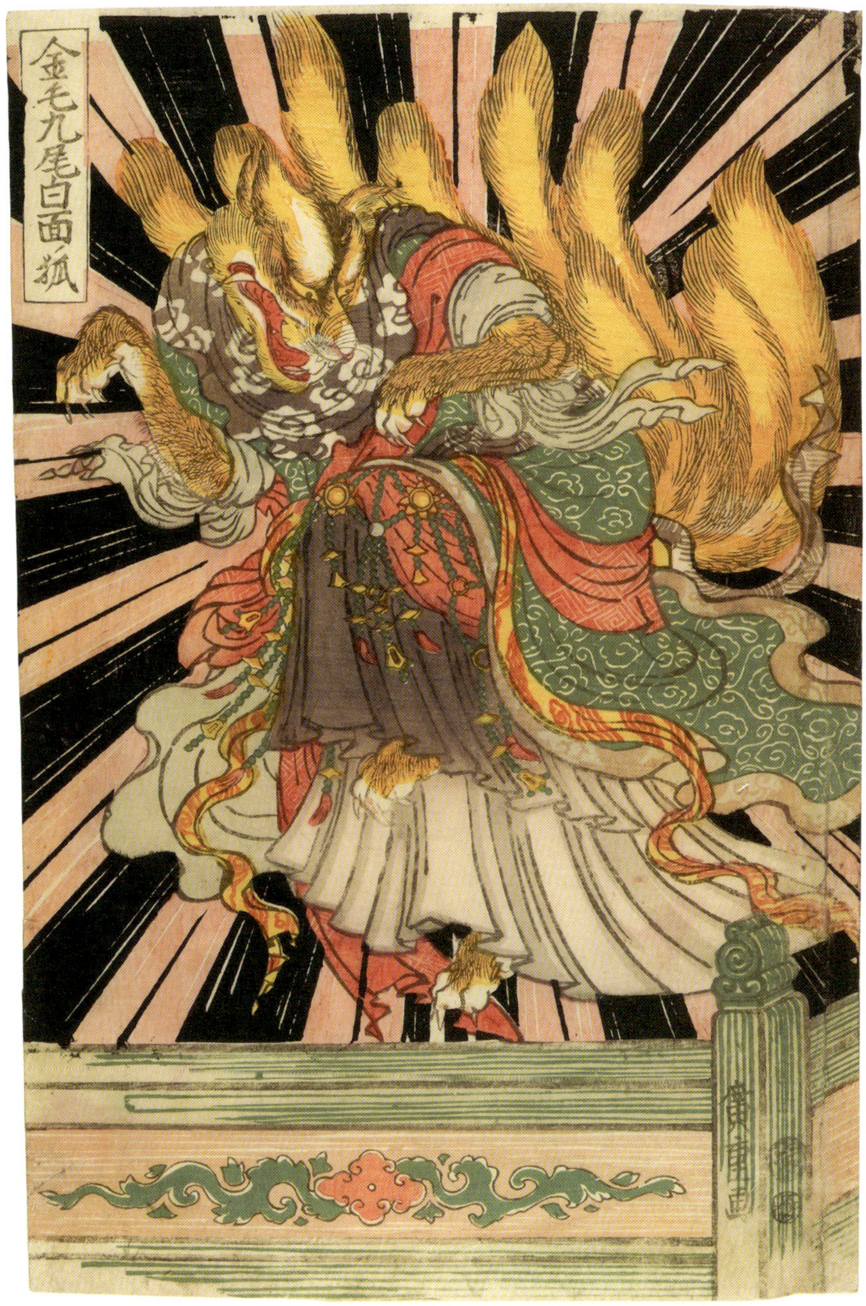

Fig. 57 Tamamo no Mae in fox form. Colour woodblock print by Utagawa Hiroshige (1797–1858) (EAX.4245)

81

Tamamo no Mae

Verso: Wind blows through the miscanthus growing beside the stone on Nasu Moor

Ivory with black and red staining
Signed: Baihōsai 貝宝齋 with seal Naomitsu 直光
Late 18th – early 19th century
Diam: 7.5; H: 3.1 cm
EA2001.101
Bequeathed by Dr Monica Barnett

Illustrated in:
Bushell. Raymond. *Netsuke Familiar & Unfamiliar*. No. 295
See George Lazarnick. *Netsuke and Inro Artists and How to Read their Signatures*. Reed Publishers, Honolulu. 1981. p. 822 where the signature is read 'Baishitsusai'

Sold at Christie's London. The Raymond and Frances Bushell Collection of Netsuke. Part 1. 27/11/1987. Lot 133

This ancient story began in India with a king's beautiful consort, in truth a cruel fox with nine tails who delighted in the killing of innocent people. The story moves to China where the malevolent vulpine creature finally becomes queen and her husband, who would do anything to please her, eventually causes the destruction of their kingdom, by ordering the death of all his subjects.

In Japan we are presented with Tamamo no Mae, a talented and beautiful courtier to the twelfth century Emperor Toba (1103–1156), or some say to Emperor Konoe (1139–1155). When the emperor fell ill, an astrologer was called in and suspicion fell upon Tamamo no Mae, for on occasion she had been seen with a strange aura of light around her. It was decided to hold a ceremony in the palace to pray for the recovery of the ailing emperor. Once again Tamamo no Mae began to emit an eerie glow and slowly she was transformed into a nine-tailed fox, showing her true malevolent identity.

Courtiers looked on aghast, and in no time she was fleeing the palace with the archer Miura Kuranosuke in hot pursuit. He finally caught up with her and shot her dead, whereupon she took the shape of a stone. This stone, in the middle of Nasu moor, was deadly to any living creature which touched, or even looked upon it. More than two hundred years later, a travelling priest named Gennō was just about to sit on the stone to rest, when it split in two revealing Tamamo no Mae, the nine-tailed fox-woman. After praying for her spirit, Gennō was able to exorcise the demon in her and she disappeared, never to return again.

Fox possession was a deep-rooted superstition in ancient Japan and one that lasted well into the Edo period. There are many stories of people, mostly women, turning into foxes (*kitsune*) to create trouble and this is perhaps one of the best known.[67] (See also cat. no. 93 for the Hatsune drum story.)

This folktale is mentioned in the the *Kagakushū* written in 1446, the first small encyclopaedia or dictionary written for ordinary people rather than scholars. It subsequently became the subject of a Nō play in the fifteenth century. Bunraku[68] and kabuki versions were launched at the end of the eighteenth and beginning of the nineteenth centuries.

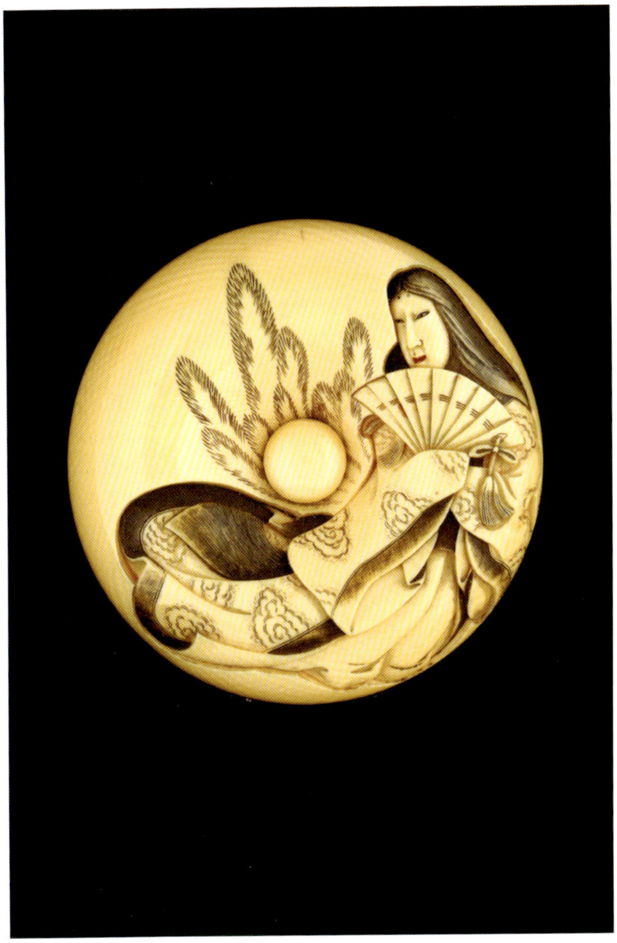

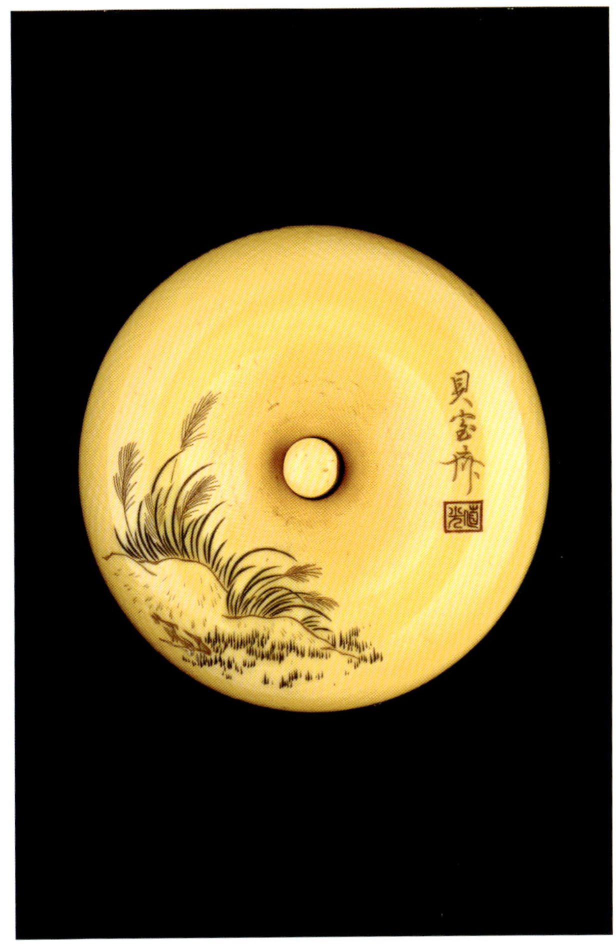

Cat. no. 81

82

Slaying the *Nue*

Verso: plain

Ivory with red and black colouring
Signed: Hakuunsai 白雲斎 with red seal reading Hakuun 白雲
Early 19th century
Diam: 7.5; H: 3.2 cm
EA2001.114
Bequeathed by Dr Monica Barnett

In 1153 the Emperor Konoe (1139–1155) was haunted by a terrible spirit. Each night, at the hour of the ox (2.00 am) a black cloud would descend over the palace and the emperor would begin to feel faint. Ceremonies conducted to rid the palace of this menace proved to be useless. As the emperor's condition deteriorated, Minamoto no Yorimasa, a skilled poet and archer, was chosen to go out to investigate. 'I have never heard of a warrior being ordered to capture an invisible monster'[69] he said as he set out. To accompany him, he took just one of his trusted retainers, a man named Ii no Hayata. As darkness fell, watching out from the veranda, the two lay in wait. Eventually a black cloud descended and 'Yorimasa saw in the cloud what appeared to be a monstrous form'.[70] Much rested on this moment, so having invoked the aid of the god of war, Hachiman, he shot one arrow into the darkness and waited. Almost immediately there was a loud thud, and the two men were faced with the most extraordinary animal they had ever seen. Ii no Hayata quickly dispatched it with his sword. A monkey's head, a badger's body, a tiger's paws and a snake for a tail were all combined in one ghastly creature, but it had sung with the voice of the golden mountain thrush (*toratsugumi*). This was the *nue*. The emperor's recovery was swift and in gratitude he presented Yorimasa with a famous sword.

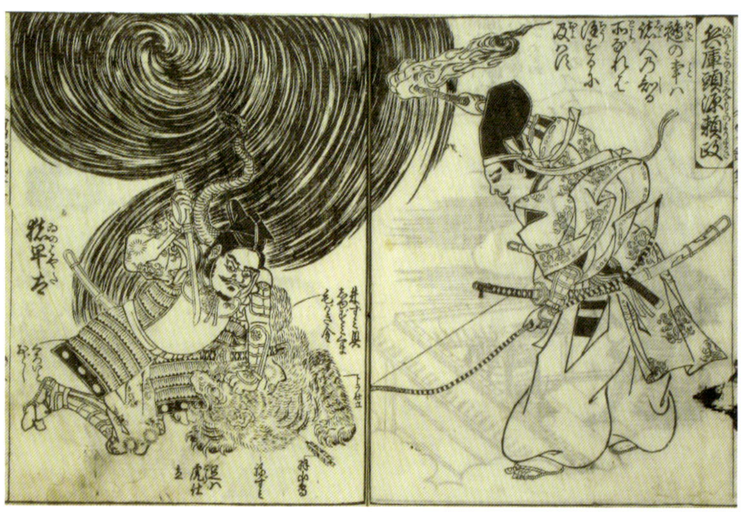

Fig. 58 Illustration from *Ehon shahōbukuro* by Tachibana Morikuni, Vol. 3, p. 5 (Waseda University Library, Tokyo, bunko 06 01293-(3))

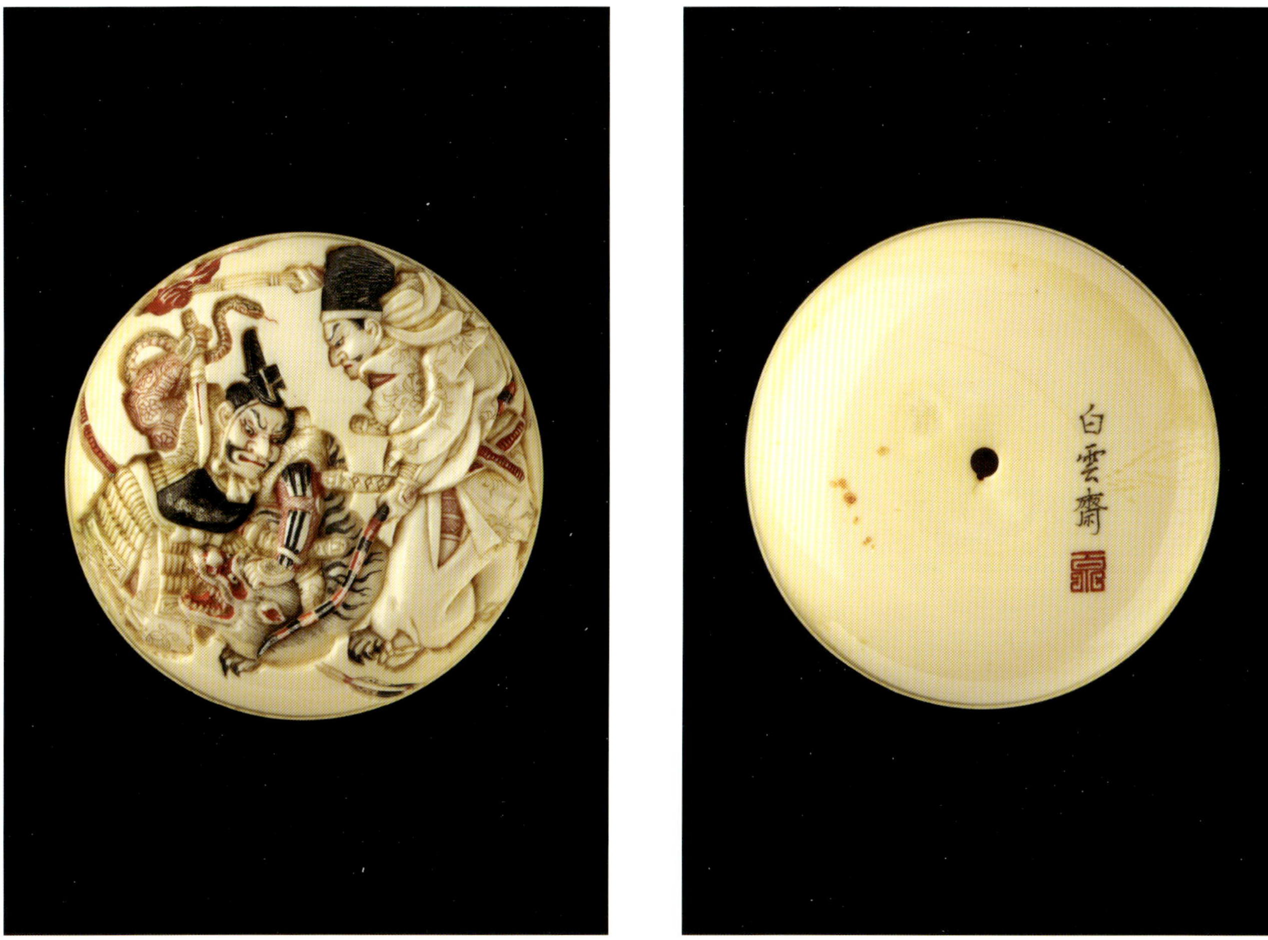

Cat. no. 82

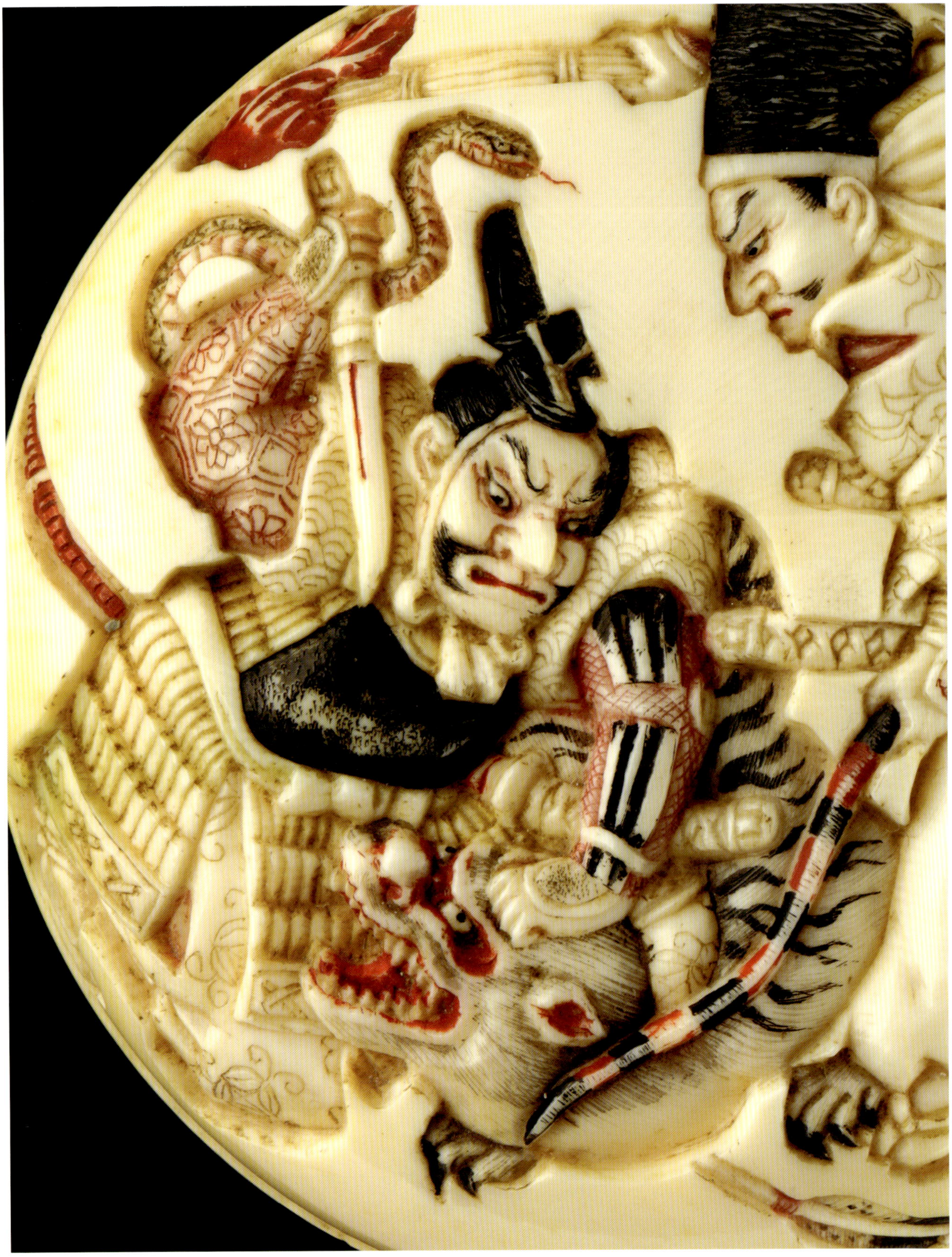

This tale is told in the *Heike Monogatari* and was transformed into the Nō Play '*Nue*' and subsequently into a kabuki play, *Yorimasa sambasō* in 1708.

The artist has cleverly adapted Tachibana Morikuni's design (fig. 58) for this netsuke. There is another *manjū* by Hakuunsai, almost identical to this, in a private collection.

Opposite: Cat. no. 82 (detail)

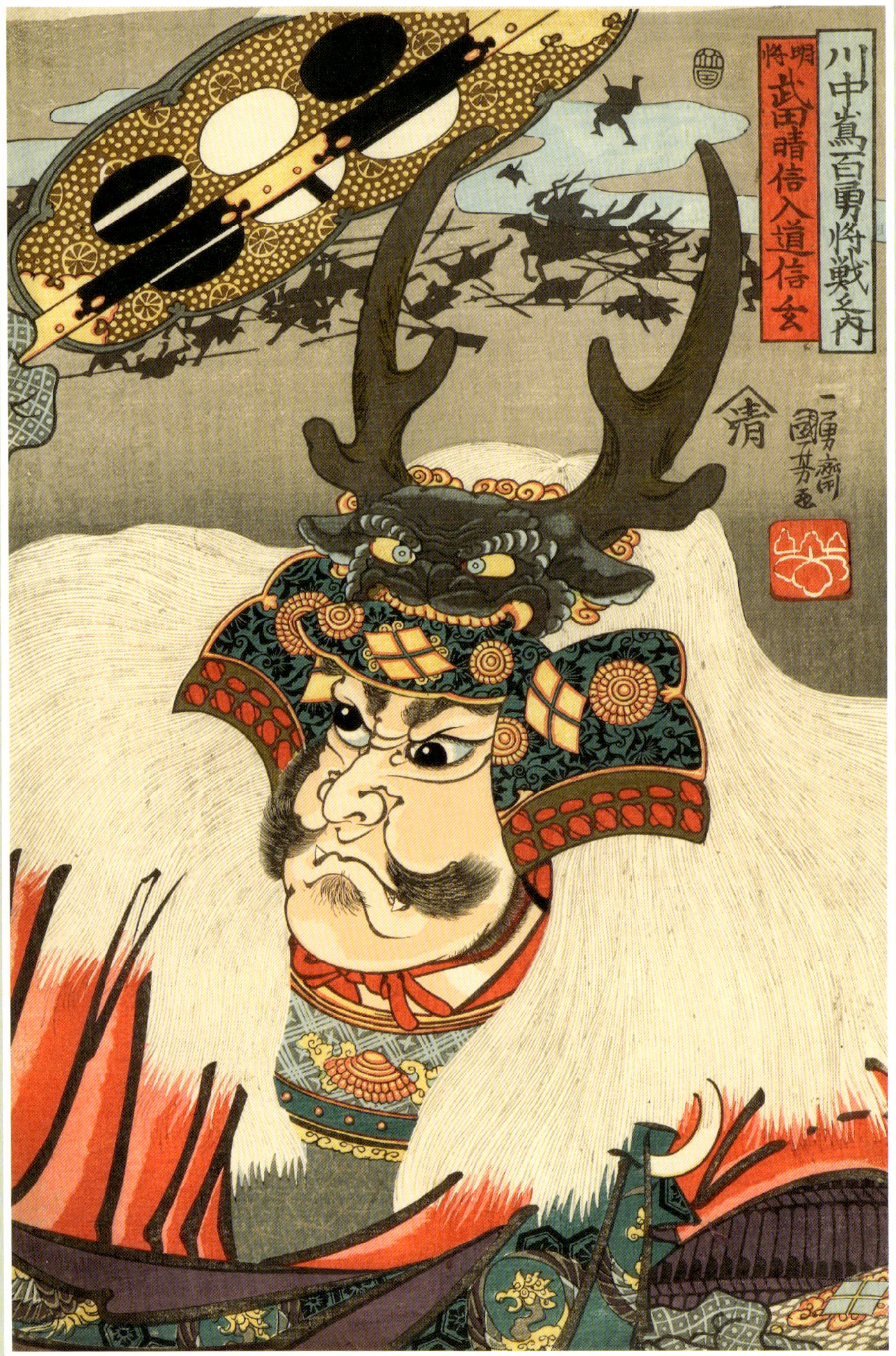

Fig. 59 The Warrior Takeda Shingen. Colour woodblock print by Utagawa Kuniyoshi (1797–1865) (EA1983.80)

Warriors

The twelfth century was a time of great military conflict. The two great clans, the Taira (Heike) and the Minamoto (Genji), were pitted against one another on many occasions. Incidents from these battles and the warriors involved in them played a significant role in literature and art. Many fictitious stories surround medieval heroes in Japan and many of these were written as plays either for the Nō or kabuki stage. These tales were extensively used by the *manjū* carvers, who used the surface as a painter would use his paper. Two particularly important military battles occurred in the twelfth century, told in the two epic tales, *Hōgen Monogatari* and *Heiji Monogatari*. The stories chart the progress of these two rebellions. At the end of the Heiji rebellion the Minamoto were temporarily defeated, but later rose up again and finally triumphed over the Taira, thanks in part to Minamoto no Yoshitsune. This later struggle between Taira and Minamoto clans, known as the Genpei wars (1180–1185), is told in the *Heike Monogatari*. Stories combining bloody conflict and romance were popular in medieval times and this popularity continued throughout the centuries that followed. Incidents from these battles became subjects in paintings, metalwork, lacquer and netsuke and these objects were especially collected and treasured by military men.

The Hōgen Incident (1156) arose because of rivalry between two retired emperors, Toba and Sutoku, who were father and son. The reigning emperor, Konoe, was a young child in very poor health, and when he died Sutoku wanted to come out of retirement and resume being emperor, but Toba had his eye on the throne for his son Go Shirakawa. Diplomatic settlement could not be reached and as Sutoku was rallying troops, Toba suddenly died. Despite being the son of the deceased Toba, Sutoku was barred from attending his funeral. This offended him so much that he sent for troop reinforcements and prepared for a fight. Warriors from both Taira and Minamoto clans answered the call to battle. Although bitter rivals, the clans were not pitted exclusively against one another but their numbers were mixed for reasons of split loyalty to the emperors. Notably, Minamoto no Yoshitomo was on the opposing side to his father Tameyoshi, who in turn was supported by his other son, Yoshitomo's half-brother Tametomo (cat. nos. 85 and 86). The result of the ensuing battle was that Sutoku's palace, the Shirakawa-den, was set alight and all within had to flee, leaving Yoshitomo triumphant. Tameyoshi and Tametomo were captured and Yoshitomo was then forced to order the execution of his own father. His half-brother, Tametomo, he exiled, but not before his arm had been disabled to prevent his ever using a bow again (see cat. no. 86).

During the Hōgen rebellion (1156), Yoshitomo had been supported by Taira no Kiyomori, who, as a result of their victory, then rose in the court ranks and began scheming to have Taira females chosen as consorts to the future emperors. Traditionally the Fujiwara clan had provided heirs to the throne.

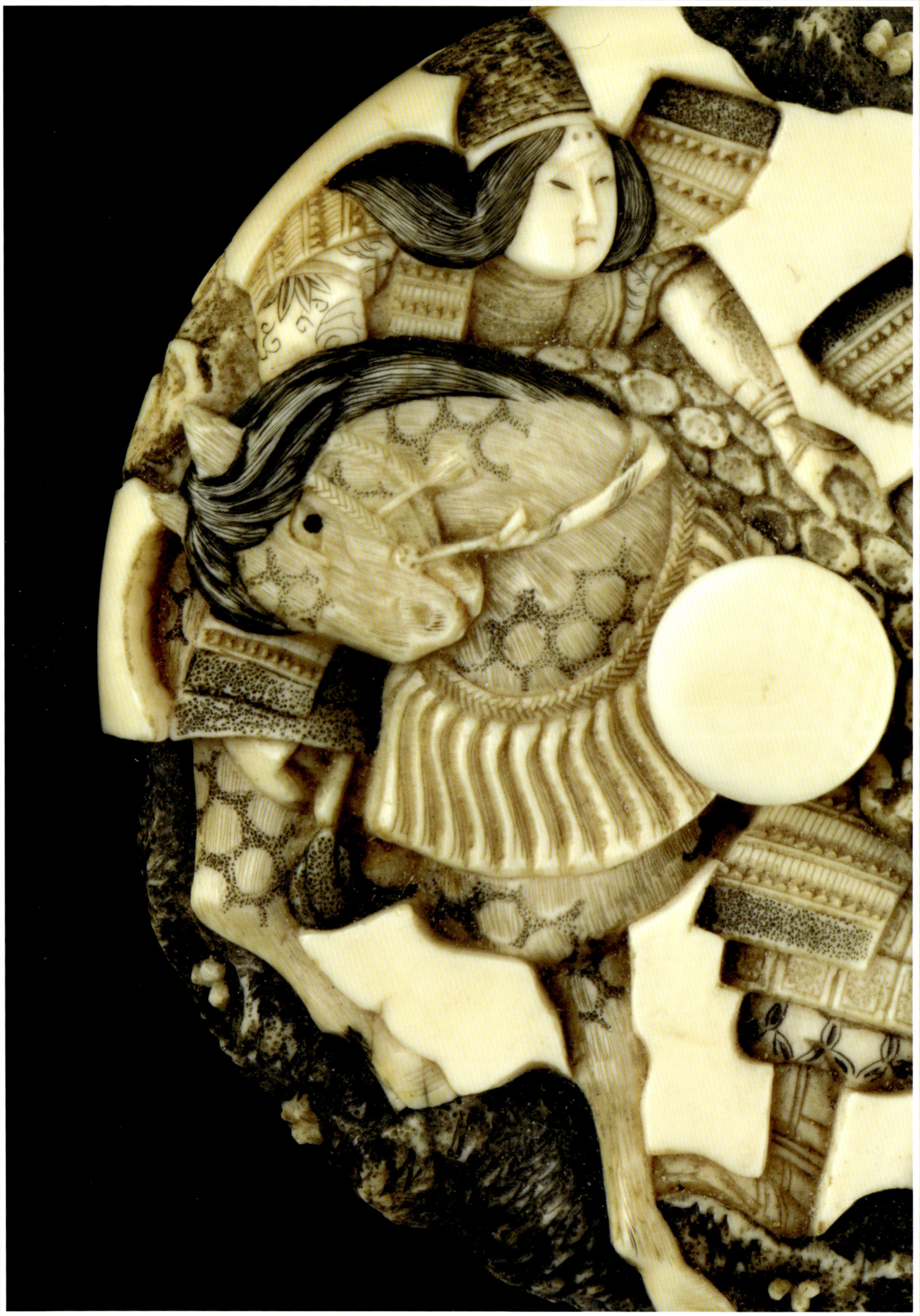

The next struggle between the Minamoto and Taira clans took place in 1160 and was known as the Heiji Insurrection, resulting in triumph for the Taira, and Kiyomori in particular. Many Minamoto were executed, including four sons of Tameyoshi. Yoritomo who had fought with his father was exiled to Izu (cat. no. 89) and the remaining three, who were very small boys, were rushed from Kyoto and into hiding by their mother, the beautiful Tokiwa Gozen. The youngest of these, still a babe in arms, was Yoshitsune, who grew to become the most famous warrior in the history of Japan.

Taira no Kiyomori was determined to find these boys and murder them, so captured Tokiwa Gozen's mother. When word reached Tokiwa that Kiyomori was torturing her mother she courageously surrendered to the tyrant. However, when he set eyes on this beautiful mother, he melted and relented on condition that Tokiwa become his mistress. To this she consented and all three boys' lives were saved. Kiyomori insisted that the two older ones should go to be educated in temples. At the age of seven, Yoshitsune, known in childhood as Ushiwakamaru, was also dispatched to a temple on Mount Kurama. It was here that he learned martial arts from the King of the *tengu*, Sōjōbō (cat. nos. 91 and 92).

Another hero who features in this collection is Minamoto no Yoshitsune's faithful companion, the warrior monk Benkei (cat. nos. 94, 95 and 96). From a very early age he was a difficult child but one of unnaturally mature physique. As a result he was given the name Oniwakamaru or 'young devil child'. He too was sent away from home to be disciplined by priests at an early age. He moved to three different temples before he finally resigned to become an independent warrior monk (*yamabushi*). At this time he gave himself the name Musashibō Benkei.

Opposite: Cat. no. 89 (detail)

83

Warrior

Verso: Samurai helmet

Ivory and dark staining
Unsigned
Early to mid-19th century
Diam: 4.7; H: 1.35 cm
EA2001.132
Bequeathed by Dr Monica Barnett

Before he dons his helmet and charges into battle, this samurai is testing the sharpness of his blade, something which could make the difference between life and death.

For the Japanese warrior, the sword was not just a functional object, it had spiritual significance. With an edge sharp enough to cut through armour, flesh and bone, it was a symbol of authority and of samurai rule. There are ancient blades, kept in Shintō shrines, which are thought to be manifestations of the gods (*kami*). It embodied the spirit of the samurai, many of whose lives were taken by the sword in battle. Made of a combination of different types of steel, each blade displays a unique pattern (*hamon*) along the cutting edge. The sword is as prized as a work of art as it is as a deadly weapon.

Loyalty to one's master was one of the most valued virtues in medieval Japan. The samurai code of ethics demanded wisdom, courage, benevolence, disdain for one's own life, impassivity under duress and maintenance of personal honour, but above all loyalty.

This netsuke shows signs of wear: the intricate patterns on the samurai's armour, carved in such detail, have been worn down in several places by repeated handling.

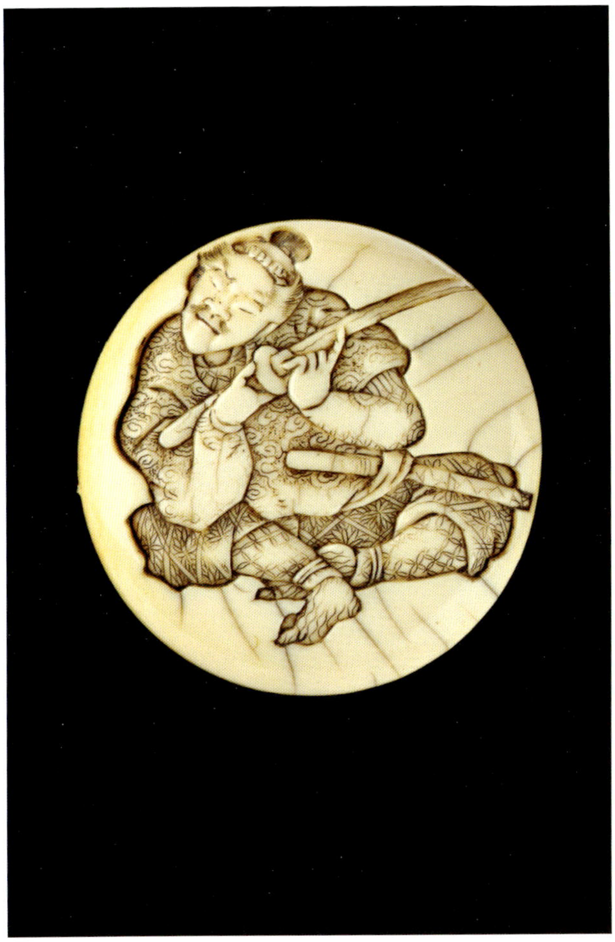

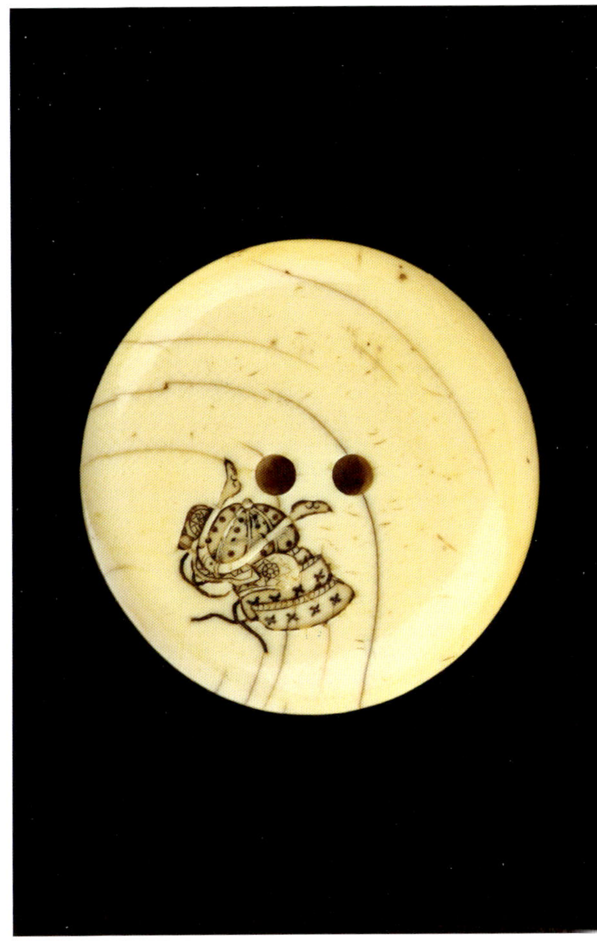

84

Warrior charging through waves

Verso: Waves and an old pine tree

Ivory
Signed: Jōkō 上幸 (unknown artist)
Mid-19th century
Diam: 5.0; H: 2.3 cm
EA2001.46
Bequest of Dr Monica Barnett

Bought 13/11/1970

This warrior, charging through water on horseback, is not part of one of the battles or incidents commonly seen on netsuke. The *maedate* (crest on the front of his helmet) is of a Chinese bellflower (*kikyō*), which was adopted as a *mon* (crest) by warriors around the thirteenth century. It was originally a wild flower which grew in the Yoshino area, near Kyoto, where many battles took place. There are several versions of bellflowers on Japanese *mon*.

This netsuke came to the collection described as Gentoku, the Chinese Emperor, who had a narrow escape from a treacherous relative, achieved by riding his horse down a castle moat wall and into a rushing torrent below.

This beautifully executed scene is by an unidentified artist, who has captured the urgency of the moment in detailed *shishiai-bori* carving with waves lashing about the figures. On the reverse, an old pine tree overhangs the dramatic waves in the ravine.

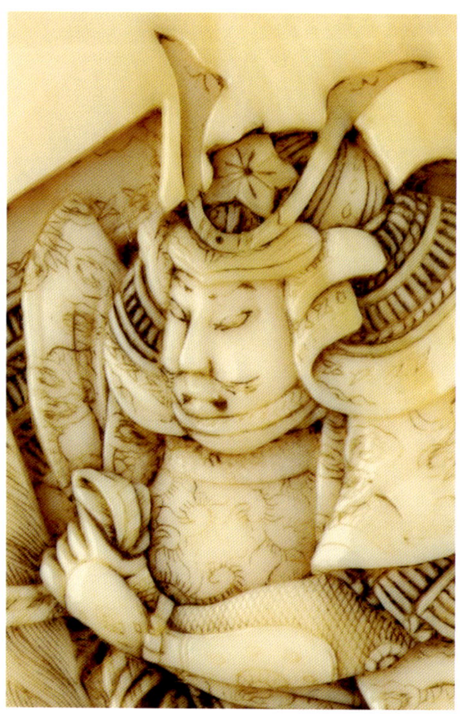

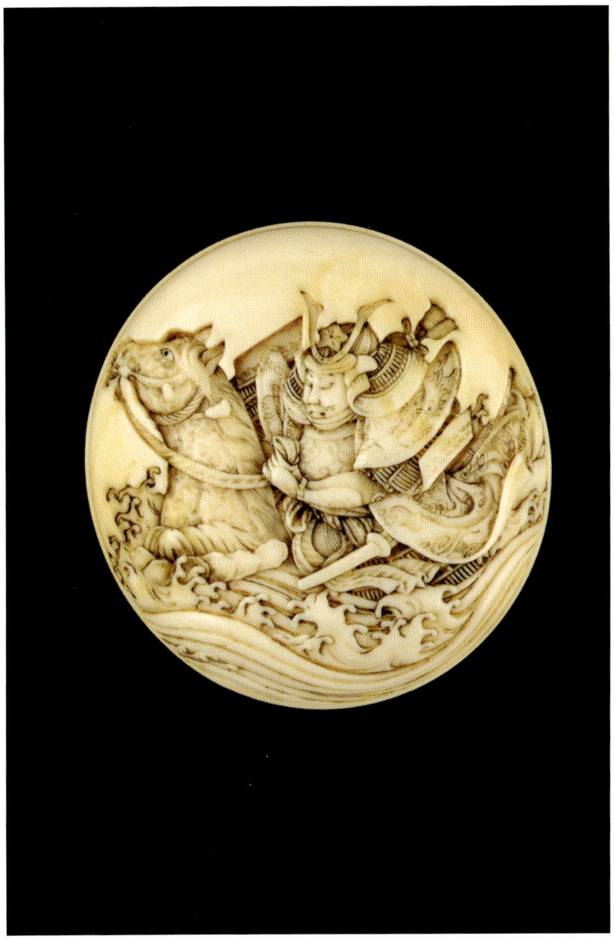

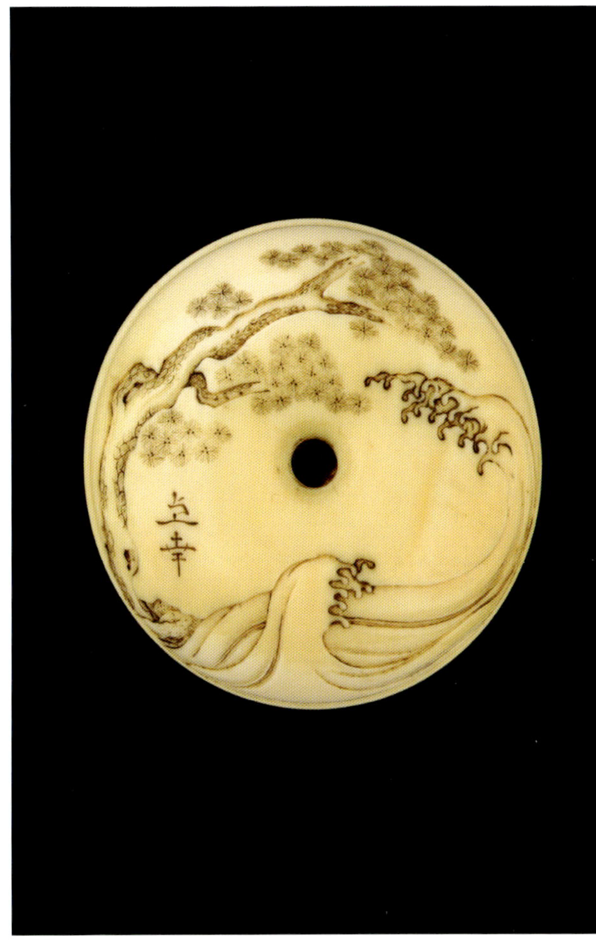

85

Minamoto no Tametomo dressed in armour with one of the 'demons' of Onigashima island

Verso: Taira Mochimitsu's ship

Pressed horn (or cross-linked casein)
Unsigned
1860–1890
H: 3.9; W: 4.4; D: 1.6 cm
EA2001.71
Bequeathed by Dr Monica Barnett

Examples of horn netsuke are common and can be seen in, Ko-ji Hō-ten Plate LX I No. 4, The Baur Collection, Geneva C 364, Henri L. Joly, *Legend in Japanese Art*, opposite p. 358 and Sotheby's, Sussex 14 & 15/10/1986, Lot 1768

Bought from Douglas J. W. Wright 28/02/1979

On this netsuke, one of the inhabitants of Onigashima island (Devil island) tries to pull the string of Tametomo's mighty bow, to no effect.

Minamoto no Tametomo (1139–1170) was the son of Tameyoshi and half-brother of the ruthless Minamoto no Yoshitomo. He was described as a seven-foot-tall giant who had one unusually long and strong arm. With this he wielded a bow of eight and a half feet in length, bringing down many an opposing warrior with deadly accuracy in the military battles that marred his teenage years. In 1156, during the Hōgen Insurrection, supporting the exiled Emperor Sutoku were Tameyoshi and seven of his sons, including Tametomo. Fighting for the Emperor Go Shirakawa was Tameyoshi's eldest son, Yoshitomo. In spite of Tametomo's great courage and skill with his bow, he and his father were on the losing side. Both Tameyoshi and one son, Tadamasa, were captured and Yoshitomo was forced to order the execution of his own father. Tametomo was exiled to the island of Izu Onigashima after his arm was dislocated and the tendons cut to prevent further mischief with his arrows. While in exile, however, the arm recovered.

These two netsuke illustrate Tametomo's final triumph in exile: the sinking of Taira no Mochimitsu's ship with a single arrow. From the shore he can be seen watching the approach of a ship, filled with Taira warriors on their way to capture him. Tametomo aimed his arrow just below the water line, holed the ship and watched it sink and all on board perish. On the back of the *manjū* there is a dramatic view of the ship's bow tilted in the water seconds before the vessel goes down. After this, Tametomo is said to have committed suicide.

As a result of Tametomo's many heroic feats in battle he became a popular figure in literature. Between 1804 and 1811 Takizawa Bakin collaborated with Hokusai to produce '*Chinsetsu yumihari-zuki*' (Strange Tales of the Crescent Moon), a romanticised version of his life which greatly enhanced his appeal. During the 1870s when this type of netsuke was being produced, there was a resurgence of interest in historical heroes. In 1874 Tametomo appeared on a bank note.

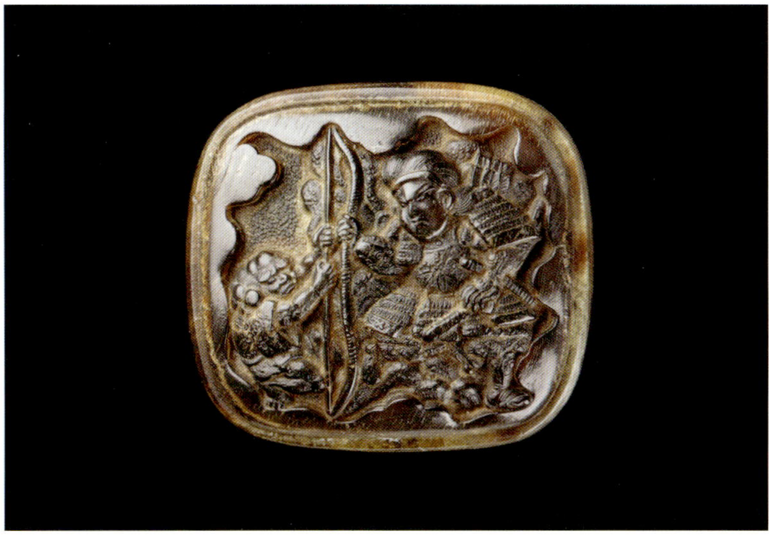

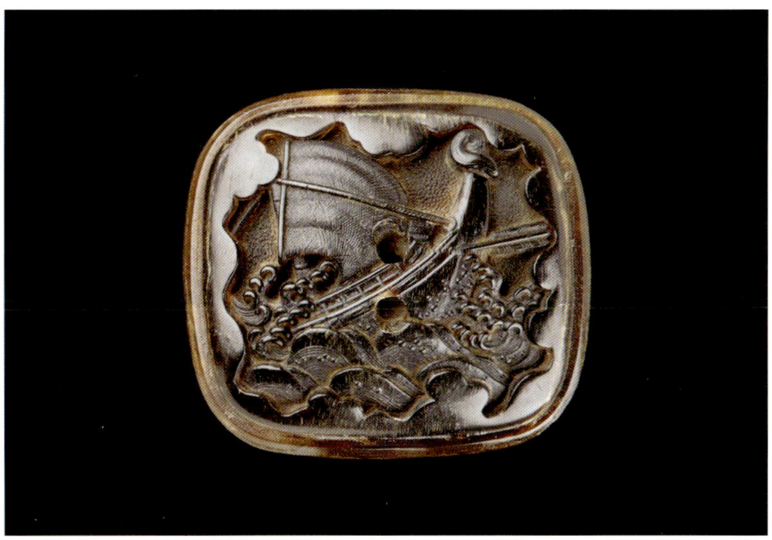

86

Minamoto no Tametomo: Tametomo is sitting on a cliff on Onigashima Island, holding his bow

Verso: Boat full of Taira warriors sailing towards the island

Ivory
Unsigned
19th century
Diam: 4.7; H: 1.9 cm
EA2001.110
Bequeathed by Dr Monica Barnett

Tametomo sits on the cliff in exile, preparing to meet a boat filled with Taira warriors coming to kill him. Greatly outnumbered, he looks pensive and resigned to his fate.

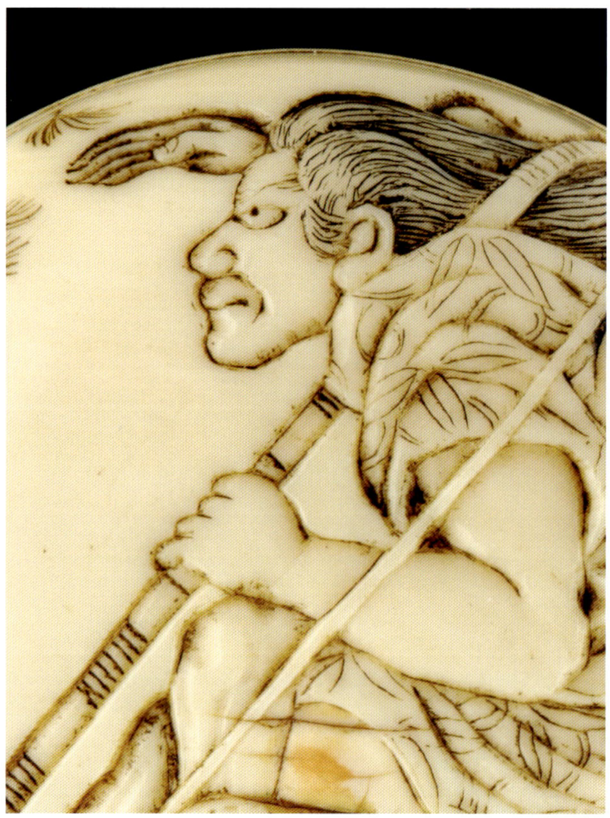

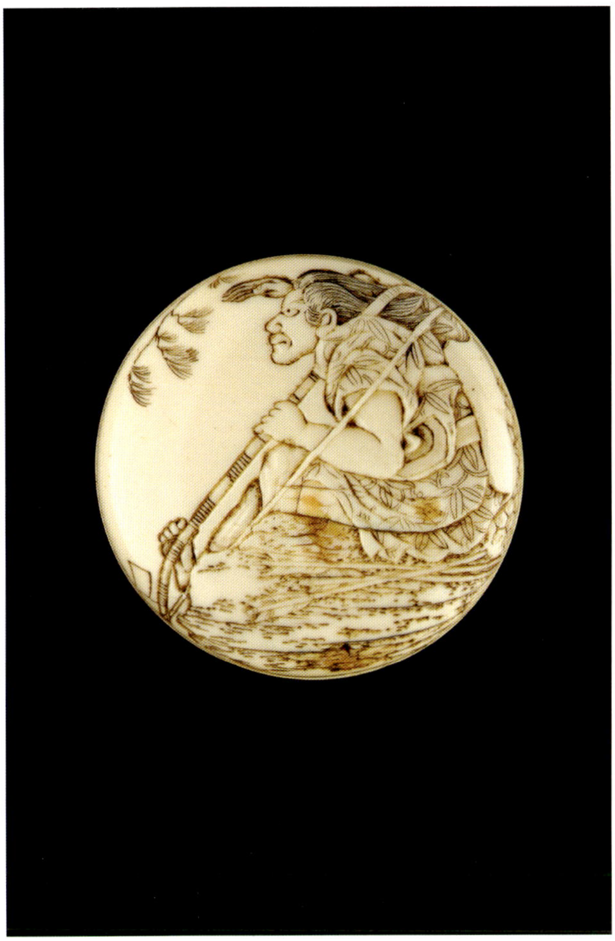

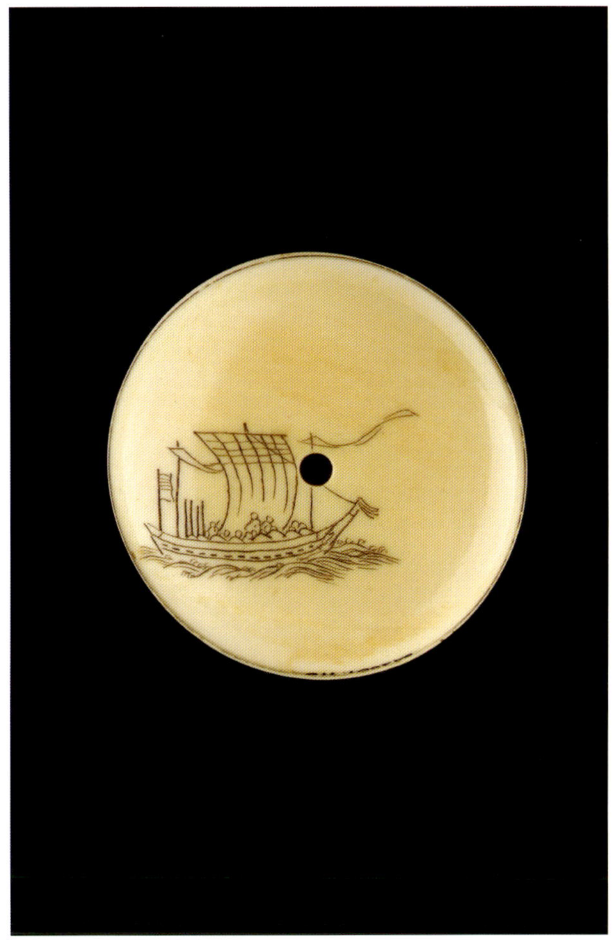

87

Tomoe Gozen and Wada Yoshimori

Verso: Pine branches and rocks

Ivory with heavy black staining
Signed: Baieisai 煤叡斎 with *kakihan*
19th century
Diam: 6.4; H: 2.2 cm
EA2001.67
Bequeathed by Dr Monica Barnett

Sold at Sotheby's 24/07/1985. Lot 41. 'Jushusai(?)'

'Tomoe was especially beautiful, with white skin, long hair, and charming features. She was also a remarkably strong archer, and as a swordswoman she was a warrior worth a thousand, ready to confront a demon or a god, mounted or on foot. She handled unbroken horses with superb skill; she rode unscathed down perilous descents. Whenever a battle was imminent, Yoshinaka sent her out as his first captain, equipped with strong armor, an oversized sword, and a mighty bow; and she performed more deeds of valor than any of his other warriors'.[71]

Tomoe Gozen was the lover of Kiso no Yoshinaka (1154–1184), and together they fought in the Genpei wars (1180–1185). After Yoshinaka's mounted warriors were reduced to five from the original three hundred, he prepared to die. He ordered Tomoe Gozen to leave him as he was ashamed to die in front her. She carried on bravely fighting for the cause despite her lover's demise.

The moment captured on this *manjū* takes place at the battle of the Uji River, in 1184 just after Tomoe Gozen, mounted on her dapple grey horse, had fought and dispatched no fewer than three other warriors. She then took on Wada no Yoshimori who attacked her with a pine tree, which somehow she grabbed and snapped in two. She was, however, captured by Wada whom legend says she later married, and bore his son, the strongman Asahina Saburō. Wada did not live to see the boy and some accounts say that Tomoe Gozen then retired to a convent in Echigo to see out her days.

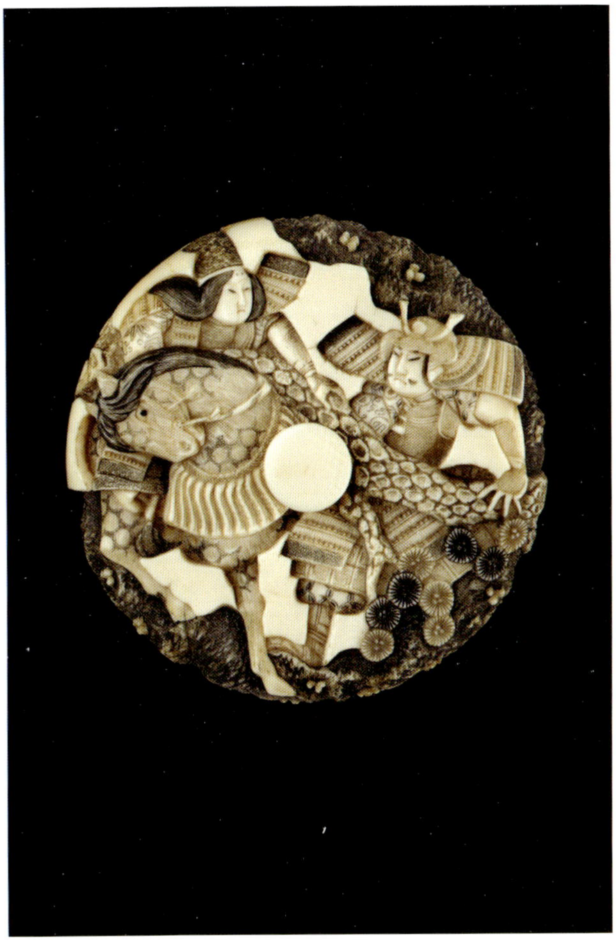

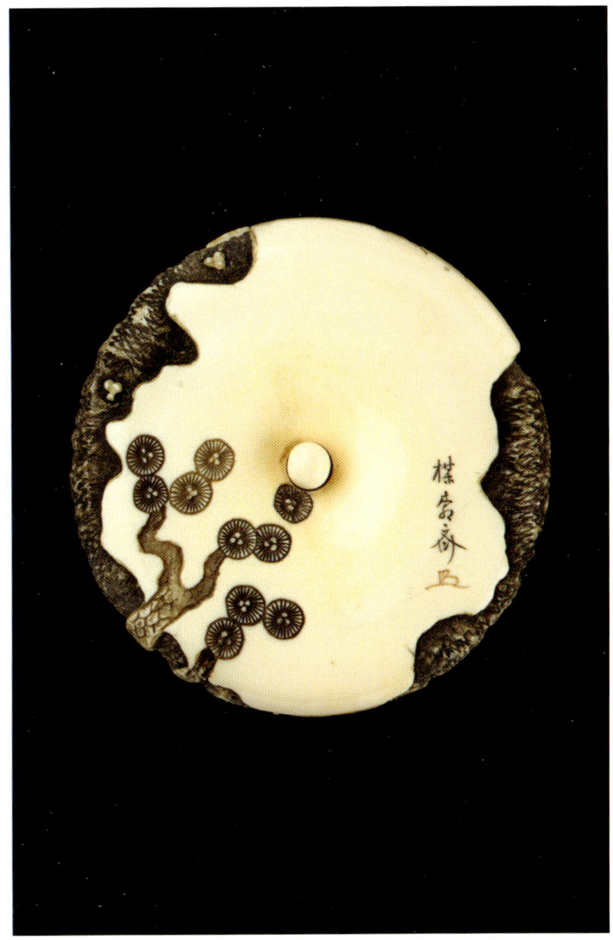

88

Sasaki Takatsuna and Kajiwara Kagesue crossing the Uji River

Verso: swimming with shield through a hail of arrows

Ivory
Signed: Ichiyūsai 一遊斎 (Naomitsu) with later red seal reading Tomochika 友親
Late 19th century
Diam: 5.2; H: 2.4 cm
EA2001.82
Bequeathed by Dr Monica Barnett

Illustrated in:
Wilhelm, G. *Manjū exégèse et appréciation*. Bulletin Association Franco-Japonaise. No. 54. Octobre, 1996. Fig. MB5 'a l'attaque'

For a similar piece by Ichiyūsai see Sotheby's *The Carlo Monzino Collection of Netsuke, Inro and Lacquer The Property of a Private Trust*, London 21/06/1995. Lot 275

See Sotheby's, London 17–19/07/1984. Lot 157 (which could be the Ashmolean's example).

Ueda Reikichi. *The Netsuke Handbook*. No. 14, p. 33 shows a further example, within a solid ivory frame but does not mention a signature.

Koryūsai Naokazu used this design on a *manjū* (Eskenazi October/November 1984 No. 10) and Ichiyūsai Naoharu also used it on an ivory *inrō*, which is illustrated in *International Netsuke Collectors Society*. Vol. 1, No. 3. p. 38

In this famous scene from the battle of Uji River in 1184, two mounted warriors, Sasaki Takatsuna and Kajiwara Kagesue were called upon by Minamoto no Yoritomo, to find a place to ford the Uji River. The enemy, Yoshinaka, had ordered his men to break down the bridges at Uji and Seta to prevent them crossing. The two warriors, Takatsuna and Kagesue, each keen to earn favour with their master by reaching the opposite bank first, raced to the river's edge: 'the two were galloping together in seeming companionship, but in reality they were racing each other to gain the lead'.[72] Kagesue was ahead at first, but the clever Takatsuna shouted to him to tighten his girth before entering the water. Kagesue slowed down to make the adjustment, which enabled Takatsuna to take the lead. Seeing that he had been tricked, Kagesue attempted to slow Takatsuna down. 'At the bottom of this river lies a net of ropes. Watch out!'[73] he shouted. But Takatsuna simply slashed the ropes with his sword and his horse, Ikezuki, pushed ahead and reached the opposite bank first, while Kagesue's horse, Surusumi, was swept further down the snow-swollen river. On the reverse of this netsuke is a warrior, his helmet gone, swimming for his life under a hail of arrows.

The image is very similar to the central panel of a triptych by Utagawa Kuniyoshi dated 1849–1853 depicting the fording of the Uji River and showing the three warriors, Hatakeyama Shigetada, Sasaki Shirō Takatsuna and Kajiwara Genda Kagesue.

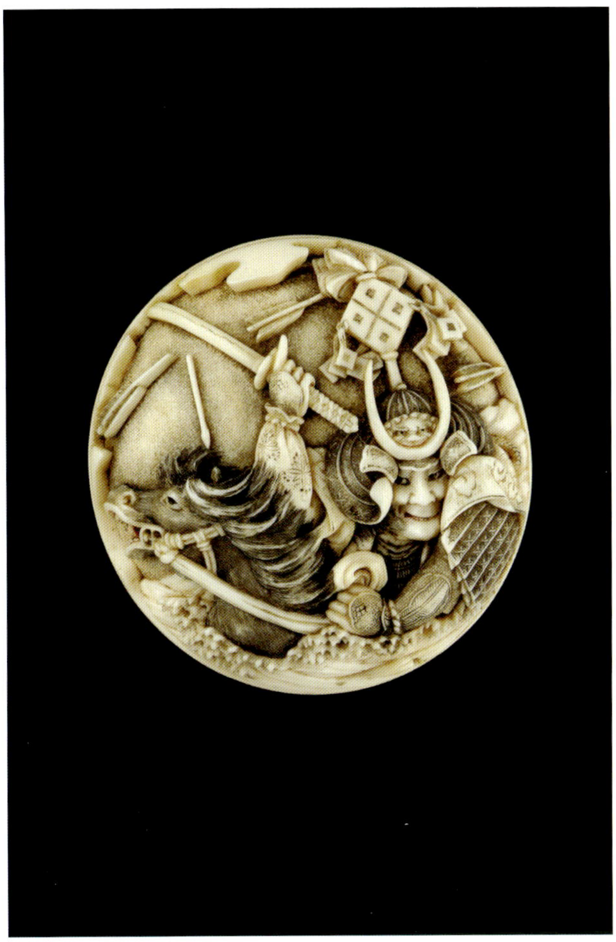

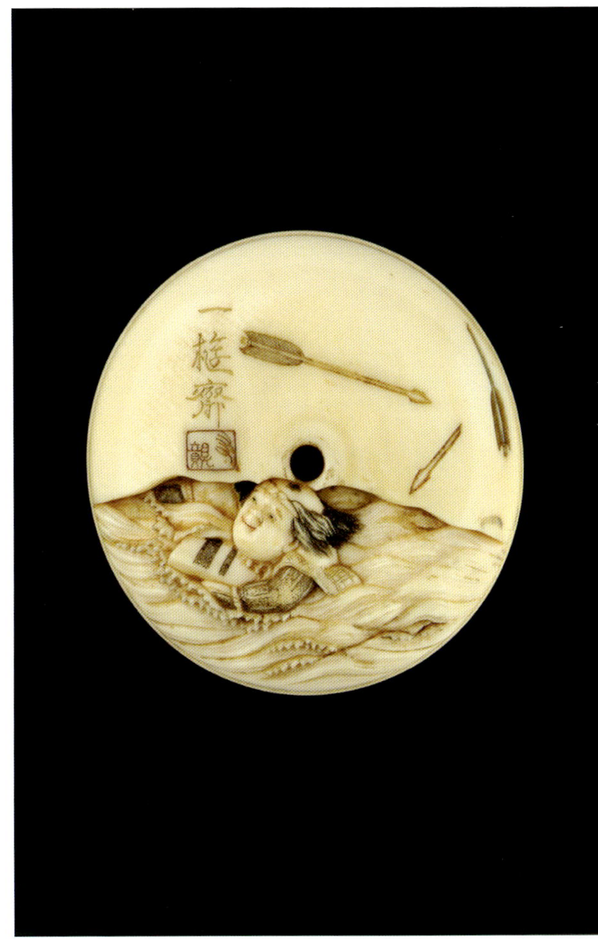
一梃齋

89

Hōjō no Tokimasa meeting Benten, disguised as a dragon

Verso: Dragon's tail disappearing above mountains in the foreground

Ivory
Signed: Kōsai Juō 光斎寿翁 with *kakihan*
Mid-19th century
Diam: 5.6; H: 1.9 cm
EA2001.112
Bequeathed by Dr Monica Barnett

Hōjō no Tokimasa (1138–1215) was a powerful warrior during the turbulent times at the end of the twelfth century. After the tyrant Taira no Kiyomori's triumph in the Heiji rebellion, he wanted the young Minamoto no Yoritomo's head. The young man had been put in the care of Itō Suechika, a member of the Taira clan, but Yoritomo had overstepped the mark in his guardian's eyes, when at the age of fourteen he fathered a child. Hōjo no Tokimasa, who was also of Taira descent, was then put in charge of the young man. Yoritomo went to stay with Tokimasa, fell in love with one of his host's daughters, and married her, eventually making Tokimasa the father-in-law of the first Minamoto shōgun.

Way back in the mists of time, on the Izu peninsula, it was said that the goddess Benten had subdued a dragon that was devastating the island of Enoshima, by playing sweet music on her *biwa* (a plucked stringed instrument). In gratitude, the islanders built a shrine dedicated to Benten near the beach and it is there where this story takes place.

Hōjō no Tokimasa went one day to the shrine to pray to Benten for the protection of his household and to his great surprise, the goddess in her serpentine form appeared to him – the moment Kōsai Juō has chosen to capture on this *manjū*. She consented to his request on condition that he refrain from unjust deeds, of which he was responsible for a large number. Otherwise, she indicated, his family would not live beyond the sixth generation. After a while she returned to the sea, leaving behind on the beach three scales from her tail. These three scales were then formed into the Hōjō family crest (fig. 60).

Fig. 60 Image from *Iroha-biki monchō* (EA2012.168) of Hōjō family crest

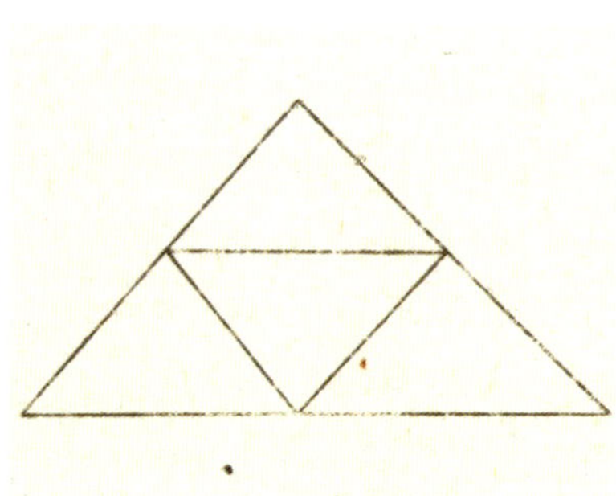

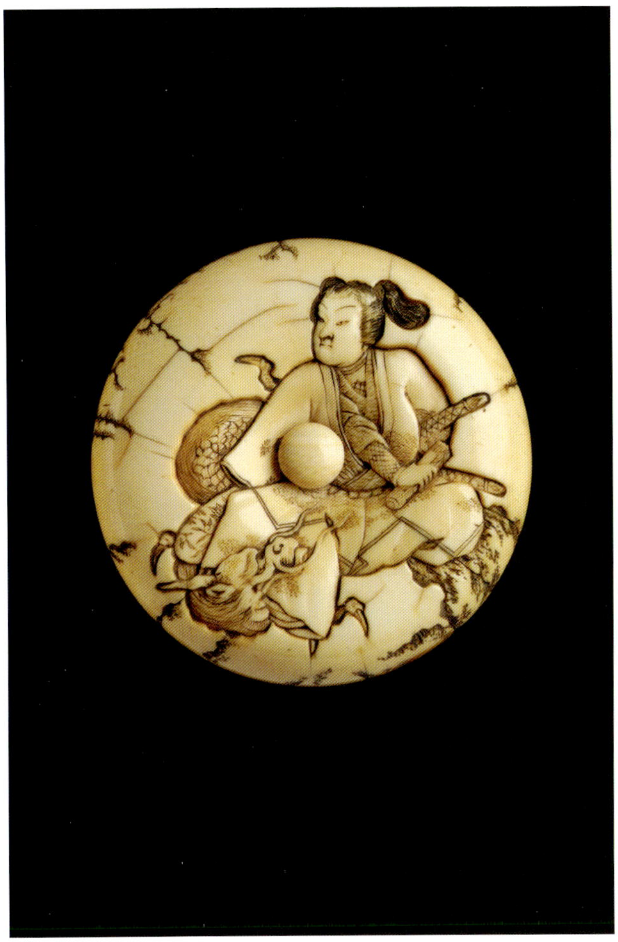

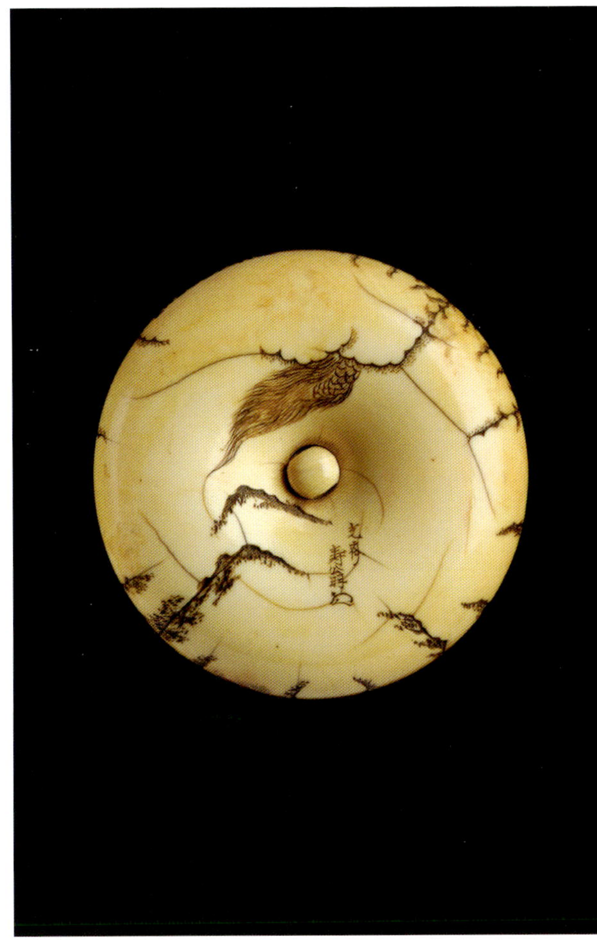

90

Satō Tadanobu fighting with the *gō* board

Verso: a slain warrior amongst scattered *gō* pieces

Ivory with red and black staining
Signed: Kōsai 光斎 with crane *kakihan*
19th century
Diam: 5.7; H: 2.3 cm
EA2001.69
Bequeathed by Dr Monica Barnett

For a dynamic rendering of this subject, by Kōgyokusai with crane *kakihan*, see Netsuke Kenkyukai, Vol. 11 No. 3, Fall 1991 Fig 11 a & b: an article by Denis Szeszler entitled *'Manju and Kagamibuta. A Look at the Valuable Qualities in These Seldom Appreciated Types of Netsuke'*.

Bought from Eskenazi 07/12/1977

Satō Tadanobu (1160–1187), was an immensely courageous retainer of Minamoto no Yoshitsune. Following a battle involving the monks of the Yoshino area in Kyoto who supported Yoshitsune's brother, Yoritomo, Yoshitsune and Tadanobu were forced to go into hiding. Tadanobu sought out his ex-lover, Koshiba Oguruma. She welcomed him and looked after him for a few days, but she had by then taken another lover, Kajiwara no Kagehisa, who was from the opposing side and whose prospects she thought were more hopeful. Unbeknownst to Tadanobu the woman betrayed his whereabouts to Kagehisa, who was at the time searching for Yoshitsune. Kagehisa secretly admired Tadanobu for his immense bravery and reproached Koshiba Oguruma for her treachery. Kagehisa thought that out of loyalty to her ex-lover she should at least help him to escape. She took no notice and promptly reported Tadanobu's whereabouts to higher authorities, which resulted in Kagehisa being ordered to arrest him. Two hundred men broke into the house where Tadanobu lay asleep. He had no weapon, for the treacherous Koshiba had tied his swords to the outside of their scabbards rendering them useless. In the heat of the moment Tadanobu seized a *gō* board to defend himself. Having knocked a number of the invaders down, he turned upon Koshiba Oguruma and killed her. Finding himself outnumbered Tadanobu fell upon his sword. He was only twenty-seven years old.

A passage in the story of Yoshitsune, *Gigeiki* sums up what Tadanobu was thinking. 'Nothing is so loathsome to contemplate, so distressing and irrational, as feminine love, which passes into nothingness more rapidly than a streak of lightning, a may-fly, or a snowflake on the water.' [74]

This version of the story possibly comes from a Bunraku play, first performed in the puppet theatre in 1680, called *Gōban Tadanobu* (Gō-board Tadanobu). In the original story in *Gigeiki* (The Chronicle of Yoshitsune) the *gō* board is not mentioned.

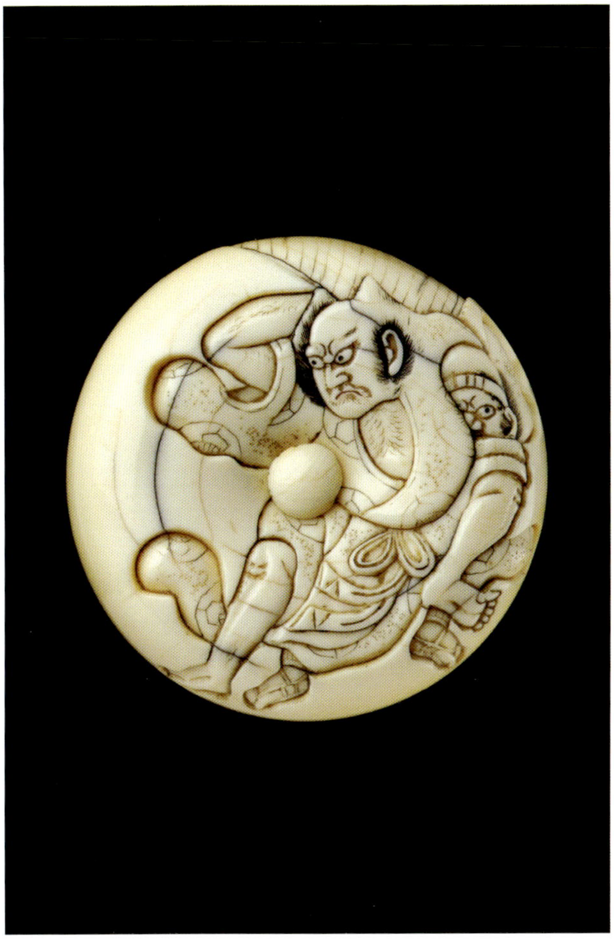

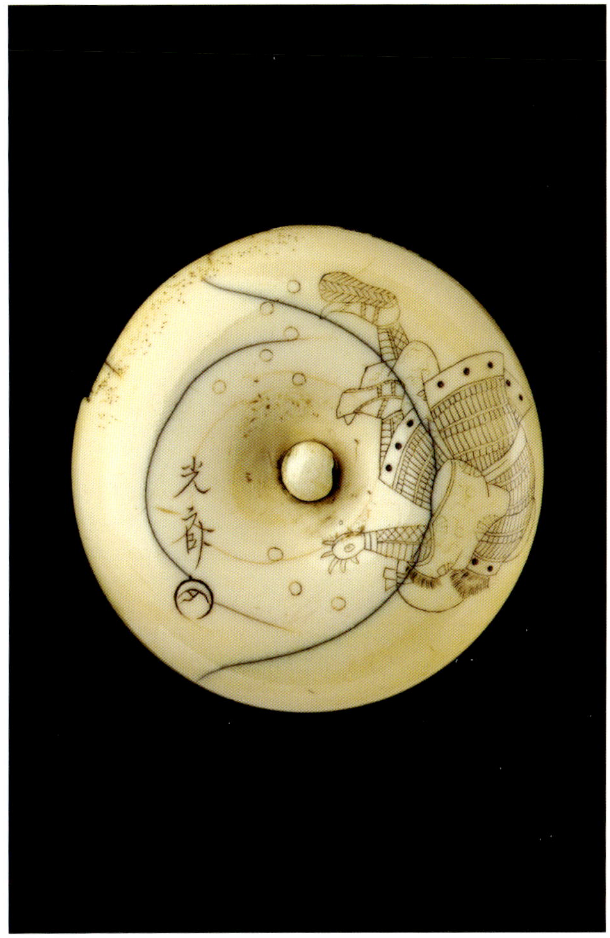

91

Minamoto no Yoshitsune learning winged combat from a *tengu*

Verso: Winged *tengu* escaping

Ivory with black and red staining
Signed: Kōsai Moritoshi 光斎守寿 with crane *kakihan*
19th century
Diam: 5.8; H: 2.25cm
EA2001.108
Bequeathed by Dr Monica Barnett

Sold to Eskenazi by Sotheby's, London on 09/05/1973. Lot 97, Plate V
Sold again at Sotheby's on 20–21/06/1988. Lot 102

This subject returns to the hero, Minamoto no Yoshitsune who, as a young boy, was known as Ushiwakamaru. By the age of eleven he was determined to take revenge on those who had killed his father, Minamoto no Yoshitomo. He went to Mount Kurama where he had lived as a young boy. There he took lessons in martial arts from the *tengu*, mountain dwelling creatures who were half-human, half-bird and whose skills in unarmed combat were legendary.

In this dynamic scene the young hero is learning fast and during a mock battle has managed to throw his opponent, a *tengu*, to the ground; on the reverse is another *tengu* apparently running away. The bamboo decorating Ushiwakamaru's robe was the emblem of the Minamoto clan.

Tengu of two types appear in Japanese art, one with a very long nose and the other, the *karasu tengu*, which has a beak and claws like that of a crow (*karasu*). One identifying feature of both is a feathered fan, seen on the side of this piece, and a small black pill-box hat, worn by the *yamabushi*, who are hermit priests of the Shingon sect to which the *tengu* belong. This training was to stand Yoshitsune in good stead when he came up against Benkei in the famous skirmish on the Gojō Bridge (cat. no. 96).

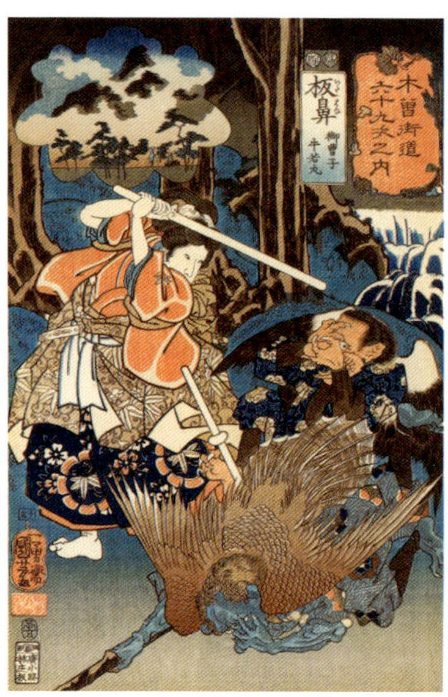

Fig. 61 Yoshitsune fighting *tengu*. Colour woodblock print by Utagawa Kuniyoshi (1797–1862) (EA1971.92)

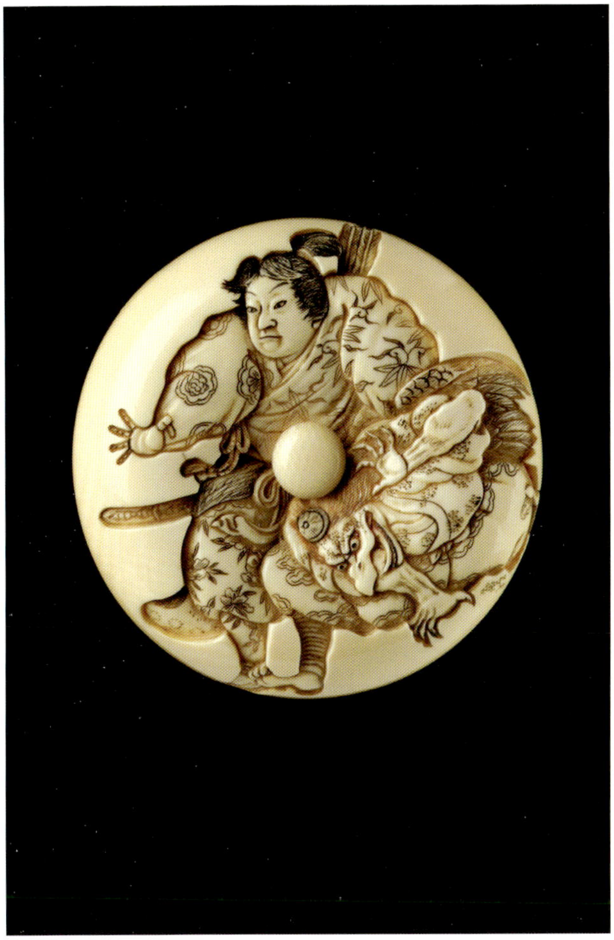

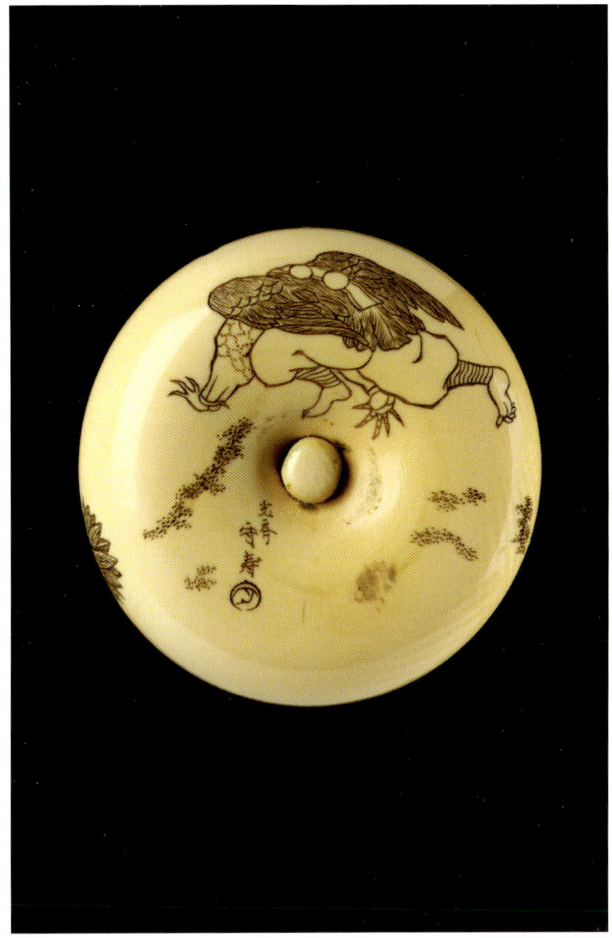

92

Long-nosed *tengu*

Ivory
Inscribed character 翁 reads Okina
Late 19th century
Diam: 5.21; H: 1.56 cm
EAX.1343
Oppenhiem gift

This damaged piece is included to illustrate a long-nosed *tengu*, who is sitting in a pine forest wearing the small pill-box hat and holding a five-part feathered war fan in his hand (Sōjōbō, the King of the *Tengu* has a seven-part feathered fan). Great feats in the martial arts were attributed to these imaginary beings, who taught Minamoto no Yoshitsune (cat. no. 91) invaluable skills and tactics to use in combat in the future.

This *manjū* was a collaboration between a metalworker and an ivory carver, but unfortunately the metal insert is now missing.

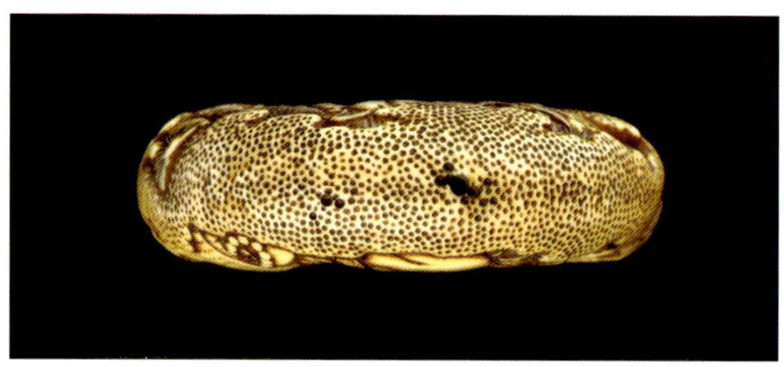

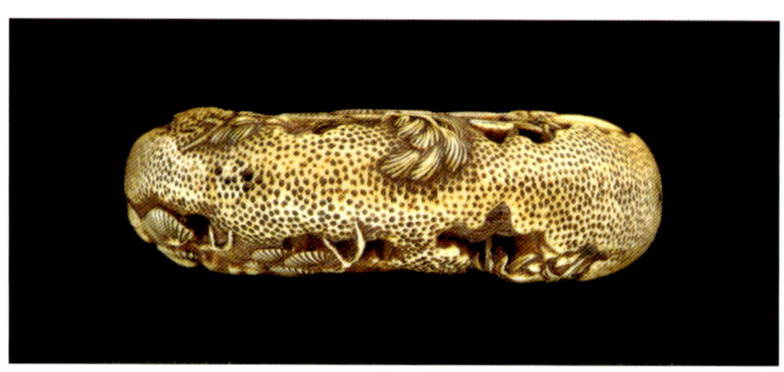

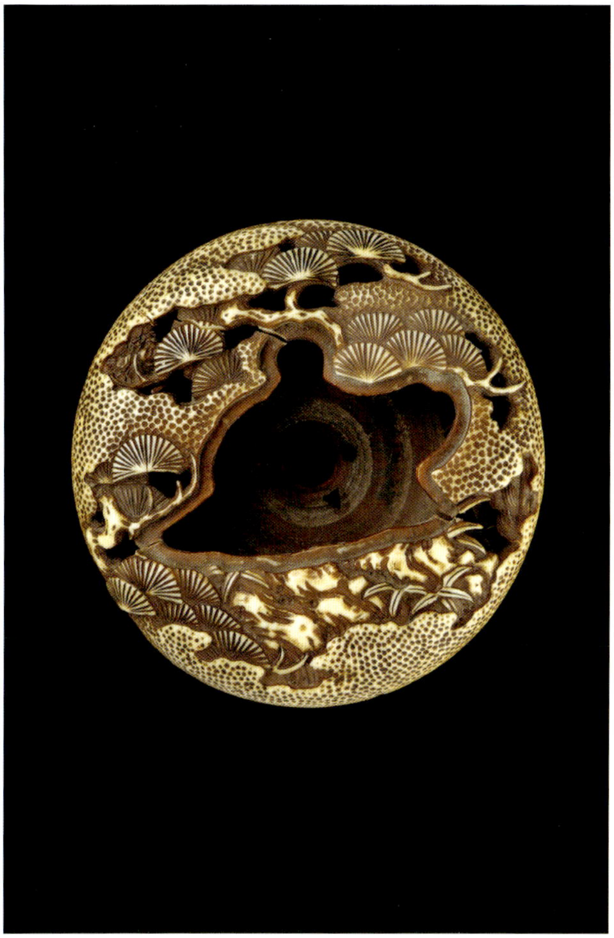

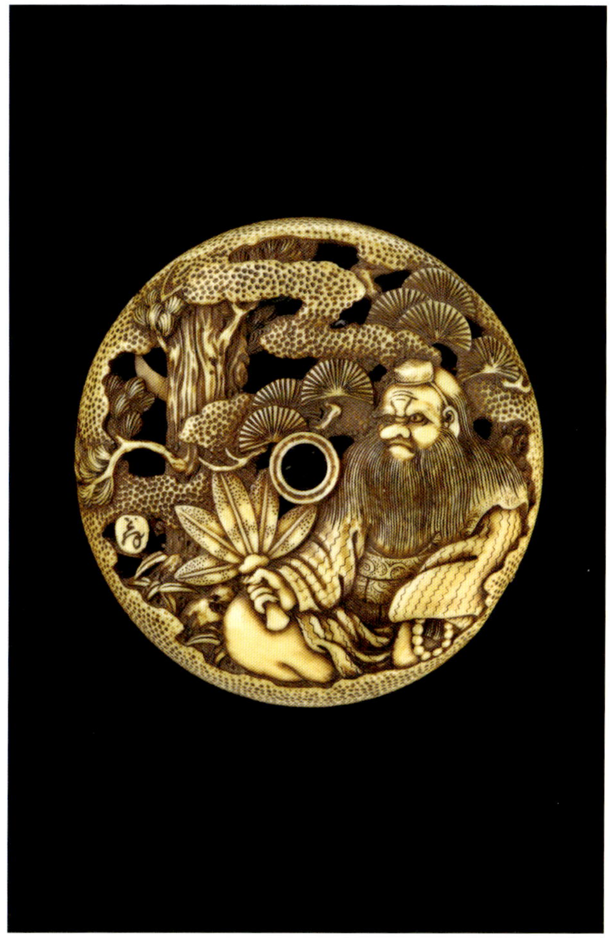

93

The drum known as Hatsune: *Karako* playing a trumpet with a drum slung on his back

Verso: Oni and fox masks and two drum sticks

Walrus Ivory with red and black staining
Signed: Ittokusai 一徳齋
19th century
Diam: 5.1; H: 2.7 cm
EA2001.49
Bequeathed by Dr Monica Barnett

For a similar piece by Ittokusai of the same subject, see Sotheby's, London 07 & 08/04/1998. Lot 613.

Bought from Crichton 20/05/1971

In the Edo period Japanese children dressed in Chinese children's clothing (*karako*) accompanied certain festival processions playing trumpets, flutes or drums. The music of the flute and drum is credited with supernatural power, for the gods were also said to play these instruments.

The fox mask and drum sticks on the back of this *manjū* reveal the meaning of this netsuke which refers to the play *Yoshitsune Senbon Zakura*, and involves the hero Yoshitsune, further stories of whom are shown in cat. nos. 91 and 96.

A drum, known as *Hatsune,* that has been kept in the imperial family for a thousand years, is given to Yoshitsune by the retired emperor. Yoshitsune is being hunted by his brother and rival Yoritomo and is fleeing accompanied by one of his trusted retainers, Tadanobu. His beautiful mistress, Shizuka, begs to go with the men, but she is told that she cannot accompany them. She resists so strongly that they are forced to tie her to a tree, while they get away. Yoshitsune gives her the precious *Hatsune* drum to appease her. Shortly after they leave Tadanobu appears and releases her and the two of them set off for Yoshino, famous for its flowering cherry trees. There they meet up with Yoshitsune, who is also accompanied by a man, also calling himself Tadanobu. When the two men called Tadanobu meet, Shizuka's companion is forced to reveal that he is in fact a *kitsune* (a shape-changing fox), who has lived for hundreds of years wanting to get close to the drum as it was made from the skins of his parents. He has never gained the respect of other *kitsune* as he has been unable to carry out his proper filial duties. The fox apologises that he has caused so much trouble. He is about to depart in shame when Yoshitsune presents him with the drum. As he skips off he hears the voices of his parents warning of an imminent attack on Yoshitsune. He is then able to use his magical powers to rout the attack and disaster is averted.

Every year, on the first Day of the Horse in February, at shrines dedicated to the fox-god *Inari*, fox masks are sold, fried bean curd

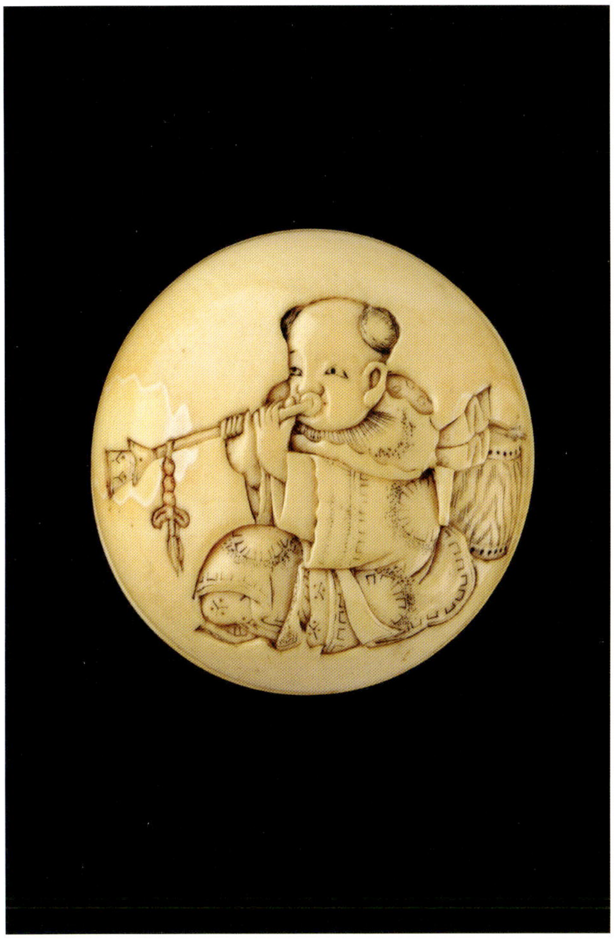

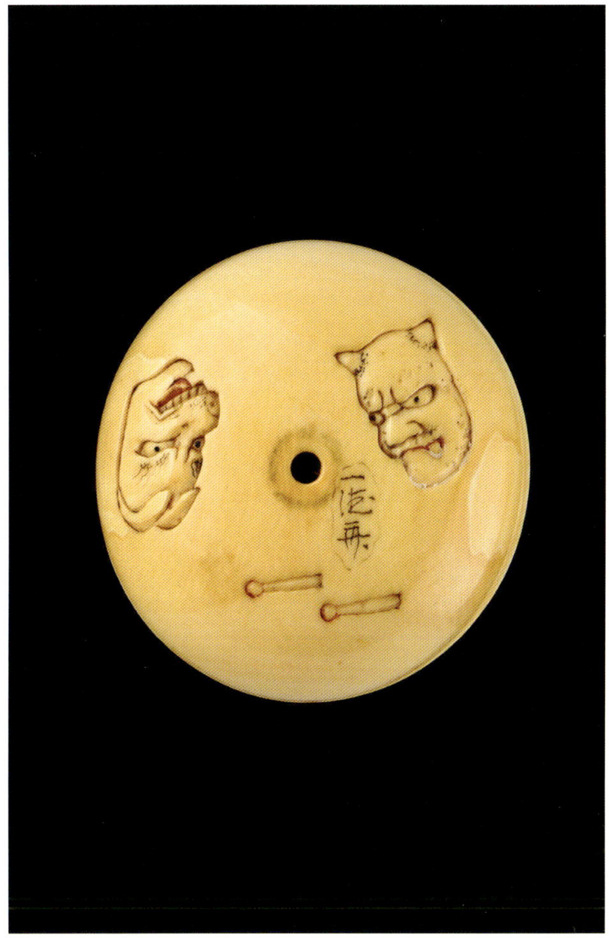

is offered to the two fox guardians of the shrines and a drum is beaten all day to keep the god *Inari* listening to supplications for an abundant rice harvest.

Ittokusai's work seems to have been exclusively carefully carved circular and square *manjū*, signed in very 'spiky' characters, sometimes enclosed in a wavy-lined cartouche.

94

Benkei killing a giant carp

Verso: Two peacock feathers and an unfurled scroll

Ivory with silver and black lacquer or horn inlay for the eye
Signed: Kikugawa *saku* 菊川作 (made by Kikugawa)
Circa 1800
Diam: 5.4; H: 2.21 cm
EA2001.42
Bequeathed by Dr Monica Barnett

This design occurs on many pieces made in the Kikugawa workshop.

See Neil K. Davey. *Netsuke. A comprehensive study based on the M.T. Hindson collection.* Faber & Faber Limited. London, in association with Sotheby Parke Bernet Publications. 1974. p. 136
F.M. Jonas. *Netsuké* (Pl. XIII, Fig. 31) for a more elaborate version by Kikugawa Masamitsu, the founder of the school.
Neil K. Davey and Susan G. Tripp. *The Garrett Collection. Japanese Art. Lacquer, Inrō, Netsuke.* Dauphin Publishing Limited. 1993 No. 135
The Baur Collection, Geneva has two of similar design not published in the catalogue, Nos. 234 and 159

See Sotheby's, 20/02/1986. Lot 23 for a large one (7.3cm) by Masatsugu
Bought from Spink & Son 19/08/1970

This subject, popular with netsuke carvers and print designers, shows Oniwaka (the young Benkei), wrestling with and killing a giant carp with his knife. The incident took place at a waterfall called Bishamon. After killing the carp he is supposed to have found in its stomach the partial remains of his mother who had drowned in the stream. Notice the enormous size of his arms, for even as a boy he was far superior in strength to his peers.

The scroll on the reverse of the *manjū* refers to an incident much later in Benkei's life when he was in the service of Minamoto no Yoshitsune. One evening Yoshitsune, Benkei and several others were fleeing from the enemy disguised as *yamabushi,* mountain priests. When they were held up at a roadblock they were asked for identification. Benkei produced a scroll from his sleeve, and proceeded to read out to the guards a plea for donations from the abbot of their temple, all of which he invented on the spot. A donation was duly given but just as they were departing, one of the guards thought he recognised Yoshitsune. Quick as a flash, Benkei chided his master for being so slow and struck him with his staff, something a retainer would under no circumstances do to his master. Witnessing this act, the guard was convinced that these were indeed *yamabushi* and the party escaped to safety.

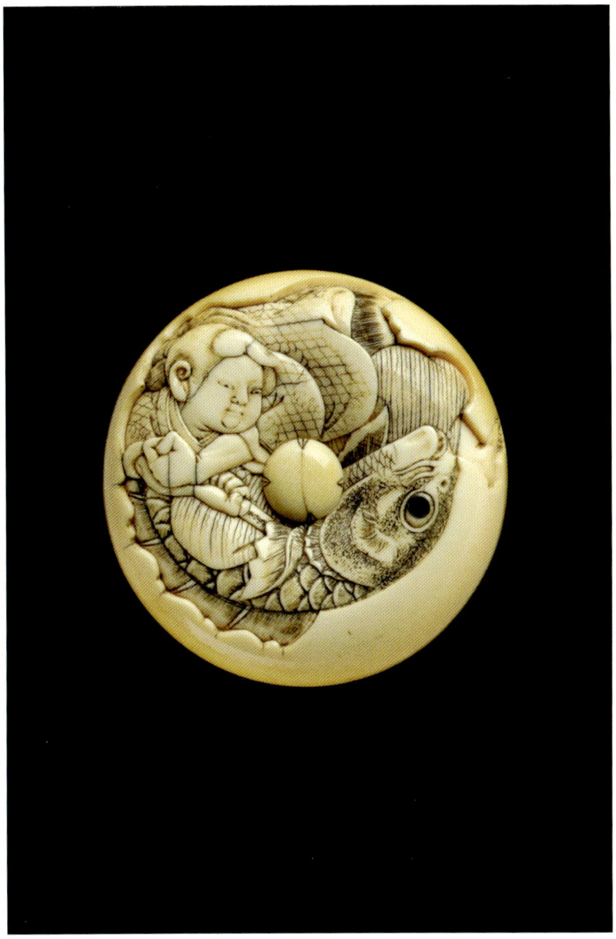

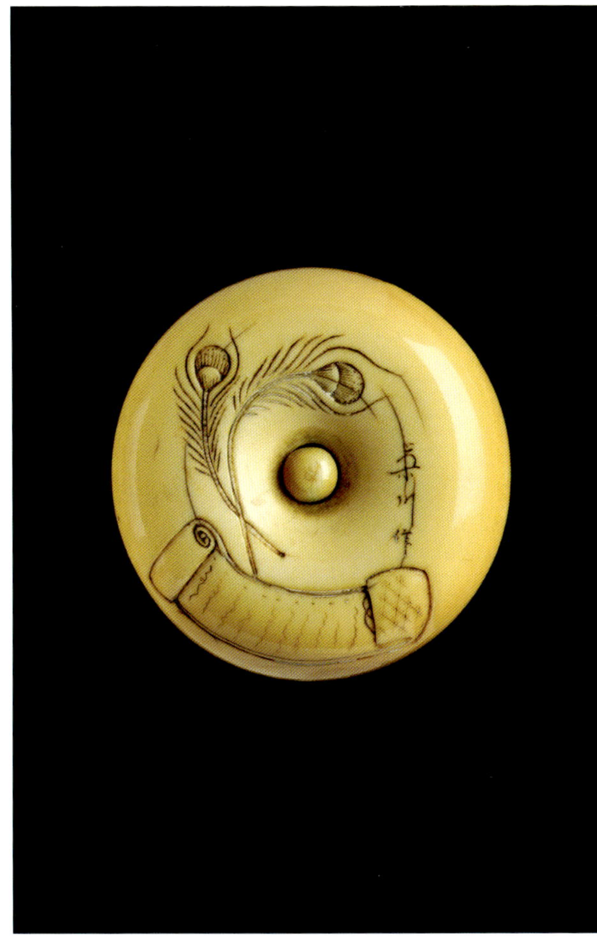

95

Benkei and Tamamushi-hime

Verso: bamboo blind and Benkei's collection of rustic weapons bound together

Ivory with dark brown and red staining
Signed: Kōgyokusai 光玉斎 with *kakihan*
19th century
Diam: 5.4; H: 1.9 cm
EA2001.96
Bequeathed by Dr Monica Barnett

While the teenage Benkei was at Enryakuji on Mount Hiei, learning the teachings and practices of the warrior monks there, he was sent to Kyoto on an errand. On the way, he came across a group of brigands, who were assaulting a very beautiful young princess, called Tamamushi-hime. Realising her plight, Benkei intervened, pulling up a pine sapling and beating the men so hard that they fled, leaving him alone with the grateful princess. Following this, Benkei formed a liason with her which in part caused the abbot of Enryakuji to consider expelling him. However, he took matters into his own hands and discharged himself from the monastery and became an independent *yamabushi* calling himself Saitō Musashibō Benkei. The name Musashibō, he took from a monk at Enrakuji who had apparently achieved rebirth at the age of sixty-one after a life of violence spanning forty years. Benkei took the 'Ben' from his father, the abbot Benshō and the 'Kei' from his teacher, Kankei. This *manjū* shows Benkei, dressed in a robe bearing his family crest, sitting with Tamamushi-hime, in front of a bamboo curtain in a moment of privacy.

Kōgyokusai belongs to the group of artists who sign with a 'crane ' *kakihan*, which includes the artist Moritoshi Kōsai.

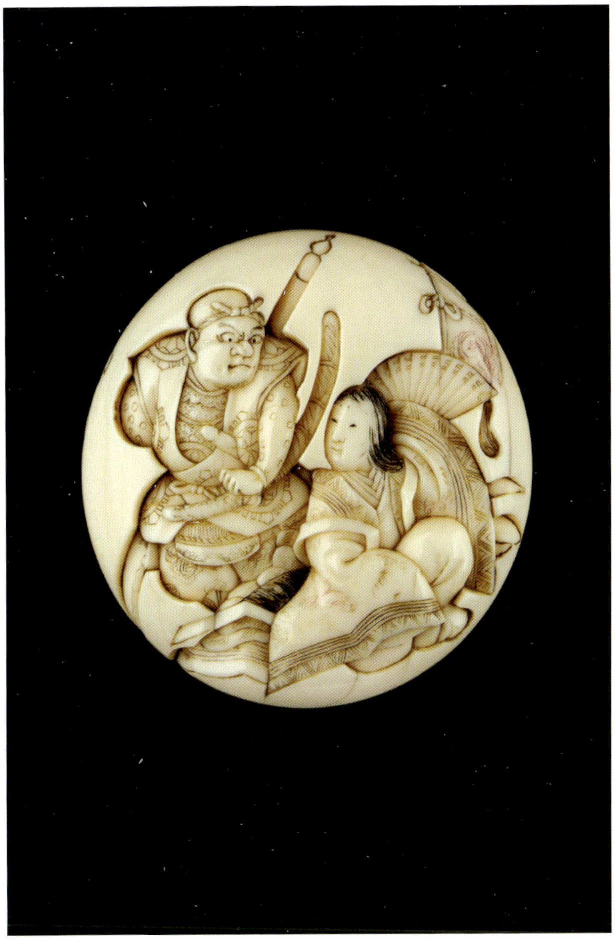

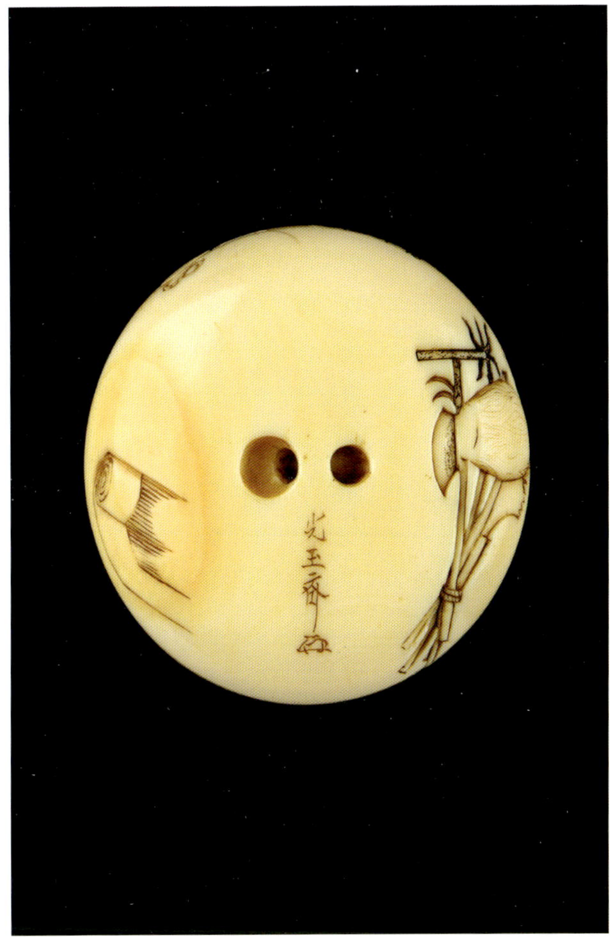

96

Fight on the Gojō bridge: Benkei leaping over Yoshitsune

Verso: Bridge post

Ivory with black and red staining
Signed: Kōhōsai 公鳳齋刻之 *(kore o koku)* engraved this, with a seal reading *Ju (kotobuki)*
Osaka School, 1860s
H: 4.6; W: 5.1; D: 1.7 cm
EA2001.51
Bequeathed by Dr Monica Barnett

The Victoria and Albert Musuem has a square version of this incident, carved in raised relief by Kōhōsai and dated 1869. (A.23-1963)[76]

Bought from Douglas Wright 18/08/1971

At the age of twenty, Benkei went to the swordsmith Kokaji Munenobu to ask if he would make him a suit of armour. The swordsmith pronounced that he would need a thousand swords in order to fulfil Benkei's wishes. So Benkei set about collecting the swords by attacking samurai and relieving them of their weapons. The night that Benkei hoped to achieve his goal of one thousand, he was walking over Gojō Bridge when a slender youth approached. He launched his attack thinking he would have the youth's sword in no time. Within seconds the young man had knocked Benkei's halberd from his hand. The fight continued with the agile youth leaping about avoiding Benkei's attempts to bring him down. This impressed Benkei so much that he shouted 'tell me your name and state.' 'I am Minamoto Ushiwaka' came the reply. Benkei immediately realised he was fighting the son of the great warlord, Minamoto no Yoritomo, who had been trained by the *tengu* in martial arts (cat. no. 91). Benkei ceased his attack and with great humility asked if he might serve the youth. In the closing speech of the Nō play *Hashi Benkei* (Benkei on the Bridge), the chorus speaking for Benkei declares:

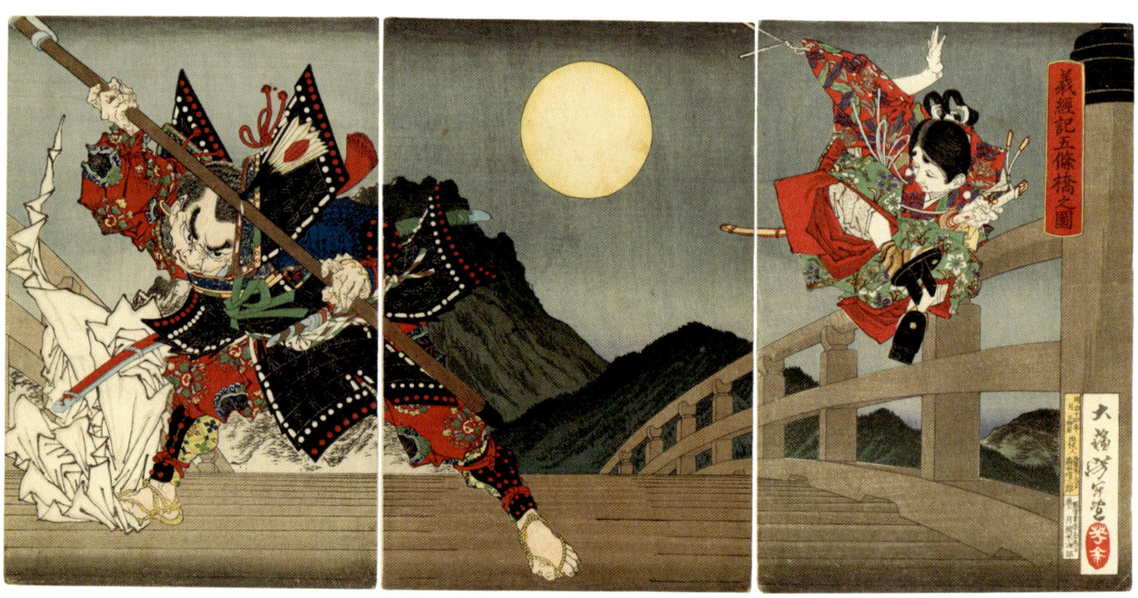

Fig. 62 Benkei and Yoshitsune fighting on the Gojō Bridge. Colour woodblock print by Tsukioka Yoshitoshi (1839–1892) (EA1983.67)

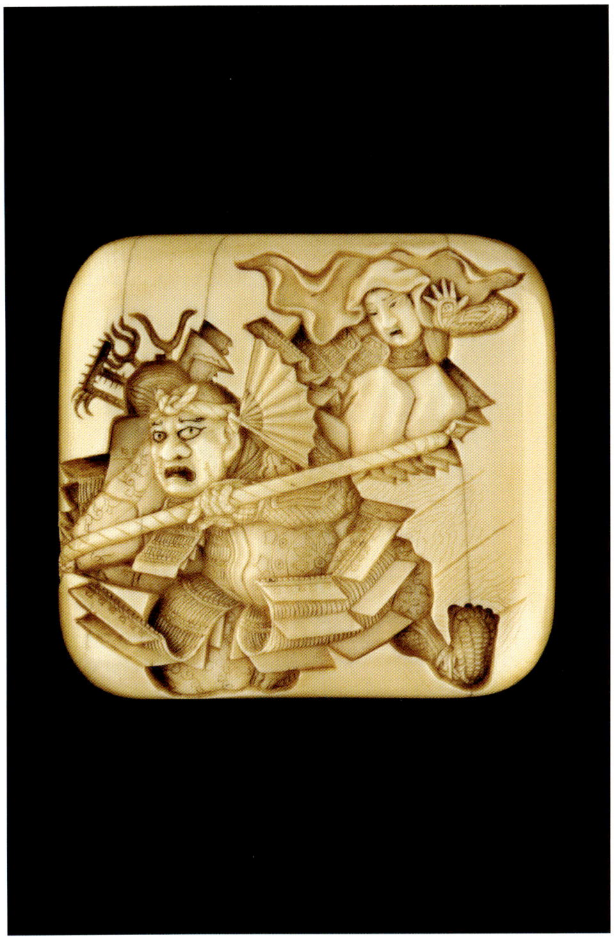

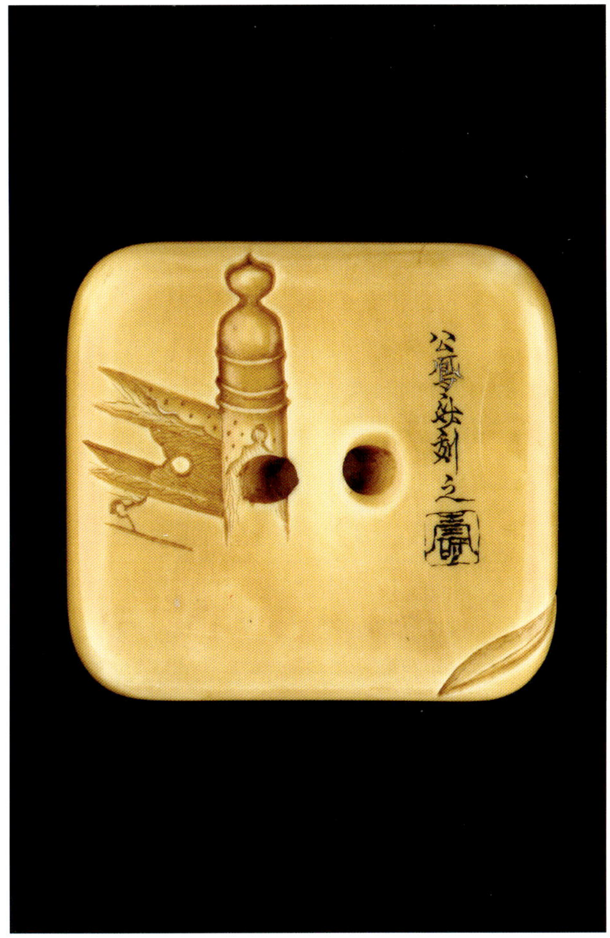

I am called Musashi Benkei of the Western Pagoda.
And now that we have told our names,
I surrender myself and beg for mercy;
For you are yet a child, and I a priest.
Such are your rank and lineage, such your prowess
That I will gladly serve you

Too hastily you took me for an enemy; but now begins
A three lives' bond; henceforward
As slave I serve you.[75]

From that day onwards Benkei undertook many brave and gallant feats of force for Yoshitsune, fighting alongside his master in the Genpei wars against the Taira clan, which finally resulted in victory for the Minamoto at the Battle of Dannoura.

This is the most familiar form of this legend, although the story of Yoshitsune's life, *Gikeiki*, does not mention the Gojō Bridge.

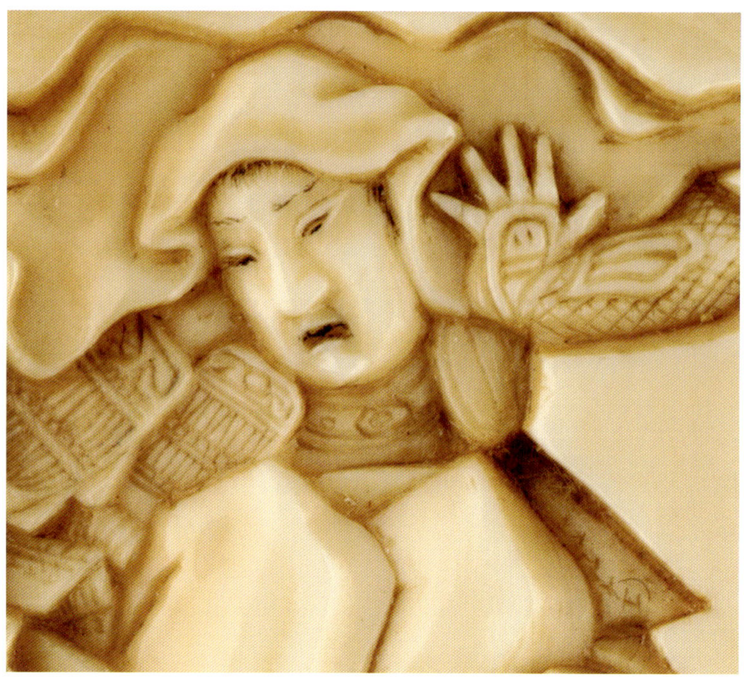

Cat. no. 96 (detail)

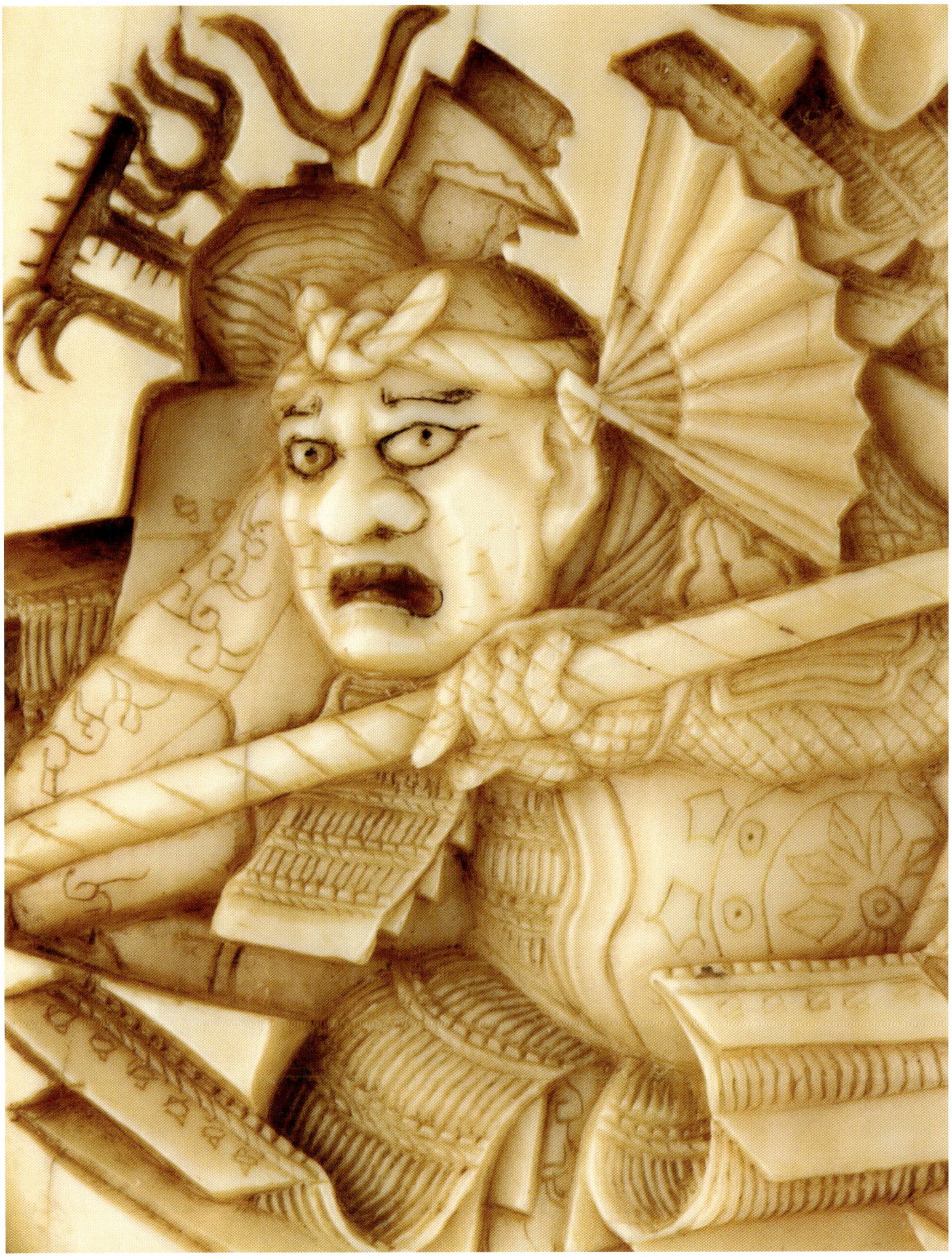

Cat. no. 96 (detail)

97

Battle of Kawanakajima: Uesugi Kenshin (1530–1578) and Takeda Shingen (1521–1573)

Verso: Pine Tree and reeds. Metal loop attachment on central peg

Ivory with dark staining
Signed: Shunkōsai Chōgetsu 春江齋朝月 (in a long oval reserve)
Active 1870s
Diam: 7.2; H: 2.9 cm
EA2001.88
Bequeathed by Dr Monica Barnett

This large, heavy *manjū* illustrates two warriors who fought in the civil wars which raged in Japan from the middle of the fifteenth century to the beginning of the seventeenth century, when peace was finally restored under the Tokugawa shogunate. This particular battle involved the warlord Murakami Yoshikiyo, whose lands had been captured by his neighbour to the south, a warrior monk named Takeda Shingen (1521–1573) (fig. 59). Yoshikiyo fled northwards to seek the help of Uesugi Kenshin (1530–1578) whose estate was now adjacent to Shingen's, to try and regain his lost territory. Kenshin agreed and battle commenced. For almost a decade these two warrior monks engaged in battles on the plain of Kawanakajima (in present day Nagano prefecture), neither side gaining a decisive victory. Many lives were lost in the process.

The incident shown on this *manjū* took place during the fourth battle, when Kenshin rode up to Shingen and slashed at him with his sword which the latter managed to fend off with his iron war fan *(gunbai)*. The attack failed so Shingen counter-attacked, large armies backing both warriors. The end result was that Kenshin's army was forced to retreat causing many to drown in the river.

For more than fourteen years this territorial rivalry continued. However, Kumasaku Tomita remarks 'although the fighting was so desperate and so prolonged, the conflict appears to have been conducted with extraordinary forebearance and courtesy on both sides'.[77] On one occasion when Kenshin heard that Shingen's supply of salt was being denied him by his neighbour to the south, he immediately offered to supply Shingen from his own estate. So when Kenshin received news of Shingen's death in 1573, he is said to have cried aloud, 'I have lost my good enemy, and have no one now to compete with me on equal terms'.[78] He then vowed never to attack Takeda lands again. He survived Shingen by five years. Both warriors displayed extraordinarily chivalrous behaviour and were held up as true examples of the spirit of *bushidō* (the way of the warrior).

At the time when this *manjū* would have been made, in the mid-nineteenth century, civil war had once again reared its ugly head in Japan and motifs referring to historical battles became popular as art motifs.

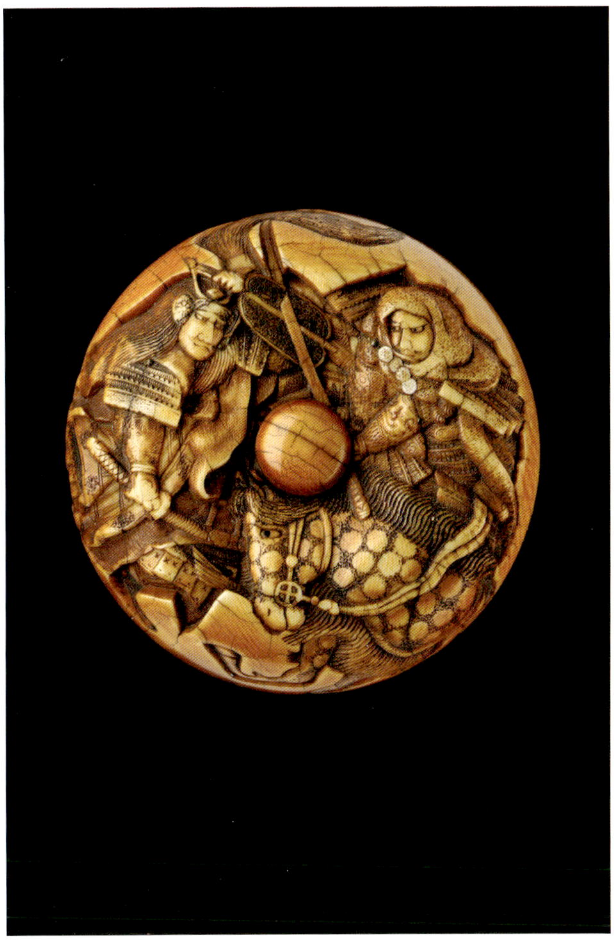

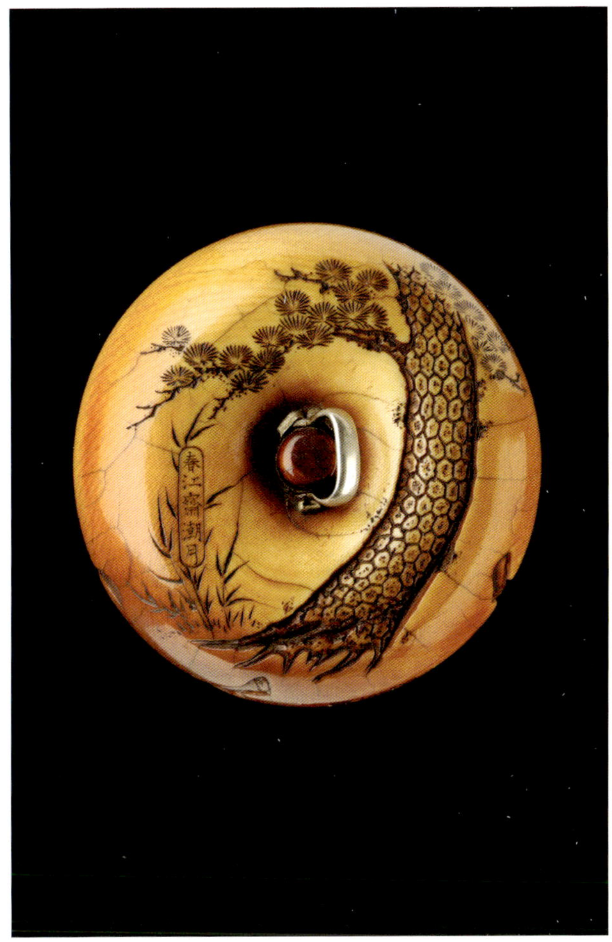
春江斎朝月

98

Katō Kiyomasa slaying a tiger in Korea

Verso: a city gate with a four-tiered pagoda within a castle

Ivory with red, brown and black staining
Signed: Shunkōsai Chōgetsu 春江齋朝月 (in a long oval reserve)
Active 1870s
Diam: 5.2; H: 2.1 cm
EA2001.81
Bequeathed by Dr Monica Barnett

Illustrated in:
George Lazarnick. *Netsuke and Inro Artists, and How to Read their Signatures.* Reed Publishers, Honolulu. 1981. Vol. 1, p. 336

Katō Kiyomasa (1562–1611) was distantly related by marriage to the great warlord, Toyotomi Hideyoshi (1537–1598), one of the three unifiers of Japan, into whose service he was taken at the age of fourteen. He grew up to be a most trusted and able general and was handsomely rewarded by Hideyoshi for his loyalty and bravery in battle. When Hideyoshi decided to invade Korea in 1592, Kiyomasa was one of the senior generals who fought against both Koreans and Chinese throughout the seven year conflict. During the winter of 1592–93 Kiyomasa was commanding his troops in the wild and snow-bound mountainous region near Korea's north-eastern border with China. Here, they met tigers for the first time, for there were none in Japan. In between skirmishes, they were obliged to hunt these beasts that were such a danger to the troops. This netsuke shows the famous incident of Katō Kiyomasa killing a tiger single-handedly with his spear. Some reports say he presented the skin to Hideyoshi. After Hideyoshi's death, Katō Kiyomasa sided with Tokugawa Ieyasu and was awarded the territory of his great rival in the Korean invasion, Konishi Yukiaga, who had backed the losing side.

This is one of two famous tiger hunting incidents portrayed in Japanese art that take place in Korea. The first involves Kashiwade no Omi Hatebe, (sometimes referred to as Hadesu). It is recorded in the Nihon Shoki in 545, ten centuries before this tiger hunt. Katō Kiyomasa's distinctive tall helmet, seen on this *manjū,* is preserved in the Tokugawa Art Museum, Nagoya. A well-known print by Kuniyoshi from around 1840, of Kashiwade no Omi Hatebe slaying a tiger confuses the issue, for he is dressed in Katō Kiyomasa's armour.[79]

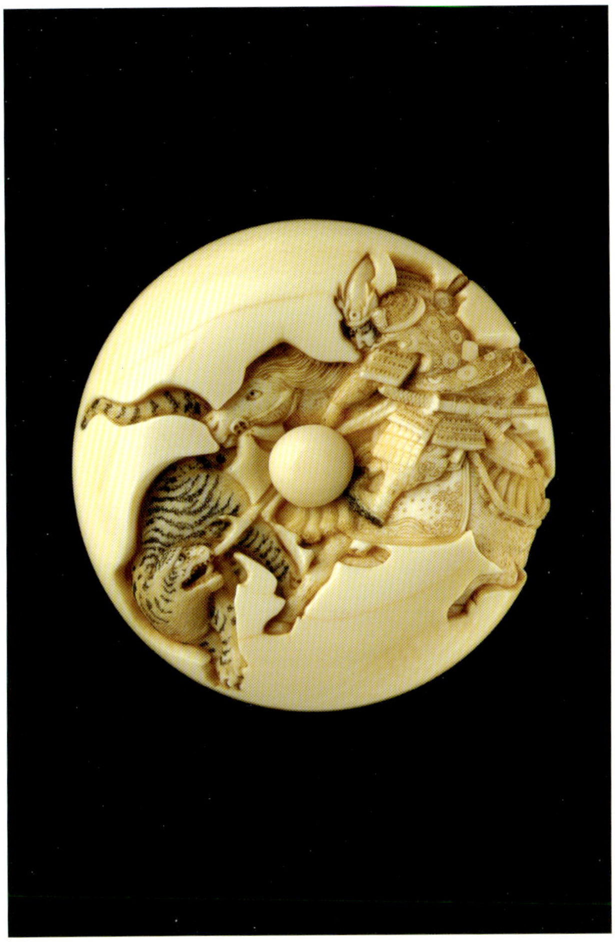

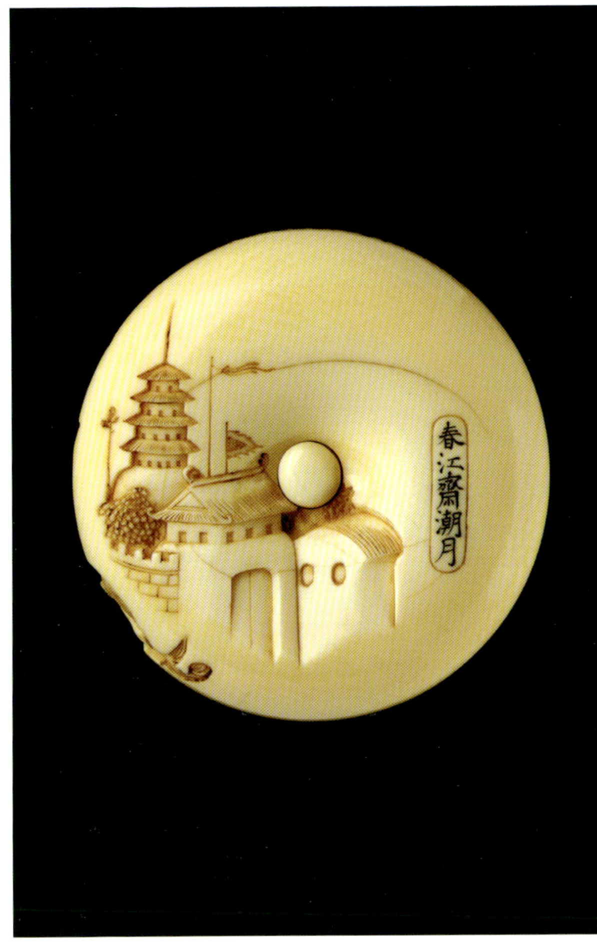
春江齋潮月

99

Ōta Dōkan

Verso: Bamboo fence

Ivory
Signed: Kōsai Moritoshi 光斎守寿
with crane *kakihan*
19th century
Diam: 4.5; H: 1.8 cm
EA2001.91
Bequeathed by Dr Monica Barnett

Sold at Sotheby's, London 12&13/11/1985.
Lot 451

This netsuke illustrates the story of Ōta Dōkan, otherwise known as Ōta Sukenaga and requires knowledge of a poem from the anthology *Goshūi wakashū* (Later Collection of Gleanings of Japanese Poems), commissioned by Emperor Shirakawa and compiled in 1086:

Nanae yae	七重八重	Though a many petalled
Nana wa sake domo	花は咲けども	flower
Yamabuki no	山吹の	the yamabuki
Mi no hitotsu dani	実の一つだに	lamentably
Naka zo kanashiki	無きぞ悲しき	has no seed

Ōta Dōkan was out hunting, wearing the hunter's *igote* (arm protector) when his party was caught by a sudden rainstorm. He had picked a lotus leaf to use as a rain hat but needed more protection. So he called in at a dilapidated inn to ask for the loan of a straw raincoat *(mino)*. A young lady went away and returned, handing to him with the greatest courtesy but without a word, a *yamabuki* (mountain rose, *Kerria japonica*). This annoyed Ōta Dōkan very much, and he stormed off.

On the way home, one of his retinue reminded him of the poem, the last two lines of which express, by the use of the pivot word '*mino*' (joining the '*mi*' and '*no*'), the sorrow that she, the mountain flower, felt at having no straw raincoat (*mino*) to offer. He was immediately filled with admiration for the girl, too poor even to have a straw raincoat, but who could express an apology with such a poetic gesture.

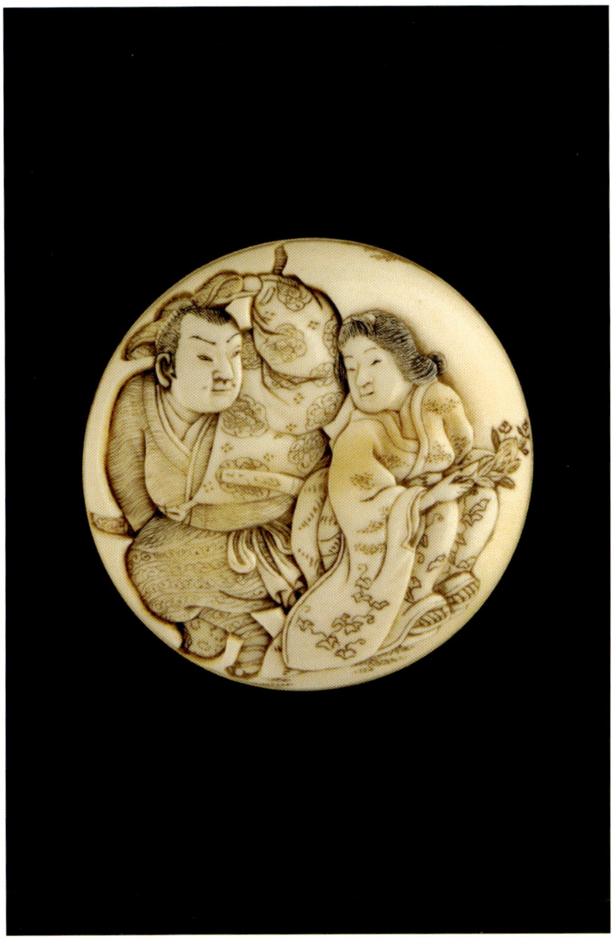

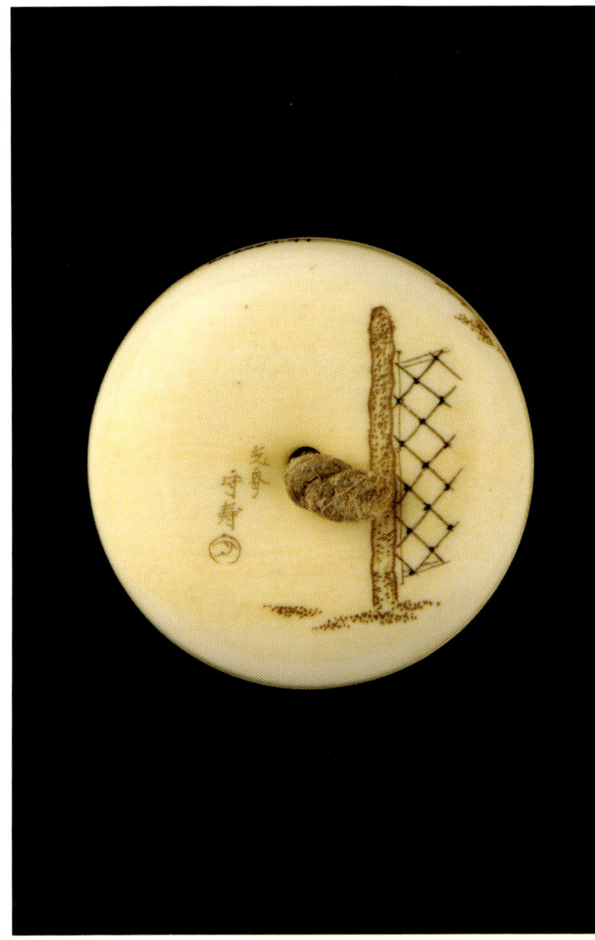

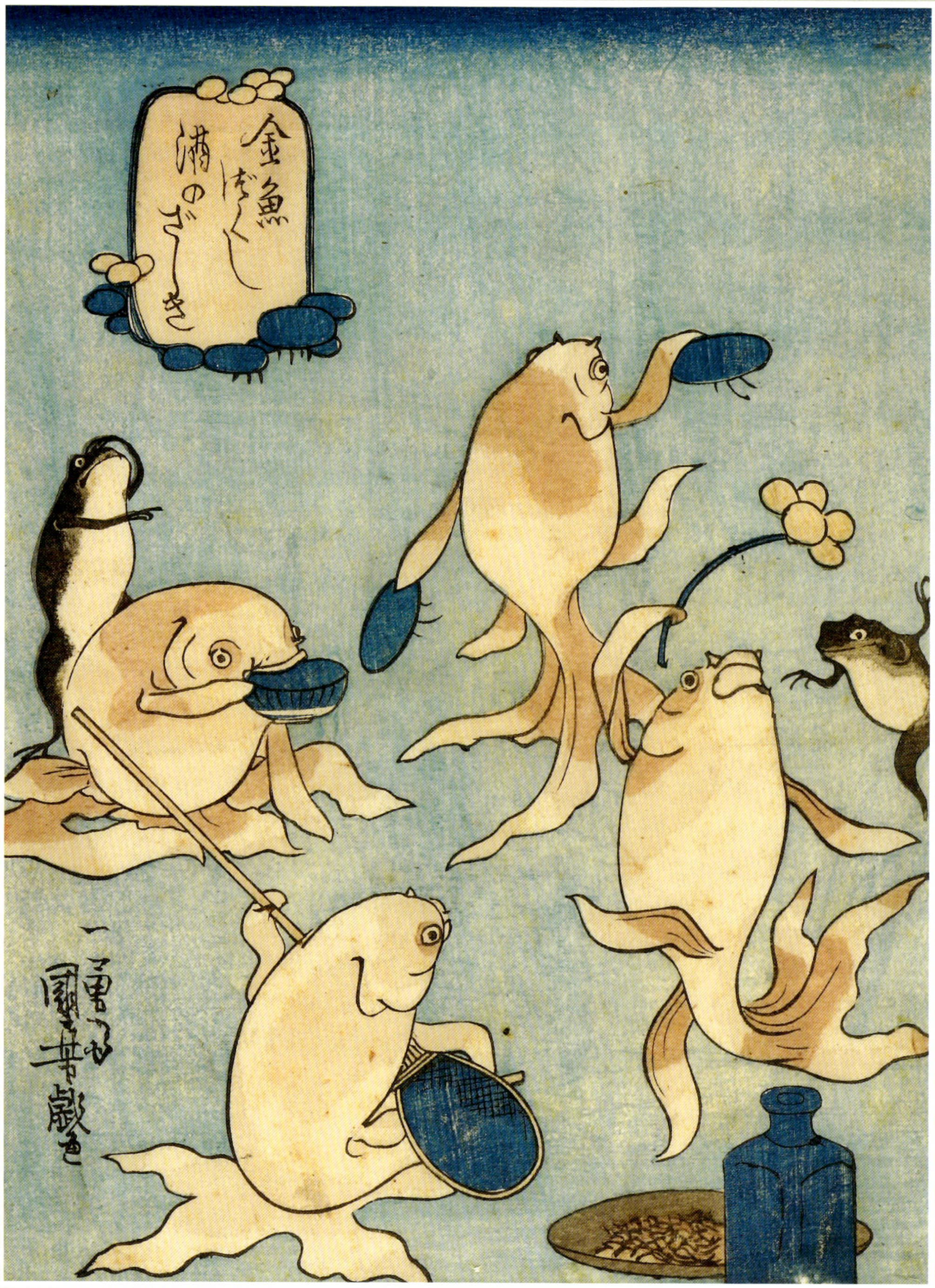

Fig. 63 Frogs and fish pretending to be human. Colour woodblock print by Utagawa Kuniyoshi (1797–1865) (EA1971.157)

Animals real and imaginary

The twelve animals of the zodiac play an important role in the life of the Japanese. Each hour of the day is associated with a particular animal, as is each year in the twelve year cycle. Each animal brings its own characteristics and meaning to its particular calendar year and auspicious occasions are planned accordingly. A special netsuke might be worn to celebrate or signify a particular occasion. The dragon, the only mythical beast in the zodiac, appears in two forms in this collection, the scaly dragon and the rain dragon (*amaryū*), a thin creature without scales. Both types of dragon were depicted in early *katabori* netsuke of the eighteenth century; for the *manjū* carver, the coiled dragon created the perfect shape and the sinuous rain dragon appeared on many *ryūsa* made by the Asakusa carvers in the late nineteenth century.

Many Japanese animals and birds were thought to have special characteristics, often on the strength of a poetic or a seasonal reference, and appear in all forms of Japanese art. For instance, a person born in the year of the rooster, (cat. no. 107) is thought to make a loyal and devoted friend. Animals are frequently given human characteristics and are usually intended to parody authority.

100

Zodiac animals

Ryūsa-type *manjū*
Ivory with dark staining
Signed: Ryūsa 龍佐
Late 18th, early 19th century
H: 2.4; W: 3.8; D: 3.2 cm
EA2001.63
Bequeathed by Dr Monica Barnett

See the Gō Collection, Tokyo National Museum, (No. 253) for a suberbly detailed rendering of the zodiac animals which is signed Ryūsa, in the same style as this piece. Gyokugasai Ryūsa was known to have carved at least three other groups of the zodiac animals.

Bought from Marchant and Son, London 06/02/1973

The Japanese calendar was devised in ancient China and later adopted in Japan. It is based on a combination of ten heavenly stems, two for each of the five basic elements of fire, wood, water metal and earth, and twelve earthly branches, represented by the twelve animals of the zodiac. These twelve (animals) multiplied by the five (elements) make up sixty, the number of years in a cycle. Into this equation come the four directions, and all together they form a method of telling time. The rat, ox, tiger, hare, dragon, snake, horse, sheep, monkey, rooster, dog and boar, in this order, are the representative animals. This calendar was used in Japan, to tell both the time and fortunes, until the late nineteenth century.

Into this intricately pierced rectangular *manjū*, Ryūsa, who was said to have invented this type of perforated netsuke carving, has with great ingenuity managed to interweave all twelve animals of the zodiac; horses (two), tiger, monkey (waving a *gohei*[80]), snake (two), rat, ox, hare (two), dragon, goat, boar, dog (two), rooster and hen. The significance of the year in which someone was born and thus its associated animal, was very important, almost more so than the day and the month. Moreover to sport a snake netsuke in the year of the boar would be sure to raise eyebrows in fashionable and educated circles. Having all the animals interwoven in one piece would give the wearer an unrestricted timetable for going out and about. Perhaps he might treat himself to a special ensemble related to his own birth year.

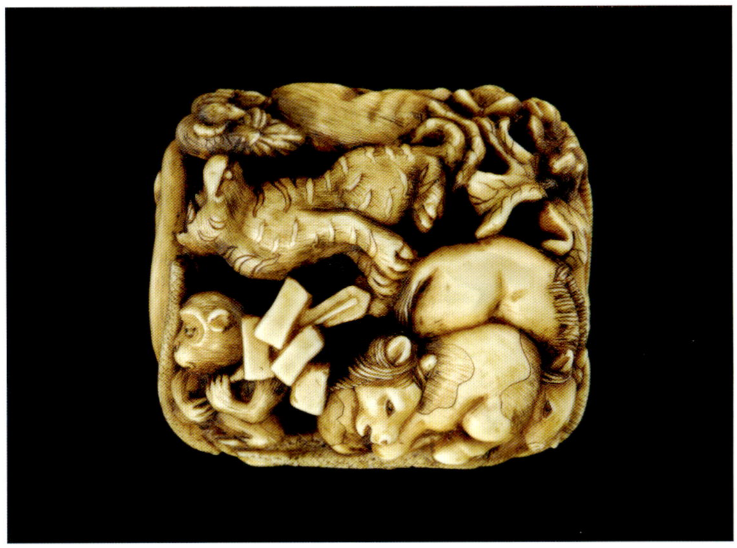

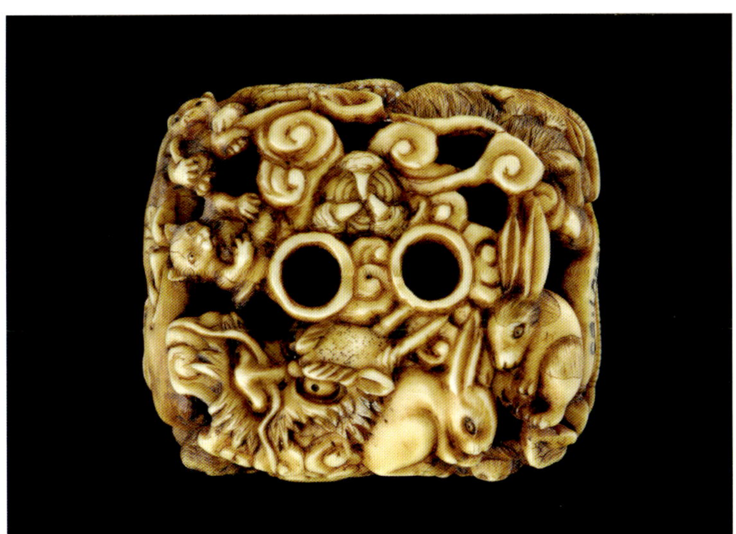

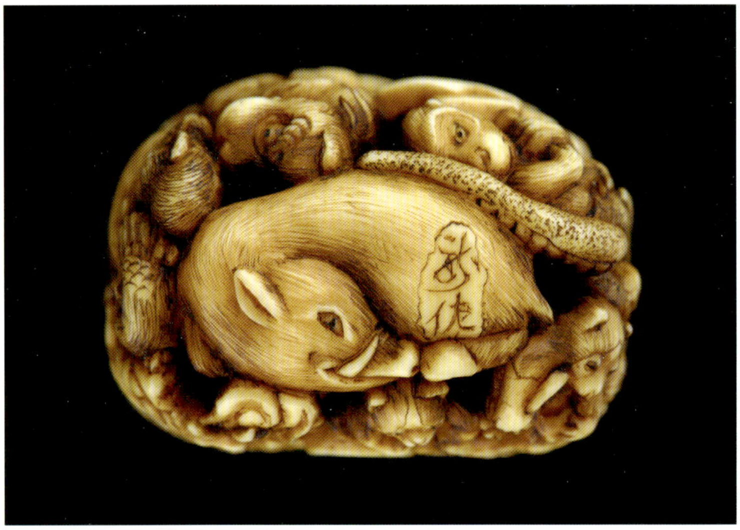

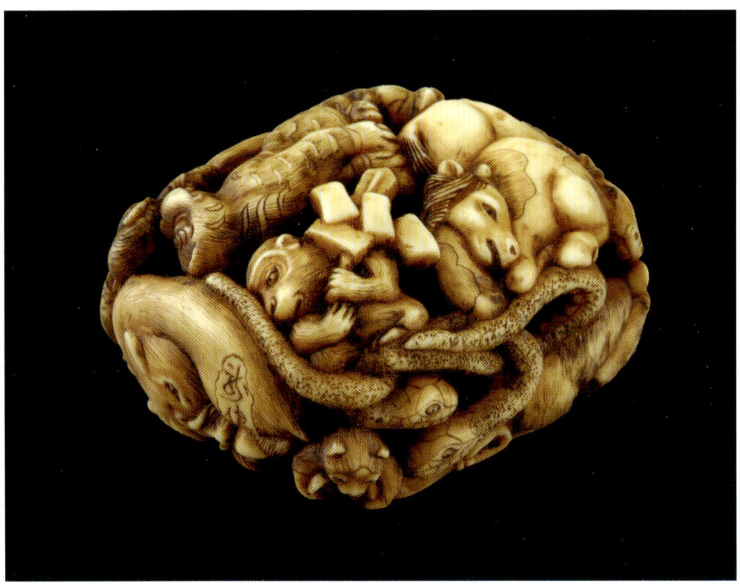

Cat. no. 100

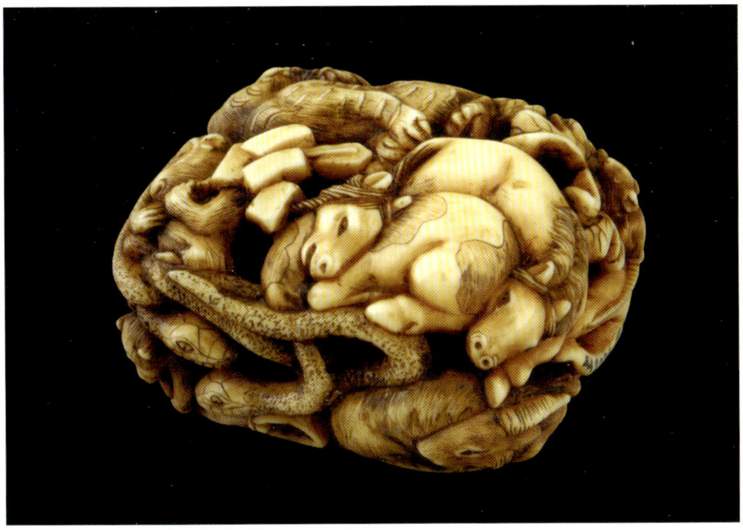

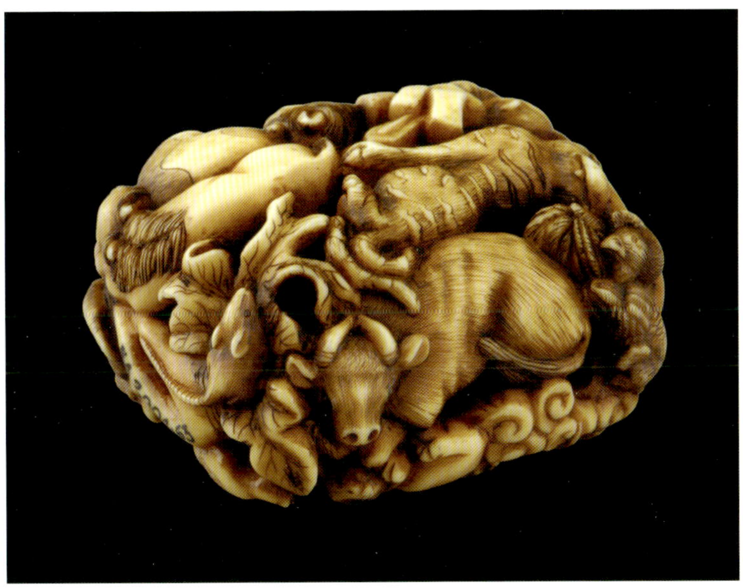

Cat. no. 100

101

Coiled dragon

Ryūsa-type *manjū*
Walnut shell and mother-of-pearl
Signed: Seimin 晴民 on a mother-of-pearl insert beside the *himotōshi*
19th century
Diam: 6.3; H: 2.4 cm
EAX.630

In China the dragon is a symbol of the emperor. Imperial Chinese dragons have five claws, whereas their Japanese counterparts only have three. They occur in stories throughout Japanese folklore and it was even believed that the emperor was descended from a dragon. Ryūjin, the Dragon King of the Sea, rules the waves.

Descriptions of a dragon's features vary but the Chinese thought of it thus: with 'a camel's head with two deer horns, eyes like a demon and ears like an ox, a snake-body with scales and tiger-legs and claws.'[81] The dragon is the most popular of the Chinese mythical creatures and is the only mythical animal in the zodiac. It is the fifth in the Japanese cycle, indicating the hours between 7.00 and 9.00 am, the south-eastern direction and the Third Month of the year. It represents the masculine (*yang*) principle. It has power over rain and wind, capable of causing both drought and flood.

Manjū netsuke carvers particularly delighted in the coiled dragon format, for it easily forms a neat circle, with no protruding parts, an essential feature of a good netsuke.

A coiled dragon is carved in great detail in walnut shell (*kurumi*), a material Seimin used on several of his netsuke, inserting his signature on a mother-of-pearl plaque on the reverse. Frederick Meinertzhagen includes an illustration in his Meinertzhagen Card Index, a similar dragon carved by Seimin, in which he states that several pieces of walnut shell were carved and were then cemented together.

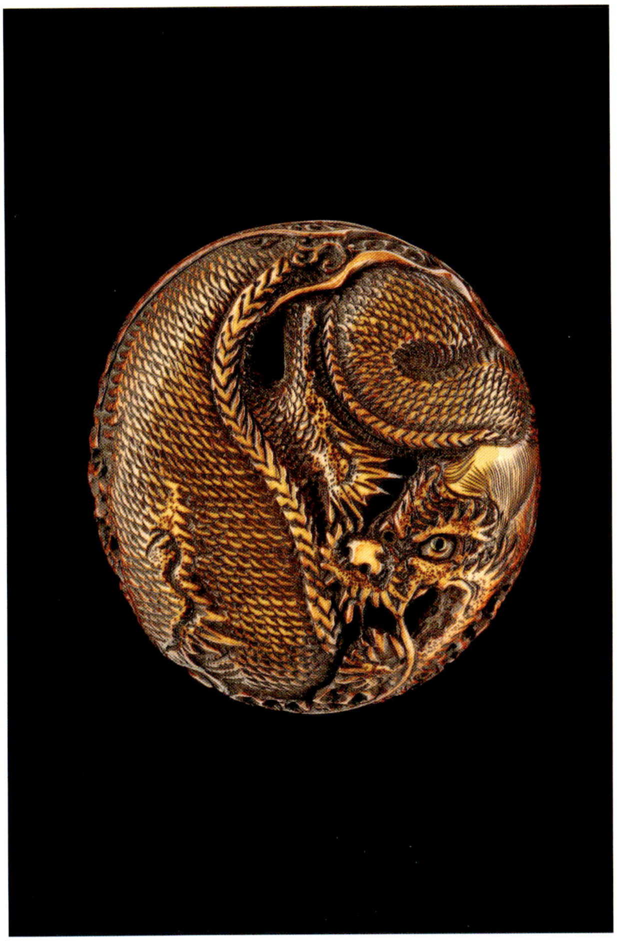

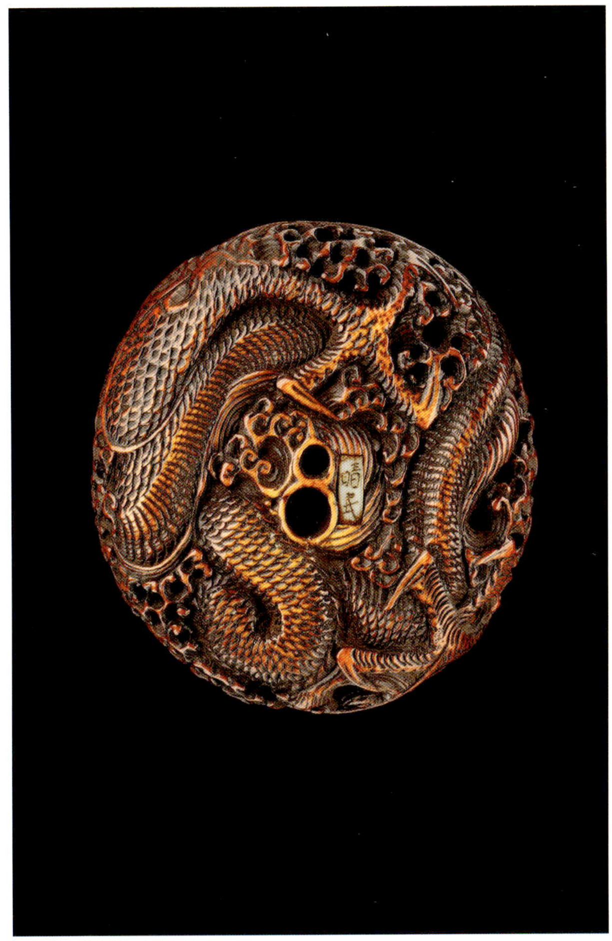

102

Coiled dragon

Ryūsa-type *manjū*
Wood
Signed: Fūshō 風昇
1830–1870
Diam: 4.9; H: 2.3 cm
EA1976.17
Presented anonymously

Published in:
Francesco Moreno, Ed., *Giappone, Terra di Incanti, Di Linea e Di Colore (Japan the Land of Enchantment, Line and Colour)*. Firenze Musei (Palazzo Pitti). Sillabe. 2012. No. I. 107

There are very few examples of work by this artist, a specialist in carving dragons. He has chosen to give central prominence to the dragon's head on the front of this compact *manjū* and on the back the body coils neatly around the *himotōshi*, giving an altogether more balanced and dramatic effect than Seimin's piece.

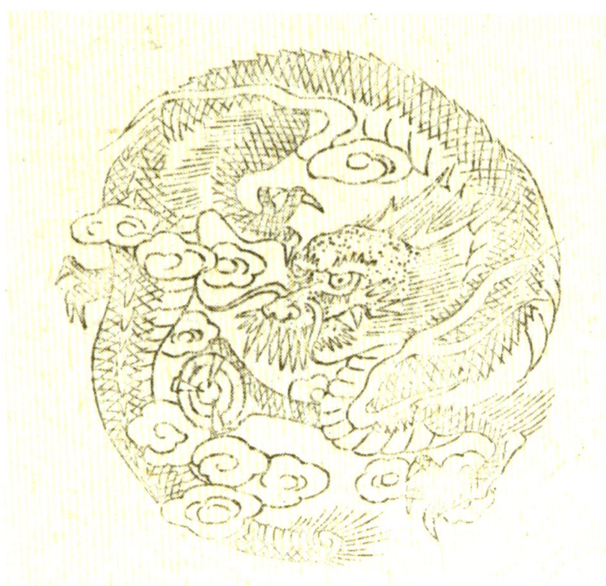

Fig. 64 Illustration from *Irohabiki monchō* (EA2012.168) of a coiled dragon

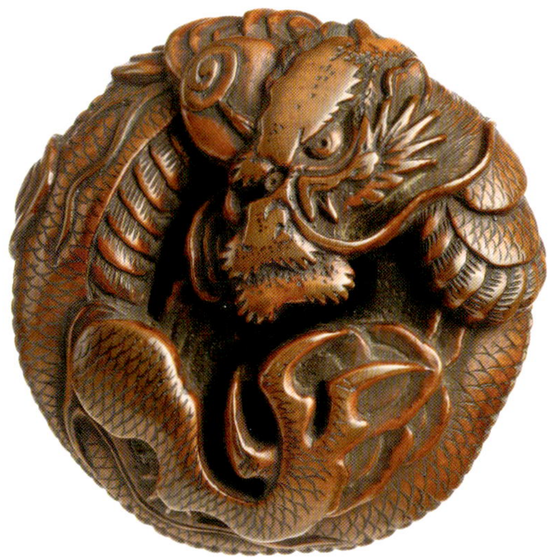

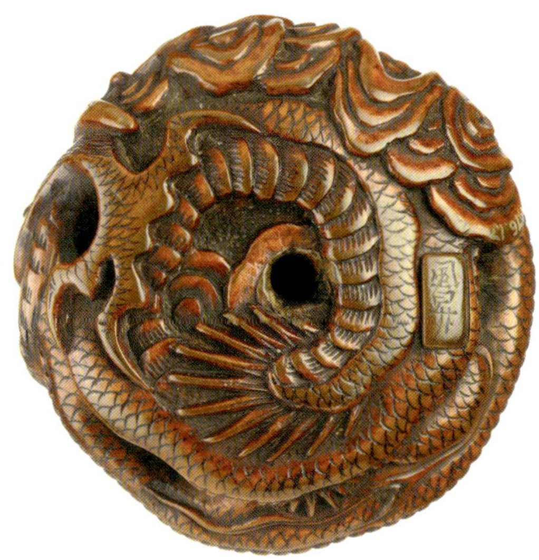

103

Mythical creature

Verso: plain

Ivory, with black staining
Unsigned
19th century
Diam: 5.2; H: 2.0 cm
EA1956.3254
Presented by Sir Herbert Ingram

The central peg on this *manjū* is surrounded by formal floral scrolling and the sides have wide wavy borders, one containing a creature which is in the shape of an elongated rain dragon with a long trunk. The other side has an archaic inscription with characters reading 斎 *sai* 止 *shi* 章 *shō*. It is uncertain what this represents.

This piece came from the collection of Sir Herbert Ingram and bears a label L.14, which probably means that it was bought in London rather than Japan, where he spent three months in 1908, immediately after his marriage. The numbering system he used for netsuke he bought in Japan in 1908 used no letters.

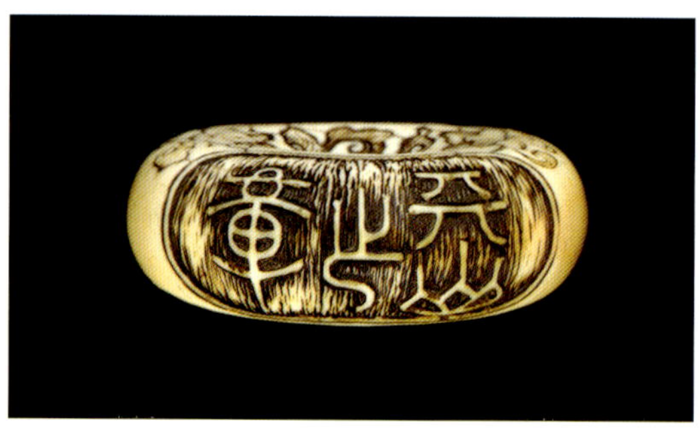

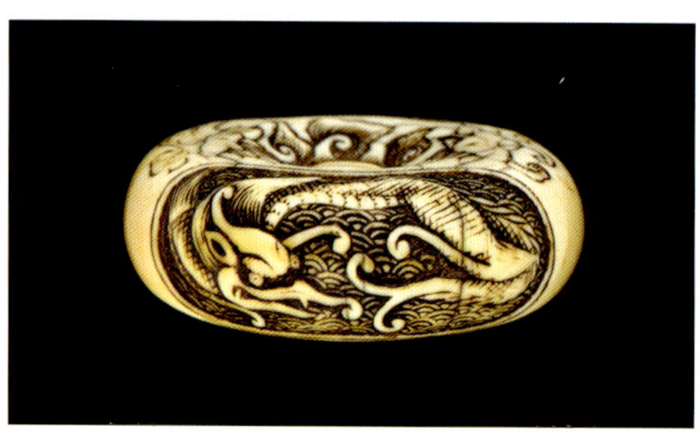

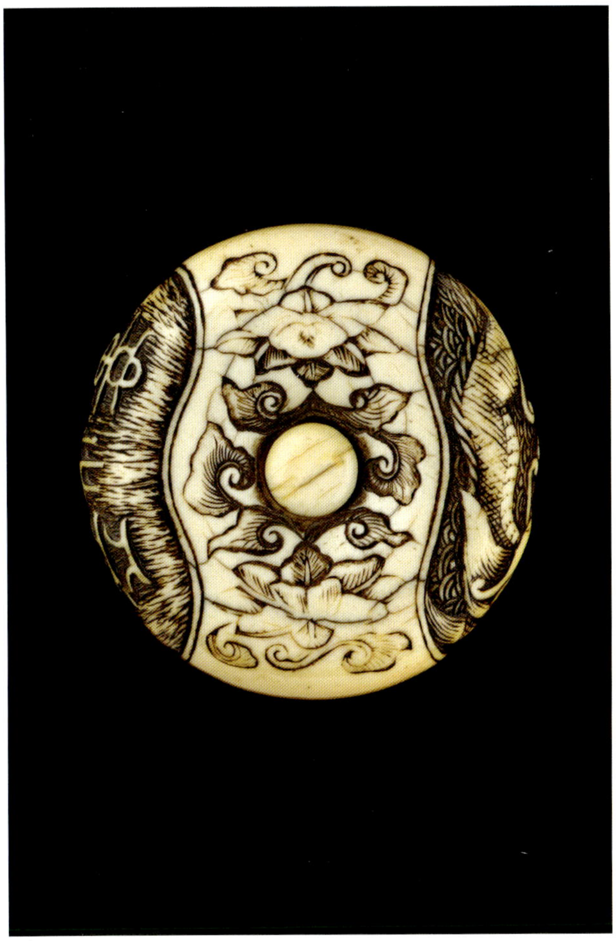

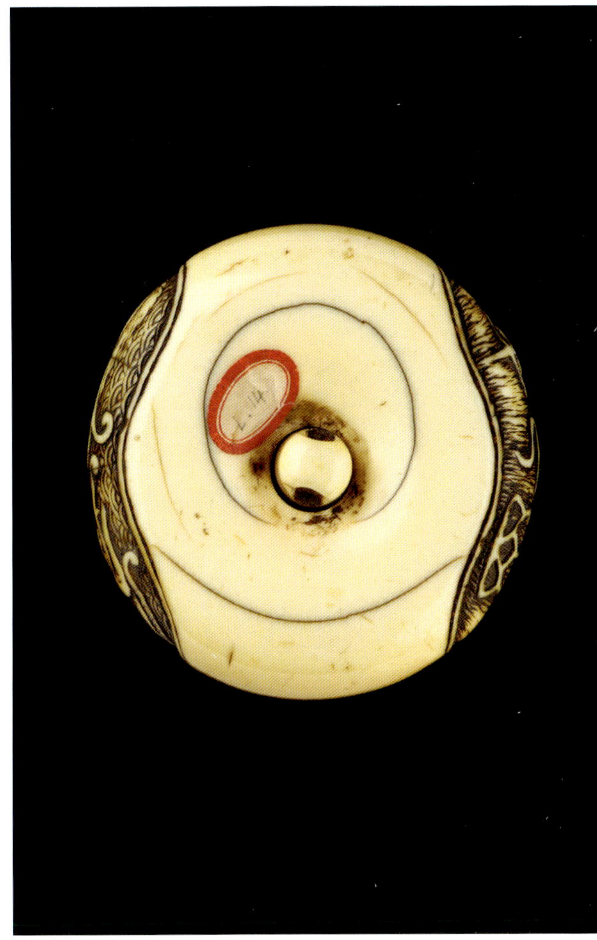

104

Intertwined mythical beasts

Coral
Unsigned
18th century
H: 1.7; W: 3.9; D: 3.2 cm
EA2001.70
Bequeathed by Dr Monica Barnett

Illustrated in:
Neil K. Davey. *Netsuke. A comprehensive study based on the M.T. Hindson collection.* Faber & Faber Limited, London, in association with Sotheby Parke Bernet Publications. 1974. p. 433 no. 1301

Ex Fairley Collection No 944
Ex Mrs Isobel Sharpe Collection
Ex M.T. Hindson Collection

See George Cohen. *In Search of Netsuke and Inrō*. 1974. Plate XXVII p. 82 No. 344, for what appears to be this piece attached to an *inrō* by Yōyūsai.

Two mythical long-tailed beasts are intertwined to form a circular shape reminiscent of the *yin-yang* symbol, or the *tomoe mon* in Japanese design which represents the male and female forces of Nature. The Confucian concept of *yin* and *yang* originated in China, where this piece was almost certainly made.

Coral was a luxury material, its use being restricted to the upper classes by the Tokugawa shogunate. This piece was probably originally a Chinese pendant and was brought to Japan to be used as a netsuke.[82] Because of its fragility, coral was rarely used for netsuke. It was more suitable for *ojime*, the beads which sit between netsuke and *sagemono*.

An article written in *The Art World* (Vol. 3 No. 3) in 1917, states that Japan was turning to a new industry, the carving of coral. Most of the harvest of crude coral prior to that had been exported to Italy to be carved. The short article concludes that colour has a great deal to do with value and the most expensive is '*boke*', the colour of a pale Japanese quince, followed by pink, white, light red and dark red in that order.

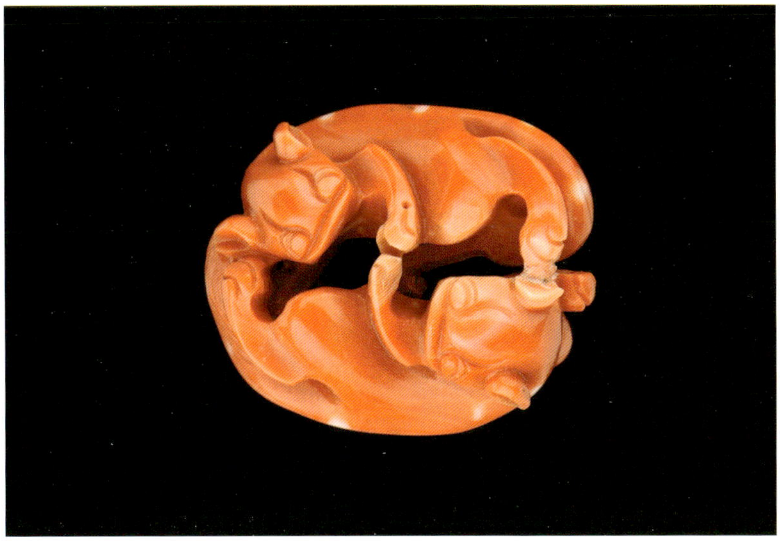

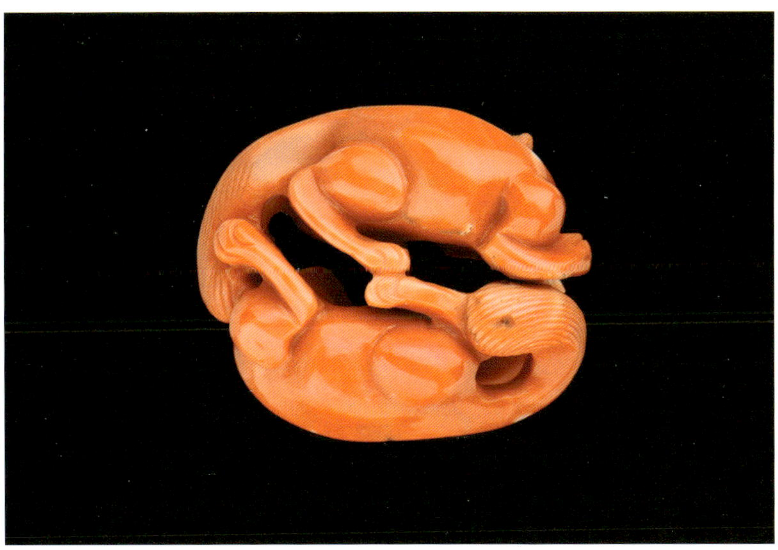

105

Squirrels and grapevines

Shakudō and silver
Signed: Funada Ikkin 船田一琴
with *kakihan*
1840–1885
Diam: 4.65; H: 1.9 cm
EA2001.40
Bequeathed by Dr Monica Barnett

Published:
Wilhelm, G. *Manjū exégèse et appréciation*. Bulletin Association Franco-Japonaise. No. 54. *Octobre*, 1996. Fig. MB20

Christie's, New York, 23/04/1991, Lot 52 illustrates 'Chinese sarigue in a grape arbour'. The note below states, 'The sarigue is a Chinese animal closely resembling the squirrel which is a member of the opossum family. The sarigue is a fruit eater which explains its feeding on grapes instead of nuts.'

The combined theme of squirrels and grapes first appeared in China in the fourteenth century. It continued to be used as a motif reaching the height of its popularity in the late Qing period, at the end of the nineteenth century. As with many Chinese themes it spread to Japan and Korea. Grapes and grapevines represent abundance, fecundity and heirs. When combined with squirrels, which in East Asian depictions resemble mice or rats, their name translates as 'pine tree mice'. These words form a rebus wishing a long life to the owner or viewer. This rebus is based on two Chinese homophones: the squirrel (*songshu*) provides the source of the word pine (*song*), while the grapes (*tao*) provide the homophone for peaches (*taozi*), both well-known symbols of longevity. Grapes are also a symbol for autumn in China.[83] 'In Japan the pairing is known as *"budō ni risu"*, literally "squirrel amongst grapes", but this in turn is a homophone which, when written in different characters, signifies efficiency in the way of the warrior'.[84] It therefore represents victory.

Onto a one-piece body of *shakudō* the artist has inlaid pieces of silver, finely crafted into very delicate grape tendrils, finishing the details with lines using the technique called *katakiri*.

Funada Ikkin's teacher, Gotō Ichijō, came from one of the finest lines of makers of sword fittings in the country. They made fittings for the court and the shoguns. During the time when Funada Ikkin was working, the wearing of two swords by the samurai was abolished, so metalworkers needed to turn their hand to other saleable articles such as netsuke, many of which found their way to foreign countries.

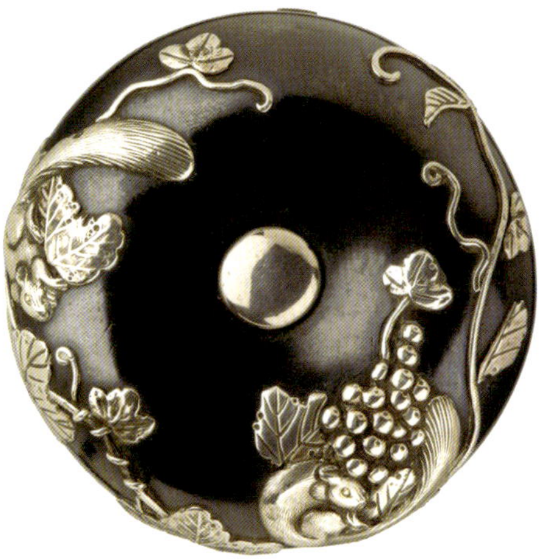

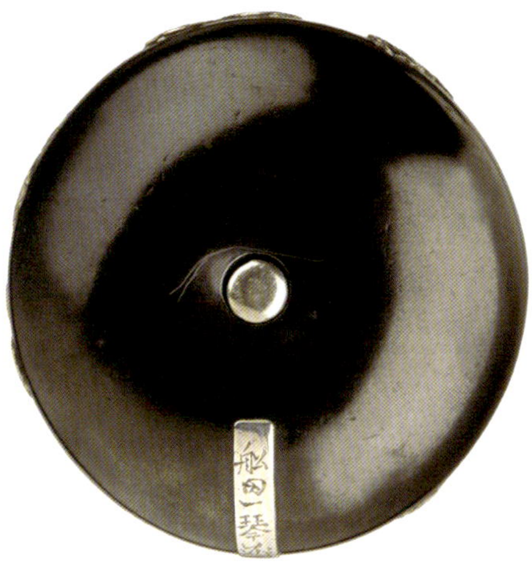
舩田一琴

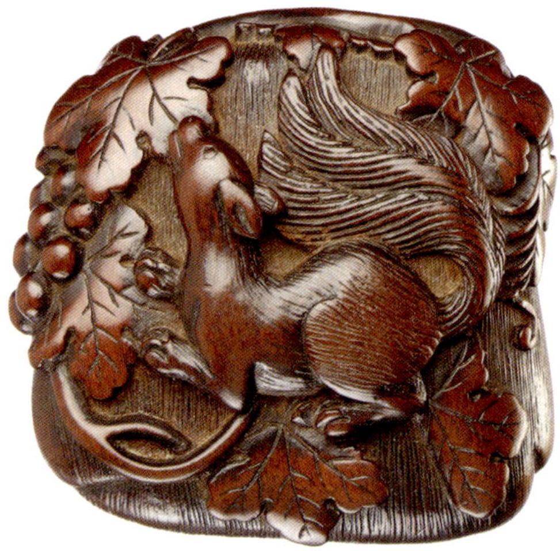

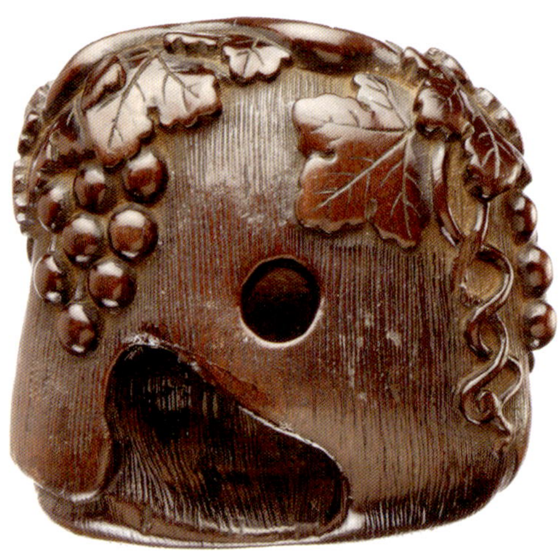

106

Squirrels and grapevines

Wood
Unsigned
Around 1800
H: 2.3; W: 4.5; D: 4.2 cm
EA2001.137
Bequeathed by Dr Monica Barnett

Published:
Francesco Moreno, Ed., *Giappone, Terra di Incanti, Di Linea e Di Colore (Japan the Land of Enchantment, Line and Colour)*. Firenze Musei (Palazzo Pitti). Sillabe. 2012. No. 116

Ex Behrens Collection

Illustrated in:
H.L. Joly. *The W.L.Behrens Collection*. Glendinning & Co., Ltd. MCMXIII–MCMXIV. No. 422. Plate VII '*Wood*, squirrel amongst grapes, the unusual feature being the tail developed into six branches three of which are visible'.

Sold at Sotheby's, London 16/11/1983. (The de Belder Collection sale). Lot 118. Bought by Eskenazi from whom Dr Barnett bought many of her netsuke.

See also Matthew Welch and Sharton Chappell. *Netsuke. The Japanese Art of Miniature Carving*. An exhibition held at The Minneapolis Institute of Arts. 1999. Paragon Publishing. Cat No. 180, for a very similar example, with a multi-tailed animal, on a netsuke of a different shape.

Both this and the squirrel on a netsuke shown in an exhibiton in Minneapolis in 1999 (cat. no. 180) have tails which appear to divide into several luxuriant branches, more a whim of the carver than a biological fact. Henri Joly, in his catalogue of the Behrens collection, mentions six branches, although only three are visible.

107

Rooster and Hen

Verso: A pattern divided by octagonal shapes

Ryūsa-type *manjū*
Stag antler
Signed: Sekisai 石蔡 unrecorded artist
Late 19th century
H: 2.8; W: 3.9; D: 1.2 cm
EAX.752
W.L. Hildburgh gift

The Asakusa school carver's preferred material was stag antler, which has been used on this piece with great skill, allowing any mottled parts of the natural material to integrate cleverly with the design. The network of blood capillary tubes in stag antler provided a challenge for the carver.

This delicate *ryūsa*-type *manjū* is rich in Chinese symbolism. The *yin* and *yang* symbols on the reverse represent the fundamental concept of Daoist philosophy: the polarity of life's forces. This is reinforced by the rooster and hen on the front. The rain dragon which appears in a circular medallion behind the fowl on the front, has Chinese origins and was a popular motif with the Asakusa netsuke makers. The bat (*fu*) shares the same sound as the word for good fortune and happiness. Sekisai has divided the pattern on the back into octagonal sections, eight being an auspicious number in Chinese. He has signed his name between the Daoist symbols in Chinese archaic characters, a practice used by some of the Asakusa carvers. Although Sekisai is not known, this delightful netsuke is typical of the Asakusa style of work in the second half of the nineteenth century.

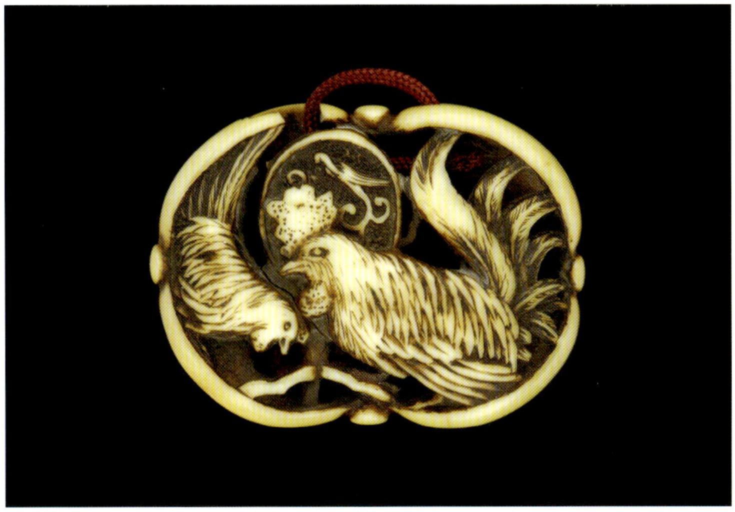

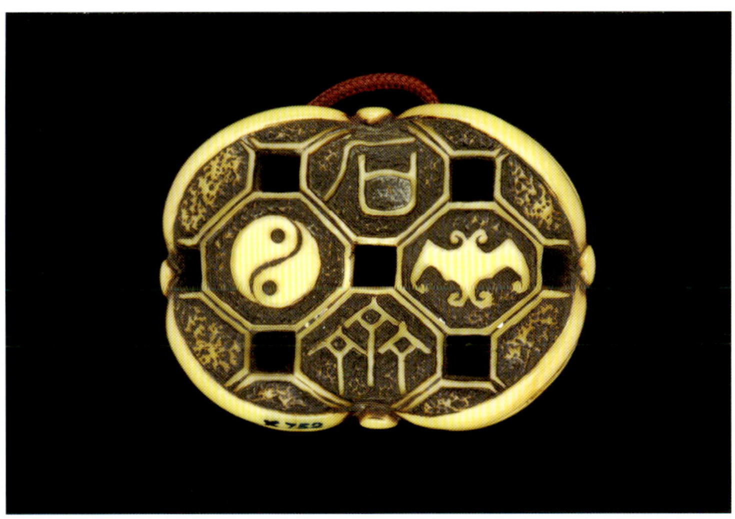

108

Bird on a perch

Verso: plain

Wood, mother-of-pearl, hornbill and green stained ivory
Unsigned
Late 19th century
H: 3.44; W: 4.05; D: 1.5 cm
EAX.1334
Oppenheim gift

With the skilful use of a section of hornbill, an artist from the Shibayama School has managed to give a good impression of a Scarlet Finch (*Haematospiza sipahi*), sitting on a fence surrounded by a plant with luxuriant white flowers, rendered in mother-of-pearl with an orange bud, also in hornbill. The fence, plant stalks and leaves are of pale green stained ivory.

Shibayama is the name of a family of several generations of artists who originally came from Shibayama, now in Chiba Prefecture, and who worked with multi-coloured inlays. Working on a lacquer or ivory base, they used a large array of inlays including shell, horn, coloured ivory, clay, coral, agates and glass to produce intricate sculpted pictures. Shibayama work was especially popular with the late nineteenth century foreign market. The successors of the founder, who created this style of inlay in the 1780s, exhibited at the National Industrial Exhibitions in Tokyo in 1880 and 1890.

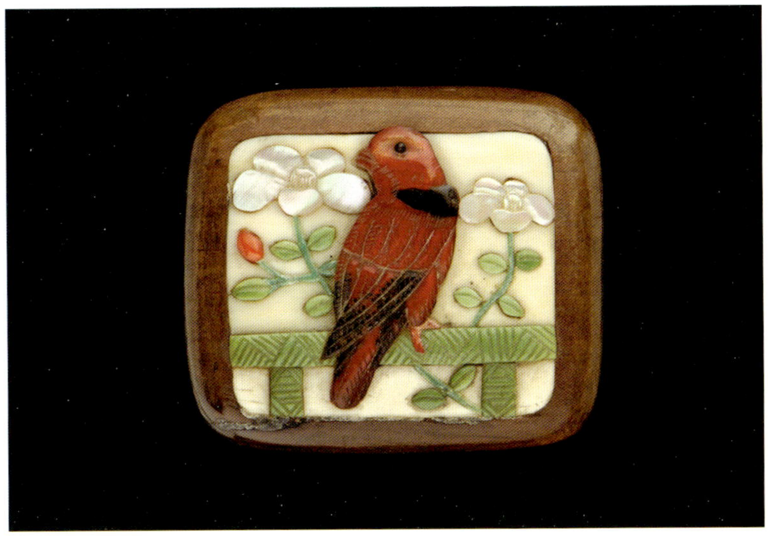

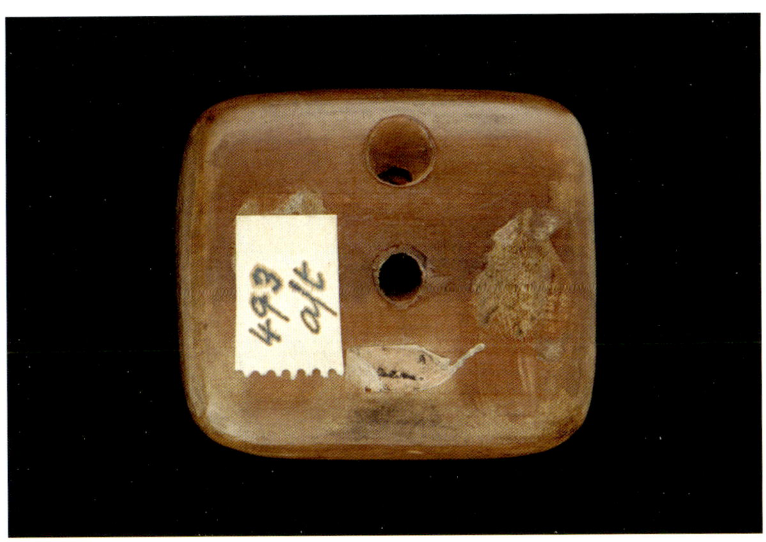

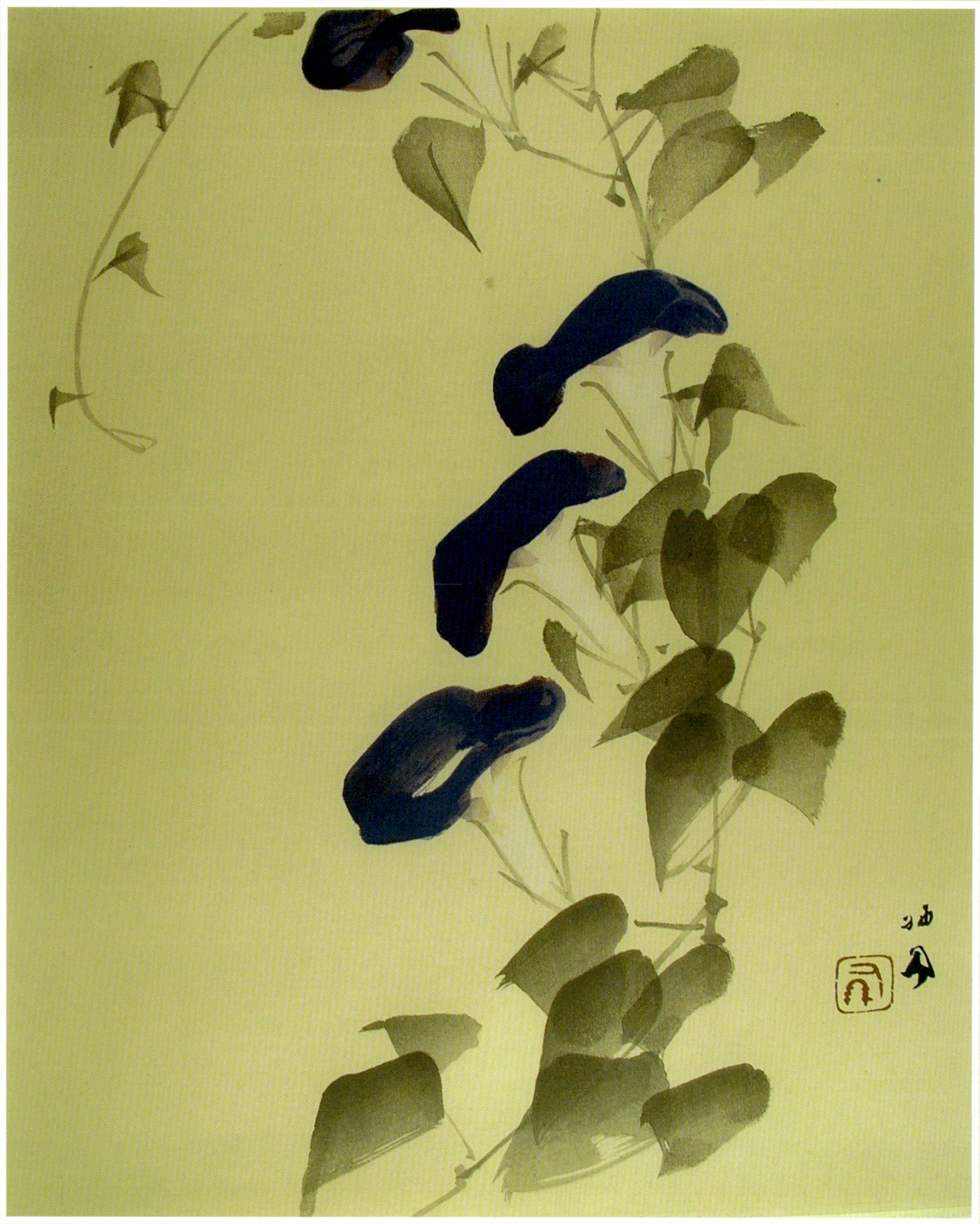

Fig. 65 Morning glory. Colour woodblock print by Takeuchi Seihō (1864–1942) (EA1963.58)

Nature and geometric patterns

Plants and insects were popular subjects for the netsuke carvers. The Japanese are acutely aware of nature and of the changing of the seasons, marking the passage of each with festivals and celebrations – the chrysanthemum festival held on the ninth day of the ninth month being one of these. Many of these seasonal occasions originated in China and were gradually assimilated into the Japanese calendar.

Plants are associated with attributes such as strength, endurance, longevity and their appearance on a netsuke signifies a wish for or admiration of these characteristics. The magnolia (cat. no. 110) for instance, which Tokoku used many times represents sweetness and feminine beauty, the peony indicates summer and prosperity, while the chrysanthemum is associated with autumn.

Geometric patterns were often used as background in textile designs. Many were formed from plants and animals, so reduced by stylization to be barely recognizable. The *guri* scrolling seen in cat. nos. 118 and 119 derives from young bracken leaves and originally came from China with Zen Buddhism as a Zen temple architectural motif.

109

Pine and vine leaves

Verso: A four-pointed star of leaves

Ryūsa-type *manjū*
Ivory
Unsigned, Asakusa School
Mid-19th century
Diam: 3.8; H: 1.02 cm
EA1956.3225
Presented by Sir Herbert Ingram

The leaves on this *ryūsa*-type *manjū* are carefully carved and the pine needles are executed in the standard decorative scored circle seen on red lacquer objects. The gnarled tree trunk is created with a geometric pattern of hexagons. The design is worn smooth in places due to handling. This is a pleasingly tactile *manjū* netsuke.

This netsuke came to the Ashmolean Museum in 1956 from the collection of Sir Herbert Ingram, who travelled in Japan for three months on his honeymoon in 1908. There he bought many decorative objects, which he gave to the museum two years before his death in 1958. He was particularly interested in lacquer, *inrō* and netsuke. However, by 1908 most of the sets of *sagemono* had been split up and this piece, although numbered 867, has no details of purchase place or price. In his catalogue he describes it simply as 'Flat ivory netsuke – leaves and plant openwork'.

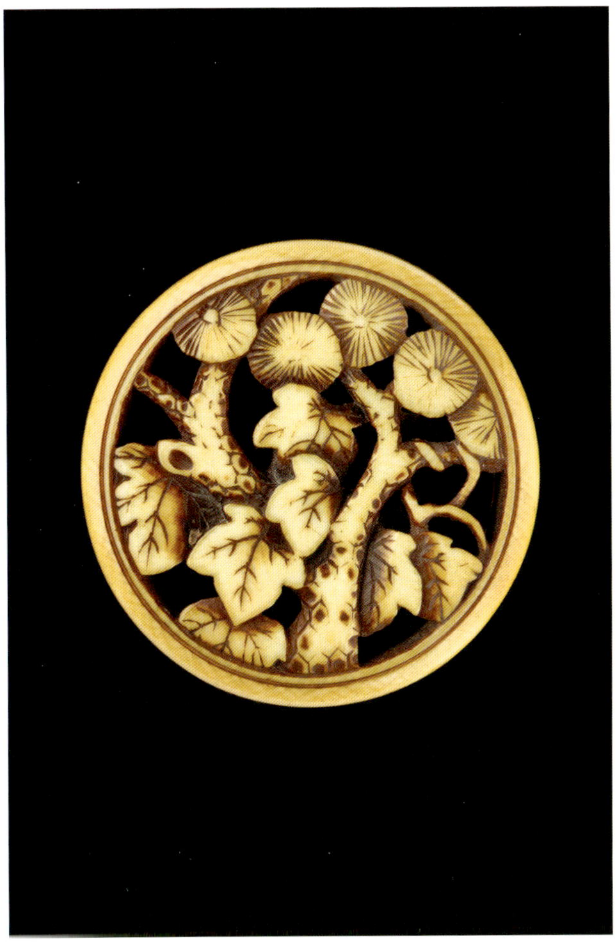

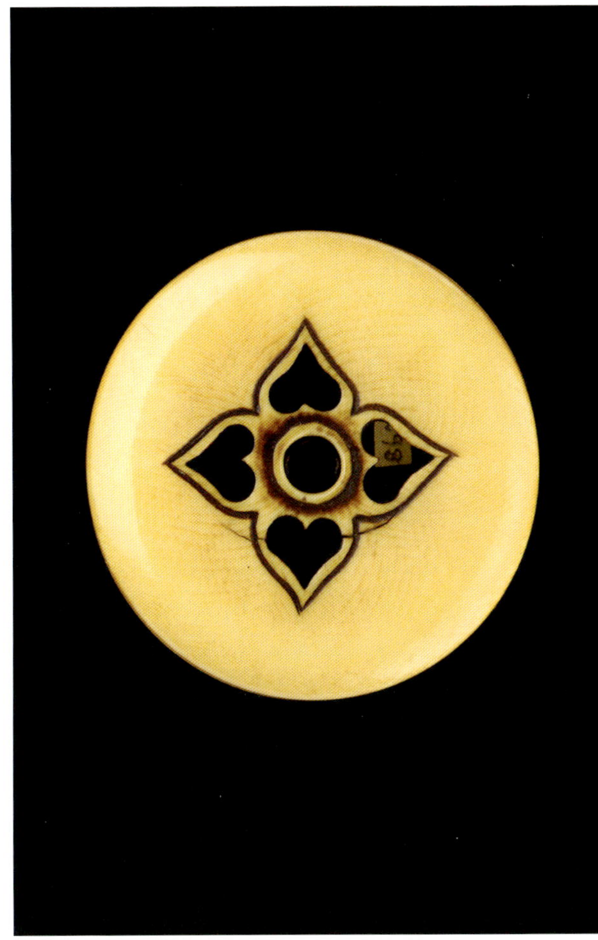

110

Flowering magnolia amongst clouds with a full moon

Ryūsa-type *manjū*
Ivory
Attributed to Tōkoku 東谷
1870–1900
Diam: 4.2; H: 2.2 cm
EA2001.94
Bequeathed by Dr Monica Barnett

Baur Collection. Geneva C 815 and Victoria and Albert Museum, London W. 247-1922 both display a very similar design with metal inlay and are signed 'Tōkoku'.

Barbara Teri Okada. *Masterpieces from The Metropolitan Museum of Art*, New York. Harry N. Abrams Inc., Publishers, New York, for a similar piece dated to the eighteenth century and attributed to Ryūsa. (10.211.1271) Cat. no. 44. P. 61.

See Joe Earle. *An Introduction to Netsuke*. Victoria & Albert Museum. 1980. Plate 68 for a very similar design, signed Kōu. 19th century. p. 40

The magnolia tree blossoms in spring, the flowers bursting forth before the leaves appear. On the reverse, clouds drift across the full moon around two *himotōshi*, one round, one oval, carved with protective rings.

Although this piece is unsigned it has been attributed to Tōkoku or his studio, for there exist several slightly different versions of the design at least one of which is signed either Tō (東) or with his full name. Paul Moss suggests it is an early work of Suzuki Tōkoku (1846–1913).[85] In later versions of these, the artist has inlaid the magnolia flowers in gold or silver. For this Tōkoku may have collaborated with a metalworker, although Paul Moss thinks he was probably capable of making his own metalwork. Many metalworkers, particularly the sword fittings makers, found it hard to make a living once the samurai privilege of wearing two swords was abolished in 1876 and samurai began to wear Western dress.

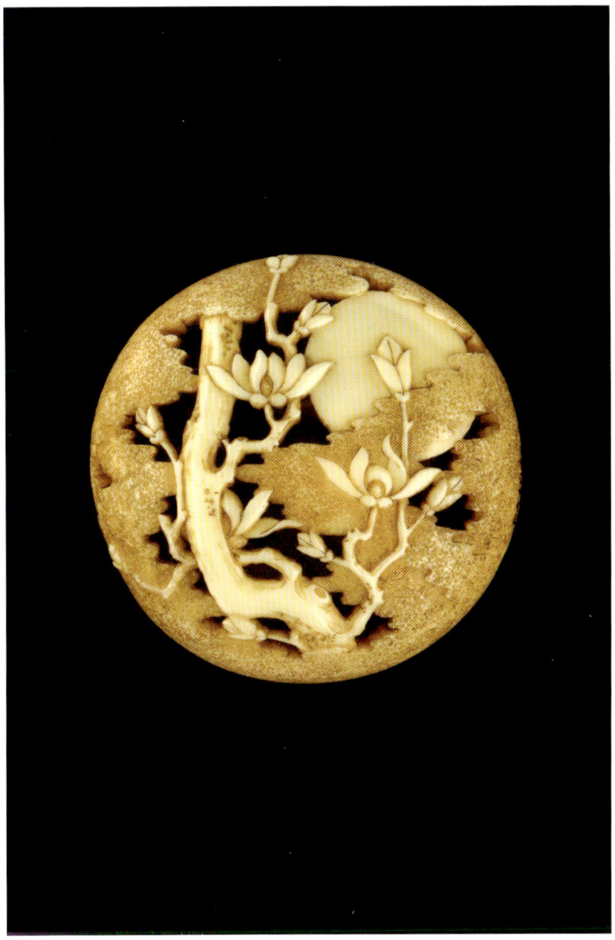

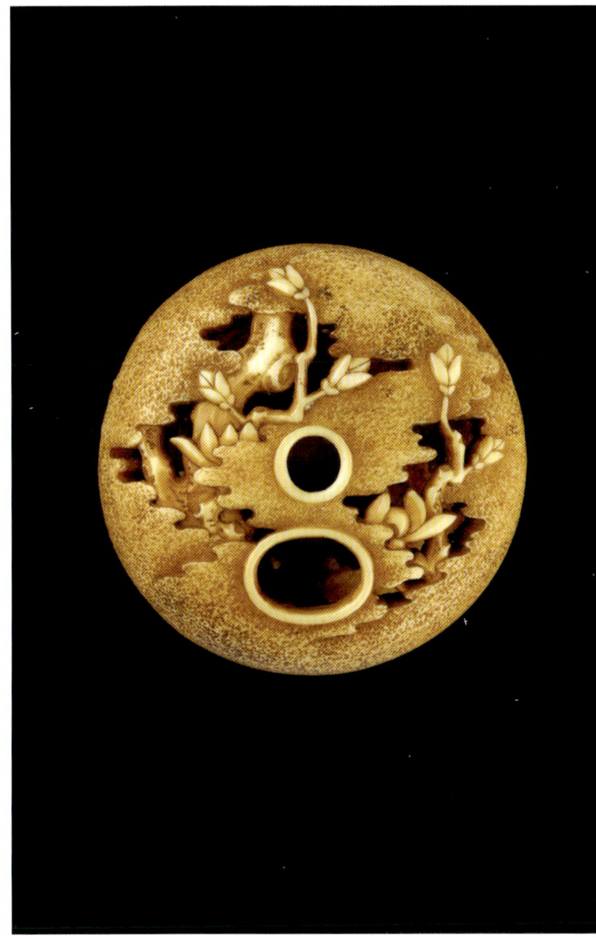

Chrysanthemum

The chrysanthemum, although not native to Japan, was brought from China in the eighth century. Soon it was appearing in paintings and verse. In the ninth century the first competition to judge different varieties of the flower was held and poems were composed as part of the contest. The tradition continues to this day of making displays of potted chrysanthemums, around the time of the festival known as *kiku no sekku,* which is traditionally held on the ninth day of the ninth month. Lovingly tended, in some cases over decades, these plants are trained into flying cranes, waterfalls and all manner of extraordinary shapes, which make a spectacular sight when in full bloom.

In the middle ages, this was the time of year, considered to be late summer in Japan, when gifts were exchanged. It was traditional for a person to visit a relative or friend whom he considered his superior and to ask after his health. During the Edo period *daimyō* visiting the shogun received in turn *sake* infused with chrysanthemum petals. It was during this era that the ninth day of the ninth month became a special festival day.

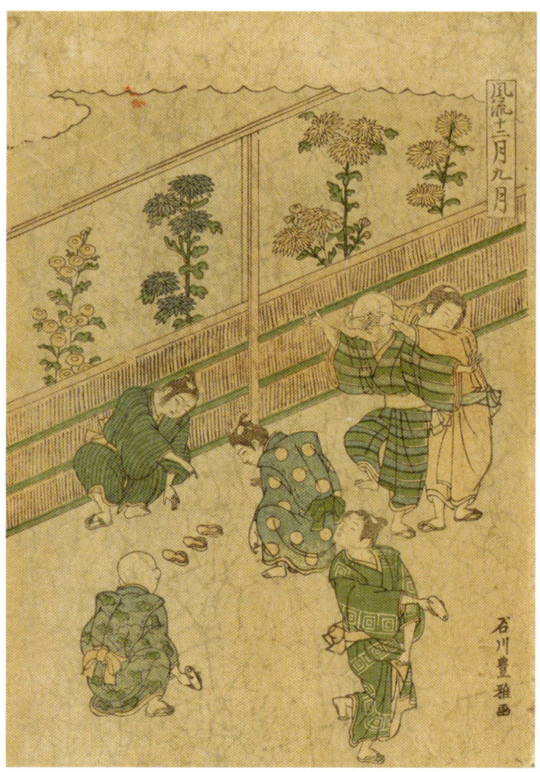

Fig. 66 Children playing in front of a display at the Chrysanthemum Festival. Colour woodblock print by Ishikawa Toyomasa (1773–1856) (EAX.4790)

In the thirteenth century the imperial family adopted the sixteen-petalled chrysanthemum as its crest. It is representative of the seasons changing from summer to autumn and although not one of the 'seven grasses of autumn' (*nanakusa*) it frequently accompanies them in painted, lacquered and textile works of art, bringing to mind the poignant association with the evanescence of life which that season evokes.

This poem by the tenth century poet, Taira no Sadafun (died in 923), was commissioned by the Emperor Uda (867–931) to accompany a floral offering to the Ninnaji, a temple in Kyoto which he founded in the year 888.

Aki o okite	秋をおきて	For chrysanthemums
Toki koso arikere	時こそありけれ	there is a season of splendour
Kiku no hana	菊の花	other than autumn
Utsurō	うつろふからに	but they increase in beauty
Iro no masareba	色のまされば	after their colour changes.[86]

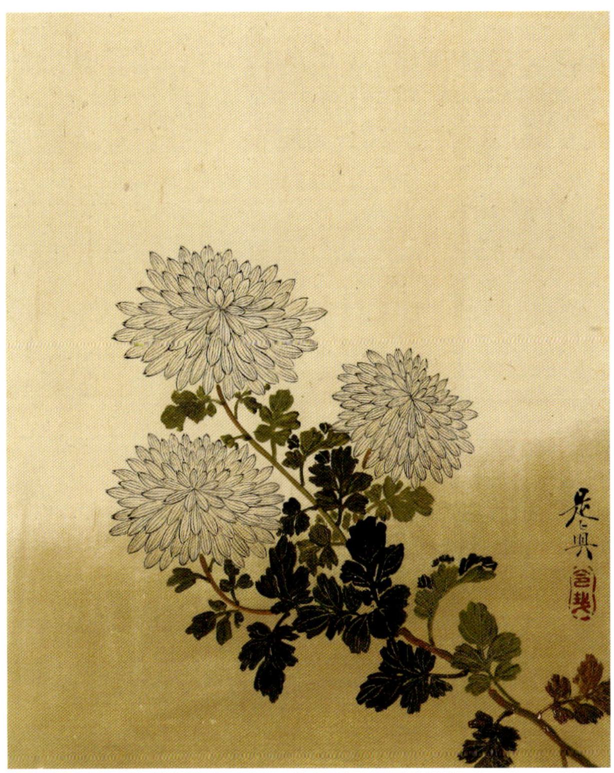

Fig. 67 Chrysanthemums. Colour and lacquer on paper attributed to Shibata Zeshin (1807–1891) (EA1966.161)

111

Stylised chrysanthemum flower

Ivory
Unsigned
Early 19th century
Diam: 4.2; H: 1.7 cm
EA2001.57
Bequeathed by Dr Monica Barnett

A rounded, compact, stylised sixteen-petalled chrysanthemum, showing four layers of concentric petals spilling over the edges onto the reverse all around a central cross-hatched stigma, which forms part of the peg.

The shape of the chrysanthemum on the reverse was adopted by the imperial family as their family crest, each branch of the family using a slightly different version.

112

Chrysanthemum

Verso: underneath view of the flower with leaves against a background of stylised waves

Carved red lacquer
Signed: Yōsei *saku* 楊成作 in gold on the black interior
19th century
Diam: 4.7; H: 2.35 cm
EA2001.43
Bequeathed by Dr Monica Barnett

Bought from Douglas J K Wright
17/05/1972

The carving of this large, open, flowering chrysanthemum surrounded by stylised leaves is carved in shallow relief. Unlike the Chinese-style examples, there is less of the elaborate diaper patterning on the underneath layer and the upper layer is in lower relief. The theme is more Japanese in flavour, depicting flowers and natural phenomena. The artist has contrasted a symmetrical approach to his design on the front with asymmetry on the reverse.

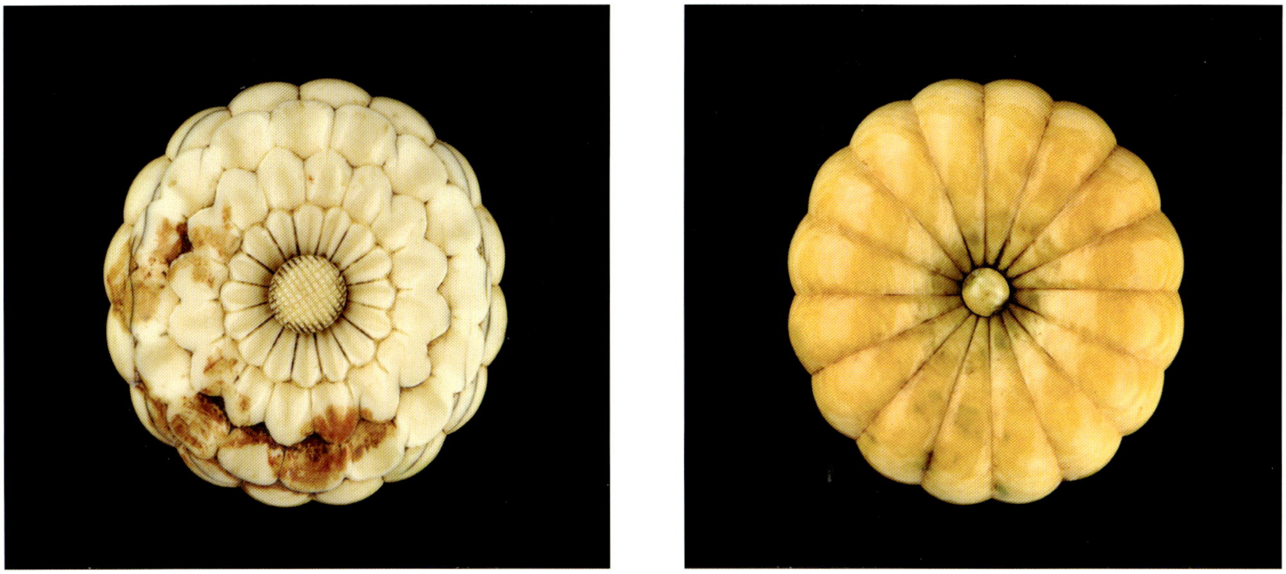

Cat. no. 111

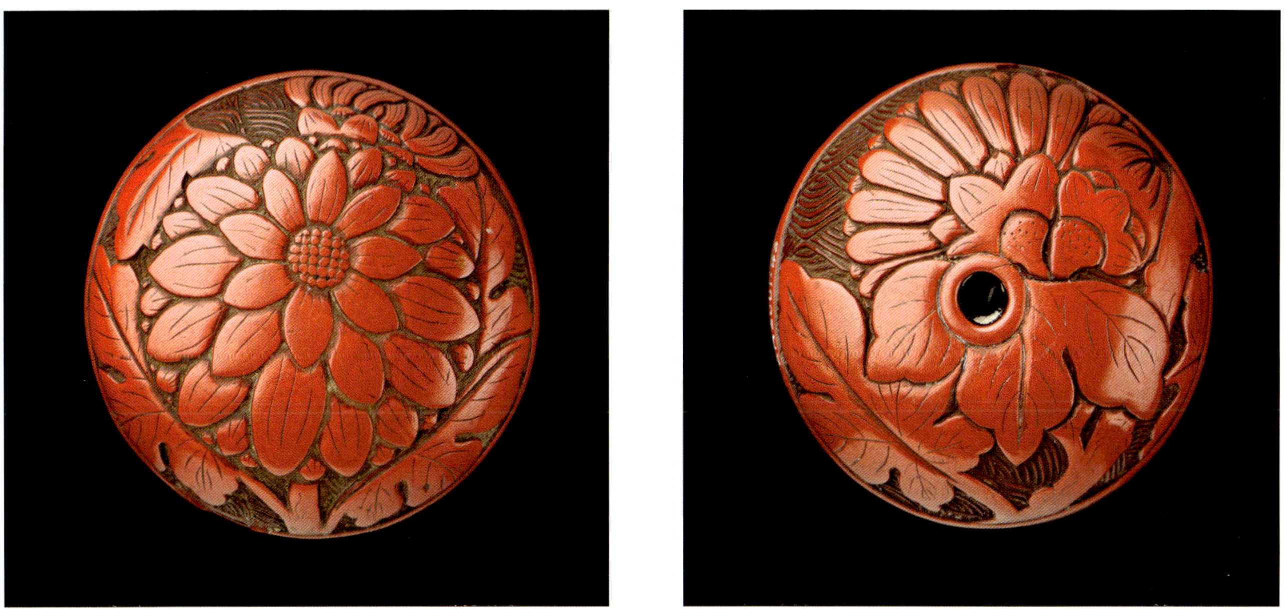

Cat. no. 112

113

Chrysanthemum and orchid

Verso: two more of the same plants

Carved red lacquer
Unsigned
18th century
H: 2.5; W: 4.7; D: 3.9 cm
EA2001.138
Bequeathed by Dr Monica Barnett

The Chinese established a number of groups of plants as metaphorical symbols and many of these ideas transferred to Japan. The 'Four Gentlemen', chrysanthemum, orchid, plum and bamboo, represent the four seasons and the virtues of the ideal gentleman. The chrysanthemum symbolises autumn and the orchid summer. It is tempting to think that this artist might have made a complementary netsuke with plum and bamboo.

Carved with graceful lines against a background of flowing water, this *manjū* is a Japanese interpretation of the Chinese style of lacquer carving seen on (cat. nos. 19 and 20).

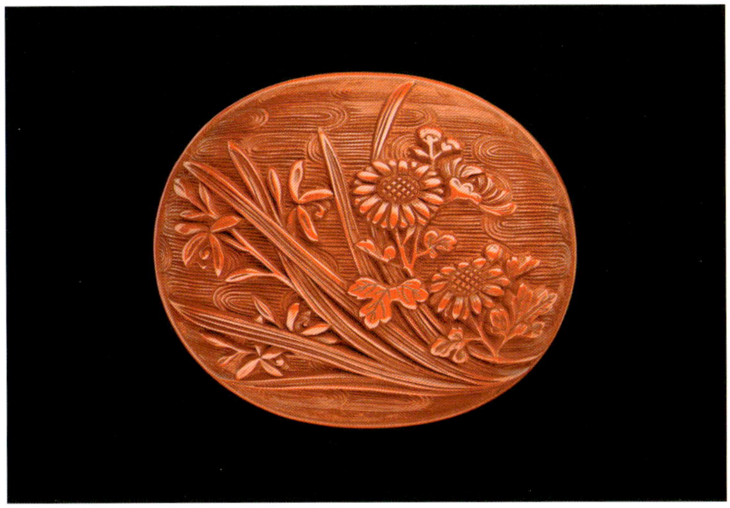

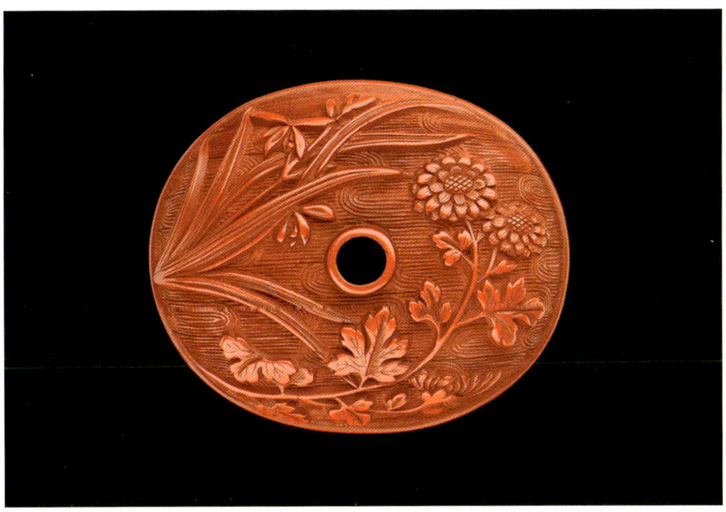

114

Peonies and scrolls

Verso: leaves and buds

Ryūsa-type *manjū*
Bone
Unsigned
Asakusa School, Tokyo
Late 19th century
H: 1.0; W: 4.4; D: 3.71 cm
EAX.1348
Oppenheim gift

A peony branch lies in the centre of a shaped cartouche, which is surrounded by a pierced foliate border. Stylised leaves and buds in four shaped panels radiate from the central cord hole.

The workmanship on this netsuke is rough and may have been the work of a student but would probably have been hurriedly made for the export market. A much more carefully and pleasingly carved *manjū* of this design carved in stag-antler and described as 'style of Kokusai' recently sold at auction in London.[87]

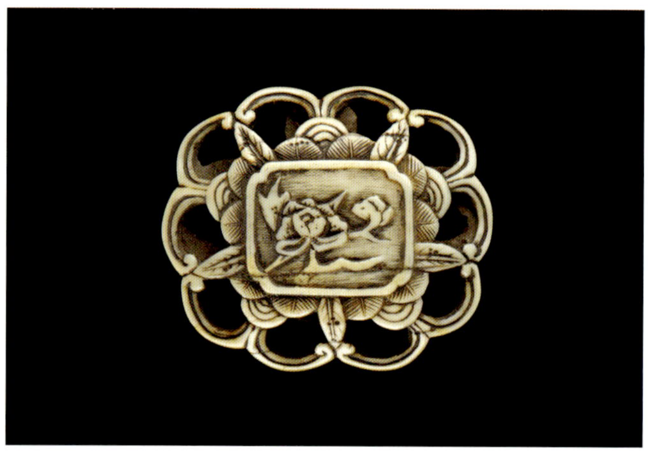

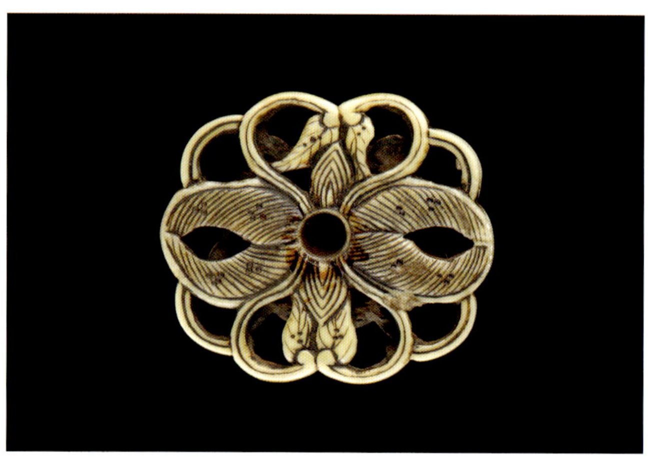

115

Wasp and berries

Verso: A leafy branch

Wood, metal, ivory, lacquer and tortoiseshell
Unsigned
Around 1800
Diam: 3.64; H: 2.0 cm
EAX.1342
Oppenheim gift

Inlaid onto wood, probably a type of rosewood, the artist has carefully crafted a realistic wasp in ivory striped with *shakudō*, with red lacquer wings and tortoiseshell legs. It is about to settle on some ivory and metal berries. A leafy plant in tortoiseshell is set to one side.

This is a lovely natural composition, suitable for summer wear. The wasp has no symbolic significance in Japanese art.

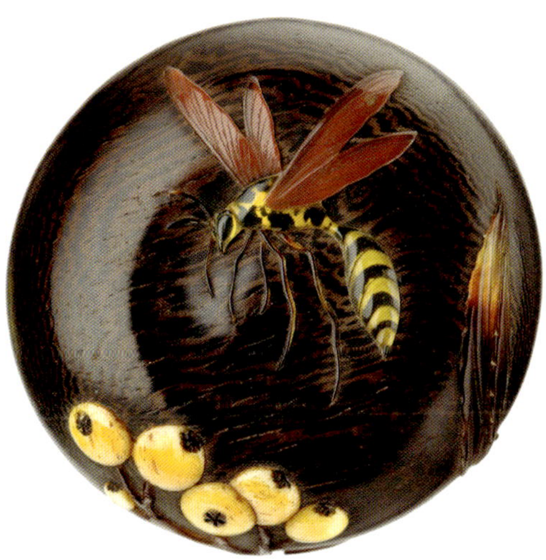

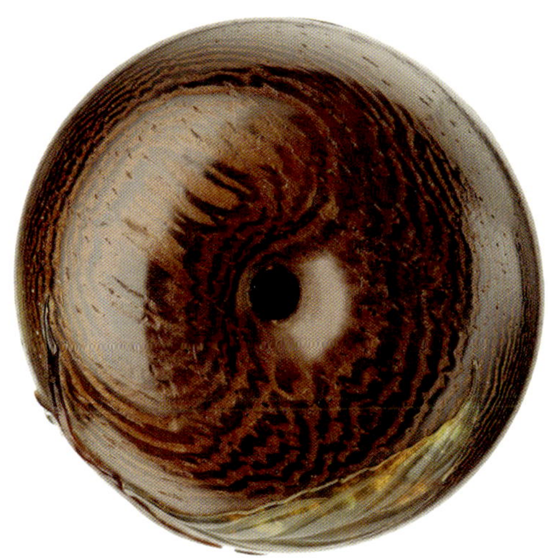

116

Vegetables

Verso: Mushrooms wrapped in straw container

Ryūsa-type *manjū*
Ivory
Signed: Gyokuhōsai 玉宝齋
1850–1870
D: 4.2; W: 1.8 cm
EA1957.265
W.L. Hildburgh gift

See Patrizia Jirka-Schmitz. *Netsuke. Gürtelschmuck aus Japan. Die Sammlung Trumpf.* Linden-Museum Stuttgart. Staatliches Museum für Völkerkunde. Arnoldsche Art Publishers. No. 746 for a similar *manjū* of a selection of vegatables by Gyokuhōsai.

A group of vegetables, radish *(daikon)*, parsnip, pumpkin and aubergine, is depicted all tightly packed with small spaces pierced between them on the front, and on the reverse Gyokuhōsai has drawn in fine *kebori* lines an elegant elongated bundle of reeds enclosing mushrooms, some of which lie on the ground beside it.

This *manjū* has Zen Buddhist overtones, for these are all vegetables which make up the strictly vegetarian diet of Zen monks and priests, many of whose duties include tending the vegetable plot within the temple precinct and cooking the meals.

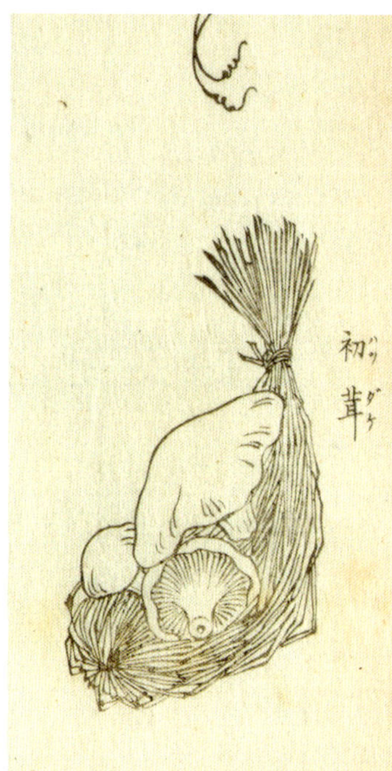

Fig. 68 Illustration from *Banbutsu hinagata gafū* (EA2012.162) Vol. 2 of mushrooms *(hatsudake)* wrapped in a similar way

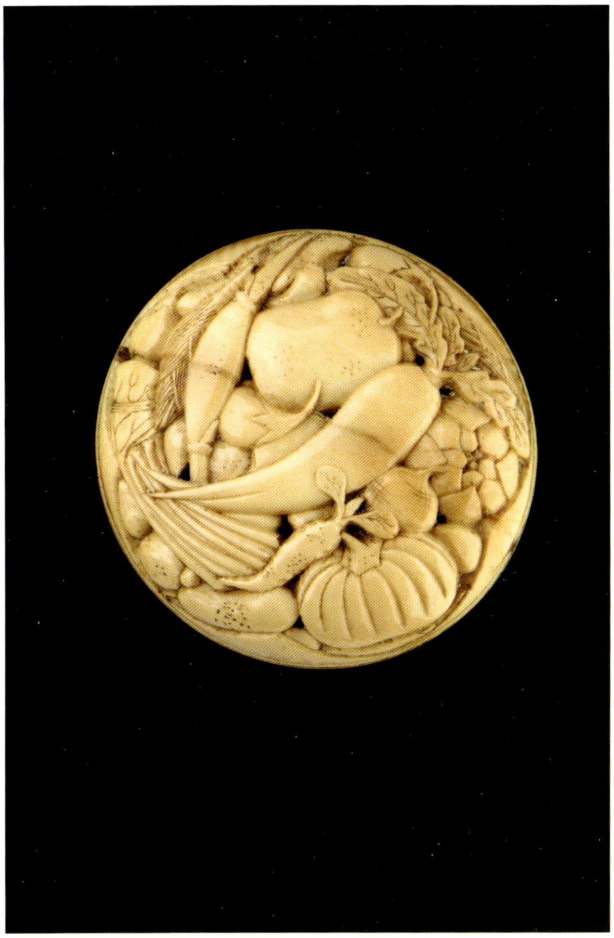

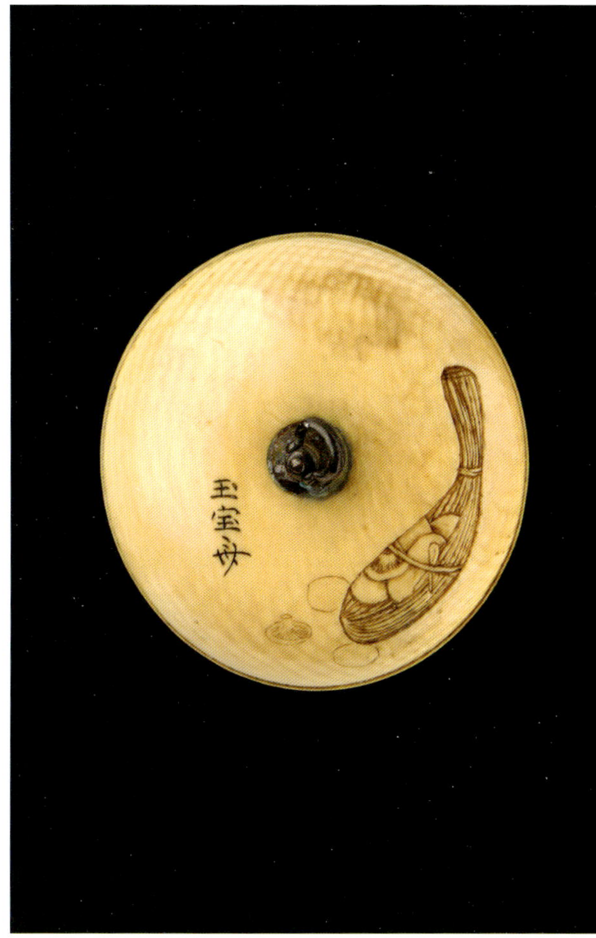

117

Birds and flower garland

Verso: plain

Tagua nut and silver inlay
Unsigned
Late 19th century
H: 3.35; W: 3.35; D: 1.8 cm
EAX.1116

This piece, attached to lacquered wooden box, probably for tobacco, shows very well the original shape of the tagua nut, from which the sides have been sliced off and polished. A metal artist has then attached a bee hovering over a garland of flowers.

Tagua nuts were occasionally used by netsuke carvers, usually after completely removing the outer brown skin, part of which remains here. It has a similar appearance to ivory and is now used by many contemporary carvers as the use of elephant ivory is now banned. The tree, from the genus *phytelephas,* grows in tropical rainforests, particularly in South America. It would have been imported and consequently regarded by the wearer as an exotic product.

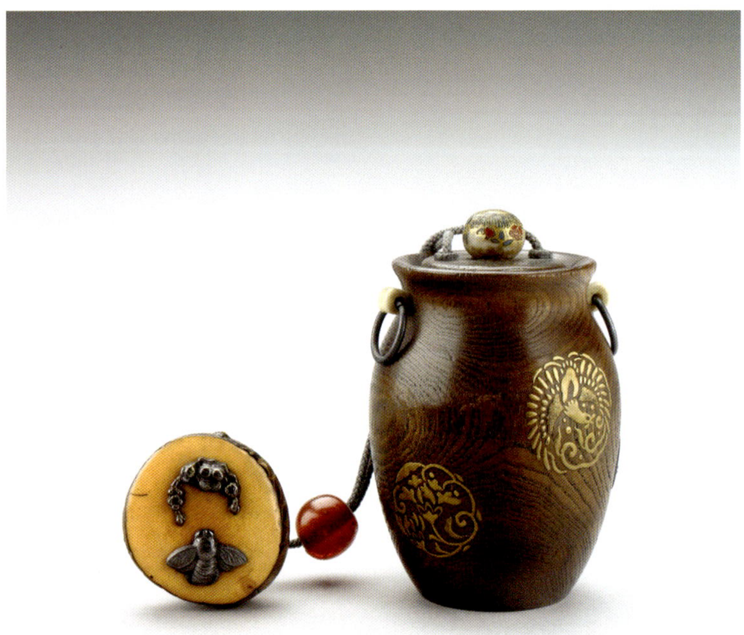

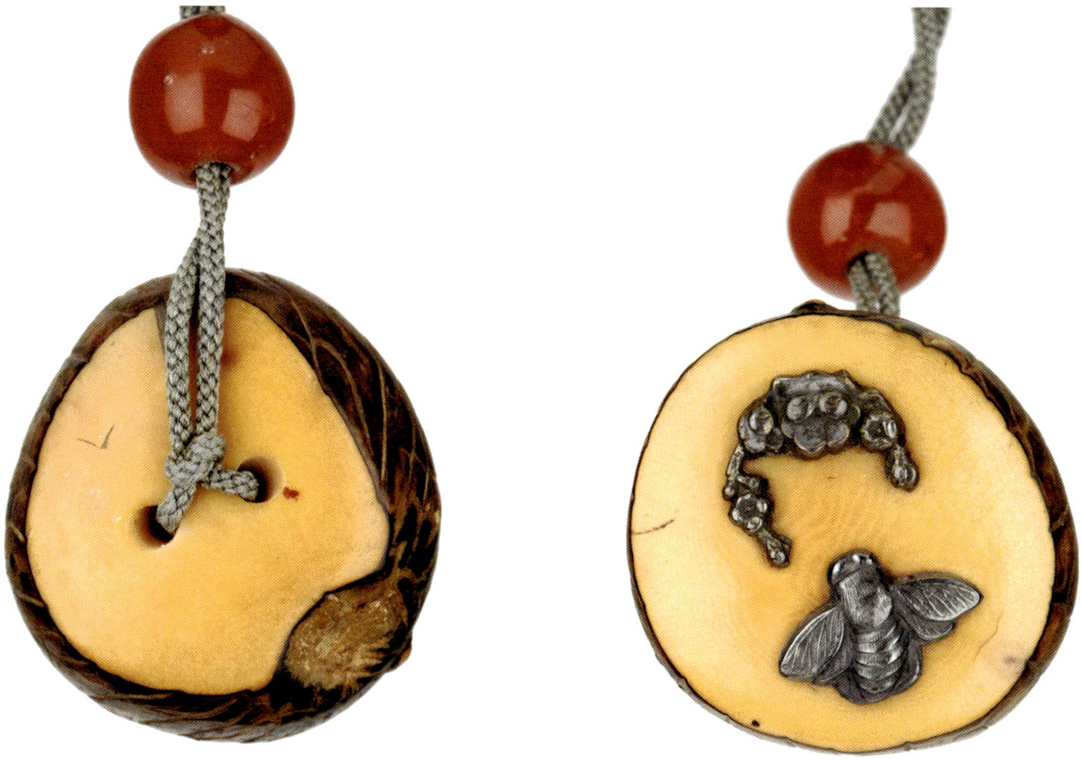

118

Geometric patterns (*guri*)

Carved lacquer
Unsigned
Mid-18th to early 19th century
Diam: 3.87; H: 2.1 cm
EAX.1333
Oppenheim gift

This *manjū* is carved in a symmetrical geometric pattern, through alternating layers of red and black lacquer. The design is divided into equal parts by four petal shapes emanating from a central circle which forms the *himotōshi* on the back.

The technique is known in Japan as *guri* and (used as decoration on lacquer) dates back at least as far as the twelfth century in China. It involves many layers of lacquer, in this case of red and black alternating colours applied to the base, after which the pattern is cut with a V-shaped knife through the layers to reveal the different colours.

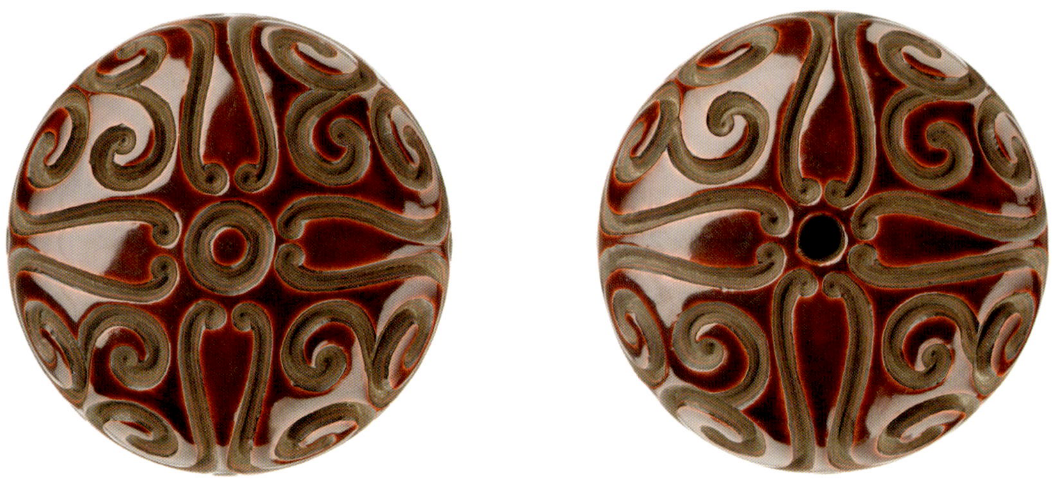

119

Geometric patterns (*guri*)

Carved metal
Unsigned
18th–19th century
Diam: 3.9: H: 1.18 cm
EAX.1331
Oppenheim gift

In this metal *manjū*, cut in the same *guri* style, the layers are in bronze and copper in a simple geometric scroll around the outer edge with concentric circles in the centre.

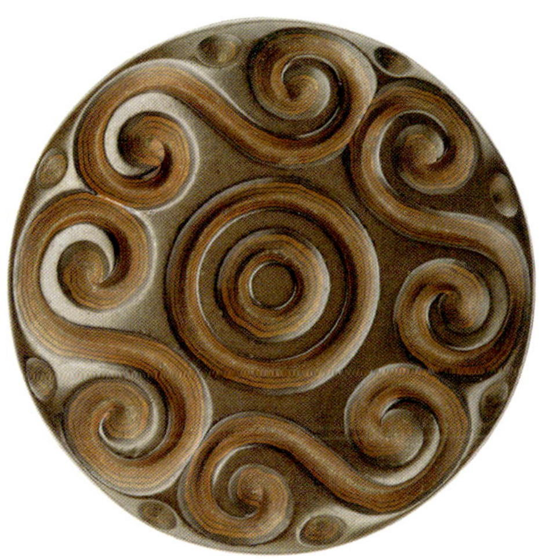

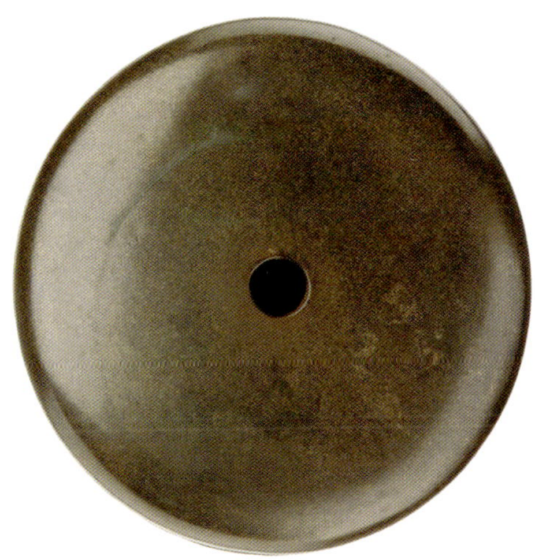

120 and 121

Basketwork

[120]
Shakudō and silver
Unsigned
19th century
W: 3.25; H: 3.15 cms
EA1956.3271
Presented by Sir Herbert Ingram

[121]
Shakudō, copper, gold and *shibuichi*
Unsigned
19th century
W. 3.3: H. 3.3: D: 1.83 cm
EA2001.115
Bequeathed by Dr Monica Barnett

See Christie's, London. *The Raymond and Frances Bushell Collection of Netsuke. Part 1.* 27/10/1987. Lot 316. Raymond Bushell attributes a similar piece from his collection to an artist called Ihei, whose other name was Toshimaya and who worked in Osaka before 1781. He was mentioned in the *Sōken Kishō*.[89] He specialised in *manjū* netsuke made from flat silver, copper and *shakudō* wire woven into geometric patterns and did not sign his work.

There are many unsigned examples dating from the nineteenth century and in particular there are five of these *manjū* in the Trumpf collection in Stuttgart.[90]

This style of squarish *manjū* woven with different basketwork patterns is quite common. The first of these two has simple stripes, closely woven in *shakudō* and silver wire. The second is a more complicated weave in *shakudō* and copper. It has inlaid on it, two purely decorative crests (*mon*): a three layered chrysanthemum in gold and a combination of bellflowers and wistaria in *shibuichi*.[88] To make these netsuke a sheet, woven with thin strips of metal was cut to size and then attached to a copper shell and bound with another stronger metal strip around the edges. They all seem to be of a very similar size.

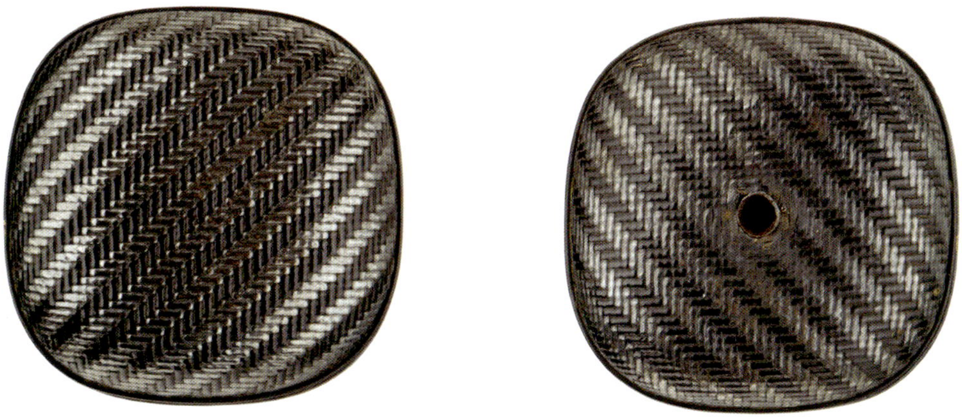

Cat. no. 120

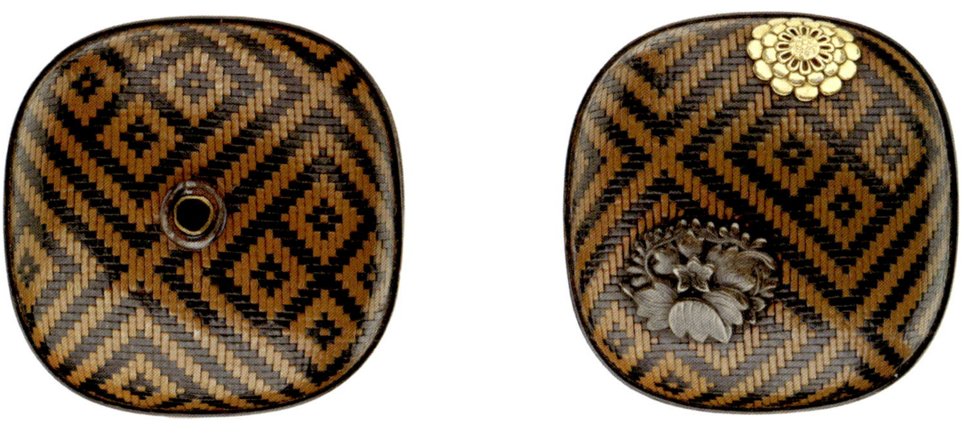

Cat. no. 121

122

Floral scrolls

A central roundel of floral scrolls in *cloisonné* enamels
Wood, metal wire and enamel
Unsigned
19th century
Diam: 3.81; H: 1.7 cm
EAX.631

A very plain *manjū* netsuke with a circular panel decorated with a *cloisonné* enamel rosette composed of a six-petalled flower surrounded by triple pine branches. This combination of wood and *cloisonné* enamel on a netsuke is unusual but not unknown. The enamel would have been fired separately and then applied to the wood.

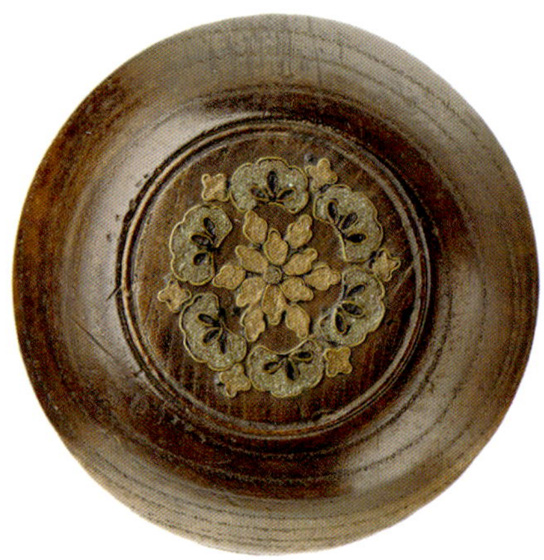

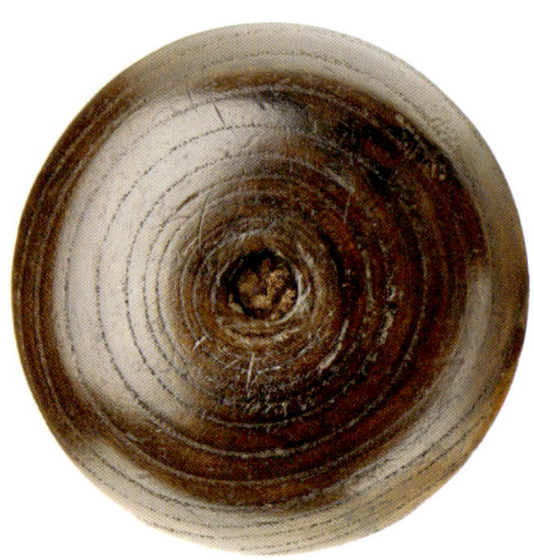

123

Plain ivory *manjū* with central peg

Ivory
Unsigned
18th or early 19th century
Diam: 3.7; H: 1.9 cm
EA1956.3214
Presented by Sir Herbert Ingram

This may be the forerunner of many of the *manjū* in this collection: completely plain and undecorated. It is also possible that it was used by a smoker, whose means did not run to decoration, but who needed an anchor for his smoking paraphernalia, such as the farmer pictured below.

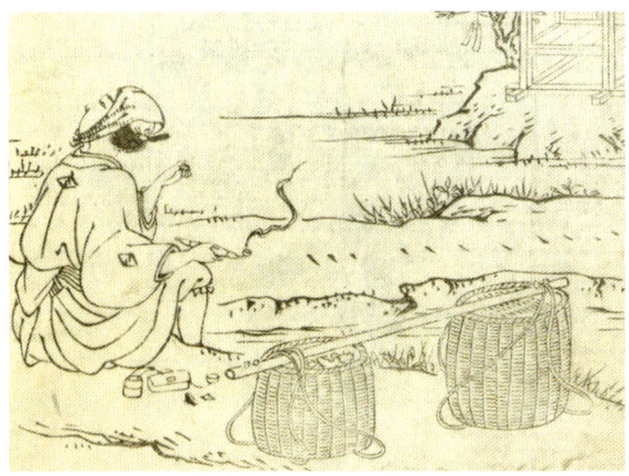

Fig. 69 Illustration from *Ehon hakuzugahara* (EA2012.35) of a farmer having a rest from his labours with his smoking paraphernalia next to him

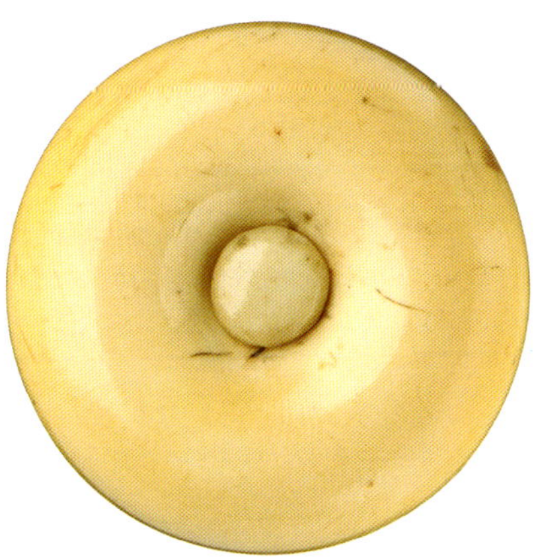

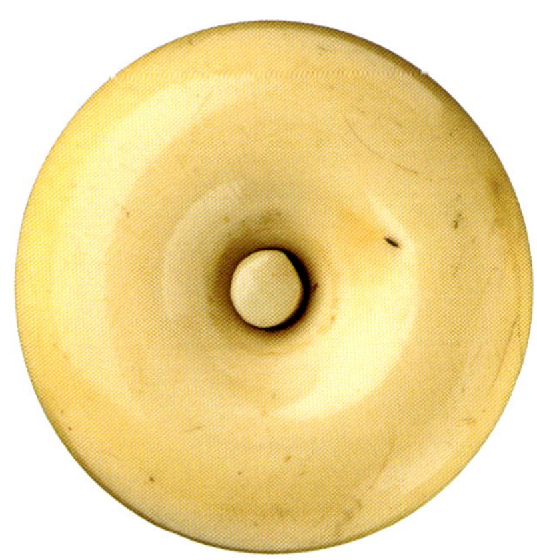

Notes to the Catalogue

1 *Kakihan*, literally a written seal mark, is a specifically designed character which represents or accompanies the signature.
2 Sekido Kengo. 'Hojitsu, un maitre de netsuke d'Edo'. *Bulletin Association Franco-Japonaise*. No. 64 Avril, 1999, p. 30. (Also translated into English in the same volume.)
3 Timon Screech. *Obtaining Images. Art, Production and Display in Edo Japan*. Reaktion Books. 2012, p. 157
4 For an article tracing the evolution of this theme see Money L. Hickman. 'On the Trail of Kume the Transcendent'. *M Bulletin* (MFA Boston). Vol. 79, 1981
5 *Sanguozhiyanyi* 三国志演义 (Jap. *sangokushi engi*) or 'The Romance of the Three Kingdoms'
6 *Diaper* is a small repeating pattern used as background. See also cat. nos. 19 and 20
7 *Shakudō* is an alloy of copper with between four and ten percent gold added. When patinated it becomes a dark blue-black colour
8 Translated by Max Rutherston
9 Shen C.Y. Fu. Translated and adapted by Stephen D. Allee. 'Puns and Playfulness in Chinese Painting'. *Asian Art & Culture*. Arthur M. Sackler Gallery, Smithsonain Institution. Fall. 1994. Humor
10 *Journal of the International Netsuke Collectors Society*. Vol. 10, No. 4, p. 26
11 Sekido Kengo. 'Hojitsu, un maitre de netsuke d'Edo'. *Bulletin Association Franco-Japonaise*. No. 64 Avril, 1999, p. 30. (Also translated into English in the same volume.)
12 Melinda Takeuchi. 'Kuniyshoshi Minamoto Raikō and the Earth Spider: Demons and Protest in Late Tokugawa Japan'. *Ars Orientalis* Vol. 17, 1987, p. 6
13 For a detailed description of the series and illustrations of many of the prints see Inge Klompmakers, *Of Brigands and Bravery, Kuniyoshi's heroes of the Suikoden*. Hotei Publishing, Leiden, 1998
14 Shi Nai'an and Luo Guanzhong. Translated by Sidney Shapiro. *Outlaws of the Marsh*. Foreign language Press, Beijing, 1980, Chapter 23. p. 355
15 Shi Nai'an and Luo Guanzhong Ibid. p. 356
16 A woodblock print of the two men fighting is illustrated in Inge Klompmakers. *Of Brigands and Bravery. Kuniyoshi's heroes of the Suikoden*. Hotei Publishing, Leiden. 1998, p. 89
17 *Wakan sansai zue* 和漢三才図会 (Illustrated Sino-Japanese Encyclopedia). Compiled by Terajima Ryōan. Tokyo, 1712
18 Richard Wolf, *Die Welt der netsuke*. F.A.Brockhaus. Wiesbaden, 1970. Opposite p. 132
19 Lafcadio Hearn. *Glimpses of Unfamiliar Japan*. Osgood, McIlvane and Co. London. 1894, Vol. 1. p. 76
20 Merrily Baird. *Symbols of Japan. Thematic Motifs in Art and Design*. Rizzoli International Publications, Inc. 2001, p. 88
21 Suzuki Rinchō. Ed. Hanabusa Itchō. *Itchō gafū*, 1770, Vol. 3
22 Jirka-Schmitz, Patrizia. *Netsuke. 112 Meisterwerke. Masterpieces. The Trumpf collection*. Linden-Museum, Stuttgart, Staatliches Museum für Völkerkunde. Arnoldsche und Autoren. 2000, No. 92
23 Luigi Bandini of Eskenazi Ltd. wrote a report on the sale of one of these pieces at Sotheby's in 1986 in Netsuke Kenkyukai Study Journal Volume 6, Number 2, 1986
24 Eitaku. *Banbutsu hinagata gafū* (A Collection of Designs based on Every Aspect of Nature). Tokyo, 1880-1882
25 Jirka-Schmitz, Patrizia. *The World of Netsuke. The Werdelmann Collection at the museum kunst palast Düsseldorf*. Arnoldsche Art Publishers, Stuttgart. 2005, No. 568
26 Miyeko Murase. *Bridge of Dreams. The Mary Griggs Burke Collection of Japanese Art*. The Metropolitan Museum of Art, New York. Distributed by Harry H. Abrams, Inc., New York. 2000, p. 115
27 Conrad Hyers. 'Humor in Zen: Comic Midwifery'. *Philosophy East and West*. Vol. 39 No. 3 Jul. 1989, p. 274
28 E.A. Wrangham. Ed. Joe Earle. *The Index of Inrō Artists*. Harehope Publications. 1995
29 It is illustrated in Bonhams, *The Edward Wrangham Collection of Japanese Art: Part III*. 15/05/2012. London, Lot 139
30 Noboru Kawaguchi 川口陟. *Tsuba Taikan* 鐔大觀 (Encyclopaedia of Sword Guards) Tokyo, 1935
31 Robert E. Haynes. *The Index of Japanese Sword Fittings and Associated Artists*. 3 vols. Nihon Art Publishers. Ellwangen. 2001, H 11413.0, p. 2233
32 Xavier Benjamin Bensky. 'Manzai: Metamorphoses of a Japanese Comic Performance Genre'. Part of an MA Thesis for the East Asian Studies Department, McGill University, Montreal. March 1998, p. 9
33 U.A Casal. *The Five Sacred Festivals of Japan*. Sophia University. Tokyo in Co-operation with Charles E. Tuttle Company, Rutland, Vermont & Tokyo, Japan, p. 35
34 Hirokazu Arakawa. *The Gō Collection of Netsuke*. Tokyo Natinal Museum. Kodansha International Ltd. Tokyo, New York and San Francisco. 1983
35 Anne Hull Grundy. 'Stagshorn and Other Quaint Netsuke, Principally of the Asakusa School'. *Oriental Art*. Vol. 6, No. 3, 1960
36 Frederick Meinertzhagen. Ed. George Lazarnick. *MCI. Meinertzhagen Card Index on Netsuke in the Archives of the British Museum*, Alan R. Liss, Inc., New York. Part A, p. 369
37 Casal, U.A. *The Five Sacred Festivals of Japan*. Sophia University. Tokyo in Co-operation with Charles E. Tuttle Company, Rutland, Vermont & Tokyo, Japan, p. 17
38 For a full explanation of the ritual see Eric E. Rath. 'From representation to apotheosis: Nō's Modern Myth of Okina'. *Asian Theatre Journal*, Vol. 17, No. 2, Autumn 2000
39 Casal, U.A. *The Five Sacred Festivals of Japan*. Sophia University. Tokyo in Co-operation with Charles E. Tuttle Company, Rutland, Vermont & Tokyo, Japan. p. 5
40 Frederick Meinertzhagen. Ed. George Lazarnick. *Meinertzhagen Card Index on Netsuke in the Archives of the British Museum*, Alan R. Liss, Inc., New York, p. 335

41 Emiko Ohnuki-Tierney. *The Monkey as Mirror. Symbolic Transformations in Japanese History and Ritual*. Princeton University Press, 1987

42 柳禮子。印路。根付。印路美術館、高山市。日本写真印刷株式会社 Yanagi, Reiko. Inro. *Netsuke. From the Inro Museum*, Takayama City. Nissha Printing Co. Ltd. September 1992, No. 252

43 Julia Meech. *Lacquerware from the Weston Collection. A Selection of Inro and Boxes*. Christie's, Inc. New York, 1995, cat. no. 49

44 Hirokazu Arakawa. *The Gō Collection of Netsuke*. Tokyo National Museum. Kodansha International Ltd. Tokyo, New York and San Francisco, 1983, Illustration Nos. 257–260

45 See Laura J. Mueller. *Adornment in Clay. Ceramic Netsuke from the Richard R. Silverman Collection*. Toledo Musuem of Art, Toledo, Ohio, 2010, cat. no. 38

46 Éva Cseh. *Netsuke. Japanese Miniature Carvings. Collections of the Ferenc Hopp Museum of East Asiatic Arts*. Budapest, Volume I, 2001

47 Minkō, Tachibana. *Saiga shokunin burui* 彩画職人部類 (Coloured Pictures of Classified Artisans) published in 1770

48 For this process see Gina Collia-Suzuki. 'Beautiful blackened smiles'. *Andon* 92, pp. 46–48

49 Published in O.R. Impey. *Japanese Netsuke in Oxford*. Ashmolean Museum. 1993, No. 56, p. 42

50 T. Volker. *The Animal in Far Eastern Art and especially the Art of the Japanese Netsuke with References to Chinese Origins, Traditions, Legends and Art*. Brill. Leiden, 1950, p. 88

51 John T. Carpenter, translated by, *(Ryokō kyōkun uta)* 旅行教訓歌, this song was inscribed in minute letters on a *manjū* netsuke listing the 53 Stations of the Tokaidō, accompanied by an *inrō* decorated with a map of Japan by the carver Ichimuken Nanka. (Ex. Weston Collection)

52 Raymond Bushell. *Netsuke Familiar and Unfamiliar. New Principles for Collecting*. Weatherill, New York and Tokyo, 1975, p. 142, Fig. 290. 'The teapot mat is usually of decorated paper or bamboo and placed under the teapot. It is an uncommom subject for netsuke.'

53 Illustrated in Neil K. Davey. *Netsuke. A comprehensive study based on the M.T. Hindson collection*. Faber & Faber Limited. London, in association with Sotheby Parke Bernet Publications, 1974, No. 394

54 For a translation of the work see McCullough, Helen Craig. *Kokin Wakashū: The First Imperial Anthology of Japanese Poetry*. Stanford University Press, Stanford, California, 1985

55 Éva Cseh. *Netsuke. Japanese Miniature Carvings. Collections of the Ferenc Hopp Museum of East Asiatic Arts*. Budapest, Vol. I, 2001

56 *Shinkokinshū*. VIII: 516

57 Hirokazu Arakawa. *The Gō Collection of Netsuke*. Tokyo Natinal Museum. Kodansha International Ltd. Tokyo, New York and San Francisco, 1983, No. 349

58 Kabuki is classical Japanese dance drama

59 William Richie Wilson, translated by, *Konjaku monogatarishū*. Volume XXV, Number VII. Translated as 'How the Noble Fujiwara no Yasumasa Faced Down the Bandit Hakadamare'

60 Will. H Edmunds. *Pointers and Clues to the Subjects of Chinese and Japanese Art*. Sampson Low Marston and Co. Ltd, 1934, p. 640

61 Melinda Takeuchi. '"Minamoto Raikō" and "the Earth Spider": Demons and Protest in Late Tokugawa Japan'. *Ars Orientalis*, Vol.17, 1987, pp. 5-38

62 Elizabeth Liilehoj. 'Transfiguration: Man-made Objects as Demons in Japanese Scrolls'. *Asian Folklore Studies*. Volume 54, 1995, pp. 7-34

63 Noriko T Reider. 'Shūten Dōji "Drunken Demon"'. *Asian Folklore Studies*, Volume 64, 2005, pp. 207-231

64 For a translation see McCullough, Helen Craig. *Kokin Wakashū: The First Imperial Anthology of Japanese Poetry*. Stanford University Press, 1985

65 Hiroshi Kitagawa and Bruce T. Tsuchida, translated by. *The Tale of the Heike*. University of Tokyo Press. 1975, Vol. 1, Book 7, p. 312

66 Alain Ducros. *Netsuke. Art, magie et médecine*. Editions Cum Turri, 2006

67 Kiyoshi Nozaki. *Kitsune. Japan's Fox of Mystery, Romance and Humor*. The Hokuseido Press. 1961 tells of this phenomenon.

68 *Bunraku* is traditional Japanese puppet theatre

69 Hiroshi Kitagawa and Bruce T. Tsuchida, translated by. *The Tale of the Heike*. University of Tokyo Press. 1977, Vol. I, Book 4, p. 281

70 Ibid.

71 Helen Craig McCullough, translated by. *The Tale of the Heike (Heike Monogatari)*. Stanford University Press, 1988, p. 291

72 Hiroshi Kitagawa and Bruce T. Tsuchida, translated by. *The Tale of the Heike*. University of Tokyo Press, 1977, Vol II, Books 7–12 and Epilogue, p. 512

73 Ibid

74 Helen Craig McCullough. *Yoshitsune: a fifteenth-century Japanese chronicle*. Stanford, California. Stanford University Press, 1966

75 Nō play *Hashi Benkei* (Benkei on the Bridge) by Hiyoshi Sa-ami Yoshikiyo. In Arthur Waley. *Nō plays of Japan*. George Allen and Unwin Ltd, London, 1950 edition, p. 120

76 Julia Hutt. *Japanese Netsuke*. Victoria and Albert Musuem, Far Eastern Series. V & A Publications, 2003

77 Tomita Kumasaku and G. Ambrose Lee. *Japanese Treasure Tales*. Yamanaka and Co., London and Osaka, 1906, p. 65

78 Ibid.

79 Robert Schaap. *Heroes & Ghosts. Japanese Prints by Kuniyoshi 1797–1861*. Society for Japanese Arts. 1998, p. 55, cat. no. 23

80 *Gohei* a wooden stick or staff, held by a Shintō priest to indicate the presence of the *kami* (god)

81 T. Volker. *The Animal in Far Eastern Art and especially the Art of the Japanese Netsuke with References to Chinese Origins, Traditions, Legends and Art*. Brill, Leiden, 1950, p. 56

82 Neil K. Davey. *Netsuke. A comprehensive study based on the M.T. Hindson collection*. Faber & Faber Limited. London in association with Sotheby Parke Bernet Publications, 1974, p. 433, No. 1301

83 Patricia Bjaaland Welch. *Chinese Art: A Guide to Motifs and Visual Imagery*. Tuttle Publishing. Tokyo, Vermont, Singapore, 2010

84 See Francesco Moreno, Ed. by, *Giappone Terra di Incanti. Di Linea e Di Colore (Japan the Land of Enchantment. Line and Colour)*. Firenze Musei (Palazzo Pitti). Sillabe, 2012, No. I.116, from the English text written by Max Rutherston and Rosemary Bandini

85 See Sydney L. Moss Ltd. *Eccentrics in Netsuke*. London, 1982

86 Helen Craig McCullough, translated and annotated. *Kokin wakashū* (The First Imperial Anthology of Japanese Poetry). With *Tosa Nikki* and *Shinsen Waka*. Stanford University Press, Stanford California, 1985, No. 279

87 Bonhams, London. 12/11/2008. Lot No. 440

88 *Shibuichi* is a metal alloy usually consisting of three parts copper with one part silver. It can be patinated to a wide range of soft colours

89 Inaba Tsūryū. Ibid.

90 Patrizia Jirka-Smchmitz. Netsuke. 112 Meisterwerke. Masterpieces. The Trumpf collection. Linden-Museum, Stuttgart, Staatliches Museum für Völkerkunde. Arnoldsche und Autoren, 2000, Nos. 809-813

SIGNATURES AND SHORT BIOGRAPHIES

Catalogue numbers are given alongside the signatures

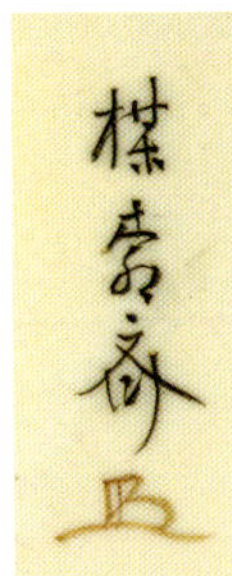
87

Baieisai 楳叡斎

There is no information on this artist. He uses a *kakihan* very close if not identical to that of Isshinsai Masayuki.

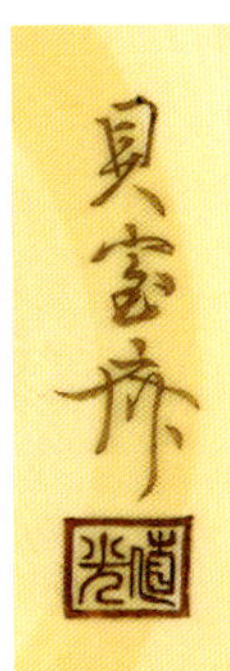
81

Baihōsai 貝宝齋

One *katabori* netsuke of a young boy appears in the Meinertzhagen Card Index under the artist Baihōsai with the seal reading Naomitsu, which Meinertzhagen describes as fine, early Meiji work. Lazarnick includes two *katabori* wood netsuke and another ivory *manjū* under the same artist and gives the earlier dates of 18th-19th century. Neither of the Lazarnick pieces uses the Naomitsu seal.

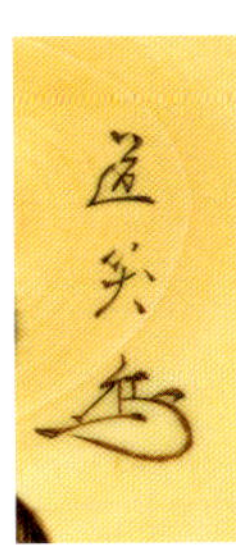
50

Dōshō 道笑 (1828–1884)

Dōshō was born in Izumo, in Western Japan in 1828 and moved to Osaka to work with Anrakusai Dōraku, whose pupil he became. He was a very fine artist, carving both *katabori* and *manjū* netsuke, always showing a flair for design, with compactness and precision in his technique. He favoured subjects from nature, carving exquisite chrysanthemum flowers, but also tackled people with equal skill and ingenuity. He sometimes signed his work Dōshōsai.

Funada Ikkin 船田一琴

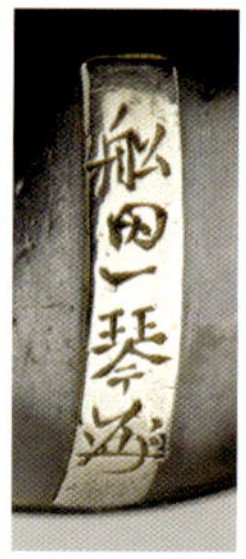

105

Funada Ikkin was born in Tsurugaoka in Dewa province, he later moved to Kyoto and then moved a second time to Tokyo. His work covers the period between around 1840 and 1885. He was the first son of Funada Ikkin I with whom he studied until the age of fourteen, when he went to Kyoto to be a pupil of Hashimoto Isshi. After four years in Kyoto he joined the Gotō Ichijō school. He worked in the Gotō Ichijō style and also learned the *katakiribori* technique. He outlived his father who died in 1863, and as a result, his output was far greater. Haynes says that 'Pieces signed Ikkin are rather common, but the majority would seem to be the work of the second generation of this name'[1]

Fūshō 風昇

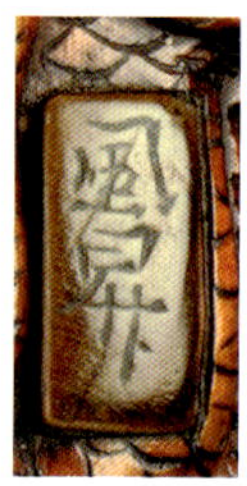

102

This artist is only mentioned as a carver of dragons in wood, at which Ueda Reikichi says he was good. He worked between 1830 and the beginning of the Meiji period (1868).

Gyokkōsai Morimasa 玉光齋守正

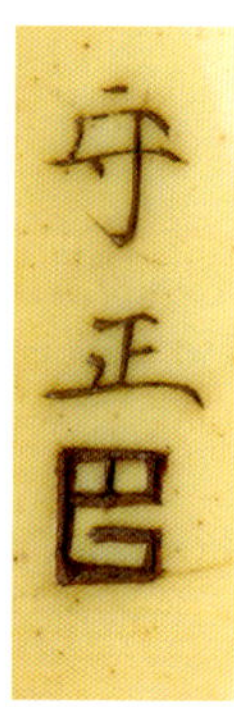

29

Morimasa is the family name of Gyokkōsai 玉光齋, who was a carver of *manjū* netsuke in Tokyo around the middle of the nineteenth century. This signature, Morimasa 守正, followed by the *'tomoe'* 巴 character, (although not surrounded by a red border as on the piece in cat. no. 49) is associated with Kikugawa Ryūgoku whom Meinertzhagen lists as Morimasa's teacher. The *kakihan* he uses on other *manjū* is the same as that used by artists signing 'Kikugawa'. His subject matter of legends and *karako* was in line with that of the Kikugawa school.

Gyokuhōsai Ryūchin 玉宝齋竜珍

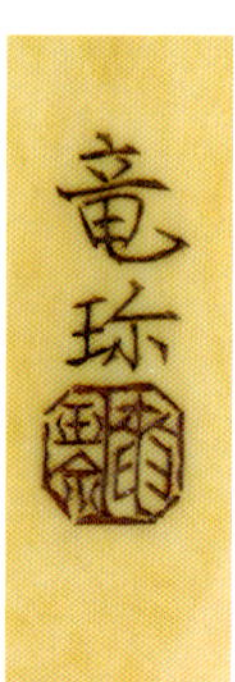

75

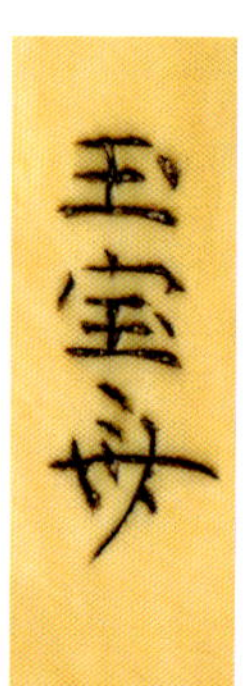

116

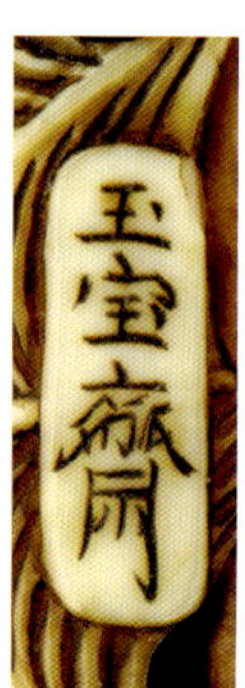

57

Gyokuhōsai Ryūchin's family name was Yamada and he worked in Tokyo between 1830 and 1860. Netsuke signed Gyokuhōsai are not uncommon and cover a wide range of subjects. His carving was done with great attention to tiny details and he excelled in putting interesting still life groups of related objects together with the greatest technical skill. These are perforated in the style of Ryūsa and it has been suggested that he was a pupil both Ryūkei and of Gyokuyōsai, giving him characters from both their names. Meinertzhagen thinks that his netsuke signed Ryūchin would be earlier than those signed Gyokuhōsai. He passed his talent to many pupils: Gyokhō, Meigyoku and Kōgyoku were three suggested by Ueda.

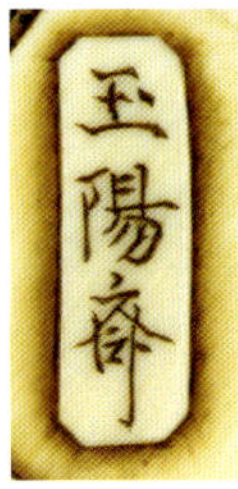

62

Gyokuyōsai Mitsuhina (Kōsō) 玉陽斎光雛 (1781–1868)

Gyokuyōsai lived in Asakusa, Fukuichō, Tokyo and was an excellent carver. According to Jonas he was originally a doll maker. He worked almost exclusively in ivory, making small, compact figures and detailed practical *manjū,* some of which include textile patterns as backgrounds. His subject matter is original and the *manjū* are interesting shapes. He seems to have been a prolific carver during the mid-late nineteenth century. The Baur Collection has many examples of his work. Gyokuyōsai was the teacher of Ozaki Kokusai, another very talented and original artist.

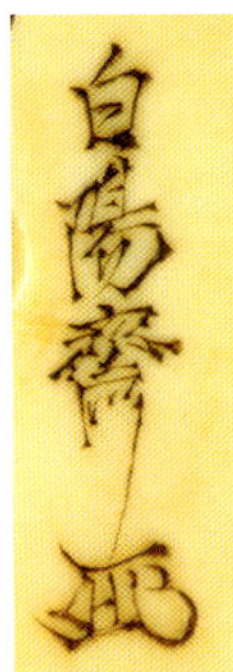

65

Hakuyōsai Kōgyoku 白陽蔡孝玉

Hakuyōsai Kōgyoku's work is uncommon, mostly *manjū* in ivory. Lazarnick illustrates a figure in wood and ivory. A *ryūsa* netsuke of Handaka Sonja is a departure from his usual style. His *kakihan* was also used by Hakuyōsai Shoraku who made similar ivory *manjū*. He was part of the Kikugawa lineage.

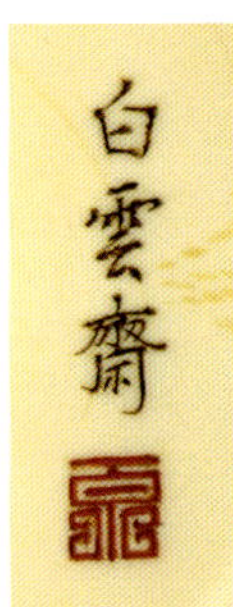

82

Hakuunsai 白雲斎

Hakuunsai worked in Tokyo around the middle of the nineteenth century and was prolific and imaginative. There were at least two carvers who signed Hakuunsai (and Lazarnick even suggests a third). Hakuunsai II, whose relationship to Hakuunsai I is not certain, was a member of the Kikugawa group of carvers and one of the finest of his time making *manjū,* groups of masks and groups of figures in ivory and occasionally in wood. He sometimes signed Hakuun and on the Ashmolean's *manjū* his seal reads Hakuun

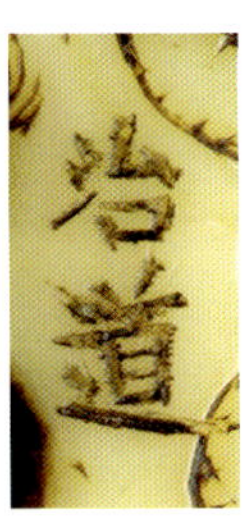

53

Harumichi 治道

Harumichi is an unrecorded artist.

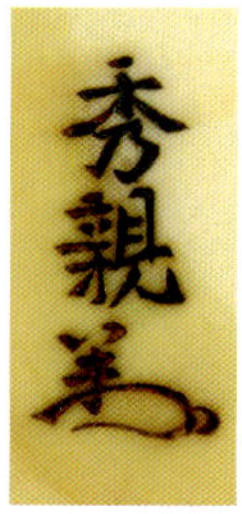

43

Hidechika 秀親

Hidechika Chōunsai was a fine carver who followed the style of Chikuyōsai Tomochika I and worked in the early and middle years of the nineteenth century in Tokyo, one piece being dated 1858. *Manjū* signed Chōunsai with the Hidechika seal frequently depict humans, whose expressive faces he has carved with great skill. Fukurokuju was one of his favourite subjects. He usually carved in sunken relief *(shishi-aibori)* on the reverse of his *manjū*, whereas many *manjū* carvers used sketchier *kebori* lines.

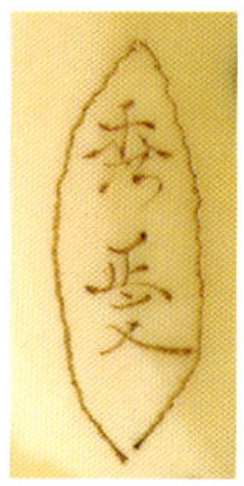

12

Hidemasa 秀政

Hidemasa lived and worked in Osaka in the late eighteenth century. He was an outstanding carver who had at least two pupils and Neil Davey suggests he had many more. His work was almost always in ivory and usually of figures, carved in minute detail some standing on a flat platform. His signature is often in a wavy reserve as on the Ashmolean's *manjū*, which appears to be an unusual shape for Hidemasa.

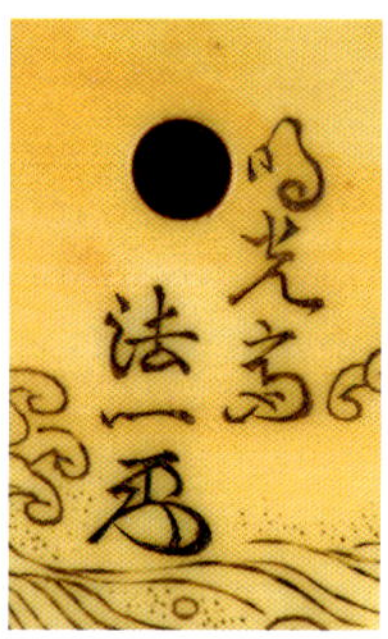

1

Meikōsai Hōichi 明光斎法一 (1808–1859)

Meikōsai Hōichi was one of Meikeisai Hōjitsu's more able pupils, but died thirteen years before his teacher. He came from the Kyoto region and moved to Tokyo to join Hōjitsu's workshop. Like his master he used ivory and wood and, carved figures, masks and *manjū* netsuke paying great attention to the small details.

Meikeisai Hōjitsu 明鶏齋法實 (*c.* 1800–1872)

Meikeisai Hōjitsu was regarded as the best netsuke carver of his time in Edo, excelling in his renderings both of *katabori* and *manjū* netsuke. He lived and worked in Edo and witnessed the social upheaval of the Meiji period and all its implications for craftsmen. He was a prolific carver of fine netsuke both in *ukibori*, where the design is raised above the surface, and sunken relief *(shishiaibori)* carving. As fashions changed in the Meiji period, he put new skills to work, using different materials and woods as inlays, particularly on his *katabori* pieces. He appears to have overseen a large workshop, with many students, evidence of which can be found engraved on his tombstone. Over twenty years after his death, a ceremony was held in 1894 at the Nichiren Sect temple, Renkyūji, to

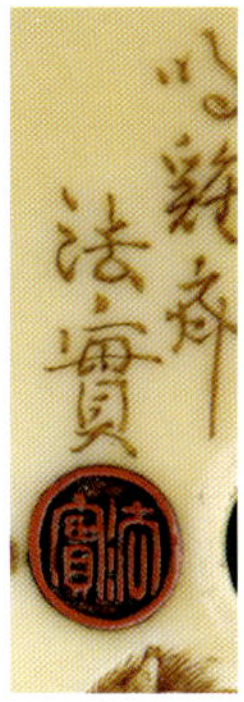

46

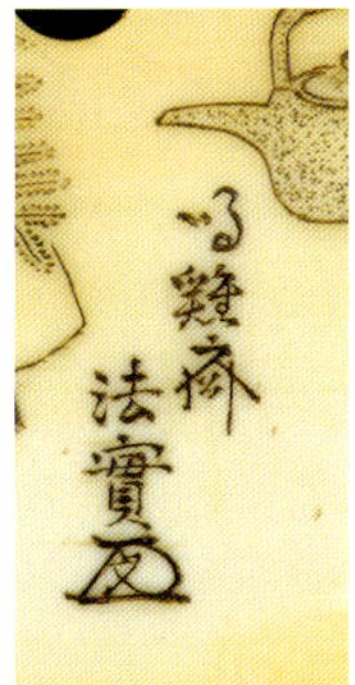

41

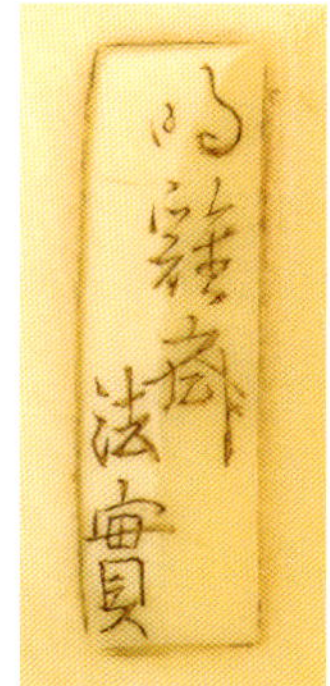

15

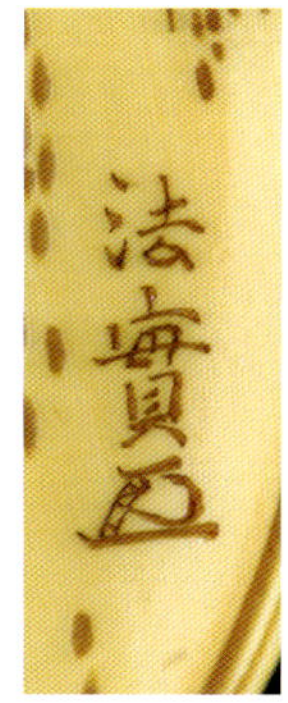

44

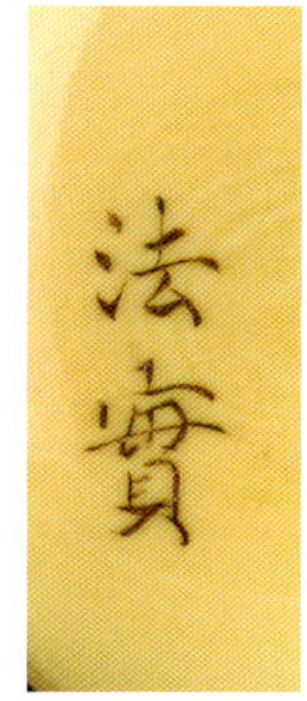

58

erect this tombstone upon which were carved the names of some of his pupils; Ippōsai, Hōichi, Kōjitsu, Hōkyō, Hōmin and Hōgyoku, the first three of whose works are represented in this collection. He made netsuke for the *daimyō* of Tsugaru and was a retainer of the Tokugawa government and it is also possible that he even carved for the shōgun. During his life he developed such a high reputation that it appears that less skilled carvers used Hōjitsu's signature, for there are a number of pieces signed Hōjitsu which are clearly not his work. Indeed Sekido Kengo does not believe these even to be the work of his pupils.[2] All five of the signatures on Hōjitsu's pieces in the Ashmolean's collection are different. The red seal after the signature on cat. no. 46 is unusual.

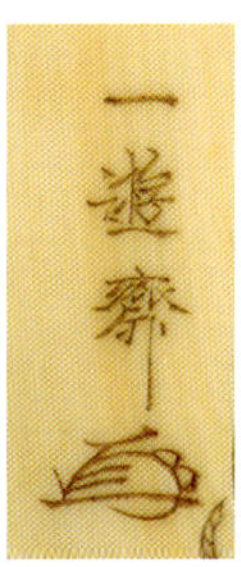

72

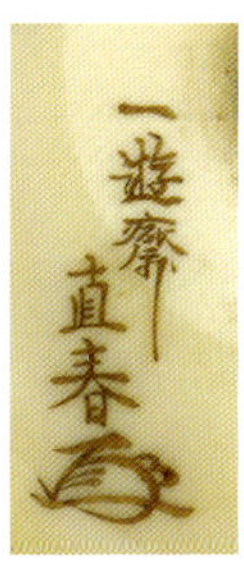

30

Ichiyūsai Naoharu 一遊齋直春

Ichiyūsai Naoharu was active in Tokyo between 1860 and 1890, although he may have worked in Osaka as well, as Ueda refers to him as Tokyo Naoharu. He was a fine carver of *katabori* figures, *inrō* and *manjū* netsuke in ivory. His workshop, which Patrizia Jirka-Schmitz suggests was large, was called Yamachō. This we know from an *inrō* which bears the shop sign.[3] On the strength of the way the 'yū' character is written on cat. no. 30, it has also been assigned to Naoharu.

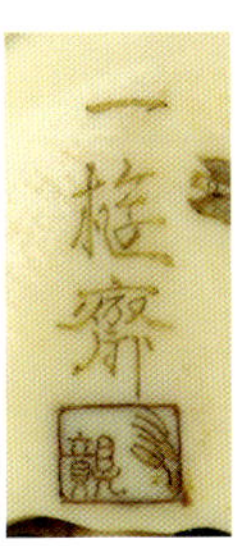

5

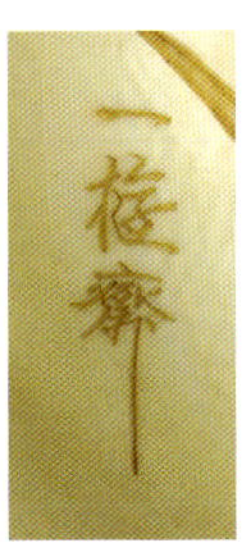

60

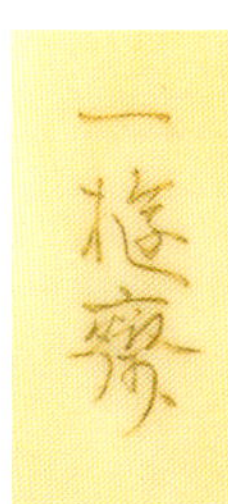

88

Ichiyūsai Naomitsu 一遊齋直光 (1868–1931)

Ichiyūsai Naomitsu was a pupil of Ichiyūsai Naoharu, possibly his only one. Despite his teacher possibly living in Tokyo at some time, Naomitsu lived and worked in Osaka. The 'yū' character in his Ichiyūsai is different from his teacher with the 'tree' element on the left, instead of in the middle. He also used the names, Murata, Isseisai and Isshōsai. The seal on cat. no. 88 may have been added later, for it appears to have no connection to Ichiyūsai Naomitsu. His chief output also seems to have been ivory *manjū*.

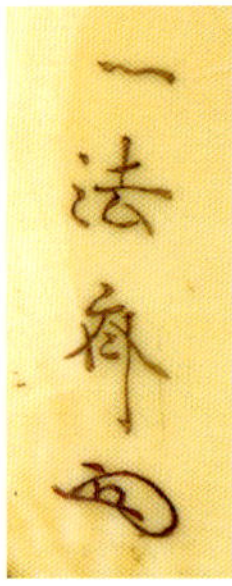

2

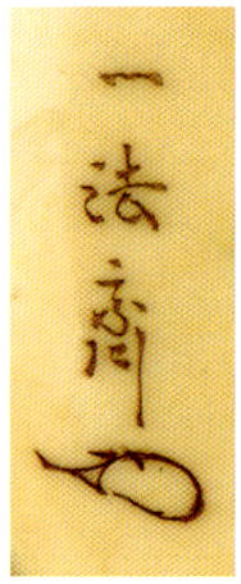

14

Ippōsai Jitsumin 一法齋實民 (1829 or 1831–1895)

Ippōsai was either born in 1829 or 1831 and lived in Asakusa, Tokyo. His family name was Hagiwara. He signed both Ippōsai and Jitsumin (實民) on some of his *manjū*, on others just Ippōsai. He seems only to have made netsuke of the *manjū* type. He was a pupil of Meikeisai Hōjitsu and carved very skilfully in the sunken relief technique. According to Ueda he was left-handed, a most unusual thing for a craftsman at the time. The 'sai' character on both the Ashmolean's pieces is the same is those in the Baur collection and in the Meinertzhagen Card Index, two of which are signed Ippōsai Jitsumin with a *kakihan*. However it is different from that on *manjū* in the British Museum, Maidstone Museum and in Karl Schwarz's book, *Netsuke Subjects*. (No.271)

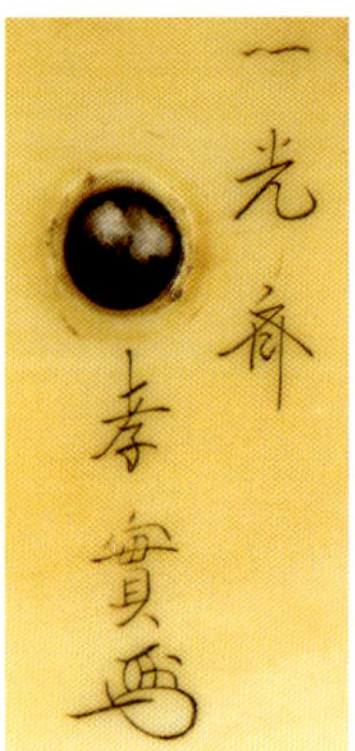

27

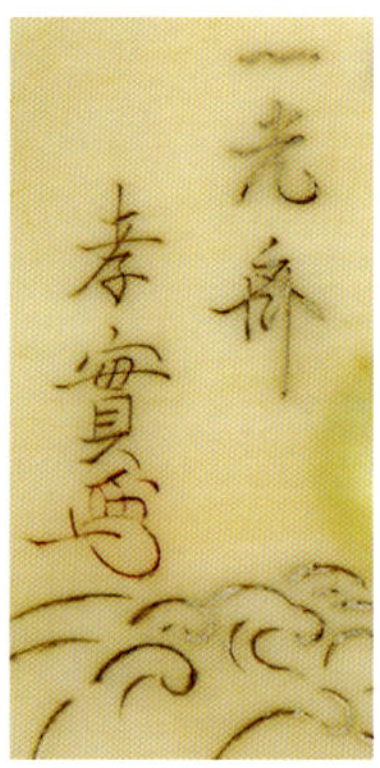

40

Ikkōsai Kōjitsu 一光斎孝實 (1833–1892)

Ikkōsai Kōjitsu was from an Osaka family, but his studies in carving were under Hōjitsu in Tokyo, where he lived in the Asakusa area. He was one of Hōjitsu's finest pupils and carved both figures in the round and a large number of *manjū* at which he excelled. For these he used the three carving techniques, *shishiaibori, ukibori* and *kebori* with equal skill. His name appeared among other fine pupils on the memorial stone of his master's grave.

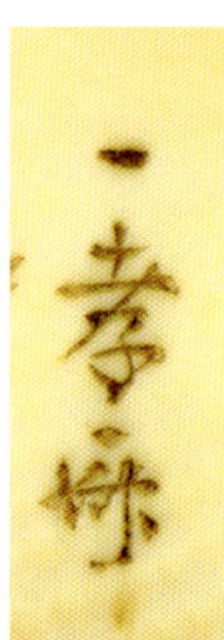

48

Ikkōsai 一孝齋

Reikichi Ueda's brief entry for this artist reads 'Ikko 一孝. Late. Ivory figures'. Lazarnick illustrates two detailed groups in ivory, and mentions a third, but no *manjū*. Ikkōsai carved in the late nineteenth century and was probably associated with Ikkōsai Kōjitsu and Hōjitsu.

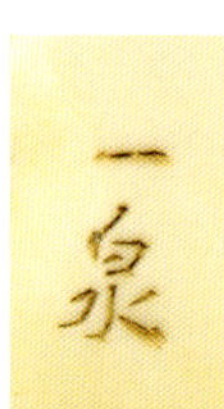

63

Issen 一泉

Issen was a skilled carver of figures, animals and groups in ivory in Tokyo in the early and mid nineteenth century. A figure of a Nō dancer from the Hindson collection very effectively combines wood and ivory. Neil Davey suggests that on stylistic grounds he was a follower of Joryū.

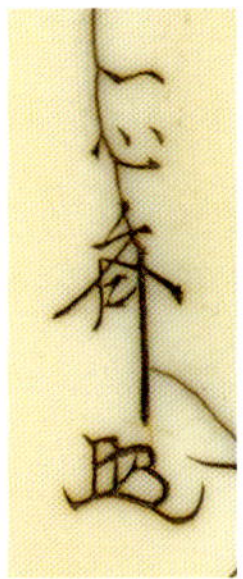

13

Isshinsai Masayuki 一心斎正之

Isshinsai Masayuki was thought to come from Osaka, and carved *manjū* netsuke in ivory. The two examples in Lazarnick have his full name and *kakihan* and are carved in low relief with figures. The Ashmolean's *manjū* shows off his skill both at the *shishiaibori* and *kebori* techniques. He has used *sumi* ink staining to further dramatise this well-known scene.

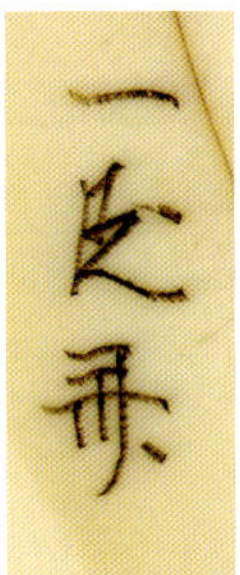

93

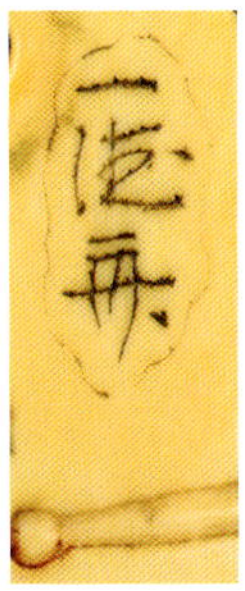

77

Ittokusai 一徳斎

Ittokusai was a carver of *manjū* netsuke in ivory. His work is not common and features *karako* and folktales, carved in shallow sunken relief with good detail especially on the clothing. On one *manjū* he has carved a most unusual beaded border.[4]

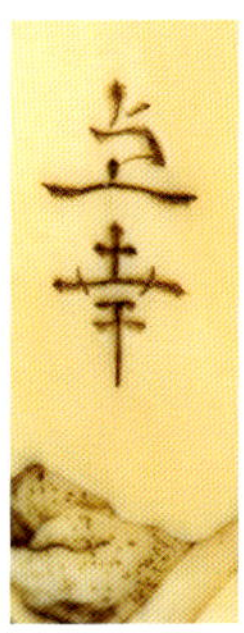

84

Jōkō 上幸

Jōkō is not recorded.

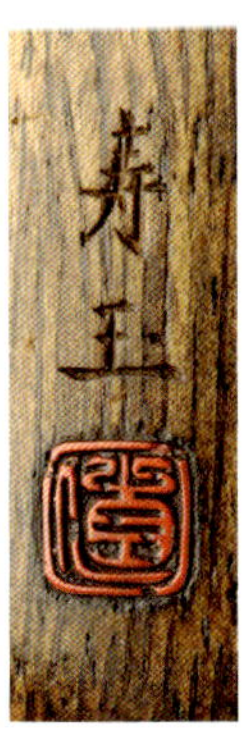

21

Jugyoku Ryūkosai II 寿玉龍光斎 (1815 or 1816–1887)

Jugyoku Ryūkosai II was a pupil of Jugyoku I. He was born in Tokyo and lived there until his death. He was a prolific and very skilled carver who used a wide variety of materials to carve *manjū* and an extensive range of figural subjects. The character 'ju' can be written with either fourteen '壽' or six '寿' strokes and both Jugyoku I & II appear to have used both versions. On the Ashmolean's bamboo *manjū* the signature is followed by a most unusual red seal which reads 'ren' 蓮. There is one other in the Metropolitan Museum, New York, (10211.1334) which has the seal on the reverse and is signed inside the netsuke within a wavy reserve with the six-stroke 'ju' character.

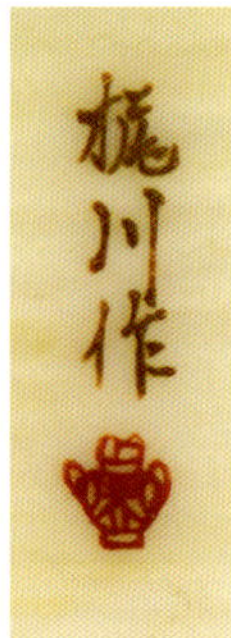

35

Kajikawa 梶川

Kajikawa was the family name of a long line of lacquerers who worked for the shogunate from the early seventeenth century to well into the nineteenth century. They made *inrō* and often *manjū* netsuke to accompany them. The red pot seal reads 'ei'.

Kikugawa Masamitsu 菊川正光

Kikugawa Masamitsu was thought to be the founder of the group of carvers which included those who used the name Kikugawa in their signature as well as those signing Hakuunsai, Hakuyōsai and Masamitsu, each of whose work features in this collection. Information is confused as to dates of their lives but all agree that they worked in Tokyo from the beginning of the nineteenth century and worked well into the Meiji period, specialising in *manjū* netsuke, many of which were larger than average and used small inlays of other materials, particularly metal beads to enhance their designs. Kikugawa Masamitsu's signature on the piece in cat. no. 55 is followed by the *kakihan* used on many other pieces signed simply 'Kikugawa'. It was also used by artists connected to the school but who were followers of Moritoshi Kōsai. The red '*tomoe*' seal on cat. no. 49 was used on pieces signed with another of the very skilled Kikugawa artsts, Kikugawa Ryūgoku. It appears that all the Kikugawa carvers at some stage in their careers carved a version of Kintarō killing the huge carp (cat. no. 94). Other favourite subjects were mothers and children, religious figures and stories from Japanese folklore.

Frederick Meinertzhagen indicates that Moritoshi Kōsai was also a follower of the school, but broke away and formed his own group of carvers, many of whom used a crane *kakihan*.

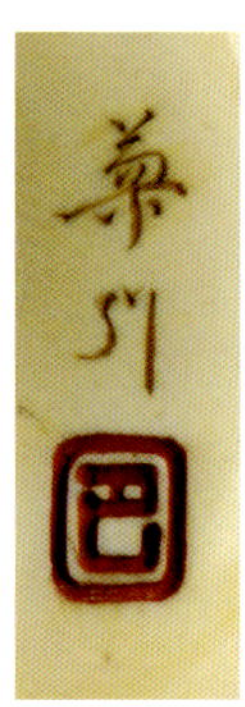

49

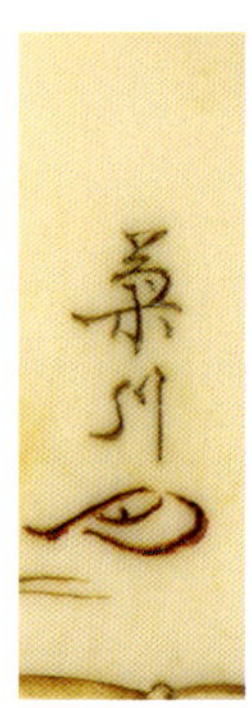

33

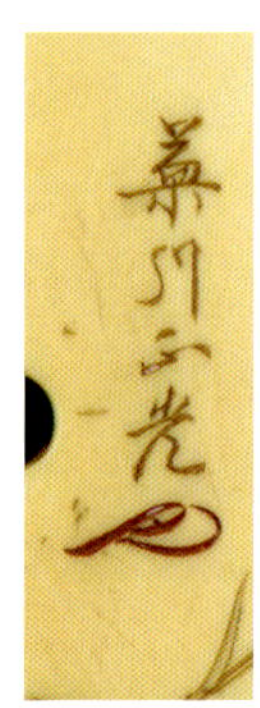

55

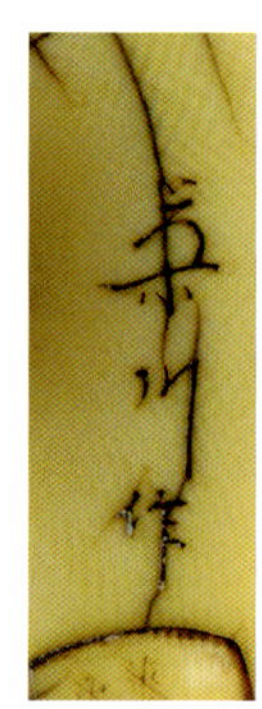

94

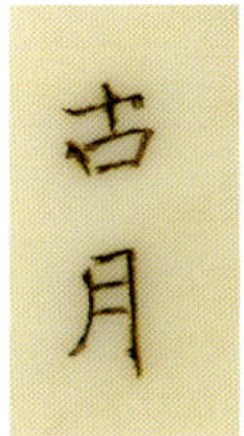

10

Kogetsu 古月

Kogetsu is not recorded. This simple signature may have been invented purely for the foreign market, to add to its value.

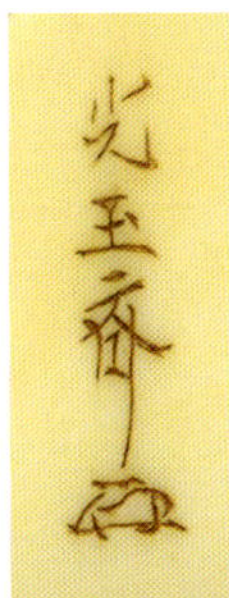
95

Kōgyokusai 光玉斎

Kōgyokusai was a Tokyo carver about whom we know almost nothing except that he worked in the late nineteenth century. His carving on *manjū* is in delicate sunken relief with coloured staining to enhance the details.

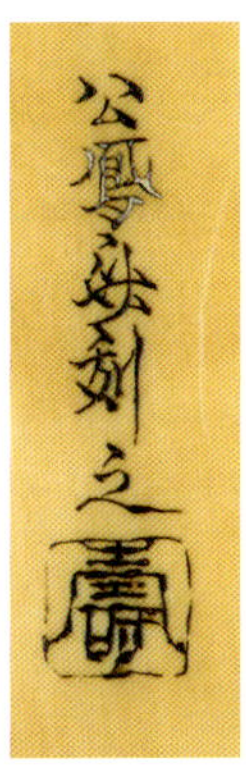
96

Kōhōsai 公鳳齋 (b.?–1907)

Kohōsai's family name was Ueda. He lived in Kawaramachi, Osaka and died around 1907. According to Meinetzhagen he enjoyed a considerable and well-deserved reputation during his lifetime. He excelled at subjects such as bulbs, fruits and flowers, but also carved fish, animals and vegetables. For his *manjū* he favoured the square shape using the *ukibori, shishiaibori* and *katakiribori* techniques to great effect. Meinertzhagen puts these square *manjū* in his earlier period and links him with Dōshōsai who also worked in Osaka.

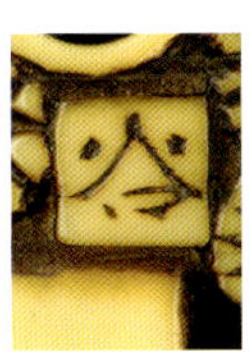

45

Kokusai 谷齋 (1830s–1894)

Ozaki Kokusai was an interesting, eccentric character and a brilliant designer and carver of netsuke, pipecases, hairpins and various other small objects in Tokyo in the mid to late nineteenth century. His name now denotes a style of perforated carved netsuke associated with the workshops in the Asakusa area. It is known as *Kokusai-bori*. Kokusai was a devout Buddhist, living close to the Sensōji temple complex, in Asakusa, which he visited frequently. In sharp contrast to his Buddhist ideals, he worked as an entertainer performing acts of buffoonery, occasionally in the nude, which gave him an income to help him support his son, Ozaki Kōyō, who was a struggling writer, but who eventually made his name as a novelist of renown.

At the age of twenty-one Kokusai began a four year apprenticeship in the technique of carving with Gyokuyōsai Mitsuhina. However, his own eccentric personality shines out in his netsuke and pipecases, for they are quite different from anything that was being produced at the time in Tokyo. His subject matter was deeply influenced by ancient Chinese Buddhist sculptural motifs and he sometimes used Chinese seal script as motifs or for his signature, which could be incorporated into a design so cleverly as not to be easily noticed. He carved in stag antler, eschewing the more malleable ivory or wood for much of his work possibly because it was readily available and it was also much less expensive than ivory.

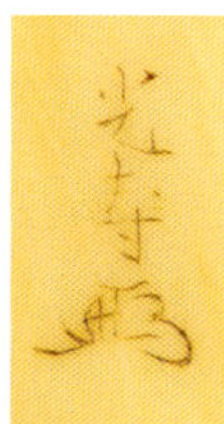

8

Kōju 光寿

Kōju was another member of the atelier of Hōjitsu in Tokyo, but mainly worked in ivory. He carved neat compact *manjū* in the style of his teacher and also carved figures. All have people with expressive faces. He worked around 1870.

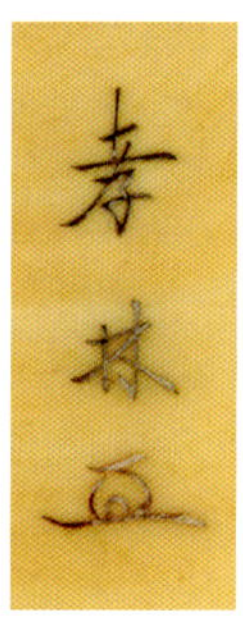

54

Kōrin 孝林

Kōrin uses the same 'kō' 孝 character as the nineteenth century Tokyo carvers Suzuki Kōsai, Ikkōsai Kōjitsu, Kōmin and Kōichi, all of whom carved *manjū*. Kōrin, whose *kakihan* was stained red, also carved masks and figures as well as *manjū*. His style is delicate and attention is paid to small details, in keeping with those artists to whom he is linked.

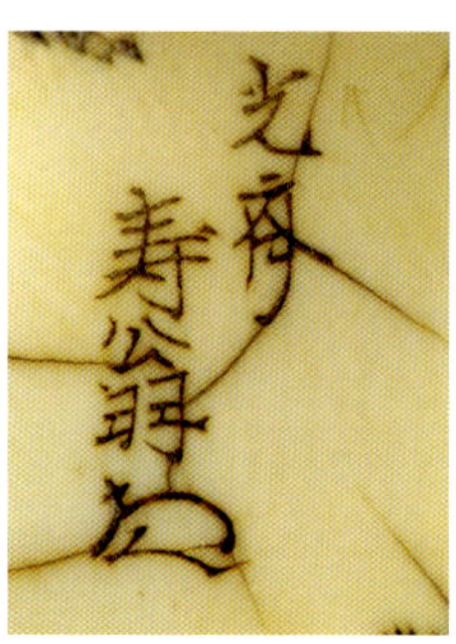

89

Kōsai Juō 光斎寿翁

Kōsai Juō shared the same Kōsai characters as the Tokyo carver Moritoshi and his known work is ivory *manjū* in Moritoshi's style. It is possible that he may have made some of the *manjū* which are just signed Kōsai (cat. nos. 28, 32 and 48). His *manjū* are however, rare.

Moritoshi Kōsai 光斎守寿

Moritoshi Kōsai was the founder of a school in Tokyo which specialised in *manjū* netsuke. He had a number of pupils who carried his style through to the end of the nineteenth century from the 1830s, when he began to carve. He and some of his pupils used the 'flying crane' *kakihan*. He was particularly good at rendering scenes from folktales, carving mostly in the *shishiaibori* technique, using coloured staining to enhance the details.

There are nine pieces in this collection, signed either with his whole name and *kakihan*, with Kōsai and *kakihan*, with Moritoshi and *kakihan* or with Kōsai and no *kakihan*. (See cat. nos. 47, 67, 32, 90, 17, 99, 28, 91, 76). Not all of these are by Moritoshi himself and are likely to be by his pupils. The characters 光斎 were also used by Kōsai Juō (see above), sometimes with a different *kakihan*. Meinertzhagen and Lazarnick both state that works signed with Moritoshi with the crane *kakihan* were the best and the earliest of his works, the later ones being signed with his whole name.

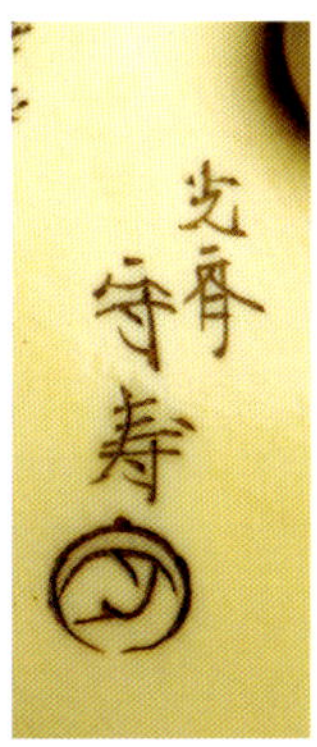

91

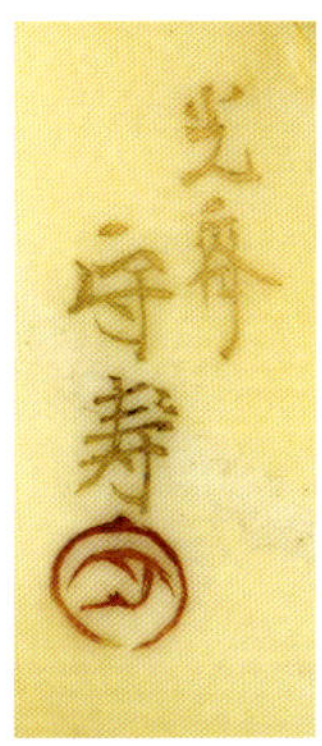

17

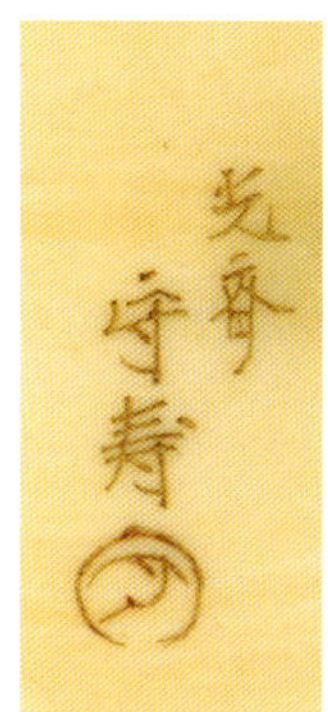

99

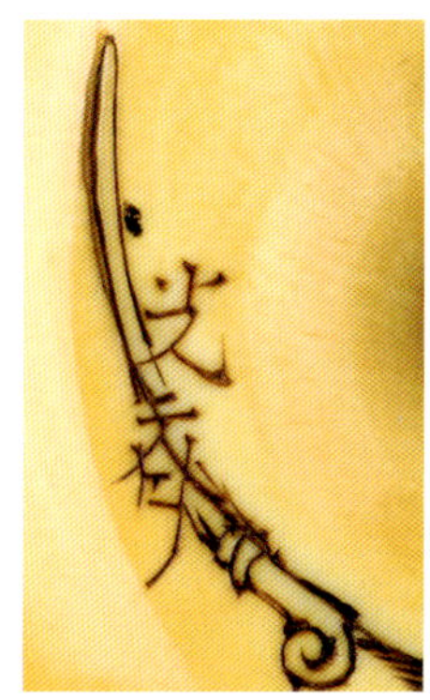

28

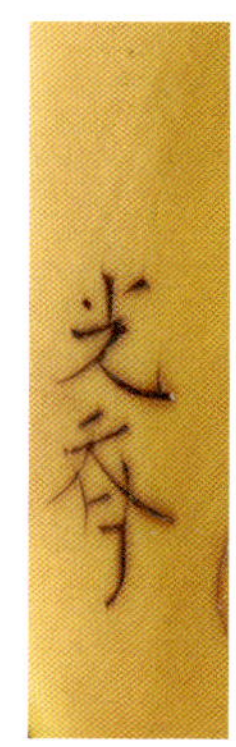

32

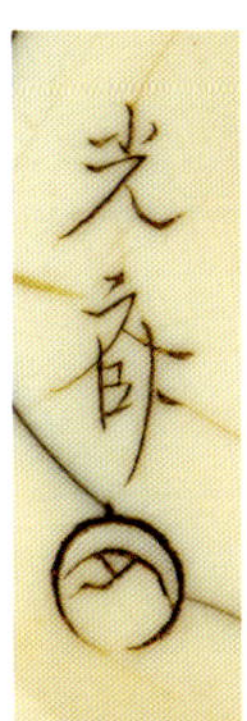

90

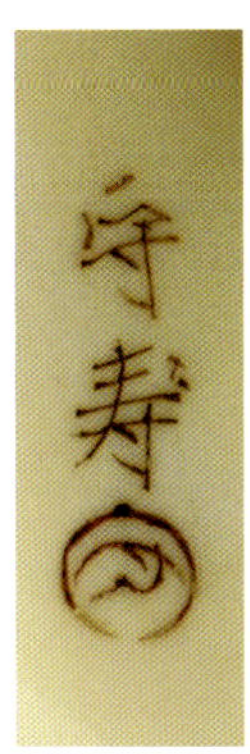

47

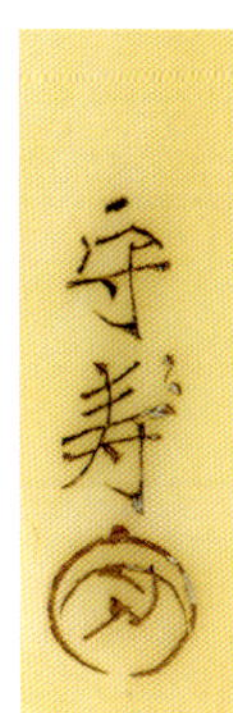

67

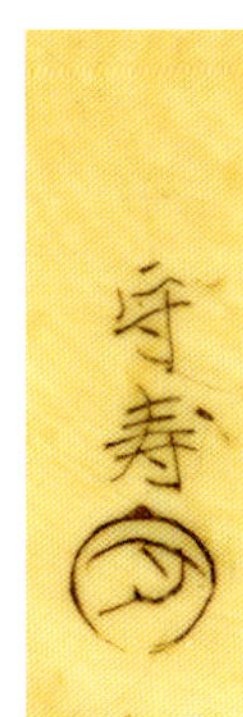

76

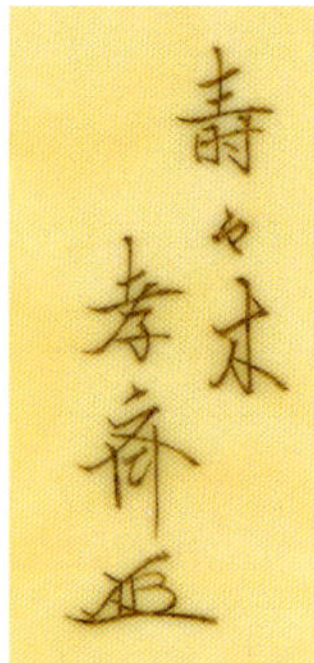

68

Suzuki Kōsai 壽々木孝斎

Suzuki Kōsai and Ikkōsai Kōjitsu shared the 孝 character in their names which probably links them together and to the Tokyo workshop of Meikeisai Hōjistu. Two almost identical *rakan*, one by Suzuki Kōsai in Maidstone Museum (42.1979.M23), the other by Ikkōsai Kōjitsu (see cat. no. 27 2001.52) also make it seem possible that the two were working in the same workshop. Suzuki Kōsai made both figures and *manjū*, the latter in a very delicate style of carving illustrating folktales and religious subjects. He was active around 1860-1880.

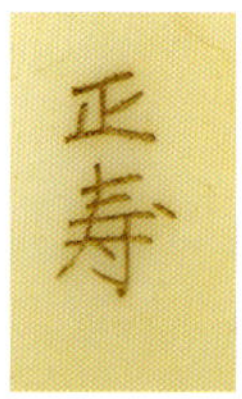

4

Masatoshi 正壽

Masatoshi was the son of Moritoshi Kōsai and seems to have followed in his father's footsteps carving *manjū* in ivory. His signature is sometimes followed by a crane *kakihan*. The Ashmolean piece's simple restrained design displays his skill with the knife in both the *shishiaibori* and *kebori* techniques.

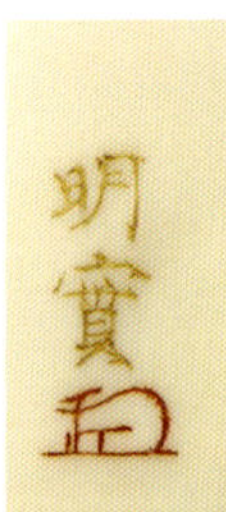

79

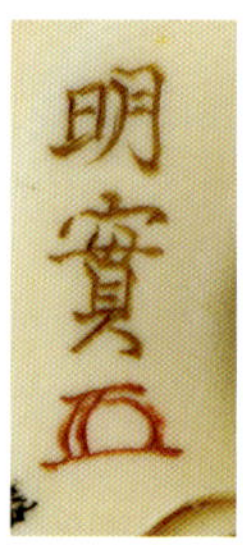

71

Hōryūsai Meijitsu 法龍蔡明實

Hōryūsai Meijitsu was one of Meikeisai Hōjitsu's more talented pupils who worked in the Tokyo workshop in the mid to late nineteenth century. He took four characters from his teacher's name. His known output was large ivory *manjū* on which he carved lively folktales and other genre scenes, with great attention to the details and liberal use of black *sumi* and coloured staining. The *kakihan* on the Ashmolean's two pieces do not match one another; however that on the shakier signature, cat. no. 71 is the more common one. Meijitsu occasionally signed his full name Hōryūsai Meijtsu and *kakihan* (See Baur Collection C 417) and sometimes added 作 *saku* (made by).

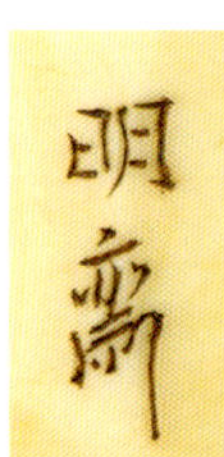

34

Meisai 明斎

Meisai was also connected with the school of Meikeisai Hōjitsu, working around 1880 in Tokyo. He carved in a shallow relief technique using dark staining to fill the lines, making scenes resembling engravings on ivory. He carved in the Meiji period when the export trade with the West was brisk. His netsuke depict folktales and other traditional motifs which would have appealed to foreign buyers.

9

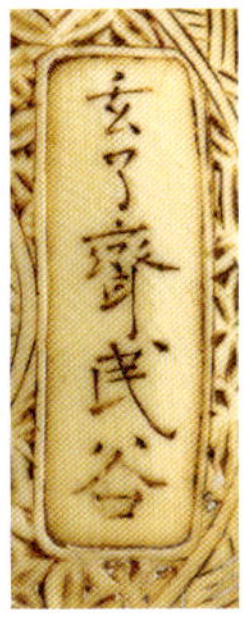

Genryōsai Minkoku 玄了齋民谷

Genryōsai Minkoku worked in the mid-nineteenth century in Tokyo carving both figures and *manjū* with great skill and particular attention to the small details of costume. Neil Davey describes him as a good worker who carved on a smaller scale than his master Minkoku I. There are many *manjū* and figural netsuke signed only Minkoku. Genryōsai Minkoku II has used his knives very delicately on this detailed piece of shallow carving. Patrizia Jirka-Schmitz notes that the style of his *manjū* is that prevalent between 1850 and 1860.

69

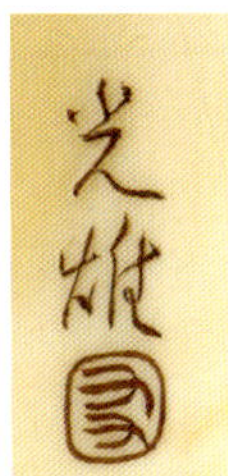

Mitsuo 光雄

There are two carvers called Mitsuo, possibly one a pupil of the other, who worked in Tokyo. The Ashmolean's piece is the only one illustrated in the Meinertzhagen Card Index. Meinertzhagen suggests this artist was associated with the school of carvers to which Gyokuhōsai and Gyokuyōsai belonged because of the treatment around the *himotōshi*. Another clue may be in the character '光' in both Mitsuhina 光雛 (Gyokuyōsai's name) and that of Mitsuo 光雄.

74

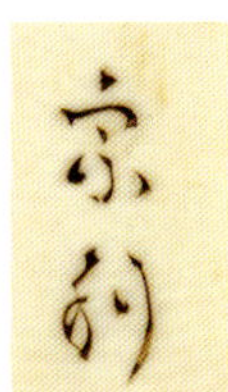

Munetoshi 宗利

This is an unrecorded artist

38

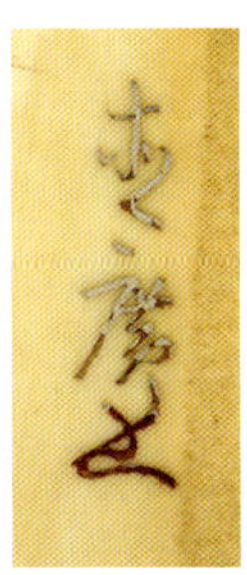

Naohiro 直廣

Nothing is known about the life of this carver who was probably from Osaka. Meinertzhagen records two *manjū* under this Naohiro, one is a group of *karako* around Fukurokuju. He dates his work to late Edo- early Meiji period (*bakumatsu*). There were other carvers of *manjū* with the character 'nao' in their names who worked in Osaka and with whom this one may have a link.

11

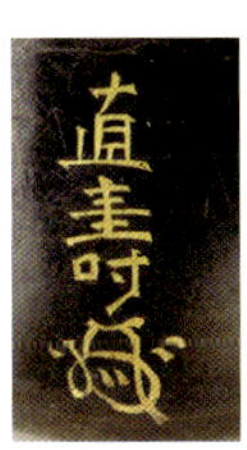

Hamano Naotoshi 浜野 直壽

Hamano Naotoshi lived in Edo and was active around 1850. He was a student of Hamano Naoyuki from whom he learned to make sword fittings using various inlay techniques, particularly *takazōgan*. He also used the names Kaikūdō 皆空堂 and Ken'yūsai 顕有斎 on sword furniture and had three similar *kakihan*, one of which he uses on this netsuke.

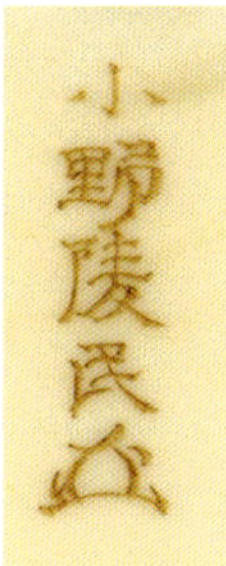

26

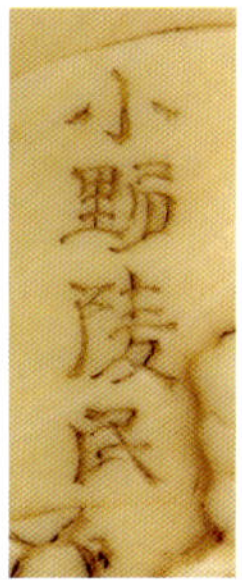

25

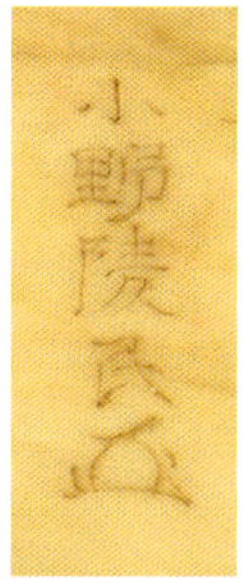

73

Ono Ryōmin 小野陵民

Ono Ryōmin lived and worked in Tokyo and was a highly skilled carver, making both *katabori* and intricately carved delicate *manjū* netsuke, some of which are dated to the early 1860s. As with many *manjū* artists, his designs were inspired by those he saw in printed books. Religious and historical figures and characters from folktales all feature on his *manjū*. Around 1880, he founded a large workshop on the banks of the Sumida River in Mukōjima, Tokyo. He had a number of pupils all of whom took the name 'Ono', his family name.

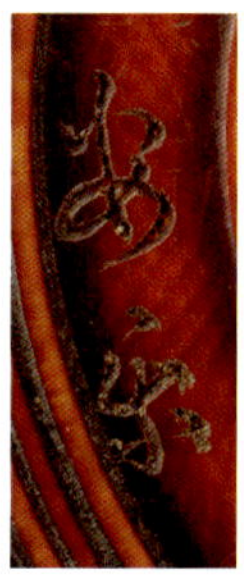

66

Ryūraku 龍楽

Ryūraku lived in Tokyo and was a follower of the style of Ryūkei. He worked in the first half of the nineteenth century and covered a wide range of subjects. He carved in wood and ivory, making mostly figures, masks and a few *manjū*.

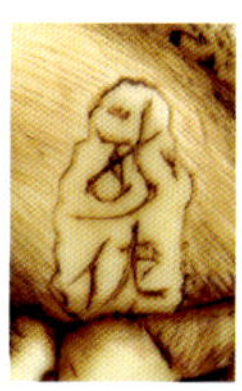

100

Ryūsa 龍佐

This Ryūsa is Gyokugasai who worked between 1830 and 1860, lived in Tokyo and was a follower of Gyokuyōsai Ryūchin and Gyokugasai Ryūchin. The original carver named Ryūsa is thought to have been the first to carve in the perforated style to which his name has now been attached. He was a wood turner, was mentioned in the *Sōken Kishō* and lived in the late eighteenth century. His family name was Ikejima. The skill in carving groups of zodiac animals, passed down through the line of carvers to Gyokugasai, is clear from the Ashmolean's piece in which all the animals have very detailed fur and feathers and are cleverly arranged in singles and pairs.

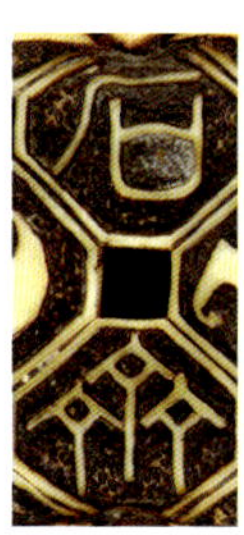

Sekisai 石蔡

Unrecorded artist of the Asakusa School

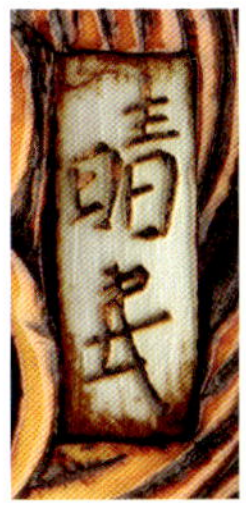

101

Seimin 晴民

This artist who lived and worked in Tokyo in the Meiji period, around 1870, was known as *kaeru Seimin*, for he was good at carving ivory frogs (*kaeru*). He used ivory, especially walrus ivory, wood and the most unusual thing about him was that he carved many netsuke in walnut (*kurumi*), of which the Ashmolean's example is one. He managed very skilfully to wrap his designs around the entire nut, when carving a whole piece, in one case including over fifty Nō masks. He also used walnut shell as a veneer, carving flatter, larger netsuke of animals, particularly dragons. He used lacquer and mother-of-pearl to highlight details and for his signature plaque.

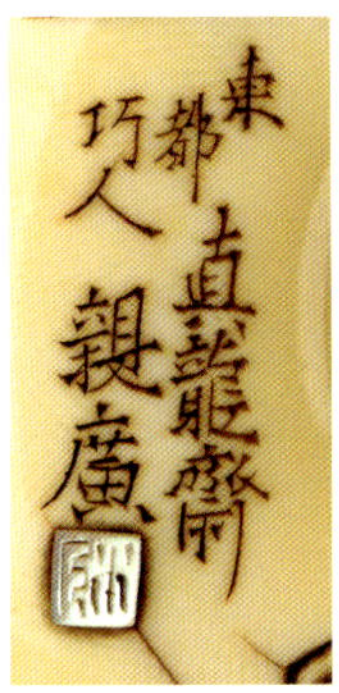

78

Shinryūsai Chikahiro 眞龍齋親廣

There is almost no biographical information on this carver, except that he worked in Tokyo, carving in ivory around the middle of the nineteenth century. There are only a few recorded netsuke by Chikahiro, this being one. At almost eight centimetres in diameter, it is a large and very heavy, but high quality piece of carving, undoubtedly made to hold a tobacco pouch and probably a collection of other items at the same time. This signature includes the bold statement 'skilful technician' and 'I am the very one'. It is most unusual for craftsmen to trumpet their own ability.

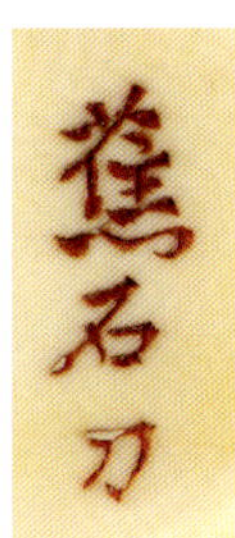

52

Shōseki 蕉石

Nothing is known of the work of Shōseki. One *katabori* netsuke of a recumbent goat in the Baur Collection bears this signature (C 1164)[5]. It is finely worked, and the animal's fur on both pieces is very detailed. The Ashmolean's *manjū* is an interesting and unusual shape.

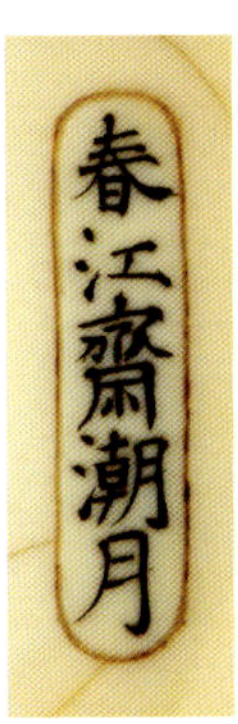

39

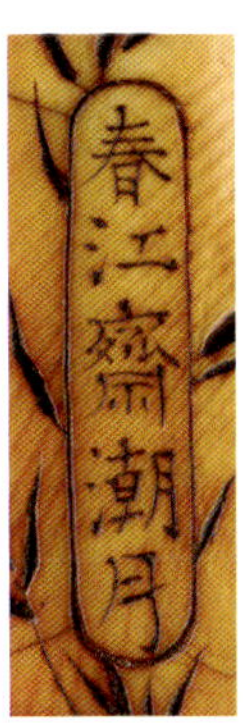

97

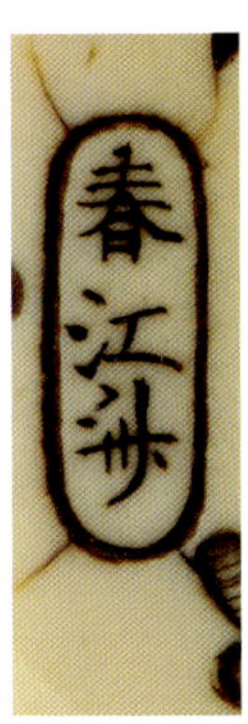

98

Shunkōsai Chōgetsu 春江齋朝月 (1826–1892)

Shunkōsai Chōgetsu was a follower of Tomochika Chikuyōsai (*c.* 1800–1850) and is known for his boldly carved *manjū*. There are two other pieces in this collection signed with his full name (Shunkōsai Chōgetsu) in an oval reserve on which he uses the deep *shishiaibori* carving technique to great effect. He was a pupil of Tokuzō, a horn carver, but abandoned the whole profession at the age of thirty-three and went to serve the shogun. He did not return to carving for almost twenty years, until 1877. He carved both figures and *manjū* netsuke and used wood, ivory and according to Neil Davey, horn. His lively renderings of legends and historical incidents are well carved with liberal use of coloured stains.

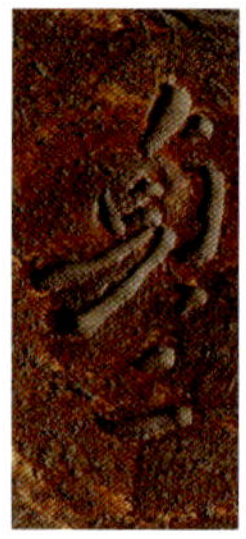

51

Teiji 貞二

Teiji, whose family name was Akiyama came from Nagoya or Gifu and worked between 1850 and 1880. He was originally a potter and a maker of lacquer boxes, which he inlaid with pottery. He was given permission to work at a kiln named Kaisuien, set up in the grounds of the Edo residence of the *daimyō* Matsudaira Yoshitake, whose domain was in Gifu prefecture. His netsuke show a sense of humour in their treatment of subjects and are made of rough earthenware with overglaze enamel decoration. He was associated with both the potters Kanji and Seiji, the latter, who shared one design with Teiji.[6]

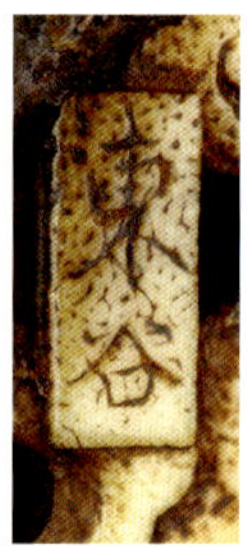

110

Tōkoku 東谷 (1846–1913)

Tōkoku, whose real name was Tetsgorō, belonged to a family which took the name Suzuki, (which Kengo Sekido suggests might have been the name of his shrine priest).[7] Tōkoku, meaning eastern country, which he adopted as his *gō*, refers to Asakusa in Tokyo where he lived. His father died when he was thirteen years old, so an antique dealer friend of his family, gave the young man work in his shop, where he became familiar with ivory carving. Tōkoku later became a dealer in tobacco pouches and smoking paraphernalia. At the age of nineteen he decided he wanted to carve netsuke and studied hard the works of the great masters of the time, Tomochika, Jugyoku, Hōjitsu and Rakumin. He seems to have been largely self-taught, at first carving in ivory, stag antler and marine ivory in a style reminiscent of Kokusai, however, he later developed inlaying techniques of precious metals and semi-precious stones which he carved himself and inlaid into both ivory and wood netsuke. He produced several versions of the Ashmolean's *manjū*, some of which had carved inlaid metal blossoms and buds. His *katabori* subject matter is very varied and intricately detailed.

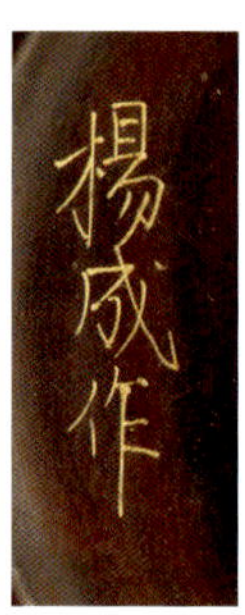

112

Yōsei 楊成

There were twenty generations of lacquerers using the name Yōsei from the fourteenth century until 1952, when the last carver died. As with the Kajikawa family of lacquerers it is hard to pin down one particular carver to this netsuke. The name Yōsei was made up from two characters of fourteenth century masters of Chinese carved lacquer: Yang (Mao) and Cheng (Zhang), which in Japanese reads Yōsei. They specialised in the technique known as *tsuishu*, seen on cat. no. 20, made objects of black carved lacquer (*tsuikoku*), also boxes and netsuke in the *guri* technique (carving a v-shaped pattern through different coloured layers of lacquer), cat. no. 118. Several different characters were used by different generations and those on cat. no. 110 are the most commonly seen. Many objects made by the Yōsei family were unsigned, for they were made for the shogunate.

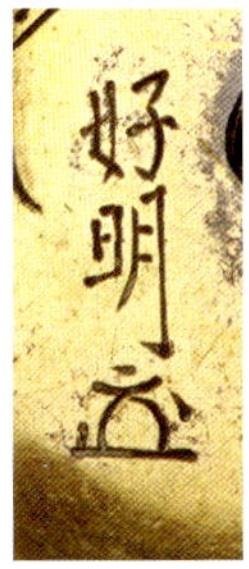

37

Yoshiaki 好明 (or Kōmin)

There is only one metalworker listed in Haynes under Yoshiaki, who worked around 1800. He specialised in the *katakiri* technique. It is not known if this is the artist of this netsuke, who uses a design from a *tsuba* maker named Yasuchika.

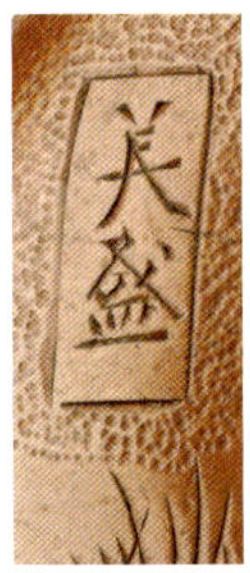

24

Yoshimori 美盛 (Unno Bisei 海野美盛 1864–1919)

Unno Yoshimori II was also known as Unno Bisei. He was the son of Unno Moritoshi and was named after his famous grandfather, Unno Yoshimori (1785-1862), who was a sword-fittings maker to the Mito branch of the Tokugawa family. He learned metalwork from Unno Shōmin and like his teacher he became a professor at the Tokyo School of Fine Arts and in 1892 was given the highest honour of Imperial Artist (*teishitsu gigeiin*). One of his great contributions to Japanese metal-working was his perfection of various casting methods. Unno Bisei exhibited at both Domestic Industrial and International Exhibitions and his work was bought by the Imperial Household.

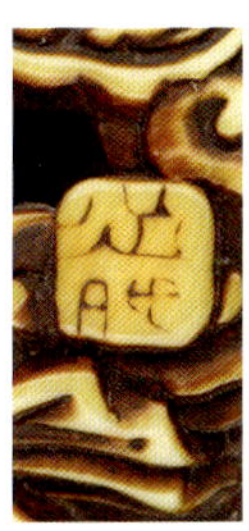

31

[Signature illegible]

Notes

1 Robert E. Haynes *The Index of Japanese Sword Fittings and Associated Artists*. Nihon Art Publishers, Ellwangen, 2001, Vol. 1, p. 385
2 *Bulletin Association Franco-Japonaise*. No. 64 Avril, 1999. 'Hojitsu, un maitre de netsuke d'Edo' by Sekido Kengo, p. 30 (Also translated into English in the same volume)
3 *International Netsuke Collectors Society Journal*. Vol. 1 No. 3, p. 38 shows an illustration
4 Sotheby's, London. 7&8/04/1998, Lot 613
5 Coullery, Marie-Thérèse and Martin S. Newstead. *The Baur Collection. Netsuke*. Genève. 1977, (C 1164), p. 365
6 *International Netsuke Society Journal*. Vol. 18 No. 1 'Kanji – Teiji – Seiji'. By Michael Dean, p. 36
7 *International Netsuke Society Journal*. Vol. 10, No. 10 'About Tokoku' by Sekido Kengo, translated and adapted by Misao Mikoshiba

Bibliography

Arakawa, Hirokazu. *The Gō Collection of Netsuke*. Tokyo National Musuem. Tokyo and New York. Kodansha International Ltd, 1983

Baird, Merrily. *Symbols of Japan: Thematic Motifs in Art and Design*. New York. Rizzoli International Publications Inc., 2001

Barker, Richard and Smith, Lawrence. *Netsuke: the Miniature Sculpture of Japan*. London: British Museum Publications for the Trustees of the British Museum, 1976

Borgen, Robert. 'Stone Bridge (Shakkyō)'. *Japanese Language and Literature,* Vol. 37, No. 2, Oct. 2003, pp. 104–116

Brinker, Helmut. *Zen in the Art of Painting*. London: Arkana, 1987

Brockhaus, Albert. *Netsuke : Versuch einer Geschichte der japanischen Schnitzkunst*. Leipzig: F.A. Brockhaus, 1905

Bulletin Association Franco-Japonaise No. 54 Oct. 1996. See Willhelm, G.

Bushell, Raymond. *Collectors' Netsuke*. New York. Walker/Weatherhill, 1971

Bushell, Raymond. *An Introduction to Netsuke*. Rutland VT. Charles E. Tuttle Co., 1982

Bushell, Raymond. *Netsuke Familiar and Unfamiliar: New Principles for Collecting*. New York, Weatherhill, 1975

Casal, U.A. *The Five Sacred Festivals of Ancient Japan. Their Symbolism and Historical Development*. Sophia University, Tokyo in co-operation with Charles E. Tuttle Co. Rutland, VT. & Tokyo, Japan, 1967

Coullery, Marie-Thérèse, and Newstead Martin S. *The Baur Collection. Netsuke*. Geneva, 1977

Davey, Neil K. *Netsuke: A Comprehensive Study Based on the Hindson Collection*. Revised edition. London. Philip Wilson Publishers Ltd, 1982

Davies, Barry. *Netsuke Classics*. London. Barry Davies Oriental Art. 1990

Davies, Barry. *100 Selected Pieces from The Netsuke Collection of Scott Meredith and 50 from another Private American Collection*. London. Barry Davies Oriental Art Ltd. 1995

Dykstra, Yoshiko K., translated by. *The Konjaku Tales 今昔物語集. Japanese Section (Honchō-Hen) (1) from a Medieval Japanese Collection*. IRI Monograph Series No. 25 Hirakata City, Osaka, Japan: Intercultural Research Institute, Kansai Gaidai University, 1998–2003

Earle, Joe. *Netsuke: Fantasy and Reality in Japanese Miniature Sculpture*. Boston. Museum of Fine Arts, Boston, MA, 2001

Edmunds, Will. H. *Pointers and Clues to the Subjects of Chinese and Japanese Art*. London. Sampson, Low, Marston & Co. Ltd, 1934

Eskenazi Ltd. *Japanese inrō and lacquer-ware from a private Swedish collection*: 12–30 November 1996, London

Eskenazi Ltd. *Japanese Netsuke from the Lazarnick collection:* 15–28 May 1990, London

Eskenazi Ltd. *Japanese Netsuke from the Carré collection:* 15 June–9 July 1993, London
Eskenazi Ltd. *Japanese netsuke, ojime, inro, lacquer-ware.* 22 October–2 November 1984, London
Eskenazi Ltd. *Japanese Netsuke from private collections:* 26 June–6 July 1979, London
Haynes, Robert E. *The Index of Japanese Sword Fittings and Associated Artists.* Vols. 1-3. Ellwangen. Nihon Art Publishers, 2001
Hickman, Money L. *On the Trail of Kume the Transcendent.* M Bulletin (MFA Boston), Vol. 79, 1981, pp. 20–43
Hinks, Marcelle A. *The Japanese Dance.* London. William Heinemann, 1910
Huish, Marcus. *The Evolution of a Netsuké.* Transactions and Proceedings of the Japan Society. Vol. III, part IV, 1895
Hutt, Julia. *Japanese Netsuke. Victoria and Albert Museum. Far Eastern Series.* London. V & A Publications, 2003
Hyers, Conrad. 'Humor in Zen: Comic Midwifery'. *Philosophy East and West.* Vol. 39, No. 3, July 1989, pp. 267–277
Jirka-Schmitz, Patrizia. *The World of Netsuke. The Werdelmann Collection at the Museum Kunst Palast Düsseldorf.* Stuttgart. Arnodlsche Art Publishers, 2005
Jirka-Schmitz, Patrizia. *Netsuke Gűrtelschmuck aus Japon Die Sammlung Trumpf.* Arnoldsche Art Publishers. Linden-Museum Stuttgart. Statliches Museum fűr Vőlkerkunde, 2000
Joly, H.L. *Legend in Japanese Art,* London. John Lane. The Bodley Head, 1908
Joly, Henri L. (edited by). *Catalogue of the H. Seymour Trower collection of Japanese Art.* Glendining & Co. Ltd. London. 1913. Reprint, Hollywood FL. Kurstin-Schneider, 1975
Jonas, F.M. *Netsuké.* Tokyo. Charles E. Tuttle Co., 1960
Joseph, Herbert S. 'The Heike Monogatari: Buddhist Ethics and the Code of the Samurai'. *Folklore,* Vol. 87, No. 1, 1976
Klompmakers, Inge. *Of Brigands and Bravery. Kuniyoshi's heroes of the Suikoden.* Leiden. Hotei Publishing, 1998
Komparu, Kunio. *The Noh Theatre. Principles and Perspectives.* New York. Tokyo. Kyoto. Weatherhill /Tankosha, 1983
Kouwenhoven, Frank. 'Meaning and Structure: The Case of Chinese qin (zither) Music'. *British Journal of Ethnomusicology.* Vol. 10, 2001, pp. 39-62
Lazarnick, George. *Netsuke & Inro Artists, and How to Read their Signatures.* Honolulu. Reed Publishers, 1982
Little, Stephen and Eichman, Shawn. *Taoism and the Arts of China.* Art Institute of Chicago. University of California Press, 2000
McCullough, Helen Craig. *The Tale of the Heike.* Stanford, CA. Stanford University Press, 1988
McCullough, Helen Craig, translated and with an introduction by: *Yoshitsune: a fifteenth-century Japanese chronicle* (Jap. *Gikeiki*). Stanford CA. Stanford University Press, 1966

Meinertzhagen, Frederick. (edited by George Lazarnick). *MCI. The Meinertzhagen Card Index on Netsuke in the Archives of the British Museum, Parts A & B*. New York. Alan R. Liss Inc., 1986

Moss, Paul. *Outside the Box. Further explorations in Japanese netsuke and lacquer.* Moss, Sydney L. Ltd. London, 2004

Murase, Miyeko. *Bridge of Dreams.* The Mary Griggs Burke Collection of Japanese Art. The Metropolitan Museum of Art, New York. New York. Distributed by Harry H. Abrams Inc., 2000

Ohnuki-Tierney, Emiko. *The Monkey as Mirror. Symbolic Transformations in Japanese History and Ritual.* Princeton NJ. Princeton University Press, 1987

Okada, Yuzuru. *Netsuke. A Miniature Art of Japan.* Tourist Library: 14. Japan Travel Bureau, Tokyo, 1960

O'Neill, P.G. *Japanese Names. A Comprehensive Index by Characters and Readings.* New York and Tokyo. John Weatherhill Inc., 1972

Pomeroy, Charles A. *Traditional Crafts of Japan, illustrated with the eighteenth century artisan prints of Tachibana Minko.* New York and Tokyo. Walker/Weatherhill, 1968

Rath, Eric E. 'From Representation to Apotheosis: Nō's Modern Myth of Okina' in *Asian Theatre Journal,* Vol. 17, No. 2, (Autumn 2000)

Reider, Noriko T. 'Shūten Dōji "Drunken Demon"' in *Asian Folklore Studies,* Vol. 64, 2005, pp. 207–231

Ryerson, Egerton. *The Netsuke of Japan. Legends, History, Folklore and Customs.* London. G. Bell and Sons Ltd, 1958

Salter, Rebecca. *Japanese Popular Prints from votive slips to playing cards.* London. A & C Black Publishers Ltd, 2006

Tanaka, Kikuo. *Iroha-biki monchō* (Book of crests and designs]. Tokyo, 1881

Takeuchi, Melinda. 'Kuniyoshi's "Minamoto Raikō" and "the Earth Spider": Demons and Protest in Late Tokugawa Japan'. *Ars Orientalis,* Vol. 17, 1987

Terajima, Ryōan. *Wakan Sansai Zue* 和漢三才図会 (Illustrated Sino-Japanese Enclycopaedia), 1712

Tomita, Kumasaku and Lee, G. Ambrose. *Japanese Treasure Tales.* Bushey, Herts. Yamanaka and Co. Printed by Andre & Sleigh Ltd, 1906

Ueda, Reikichi. *The Netuske handbook of Ueda Reikichi.* Adapted from the Japanese by Raymond Bushell. Rutland VT. Charles E. Tuttle Co., 1961

Varley, H. Paul (translated by). *A Chronicle of Gods and Sovereigns. Jinnō Shōtōki of Kitabatake Chikafusa* New York. Columbia University Press, 1980

Volker, T. *The Animal in Far Eastern Art and especially in the Art of the Japanese Netsuke with References to Chinese Origins, Traditions, Legends and Art.* Leiden. E.J. Brill, 1950

Welch, Matthew & Chappell, Sharon. *Netsuke. The Japanese Art of Miniature Carving.* The Minneapolis Institute of Arts. Minneapolis MN. Paragon Publishing, 1999

Welch, Patricia Bjaaland. *Chinese Art: A Guide to Motifs and Visual Imagery.* Tokyo, Vermont, Singapore. Tuttle Publishing, 2010

Wilhelm, G. *Manjū exégèse et appréciation.* Bulletin Association Franco-Japonaise. No. 54, Oct. 1996
Wrangham, E. A. *The Index of Inrō Artists.* Edited by Joe Earle. Alnwick, England. Harehope Publications, 1995
Yetts, W. Perceval. The Eight Immortals. *Journal of the Royal Asiatic Society of Great Britain and Ireland.* October 1916,. pp. 773–807

Concordance

EAX.608	61
EAX.626	23
EAX.627	45
EAX.628	53
EAX.629	76
EAX.630	101
EAX.631	122
EAX.633	42
EAX.752	107
EAX.753	24
EAX.757	64
EAX.1116	117
EAX.1331	119
EAX.1333	118
EAX.1334	108
EAX.1340	19
EAX.1342	115
EAX.1343	92
EAX.1348	114
EA1956.3198	51
EA1956.3214	123
EA1956.3223	20
EA1956.3225	109
EA1956.3254	103
EA1956.3271	120
EA1957.265	116
EA1976.17	102
EA1976.26	29
EA2001.35	36
EA2001.36	54
EA2001.37	47
EA2001.38	67
EA2001.40	105
EA2001.41	49
EA2001.42	94
EA2001.43	112
EA2001.45	9
EA2001.46	84
EA2001.47	52
EA2001.48	32
EA.2001.49	93
EA2001.50	7
EA2001.51	96
EA2001.52	27
EA2001.53	2
EA2001.54	30
EA2001.55	69
EA2001.56	37
EA2001.57	111
EA2001.58	38
EA2001.59	12
EA2001.60	71
EA2001.61	33
EA2001.62	35
EA2001.63	100
EA2001.64	39
EA2001.65	43
EA2001.66	77
EA2001.67	87
EA2001.68	11
EA2001.69	90
EA2001.70	104
EA2001.71	86
EA2001.72	6
EA2001.73	60
EA2001.74	10
EA2001.75	72
EA2001.76	78
EA2001.77	3
EA2001.78	18
EA2001.79	44
EA2001.80	58
EA2001.81	98
EA2001.82	88
EA2001.83	79
EA2001.84	17
EA2001.85	14
EA2001.86	59
EA2001.88	97
EA2001.89	22
EA2001.90	15
EA2001.91	99
EA2001.93	50
EA2001.94	110
EA2001.95	73
EA2001.96	95
EA2001.97	5
EA2001.99	28
EA2001.100	40
EA2001.101	81
EA2001.102	65
EA2001.103	48
EA2001.104	1
EA2001.105	74
EA2001.106	63
EA2001.107	25
EA2001.108	91
EA2001.109	16
EA2001.110	85
EA2001.111	70
EA2001.112	89
EA2001.114	82
EA2001.115	121
EA2001.116	55
EA2001.117	4
EA2001.118	66
EA2001.119	31
EA2001.121	57
EA2001.122	75
EA2001.123	21
EA2001.124	8
EA2001.126	46
EA2001.127	34
EA2001.131	41
EA2001.130	13
EA2001.132	83
EA2001.133	26
EA2001.134	56
EA2001.135	62
EA2001.136	80
EA2001.137	106
EA2001.138	113
EA2001.139	68

Index